THE MASS OBSERVERS

Praise for Nine Wartime Lives

'The life stories are moving and beautifully described.'
Vernon Bogdanor, *New Statesman*

'[A] welcome, scholarly and illuminating installment in the story without end of the "People's War".'
Juliet Gardiner, *Financial Times*

'An absorbing volume packed with illuminating detail and convincing analysis.'
Sue Bruley, *History Today*

'A compelling account that presents much that is unexpected about the lived experience of the war. Hinton is to be congratulated on demonstrating the value of a welcome and overdue "biographical turn" in historical studies.'
Penny Summerfield, *BBC History Magazine*

'Elegantly written and subtle in its analysis, this book will offer much to those interested in the social history of the war, those new to using personal sources, and more generally to those interested in existential questions about life.'
Hester Vaizey, *Times Higher Education*

'[An] absorbing and sophisticated exploration of how the public demands of war intruded into the private sphere and moulded new identities.'
Literary Review

'Skilfully synthesising a dense conceptual literature on themes of modernity, identity and the self, Hinton makes a powerful case for the value of diary-writing to the historian . . . an immensely enjoyable read.'
Reviews in History

THE MASS OBSERVERS

A HISTORY, 1937–1949

JAMES HINTON

OXFORD
UNIVERSITY PRESS

OXFORD
UNIVERSITY PRESS

Great Clarendon Street, Oxford, OX2 6DP,
United Kingdom

Oxford University Press is a department of the University of Oxford.
It furthers the University's objective of excellence in research, scholarship,
and education by publishing worldwide. Oxford is a registered trade mark of
Oxford University Press in the UK and in certain other countries

First Edition published in 2013
Impression: 1

British Library Cataloguing in Publication Data
Data available

ISBN 978-0-19-967104-5

Printed in Great Britain by
MPG Books Group, Bodmin and King's Lynn

For Dorothy

Preface

A full history of the original Mass-Observation (MO) project has long been overdue. Since the opening of the archive at Sussex University in 1975 interest in MO has grown exponentially and it shows no sign of flagging. For nearly 40 years now historians have been mining the archive's vast accumulation of material bearing on everyday life before, during and immediately after the Second World War. Our understanding of the social history of mid-20th century Britain has been immeasurably enriched by the reports written by MO's full-time investigators, the questionnaire responses of its volunteer observers and the diaries that many of them wrote. Edited collections of MO material have delighted the general reader, opening a window onto a period of history that remains, for better or worse, central to British national identity.

But the history of MO itself—the organization, the people, the methods, MO's characteristic 'voice', its role in the cultural and political life of the period—has remained relatively under-researched. Most of what has been written about MO has focussed on its early years, and has tended to treat the period after the outbreak of war—when MO was actually at its most productive—as a rather disappointing coda to a promising beginning. Looking at the enterprise over a longer period shifts perspectives on the early years, and changes judgements about the relative contributions of its two leading personnel. Some recent work has sought to put Charles Madge at the centre, but, although his contribution was crucial to what MO became, he himself dropped out in 1940, leaving Tom Harrisson in sole control. Existing narratives usually represent Madge's departure as a key moment in the degeneration of MO, from an exciting cultural experiment into a servant of the state on the road to mere market research. Given the centrality of market research to the ways in which culture operates in contemporary Britain, one could rewrite the history non-judgementally to trace MO's role in its development. But that would be to lose the uniqueness of what MO was in what I will argue was its prime during the war years: a successful enterprise designed to construct an archive appropriate to the creation of a people's history of the war.

This book should have been written by Angus Calder, author of what remains the best social history of Britain during the Second World War. Calder, who had been instrumental in bringing the archive to Sussex, made a start on the history in the late 1970s, interviewed many of the leading personnel, published a characteristically brilliant article, and drafted an (unpublished) introductory chapter. But other interests took precedence, the project languished and he did not return to it before his untimely death. It is more than ten years now since Dorothy Sheridan—in charge of the archive from 1974 until 2010—asked me if I would be interested in taking on the project. I decided that I could not approach the history of the organization without understanding more about the diarists who were empowered by MO to write so intimately about their everyday lives. So I spent some years studying the diaries, resulting in my book *Nine Wartime Lives: Mass-Observation and the Making of the Modern Self.* That done, I turned my attention to the history of the organization.

Being very much the personal creation of its two founders and lacking any formal constitutional set-up, MO failed to generate the kind of internal records that make it easy to reconstruct the history of an organization: there was, for example, no executive committee to provide the historian with its minutes (except during a brief interregnum in 1942–3). The material for reconstructing MO's history is scattered through an archive organized largely around its output rather than its internal routines, as well as in the archives of other organizations and individuals who had dealings with MO.

Proceeding chronologically, I have tried to describe the everyday functioning of the organization; to discuss the evolution of its aims and its methods of work; to explore the MO 'voice' and the core themes running through its output during these years; and, whenever the records allow, to assess the contribution of successive generations of MO staff—the impact of war ensured a rapid turnover—whose identities, attitudes, and personalities have to date been largely hidden from history by MO's habit of indicating authorship of reports with the initials rather than the full names of their writers.

Working my way through the archival material and putting together a comprehensive account, I have found myself correcting a good many errors and misunderstandings in much of the existing historiography. The more trivial of these corrections, where mentioned, I have confined to the notes. Among the larger reassessments of the received picture, I argue that:

- MO had two founders (Tom Harrisson and Charles Madge), not, as all existing accounts assert, three—the influence of Humphrey Jennings has commonly been exaggerated;
- those who write about MO as though it were some kind of failed revolutionary project misunderstand its nature—indeed Harrisson's ongoing connection with the radical wing of the Liberal Party was considerably more important to MO's development than Madge's engagement with Marxist or surrealist ideas;
- characterizations of MO's pre-war team in Bolton as a bunch of public school boys engaged in a quasi-colonial encounter with the working class are misconceived;
- work for the Ministry of Information during the early years of the war did not fundamentally compromise its independence, nor was it the primary reason why Madge decided to quit;
- post-war changes in the political context, with the election of a Labour Government, did not undermine MO's *raison d'être*; indeed there was a major upsurge of MO activity in 1946–7 which could well have continued had Harrisson not decided to return to anthropological work in Borneo.

In the course of writing this history I have incurred many debts, the greatest of which is to Dorothy Sheridan who not only asked me to do it in the first place, but also gave me wise advice about how to approach the archive, constant encouragement, and a great deal of practical help in facilitating my work. Fiona Courage, the current archivist, and her staff have been unfailingly helpful; the staff uncomplaining as they fetched up an unprecedented number of boxes per day to enable me to sift through topic files for the occasional relevant item of correspondence. Fortunately, the excellence of the archive's catalogue did much to compensate for the absence of any easy route into the organizational history, as did the archive's policy of collecting the papers of individuals involved with MO, most notably those of Charles Madge, Mary Adams, Henry Novy and Richard Fitter. I have also been enormously helped by the interviews conducted by Angus Calder and Nick Stanley in the late 1970s and early 1980s with surviving members of the MO staff. Without this personal testimony—almost all of it no longer accessible by the time I got to work on the history—the account would have been very much thinner. I am grateful also to the staff of the many other archives which have thrown light on MO's operations, most significantly the National Archives, the Brumwell papers in Tate Modern, the Malinowski papers in the British Library of Economic and Political Science, and the Trevelyan papers at Trinity College, Cambridge. I also thank the Trustees of the Mass-Observation Archive for permission to quote MO material.

James Hinton
Les Trémoulèdes

Contents

List of Abbreviations

ADM	Admiralty (National Archives)
ARP	Air Raid Precautions
ASG	Advertising Service Guild
ATS	Auxiliary Territorial Service
BIPO	British Institute of Public Opinion
BLEPS	British Library of Economic and Political Science
BMpap	Bronislaw Malinowski papers (BLEPS)
CAB	Cabinet Papers (National Archives)
CM	Charles Madge
CMpap	Charles Madge papers (University of Sussex)
DNB	Oxford Dictionary of National Biography
DR	Directive Reply (MO Archive)
DS	Day Survey (MO Archive)
FR	File Report (MO Archive)
GBpap	Graham Bell papers (Tate Gallery Archive)
HNpap	Henry Novy papers (University of Sussex)
HO	Home Office
INF	Ministry of Information (National Archives)
JTpap	Julian Trevelyan papers (Trinity College, Cambridge)
LSE	London School of Economics
MApap	Mary Adams papers (University of Sussex)
MO	Mass-Observation
MOI	Ministry of Information
MRC	Modern Records Centre (University of Warwick)
NIESR	National Institute of Economic and Social Research
PEP	Political and Economic Planning
RAF	Royal Air Force

RCA	Railway Companies Association
SRP	Social Research Publications
TC	Topic Collection (MO Archive)
TH	Tom Harrisson
W	Worktown (MO Archive)
WEA	Workers' Educational Association

List of Tables

Note to the Reader

The books published by MO, listed in the bibliography, are referred to throughout by their short titles.

All interviews cited are in the MO Archive Former Personnel boxes, unless otherwise noted.

I

Origins

I

Mass-Observation (MO) originated from the meeting of two young men—Tom Harrisson (aged 27) and Charles Madge (aged 26)—early in January 1937. For some weeks prior to this Madge, together with a group of metropolitan artistic and literary friends, had been discussing ways of accessing the 'collective unconscious'; to this end he had written to the *New Statesman* inviting volunteers to participate in the creation of a new science of 'mass observation', an 'anthropology of our own people'.[1] Meanwhile Harrisson, in the very different atmosphere of the northern textile town of Bolton, was setting up an anthropological project of his own: a study of everyday working-class life. Intrigued, he contacted Madge and was invited to the next meeting of the London group in Madge's Blackheath flat.

The occasion was not a great success. Harrisson, whose ideas about observing the masses were very different from those being discussed in the Madge group, found himself confronting a man whose conviction and loquaciousness were equal to his own: the documentary film-maker Humphrey Jennings:

> What I chiefly remember of the evening [wrote one of those present] is the picture of Humphrey, with his elbow on one end of the mantelpiece, and Harrisson, with *his* elbow on the other end of the mantelpiece, both talking loudly and simultaneously...without either of them paying the slightest attention to what the other was saying.[2]

---

1. *New Statesman*, 2 January 1937.
2. David Gascoyne, cited in Judith Heimann, *Most Offending Soul*, 1997, 129; CM, 'Autobiography', 68. Harrisson's view of Jennings' eloquence was that 'he talks too much about too little' (TH to Trevelyan, 28 February 1938, JTpap).

It must have taken all Madge's tact to convince Harrisson in the days following this meeting that there was something to be gained by pooling their
two very different approaches to the study of popular culture. Harrisson
remained suspicious and he was careful to preserve the autonomy of his
own project in Bolton. Nevertheless within a month the two men had
drafted MO's founding manifesto, although this was not to see the light of
day until the summer, when it was published as the first two sections of their
pamphlet *Mass-Observation*.[3] By the end of January Madge and Harrisson
had announced the formation of the new organization in a letter to the
New Statesman. Jennings, who had not seen the final draft, was angry that his
name was attached to this letter.[4] 'Attempting to write in collaboration
with Harrisson was one of the most stimulating and difficult tasks one
could imagine,' Madge remarked later that year.[5] It was hard enough to find
common ground with one prima donna: with two the project would have
been impossible.

When a few months later Madge sought to distinguish his approach from
Harrisson's, he represented himself as the detached empiricist for whom
MO was simply 'an instrument for collecting facts, not a means for producing a synthetic philosophy, a super-science or a super-politics.'[6] This was
disingenuous. In fact it was Madge, if anyone, who was drawn to 'super-
science or super-politics'—or, as Harrisson saw it, 'dogmatic faith'—in the
shape of Marxism, and this was a bone of contention between the two men
from the outset. Shortly after their first meeting Harrisson wrote to Madge
expressing anxiety about his 'prejudiced approach via Marxism.'[7] While
Madge was a member of the Communist Party, Harrisson's political affilia-
tions lay with the radical wing of the Liberal Party, and it was misleading
of Madge to describe the 'new synthesis' that his collaborator hoped for
as a 'super-politics'. What Harrisson had in fact expressed was a modest
social democratic hope that, in time, MO would facilitate 'something less
fierce, more understanding and permanent, than the present miserable conflicts of dogmatic faiths in race, politics and religion.'[8] 'Black shirt or red are

3. *Mass-Observation*, 1937, 28.
4. *New Statesman*, 30 January 1937; TH to CM, 18 January 1940, 5, Org&Hist 1/1.
5. CM to Malinowski, 3 December 1937, BMpap.
6. *Mass-Observation*, 47–8.
7. TH to CM, January 1937, reproduced in CM, 'Autobiography', 68. Tom Jeffery, *Mass-Observation—
   A Short History*, 1978, 23 correctly identified the pamphlet's curious effect of inverting the two
   men's positions.
8. *Mass-Observation*, 47–8.

transitory furies', he had written elsewhere, advocating a humanism rooted in 'the steady core of man and mind which weathers all things.'[9]

Political differences, however, were the least of their difficulties. In the popular front atmosphere of the late 1930s it was easy enough for Liberals and Communists to find common ground in the defence of democracy against fascism; it was in this wide and flexible political space that MO situated itself. As a political project, MO's aim was to enable the masses to speak for themselves, to make their voices heard above the din created by press and politicians speaking in their name. In this way the organization—bridging the gulf between elite and popular culture—would help to place democracy on a firm and sustainable footing. In the spirit of popular frontism, MO's political aims were sufficiently vague and open-ended to elide the difference between giving existing elites the knowledge of the masses necessary to rule them effectively, and empowering the masses to overthrow those elites. For most of its career MO, like the popular front itself, existed somewhere between these two extremes: anti-fascist unity, depending on circumstances, could be seen either as an opening towards genuine democracy (whether at the Communist or Liberal end of the imagined utopia), or as a means, as the poet Cecil Day Lewis had put it, of 'defending the bad against the worse', enabling what passed for democracy in capitalist Britain to weather external and internal threats in difficult times. The question of whether MO was doing more to empower the masses or to facilitate their manipulation by existing elites was one that hovered over its activity throughout the period covered by this book. The answer, if there is one, depends as much on how one sees the larger historical picture as on anything intrinsic to MO's own operations. The popular front strategy of enhancing democracy through anti-fascist unity seemed to many on the left to have a compelling logic; but it would be easy, in retrospect, to exaggerate the degree to which that strategy delivered its intended results. Which is not to say that any alternative revolutionary politics would have achieved more: indeed it might well have been disastrous in the face of the fascist threat. By 1944, if not earlier, it was clear even to the most eloquent advocate of the popular front—the late convert George Orwell—that the forces of capitalist reaction were simply too strong to be overcome by either approach.[10]

---

9. Tom Harrisson, *Savage Civilisation*, 1937, 366.
10. George Orwell, 'London Letter', *Partisan Review*, December 1944, in Sonia Orwell and Ian Angus, *The Collected Essays, Journalism and Letters of George Orwell*, 3, 1970, 335–6.

II

Cooperation between the Liberal and the Communist was further enhanced by the fact that the two men approached the investigation of popular culture from a common class position. Born in Argentina in 1911, Harrisson had arrived in Britain aged three, when his father, a railway engineer, came home to fight in the First World War, from which he emerged a brigadier general.[11] After the war his parents returned to Argentina abandoning eight-year-old Tom and his younger brother to the care of preparatory school and vacations spent as paying guests in loveless guest houses, interrupted only by one happy year (when he was 11) spent among affluent British ex-patriots in Argentina. By the time his parents returned to Britain, Tom, now 16, had found a substitute father in his housemaster at Harrow—the Reverend Kittermaster—who had been in Argentina before the war and was actually Tom's godfather. With Kittermaster's support Harrisson weathered his adolescence, avoiding team games, gaining a reputation for daring and physically challenging exploits, and establishing what was to become a lifelong daily habit of recording (in largely unintelligible handwriting) detailed observations of the world around him. Developing a childhood fascination with natural life, Harrisson took to birdwatching, publishing, while still at school, a booklet on *Birds of the Harrow District* and launching (with a friend at another public school) the first nationwide census of the great crested grebe, whose mating habits had been the subject of a famous 1914 article by Julian Huxley which pioneered the new science of ecological ornithology.[12] The organization of large numbers of volunteers (eventually 1,300 of them on the grebe census) to observe and record everyday local occurrences, and to send in their findings for collation and analysis at national level, was—it has been convincingly argued—symptomatic of the emergence of a new kind of scientifically inspired active citizenship during the 1930s: birdwatching, aircraft spotting, and, with MO, people-watching all belonged to a democratization of science, the 'creation of a band of socially-minded and scientifically-minded people within the

---

11. Unless otherwise noted the biographical details in this and the following paragraph are taken from Heimann, *Most Offending Soul*.
12. M. Toogood, 'Modern observations: new ornithology and the science of ourselves, 1920–1940', *Journal of Historical Geography*, 37, 2011, 354.

community at large', as Huxley, welcoming the establishment of MO in 1937, was to put it.[13] It was through his ornithological activities that Harrisson got to know the leading figures in the field: James Fisher and Richard Fitter were both to bring their experience in the birdwatching movement to bear on the management of MO; and, most importantly, the environmentalist Max Nicholson, seven years Harrisson's senior, whose combination of scientific observation, adventurous fieldwork, and involvement in public affairs (he was a leading member of Political and Economic Planning in the 1930s) made him an ideal mentor for Harrisson's future career.[14]

In the summer of 1930, before going up to Cambridge to read natural sciences, Harrisson had already been on his first overseas scientific expedition, observing bird habits on a two-month trek in the Norwegian arctic as part of a team organized by the Oxford University Exploration Club (established the previous year by Max Nicholson, among others). Cambridge was dull by comparison, and after little more than a year—in which he used excessive drinking and dangerous escapades to compensate for unimaginative teaching and a college full of boorish 'hearties'—he abandoned his degree and fled to friends in Oxford where he spent the next ten months recruiting and raising money for a six-month undergraduate expedition to explore the flora and fauna of Sarawak, a British protectorate in north-west Borneo. The success of this expedition under Harrisson's leadership paved the way for his selection as the ornithologist on what was planned as a year-long expedition to the South Pacific islands of the New Hebrides led by an Oxford zoologist, John Baker. While in Oxford he lived a riotous and bohemian life. Reacting with disgust to the notorious declaration by the privileged young gentlemen of the Oxford Union that they would 'under no circumstances fight for king and country', Harrisson published a wildly polemical tract lashing out against what he saw as timidity and apathy among a post-war generation too bored and ineffectual to fight for anything at all.[15] In the New Hebrides, after a passionate affair with Baker's wife, Zita, Harrisson stayed on alone exploring, living in close contact with the native people, and shifting from ornithology to anthropology. When he came back

13. Helen Macdonald, ' "What makes you a scientist is the way you look at things": ornithology and the observer 1930–1955', *Studies in the History and Philosophy of the Biological and Biomedical Science,* 33, 2002, 53–77; D. Matless, *Landscape and Englishness,* 1998, 259; J. Huxley, preface to *Mass-Observation,* 1937; Tom Harrisson, *Britain Revisited,* 1961, 20.
14. DNB entry on Nicholson.
15. Tom Harrisson, *Letter to Oxford,* 1933.

to England in December 1935, after two and a half years in the Pacific, he immediately set about preparing a new expedition to study 'stone-age man' in New Guinea. But he was also already thinking about doing anthropology among the British, and when the manuscript of his book on the New Hebrides was complete he went north to go native in working-class Bolton.

Like Harrisson, Madge was also a child of empire: he was born in South Africa in 1912 where his father, who had been a colonel in the Boer War, had subsequently worked in the administration organizing white immigration before returning to fight in France, where he was killed in 1916.[16] Educated at Winchester, Madge took to writing poetry, read his way into contemporary literary debate, anthropology, and psychology, before going up to Cambridge in 1931, where communist politics and Auden's poetry turned his world upside down. On the fringes of the revolution in English studies wrought by Leavis and I. A. Richards, Madge imbibed Richard's belief that 'poetry is capable of saving us, it is a perfectly possible way of overcoming chaos',[17] and fell in love with the poet Kathleen Raine, four years his senior. Quixotically, he undertook to rescue Raine from an unhappy marriage, abandoning his studies, and his selection as the next secretary of the Communist Party branch, to elope with her. By June 1934, still aged only 21, he had become a father. For a time the couple got by with occasional fees for reviewing and financial support from Madge's mother, until T.S. Eliot, who rated Madge's poems, persuaded a journalist friend to find him a job as a reporter on the *Daily Mirror*. It was this job, Madge later remarked, which brought him into contact with 'the real concerns of life'.[18] At the same time, early in 1936, the Madges moved into an elegant 18th-century house in Blackheath (6 Grotes Buildings) which was to become MO's first London headquarters. Alongside his work as a reporter, Madge wrote poetry—*The Disappearing Castle*, his first volume of poems, was published in May 1937—and read Darwin and Marx.[19] In Blackheath the Madges found congenial, like-minded friends, including Humphrey Jennings and his wife Cecily, and the documentary film-maker Stuart Legg

---

16. The biographical details in this paragraph are taken from CM, 'Autobiography', unless otherwise noted.
17. Nick Hubble, *Mass-Observation and Everyday Life*, 2006, 40.
18. CM, interviewed by Calder, March 1976.
19. CM, 'Autobiography', 62.

and his wife Margaret. This was the core of the group whose meeting Harrisson attended in January 1937.

Upper middle class and public-school educated, Madge and Harrisson both approached the investigation of working-class, and indeed lower middle-class, life as social explorers venturing into alien territory. The fact that both had been born outside Britain and that neither had a secure income of their own may have contributed to their capacity to view this alien territory without the crasser prejudices of their class, but there the similarity ended. The approaches that the two men brought to the task of social exploration could scarcely have been more different.

III

It was the behaviour of the press during the abdication crisis of 1936 that, Madge recalled, 'precipitated' him 'in the direction of Mass-Observation'. For months, protected by a press embargo, the constitutional crisis over Edward VIII's desire to marry a divorcee had mounted behind closed doors. When the embargo broke down, ten days before the abdication, the claims made by rival newspapers about public feeling for and against the king were manifestly products of editorial invention. For Madge, personally involved as one of the reporters waiting outside Mrs Simpson's house, this 'massive piece of falsification' provided an object lesson in how the masses were being misrepresented and excluded.[20] At the same time, by destabilizing the monarchy (the central symbolic pillar of the British state) the crisis held a deeper subversive potential, a potential surely enhanced by the coincidental burning down, a few days before the abdication, of the Crystal Palace (built for the Great Exhibition of 1851 and symbol of Victorian ideas of progress). The destruction of two such icons of British identity within hardly more than a week could, Madge believed, hardly fail to stir up hidden depths in the national psyche and lay open to challenge the disempowering assumptions and superstitions (like those surrounding kingship) that held the masses in thrall.[21]

During the autumn of 1936 the Madges had been meeting with friends in their Blackheath house, discussing how best to discover 'the unconscious

20. CM, interviewed by Stanley, 26 May 1978.
21. CM, *New Statesman*, 2 January 1937.

fears and wishes of the masses.'[22] As well as the Jennings and the Leggs, the group included Guy Hunter, a Communist friend from Madge's Cambridge days, and David Gascoyne, a poet who, like Humphrey Jennings, had been on the organizing committee of London's sensational Surrealist Exhibition in June 1936.[23] Surrealist techniques for probing the individual unconscious could, the group believed, be adapted to access, and potentially to liberate, the repressed wishes of the masses. The process—apparently random and merely coincidental, by which, for the Parisian surrealist, André Breton, an individual might stumble upon an *objet trouvé* which embodied his unconscious desires—could also be seen to be operating at a collective level. Themselves experts in the manipulation of images, Jennings and Madge, film-maker and poet, sought webs of hidden meanings embodied in symbols or images surfacing from the collective unconscious; images which, Madge tried to explain, not altogether helpfully, were to be understood as 'something between an idea and a sensation. It is more vivid than an abstract idea; it is more intangible than a concrete sensation.'[24] There was a poetry, a visual collage, to be found even in the juxtaposition of sex, scandal, and crime on the pages of the popular press, put together by layout men with an intuitive feeling for the 'mass-wish'.[25] Madge, swept along in what his wife described as a state of 'imaginative poetic exaltation', saw in the 'Crystal Palace–Abdication symbolic situation' an opportunity to probe 'the ultra-repressed condition' of the British people.[26] Geoffrey Pyke, a Cambridge anthropologist, expressed a similar thought—although in rather less exalted language—in a letter to the *New Statesman*, and it was Madge's response to this that alerted Harrisson to the existence of the Blackheath group.[27]

How to proceed? Madge had earlier played with ideas of reproducing versions of the Blackheath group as 'Coincidence Clubs...in colleges, factories and localities' to tease out the 'popular poetry' embedded in newspapers and advertising.[28] By the end of December the group had prepared a questionnaire intended to explore 'scientifically' the 'mechanism of repression'.[29] Alongside questions on the abdication and the Crystal Palace, volunteers were

22. CM, 'Press, radio and social consciousness', in C. Day-Lewis (ed.), *The Mind in Chains*, 1937; Kathleen Raine, *The Land Unknown*, 81; Hubble, *Mass-Observation and Everyday Life*, 77.
23. Kevin Jackson, *Humphrey Jennings*, 2004, 159.
24. *Mass-Observation*, 38.
25. CM, 'The Press and Social Consciousness', *Left Review*, 5, 1937, 153–4.
26. CM, *New Statesman*, 2 January 1937; Raine, *The Land Unknown*, 83.
27. *New Statesman*, 12 December 1936.
28. Hubble, *Mass-Observation and Everyday Life*, 77.
29. CM, *New Statesman*, 2 January 1937.

asked to collect spontaneous responses to questions such as: 'What are your superstitions?'; 'Are you religious?'; 'Do you...hate your Father...your Mother...your boss?'; 'What are you frightened of?'; 'Do you welcome or shrink from the contact by touch or smell of your fellow men?'[30] The responses, if any, have not survived, but the psychoanalytically inspired agenda was to be central to the issues that MO was later to raise with its panel of volunteers. Less important for the future, but central to Madge and Jennings' thinking at the time, was the notion that the collective unconscious could be accessed via the 'images' which, they believed, could be found arising seemingly coincidentally in the minds of disparate individuals, and in search of this they asked the first volunteers to keep a record of each day's 'dominant image'. 'The observer', Madge explained, 'is to ask himself at the end of each day what image has been dominant in it. The image should, if possible, be one which has forced itself on him and which has confirmed its importance by recurrence of some kind.'[31] The images that came in, like the dreams that volunteers were also asked to record, were no doubt suffused with meaning for the individuals concerned—one of them, indeed, welcomed the process as a substitute for the psychoanalysis that he could not afford to pay for—but 'collective image' came there none, and, as one puzzled respondent remarked, it was very hard to see what public significance his private images might have.[32] Herbert Howarth, a leading light among Oxford's student literati who was swept up in the excitement of the enterprise, did his best to find confirmation of his private images in newspapers and public events.[33] He also

---

30. 'Questionnaire', December 1936, FR A4. A circular sent to members of the panel asked them to 'send in questionnaires' by the end May ('Mass-Observation Circular', April 1937, FR A4).
31. CM, 'Magic and Materialism', *Left Review*, February 1937, 34.
32. Munro to Madge, 7 May 1937; Bradfield, 'Notes on Image of the Day', TC 28/1/A. See also Jeremy MacClancey, 'Mass-Observation, Surrealism, Social Anthropology: a Present-Day Assessment', *New Formations*, 44, Autumn 2001, 97–8.
33. Howarth, daily tabulation of 'Image' and 'Confirmation', 10 January to 4 February 1937, TC 28/1/A. On Howarth see John Waller, 'Disillusionment', *Poetry Review*, April 1940: 'Over all played the influence of Herbert Howarth. A slender, dark haired man with something of the detached air of a critic he had come to Oxford [in 1936] with a scholarship to Christ Church. He was the most alive of anybody, and it was his fire and energy that kept intellectual Oxford awake...an intellectual daring beyond his contemporaries...Through his inspiration Oxford accepted Auden and the moderns, Paul Eluard, Surrealism, French films, Kafka, Deanna Durbin (!) and Mass-Observation...In his last year, after dragging the intellectuals panting after him for the previous three, he surprised everybody by attacking Auden, getting a first, marrying, and leaving for Egypt as lecturer in English at the Faud I university in Cairo.' Howarth spent most of the war in Middle East and later held academic posts in United States. Before his early death in 1971 he had published books on Yeats, Joyce, Eliot, and Shakespeare (Obituary, *The Times*, 17 July 1971).

organized a group of enthusiasts from the English Club to pool their 'dominant images' in a collective poem capturing, he claimed, 'the sense of decay and imminent doom which characterises contemporary Oxford.' The publication of this poem did much to open the new organization to ridicule among the uninitiated or the merely sceptical, and it ends in triumphant cliché:

> And on our heads the crimes of our buried fathers
> Burst in a hurricane and the rebels shout.[34]

The most important request to the early volunteers was to write a detailed diary on the 12th of each month, starting in February 1937; a date chosen because the coronation was due to occur on May 12. Reflecting on responses to the first of these 'day surveys', in February 1937, Madge and Jennings found in them an authenticity of language and a poetic quality quite absent from the self-consciously literary work of proletarian novelists (or indeed the Oxford students); qualities which continue to impress readers of the MO diaries. But their misleading presentation of this writing as predominantly proletarian belongs to a conventional 1930s upper class leftist romanticism which continued for some time to befuddle Madge's understanding of *whose* voices were actually being empowered by MO to 'speak for themselves, about themselves'.[35] It was not until the war years that MO publicly acknowledged that its volunteer panellists were predominantly drawn from the educated middle class, not from the proletarian masses who had left school at 14.

IV

Despite being impressed by the intellectual brilliance of Madge's circle, Harrisson had no time for most of their ideas. Drafting the statement of aims with Madge during January 1937, he felt under 'constant strain', resisting the influence not only of Jennings, but also of Madge's Communist friend, Guy Hunter, who, Harrisson suspected, wanted to use the emerging organization as an instrument of Communist propaganda.[36] One of MO's great virtues, he explained to the anthropologist Malinowski later that year,

---

34. CM, 'Oxford Collective Poem', *New Verse*, 25, May 1937.
35. CM and Jennings, 'They Speak for Themselves. Mass-Observation and Social Narrative', *Life and Letters Today*, 9 February 1937. See also *First Year's Work*, 1938, 68–79.
36. TH to CM, January 1937, reproduced in CM, 'Autobiography', 68.

was that 'though our methods may be amateur our intentions are honest, and, what is even more unusual in these difficult time[s], unMarxist.'[37] Harrisson, who had read neither Marx, Freud, nor even Darwin at the time, was proud of having developed his own 'scientific approach' independently, working it out for himself in the course of his various expeditions.[38] He was not going to compromise what he saw as scientific empiricism with any Marxist or surrealist mumbo-jumbo. Rather than allow that to happen, he told Madge, he would abandon the joint project and pursue his own line independently: 'simply and solely a British anthropology'.[39]

The nature of Harrisson's anthropological stance was clearly expressed in the title of his book on the New Hebrides—*Savage Civilisation*—the publication of which coincided with the launching of MO. The first step for the explorer of an alien culture was to abandon 'our belief that we are the only civilised ones'.[40] 'Are you so superior to these savages?' he teased the privileged white boys, lecturing at Harrow: 'If you were put in their environment you would be stupid, ludicrous, not worth hitting on the head. You couldn't make a fire, a house, a comb…[or] clean your teeth with sand. What good are you?'[41] Attacking 'the anthropologist's custom to detach his daily life from the people among whom he is working, to eat his own foods', Harrisson insisted that the only reliable route to understanding an alien culture was to immerse oneself in it, to live it: 'Dancing and war are the Malekulan approaches to understanding. So it is necessary to dance and to fight before you may understand fully.'[42] Rather than emphasizing his outsider status by paying native informants to 'tell their stories' and scribbling them down in notebooks, the anthropologist should go native: 'Most of the time I wrote down nothing, being too busy eating, sleeping, drinking *kava*, living hard and good until I became almost part of the landscape.'[43] Making himself as unobtrusive as possible, Harrisson could watch and learn—a birdwatcher's approach to observation. It was never enough to ask people about their beliefs and values; only by direct observation of behaviour could one hope to understand how a culture operated in practice. 'What oceans of error we should have been spared if those who wrote

37. TH to Malinowski, 31 November 1937, BMpap.
38. TH to CM, 18 January 1940, 4–5, Org&Hist 1/1.
39. TH to CM, January 1937, reproduced in CM, 'Autobiography', 68.
40. Harrisson, *Savage Civilisation*, 343.
41. Heimann, *Most Offending Soul*, 135.
42. Harrisson, *Savage Civilisation*, 342–3.
43. Heimann, *Most Offending Soul*, 84.

about the "savage," primitive mentality, had done more primitive living.'[44] Summarizing his approach ten years later, thinking as much about his work in Britain as in the Pacific, Harrisson wrote:

> Much of what I have seen and heard I would not have seen and heard (1) if I had *not* been there a long time; (2) if I had *not also* won and rewon the confidence of most of the people... (3) if I had *not* shown a positive sympathy with their culture and an *active* participation in a large part of it; (4) If I *had* been visibly interested in all I saw and heard; (5) If I *had* displayed any prejudices antipathetic to their culture and race.[45]

At the core of Harrisson's anthropology, and his politics, was a refusal to essentialize human differences, whether of race or of class (gender, however, was another matter). He had no sympathy with the agonized introspection about the 'class difficulty' paraded in *The Road to Wigan Pier* by that other public-school explorer of the northern working class, George Orwell. Going native in Bolton, Harrisson insisted that there was nothing in his upbringing, education, or accent to prevent him from mixing on equal terms with working-class people, and he was never more at ease than when drinking in masculine company, whether in Malekula, Bolton, or the East End of London.[46]

But for all his capacity for living rough and mixing in easy companionship with the poor or the primitive, Harrisson never stopped thinking of himself as part of the social elite, whose duty it was to provide leadership to the less privileged. Hierarchy, and what he took to be the innate desire of individuals to rise up whatever social ladders their culture provided, was a natural part of the human condition, as apparent in the bizarre status gradations operating among Harrow schoolboys as in the accumulation of pigs in the gift economy of the Pacific islanders or, he was later to observe, in the upward-striving individualism characteristic of the British working class. In the words of his biographer, Harrisson 'had no wish for an egalitarian society. He liked hierarchy and was comfortable with inherited privilege. He felt that the privileged classes, of which he was a member, had a duty to lead', but to do so disinterestedly and intelligently. Loathing the rapacious arrogance of colonial planter society, he had found no problem in reconciling

44. Harrisson, *Savage Civilisation*, 342.
45. Heimann, *Most Offending Soul*, 256.
46. Tom Harrisson, *A World Within. A Borneo Story*, 1959, 159–60; Walter Hood, memoir, 1974, 15, Personnel/Hood; Nick Stanley, 'Extra Dimension', CNAA PhD thesis, 1981, 204–5, 207.

his anthropological stance with a six-month tour of duty as the acting colonial district agent on a remote Pacific island. Back in Britain, making democracy work was, for Harrisson, not a question of abolishing hierarchy, but of fostering intelligent leadership. To lead well, writes his biographer, 'leaders needed to be in active dialogue with the common people, to learn from them their hopes and fears, and to teach them better ways of thinking about the world and coping with its challenges.'[47]

V

While the Liberal and the Communist might have radically different ideas about the ultimate goal, they could agree on the urgent need to raise the consciousness of the masses. For Harrisson, MO's role was not itself to act as the educator, but to find out how the masses thought so that those who aspired to enlighten them might be better able to connect with their actual hopes and fears. How far, at this time, Madge looked to the Communist Party to undertake this task is unclear. Leninist notions of the vanguard party must have sat uneasily alongside the project of inducing 'self-realisation' among the masses through their participation in the therapeutic practice of mass observation. Like so many 1930s intellectuals, Madge inhabited a zone where Marx and Freud intersected, and his attempts to reconcile the two were no more successful than anyone else's. Where, as they talked during January 1937, the two men found common ground was, as Madge put it when announcing MO's formation to the readers of *Left Review*, in 'the application of materialism to superstition'.[48]

It was 'the sway of superstition in the midst of science', they argued, that lay at the core of the contemporary problem; the sinister symbiotic relationships being established between technologies made possible by modern science and an undiminished, or even enhanced, tendency of the mass of the population 'to ascribe phenomena which admit of a natural explanation to occult or supernatural causes.' Advertising agencies and the press were employing 'the best empirical anthropologists and psychologists in the country' to target their propaganda 'at that part of the human mind in which the superstitious elements predominate.' Mass literacy, which potentially

47. Heimann, *Most Offending Soul*, 125.
48. CM, 'Magic and Materialism', *Left Review*, February 1937, 33–4.

opened the way to an age of science and reason, was being subverted by 'staffs of technical experts' hired to use the vehicles of mass entertainment—radio, film, newspapers—to bypass resistance to more open forms of propaganda, bringing 'to final perfection' techniques for manipulating 'the superstitiousness of a literate but suggestible majority'.[49] In Germany the fascist propaganda machine linked atavistic racist beliefs to the military power provided by modern physics, chemistry, and engineering. And as crisis followed crisis, confronting humanity with the most suicidal achievement of modern science—the threatened combination of aeroplane, high explosive, and poison gas—the masses were losing whatever faith they had ever had in science, progress, and democracy, retreating into political apathy and fatalism, a state of mind readily exploited by that paradigmatic growth industry of the inter-war years: newspaper astrology.

It was against this unholy alliance of science and superstition that Harrisson and Madge pitched the MO project. Just as the voyage of the *Beagle* had enabled Darwin to lay the empirical foundations for the theory of evolution which brought the study of man into the realm of science, so MO's 'anthropology of ourselves' would bring into the light of scientific enquiry the facts of everyday social existence which until now had been known only through the 'the intuition of men of genius', writers and artists whose grasp of the mass life was 'to a human science of the future what cookery is to chemistry.'[50] One thing that facilitated cooperation between the poet and the anthropologist was the fact that both men, while aspiring to a science of society, saw the artist as having a vital role to play. Citing the 19th-century novel's 'illumination of the inner man' as 'a pre-scientific parallel to the successive discoveries about the unconscious mind made in the course of Freudian psycho-analysis', they argued that the role of the artist was to lay out terrain which science would eventually colonize:

> Whenever it becomes historically necessary for man to view the world in a new way, artists will arise who are sensitive to the change and will display to man the world which science will then proceed to classify and interpret.

On this view it was absurd for 'post-Freudian surrealists and painters' to try to compete with psycho-analysis now that Freud, however controversially, had brought the inner man into the realm of science. It was as social realists,

49. *Mass-Observation*, 19, 20, 28.
50. *Mass-Observation*, 10.

not surrealists, that post-Freudian painters could best contribute to the growth of human knowledge, converging with science on 'the field of human behaviour which lies immediately before our eyes.'[51] This was an analysis which spoke more to the ways in which Harrisson was to seek to involve artists in the MO project, than it did to the surrealist origins of Madge's ideas about uncovering the popular poetry of the collective unconscious.

Although the common ground was substantial, the contrast between the two men's approaches to social exploration remained stark. Drafting a radio broadcast about MO in June 1939, Harrisson summarized his own understanding of the difference:

> Charles is a poet...interested in people's feelings, what goes on in their minds and for this purpose the system of Mass-Observers is very useful. But I started as an ornithologist, a bird-watcher and I went on to be an anthropologist, a man-watcher. My interest was to describe as accurately as possible how people behave.[52]

During the early months of 1937, while Madge sat in his well-appointed house in Blackheath, sifting through growing piles of material from the panel, searching for ways to understand the poetry of everyday life, Harrisson was toughing it out in grimy Bolton, building a team of full-time observers trained in what he liked to refer to as 'objective' fieldwork. Three years later, as the collaboration between the two men approached its final breakdown, Harrisson looked back to these origins: 'Does it all go back to a difference in approach...between the artist and the scientist? Between the panel of anonymous people writing in to the man in his home, and the team of anonymous observers going out to see, describe, analyse.' While 'artist' versus 'scientist' was an oversimplification of their respective stances, their differences were certainly profound. But it was precisely these differences between their initial starting points that made their collaboration, while it lasted, so productive. There was plenty for them to learn from each other.

What complicated the mutual learning process had less to do with the difference between the poet and the anthropologist, or the Liberal and the Communist, than with differences of temperament. Within days of their first meeting, Harrisson, in a characteristic rush and jumble of words,

---

51. *Mass-Observation*, 26–8.
52. 'They Speak for Themselves', 1 June 1939, 4, FR A26. The first sentence is crossed out in the draft script.

unloaded his anxieties about his capacity to work cooperatively in a letter to Madge:

> I am . . . a fiendishly energetic, jumping person, used to organising everything I do for myself, and never working under anyone, always free . . . All the untamed horses are waving my blood, Bolton, to my book, to myself. I'm not ambitious or power-wanting. I just believe in life. How can we work that in and keep together? . . . It is useless for me to try and play down myself for long; I can't help it, and it is my up and up that makes me pamphlet, explore, work in cotton mills. It's lousy in me, I suppose. Work it out . . . I say all this to you as the diplomat and correlator! It is not confidential. . . . It should be filed against me![53]

And it was. Harrisson may have been 'the most offending soul alive',[54] but Madge could be difficult in his own way. If Harrisson's denial of being power-hungry should be taken with a pinch of salt, then so too should Madge's reputation as a gentle soul.[55] 'Diffident and self-effacing' he might appear, but, in the words of a post-war academic colleague, the 'charming and tentatively friendly' face that he presented to the world 'hid a passionate and impulsively radical nature'.[56] In the contest of wills, as we shall see, he could be as self-absorbed as Harrisson. And, if Madge complained of his partner's insecurity and irascibility, Harrisson for his part had reason to complain that Madge allowed his over-complicated love life to disrupt his work for MO, leaving work unfinished and staff unsupervised.

The Jennings–Harrisson confrontation that had marked the beginning of MO provided a foretaste of the tempestuous relationship between Harrisson and Madge which stood at the organization's centre during its first three years until, finally, their differences blew them apart. From 1940 MO was to become Harrisson's property and project. But it was not a project that Harrisson could ever have created by himself and, without Madge's involvement, nothing like MO would ever have emerged.

---

53. TH to CM, January 1937, reproduced in CM, 'Autobiography', 68–9.
54. Heimann's title is taken from Henry V: 'But if it be a sin to covet honour/I am the most offending soul alive'.
55. 'A gentle, quiet man with a marked public school accent,' recalled one of the early MO staff (Brian Barefoot, memoir, 1979, Personnel/Barefoot).
56. A. H. Halsey, *A History of Sociology in Britain*, 2004, 22, 24.

2

Harrisson's Worktown

I

When Tom Harrisson returned from the South Pacific in December 1935, he was already thinking of applying anthropological techniques to the study of industrial society in England.[1] Bolton—or 'Worktown' as it was to be named in Mass-Observation (MO) publications—was suggested to him by John Hilton, a popular broadcaster and journalist as well as professor of industrial relations at Cambridge, who had been born into the Bolton working class. The two men hit it off, Hilton enjoying Harrisson's radio talk about the role of the pig in Malekula's gift economy, and Harrisson impressed by the older man's readiness to engage non-judgementally with working-class culture— demonstrated in a 1936 pamphlet on the pools based on letters from working men.[2] Harrisson was all the more responsive to Hilton's suggestion because Bolton was also the home town of William Lever, founder of Unilever, whose economic empire touched even the New Hebrides ('buying copra, selling soap'), providing a pleasing link between Harrisson's anthropological efforts at home and abroad.[3] Perhaps it was more than that. It was rumoured that his original project had been an exposé of Unilever's profiteering, but that the manuscript was so libellous that it failed to find a publisher.[4] The story is plausible, and it seems to be confirmed by an unsigned and inadequately dated letter in the Worktown archive, probably written by Harrisson imme- diately after he had finished work on the manuscript of *Savage Civilization* in

1. Heimann, *Most Offending Soul*, 113.
2. 'Why I Go In For the Pools. By Tom, Dick and Harry-also Peggy, Joan and Kate. Letters writ- ten to John Hilton,' 1936; John Hilton, 'Pigs and Battleships', *New Statesman*, 16 May 1936; E. Nixon, *John Hilton*, 1946, 258; Mathew Hilton, DNB entry on John Hilton.
3. Harrisson, *A World Within*, 159; Harrisson, *Britain Revisited*, 25–6, 86.
4. Thomas, interviewed by Stanley, 26 November 1979, tape in MO Archive.

late July 1936,[5] in which he set out an agenda for research on the organization of the food trade in Bolton, including 'where the food comes from and the profit process along the line... The influence of individual combines like Unilever, etc, in creating artificial price conditions.' The letter was addressed to 'Jack', who was being asked to do much of the research, and informed him that 'Albert' was 'collaborating in a book I'm doing for Heinemann's on the whole idea.' Jack Fagan and Albert Smith were, as we shall see, two of Harrisson's earliest collaborators in Bolton.[6]

Whatever his original purpose Harrisson quickly came to think of Bolton as the archetypal industrial town, cradle of the industrial revolution, 'representative of the industrial life-pattern which prevails for the majority of people in Britain.'[7] This was not strictly true, since, like other Lancashire textile towns, Bolton had an unusually high proportion of women workers. But for bad housing, poor health, air pollution, and a largely absent middle class, Bolton was characteristic enough of the industrial north.[8] 'The ugliness', wrote J. B. Priestley, 'is so complete that it is almost exhilarating.'[9] Southern visitors were appalled by the 'perpetual delicate mist of soot', which would leave a visible layer on a sheet of paper left by an open window within an hour. Even an observer who had grown up in the hardly salubrious environment of a Durham mining village found the grime created by hundreds of factory chimneys hard to tolerate: 'You always felt as if you should be washing your hands and face'.[10]

Harrisson arrived in Bolton in August or early September 1936, and spent several months working as a lorry driver, shop assistant, labourer, ice-cream man, and newspaper reporter, while passing his evenings 'at the fireside of prosperous Lever relatives, feeling slightly guilty but softly elated' by his own ability to vault the gulfs of class with nothing more than a sprinkling of eau de cologne to disguise the labours of the day.[11] Most useful

5. Heimann, *Most Offending Soul*, 120.
6. Letter to Jack, unsigned. Pencilled on the top '29 July', W 29/A.
7. 'M-O in Bolton: A Social Experiment', 2, W 1/C.
8. Sam Davies and Bob Morley, *County borough election results, England and Wales, 1919–1938: a comparative analysis. Vol. 1. Barnsley—Bournemouth*, 1999, 465.
9. J. B. Priestley, *English Journey*, 1934, 262.
10. 'The Voter's Skull', W6/E; Barefoot memoir, 1979; Hood memoir, 1974.
11. Harrisson, *World Within*, 159. In 1942 Harrisson wrote that he had been working in Bolton for six months before January 1937 when he first met Madge: 'trying to pick up the threads of mass life in Britain in much the same way as one does when visiting a little known country' (*The Pub and the People*, 7). This is difficult to square with Heimann's account of his movements in 1936: she does not place him definitively in Bolton until October, three months before he met Madge.

among the 'Lever relatives' was W. F. Tillotson, husband of one of William Lever's nieces and, as the Liberal owner of the main local newspaper, an invaluable ally for Harrisson throughout his time in Bolton.[12] If he was, in 1936, simultaneously working on the exposé of Unilever profiteering, this was espionage of a high order. The beginning of November found him living in a Bolton pub and working 11 hours a day in a cotton mill,[13] and by the time he met Charles Madge in January 1937 the project initially known as 'The South Lancashire Cultural Survey' was beginning to take shape.[14]

The first need was for money. Since quitting Cambridge in 1931 Harrisson had received little money from his wealthy father and was eventually disinherited altogether in favour of his younger brother on his father's death in February 1937. After returning to Britain he had scraped a living with journalism and radio talks, and at the outset of the Bolton project all he had was the income from *Savage Civilisation*, published in January 1937.[15] This was soon supplemented by Gollancz, who provided £500 in monthly instalments as an advance on four planned books dealing with politics, religion, pubs, and holidays.[16] Income from publishers alone, however, could not have sustained the enterprise, and Harrisson raised at least another £1,000 from a variety of sources, most of it from two Lancashire industrialists, Sir Thomas Barlow and Sir Ernest Simon, both of whom were leading figures in the non-partisan social reformism characteristic of much 1930s 'middle opinion'. Barlow was active in Political and Economic Planning; and Simon, a one-time Liberal MP and treasurer of Manchester University, had co-founded the Association for Education in Citizenship to promote the teaching of citizenship in schools in 1934.[17] By March 1937 Harrisson had raised enough money to rent a terraced house in Davenport Street and to pay living expenses (but not wages) to five investigators who, he claimed, with characteristic exaggeration, 'had given up other jobs' to work full-time in Bolton.[18]

---

12. Paul Harris, 'Social leadership and Social Attitudes in Bolton, 1919 to 1939', Lancaster PhD, 1973, 6, 14, 445; TH to Julian, March 1938, JTpap.
13. Heimann, *Most Offending Soul*, 124.
14. The earliest contemporary reference I have found to the existence of a group of researchers under Harrisson's direction in Bolton is in a letter to TH from W.J. Havelock Davidson, Vicar and Rural Dean of Bolton, dated 3 January 1937, W 1/E.
15. TH conversation with Hood, 4 May 1972.
16. Lee to Wainwright, 24 April 1976; Barefoot memoir, 1939, 56.
17. TH to Collins, 26 February 1940, Org&Hist 3/10.
18. TH to CM, 18 January 1940, 8, Org&Hist 1/1; *First Year's Work*, 7. In fact at least three of the five were unemployed at the time that he recruited them.

Three names were listed alongside Harrisson's on the notepaper of the South Lancashire Cultural Survey: Albert Smith, Walter Hood and Joe Wilcock. Smith, son of an insurance agent, had grown up in Bolton, gone to Oxford on a scholarship, graduated in history in 1925, and subsequently returned to Bolton where he worked as a Workers' Educational Association (WEA) tutor, describing himself as an anthropologist and running such invitingly entitled classes as 'Striptease to Shakespeare. An anthropological study of the Drama'.[19] Smith had represented the WEA on the Bolton Unemployed Welfare Association—a charitable organization set up by the local great and good to provide 'for the best use of leisure time' for the unemployed—and ran classes in the Association's club house.[20] In the autumn of 1937 Smith launched a class on the 'History of the People of Bolton from 1900 to 1937', announced—very much in tune with MO—as an opportunity 'to work out a new way of studying ourselves.' 'History is criticism,' Smith told the introductory meeting, instructing the students that rather than reading 'vast and dull books about the industrial revolution' they would bring their own life experiences to the class. 'No one', he said 'has ever written a short history of the English people—and it was up to them to do so.'[21] Whether or not Smith had co-authored an unpublished book with Harrisson in 1936, what seems certain is that the existence in Bolton of a group of working-class men familiarized by Smith's teaching with anthropological ideas played an important part in the early stages of the MO project: it was one reason, Harrisson wrote at the time, why he chose Bolton as the site for his 'anthropology at home'.[22] Smith himself seems to have been an opinionated and curmudgeonly anarchist, and he soon fell out

19. Bolton WEA leaflet, 9 September 1937, TC 36/1/A. I am indebted to the archivists of the Goldsmith's Company (who gave Smith his scholarship) and of Jesus College library for information about Smith.
20. Bolton Unemployed Welfare Association, minutes, 13 February, 17 April 1934, 3 September 1936, 18 February, 5 August 1937, 10 February 1938, Bolton Archives, FZ/36.
21. Bolton WEA leaflet, 9 September 1937; Hood's report of WEA meeting, 22 September 1937; Taylor's report on the Bolton Unemployed Welfare Association, 23 November 1937. See also Zita Baker's report on the working-class composition of the class, quite unlike the adult education classes she was familiar with in Oxfordshire, 2 November 1937; all in TC 36/1/A.
22. '… in consequence [of Smith's classes] there were in Bolton a considerable number of people who had a really astounding knowledge of anthropology and psychology…They offered to help, and this was one of several reasons that caused me to select Bolton …' (TH, 'M-O and the WEA', *The Highway*, December 1937).

with Harrisson,[23] but several of his admirers continued to work with
MO, including two unemployed men: Peter Jackson, who 'made a special
study of how people use their leisure on Saturday afternoons',[24] and Eric
Letchford, a one-time iron miller and a militant atheist who was happy
to put his exceptional capacity for beer consumption at the disposal of
MO's work on pub culture.[25] Other members of Smith's WEA classes
who participated included Tom Honeyford, a former spinner now running a small beer-house, who was described by Harrisson as 'a constant
helper';[26] and Tom Binks, an ex-Catholic, atheist piecer who wrote some
vivid accounts of his 'long, slow, dreary' wasted days in the mill.[27]

None of these men, however, worked full-time for MO, and Harrisson
looked elsewhere for people to lead the main areas of research. Walter Hood,
five years his senior, was an experienced Labour Party activist. He had been
born in a Durham mining family and started work as a miner himself before
making his name as a socialist orator. The village clubbed together to send
him to the Quaker-run college, Fircroft. A classic autodidact, Hood was
proud of his own achievements and believed passionately in the capacity of
working people to produce their own poetry, literature, and, in his case,
drawing and painting. While studying at Fircroft he also took classes at the
Birmingham School of Art, going on to Oxford for two years at Ruskin,
where he learned to mix with left-wing public school boys, some of whom
joined him during vacations in the Clarion Rural Campaign—a Labour
Party offshoot—to preach socialism to agricultural workers. He also drew
cartoons for the student newspaper *Isis* and was taken up as a proletarian
artist by the painter Julian Trevelyan. Down and out after he left Ruskin in
1936, he spent some time living off Trevelyan and his circle in London,

23. TH note on card, 2 December 1937: 'LT reports Albert Smith, WEA, as discussing public
schools in class, and saying: "In Bolton we only know one and he's a bloody fool. But that
doesn't mean they all are." He also said that the Bolton unemployed could raise a rowing eight
to lick Oxford. (Typically irresponsible remarks.)' TC 36/1/A. See also Leslie Taylor's amusing
account of one of his classes, 23 November 1937, TC 36/1/A; and Smith's rumoured response
to a police request to see his identity card in July 1940: 'I haven't got one, don't want one, and
have no intention of getting one' (GT [Geoffrey Thomas], 'Spy story: Bolton', 4 July 1940, W
52/A).
24. Draft for *First Year's Work*, 39, BMpap; Bolton WEA leaflet, 9 September 1937, TC 36/1/A.
25. EL, 'Class distinctions in our street', 21 September 1937, W 44/B; letter from Letchford, *The
Bolton Citizen*, March 1938; EL, 'Survey of pubs', 7 May 1937, W 3/B; Calder and Sheridan,
Speak for Yourself, 1984, 16–19, 44.
26. *First Year's Work*, 27.
27. See Bink's Day Surveys for February, March, and April 1937, reproduced in *May the Twelfth,
Mass Observation Day-Surveys 1937 by over two hundred observers*, 1937, 351ff.

before taking off for the summer to France with an Oxford student he had
met on the Clarion Rural Campaign and who had come home with him
'to see how miners lived'. The two friends made plans to spend the winter
months writing a book on 'the English in the 1930s', for which Hood
would do the illustrations.[28] Looking for an advance to live on, they took
the idea to Gollancz, who put them in touch with Harrisson:

> And then he... took me off for one of these Soho meals, and I sat there, not
> necessarily picking me nose and eating it, but just a little bit 'what was all this
> about'. [Harrisson] talked about the art work that could be done... and the
> effect [that MO would have] on my future... He was very anxious to bring
> me in and I, after about two or three hours, agreed to join.[29]

While Hood, with his background in Labour politics, was to lead the work
on political life in Bolton, Joe Wilcock, a working-class Christian activist,
had already been recruited to run the parallel project on religion. Born in
1895 to a weaving family, Wilcock had grown up in Lancashire and been
apprenticed to a blacksmith.[30] At some point he broke free from life as a
wage earner to become 'Brother Joe', 'one of the small sect of tramp preachers who have for years walked the highways and byways of Britain, taking
no thought for the morrow, sleeping in casual wards and haystacks, preach-
ing a social gospel.'[31] For several years he worked in London's East End as
warden of a hostel rescuing destitute young boys from crime and prostitu-
tion, and it was there that Harrisson—helping out during school holidays
while at Harrow—had first got to know him.[32] Some of Wilcock's colleagues, who did not share his Christian faith, found him introverted and
oversensitive, but he seems to have inspired confidence in the sectarian
world of Bolton Christianity.[33]

---

28. TH conversion with Hood, 4 May 1972; Hood memoir, 1974; and the transcript of his taped
    memoir (1974). The painter Graham Bell, who took a pretty jaundiced view of the whole MO
    enterprise, dismissed Hood's drawings as 'the sort of work which would make even the Daily
    Worker blanch a bit.' He also thought Hood went on at excessive length about his own pre-
    cocity as a 'boy orator': 'he tells me every day several times that when he was 18 he was union
    secretary over 1800 men ...' (Bell to Popham, 5 May 1938, GBpap). On the Clarion Rural
    Campaign see material in MRC 292/69/1.
29. Hood memoir, 1974.
30. Census of England and Wales, 1901 and 1911.
31. Draft for First Year's Work in BMpap, 29.
32. Harrisson, World Within, 158; Calder and Sheridan, Speak for Yourself, 23–8; Christianity in
    Industrial Bolton, 1, W 14/C; JW, 'Labour Exchange', 2 February 1937, W 42/C.
33. Barefoot memoir, 1939, 70; 'He is the only man who can touch Beulah' (undated, unsigned
    note, by TH?, in W 14 C).

After politics and religion, the third major area of MO's work in Bolton was working-class leisure, particularly as displayed in the pub. The fieldwork here was led by the Communist novelist John Sommerfield. Son of a newspaper editor and educated at public school in Hampstead, Sommerfield had left school at 16 and worked as, among other things, a carpenter's labourer, a stage hand, and a dishwasher on transatlantic steamers. He joined the Communist Party shortly before publishing his first novel in 1930. After his best known novel, *May Day*, was published in 1936—itself a kind of mass observation of an imagined revolutionary upheaval in London—he fought with the International Brigade in Spain, returning at the end the year.[34] Soldier, adventurer, social explorer, and writer, heavily built and with a rugged way of speaking, Sommerfield, aged 29 in 1937, deeply impressed the younger middle-class investigators who worked alongside him in Bolton. 'He had an aura of toughness about him', one of them recalled, identifying precisely the quality that Harrisson valued above all else. 'Toughness', and their shared experience as upper middle-class men prepared to rough it in working-class conditions, made him, despite their different politics, the most trusted of all Harrisson's recruits.[35]

Apart from Hood, Wilcock, and Sommerfield, the other two full-timers were both unemployed shop assistants: Leslie Taylor, who had worked for a pharmacist, and Eric Bennett, a Labour Party activist who had been sacked for his trade union activity and was listed in January 1938 as a co-author of the politics book.[36] A number of other local working-class people cooperated as volunteers. Jack Fagan had worked with Harrisson 'from the very first days', and was probably the 'Jack' involved with the 1936 project on the food trade. At one time a Communist and secretary of the local Unemployed Workers Movement, by 1937 he had become 'one of [the] six people who are active and militant' in the Bolton Labour Party.[37] Harry Gordon, an

34. John Sommerfield, *Volunteer in Spain*, 1937; Andy Croft, introduction to J. Sommerfield, *May Day*, 1984. Jack Hugo Sommerfeld [sic], birth registered at 3 Crescent Mansions, Kensington, 25 June 1908. He died in August 1991, the death registered as John Hugo Sommerfield. His father may have been the Vernon Sommerfield who published extensively on the British transport systems in the inter-war years.

35. Barefoot memoir, 1939, 70. Towards the end of the war TH wrote, in an obituary of another MO full-timer, Brian Allwood, whose 'toughness' he had also admired, that 'there was no one I more wanted back after the war (except perhaps John Sommerfield) ...', *New Saxon Review*, 4, nd (1945?), copy in Personnel/Fitter.

36. Barefoot memoir, 1939, 71; *First Year's Work*, 24.

37. TH, 'Discussion with Fagan in The Royal Arms over Five Gills of Mild', 4 November 1937, W 7/C; Novy to Allwood, 9 February 1940; Novy to TH, 11 April 1940, HNpap.

unemployed fitter, translated for outside observers unable to penetrate the Bolton dialect.[38] Joyce Mangnall, a weaver who Harrisson had met during his brief spell working in a mill in 1936, helped with introductions to people in her circle.[39]

As should be clear by now the characterization of the Worktown project in some of the secondary literature as essentially an encounter between middle-class intellectuals and the Bolton working class is fundamentally misleading.[40] If MO's reports sometimes appear to patronize the ordinary worker this was more likely to reflect the mentality of working-class activists who had bettered themselves through education, than that of voyeuristic middle-class observers.[41] As Harrisson rightly recalled 'our main asset was that all the people who began this job had direct experience of working-class life,'[42] and the middle-class observers who came to work in Bolton were joining a project already shaped by such people. Brian Barefoot, son of an architect, had graduated in languages and psychology from Cambridge in 1936. Marking time while waiting to start medical training in Edinburgh in October 1937, he advertised for a summer job in the *New Statesman*. To his advertisement, which specified 'non-academic, proletarian employment preferred', Harrisson replied with characteristic verve: 'There ain't no academia about here in this universal smokey cobbleclog'.[43] As a 23-year-old middle-class socialist in search of the workers, nothing could have suited

---

38. Humphrey Spender, *Worktown People. Photographs from Northern England, 1937–38*, 1982, 125–8.
39. During the war she and her husband worked in the Royal Ordnance Factory at Chorley. Later she became a social worker in Australia. Chapman to Sheridan, 3 December 1997, Personnel/Mangnall. Another Bolton full-timer wrote of Mangnall in 1940 that she 'has been coming in for over a year. She is a weaver and literally hundreds of her conversations have been recorded, especially during the period when Charles was in Bolton. Last summer she did a lot of voluntary work…and [she] is an extremely useful contact since she brings in other people and will always do half a dozen or more questionnaires in her own circle…She is currently our cook' (Cornhill to TH, 23 February 1940, Novy Papers).
40. Peter Gurney, '"Intersex" and "Dirty Girls": Mass-Observation and Working-Class Sexuality in England in the 1930s', *Journal of the History of Sexuality*, 8, 2, 1997, 256–90; Mark Abrams, interviewed by Stanley, 9 September 1982.
41. See, for example, Jack Fagan's dim view of the more impoverished sections of the Bolton working class: 'In the East Ward Labour Club shawled women, and many men sit and drink through the afternoon. The place reeks, There are bugs. There is no political interest. The atmosphere is one of stupidity and degradation.' GT, 'The change in psychology of workers caused by change in environment…summary of a talk with Jack Fagan', 2 February 1939 (misdated as 1937 in the MO catalogue). Graham Bell characterized Joe Wilcock as 'a working man originally who has turned into a dreadful snob' (Bell to Popham, 5 May 1938, GBpap).
42. *The Pub and the People*, 329.
43. Barefoot memoir, 1979.

Barefoot better. He quickly became good friends with Wilcock and Hood, and enthusiastically recommended MO to fellow students in Edinburgh as 'the finest plan yet invented for bringing the remote intellectual into contact with real life.'[44] He came back to Bolton during vacations, spending a final four weeks there in the summer of 1938 helping to write up the politics book.[45] Two other middle-class full-timers were briefly employed during Harrisson's period in Bolton. Frank Cawson was born in Lancashire and did a diploma in education in Liverpool in 1937 after graduating in English from Oxford the previous summer. Enthused by a visit to MO in Bolton, he got Harrisson over to talk to the students' union and set up a short-lived MO project in Liverpool.[46] When a temporary teaching job ran out in the winter, Harrisson took him on full-time in Bolton where, like Barefoot, he worked with Hood on the politics book, leaving after four months (somewhat disillusioned, as we shall see) to take up another teaching post.[47] Sheila Fox, in her mid-20s, possessed a sports car and, apparently, Trotskyist views. She worked in Blackpool and Bolton between August and November 1937 before being sacked by Harrisson, whose autocracy she refused to accept.[48]

Many of the middle-class volunteers were the students from various universities who spent their vacations working for MO. In August 1937, 25 Oxford students descended on Blackpool, joining full-timers and volunteers from Bolton and elsewhere to conduct an intensive study of the seaside resort during the week of Bolton's annual holiday. The students were led by Herbert Howarth, who had grown up in Blackpool and been educated at the grammar school.[49] Howarth, as we have seen, had been recruited by Madge in Oxford early in 1937. On his return from Blackpool in the

44. Barefoot memoir, 1939. He had canvassed for the Labour Party in Suffolk, and had been on the Clarion Rural Campaign just before coming to Bolton.
45. Barefoot was briefly a member of the panel in the autumn of 1937. He worked as a volunteer occasionally in Blackheath during 1938–9, and for two weeks at Ladbroke Road in the summer of 1941, irritating TH with his hesitation about whether or not he wanted to work full-time for MO. Joined the army in 1943. Did two reports for MO just after the war. He did not qualify as a doctor. He wrote a novel set in post-war Hamburg. In 1974 he was running a small translation business (*The Times*, 19 December 1974, 18).
46. The Liverpool group comprised half a dozen people including John Garrett, a gifted teacher who had collaborated with Auden on *The Poet's Tongue* and later became headmaster of Bristol Grammar School (Cawson, interviewed by Calder, 29 February 1980; DNB entry on Garrett).
47. Cawson, interviewed by Calder, 29 February 1980.
48. Barefoot memoirs, 1939 and 1979.
49. *Blackpool Gazette and Herald*, 7 August 1937, cited by J. K. Walton, 'Mass-Observation's Blackpool and some alternatives', in Gary Cross (ed.), *Worktowners at Blackpool. M-O and popular leisure in the 1930s*, 1990, 237–8.

autumn of 1937, encouraged by a big response to Harrisson's visit to the Oxford English Club, Howarth and a fellow student, Bruce Watkin, drew up an ambitious plan for an MO project among their peers. Although little came of this, it does clearly demonstrate that for them MO was not just a top-down exercise in observing working-class behaviour: they intended to apply techniques they had learned in Blackpool to everyday life in Oxford. By systematically recording overheard conversations in the street, they hoped to demonstrate that, far from being a hotbed of intellectual discussion, the university town was no less a pleasure resort than Blackpool.[50] Subsequently Howarth, together with his school friend Richard Glew (who threw up his job with a local surveyor to work for MO), wrote up the Blackpool material,[51] while Watkin helped Sommerfield with the pub investigation and briefly worked full-time for Harrisson in London during the summer of 1939.[52]

Other middle-class volunteers who made substantial contributions to the Bolton work included Stanley Cramp, an accomplished mathematician who did the statistical work for the politics book. He was a civil servant in Cheshire, a Fabian and a birdwatcher, who knew of Harrisson from his work on the great crested grebe, and made contact after reading *Savage Civilisation*.[53] Reynold Bray, another ornithologist, worked on the religion book before losing his life on a scientific expedition to the Arctic in 1939. Bray had been one of Harrisson's closest friends since Harrow, where his escapades had gained him a reputation as the toughest boy in the school, and Harrisson had moved into his rooms in Balliol after abandoning his Cambridge degree.[54] Derek Kahn, a London School of Economics (LSE) anthropologist who helped to plan the work on religion and was later commissioned to write the introductory chapter, had also known Harrisson in

50. HH and BW, synopsis of survey of Oxford University, November 1937, TC 31/1/C.
51. Herbert Howarth, 'Mass-Observation and the Higher Criticism', *Fords and Bridges*, February 1939; *First Years' Work*, 45; Howarth to TH, nd, W1/B.
52. Before going on to Bolton and Blackpool, he had worked for Madge in Blackheath (Watkin to MO, 21 January 1995). A publisher's blurb, probably from the cover of Watkin, *A History of Wiltshire*, 1989, describes him as having been 'in turn a meteorologist, research engineer, [town] planning officer, field advisor to the National Parks Commission and advisor and deputy secretary to the Royal Fine Art Commission.' Watkin also published Shell guides to Surrey (1977) and Buckinghamshire (1981).
53. He continued to work for MO in his spare time for several years after moving to London in April 1938. Cramp, interviewed by Calder, 17 March 1980; *Ibis, the International Journal of Avian Science*, 131, 4, 1989, 612–14.
54. Bray also paid for the printing of Harrisson's 1933 *Letter to Oxford*; Heimann, *Most Offending Soul*, 24, 40–1; Obituary in *Nature* 143, 4 March 1939, 367.

Oxford.[55] Bill Lee, a schoolteacher who became, after the war, a leading figure in the development of the teaching of English as a foreign language, also spent several short periods in Bolton working on religion and later worked editorially in London on the book.[56] Ralph Parker, a journalist who became *The Times* Moscow correspondent during the war (and subsequently did the same job for the *Daily Worker*), liaised with the local press and radio during MO's blitz on Blackpool in the summer of 1937, before running off to Prague on a sexual adventure with the alluring Sheila Fox.[57] Penelope Barlow, daughter of MO's benefactor, was studying Social Science at LSE. As part of her preparation for a career in personnel management she worked incognito for a fortnight in April 1937 in one of her father's spinning mills, subsequently writing up the experience for MO and undertaking further shop-floor observation in another mill at the end of the year.[58] John Martin-Jones, a documentary film-maker, systematically photographed church buildings and religious rites, as well as acting for a few months in the autumn of 1937 as a one-man 'Cinema Research Unit' in Bolton. According to Harrisson he was a fascist, which must have made for some interesting conversations in Davenport Street.[59] His presence in the team studying religion was balanced, no doubt, by Philip Harker, described by Harrisson as a one-time Unitarian minister, who 'took up politics, has several times been in prison for political activity and is just [in 1937] returned from Spain'.[60] Among the many local clerics who helped Wilcock with his work on religion, the Unitarian minister John Bright, a member of the local Left Book Club, came to see himself as the 'Hedge Priest' of Davenport Street, although,

---

55. 'Christianity in Industrial Bolton', W14/C; Harrisson, *Letter to Oxford*, 87. In his draft for *First Year's Work*, 29–30, (BMpap), TH described Derek Kahn as an 'anthropologist from Cambridge and the LSE well known for his writings on social matters in progressive papers. He has specially trained himself with the idea of studying anthropology of ourselves [under Malinowski and Firth] who recommended him for the job' (29–30) Khan reviewed the *Mass-Observation* pamphlet in *Left Review*, 1 July 1937.
56. Obituary in *The Independent,* 26 February 1996.
57. TH to Julian and Ursula Trevelyan, September 1937, JTpap; Bloomfield to Parker, 3 September 1937, TC 58/1/B; I. Macdonald, *History of The Times*, Vol. 5, 1984, 80–5.
58. Barlow to TH, nd; PB, Cobden Mill, 17 April 1937; PB, observations at Musgrave's Spinning Company, November 1937, all in W 40/B; interview in 'Stranger than Fiction', MO Archive. Her plan to work as a welfare supervisor never materialized. After a wartime spell in the civil service she married and did not work again.
59. TH, 'Christianity in Industrial Bolton', 1, W 14/C; PMJ, 'The Cinema', 18 November 1937, W 36/A; BFI website; Jeffrey Richards and Dorothy Sheridan (eds), *Mass-Observation at the Movies,* 1987, 4–5.
60. TH, 'Christianity in Industrial Bolton' 1, W 14/C.

as he wryly admitted when he left town in June 1939, 'perhaps they'll be happier without benefit of clergy.'[61]

II

Despite appointing Hood, Wilcock, Sommerfield, and Howarth as leaders of the fieldwork and announcing them as authors of the planned books, Harrisson had no intention of leaving them to their own devices. For much of the 18 months that the project lasted, he lived in the Davenport Street house directing operations from day to day. Inhabited mainly by undomesticated males, the headquarters of the Bolton 'experiment'—as Harrisson liked to call it—was a squalid place. Although the large terraced houses of Davenport Street had seen better times, and many were now multi-occupied, an air of respectability remained; the houses set back from the pavement behind tiny well-tended front gardens.[62] The neglected state of the garden at No.85 advertised the bug-ridden wilderness within. One young intellectual, invited by Harrisson to help write up some of the accumulated material, recalled his visit to Davenport Street:

> When I got to Bolton he showed me into the room that was to be my office and bedroom. "Here are your files", he said tapping a small chest of drawers. "You might like to have a dip into them before we eat..." There was one chair in the room with a large tin of Keating's insect powder on the seat. I removed that and sat down to begin dipping.

Unable to make head nor tail of the material, and sickened by the need to throw insect powder on the sheet before going to bed, he quit after a couple of days.[63] There was sufficient space for each of the four or five regular inhabitants to have their own bedroom ('but rarely clean sheets'), doubling up with mattresses on the floor when visitors were staying, but the only communal space was the kitchen.[64] A typical Davenport Street day would start with breakfast at 9 or 10 a.m. (bread, jam, a fried egg); the morning out observing; back for the main meal of the day at lunchtime (one of the two or three menus provided by the daily help, who also washed up, did the washing, and saw to whatever cleaning was possible amid papers piled on the floors); out again or typing up reports

61. Bright to TH, 1 June 1939, W1/E; Bright, interviewed by TH, 7 November 1937, W21/C.
62. Spender, *Worktown People*, 121; Barefoot memoir, 1979.
63. Anthony West, *New Statesman*, 13 April 1973.
64. Barefoot memoir, 1939; Hood, interviewed by TH, 4 May 1972.

.around the kitchen table in the afternoon; more bread and jam for tea at 5 p.m.; going to report a meeting in the evening, maybe a trip to the pub; fish and chips from the shop on the corner for supper (the lingering smell of which never left the house[65]); and, because immediate recording of the day's observations was insisted upon, more writing up possibly into the small hours.[66] Harrisson paid the rent, the daily help, and ran up debts with tradesmen.[67] Bill Rigby, an unemployed ex-miner in his sixties who produced several reports for MO and did odd jobs around the house, complained that he was hardly ever paid for his work.[68] When funds ran low Harrisson dispensed with the daily help, providing, when reminded, cash for food instead. Hood recalled:

> Tom used to get so involved with his writing and what he was doing, he never bothered at all whether there was anything for us to eat ... so it was my job to have a word with him and say: 'Look Tom, what about it? I mean there's not even a bloody tin of bully beef for us to have a go at.' And Tom would fork out a couple of quid and I would go around and do a bit of shopping...'[69]

Observers were given their board and keep, and for the first few months, when the finances were relatively healthy, pocket money for expenses, but there was no regular pay. Hood, promised a pound a week when recruited, claimed never once to have received it, although cash would be found for emergencies, to buy books, or, as Hood recalled with some bitterness, for Harrisson's own extravagant taxi rides when he went into Manchester to do a broadcast or meet a potential funder.[70]

---

65. One visitor in May 1938, throwing open all the windows while the others slept, claimed to have 'reduced the smell of his house by half—i.e. we banished stale sweat and about half the smell of onions and vinegar. We were powerless against his drains' (Bell to 'My dear family', 10 May 1938, GBpap).
66. Barefoot memoir, 1939; Barefoot memoir, 1979; Wagner, interviewed by Sheridan, 27 April 1988. Hood recalled that Harrisson insisted that notes were written up immediately after the interview, not four or eight hours later, even if this meant stopping up all night (Hood memoir, 1974).
67. Greenhagh to Harrisson, 28 October 1938, W1/B; Chapman (interviewed by Stanley, 23 February 1979) described Harrisson as 'very, very careless about money, and totally contemptuous of the interest of the small tradesman. He ran up bills everywhere and never paid them, which was the antithesis of the working-class ethic he was supposed to be studying.' He illustrated this with a story of a radio set in Davenport Street bought on the never-never. Warned by Madge that it was about to be repossessed because he had failed to keep up the payments, Harrisson came post-haste from London on a first-class sleeper (with a lady friend), and took the radio back with him so that it could not be repossessed.
68. Barefoot memoir, 1939.
69. Hood, interviewed by Harrisson, 4 May 1972.
70. Hood memoir, 1974.

Harrisson ran Bolton as a charismatic autocracy: 'He had an almost hyp-
notic power over those who worked for him; he would ask the most impossible things of us and we would willingly do them.'[71] For the young
middle-class recruits, Harrisson was an overwhelming presence,

> an engaging, remarkable sort of charisma...explosive, irascible...wonderful
> at firing people with his ideas and enthusiasm. He could take up an idea and
> out of nothing build it up into something rather exciting. He would fantasti-
> cate it and embroider it and put dynamism into it...[72]

On first meeting Brian Barefoot, he explained that 'it was necessary for
him to be rather autocratic at times, in order to keep the experiment
going'.[73] 'They never had meetings,' another observer recalled, 'Harrisson
decided everything.'[74] Harrisson himself admitted that during the first
year in Bolton he had 'set too high a standard...all private life was killed
and MO was the only thing anyone was allowed to think about from
dawn till dream.'[75]

Madge, in the midst of one of their many rows, affectionately described
Harrisson as 'the most perfect living example of disordered "genius", perhaps starting a new type, that of Bohemian scientist.'[76] No one found it easy
to be around such genius. For one thing he liked noise, complaining 'that he
could not really sleep unless he could feel through the wall the people next
door going to bed; could not work unless the radio was turned on full
blast.'[77] Mark Abrams, the opinion pollster, found meeting Harrisson 'a bit
of an ordeal because [he] kept his gramophone playing throughout.'[78] Hood
never forgot the misery of trying to write up his notes in the kitchen, desperately searching his pockets 'for a fag end I knew wasn't there', while
being subjected hour after hour to George Formby's 'When I'm Cleaning
Windows', which Harrisson played again and again, the better to absorb the
tones of Lancashire popular culture, while the 18-year-old Woodrow Wyatt,
a favoured Oxford visitor, devotedly turned the handle of the wind-up

71. Julian Trevelyan, *Indigo Days*, 1957, 82.
72. Cawson, interviewed by Calder, 29 February 1980, 10.
73. Barefoot memoir, 1979.
74. Wagner interviewed by Sheridan, 27 April 1988.
75. TH to CM, 18 January 1940, Org&Hist 1/1.
76. CM to TH, 21 January 1940, 16, Org&Hist 1/1. Harrisson enjoyed this and put a tick
    against it.
77. Trevelyan, *Indigo Days*, 82.
78. Mark Abrams, interviewed by Stanley, 9 September 1982.

gramophone.[79] Harrisson usually got up late, having worked half the night. Barefoot remembered him on more than one occasion typing for 14 hours non-stop, kept going with fish and chips, and cups of tea supplied by observers who did not dare to speak to him: 'At the end of this long slog he was surrounded by a little cloud of halitosis and bad air'.[80] It was, no doubt, Harrisson's indifference to personal hygiene—shaving irregularly, seldom washing his hair, bathing rarely ('which made him not particularly nice to be near')—that informed his contempt for Orwell's fastidious sensitivity to the smell of the great unwashed.[81] But none of these irritants prevented the 'Bohemian scientist' from remaining a continuing source of inspiration to those who chose to join the Worktown 'experiment' under his autocratic leadership.

III

The first principle of Harrisson's method was a relentless empiricism, an insistence that the starting point of any research was not conceptual clarity about the hypothesis to be tested but an almost passive stance of pure observation, 'wallowing about in a maze of fact, rather than . . . bee-lining for a conclusion'[82] with mind, eyes, and ears open to whatever the social terrain presented:

> We could not ignore who did and did not drop their tram tickets into the litter bins. The pattern of saliva round a spittoon could not be dismissed as irrelevant . . . For the first two months we wrote down everything we could observe or find. It was important to avoid falling into the old accepted categories.[83]

Trying in retrospect to be positive, Madge justified the seemingly unsystematic collection of often trivial observations in Bolton on the grounds that

79. Hood to Mrs Ree, 4 February 1972; Hood memoir, 1974; Woodrow Wyatt, *Into this Dangerous World*, 1952, 33–5.
80. Barefoot memoir, 1979.
81. Barefoot memoir, 1979; Hood memoir, 1974.
82. TH to Gorer, nd (October 1937?), Org&Hist 1.
83. Draft for *First Year's Work*, BMpap. These examples were not casually chosen. Frank Cawson later recalled being instructed by Harrisson to imitate the methods of 'some surrealists in Paris [who] had come to conclusions by the pattern which had been taken up by discarded tram tickets along the streets of the Champs Elyse . . .' (Cawson, interviewed by Calder, 29 February 1980).

'some sort of net had been spread to catch that fleeting, glinting apparition, the essence of the time'.[84] Other critics, less charitably, complained that Harrisson spread his net far too wide, making it virtually impossible to pull the resulting material together into a coherent analysis, a criticism apparently endorsed by Barefoot who asserted that Harrisson 'did not really know what we were trying to find out; so in general we just observed everything that went on.'[85] Humphrey Spender's retrospective account of his time at Davenport Street feeds this perception:

> There were never any written directives... there was a daily session which usually took the form of Tom seizing about half a dozen national newspapers, reading the headlines, getting us laughing and interested, and quite on the spur of the moment, impulsively, hitting on a theme that he thought would be productive. For instance, how people hold their hands, the number of sugar lumps that people pop into their mouths in restaurants, how people steal things like teaspoons in restaurants, matches, bits of paper. Anything. Every day started with a kind of lead, and then you were working on your own.[86]

While, no doubt, there were days like these, they were far from typical. After the initial period of soaking up the local atmosphere, the observation became more selective, if only because of the discipline imposed by the promised Gollancz books. As Barefoot himself explained, contradicting his own remark quoted above: 'It worked more or less like this. Tom Harrisson decided on an event to be covered; he would draft a "directive"... [And] each paragraph in the report answered a question in the directive.'[87] A few of these 'directives' survive in the archive, most of them addressed to Lee who was working with Wilcock on religion and superstition, and the impression they give is hardly that of a man who 'did not really know what we were trying to find out'. A February 1938 directive on 'Sunday Behaviour', for example, included:

> You know some of the times at which [church bells] will ring. Can you send out observers to get as much information as possible... Do people notice; do

84. Harrisson, *Britain Revisited*, 280.
85. Barefoot memoir, 1979; Laura Marcus, 'The Project of Mass-Observation', *New Formations*, 44, Autumn 2001, 11.
86. Spender, *Worktown People*, 15. Spender, however, went on to qualify this impression of inspired serendipity by recalling how Harrisson specified exactly what pictures he needed for the religious study.
87. Barefoot memoir, 1939, 5–6.

they walk faster or slower; do they look up; do they hum; do they notice when hymn tunes are played? What do they say – not only about the bells, of course.

'I am eager', he wrote on the same day, 'for religious bog-graphiti, and on hearing from you will make out a scheme for studying stuff on walls.'[88] A month later, when attention had turned to popular superstitions, Lee was told to post observers close to ladders with detailed instructions on what to look for; or to watch for children attempting to avoid stepping on the cracks between paving stones: 'choose a good crack and stand by it . . . or follow children in turn over a fixed stretch'. Helpful hints followed on how, using dried peas and several pockets, one could simultaneously count both the number of the cracks and the number stepped upon. 'If this yields anything', Harrisson concluded, optimistically, 'then further and more detailed directives can be sent, including one on Conversation while Crack-stepping.'[89] A control freak in danger of taking himself too seriously, perhaps; a researcher more concerned to establish *what* people actually did than to investigate *why* they did it, certainly; but emphatically not a man without a research agenda.

Young men systematically following children on their way home from school might be construed as a problem, but at least they were not stopping the kids to ask them why they avoided stepping on the cracks. For Harrisson, the ornithologist, the key to objective reporting was watching and listening, observing the masses as if they were birds. And even the listening was suspect, since people seldom articulated, or even knew, the reasons for their behaviour. Direct interviewing was almost designed to solicit what the respondent thought his interrogator wanted to hear, rather than his real, private, opinion. The ideal equipment, Harrisson used to tell his observers, was the ear plug.[90] In pursuit of purity in observation he sometimes even sought to disaggregate the evidence of sight and sound. Thus a note on observing church services included separate questions on 'What does Christianity sound like?' and 'What does Christianity look like?', suggesting that the first 'might be done as if the Observer was deaf' while for the second 'he will be able to hear, but the poor fellow will be blind.'[91] These were all distancing techniques: 'doing this,' Harrisson

88. Directive II, 2 February 1938, W14/A.
89. Directive on Superstitions, 15 March 1938, W14/A.
90. Harrisson, *Britain Revisited*, 19.
91. 'Christianity in Bolton', W14/A.

explained, 'made it possible to be objective about things that were close to some of the observers'.[92]

The staple of MO's work in Worktown was 'observation without being observed.'[93] One of the Blackpool volunteers recalled the team-work involved in following people in the street: if you passed another observer you exchanged 'quarries' to avoid being spotted.[94] As a spying technique this was elementary, but MI6 could not have bettered the positioning of multiple observers to record precise details of a couple's behaviour on a seafront bench in Blackpool: 'We sat on seat adjacent, twenty yards south. TH commentated, RP screened him, HH wrote down from dictation, RG screened him, TIR pretended to be sick over the railings.'[95] A similar technique was used to record the speed at which groups of drinkers finished their beer: 'it takes two, or preferably three trained observers, one watching, one timing, one writing down and checking to secure 40 or 50 timings a night.'[96] Work like this produced the endless 'counts' that litter MO's reports. Imagining how the work might develop, Harrisson fantasized about setting up museums of sounds, smells, foods, and recorded dialect to enable observers to familiarize themselves with the local culture before going into the field, or a 'field wardrobe' from which they could borrow 'the necessary outfit of cloth-ing for effective assimilation.'[97]

Despite Harrisson's boast in his introduction to *The Pub and the People* that all the material had been gathered without a single direct interview,[98] observation was by no means the whole story. In the pub it was easy to progress from listening in to other people's conversations to participating directly, steering conversation to the issues one wanted to probe without revealing one's identity as a researcher. Faced, for example, with the puzzling

---

92. Draft for *First Year's Work*, BMpap.
93. *Pub and the People*, 11.
94. Sheridan, interview with Ursula Mommens, 1983.
95. The results, each kiss and grope measured to the nearest second, are reproduced in Calder and Sheridan, *Speak for Yourself*, 48ff, which also has details of searching for copulation among couples in the sand dunes by the simple device of falling over them to see what they were up to. In prepar-ing their Oxford study Howarth and Watkin took this prurient sexual spying one step further: 'Bruce and I did a wonderful joint observation of a man masturbating in his bath for twenty minutes,' adding, prudently, that such 'bath prying' should always be undertaken by two observers 'for support both moral and physical' (Herbert to TH, nd (November 1937?), TC 36/1/C).
96. *Pub and the People*, 175.
97. *Mass-Observation*, 35.
98. *Pub and the People*, 10.

observation that holidaymakers in Blackpool seldom looked at the sea, the next step, Hood recalled, was to 'talk to some people, try to get them in depth when you got to know them and buy them a couple of pints…we began to understand much more.'[99] Much Worktown evidence was gathered in this way, from Penelope Barlow's participant observation in the cotton mill to the even more participant methods used to research pick-up behaviour. Zita Baker stood under the Blackpool Tower, whose phallic significance was all too apparent to the mass observers, inviting attention from passing males, undeterred by the directness of her first middle-aged, bowler-hatted interlocutor: 'Will yer come to bed with me, love? 'Ave yer done it before?'[100] Some of the male observers went a good deal further, picking up local girls for a kiss and a cuddle in the back row of the cinema, or, in at least three documented cases, a 'knee-trembler' in a back alley.[101] As 'anthropologists [we] were apparently relieved of certain moral restraints', Dennis Chapman recalled; and, in Savage Civilisation, Harrisson had come close to recommending sleeping with the natives as a means of understanding an alien culture.[102] Unfamiliarity with local working-class rules of the game could, of course, lead to misinterpretation of behaviour, as Peter Gurney has argued in relation to what he sees as Sommerfield's fascinated disgust at the conduct of 'dirty girls' flirting in the pub, or, as Mark Abrams argued more generally, contrasting the short-lived sallies of some of MO's public school volunteers into northern working-class culture with the long-term participant observation carried out by sensitive researchers like Mark Benney or Pearl Jephcott.[103] But Gurney is almost certainly wrong about Sommerfield, whose thinly disguised contempt for the 'dirty girls' reflected masculine arrogance rather than a middle-class fastidiousness long since abandoned in his exploration of working-class life.[104] Harrisson's key men, and his local helpers, had all been recruited as 'native informants', familiar with the cul-

99. Hood memoir, 1974.
100. Calder and Sheridan, Speak for Yourself, 54; Heimann, Most Offending Soul, 142.
101. Calder and Sheridan, Speak for Yourself, 60, 39; Cawson, interviewed by Calder, 29 February 1980, 8.
102. Chapman, interviewed by Stanley, 23 February 1979, 11; Mass-Observation, 36; Malinowksi, critiquing this stance in First Year's Work, 97–100, clearly felt that such behaviour was a threat to white civilization.
103. Gurney, ' "Intersex" and "Dirty Girls" '; Mark Abrams, interviewed by Stanley, 9 September 1982.
104. This is borne out by Sommerfield's novel, May Day, which combines a realistic (if over-politicized) account of working-class life with a relentlessly sexualized treatment of the female characters.

ture they were studying. Nothing produced on working-class youth by Jephcott, for example, could surpass in empathetic insight the interview that Wilcock conducted with a petty criminal he bumped into in Blackpool, a lad who, as a former inmate of Wilcock's East End hostel for juvenile delinquents, clearly knew and trusted him.[105] Sommerfield, Wilcock, and Hood could talk with familiar ease with the drinkers, Christians and labour movement activists that, respectively, they were studying. There was, undeniably, a source of systemic distortion in Harrisson's team. It lay, however, not in their class origins, but in their gender. They were almost all men, and it was with working-class masculinity that they empathized. Women, when they were discussed at all, were usually cast as objects of more or less predatory male desire (including that of the observers). Sommerfield led the field in constant smutty talk about 'women, copulation, etc', much to the disgust of more sensitive souls like Spender.[106] Unlike much of MO's wartime and post-war work, the early Bolton material seldom captures the world through feminine eyes.

In 1942 Harrisson claimed that,

> for the first two years we were practically unnoticed, and investigators penetrated every part of local life, joined political, religious and cultural organisations of all sorts, worked in a wide range of jobs and made a great circle of friends and acquaintances at every level of the town structure from the leading family though the Town Council to the permanently unemployed and the floating population of Irish doss house dwellers.[107]

'Practically unnoticed' is certainly an exaggeration. Many of those 'friends and acquaintances' knew that the young men from Davenport Street were up to something. Wilcock, for example, drafting an appeal to individual churchgoers to write about 'the part that religion plays in personal life', early in 1938, already assumed that: 'You probably know that a number of people have been making a special study of Christian churches in Bolton during the past year'.[108] Despite the cult of invisibility, MO repeatedly broadcast invitations to local people to make their own writ-

---

105. JW, 'Larkhill Lodging House', 11 September 1937 (?), W 55/B.
106. Bell to Popham, 28 April 1938, GBpap.
107. *Pub and the People,* 8.
108. Untitled page in W14/A; see also Tony Kushner's discussion of Wilcock's (and Harrisson's) open involvement with the care of Spanish refugee children in Bolton in the summer of 1937, Kushner, *We Europeans,* 66–9.

ten contribution to the research, soliciting—Harrisson wrote defensively and rather portentously, embarrassed perhaps by this departure from his 'objective' methods of observation—the kind of 'subjective data that is often mistakenly called unscientific' to illuminate 'the darkest territory of all social science—what people think.'[109] A draft addressed to the inhabitants of Bolton called on them to contribute to 'an increased scientific knowledge of human affairs... by entering for the competitions which MO will announce from time to time in the advertising columns of the *Bolton Evening News*.'[110] The idea may have derived from James Whittaker, a self-educated journalist from a working-class background who had made it his business as an independent investigator to compile evidence for the official committee examining the case for legislation on Holidays with Pay.[111] Whittaker had offered a £5 prize for the person who sent in the best statement on what they would like to do on holiday, and subsequently cooperated with MO in a follow-up questionnaire.[112] MO used the same technique to solicit opinion on the pools, on 'Why I drink beer', 'How I spend Sunday', and most importantly, on 'What is Happiness?':

> Once more 'Competitions' are trying to find out what Bolton thinks. What does HAPPINESS mean for you and yours. Write down what you think – Never mind about style or grammar – It's your own opinion that is wanted.[113]

Hilton agreed to judge the entries. In a few cases diaries provided by local informants were used, though the systematic trawling of diary material was

---

109. Cross, *Blackpool*, 40–1.
110. 'M-O in Bolton: A Social Experiment', 6, W1/C.
111. Prize essay competitions had also been used in the *Marienthal* study, and Harrisson may have got the idea from there independently of Whittaker. On Whittaker's project see: Committee on Holidays with Pay, minutes of evidence, 2 November 1937, 268, 270, in Bevin papers, MRC 126/EB/HP/6. Cross (*Blackpool*, 8, 40–1) describes him as 'a BBC journalist and author of a well-known book about Lancashire'. But when Whittaker begged TH to 'wangle' a spot for him on the radio he warned that 'I'm not "mike" conscious' (Whittaker to TH, 3 September 1937, TC 58/1/E). I have been unable to trace the 'well known book about Lancashire', but he had published an autobiography—*I, James Whittaker*, London, 1934—at the age of 27. Whittaker subsequently published a pamphlet, with a preface by Lord Horder, based on responses to letters he had written to employers (James Whittaker, *Holidays with Pay*, nd (1938?), copy in BLEPS).
112. Hood to TH, 2 and 3 September 1937; 'Holidays with pay investigation', 14 September 1937, TC 58/1/E.
113. Leaflet: 'Happiness. What is Happiness?', TC 7/1/A; *Pub and the People*, 24, 42; Kahn to Harrisson, nd, W1/B.

not developed until the war years.[114] The investigators also used more conventional techniques where appropriate. Barefoot, for example, on his first
day in Bolton, found himself accompanying Hood in door-to-door interviews asking people why they didn't vote.[115]

IV

The pursuit of the non-voter was central to Harrisson's Bolton agenda. All
those involved in the politics project (apart from Harrisson himself) were
socialists of one hue or another, and they quickly established close working
relations both with the local Labour Party—to which Hood, already well-
known in Labour circles, was recommended by the national party[116]—as
well as with the Communists, Left Book Club, and other left organizations
in the town. But Bolton was not a good place to be a socialist in the later
1930s. The Conservative Party, sustained by large numbers of working-class
votes, remained firmly in control of the local council. For ten years from the
mid-1920s Labour's position had steadily improved, but their council membership peaked in 1935. Thereafter the Labour vote fell sharply, and by 1938
more than half the Labour councillors had lost their seats. At the same time
electoral turnout fell towards 50 per cent, compared with well over 60 per
cent during the 1920s. The Labour Party, reports the historian of interwar
local elections, 'ended the decade almost as far away from power in Bolton
as it had been in 1919, and apathy and disillusionment had to a large degree
replaced the confident hopes of 20 years earlier.'[117] Labour suffered similar
setbacks in many parts of the country in the late 1930s, but things were
especially bad in Lancashire where, in the words of one historian, the 'working class remained stolidly politically apathetic and conservative in all senses
of the word.'[118] Harrisson could not have chosen a better place to probe the
causes of working-class political apathy, and his team quickly picked up on
the general air of despondency among Labour activists, and the limited
appeal of the more radical groupings.[119]

114. e.g. a quote from a diary that one of the Labour Party workers 'kept for me ... M-O now has
    a unique and tremendous collection of such native documents' (Harrisson, 'Poverty of
    Freedom', 106); see also Cross, *Blackpool*, 21, 185.
115. Barefoot memoir, 1939, 2.
116. Hood memoir, 1974; draft of *First Year's Work*, 36–7, BMpap.
117. Davies, *County borough election results*, 478.
118. Walton, cited in Davies, *County borough election results*, 474.
119. Barefoot memoir, 1939: 'Analysis of political material available', 28, 32.

But to answer the question of why the forces of progress were unable to connect more effectively with Bolton's workers, MO needed to look beyond the world of the activists to the world with which they were trying to engage. That meant putting aside conventional socialist condemnation of the apathetic masses and starting from the assumption that the non-voter 'is every bit as much a human being, with hopes and fears and social feelings, as the voter, and often has as good a reason for not voting as the voter has for using his vote.'[120] For Hood, instructed by Harrisson in techniques of anthropological distancing, this came as a salutary revelation:

> I was very excited...and for the first time in my life since I was a boy of 16 or 17, I was looking at politics, I was looking at Socialism, I was looking at Trade Unionism, I was looking at the Labour Party as it really was, not what I romantically thought it was...Now I was wanting to know what people thought, why they thought the way they did, and how they thought about politics, and this was...really fascinating...Up till then you had this feeling, as a socialist, that your influence was much greater than it was in the community.[121]

Hood learned to look at the political life he was familiar with in new ways: mapping where people chose to sit in meetings—'the distance between people...the whole problem of the physical reactions of one person to another'—or trying to classify the language of gesture employed by platform speakers.[122] His earlier 'romantic' belief in the revolutionary potential of the working class was tempered by a growing realization that, as he put it many years later,

> People are not economic; they have love for their children...even men who are unemployed...you say 'Oh they'll struggle against it'. Of course not! They for the first time have the opportunity of a good deal of sunshine and walk out and pick blackberries and take them to their wives...

Nothing impressed him more than 'the excitement and pride and joy and sense of relief that ran through Bolton station' at the beginning of the annual trip to Blackpool:

> the worker has money in his pocket to buy his wife things, to buy ice-cream for the kiddies, and also with his mates and his wife to sit in these bars and enjoy food or enjoy a pint...and live a life he hasn't lived for 51 weeks of the year he's

---

120. *First Year's Work*, 32. See also 'They Speak for Themselves', 1 June 1939, 5, FR A26, and *Britain*, 227–9.
121. Hood memoir, 1974.
122. Draft for *First Year's Work*, 11; 'Analysis of Gestures', nd (February 1938?), W12/H; Hood, interviewed by Harrisson, 4 May 1972.

been saving up for this... He felt his arse pocket and he knew he had thirty quid there and he could do what he wished with it. You could see his glowing with excitement for the following week... Now of course this was a long way from... a WEA series of talks on Shakespeare. This was working-class people in the raw enjoying themselves. And we tried to understand what made them enjoy themselves... why did they spend their money on this kind of thing.[123]

MO's exhaustive investigations of working-class leisure—in the interstices of the working week in Bolton as much as in the annual holiday in Blackpool—was primarily intended to map out and describe what work-ing-class people actually did with their spare time. This work, rich in detailed observation, provided much of value for future social historians of northern working-class culture. When it came to explaining why they spent money and free time 'on this kind of thing', one main line of argument relied on a functionalist model in which the colour and excitement of holiday Blackpool, the excesses of drunkenness or flirtatious sexuality, provide a necessary counterpoint to the repressions, the colourless monotony of the working day: 'the machinery to preserve the stability of the society must include safety valves, that allow a partial release of accumulating tensions.'[124] Whatever its limitations, this approach at least allowed the mass observers to approach spare time excess, notably drunkenness, not through the moraliz-ing category of 'social problem', but as 'a... regular social process of self-liberation from the... time-clock factory-whistle dimension of living'. 'Social intoxication', variously facilitated by alcohol, music, dance, drugs, or religious ritual, was, after all, a feature of all known societies; a process inte-gral to their stability, not a symptom of breakdown and decay. Reflecting on the unnatural rhythms of industrial life, in ways that anticipated by 20 years a famous essay of the 'new social history', Harrisson, with characteristic intellectual bravado, suggested that social science would gain predictive power when it found its Einstein or Plank, a theorist capable of explaining the social relativity of time.[125]

The mass observers' detached anthropological distancing threatened to desert them, however, when they turned to what they took to be the central dynamic of contemporary change in the forms of working-class leisure: the contrast between the face-to-face companionship of the pub and new forms

123. Hood memoir, 1974.
124. *Pub and the People*, 337.
125. *Pub and the People*, 198, 338–9. Edward Thompson, 'Time, Work Discipline and Industrial Capitalism', *Past & Present*, 38, 1, 1967, 56–97.

of commercial exploitation of working-class leisure, which tended to promote social attitudes at once more individualistic, more fatalistic, and even
more resistant to the appeals of socialism than the older culture they were
displacing. It was in the exploration of this contrast that the political concerns most eloquently expressed by Hood, but shared by all the main
observers, did most to shape the investigation. Sommerfield's work on pubs
focussed on the taproom—where regulars could sit down to talk, play dom-
inoes and darts, or read the paper—and the stand-up vault where anyone
was welcome to join in the conversation. It was the informal community of
these working-class male preserves that embodied, for MO, the fundamental
social value of the pub, far more than the lounge, where men could take
their women, and people tended to arrive in pre-constituted groups and
stay together for the evening. Discussing the games, clubs, and hobbies that
flourished in the pub, Harrisson and Sommerfield were at pains to stress
how satisfactorily the ethos of the pub handled the abiding human tension
between, on the one hand, the individualistic competitive spirit, the motive
of personal advancement, the striving to be top of the heap, displayed, for
example, in the intricate mock-archaic hierarchies of the pub-based friendly
societies; and, on the other hand, the egalitarian spirit of fraternity and
companionship:

> the democracy of drinking... manifests itself both in the merging of individu-
> als into groups, and also in the basic ritual of drinking, that of standing rounds.
> This, the most fundamental and regular of all the pub rituals, is based on an
> assumption that all the members of the drinking group have the same amount
> of money to spend, a truly 'democratic' assumption in a wage-earning, per-
> sonal-advancement society.[126]

Just as in the middle-class public sphere of the 18th-century coffee house,
famously portrayed by Habermas as underpinning an emergent 'public
opinion' free from feudal chains of dependency or the attentions of the
absolutist state, so the democratic egalitarianism of the pub sustained the
autonomy of, in this case, a working-class public sphere functioning with a
minimum of organization: 'an essentially communal, egalitarian, leaderless
drinking group.'[127] More Bolton people met in the pub than in all the other
public buildings of the town put together, and, most significantly, the pub
was 'the only kind of public building used by large numbers of people

126. *Pub and the People,* 312, 117.
127. *Pub and the People,* 312; Harrisson, 'Poverty of Freedom', 126–8.

where their thoughts and actions are not being in some way arranged for them.'[128]

But the pub was in decline, its centrality assaulted by new forms of commercial exploitation of working-class leisure. The popular press, football pools, cinema, radio, even the dance hall, argued MO, all served to

> shift the emphasis of people's leisure from active and communal forms to those that are passive and individual. . . . The pub stresses the fact that you are living among your fellow men, that the issues of life, whether faced or escaped, are not solitary but communal. The Church and the political party say the same thing in a different way. The films and pools do not . . . they emphasise the separateness of the individual, and they do not ask him to know anyone. They do not suggest that he has a duty to help anyone else but himself, and maybe his wife and kids and old sick mother.[129]

The new cultural entrepreneurs, unlike the pub landlord, the cleric, or the political activist, had no need to bring people into 'active physical and verbal communication with one another . . . Though all share the same experience, the emphasis is on each individual experiencing it, not on any common feeling, interest or talk.'[130] Interested only in profit, these entrepreneurs were unconcerned with the antisocial consequences of their innovations: indeed they thrived on the popular appetite for escapist fantasy and the irrational trust in 'fate' and 'luck' catered for by newspaper astrology and the pools.[131]

There was, MO suggested, a correlation to be made between the spread of this new commercial culture and the indifference of so many working-class people to politics. Active citizenship dwindled as the older institutions declined. Discovering that churchgoers had a higher than average propensity to vote, MO commented: 'people who care for organised religion also care for organised politics. They were in fact "socially conscious"; they are not people entirely concerned with spending their public leisure in the newer profit organisations.' 'Political apathy', Harrisson concluded, 'is only the index of a general *social apathy*.'[132]

In passages like this MO came close to endorsing a simple contrast between a degenerate modernity and a lost golden age of social responsibility

128. *Pub and the People*, 17.
129. *Pub and the People*, 218–19; Harrisson, 'Poverty of Freedom', 32–3.
130. *Pub and the People*, 77–8.
131. Harrisson, 'Poverty of Freedom', 293, 300.
132. Harrisson, 'Poverty of Freedom', 281, 287.

and active citizenship. Usually, however, their analysis was a good deal more nuanced, avoiding the extremes of cultural pessimism indulged in by much of the contemporary intelligentsia.[133] For one thing the pub, though in decline, was resilient and still held far more appeal than church or political party.[134] Moreover, even on Bolton's publess new council estates, the proliferation of tenants' associations, they argued, demonstrated that 'it takes more than a semi-detached house and a small piece of garden to destroy the Worktown workers feeling for fraternization.'[135] More importantly, though, MO was well aware that the fraternity of the pub was not, and never had been, a highly politicized culture. The new individualized forms of leisure certainly made it more difficult to tackle the roots of 'social apathy', but those roots lay in older and deeper soil.

Even before arriving in Bolton Harrisson had been speculating about the relationship between happiness and politics.[136] Now, listening to what Bolton people had to say in answer to the question 'What is Happiness?', what impressed him most was the working-class capacity to adjust expectations to circumstances; the modesty of desire. It was not, he insisted, that working people lacked the capacity to appreciate life's richer pleasures: 'You only need to study working-class gardens to know that however poor, ignorant or apathetic most men and women have in embryo the...sensibility...for the appreciation of anything beautiful.'[137] But the conditions of working-class life gave little opportunity for the cultivation of such sensibilities. The desire for beautiful things—as for so many of the other desiderata of good living—was crushed by a realistic sense of their unavailability. Despite the best efforts of Labour and the trade unions, most people could not even be persuaded that they had a right to holidays with pay, let alone to larger social changes. 'Working-class people', wrote Harrisson, 'recognise the boundaries of their lives, set by the atmosphere of smoke, the horizon of factories and the future of doubtful employment.' This did not, however, mean that they were miserable. The well-off southern visitor might find it impossible to imagine anyone being happy living in Worktown's appalling

133. John Carey, *The Intellectuals and the Masses: pride and prejudice among the literary intelligentsia, 1880–1939*, 1992.
134. *Pub and the People*, 79.
135. *Pub and the People*, 333–4.
136. Heimann, *Most Offensive Soul*, 74. Heimann wrongly assumes that this was a concern which went nowhere.
137. Harrisson, 'Poverty of Freedom', 355.

conditions, but in fact the great majority of Boltonians were not only incomprehensibly proud of their home town, but also claimed to be happy often, generally, or all the time. The key to happiness, they explained again and again, was to be found within: 'Make the best of what you've got, is the reiterated cry of two out of every three.' Evidence that millionaires could be unhappy was seized upon eagerly: 'a negative wish-fulfilment for poorer people, curtail[ing] ambition and discontent.'

> 'It is immoral to want much.' That is hardly the cry of a dynamic or progressive nation. It must tend to mean an easy acceptance of the status quo, a tendency towards complacency, apathy; the reverse of political or citizen enthusiasm.[138]

The point, for Harrisson, was not only to understand the causes of apathy, but also to put this understanding to practical use in challenging popular indifference to the political process. This was, indeed, a goal shared by all MO's sponsors: the liberal industrialists as much as Gollancz and his Left Book Club. Characteristically tactless, Harrisson pulled no punches in attacking both. He dismissed Ernest Simon's Association for Education in Citizenship as the well-meaning folly of a man 'who lives in an enormous house and has not much idea how the problem looks when you live in a row', while being equally rude about the Left Book Club's efforts to spread enlightenment 'in the most traditional and formal way, with little use of contemporary language, technique or symbolism suitable for the working classes.'[139] As for the main political parties, their propaganda methods were positively archaic: a fact dramatized by Harrisson in a play intended for the amateur theatre groups in which

> a character on one side of the stage reads out an actual Worktown election address for 1838, while on the other side of the stage another character reads out an election address from 1938 ... It is practically impossible to tell the difference between the two addresses.[140]

In Bolton for a by-election in January 1938, the remoteness of Labour's national leaders from popular culture was apparent in Herbert Morrison's use of language incomprehensible to a working-class audience (MO had

---

138. Harrisson, 'Poverty of Freedom', 43–4.
139. Harrisson, 'Poverty of Freedom', 301–2, 48.
140. Harrisson, 'Poverty of Freedom', 162. There is a copy of this play—'Swelling the Labour Vote'—in TC 46/2/A.

observers in the audience of his meetings counting the numbers of unintelligible or ambiguous words), and in Clement Attlee's admission, when shown a pools coupon by a mass observer, that he had never seen one before.[141]

The pools coupon was symbolic, providing for millions a more compelling hope for change than that offered by the labour movement. Nearly half the people who took a flutter once a week by marking up a complicated pools coupon were non-voters, unpersuaded by the politicians of the value of putting 'a cross on a piece of paper once a year at no expense to themselves, in order to help decide [in municipal elections] who shall control their rates and bus fares and gas bills.'[142] Putting to one side the deeper causes of apathy (which MO was not in any position to affect directly), Harrisson denied that 'the masses are too "dumb" to take any notice of politics', insisting rather that the politicians—'too "dumb" to take any notice of the masses'—fostered popular indifference to politics by continuing to present their messages in language 'which advertisers, film-producers, sub-editors have long since rejected'.[143]

MO set out to demonstrate that the language and techniques of the new cultural entrepreneurs could be put to good use in mobilizing people for the older virtues of active citizenship, using propaganda methods drawn from the commercial world to stimulate the non-voter into active citizenship.[144] 'It ought to be possible', Barefoot had written in August 1937, 'to ... discover ... which sort of appeal is the most effective ... by sending out different forms of election address to each section [of a ward], and finding how each section voted'.[145] For the municipal elections of November 1937, MO produced three non-party leaflets based on pools coupons, comic strips, or dance-tune lyrics urging people to use their votes, distributing them to every other house in a number of streets.[146] Monitoring the subsequent voting they found that the 3,000 people in households that received the leaflets were 10 to 15 per cent more likely to vote than their un-leafleted neighbours.[147]

141. *First Year's Work*, 44–5; Harrisson, 'Poverty of Freedom', 345–7.
142. *First Year's Work*, 32, 44–5.
143. Harrisson, 'Poverty of Freedom', 289.
144. Harrisson, 'Poverty of Freedom', 162, 277–8, 347–8.
145. Barefoot memoir, 1939, 'Analysis of political material available', 46.
146. The pools leaflet is reproduced in *Britain Revisited*, 78–82.
147. 'Personification Processes—(You)', 10 October 1940, FR 448; Harrisson, 'Poverty of Freedom', 286–7.

While this intervention could be justified in the name of research, MO took things further in one ward, taking over the Labour campaign in an 'experiment... designed to see what pep and vigour and militancy would do in local politics'.[148] They distributed their own colloquially phrased (but unattributed) leaflets and shouted down the Tories with a super-powerful loudspeaker van broadcasting a mixture of George Formby, political insults, and Tom Harrisson crooning 'voodledoddledo and hatchacher noises' to the astonishment of bystanders who 'seemed to laugh and look as if it was a pro-fane action, the voice of god gone gay.' For good measure a cameraman from the left-wing film news team 'March of Time' arrived to record events.[149] The local children loved the razzmatazz, joining in enthusiastically with chants of 'vote, vote, vote for Mr Hadley'. But while MO's intervention increased the Labour vote (against the trend), it raised hackles among local Labour Party activists who 'resented what they thought of as the vulgarity of the cam-paign.'[150] 'The Conservatives', one disapproving Labour delegate complained, 'can at least behave like gentlemen.'[151] Harrisson was by this time so closely associated with the Labour Party that one of his contacts proposed to nomi-nate him for the local executive, another announced the formation of a 'Labour Research Group' under his direction, and a third tore up his draft editorial for the Party's local propaganda sheet when Harrisson complained that it was 'written in language that only politicians can understand'.[152] Harrisson himself described the relationship as 'a community of interest between our Mass-Observation work and the Labour movement.'[153]

During the Farnworth parliamentary by-election two months later, Harrisson went even further in compromising MO's independence. In order to assess the impact of canvassing on the propensity to vote MO needed access to the canvass returns of the two main parties. There was no difficulty getting hold of the Labour Party returns, but MO had no such close relations with the Conservatives.[154] To this end Frank Cawson joined

148. TH, 'Great Lever', October 1937, W 11/I.
149. CM to TH, 17 September 1937, Org&Hist 1/9.
150. Barefoot memoir, 1979; Barefoot memoir, 1939; 'Delegate Meeting', 3 November 1937, W 7/C; Davies, County borough election results, 513–14.
151. 'Delegate Meeting', 3 November 1937, W 7/C.
152. TH, 'In Labour Party Office, Spinners Hall', 8 November 1937, W 7/B; EB, 'Labour Party Re-Organisation Committee', 29 November 1937, W 7/C.
153. 'West Fulham March 1938', nd (July 1938?) FR A7, 5.
154. Harrisson himself had briefly joined the local Conservative Party in a futile effort to redress the Labour bias of his team, but rapidly concluded that since it was 'impossible to preserve

the party, infiltrated their committee rooms, and 'borrowed' their returns for the team at Davenport Street to work on overnight. Uncomfortable about the deception, which had included dating a female election worker under false pretences, he sternly reminded himself of Lenin's purported declaration that 'he would wear knickers in the cause of the Revolution.'[155] While the subterfuge, which showed clearly that canvassing did increase the propensity to vote, could be justified in the name of science, Cawson was horrified to learn a few weeks after the election that Harrisson had sold the pirated canvass returns to his contacts in Transport House.[156] Lacking the courage to confront Harrisson directly over this, he decided to leave MO as soon as he found another teaching job.[157]

In August 1937 Madge told the panel that 'politicians and advertising agencies' who had approached MO 'have been told that any results which MO may get must be published or made available simultaneously to everyone. If, on these conditions anybody still agrees to contribute to the finances of MO such a contribution has the status of a scientific grant and can be accepted.'[158] No evidence survives about who had made these approaches, or which of them, if any, were accepted, but Harrisson seems to have been taking money from the Labour Party during the winter of 1937–8 on terms that breeched the principle that the results of commissioned research should be 'published or made available simultaneously to everyone'. In the light of this it is difficult to know how to interpret an apparently firm statement in the April 1938 Bulletin:

> Mass-Observation has been approached by political bodies and advertising agencies which were willing to pay for exclusive information. To accept such offers would be injurious to the value of the work. Mass-Observation can only accept subsidies on the understanding that its organisers decide how the

for practical purposes an equal impartiality' the politics book would have to be 'written mainly for the Labour angle' (draft for *First Year's Work*, 37).

155. I can find no trace of Lenin making this bizarre remark.
156. We only have Cawson's word for it that Harrisson took money from Labour. His relationship with the national Labour Party at this point remains obscure. He claimed 'support for our ideas from Mr Attlee and others', (draft for *First Year's Work*, BMpap), and Michael Higgins, who was to act as an intermediary between Harrisson and Transport House later in 1938, was active in the Bolton municipal election campaign in November 1937 (list of helpers during the election in Great Lever, W 11/1.) Higgins was later identified by Harrisson as one of MO's early benefactors in Bolton (*Pub and the People*, 8). See also FR A7. Attlee was among those who in 1936 had agreed to have their names on the letterhead of TH's anticipated expedition to New Guinea (Heinmann, *Most Offending Soul*, 119).
157. Cawson, interviewed by Calder, 29 February 1980, 5, 8.
158. 'A Thousand Mass Observers', August 1937, FR A8.

investigation is to be carried out, and retain the right to publish all results. The organisers pledge themselves to retain this independence, or dissolve the organisation.

Despite the apparent firmness of this pledge—designed, presumably, to head off discontent from staff or panel members—Madge and Harrisson were using weasel words: 'retain the right to publish' dilutes the August 1937 condition of making results 'available simultaneously to everyone'. At the time this statement was made Harrisson was promising his Labour Party sponsors to delay 'for several years' publication of the results of work they had commissioned.[159]

V

Harrisson's interventionist spirit was not restricted to the political sphere. From the outset he was keen to supplement sociology with art, badgering leading London painters to come north and participate in the project. Trevelyan, Hood's benefactor who was friendly with both Madge and Harrisson, first visited Bolton in June 1937 and made several visits thereafter.[160] Michael Wickham came with him, setting up his easel in the street.[161] In April 1938, shortly after debating the relative merits of surrealism and realism with Trevelyan at the leftist Artists' International Association in London,[162] two of the leading members of the Euston Road school of realist painters went north to put theory into practice. William Coldstream and Graham Bell spent three weeks in Bolton, painting factory chimneys from the roof of the Bolton art gallery, sketching in the street and from the

159. TH to CM, 25 Jan 1940, 5, Org&Hist 1/1.
160. TH to Trevelyan, 7 June 1937, 16 March 1938, JTpap; Hood, interviewed by TH, 4 May 1972.
161. Wickham interviewed by Stanley, 8 February 1980. Wickham, who was later to be influential in the development of Habitat, was described by Terence Conran as 'a larger than life raconteur and bon vivant' (Obituary, *The Independent*, 7 February 1995). In his interview with Stanley he claimed to have spent several months working with MO (and sleeping with most of the women involved) in both Bolton and Blackpool, some of which may be true although the only trace I have been able to find of him in the archive is as the owner of a Bentley used to give rides to local children singing jingles in support of the Labour candidate in a municipal election ('Great Lever', November 1937, W 11/I). According to TH, Wickham 'spent only the shortest time with us, and he had a big car and didn't mix much with the people' (quoted in Stanley, *Extra Dimension*, 143).
162. Robert Radford, *Art for a Purpose. the Artists' International Association, 1933–1953*, 1987, 89.

balcony of the palais de dance, and all the time complaining bitterly about the food, the filth, and what they saw as the slovenly disorganization of everyday life in Davenport Street.[163] Harrisson, unsure about the relative merits of rival surrealist and realist approaches in painting, was pleased with their work: 'decent straight stuff' he told his friend Trevelyan, apologetically, and well suited for the visual ethnography with which he was intending to illustrate the planned books.[164]

To this end he also invited Humphrey Spender—a pioneer of documentary photography employed at the time by the *Daily Mirror*—to come and work in Bolton, and to supervise photography by other visitors. Spender, swept off his feet by Harrisson's charisma, made four extended visits, working unpaid, photographing everyday life in Bolton and Blackpool. Instructed to work unobserved, he was ill at ease with the class gulf, feeling 'like a man from another planet', and, unlike the full-time investigators, unable to make contact with the subjects of his enquiry. The pictures themselves have been controversial, seen by some as patronizing, voyeuristically objectifying their subjects, but by others as displaying 'a rare feeling of equality between photographer and photographed.'[165]

While Spender was instructed to work unobserved, Harrisson had a quite different agenda for the painters. 'The man in the street', he wrote in the *Mass-Observation* pamphlet, 'is apt to complain of art that it is not useful to him...yet every ornament on his mantelpiece is a proof [that he has aesthetic needs]...Mass-Observation is going to try to find out what this basic need is, and then if possible to get the artists to satisfy it.'[166] By facilitating dialogue between worker and artist Harrisson sought to rescue the former from aesthetic deprivation and the latter from ivory-tower isolation. As things stood, Boltonians had little opportunity to appreciate art. The art gallery, he told a gathering of local businessmen, 'is tucked away in a remote place...shut on Sundays' and, in any case, possessed 'only one picture...which

163. Coldstream, interviewed by Stanley, 19 May 1980; GBpap, *passim*.
164. Stanley, *Extra Dimension*, 117; TH to Trevelyan, nd (May 1938?), JTpap; see also Bell to Popham 4 May 1938, recounting a dinner with Harrisson: 'We all parted best of friends after Harrisson had said that our kind of painting could be correct and surrealism could only be retrogressive.'
165. Jeremy Mulford (ed.), *Worktown People. Photographs from Northern England 1937–38*, Bristol, 1982, 9, 15–16; Gurney, '"Intersex" and "Dirty Girls"', 261, 265–6, 271; Tony Bennett and Diane Watson (eds), *Understanding Everday Life*, Oxford, 2002, 195; draft for *First Year's Work*, 14, BMpap.
166. *Mass-Observation*, 37.

anyone with any sensibility could possibly enjoy.'[167] Bell and Coldstream
hoped that their realist paintings would have sufficient popular appeal to
encourage some wealthy local benefactor to commission more work from
them for the art gallery. Success in the Bolton experiment could, Bell wrote,
'revolutionise the art galleries in England', bringing art to the people and
income to artists producing the realist portrayal of local scenes that, he
assumed, ordinary people would be most likely to appreciate.[168]

It may have been with some such idea in mind that, in the summer of
1938, Harrisson took copies of the paintings he had solicited onto Bolton's
streets, writing to Trevelyan:

> I am...having fun showing all you boyses pictures of Bolton (you, Michael,
> Coldstream, Bell) to workers and getting their votes. Also getting comparative
> comments on Picasso and Rivera...As usual the old M-O method plays hell
> with sententious generalisations. For example everyone – contrary to Blunt's
> bet – recognised exactly where your picture was done...Michaels' work they
> think was done fifty years ago when the streets weren't safe to walk in by
> night. ALL are criticised, as I expected, for LACK OF LIFE...It's this business
> of LIFE...that is emerging so much. But I am more and more certain that
> ordinary workers have keen interest in and wish for good pictures.[169]

He reported the outcome of this experiment in a radio talk on 'Art and the
Ordinary Chap', insisting that it demonstrated that the masses were perfectly capable of appreciating the best in modern art (e.g. Picasso's *Guernica*),
and that British realist painters would widen their appeal if they put some
human beings in the streets among the mills and chimneys they painted so
evocatively.[170]

---

167. 'Too Apathetic. Anthropologist and Social Habits. Mass-Observation as remedy', unidenti-
     fied newspaper report of speech by TH to Bolton Rotary Club, August 1938. Press cuttings.
168. Bell to Popham, 30 April 1938, 4 May 1938; Bell to My dear family, 10 May 1938, GBpap;
     Stanley, *Extra Dimension*, 118–19.
169. TH to Trevelyan, August 1938, JTpap.
170. *The Listener*, 25 August 1938; Hood, interviewed by Harrisson, 4 May 1972; Harrisson, *Britain
     Revisited*, 132; Harrisson, 'Poverty of Freedom', 348–9; Stanley, *Extra Dimension*, 143. This was
     to be a continuing theme in Harrisson's writing. In 1943, for example, in a talk delivered to
     the Design and Industries Association, he recycled his pre-war Worktown experiments with
     paintings and, ranging across wartime evidence of popular taste in everything from radio
     drama to housing design, argued that far from producing a 'democracy of popular design',
     lazy commercial pandering to the lowest common denominator served only to give public
     sanction to habits of bad taste; habits often at odds with aesthetic sensibilities for which
     ordinary people could find no outlet. Down in private opinion there was an untapped audi-
     ence for good things. 'Humanity', he insisted, 'has basic good taste' (TH, 'Public Taste and
     Public Design', *Art and Industry*, September 1943).

But bridging the gap between art and the masses was not so easily done. No local benefactor appeared, and for Bell—at the time the leading British theorist of realist painting[171]—the Bolton experience did nothing to foster respect for his potential working-class audience. 'The people are all very nice,' he wrote to his girlfriend, 'but their stupidity is fantastic':

> The real trouble about this town is that class distinction is unknown. It really is like Soviet Russia an absolute hell of incompetence and awful food with a great deal of work going on and very nice people leading a very unpleasant life. The unpleasantness of the life has had an extraordinary effect upon the intelligence of the people which is just about as low as could be.[172]

For his parents in South Africa he chose a different comparison: 'the people here have less intelligence than any others I have ever met, even in Zululand.'[173] Bell's relief at returning, after three weeks in 'the hideous north', to his 'dear blessed haven of intelligence, comfort etc' in the metropolis[174] goes some way to explain the contempt with which the surrealist critic Herbert Read dismissed 'our English Realists...not the tough guys they ought to be but the effete and bastard offspring of the Bloomsbury school of needlework.'[175] Harrisson—whose toughness no one could deny—was inclined to agree.[176]

While Coldstream and Bell had nothing more to do with MO, Harrisson redirected his search for a genuinely popular aesthetic from professional artists to the work of amateur working-class painters. Since 1934 a group of enterprising amateurs in the Northumberland mining town of Ashington had turned a WEA art appreciation class into a painters' workshop, representing their everyday work and leisure in a primitive style untouched by the protocols of art school education.[177] When Harrisson got wind of the Ashington group—alerted by an article in *The Listener* written by one of Madge's Cambridge friends now living in the north-east—he quickly made contact, excited by the subject matter, the style, the conditions of production,

---

171. DNB entry on Bell; Bell, *The Artist and his Public*, 1939; Bell, 'Escape from Escapism', *Left Review*, January 1938.

172. Bell to Popham, 22 and 25 April 1938, GBpap.

173. Bell to 'Dear Family', April 1938, GBpap.

174. Bell to 'My Dear Family', 10 May 1938, GBpap.

175. Cited in Radford, *Art for a Purpose*, 89–90.

176. By October 1938 he was writing off 'the well-meaning Social Realist school' as phoney left-wing revolutionaries 'who paint portraits of rich women, Charlotte Street cafes and Sussex landscapes' (cited in Stanley, *Extra Dimension*, 120).

177. William Feaver, *Pitman Painters. The Ashington Group, 1934–1984*, Ashington, 2009.

and the painters' indifference to the art market; all of which, he believed, combined to provide a fresh and genuinely popular point of entry into the ongoing metropolitan debate about the social relevance of art. Trevelyan, himself shifting away from surrealism and intrigued by the naive realism of the amateurs, was equally enthusiastic, and in September 1938 the two men went to Ashington to meet the group.[178]

In the early months of 1938 Harrisson and Trevelyan had been discussing plans for an exhibition to coincide with the anticipated publication of Sommerfield's book on the pub. Alongside photos and paintings, the exhibition would feature reconstructions of 'a bit of a pub...part of a street...the graphiti of one lavatory wall...' and a mock-up of that MO standby of popular aesthetics, a mantelpiece. There would be Bolton smells, 'fish and chips frying continually, and soot falling constantly'. Typical meals would be served to the visitors, 'with readings aloud on how to eat them'.[179] In their excited imaginations, Harrisson and Trevelyan were conjuring up a cultural event to rival the surrealist exhibition of 1936. Fortunately for MO's reputation, perhaps, the delay in publishing *The Pub and the People* put paid to these plans, and Ashington seemed to provide the two men with an alternative, and rather less patronizing, way of putting MO on the cultural map.

By the end of their week in Ashington, Harrisson and Trevelyan had arranged to organize an exhibition of 'Unprofessional Painting' in a Gateshead community centre during October, featuring the work of the Ashington group alongside work by other amateur artists from around the country.[180] To accompany the exhibition they set up a series of lectures, including Harrisson on social realism and Madge on 'poetry and everyday life', culminating in a debate on the proposition that 'anyone can paint.' Mobilizing a miscellaneous collection of metropolitan intellectuals, avant-garde painters, and modernist architects to make the trip north for the debate,[181]

178. CM, interviewed by Stanley, 26 May 1978; *The Listener*, 28 April 1938; Stanley, *Extra Dimension*, 144; DNB entry on Trevelyan. Janet Adam Smith had been Arts Editor of *The Listener* before moving to Newcastle where her husband, the poet Michael Roberts, taught at the grammar school (Feaver, *Pitman Preachers*, 67 predates *The Listener* article by a year).

179. TH to Trevelyan, February and March 1938, JTpap.

180. For details of the exhibition see Feaver, *Pitman Painters*, 77 and material in TC 33/1/E.

181. Including Penguin's Allen Lane; Jean Varda, a Greek artist living in London, who had exhibited in the 1936 surrealist exhibition; the American/French surrealist Henri Goetz; and two modernist architects, Serge Chermayeff and Denis Clarke Hall.

the two men looked forward to a weekend of cross–class mingling, facilitated by the sleeping arrangements:

> FAR BEST [wrote Harrisson to Trevelyan] if most of us can stop on mattresses on floor...mixed up with Ashingtonians, this would be ideal...All have come to mix in with Ashington chaps, and that is what they want to do – not have elaborate meals with [middle-class] hosts, and have to be in at a certain time...

He did allow, however, for 'a few beds in houses for those who don't stand that sort of thing because they are afraid to undress in public', notably his friend the critic and writer Geoffrey Gorer—a 'tough explorer but also a soft civilised creature'.[182] It did not occur to Harrisson that the Ashington men might be equally 'civilised', and Trevelyan remembered a comic mismatch of sartorial manners in the dormitory—the Ashington men having brought their best pyjamas while the wild artists from the south 'had only a few rags if anything to sleep in.'[183]

Despite such cultural misunderstandings, the Ashington men seem to have been pleased to meet the professionals on something approaching their own ground, and the debate, chaired by Tom Driberg, attracted around 60 people. Gorer spoke against the motion, as did George Downs, a self-taught painter who made a living selling lingerie in the Caledonian Road market and whose paintings of Blackpool were among those Harrisson was intending to use in the Gollancz books.[184] Despite having some of his own pictures in the exhibition, Downs insisted that years spent struggling to paint without an art school training had convinced him that the motion's proposers were wrong to suggest that 'painting offers the simplest technique of self-expression', requiring, unlike music-making, no special training. Sweeping aside such reservations, Harrisson and Trevelyan carried the day for democracy: by a two to one majority it was agreed that 'anyone can paint a good picture'.[185]

So far as Ashington was concerned, Gateshead was an end rather than a beginning. While the affinities between MO's practice and their own

---

182. 'Persons coming to weekend school', nd, TC 33/1/B.
183. Feaver, *Pitman Painters*, 80.
184. TH to Trevelyan, August 1938, JTpap. The two men took a continuing interest in Downs (TH to Trevelyan, 5 June 1941) and on 19 August 1944 TH, writing from Australia, urged the Trevelyans to 'keep art alive and Downs off the drink'.
185. Feaver, *Pitman Painters*, 79–82.

documentary representation of the everyday may have encouraged
Harrisson to fantasize about using the Ashington men as the nucleus of a
second Worktown-style project,[186] they had their own agenda and no
interest in becoming mass observers. In any case, by the end of October,
Harrisson had moved his centre of operations to London, and his continuing interest in Ashington reflected his concern, not to colonize the group,
but to promote it as a model to encourage similar initiatives in other parts
of the country. To this end he and Trevelyan arranged for the 'Unprofessional
Painting' exhibition to go on tour to the Peckham health centre, the
Fulham public library and the Mansfield art gallery in the Nottinghamshire
coalfield. On each occasion visitors were invited to sign up if they were
interested in forming a group of their own, but despite Trevleyan's declaration that 'there is no town or community where it would not be possible
to form a group somewhat on the same lines [as Ashington] and achieve
very much the same results' nothing came of these initiatives.[187] Equally
abortive was the plan Harrisson put together for a book that he and
Trevelyan were going to write to accompany a 'permanent touring collection' of 'the working class art which…goes on unnoticed in England.'
Elaborating on the brochure Harrisson had written for Gateshead, the
book was to discuss Ashington and the 50 or so 'ordinary painters, painting
ordinary life' with whom the two men claimed to be in contact, setting
their work in the context of different 'ways of seeing', from primitive art in
Melanesia to MO's own researches on popular reactions to contemporary
painting.[188] Early in 1939 they took the proposition to Faber and Faber
where Read turned it down, effectively putting an end to Harrisson's
attempt to deploy his entrepreneurial skills in the world of art. Many years
later, reflecting on these events, Trevelyan pointed out that although the
Ashington group still existed,

> it has become the antithesis of what Tom thought it. He conceived of it as
> working-class people painting their own lives, with an admiring audience
> around them. Now they lead rather a life apart, nobody much sees their work,
> and they have no effect on the community. At that time we all encouraged

186. TC 33/1/A contains an outline for a 'Study of a Mining Town' based on Ashington; and an
      undated document from late 1938 includes a reference to 'a group of 20' in Ashington who
      'are co-operating' in M-O's work ('Outline of Social Factors in Economics', nd, W1/C).
187. Feaver, *Pitman Painters*, 83; Stanley, *Extra Dimension*, 121; BB, 'Fulham exhibtion', 4 January
      1939, TC 33/1/A.
188. Book outline, TC 33/1/A.

everyone to paint, but now the world is full of mostly rather bad amateur painters, and they need discouragement if anything.[189]

VI

All four of the books commissioned by Gollancz were originally scheduled for publication in the autumn and winter of 1938.[190] When Barefoot returned to Bolton in July 1938 he found everyone furiously involved in writing up the politics material, with a deadline looming at the end of August.[191] By the end of the year Harrisson was claiming that complete drafts of the planned volumes on politics, Blackpool, and the pub were ready for the publisher; and that the fourth volume, on religion, was close to completion.[192] In the event the only book that Gollancz published was *The Pub and the People*, and that not until 1943. What went wrong?

Harrisson's wartime correspondence with Gollancz goes some way to explain what happened. Sommerfield's draft of the book on the pub was ready by the autumn of 1938, but neither Gollancz nor Harrisson were satisfied with it, and subsequent revisions and rewriting delayed the final draft until shortly before the war. After some further last-minute adjustments the proofs finally emerged in March 1940, at which point Harrisson insisted on rewriting the preface, now 'flagrantly out of date and . . . out of line with the latest development of our own work . . . giving a misleading idea of our methods and scope.'[193] A year later, when Gollancz, assuming that MO had decided to abandon the book, asked if it was safe to scrap the type, Harrisson was spurred into renewed action, working with Sommerfield and Watkin (both now in the army) to produce a much shorter version of the

---

189. Trevelyan to Sheridan, 16 November 1982, Personnel/Trevelyan.
190. FR A7, March 1938.
191. Barefoot memoir, 1939, 158, 172.
192. Harrisson to Simon, nd (December 1938?), W1/B. In November he had reported that all four books were already with the publisher (M-O Bulletin, FR A8, November 1938).
193. TH to Horsman, 4 April 1940; TH to Collins, 7 September, 4 December 1939; Sommerfield to TH, 20 January 1940; TH to Collins, 14 February 1940; Collins to TH, 23 February 1940, all in Org & Hist, 3/Gollancz. See also TH to CM, 18 January 1940, 16; TH to CM, 25 January 1940, 3–4 both in Org & Hist, 1. I have found no evidence to support Liz Stanley's assertion that Gertrude Wagner played a key role in writing the book (Liz Stanley, 'It has always known, and we have always been "other": Knowing capitalism and the "coming crisis" of sociology confront the concentration system and Mass-Observation', *Sociological Review*, 54, 6, 2008, 549).

manuscript.[194] Finally, in February 1942, lobbied by Basil Nicholson (who had written the section on drink in the 1935 volume of the *New Survey of London Life and Labour*), Gollancz agreed to publish the book and Harrisson sent in corrected proofs a month before he was conscripted into the army in July 1942.[195] *The Pub and the People* finally appeared in January 1943, though shorn of the photographs Spender had taken to illustrate it.

The draft of the Blackpool book, submitted 'under the utmost pressure' sometime in 1939, seems to have languished unread at the publishers until war broke out, at which point 'we were finally left to take it away again'.[196] By 1942 it was clear to Harrisson that publication would have to wait until after the war, when he hoped to be able to update the manuscript with new research.[197] He did do a bit more work on it before his death in 1976, and a version was eventually published in 1990, pieced together by Gary Cross from material in the archive.[198]

No one, as yet, has tried to rescue the book on religion, perhaps because Nick Stanley, MO's first historian, judged that it was hard to see from the remaining material what the book would have looked like.[199] There were ambitious plans to incorporate photographs (by Martin-Jones), paintings (by Trevelyan), and drawings (by Hood), and a draft of the opening chapter, clearly drawing on Harrisson's experience, is constructed as an account written by a Melanesian sent to Bolton by his cannibal tribe:

> The tribe are on the fringe of Missionary activity, which is pressing inland. They must decide between either preserving their own beliefs and dying out from introduced disease, or accepting the new way of life which they do not

194. TH to Fitter, 21 May 1941, TC 25/12/a; Gollancz to TH, 27 May 1941; Horsman to TH, 19 August 41; TH to Horsman, 26 August 1941; TH to Gollancz, 2 October 1941 all in Org & Hist, 3/Gollancz.
195. TH to Gollancz, 13 May, 8 June 1942, in Org & Hist, 3/Gollancz.
196. TH to Collins, 26 February 1940, Org & Hist, 3/Gollancz. Stanley Cramp believed that publication of the politics volume was held up because the local authority threatened to sue over what it said about sewers (Cramp, interviewed by Calder, 17 March 1980). This seems more likely to be a confused memory of the Blackpool book, whose opening passage describing the discharge of sewage on the beach can hardly have pleased local worthies in a resort that promoted itself as home of goof health (Cross, *Blackpool*, 75).
197. *Pub and the People*, 9.
198. Cross, *Blackpool*, 62.
199. Stanley, *Extra Dimension*, 22. However, since Stanley wrote this, more material seems to have come to light, and it might well be possible for someone to reconstruct the book on religion as Gary Cross did for leisure, and Liz Stanley for M-O's 1949 report on sexual attitudes and behaviour.

understand. So they send [a] delegate...over to the 'Geneva of the North', that he may report on What is this Christianity. Does it do among white men what the missionary says it will do among the black men?[200]

An early sketch for this chapter included the Melanesian's observation of churchyards: 'you walk across a belt of stones over corpses to enter the service of eternal life', and a description of 'communion from the cannibal point of view'.[201] By the time drafts of the other three books were finished in the autumn of 1938, however, Harrisson had run out of money, and Wilcock, the chief researcher, had to find another job.[202] In December 1938 Harrisson was still discussing a 'working synopsis for [the] religion book' with Lee[203] and he commissioned Derek Kahn to write the introductory chapter.[204] The 273-page draft that survives in the archive took another year to produce.[205] In January 1940 Harrisson was intending to have a final manuscript ready by the spring, but Gollancz had probably lost interest by then and MO's work for the wartime Ministry of Information left Harrisson with little time to pursue an alternative publisher.

One reason the religion book found itself at the back of the queue may well have been tension between Wilcock and Harrisson over the approach to be taken. Wilcock himself was no writer and, despite designating him as author of the forthcoming book, there is little doubt that Harrisson intended all along to write it himself, with help from his educated, middle-class associates.[206] Introducing the study, Harrisson explained that finding out 'how religion works or doesn't in a large industrial town' was equally important for those who 'are interested in insuring its future survival and to all those who are interested in securing its immediate destruction.'[207] But this stance of impartiality must have been difficult to sustain, since Harrisson (a non-

200. 'Christianity in Industrial Bolton', W14/C. This is undated, but early in 1938 Harrisson had been anticipating a fifth book, summing up the findings of the whole Worktown project, to be entitled *A Cannibal looks at Britain* and to be written entirely by himself ('and fireworks are therefore to be expected to go off every other paragraph'). The publisher, he reported, expected the book to be a best seller (draft of *First Year's Work*, 46, BMpap).
201. 'Christianity in Industrial Bolton', W14/C.
202. TH to CM, 25 January 1940, 21, Org&Hist 1.
203. Lee, 'Working Synopsis for Religion Book' 2 January 1939, W 14/B.
204. Sensibly Kahn—'as someone who hopes eventual to assist his livelihood by writing'— demanded a written contract specifying both payment for his work, and, aware no doubt of the fate of others, his acknowledgement as an author: Kahn to TH, 31 December 1938.
205. Typescript in W 14/B. See also TH to CM, 25 January 1940, 21, Org&Hist 1.
206. Barefoot memoir (1939). Already in February 1938 TH seems to have taken charge of the writing: 'Questions for Clergy, etc' 20 February 1938, W14/A.
207. 'Christianity in Industrial Bolton', W14/C.

believer) saw Wilcock as 'a far-out fundamentalist' easily taken in by par-
sonic sentimentality, and Wilcock (whose capacity to get on with the local
clergy was critical to the success of the project) worried that Harrisson was
going to make 'some blasphemous use of the material.'[208] Such incompatible
viewpoints must have made it difficult to move from the collection of information to the framing of a coherent analysis.

It was with the book on politics that Harrisson's compulsion to supplant
those he had earlier named as authors of the Gollancz books was at its most
blatant. Watkin later wrote angrily of the exploitation of MO's 'less educated' workers, who Harrisson had seduced into working for nothing 'by
feeding them promises of future fame' as authors of forthcoming books. He
had in mind Wilcock, but the remark might equally have applied to Hood.[209]
Barefoot realized from his earliest days with MO that 'while Tom Harrisson
would make his name from Bolton, no-one else was likely to make a career
from it.'[210] In an account of his time in Bolton, written in August 1939,
Barefoot commented:

> As for the books...they were originally supposed to have been published by
> Gollancz last autumn, then the dates were postponed to spring and then sum-
> mer; the latest I heard was that Harrisson was going to take them to another
> publisher. Perhaps he is trying to buy off or otherwise eliminate the 'part
> authors', so that he may rewrite all the books himself; perhaps persecution
> mania has something to do with it; but it's certainly queer that with all the
> material ready and the books (except perhaps the religious book) fit for the
> printer, nothing ever happens about them, and no one ever hears.[211]

Some people even suspected, according to Barefoot, that Harrisson's paranoia about other people sabotaging the work led him to engineer a fire
'which destroyed a large proportion of the political material'.[212] Be that as

208. Hood, interviewed by TH, 4 May 1972; TH interview with Rev J Bright, 7 November 1937,
     W21/C; Kahn to TH, November 1937, W1/B.
209. Watkin to Sheridan, 28 January 1995.
210. Barefoot memoir, 1979.
211. Barefoot memoir, 1939.
212. Humphrey Spender, less conspiratorially, attributed the fire to the 'endless smoking'
     (Heimann, *Most Offending Soul*, 138). This was not the only disaster to befall the political
     material. Early in 1938 Harrisson wrote that: 'One Saturday evening some persons burgled
     the house and destroyed a considerable party of the results of the non-political [i.e. non-
     voter] part of the work, some of which cannot be replaced. Of course we expect this type of
     opposition, everyone who is trying to report truly and accurately what happens in modern
     life must expect this sort of thing. £300 went down the drain that burgle' (draft for *First Year's
     Work*, 38, BMpap). Graham Bell reported that the staff had 'a ridiculous persecution mania.

it may, he certainly took over the authorship, leading the Labour Party agent in East Fulham (with whom, as we shall see, Harrisson had by then worked closely) to warn a new recruit in November 1938: 'Please look out for Tom Harrisson and for heaven's sake do not start to work on the understanding that you will be part author of a book for on that road lies disappointment and disillusionment. This from Walter Hood and he knows.'[213]

What seems to have happened is that, in order to free himself from any possible interference from his erstwhile colleagues, Harrisson put the non-voter manuscript on a back burner, while forging ahead with a book of his own, 'The Poverty of Freedom', which made full use of the Bolton material while not presenting itself as an MO study.[214] This book was completed in June 1939 and was due to be published in August by the Liberal Book Club, a choice of publisher that marked a significant shift in Harrisson's politics away from his close identification with the Labour Party during the first half of 1938. At the last moment, with the book in proof, the Liberal Book Club collapsed, and a subsequent attempt to get Chatto and Windus to take the book on came to nothing.[215] During 1939 Harrisson had been intending to go ahead with the non-voter book for Gollancz as well, and as late as May 1941 he was intending to publish some of the material in another context.[216] But by August 1942, when he wrote the preface to *The Pub and the People*, Harrisson had given up any hope that any of the other volumes would see the light of day until they could be updated post-war.[217]

The disappointingly thin results of Harrisson's 'experiment' in Bolton have sometimes been ascribed to the vagueness of his research agenda or to his chaotic style of managing the work. In the light of the evidence presented here, however, it seems more reasonable to attribute the non-appearance

---

They believe that fascist ROUGHS and other lawless elements are continually hoping to break in and bust up the house. Consequently the house is locked and barred, and every room has its padlock and everyone in the house locks his room religiously as he comes out of it' (Bell to 'My dear family', 10 May 1938, GBpap).

213. Jackson to Thomas, 30 November 1938, Personnel/Thomas.
214. Proofs of the 'Poverty of Freedom' were deposited in the MO Archive by Richard Fitter in 1992.
215. Dougal to TH, 20 November 1939, Org&Hist 3/1.
216. TH to Simon, nd (December 1938?), W1/B; see also 'Poverty of Freedom', 162. In 1941 Stanley Cramp wrote a well-researched chapter for a Penguin that never appeared placing the Bolton material alongside published studies of non-voting from America and continental Europe (Cramp to TH, 16 May 1941, W6/D; RF 'Progress Report on Penguin' 4 April 1941, TC 25/12/A).
217. *Pub and the People*, 9.

of three of the four commissioned volumes to circumstances beyond his control. However badly Harrisson treated his putative authors, it is quite clear from MO's subsequent publication record under his management that he knew how to turn wide-ranging research materials into marketable books. His failure to do this with the Bolton material was mainly a result of shifting priorities caused by the international crisis both for the publishing industry and for MO itself. In the autumn of 1938, with the Bolton research apparently complete, Harrisson joined Madge in London to investigate popular attitudes during the Munich crisis. It was this work, for the first time bringing their divergent approaches into effective collaboration, which was to secure MO's public reputation and pave the way for its subsequent wartime career. Before examining these developments, however, we must turn our attention from the anthropologist to the poet, from Bolton to Blackheath.

3

Madge's Observers

I

While Tom Harrisson organized his 'objective' fieldwork in Bolton, Charles Madge concentrated on building up the national panel of volunteers, and on developing appropriate analytical tools for making sense of the 'subjective' accounts of everyday life, attitudes, and feelings sent in by the volunteers. During the first phase of his work in Bolton, as we have seen, Harrisson was anxious to work incognito, establishing background information and the ground rules of detached, objective fieldwork before the subjects of Mass-Observation's (MO's) investigation became aware that they were being observed. Madge, on the other hand, needed publicity. While he was at one with Harrisson in the belief that 'slow development, gradual mobilisation, and avoidance of emotional or revivalist appeal, are essential to the building up of a scientific organisation,'[1] it was only by advertising the project that he would be able to recruit more volunteers, and widen the social and political range of the panel. Articles in the *News Chronicle, Daily Herald* and *Daily Express* did something to broaden the base and the widespread press coverage that followed the publication of Madge and Harrisson's *Mass-Observation* pamphlet in June 1937 brought a flood of new offers of help.[2] Assiduous in cultivating endorsements from the great and the good, the two men set up an advisory committee—it probably never actually met—which included H. G. Wells, Julian Huxley (perhaps Britain's best known scientist, and author of the preface to the *Mass-Observation* pamphlet), Bronislaw Malinowski, John Hilton, J. B. Priestley, Olaf Stapeldon (philosopher, pacifist, and science-fiction writer), George Catlin (Fabian,

1. *Mass-Observation*, 46.
2. *News Chronicle*, 30 January 1937; CM, interviewed by Calder, March 1976, 19; *May the Twelfth*, iii.

political scientist, campaigner for Indian independence, and husband of Vera Brittain), and Canon F. R. Barry (who had published on psychology and Christianity).[3]

By the end of the first year there were about 600 observers, three-quarters of them recruited via the *New Statesman*. Of the latter, half were from London and the Home Counties, but over a hundred were from industrial parts of the North, Midlands and South Wales. The panel remained overwhelmingly middle class, though covering the whole range from substantial businessmen, scientists, and intellectuals to clerks and shopkeepers. No more than 10 per cent were in working-class occupations.[4] By the end of 1938 over 900 people had responded to MO's appeals for voluntary observers, but one-third of these dropped out after a single response, and another 100 after two responses. Little more than 300 people sent in more than five responses during these two years, and only 100 more than ten. Responses to individual directives, which had grown to nearly 100 by June 1937, doubled in July following the publication of the *Mass-Observation* pamphlet, and stayed well above 200 until November. But during 1938 numbers seldom exceeded 100, except when the dead-line was extended over several months, and around the time of the Munich crisis when they peaked at 172.[5]

But numbers were never an end in themselves: the quality of the observers mattered as much as the quantity, and Madge devoted much care and attention to training his recruits. Whatever the future might hold, the very process of constructing this 'elementary piece of human organisation and adaptation' would 'effectively contribute to an increase in the general social consciousness' by encouraging its members 'to look more closely at their

3. *First Year's Work*, 62. There were three other academics on this panel: H. J. Fleure, professor of geography at Manchester and an influential figure in the development of community studies, who encouraged his students to work for Harrisson in Bolton (TH to Malinowski, 31 November 1937, BMpap; R. Pahl, review of Mike Savage, *Identities and Social Change since 1940*, *Sociological Review*, 59, 1, 2011); Philip Sargant Florence, an industrial economist who was later to preside over the establishment of sociology at Birmingham, and whose support for MO continued during the war (Consultative Committee, minutes, 10 October, 2 December 1942, Org&Hist 4/3); and T. H. Pear, professor of psychology at Manchester, discussed later in this chapter.
4. Stanley, *Extra Dimension*, 152; 'New Statesman Panel Composition, 1937–47', FR 2479, 1947; *First Year's Work*, 64–5; 'Directives', April 1937, FR A4.
5. These figures need to be treated with caution since they are based on extant material catalogued in the archive. The number of extant responses, particularly before the war, often differ from the numbers claimed in contemporary MO sources, most notably for the smoking and mantelpiece directives.

social environment than ever before'.[6] As the scientist Huxley put it in his preface to *Mass-Observation*, the new organization was creating 'a band of socially-minded and scientifically-minded people within the community at large.'

As the number of observers increased the work involved in communicating with them and in filing and analysing their reports also grew. In the spring of 1937 Madge expected the composition of the Blackheath team to 'remain fluid until we can employ the best people for the job. Some members of it will be whole-time workers, others will act as advisers.'[7] Less information has survived about the personnel in Blackheath than in Bolton, but it seems unlikely that Madge had the resources during 1937–8 to employ anyone on a full-time basis. Much of the work was done by Madge and Kathleen Raine, aided by a fluctuating body of volunteers drawn mostly from among observers resident in London.[8] In October 1937, for example, he had six people beavering away analysing the latest day survey. Many years later Madge recalled having had initial help from up to 20 such people 'who just turned up and just worked for a day on some fairly mechanical job'.[9] At the time, he could be equally dismissive of the contribution of these helpers, confiding to his mistress in August 1938: 'I have three people working away in the big room today while I sit here in M-O office writing to you. They are slow, incompetent and stupid.' But the next day things looked up:

> Blackheath is buzzing with people. A marvellous coal-bagger and all-in-wrestler arrived for breakfast, having come down from Bolton on a lorry all night. One of the nicest people I've met for a long time [Bill Naughton]. Also a crippled schoolteacher from Northumberland in a chair who is very good. And a boy and a girl from Lewisham. Not to mention Ralph Parker [the *Times* journalist] and Joe Wilcock [who had recently moved back to London]. I set them all to work and then retire. And I too work.[10]

Among Madge's more regular helpers was Bruce Watkin, a leading member of the Oxford group of observers, who managed the office for a time and helped with the writing of reports, and 19-year-old Priscilla Feare (probably the 'girl from Lewisham'), who came to work (unpaid) as a typist and filing

6. *Mass-Observation*, 47–8, 29.
7. *Mass-Observation*, 43.
8. MO *Bulletin*, February 1945, FR 2213.
9. CM, interviewed by Stanley, 23 March 1978; MO *Bulletin*, October 1937, FR A4.
10. CM to Inez, 2 and 3 August 1938 to Inez, CMpap, 8/3.

clerk. The atmosphere in Blackheath, as Feare remembered it from the summer of 1938, could hardly have been more different from what we know of Bolton: laid-back working lunches on the terrace, and Madge himself 'rather languid... most charming and wonderful to work for.'[11] In fact, by then, Madge's marriage, and with it the viability of the Blackheath house as a base for MO, was on the point of collapse. While Feare was not privy to Madge and Raine's marital difficulties, another volunteer, Gay Taylor, quickly became intimately involved. Taylor, a middle-aged writer, astrologist, and mystic, was described by Raine as one of 'the many "dotty" correspondents who answered Charles' advertisements', and came to address envelopes. In appearance she was 'a caricature of a lady novelist of the twenties with her brow curtained by her long fringe, her dangling earrings, her cigarette-holder, her verbal underlining's'. Deeply scarred by an unhappy love affair, 'her life... as totally catastrophic as my own was fast becoming', Taylor formed the closest of bonds with Raine. Madge disliked her, perhaps sensing that she was 'one of those women allies of other women who are so dangerous to marriages.' Taylor did much to sustain Raine during the break-up of the Madges' marriage and in later years the two women were to become 'fellow pilgrims' in the search 'for a self that is fit to look for a God.'[12] But Taylor also graduated from addressing envelopes to become an enthusiastic interviewer who worked on and off for MO into the 1950s.

From this complicated and fluctuating ménage in Blackheath, Madge set out to foster the skills of his dispersed observers. The amateur status of the panellists—'he will not need to have received scientific training in order to make his observations'[13]—was crucial to MO's democratic aspirations; but it did not mean that the observers were simply left to their own devices. From the outset, rather than just inviting them to send in accounts of their day, Madge gave them detailed instructions on how this should be done. In March, for example, they were told to keep their feelings for a final section, and stick to facts in the body of the report. Information about their health, the weather, and the background of local events should be followed by a

11. Macnamara (née Feare), interviewed by Calder, 10 January 1980; Watkin to MO, 21 January 1995.
12. Raine, *The Land Unknown*, 86–91; Loran Hurnscot, pseud. [Gay Taylor], *A Prison, a Paradise, etc. Reminiscences in the form of a diary*, London, 1958, 177. The 'life-enhancing' sense of fun which Raine so appreciated in Taylor is apparent throughout this book, including her accounts of MO, thinly disguised as *Bomp*. Taylor had been involved from the outset, sending in reports of dreams full of predictive coincidences and Freudian sexual references (TC 28/1/A).
13. *Mass-Observation*, 31.

factual (later versions specified 'hour by hour') report of their own day. When recording conversations they should indicate the class of the speaker (and what criteria they had used to determine it), and they were warned to be wary of reporting conversation in direct speech ('very often incorrectly remembered') unless written down almost immediately.[14] By June 1937 Madge was asking new volunteers to write a 500-word self-report— 'everyone has his own individual background, which is likely to affect his observations, and which must be taken into consideration in dealing with his reports'—and to train their powers of observation by submitting an account of the contents of their mantelpiece and those of their friends and relatives. Only after they had sent in two or three day surveys could their initial training be thought complete.[15] From the start Madge circulated volunteers with mimeographed examples of the most interesting observer reports, and from August 1937 he produced a printed monthly bulletin presented as 'an experiment in co-operative newspaper-making, since those who read it will also help to write it.'[16] He also did his best to respond individually to observers with praise and constructive criticism of their work.[17] In May he noted approvingly that the observers' reports were 'showing a marked increase in accuracy and control of the subjective elements over their earlier efforts.'[18] No doubt the extensive training package helped to deter many of the 1,000 new volunteers who had offered to help in June, and by October Madge was asking those who had expressed an interest but not contributed if they would be interested in joining a 'second line' of observers with less stringent obligations. But his sights were set on building the front line, the shock troops of the 'democratic science' which, he wrote in October, would open the way towards the eventual transformation of Britain into 'a scientific democracy'.[19]

Had the *Mass-Observation* pamphlet put more stress on the element of training involved this might have gone some way to deflect MO's critics, many of whom focussed on the unreliability of untrained observers. While Madge accepted that the observers were indeed 'subjective cam-

14. *May the Twelfth*, 350–1.
15. 'Directive to new observers', June 1937, FR A4; *Mass-Observation*, 31–2.
16. *Mass-Observation*, 41; 'MO Circular', April 1937, FR A4 370800 A8 'A Thousand Mass Observers', August 1937, FR A8.
17. Although no such letters have survived, there are appreciative replies to Madge thanking him for his advice among the day surveys.
18. *May the Twelfth*, 89.
19. MO *Bulletin*, October 1937, FR A4.

eras' who reported not 'what society was like, but what it looks like to them', he was keen to make a distinction between the private feelings and opinions of his informants and their capacity to report accurately on the facts of their everyday lives. With training, the distortions introduced by their own feelings could be reduced; hence the advice to keep their private feelings and opinions to the end of their day surveys. Moreover the very fact that they had volunteered to work for MO meant that they were likely to be people with 'some extra degree of detachment which makes them want to stand back from . . . normal life and describe it', as well as being 'above average in their ability to . . . express themselves on paper.'[20] Huxley agreed, reporting that 'some of the "day surveys" I have seen . . . would put many orthodox scientists to shame in their simplicity, clearness and objectivity.'[21]

II

The date for the day surveys had been selected because the coronation was fixed for 12 May, and, from the outset, Madge and Humphrey Jennings were planning to compare the experience of Coronation Day with those of a normal day. The heightened collective fantasy to be expected on Coronation Day provided a perfect opportunity to subject to scientific analysis a relatively harmless version of the kind of collective hysteria—'these forces of the lower mind'—whose more sinister forms it was MO's task to find ways of combating, as they explained in a leaflet distributed ahead of the coronation to solicit reports from the general public. The 77 responses, along with 43 day surveys sent in by established observers, and a mobile squad of 12 people deployed in London on the day, provided the raw material for MO's first book, *May the Twelfth: Mass-Observation Day-Surveys*, a scissors and paste job completed by Madge and Jennings in little more than two weeks and published (at T. S. Eliot's insistence) by Faber in September 1937.[22] Over 400

20. *First Year's Work*, 66.
21. *Mass-Observation*, 6.
22. Draft for *First Year's Work*, BMpap, 47; Hubble, *Mass-Observation and Everyday Life*, 66. Madge and Jennings were assisted in this work by several other people, notably the poet and critic William Empson who had been part of Jenning's circle in Cambridge and who also visited Bolton around this time with Trevelyan, where he was sent by Harrisson to report on the contents of sweet shop windows (John Haffenden, *William Empson: among the Mandarins*, 2005, 428–9).

pages long, the book was expensive and did not sell well.[23] The material on Coronation Day, edited by Jennings, was presented in documentary-style press cuttings juxtaposed with one another, and the divergent images supplied by the three different kinds of reports providing 'close-up and long shot, detail and ensemble.'[24] But the evocative manipulation of images that Jennings did so brilliantly in film worked less well in this huge and sprawling text, and the book was as likely to evoke boredom as emotional involvement. Most of it dealt with the preparations for 12 May and the events of the day, but a final section, written by Madge, attempted a scientific analysis of the day surveys from 12 March, a normal day, by way of contrast to the documentary treatment of 12 May. The book had a mixed reception. Some found the material fascinating: 'a social document of real importance'.[25] But to the sociologist T. H. Marshall it appeared 'so completely devoid of interest that even the most well-intentioned reviewer is at a loss to find anything to say about its contents.'[26]

These divergent views are partly a result of an ambiguity running through the text. David Pocock, who supplied an afterword to the re-publication of the book in 1987, recalls his schoolboy delight, surreptitiously reading under his desk, in its 'magnificent subversion of authority'.[27] The juxtaposition of press cuttings detailing official preparations for the celebrations with stories of outraged Scottish protestants threatening to burn the Pope (who had been invited to attend) in effigy, Hindu subjects of Raj protesting at plans for public ox-roasting, and London catering workers, musicians, and busmen planning to disrupt proceedings in pursuit of higher pay, serves to deflate the high-flown rhetoric of national and imperial unity. Evidence that for many the main attraction of the day was not the rituals of kingship but just the excuse for a holiday has a similar effect. And the book's subversive intent was revealed most explicitly by the placing of an overblown *Times* leader (ridiculed in a footnote as displaying a 'primitive animism' in its claim that 'the Crown is the necessary centre, not of political life only, but

23. David Pocock, 'Afterword', *May the Twelfth*, 2009 edition, 417; Calder and Sheridan, *Speak for Yourselves*, 62.
24. *May the Twelfth*, 90. Madge and Jennings had already carried out a similar exercise on the February day surveys, which got as far as being typeset but was never published (draft of *First Year's Work*, 47, BMpap).
25. [I. A. Williams] 'A clown of Witnesses', *Times Literary Supplement*, 2 October 1937; *Yorkshire Post*, 15 October, cited in *First Year's Work*, 61.
26. T. H. Marshall, 'Is M-O Moonshine', *The Highway*, December 1937.
27. David Pocock, 'Afterword', *May the Twelfth*, 2009 edition, 415.

of all life') alongside a declaration from the Communist leader, Harry Pollitt, that this attempt by the class enemy to gild the workers' chains with a day of 'cheap bunting and flags' would not long delay the revolution which would transform Britain into 'a paradise in which the sun of joy will never set', a claim on whose extravagance Madge and Jennings saw no need to comment.[28]

These moments of subversion, however, are contained within a day infused with a sense of national occasion, and the story *May the Twelfth* tells is of a kind of unofficial national unity running alongside the official celebrations. The 'peculiar quality of the day' penetrated everywhere, even into the dream life of the observers, and whatever doubts the abdication crisis may have raised about the mystery of monarchy seem to have disappeared by the time of the coronation. Harrisson, who thought Madge crazy to give Jennings free rein in editing the material, and deplored the picture it painted of MO's work, nevertheless found the book of value in showing how 'everyone, even extreme anti-royalists and Communists, were [sic] drawn on May 12th somewhat into the spirit and feeling of the occasion... differences in outlook... were overwhelmed by a common bond and focus which is apparently the strongest of any that can be presented to Englishmen.'[29] Turning its gaze from the pomp of the procession to the behaviour of the crowd MO found not the regimented hysteria of the Nazi rally but the same quirky individualism and the same comforting capacity to domesticate and gently laugh at the pretentions of power (throwing sweets to the soldiers who 'at such times are regarded as pets, and you feed them as you give sugar to horses'[30]) that Orwell was later to celebrate in the *locus classicus* of unofficial English patriotism, *The Lion and the Unicorn*. Jennings' presentation of the crowd anticipates editing techniques he was to deploy to much greater effect in his documentary films, where shots of collective activity (a dance floor, a football crowd, an audience at a concert) are intercut with private individual moments (adjusting a shoe strap, a whispered exchange, or just a shy glance at the camera).[31] A repeated theme in *May the Twelfth* was of young women in the crowd flirting with policemen, a perfect image of the informal nation at ease with power, culminating in

28. *May the Twelfth*, 38–41, 74–6, 83–5, 91.
29. TH to Gorer, nd (October 1937?), Org&Hist 1.
30. *May the Twelfth*, 147.
31. Dai Vaughan, *Portrait of an invisible man: the working life of Stewart McAllister, film editor,* 1983; Hubble, *Mass-Observation and Everyday Life*, 86–7.

Jennings' own improbable observation—he was one of the mobile squad—of 'a girl lying on the ground in the arms of a policeman. He says: "Open your eyes—let me see you open your eyes." '[32]

Jenning's poetic evocation of an unofficial Englishness came into its own as an ideological defence against fascism once England was at war with Nazi Germany. Whether this is seen as a containment of official patriotism within a transcendent popular identity, or the effective subordination of popular identity to a script determined by the state, remains a matter of contention. *May the Twelfth* has been placed in the context of a late modernism in which the treatment of the everyday, undertaken so subversively by James Joyce and Virginia Woolf, had become tamed and softened: 'an aesthetic whose newly learned hospitality to national traditions and resonances was impelling it toward figurations of cultural authority from the perspective of which a nation's factions might appear, as T.S. Eliot would put it, "united in the strife which divided them." '[33] Others have seen it as a text which holds open the possibility of 'the philosophical independence of the masses'.[34] But, however *May the Twelfth* is read, it is difficult to see how its findings served to advance MO's fundamental goal of combating superstition in the name of science.

Madge apologized for Jennings' use of a documentary technique designed to appeal on a poetic and emotional level, reminding his readers that MO was 'more than journalism or film documentary because it has the aim in view not only of presenting, but of classifying and analysing, the immediate human world.' To explain what might appear, from a scientific point of view, to be premature publication of material not yet 'reduced to scientific shape' he pointed out that MO, unlike orthodox science, had to publish its findings

32. *May the Twelfth*, 144.
33. James Buzzard, 'Mass-Observation, Modernism and Auto-Ethnography', *Modernism/Modernity*, 4, 3, 1997, 93–122. See also Marina Mackay, *Modernism and World War II*, Cambridge, 2007; and Ben Highmore, *Everyday Life and Cultural Theory: an introduction*, 2002, 91–2.
34. Hubble, *Mass-Observation and Everyday Life*, 211, 126–7; Jeremy MacClancy, 'Mass-Observation, Surrealism, Social Anthropology: A present-day assessment', *New Formations*, 44, Autumn 2001, 98. Hubble's reading is idiosyncratic—framed rather speculatively by what is *not* there in the text, MO's 'unwritten questions' and 'unwritten answers' (120). Laura Marcus ('The Project of Mass-Observation', *New Formations*, 44, 2001, 10–11) has read it as a post-modern text not attempting a unified point of view (10–11), the collage forcing the reader to make up their own minds. Liz Stanley makes a similar point, adding that the interestingly structured index, compiled by Ruthven Todd, invites the kind of non-linear reading that an electronic text with hypertext now enables, undercutting editorial authority ('MO's Fieldwork Methods', in Paul Atkinson et al (eds), *Handbook of Ethnography*, 2001, 99, 105). Less charitably one might see it merely as an attempt to export the work of making sense of the data to the reader.

as soon as possible in order to sustain the interest of its volunteers. Moreover, rather than treating the observers as 'mere recording instruments', MO wanted to operate 'on a truly democratic basis' by involving them actively in the development of scientific techniques of analysis of the material.[35] 'Our model', he told observers in August, 'must be the patient work of scientists like Darwin, who for over twenty years was collecting facts to confirm his epoch-making theory. But in our case there are hundreds of Observers whose enthusiasm is needed to bring new facts to light.' Counselling patience, Madge, in grandiloquent mood, predicted that eventually MO would 'produce of itself a scientific theory as useful to mankind as the atomic theory or the theory of natural selection; but in this case the discovery will be due not to the labours of a few people only, but of a great number.'[36] In the final section of the book, dealing with the day surveys from a 'normal day' (12 March), Madge turned from the documentary to put forward what he described as 'the first tentative approach to a new set of scientific problems.'[37]

Before tackling the coronation material, he had been inclined to postpone analytical questions to the distant future: 'the task of collecting data is long and difficult. On these data science will one day build new hypotheses and theories. In the meantime we must patiently amass material, without unduly prejudging or preselecting from the available facts.'[38] While the resulting 'bombard[ment] with...fact' proved to be 'a salutary process for the removal of preconceptions', it did nothing to fill the conceptual black hole left by his retreat from the surrealist search for 'dominant images' and the churnings of the collective unconscious.[39] And nothing was going to emerge spontaneously from the 'inexhaustible and boundless' reservoir of data about everyday life; an 'archive', as Ben Highmore has remarked, 'that resists cataloguing.'[40] As they contemplated the accumulating material—facts, as one critic put it, 'multiplying like maggots in cheese, leaving no shape behind'[41]—the excited but undisciplined brainstorming of the Madge group gave way to a rather more modest attempt to clear the decks for some

35. *May the Twelfth*, iv, 347, 413–14.
36. MO *Bulletin*, August 1937 FR A4.
37. *May the Twelfth*, 413.
38. *Mass-Observation*, 29.
39. *First Year's Work*, 47.
40. Highmore, *Everyday Life*, 161.
41. *The Listener*, 17 November 1937, cited in *First Year's Work*, 58.

future yet-to-be-imagined social theory by setting up a schema—dryly described as 'the three social areas'—with which to classify the various ways in which society impacted on the individual.

Area 1 included family, friends, immediate neighbours, regular tradesmen (or customers), work colleagues, or people regularly met in political, religious, or other civic activity. Area 2, a somewhat residual category, encompassed an outer circle of people with whom an individual might come into direct contact in the course of a day: strangers, public figures, and chance acquaintances, irregular tradesmen (or customers). Area 3 consisted of people with whom the individual had no direct contact, but who nevertheless had 'peculiar power in influencing his life' through radio, cinema, newspapers, and books: celebrities, politicians, writers, kings, and 'mythical heroes'; and alongside these the abstract categories of identity offered by discourses of nation, ethnicity, class, etc. or the clamour of advertising slogans. In order to analyse the day surveys in these terms, Madge distinguished between descriptions of unchanging everyday routine (Pavlovian conditioned reflexes, he suggested, automatically reproduced) and accounts of 'social incidents'—for example an encounter, a conversation, something read in the paper, or heard on the radio—which made sufficient impression on the observer to seem worth recording at the end of the day. It was by focussing on these 'social incidents' that MO could map the ways in which influences from areas 1, 2 or 3 impacted on the individual, enhancing, to however small a degree, his 'social consciousness'.[42] The distinction between the private individual and the everyday intercourse with others through which he was constituted as a social being was central to Madge's thinking. However unrepresentative an observer's private opinions might be, Madge argued, his 'everyday relations with other people... will tend to be normal... So we can place more reliance on his description of such relations than on the normality of his private opinions.'[43] While Harrisson's fieldworkers studied the social and institutional environment, Madge studied society from the standpoint of the individual observer, working outwards 'from the individual... into their social surroundings.'[44] Trained to report on the 'social incidents' in their day, rather than simply on their own inner life, the observer's testimony would provide the material necessary to understand 'how, and

42. *May the Twelfth*, 345, and see footnotes on 353, 374.
43. *First Year's Work*, 66–7.
44. Draft for *First Year's Work*, 8, BMpap.

how far, the individual is linked up with society and its institutions.'[45] That, at least, was the theory.[46]

Although Madge deployed the three social areas in analysing the 12 March day surveys, he made no attempt to draw any conclusions about the impact of society on the individual, and freely admitted that he remained none the wiser about the degree to which area 3 imparted to 'normal days' anything like the underlying unity apparent on the day of the coronation.[47] Instead he presented lengthy extracts from the day surveys with marginal annotations whenever an observer mentioned a 'social incident indicating to which area this incident belonged. Occasional footnotes highlighted incidents representing a 'break in routine', a 'shift in social consciousness' or a disturbance of the boundary between area 1 and area 2. Madge also added such footnotes earlier in the book to Jennings' text, which had the disconcerting effect of confronting the hapless reader with the language of the three social areas before it had been properly explained. It is difficult not to see some of these as exercises in self-parody, like the gloss he provided to one observer's account of his pursuit of a girl he fancied in a dance hall: 'She seemed to be in area 1 for other men, and he wanted her to

45. *May the Twelfth*, iv–v.
46. My understanding of the 'three social areas' differs markedly from that offered by Hubble. This is arcane territory, but for any reader who might want to enter into it more fully I provide here some signposts to the differences between myself and Hubble. The central argument of Hubble's book concerning the promise and the degeneration of MO appears to turn on what seems to me to be an inaccurate reading of what Madge meant by Area 2. Hubble equates it with the 'public sphere', with 'public contact in streets and workplaces' (154). But much of what would normally be thought of as belonging to the public sphere (political, civic, and religious life, in so far as it is conducted with familiar people; the company of regulars in the pub; relations with colleagues in the workplace) are actually located by Madge in Area 1. The residual character of Area 2 is clear in all three published accounts of the theory (in *A Thousand Mass Observers*, *First Year's Work* and *May the Twelfth*.) In *A Thousand Mass Observers*, for example, Area 2 gets only three words: 'meetings with strangers'. Citing this, Hubble asserts (127) without argument or evidence that 'it can be deduced' from the discussion in *May the Twelfth* that the difference between Area 1 and Area 2 is that the latter is 'governed by social conventions' while the former is not. I can make no such deduction from the text cited. MO was certainly arguing that moments of national unity tended to break down the barriers between Areas 1 and 2 'temporarily at least' (*May the Twelfth*, 18, 42). But I can find no justification for Hubble's assertion (151) that Madge's original insight about the 'natural tendency to conform, by agreement or by imitation with other members of his social group' was abandoned, thereby representing the masses as passive victims of manipulation from Area 3. Hubble bases this assertion on a change made early in 1938 between the draft of *First Year's Work* (in the BMpap) and the published version. The tendency to conform, he reports, is presented in the later text as 'an assumption held *only* [my emphasis] by political propagandists and advertisers'. But that is not how the published text reads to me: and, in any case, it echoes a very similar passage on page 20 of the *Mass-Observation* pamphlet written a year earlier.
47. *May the Twelfth*, 347.

be in his area 1.' Evelyn Waugh can hardly be blamed for dismissing all this as 'a great deal of pseudo-scientific showmanship'.[48] Halfway through the chapter on 12 March Madge felt it 'necessary to emphasise . . . that the analysis and classification which we have given are no more than an experimental and tentative try-out'.[49] When one observer is caught by a shower and runs home for his umbrella, Madge footnotes: 'There is break in routine here without any human intervention. Possibly such incidents, involving external physical factors (weather, animals, plaster falling from ceiling, etc.) should form a separate area, 4.'[50] Since the areas were intended to classify the ways in which *society* impacted on the individual this proposition only needed to be stated for its absurdity to be apparent.

Despite its inconclusive deployment in *May the Twelfth*, Madge continued to hanker after putting the notion of the three social areas to use. Over the summer of 1937, in line with his aim of involving observers as active participants in the development of the new science, he asked some of the longer standing ones to classify the 'social incidents' in their own days, and to give details of their areas 1 or 2 or 3, promising that 'their work is going to be the basis of a scientific theory of the areas, which we hope will light up the whole nature of our society.'[51] Some responded with exhaustive character sketches of each of their relatives, friends, and work colleagues, fascinating material for anyone concerned with the biographies of individual observers[52] but of very little use for MO's declared purpose of focussing on 'collective habits and social behaviour' rather than 'the private life of any individual'.[53] In October Madge changed tack, using the day surveys over successive months to collect data on behaviour at different times of day, until discontinuing them altogether in January 1938. At this point he announced his intention of compiling a 'structural index' of 'social incidents' described in the 1,700 reports (2.3 million words) in order to 'work out definitions, from concrete examples, for the theory of Social

48. Evelyn Waugh, *Night and Day*, 14 October 1937, cited in *First Year's Work*, 60.
49. *May the Twelfth*, 370.
50. *May the Twelfth*, 367.
51. MO *Bulletin*, FR A4; draft of *First Year's Work*, 47.
52. Notably DS 220, 269 and 031 (Mary Clayton, who is discussed in James Hinton, *Nine Wartime Lives*, 2010).
53. *Mass-Observation*, 30. This objective clearly determined the way the day surveys were filed. Despite the request for brief self-reports to be used to make allowances for probable observer bias in using the day surveys, they were filed in such a way that, as Harrisson later complained, 'the cross-correlation of material from the same individual would be an appalling task' (TH to CM, 18 January 1940, 15, Org&Hist 1/1).

Areas', a task he expected to take at least another year.[54] But in the course
of the next year Madge made little progress on either the structural index
or the promised 'analyses of everyday activities in the British isles',[55] leaving Harrisson to announce, when he took over at Blackheath in November
1938, that 'the enormous and enormously interesting day-survey material
is now being organised into "the English Day"'.[56] This was a project that
continued to surface from time to time in various guises over the next
three years, but, in the end, nothing actually materialized.

Madge's collaboration with Jennings did not survive the completion of
May the Twelfth.[57] Harrisson hated the book, and told Geoffrey Gorer that he
was 'insisting in future that Blackheath publishes nothing of that sort except
in conjunction with intensive, whole time research into objective aspects of
the same problem.'[58] Madge accepted this, telling his observers that their
September day surveys, which fell on a Sunday, would be used as 'part of a
big book on religion and its role in social life': i.e. one of the books that
Harrisson was planning for Gollancz.[59] Already in November 1937 Madge
was describing *May the Twelfth* as representing 'a stage of M-O that has now
been left behind',[60] and two years later, writing to Harrisson, he remarked
that the book, 'produced in the very first flush of M-O', had served as 'a
deterrent to indiscriminate publishing' of material from the panel.[61] Early in
1938 Harrisson felt sufficiently confident to remark in print that 'Madge

54. *First Year's Work*, 47.
55. MO *Bulletin*, FR A4, December 1937. In January 1940 Madge admitted that the day surveys,
which TH believed 'would have justified a really important book on The Day', were
'never...properly digested' (TH to CM, 18 January 1940, 22; CM to TH, 18 January 1940,
Org&Hist 1/1).
56. MO *Bulletin*, November 1938, FR A8.
57. The assertion (in Kevin Jackson, *Humphrey Jennings*, 2004, 181) that Jennings quit MO 'after a
series of angry confrontations with Tom Harrisson, early in 1938' is incorrect. In his autobiography Madge made it clear that Jennings 'took no further part' in MO after completing his
part of *May the Twelfth*—i.e. at the end of June 1937—because 'he was out of sympathy with
the direction taken by M-O as a result of Tom's own initiatives or those which I took in an
attempt to adapt my own initial approach to that of Tom' (CM, 'Autobiography', 71). Nick
Hubble's assertion (*Mass-Observation and Everyday Life*, 115–16), based on a remark in the preface to *May the Twelfth* (iv), that MO functioned between January and September 1937 through
a 'tripartite operational division' in which Harrisson ran Bolton, Madge the panel, and
Jennings had responsibility for 'the business of presenting the results' greatly exaggerates
Jennings' role. It is inconceivable that Harrisson would ever have consented to such a division
of labour.
58. TH to Gorer, nd (October 1937?), Org&Hist 1.
59. MO *Bulletin*, September 1937, FR A4.
60. MO *Bulletin*, November 1937, FR A4.
61. CM to TH, 21 January 1940, 6, Org&Hist 1.

and myself now work on a common programme and are no longer concerned with literature—he got rid of that in the Coronation book.'[62]

This 'common programme' was outlined in MO's second book, a report on their *First Year's Work*, presented as 'dispatches home' from 'a party of explorers which has barely got a foothold in its island' but has to show results if it is to secure the support needed to continue.[63] Alongside chapters derived from Harrisson's work in Bolton and Blackpool, an account of the social composition of the panel, and an analysis of press responses to the earlier publications, Madge opened the book with an essay on 'Smoking as a Social Habit', based on 336 responses to a special directive. Although the essay began with another rehearsal of the social areas theory, the theory contributed little to the analysis that followed. Dismissing smokers' claims that their need for cigarettes was an addiction with a physical basis, Madge asserted the 'overwhelming importance' of social factors 'invisible' to the smoker: 'as the habit grows, people forget that it has a social function'.[64] In pursuit of the 'unwritten laws and invisible pressures and forces' which govern 'how new habits are learnt and why old habits are maintained',[65] the smoking report revealed the power of imitative behaviour. A surprising absence from the report was any analysis of the impact of advertising.

Madge followed up the smoking report with a directive, in June 1938, on prejudices about margarine. An interim report found that while most people had no very strong feelings against the taste of margarine, the overwhelming majority would hesitate to offer it to their friends.[66] This work was paid for by Unilever's advertising agency, Lintas, whose director, T. O. Beachcroft, had earlier worked with Madge on *May the Twelfth*.[67] Later in the year, faced with rumblings of discontent from observers suspicious that the organizers were taking on 'jobs for business firms' exploiting the volunteers to make money for themselves, Madge and Harrisson responded by repeating the mantra that 'Mass-Observation undertakes no research that will not be published, that is not open to everyone', adding that the £2,000

---

62. *Light and Dark*, 3 February 1938. CM dismissed TH's suggestion that he should give up writing poetry as 'an amiable kind of nonsense...letting off steam in undergraduate papers', but did not contradict the denigration of *May the Twelfth* as mere 'literature' (*New Statesman* 5 March 1938). The exchange is cited in Hubble, *Mass-Observation and Everyday Life*, 143–4.
63. *First Year's Work*, 22–3.
64. *First Year's Work*, 23.
65. MO *Bulletin*, November 1937 FR A4.
66. 'Interim Report on Margarine Survey', July 1938, FR A9.
67. CM, interviewed by Nick Stanley, 26 May 1978.

or so that MO had spent since its foundation had come either from 'wholly disinterested people' like Sir Thomas Barlow and Sir Ernest Simon, or from their own private incomes. At the same time, while avoiding any mention of the Lintas contract, they explained that the purpose of the margarine survey was 'to see whether margarine versus butter was a social cleavage running right through society in the same sort of way' as the similarly irrational division between smokers and non-smokers.[68] By the time this report was written Madge, as we shall see, had moved to Bolton to study 'the economics of everyday life', one objective of which was to illuminate 'social prestige and food habits' including the 'prejudices and habits which decide (i) the bread—white or brown (ii) the spread—butter or margarine (iii) jam (iv) the milk, fresh or tinned (v) the ritual of tea'.[69] Unilever made a substantial contribution to the cost of this work, as did another advertising agency, the London Press Exchange.[70] Such funding, MO's leaders believed, could be reconciled with MO's stated policy of refusing to undertake work the results of which could not be freely published since 'big combines like Unilever [had] research departments [which] were interested in such a wide range of products that they were willing to help M-O financially without asking for exclusive information or otherwise limiting its independence.'[71] Nevertheless MO's leaders' readiness to cultivate advertising agencies as a source of funding sat uneasily with their earlier declaration that 'whereas commercial research wants to find out how to sell more things to more people, MO wants to find out why human beings are suggestible, and how they can protect themselves against suggestions which do not help them to survive.'[72]

---

68. MO *Bulletin*, November 1938, FR A8.
69. 'Spending and Saving in Worktown', nd, W/1/C. TH's very first plans for research in Bolton had flagged up a similar agenda: 'things about food that the ordinary person would not suspect, and about the irrational and archaic factors that influence food and food habits' (TH to Jack, 29 July (1936?), W29/A).
70. CM to Max Nicholson, 23 August 1939, TC 43/2/B; TH, 'Emergency Problems and Mass-Observation', 29 August 1939, FR A22. In February 1939 Geoffrey Thomas wrote in his diary: 'On Tuesday Charles had gone to London again to see about the money situation since it had become serious. We were broke and being dunned. He came back on Friday with 50 quid from LPE in hand and 100 promised from Unilever for the 21st.'
71. Undated note referring to meeting of the MO Advisory Committee in February 1939, Org&Hist 1. Shell, Cadbury, the Co-operative Wholesale Society and the London Passenger Transport Board were also successfully approached for money on this basis (TH, 'Emergency Problems and Mass-Observation', 29 August 1939, FR A22). See also 'employers of MO', nd (1940?), MApap, 4/f.
72. MO *Bulletin*, June 1937, FR A4.

III

In June 1937 Madge made 'a small expedition into objective fieldwork', organizing MO's first by-election study in Ilford.[73] His report, anticipating Harrisson's focus on the non-voter, concluded that the results 'fairly clearly indicate...a paralysis of the political faculties of the people of Ilford...a failure to link up political issues with their daily needs and troubles.' So long as politicians remained ignorant of the deeper forces determining popular attitudes they would continue to put out inappropriate propaganda, hence the need for MO's fundamental research on 'class distinction, social areas and the social response to stimuli (advertisements, propaganda, newspapers, sporting events, public ceremonies etc.).'[74] It was the 'social response to stimuli' that was to move to the centre of Madge and Harrisson's 'common programme' over the next few months. In June 1937 observers had been instructed as part of their next day survey to 'state what (a) news item and (b) advertisement struck you most in the newspapers or elsewhere and say what effect it had on you.'[75] Plans were flagged up in August 'to go on to the study of what people read and how their mental habits are formed.'[76] This was followed up in October with a questionnaire asking people what books they had read recently; whether they bought them or borrowed from libraries or friends; how much time they spent reading; with whom, if anyone, they discussed their reading; and what periodicals they took.[77] During the first six months of 1938 the day surveys were replaced by successive directives on opinion formation—two more on book reading, one on advertising, and one on newspapers—flagged up as 'an extensive study of modern propaganda and how it is used to change the social conformities of adult social life.'[78] While observers willingly responded, setting 'forth their views at considerable length and often with considerable lucidity', there were limits to what could be discovered by asking people directly what effect different

73. TH to CM, 18 January 1940, 10, Org&Hist 1.
74. CM, 'Ilford by-election', June 1937, TC 46/1/A.
75. MO *Directive*, June 1937, FR A4.
76. MO *Directive*, August 1937, FR A4.
77. At the same time observers were asked to rank in order of preference a further eight possible 'new subjects for investigation', among them 'a study of the way in which the mass of people are being affected by three propaganda campaigns on a national scale: the National Fitness Campaign, Mr Therm and the Left Book Club' (MO *Bulletin*, October 1937 FR A4).
78. *First Year's Work*, 13; MO *Directives* in FR A8.

media had on their views.[79] Madge, less enamoured of this rather positivistic approach than Harrisson, later described the focus on opinion formation as 'a snare and a delusion', and the responses as 'the most barren of any we have had':

> If we ask people 'How do you form your opinion?' we are asking them to perform a feat of introspection from whose results it would be difficult to generalise. We may only be told the fact, interesting in itself but incomplete, of how intelligent-ish people *think* they form their opinion.[80]

To properly investigate the unconscious processes involved would need individual psychological work, something which Harrisson toyed with undertaking in the winter of 1938-9, with help from Geoffrey Gorer and other 'qualified experts', using techniques of 'Individual Psychology and association of ideas'.[81]

IV

MO's relationship with 'qualified experts' was always a difficult one. Having both left Cambridge without finishing their degrees, Harrisson and Madge shared an ambivalence towards academia: on the one hand dismissive of academic pedantry and, on the other, yearning for the intellectual respect-ability accorded to university scholarship.[82] In an era when professional anthropologists and sociologists were still struggling to establish their pur-suits as reputable academic disciplines, the academics were unlikely to warm to MO's cultivation of amateur volunteers and still less to the anti-academic rhetoric with which Madge and Harrisson presented their enterprise.[83]

---

79. MO *Bulletin,* December 1938, FR A10.
80. CM to TH, 18 January 1940, 5, Org&Hist 1. Raymond Firth had made the same point force-fully in 'An Anthropologist's View of Mass-Observation', *Sociological Review,* 31, 2, 1939, 180–1.
81. TH, Outline, 7 December 1938, TC 20/2/B.
82. For Harrisson this was an abiding ambivalence—contempt tempered by yearning for accept-ance—eventually appeased when he became an honorary professor at Sussex. Much sooner Madge had made terms with the academy as one of Britain's first professors of sociology, but he continued to chaff at the narrowness of the academic life and was never content in this role.
83. Henrika Kuklick, *The Savage Within. The Social History of British Anthropology, 1885–1945,* 1991; Martin Bulmer, 'The development of sociology and of empirical social research in Britain', in M. Bulmer (ed.), *Essays on the History of British Sociological Research,* 1985; M. Bulmer, K. Bales, and K. K. Sklar, *The Social Survey in Historical Perspective, 1880–1940,* 1991.

In the *Mass-Observation* pamphlet the two men laid about them enthusiastically, rubbishing academic philosophy, condemning anthropological
practice as carelessly subjective, and condescendingly suggesting that sociology, after a faltering start, might be beginning to move towards the path
being pioneered by MO.[84] Elsewhere Harrisson expressed contempt equally
for the head-in-clouds theorists at the London School of Economics (LSE)
(Britain's leading sociology department), which did little empirical work,[85]
and for the merely empirical British tradition of social survey: 'administrative sociology', theoretically uninformed and designed only 'to do minor
things here and there to adjust different groups of people to the social
framework.'[86] Privately, Harrisson was scathing about the social survey tradition, conceding that while Charles Booth, despite the 'moral angle' of his
approach, had made 'a powerful start' in *London Life and Labour,* his interwar
successors had sidetracked the tradition into 'adminstro-ameliorative ball-
sachers like the Merseyside and New London surveys.'[87] American sociology, Harrisson argued, was 'streets ahead' of its British counterpart,
particularly in the ethnographic work of the Chicago school which had
shown how empirical observation and conceptual innovation could fruitfully be combined.[88] In contrast to the British social surveys, which dealt
exclusively with the condition of the working class, the Lynds' study of a
mid-western town, *Middletown* (1929), provided a portrait of a whole community. Produced by a team of five investigators living in the town over
several months, *Middletown* provided a model for the Wortktown project,
although Harrisson was critical of its underlying assumptions about 'class,
morals, progress, etc' and its neglect of more intimate topics such as 'superstition or love.'[89] But it was Paul Lazarsfeld and Marie Jahoda's study of an
Austrian textile village devastated by unemployment, *Marienthal* (1933), that
came closest to the kind of excavation of 'ordinary behaviour, superstition
and ideas' that Harrisson aimed to achieve in Bolton.[90] The 12 members of
the *Marienthal* team—psychologists, doctors, and students of law, social work,
and economics—positioned themselves as participants, not mere observers, in

---

84. *Mass-Observation,* 21, 35–6.
85. '. . . nearly all these University sociologists seem to be dead from the neck sideways', TH to
   Malinowski, 31 November 1937. See also Harrisson, *Britain Revisited,* 162.
86. Draft for *First Year's Work,* 9, BMpap.
87. TH to Trevelyan, September 1937, JTpap.
88. TH review of *Poverty and Progress,* cited in Stanley, *Extra Dimension,* 193.
89. TH, 'Mass-Observation and the WEA', *The Highway,* December 1937, 46.
90. *Mass-Observation,* 36.

the life of the town, putting on classes in dressmaking and gymnastics, providing a clothes laundering service and free medical and vocational advice.
They recruited the local teacher to collect statistics, trained some unemployed people to act as researchers, invited participation by others through
diary-keeping exercises and prize essay competitions. As in Bolton, the
work began with the vaguest of objectives, simply, Jahoda recalled, wanting
'to know "everything" related to the impact of unemployment on the community' and 'relying on hunches rather than formulated concepts'.[91] The
open-ended approach, the opportunistic use of whatever research methods
came to hand, the juxtaposition of quantitative and qualitative data, all contributed to an ethnographic masterpiece which set the standard for future
research on the psychological impact of unemployment in the 1930s and
beyond.[92]

Despite Harrisson's colourful language and his inability to resist 'the
acute but short-lived pleasure of irritating the academic bourgeois',[93] his
assessment of the state of sociology in Britain was broadly in line not only
with later authoritative accounts,[94] but, more importantly, with the views of
a number of leading contemporary academic psychologists. Having established a toe-hold in the universities by positioning themselves as experimental scientists, some academic psychologists were now anxious to break
out from the artificial environment of the laboratory. In 1935 the Cambridge
Professor of Experimental Psychology F. C. Bartlett took the initiative
in convening an informal 'social psychology discussion group' which met
regularly over the next three years with the aim of producing an authoritative account of fieldwork methods in social psychology, which could
advance the study of complex modern societies in much the same way that
the British Association's *Notes and Queries on Anthropology* had fostered good
practice in the study of primitive societies.[95] Harrisson was already in contact with at least one member of this group, Oscar Oeser, when, in the *Mass-*

91. Marie Jahoda, 'Reflections on Marienthal and after', *Journal of Occupational & Organizational
    Psychology*, 65, 4, 1992.
92. David Fryer, 'Introduction to Marienthal and Beyond', *Journal of Occupational & Organizational
    Psychology*, 65, 4, 1992.
93. Bronislaw Malinowski, 'A Nation-Wide Intelligence Service', *First Year's Work*, 103. Writing to
    CM in 1940 TH confessed to his 'compulsion to attack and deflate those in authority' (TH to
    CM, 18 January 1940, Org&Hist 1).
94. See, for example, Bulmer, 'The development of sociology and of empirical social research in
    Britain', M. Bulmer (ed.), *Essays on the History of British Sociological research*, 1985, 5–8, 14–18.
95. F.C. Bartlett et al, *The Study of Society. Methods and Problems*, 1939, vii–viii.

Observation pamphlet, he and Madge called for 'the assistance of trained scientists in drawing up the ground plan for our long-term researches. It is for them to help in framing well-constructed hypotheses to be tested by Mass-Observation methods, and to suggest subjects for detailed enquiry ... we offer them a new instrument, with every opportunity to use it to the full.'[96]

Oeser was a social psychologist at St Andrews directing a Pilgrim Trust funded project on juvenile unemployment among Dundee Jute workers. At the British Association annual conference in September 1936, held in Blackpool, he expounded his own version of 'anthropology at home'. Social psychology, he declared, 'if it is to become a science at all, must turn away from philosophy ... and must apply itself wholeheartedly to fieldwork.' Harrisson, already in Bolton developing ideas for his own anthropology at home, was probably in the audience, and he would have eagerly responded to Oeser's rejection of questionnaires in favour of the indirect approach: 'the questions to be asked are ... introduced into conversations as they arise, and the answers are noted as soon as is physically possible.'[97] The two men probably first met on this occasion. A year later, Oeser paid a visit to Davenport Street where he grilled Walter Hood on MO methods before going on to meet Harrisson the next day (staying in Blackpool at the time). 'Who is this Oeser, Tom?', Hood wrote anxiously, 'He certainly was interested and asked a hell of a lot of leading questions on our method ... Honest I think I came through well and created a good impression ... I told him how we wrote up everything the same day, etc.'[98] Oeser's central idea, which he drew from the

96. *Mass-Observation*, 34. The existence of the 'Social Psychologists Group' was noted in the pamphlet, 61.
97. O.A. Oeser, 'Methods and Assumptions of Fieldwork in Social Psychology', *British Journal of Psychology*, General Section, 27, 4, 1937, 344, 353. This article is cited in the *Mass-Observation* pamphlet, 61. Bartlett, who edited the journal, hailed Oeser's methods and ideas as of fundamental importance, and hoped the article would stimulate discussion and research over a wide field. Stanley overstates the case when he describes Oeser's paper as 'the template for M-O' (*Extra Dimension*, 49). Hubble (*Mass-Observation and Everyday Life*, 118) correctly points up aspects of Oeser's approach which were incompatible with MO's practice, although he is probably wrong in assuming that the first Harrisson knew of Oeser's work was the publication of his paper in April 1937.
98. Hood to TH, nd (3 September 1937?), TC 58/1/B. Talking to Stanley in 1980 Oeser said that he had been shown around by MO in 1936 at the time of the British Association meeting in Blackpool, which was impossible since MO had not been formed by then. Probably he had merged his memory of the visit to Bolton in 1937—on his way to deliver a paper at the British Association which met in Nottingham that year—with his memory of meeting Harrisson during the 1936 meeting in Blackpool (Oeser, interviewed by Stanley, 4 June 1980).

Marienthal study, was that fieldwork required investigators to approach peo-ple 'not as reporters with notebook and camera, but as far as possible as accepted members of [the] community', thus enabling them to gain access not only to 'conventional (public) attitudes' but also to 'central (private) attitudes'. What he described as the 'functional penetration' that would make this possible fell in fact a good deal short of the kind of participant observation that Harrisson encouraged in Worktown. As in *Marienthal*, the penetration pursued by Oeser's team of experts seems to have been limited to such top-down activities as offering vocational guidance, shadowing medical consultations, rent collecting, and giving lectures in unemployed clubs.[99]

In public Oeser kept his distance from MO, but a second member of the social psychology group—T. H. Pear, professor of psychology at Manchester—was happy to give them his endorsement, joining their Advisory Committee, praising them in print, and encouraging his only full-time colleague at Manchester, Harold James, to embark on a study of class distinction in collaboration with MO.[100] Pear's trenchant advocacy of fieldwork as an antidote to the desiccated activities of laboratory-bound colleagues, had been partly inspired by an influential 1934 article on 'The Social Psychology of Everyday Life' in which the American psychologist Hadley Cantril roundly took the discipline to task for its focus on 'control-led laboratory experiments on problems which have no relation to life itself', and laid out a wide-ranging and exciting agenda for psychological fieldwork, which Harrisson and Madge reproduced in the *Mass-Observation* pamphlet, and whose agenda of qualitative research into 'various types of social stimuli on attitudes' clearly informed their own approach to opinion forma-tion.[101] Cantril's article, Pear's insistence that it was time for psychologists to

99. O. A. Oeser 'The value of team work and functional penetration as methods of social investigation' in Bartlett et al, *The Study of Society*, 411–12; Oeser, 'Fieldwork in Social Psychology', 354.

100. *First Year's Work*, 62; T. H. Pear, 'Psychologists and Culture', *Bulletin of the John Rylands Library*, 23, 1939, 427–8; *A Thousand Mass Observers*, August 1937, FR A8. James's study came to noth-ing, but it is possible that Pear contributed to the drafting of MO's June 1939 directive on 'class', which closely reflected many of his social psychological interests. On Harold James and Pear's department see Alan Costall, 'Pear and his peers', in G.C. Bunn, A.D. Lovie, and G.D. Richards (eds), *Psychology in Britain: historical essays and personal reflections*, 2001. In 1939 Marie Jahoda, now a refugee in Britain, was also associated with the department.

101. Hadley Cantril, 'The Social Psychology of Everyday Life', *The Psychological Bulletin*, 31, 5, May 1934. Pear remarked that this article 'changed my life' (Costal, 'Pear and his peers', 201).

investigate real-world topics like class distinction and the impact of propaganda, and his own published work on the class coding of radio voices and the psychology of conversation, all helped to situate MO's concerns in the mainstream of late 1930s social psychology.[102]

Pear's enthusiasm for MO was not shared by some of the other contributors to the social psychology group's 1939 book of essays who insisted that 'there seems to be no foundation for the opinion that the collection of social facts is so easy that social science can be advanced by the accumulation of observations by enthusiastic but untrained observers.'[103] Bartlett was prepared to countenance a role for 'intelligent observers who have not received any special psychological training' in the 'preliminary collection and sorting of facts', and he floated the idea of fostering such work by setting up

> one or more central 'clearing-houses'...to which they could report from time to time. Through these they could be informed of results of similar work in other areas which would give point and meaning to their own research, and be kept in touch with the psychologists who wish to utilize their field data, and who could assist them in developing new lines of approach.

His failure to note that something very like one such 'clearing house' was already in well-publicized existence can only have been deliberate; but any attempt to establish a rival 'clearing house' would have been unlikely to succeed given the dull and abstract quality of the topics he deemed suitable for amateur research.[104] The five members of the Psychological Society who, in September 1939, offered to collaborate with MO probably understood this, but Harrisson was wary, writing to Madge: 'I presume they will be useless, but I suppose one must keep an open mind even about someone who has been trained by Bartlett, provided they don't expect to be paid for one to keep it open.'[105] Bartlett was anxious to restrict psychological fieldwork to narrowly defined topics suitable for refinement in the laboratory, seeing the

---

102. Pear, 'Some problems and topics of contemporary social psychology' in Bartlett et al, *The Study of Society*, 1939, 2; TH, report on the Social Psychology Section of the British Psychological Society, Brighton, 9–18 April 1942, FR 1214; Pear, *Voice and Personality*, 1931; Pear, *The Psychology of Conversation*, 1939.

103. R. H. Thouless, 'Scientific method and the use of Statistics', Bartlett et al, *The Study of Society*, 126.

104. Bartlett et al, *The Study of Society*, 24, 42–4.

105. TH to CM, 27 September 1939, TC 42/1A. But at least one of the five, Celia Fremlin, turned out, as we shall see, to be far from useless.

ethnographic urge to present 'a picture of a culture, or of the intertwined activities of a whole social group' as a threat to the scientific basis of the discipline, and best left to sociology and anthropology.[106] While Pear became increasingly interested in probing 'patterns of culture', Bartlett, with his eye on the funding available for experimental psychology, turned his back on the social agenda. In the 1950s and 1960s, when Bartlett's students dominated British psychology departments, social psychology was at a low ebb and the work of Pear and Oeser, like that of MO, was largely forgotten.[107]

MO, of course, was not a branch of academic social psychology. Where *Marienthal* and Oeser had employed trained experts, Harrisson's Worktown team had no pretensions to academic expertise. And the academics' concern to develop scientific methods of enquiry was far more rigorous than anything that Harrisson or Madge—who needed substantive results quickly to finance the work—could afford to entertain. More surprising than hostility from the academics was the readiness of some of them to lend their support, most notably the central figure of British anthropology at the time, Bronislaw Malinowski. When, in the autumn of 1937, Harrisson berated an audience at the Institute of Sociology with his usual abuse of all things academic, Malinowski found his initial irritation giving way to admiration for these 'enthusiastic youngsters without the hall-mark of academic status or the paraphernalia of its pomp ... [rushing in] where Dons have feared to tread'.[108] By the beginning of December, Madge had acquitted himself well at Malinowksi's research seminar, attended by all the coming leaders of British anthropology, and Harrisson, sending details of the Worktown project, was effusive in his appreciation of the fact that the great man was 'interested and vigorously sympathetic to our work', unlike the sociologists who had returned insult for insult at the autumn meeting.[109] Malinowski, proclaiming that 'from the start of my own fieldwork, it has been my deepest and strongest conviction that we must finish by studying ourselves through the same methods and with the same mental attitude with which we approach exotic tribes', agreed to contribute an assessment of MO's project for the book Harrisson and Madge were putting together on their *First Year's Work*.[110] MO's initial unselective

106. Bartlett et al, *The Study of Society*, 39.
107. Costall, 'Pear and his peers'; Alan Costall, 'Why British psychology is not social: Frederic Bartlett's promotion of the new academic discipline', *Canadian Psychology*, 33, 1992, 633–9.
108. Malinowski, draft for 'A Nation-Wide Intelligence Service', BMpap, 21; *First Year's Work*, 84.
109. TH to Malinowski, 31 November 1937, BMpap; CM, interviewed by Stanley, 23 March 1978; CM to Malinowski, 3 December 1937, 19 January 1938, BMpap.
110. *First Year's Work*, 103.

data collection conformed to his own practice—'note down everything you see and hear, since in the beginning it is not possible to know what may or may not be significant'[111]—as did Harrisson's focus on observing what people actually did rather than being satisfied with what they said they did.[112] Putting to one side the anti-academic rhetoric, and praising MO's leaders for their readiness to cooperate with experts and to learn from criticism, Malinowski predicted that the organization 'bids fair...to grow' into 'a nation-wide intelligence service' fostering 'national self-knowledge'.[113]

However flattering this was, Madge and Harrisson cannot have been entirely pleased with the great man's embrace, not only because (as Madge later admitted) 'we weren't quite up to what he thought we might be', but also because Malinowski, becoming increasingly conservative in the face of the 'newly manufactured pseudo-mysticisms' of fascism and communism, sought to position MO as a 'powerful stabilising force' alongside monarchy and traditional religion.[114] The subversive intent of *May the Twelfth* seems to have been completely lost on Malinowski, who believed it was simple error that led the editors to neglect the function of the central ceremony as a symbolic affirmation of the 'permanence of the British Empire', and to give the impression that for many people the coronation was nothing more than an excuse for a holiday.[115] Moreover Harrisson never accepted Malinowski's indignant dismissal of his claim that anthropologists, partly because of the remoteness and illiteracy of the cultures they study, 'make [their] observations unchecked'.[116]

Malinowski's (qualified) endorsement certainly helped to establish MO's credibility with the wider community, but it did little to establish a constructive dialogue with British anthropologists, some of whom saw the old man's flirtation with 'the Mass-Observation bilge' as confirmation of his intellectual decline.[117] Harrisson soon fell out with Malinowski and by June

---

111. Hortense Powdermaker, one of Malinowski's first graduate students, cited in Buzzard, 'Mass-Observation, Modernism and Auto-Ethnography', 95.
112. Adam Kuper, *Anthropologists. The Modern British School*, 1983, 14–15.
113. *First Year's Work*, 83.
114. CM, interviewed by Stanley, 23 March 1978; *First Year's Work*, 104–5, 109.
115. *First Year's Work*, 114–15. His enthusiasm for the Peace Ballot (*First Year's Work*, 107–9), very apparent in his marginal notes on the draft of *First Year's Work* (BMpap), belongs to a similarly conservative 'imperialist pacifism' (on which see James Hinton, *Protests and Visions*, 1989).
116. CM and TH, *Mass-Observation*, 36; TH, 'Mass-Observation and the WEA', *The Highway*, December 1937, 46; *First Year's Work*, 98–103. TH returned to this issue in his notebooks after his return to Borneo in 1947 (Heimann, *Most Offending Soul*, 255–60).
117. Correspondence between Evans-Pritchard and Fortes, cited in Goody, *The Expansive Moment*, 1995, 74.

1938 was privately dismissing him as just another 'university gabbler' whose essay he had never wanted to publish; while Malinowski, for his part, had concluded that Harrisson was a 'crook'.[118] Raymond Firth, a colleague of Malinowski's at LSE, had invited Harrisson to address his students (at least one of whom, Edmund Leach, had arranged to visit Bolton at the end of 1937) and, as secretary of the Royal Anthropological Institute, Firth arranged for Harrisson to give an illustrated lecture in February 1938, at which he presented preliminary findings, with Humphrey Spender on hand to explain how the photographs were taken.[119] But the assessment Firth published in April 1939 reinforced Malinowski's criticisms with a forensic attack on *May the Twelfth*, Madge's 'three areas' theory, and the shoddy handling of statistics and questionnaire results in MO's most important pre-war publication, *Britain by Mass-Observation*.[120] Despite this, Firth did not entirely write off MO. Like the sociologist T. H. Marshall, he saw many of the weaknesses as a product of MO's financially driven need for hasty publication and journalistic appeal, and remained hopeful that the Worktown volumes—when they eventually saw the light of day—would make a serious contribution to 'anthropology at home' free of such distractions.[121]

Although Madge had invested a good deal of time and energy in securing Malinowski's chapter in *First Year's Work* he came off worse than Harrisson in these early encounters with academia. During the spring and summer of 1938 work at Blackheath continued on indexing the day survey material, but nothing much seems to have been achieved. Harrisson later complained that during this period

> trunkloads of panel reports ... were put together in any order at Blackheath, tied round with string, and simply put away after M[adge] and Kathleen [Raine] and others had read through the quotations, typed out some, been

118. TH to de Casseres, 20 June 1939, Org&Hist 2/5; CM, interviewed by Stanley, 23 March 1978.
119. R. Firth, 'An Anthropologist's view of Mass-Observation', *The Sociological Review*, 31, 2, 1939, 169–70; Derek [Kahn] to TH, nd (1937?), W1/B; *The Journal of the Royal Anthropological Institute of Great Britain and Ireland*, 68, July–December 1938, 415; TH, 'Fieldwork in Northtown,' *Man*, 33, March 1938. TH had already lectured at LSE in June 1937 (TH to Trevelyan, 7 June 19 37, JTpap).
120. Firth, 'Anthropologist's view', *passim*.
121. Firth, 'Anthropologist's view', 192; Marshall, 'Is M-O Moonshine', *The Highway*, December 1937: 'unfavourable criticism of this book [*May the Twelfth*] does not imply condemnation of the other venture of MO, the intensive study of a single town. Here, we are given to understand, a team of trained men is at work studying selected problems. That is a most helpful experiment, and the results will be eagerly awaited.'

stimulated, and put two or three in the private observer bulletin. Most of this work has been utterly unproductive, not only on fact and publication, but also on theory.

True, a book on the environment had been prepared, but this was 'without any apparent background ideas...simply collected quotations; but (happily?) nothing was done about getting it published.'[122] The manuscript of this book, *Historic England*, survives in the archive: a compilation of the descriptions panellists were asked to send in of the places where they lived and worked, totally devoid of editorial content apart from snappy subheadings for each of the extracts.[123] At some point plans had been made to do rather more with this material, adding footnotes and a detailed index (as in *May the Twelfth*), and a draft exists of an intriguing introduction on housing, happiness, and human ecology probably written by Harrisson.[124] But nothing came of this. Similarly unproductive were Madge's attempts during 1937–8 to organize panellists living in the London area to work as part-time fieldworkers in surveys of visitor behaviour at London Zoo and Kew Gardens: 'insufficient return', he wrote later, 'for the effort involved'.[125]

In August 1938 Madge threw himself enthusiastically into observing a new dance craze in London, and travelled north to witness the totemistic ritual of 'Keaw Yed' in West Houghton, a mining town near Bolton, on which he later wrote a brilliant essay.[126] At the same time he re-engaged with the Communist Party, which he had neglected since leaving Cambridge four years earlier, seeking (and apparently securing) the blessing of the Foreign Commission of Moscow's Writers Union for MO, while canvassing blocks of south London flats in order to 'consolidate myself locally in party work so as to be able to take a very tough line with Writers Fractions and

122. TH to CM, 18 January 1940, 16, Org&Hist 1/1.
123. TC 66/20/G.
124. TC 1/1/B. It seems odd that Harrisson should have written: 'As a zoologist, the aspect that has interested me most has been ecological. An anthropologist would probably have picked out another set of facts for comment'. But he adopted a similarly zoological identity in *People in Production*, 68.
125. CM to TH, 18 January 1940, Org&Hist 1/1; MO *Bulletin*, June 1938, FR A8; CM to Inez, 2 August 1938, CMpap 8/3; Box to CM, 30 October 1937 (DS 18). Julian Huxley and James Fisher facilitated the work at the zoo, where they were respectively secretary and assistant curator. The Kew survey was suggested by an assistant director at Kew, John Gilmour, who had been an early member of the panel (Madge, interviewed by Stanley, 26 May 1978; chronology, 29 November 1937, CMpap 71/1/5). Copious material—now lost—was gathered, but, as Madge later admitted, 'its diffuseness would have made it difficult to present coherently' (CM, 'Autobiography', 75, CMpap).
126. Angus Calder, 'Introduction', *Britain by Mass-Observation*, 1986 edition, xi.

nonsense of that kind'. 'I hope I am not being regressive', he wrote to his lover, Inez Spender: but in fact he was.[127] The work in Blackheath was in disarray, affected by the backwash from the crisis of his marriage,[128] and Madge was losing faith in the value of the panel, which had not grown significantly over the previous year and provided less reach into the work-ing-class experience he wanted to investigate than Communist Party can-vassing, where he was able to visit working-class people in their homes and talk 'not about politics as such but about fights between families, stinking rubbish chutes, children, distance to markets, and other things that political agitations should start from'.[129] This, however, was a poor substitute for research, and within a few months Madge had decided to drop out of com-munist politics on the grounds that such involvement was incompatible 'with trying to be detached as a social scientist.' By then, having swapped places with Harrisson, he was engaged on a quite new project in Bolton, 'heading', as he was later to put it, 'in the direction of sociology'.[130]

127. CM to Inez 15 and 20 August 38, CMpap 8/3; CM, interviewed by Calder, March 1976; CM, interviewed by Stanley, 23 March 1978.
128. Raine came to believe that Madge was wasting his talent on MO, and that Harrisson was 'as bogus and unsound as anyone that you could pick for a collaborator' (Raine to CM, 10 November 1939, CMpap 71/1/6).
129. CM to TH, 18 January 1940, Org&Hist 1/1; CM to Inez, 20 August 38, CMpap.
130. CM, interviewed by Stanley, 23 March 1978.

4

Metrop

I

Moving to London at the beginning of September 1938 Tom Harrisson was immediately swept up in the escalating international crisis. Over the next two months, working in closer collaboration than they ever had done before or were to do again, Harrisson and Charles Madge produced the book which, more than any other, put Mass-Observation (MO) on the map. *Britain by Mass-Observation*—published as a Penguin Special in January 1939—sold 100,000 copies in ten days, stimulating recruitment to the MO panel and alerting key players in Whitehall to the potential value of MO as an instrument for monitoring public opinion under war conditions.[1] An extremely positive review in *The Times* concluded:

> This is a book above all for ' intellectuals' and men of affairs, for all those who confuse their own interest with those of the vast majority of ordinary people . . . an excellent corrective for those inhuman generalisations which so often pass muster as judgements of how the English people think and behave.[2]

The book presented a detailed analysis of public opinion during the weeks of the Munich crisis, largely based on random interviews in London and responses from the panel, alongside an outline of MO's work as a whole, and discrete chapters discussing diverse aspects of British life, including all-in wrestling in Bolton; an anthropologically informed account of West Houghton's ancient annual 'Keaw Yed' festival (written by Madge[3]); and a multi-layered account of the processes by which a song and dance routine

1. CM, 'Autobiography', 82; Calder (ed.), *Britain by Mass-Observation*, 1986, vii.
2. *The Times*, 20 January 1939.
3. CM to Inez, 24 August 1938, CMpap 8/3; CM, interviewed by Calder, March 1976.

(the Lambeth Walk) from a West End musical became all the rage in dance halls up and down the country during the early summer of 1938.

By the time *Britain* was published, the organization of MO had been radically reshaped. By the summer of 1938 Madge's romance with Kathleen Raine was in terminal crisis. In the spring he had quit his job on the *Daily Mirror* to devote himself full-time to MO, leaving him with no means of support for Kathleen and the children. She found the chaos created by MO in their Blackheath house intolerable, while he was carrying on simultaneous affairs with two other women, James Fisher's wife, Angus, and Stephen Spender's wife, Inez, who Madge was later to marry. In an effort to relieve the pressure, Harrisson proposed an exchange of places. With *Britain* substantially drafted, and thankful for the escape route, Madge went to Bolton at the end of October, while Harrisson moved into Grotes Buildings to take charge of the London operation.[4]

Harrisson's motives for proposing the switch were not entirely altruistic. Having done his time in the remote North he was now delighting in the excitements of metropolitan life. In March 1938, at the invitation of the Labour Party, he had temporarily moved the whole Bolton team to work on a by-election in Fulham, a move which he was later to describe both as 'a natural reaction after a year of slave work in Bolton' and as symptomatic of his growing taste for direct political engagement.[5] During the Munich crisis he had access to the fringes of high politics through his friend and patron, Mary Adams, whose husband, Vyvyan, was a dissident Tory MP. At parties in the Adams' Regents Park household Harrisson could pick up the latest anti-appeasement gossip, some of which surfaced in his account of the crisis in *Britain*.[6]

But it was not only politicians who it was easier to cultivate in the metropolis. From the summer of 1938, as Harrisson set out to build up a new team of full-timers in London, Fulham—referred to as 'Metrop' in MO publications—was flagged up as the metropolitan counterpart to Worktown. To a degree 'Metrop' was, as Madge later remarked, merely a rhetorical device: 'a very approximate framework that Tom Harrisson dreamed up to keep people ticking over... no really comprehensive plan... little bits here and little bits there of quite an opportunistic kind.'[7] In the autumn of 1938,

4. CM, 'Autobiography', 70, 80–1; TH to CM, 18 January 1940, 18–19, 21–2, Org&Hist 1/1.
5. TH to CM, 18 January 1940, 13, Org&Hist 1/1.
6. *Britain*, 35; Heimann, *Most Offending Soul*, 38–9, 118; Lord Taylor of Harlow, *A Natural History of Everyday Life. A biographical guide for would-be doctors of society*, 1988, 260.
7. CM, interviewed by Stanley, 23 March 1978.

for example, MO's work in Fulham included a survey of the voting habits of shopkeepers, work on the leisure activities of young people, and some observation of pubs and churchgoing, although nothing of the latter survives in the archive.[8] But there was never the money to repeat the kind of in-depth study that Harrisson had organized in Bolton; by the outbreak of war MO still had little reliable information about either the class composition or the denominational make-up of the area.[9] Nevertheless, by flagging up a local MO presence in the capital, Harrisson was able to tap into some significant new sources of support and finance, notably in the overlapping worlds of advertising and architectural innovation.

II

Methodologically, the essay on the Lambeth Walk was the high point of *Britain*, a path-breaking study of the dynamics of popular culture 'nobly' anticipating 'by some two decades', Angus Calder remarked, 'the first large stirrings of "serious" interest in popular culture.'[10] While giving full weight to the initiative of shrewd cultural entrepreneurs, professional songwriters, and dancing instructors, Madge and Harrisson argued that the key to the Lambeth Walk's success was the fact that, reversing the usual top-down direction of cultural diffusion, it both drew on popular sources (Cockney humour, singing, and dancing), and catered to an unmet popular demand for the mix of individual self-expression and communal togetherness summed up in the words of the song:

> Any time you're Lambeth way,
> Any evening, any day,
> You'll find us all doin' the Lambeth walk.
> . . .
> Ev'rything free and easy,
> Do as you darn well pleasey,
> Why don't you make your way there?
> Go there, stay there.

8. TC 66/7/D and E.
9. 'Report on ARP in Fulham', 3 September 1939, 9–10, 12, FR A24.
10. Calder, *Britain by Mass-Observation*, xii.

Taking the lyricist at his word, in August 1938 Madge had taken himself off to Lambeth, delighted to discover the 'free and easy...do as you darn well pleasey' high jinks of a Sunday night get together in a working-class home:[11]

> Christ! what an evening. We had the most wonderful party till two in the morning. Tremendous dancing. Tremendous people. All playing piano or accordion by ear. All handing round their glass of beer for others to drink. Transvestism and fine class conscious songs...[12]

If the class consciousness suited Madge's political mood at the time, the transvestism (not an uncommon feature of popular revelry, as MO had noted in *May the Twelfth*) rang interesting anthropological bells.[13] Ursula Mommens, perhaps with the same occasion in mind, remembered accompanying Harrisson to 'drag parties in the East End. Masc[uline] drag not at [all] pansy',[14] and Harrisson himself was quick to exploit the money-raising possibilities of all this fun, proposing a television documentary on the new dance featuring, among other things, 'a Sunday night at the Page family home with song, talk and refreshments.'[15] Other observations followed, in a park in Wapping—the London County Council (LCC) was experimenting with summertime dancing in the parks—and a mass turn-out in Highbury Fields where 20,000 dancers and spectators 'got completely out of hand'.[16]

Far from being a trivial sideshow to the serious work on political attitudes, the study of popular culture, Madge and Harrisson insisted, could yield vital insights into trends in the underlying social attitudes on which the future of democracy depended. While the popularity of football pools and horoscopes pointed to an 'each-for-his-own self, individualist pattern', the Lambeth Walk represented a reassertion of 'social feeling and activity', a revolt against the 'world of personal superstition and magic' promoted by American dance tunes:

---

11. *Britain*, 144–7.
12. CM to Inez, 2 August 1938, CMpap 8/3.
13. *May the Twelfth*, 32, 434.
14. Mommens, interviewed by Sheridan, 1983. Lambeth, of course, is not in the East End; but memory plays tricks.
15. Adams to Tel, 28 August 1938, TC 38/6/E. The programme was broadcast: Harrisson, *Britain Revisited*, 206.
16. CM to Inez, 5 and 12 August 1938, CMpap 8/3; *Britain*, 177–80; Woodford to Wilcock, 12 August 1938, TC 46/2/A.

the dream-sex of the dance lyric...is no more about reality than Hitler's speeches are. Ballroom dancers sleep-walk to its strains with the same surrender of personal decision as that of uniformed Nazis. These Lambeth Walkers are happy because they find they are free to express *themselves* without the hypnosis of a jazz-moon or a Fuhrer.[17]

And because it promoted genuine community, rooted in individual self-expression, not the ersatz community of automatons constructed in their different ways by Hollywood and fascism, the Lambeth Walk showed how the left could engage in positive ways with popular culture. Harrisson did his best to explain this to Labour's 'propaganda experts' at Transport House and even got them to produce an electioneering song to the Lambeth Walk tune, although it was never used.[18] It was, Harrisson argued, a mistake for the left to dismiss the professional expertise of what he was later to call 'marginal creative personnel' as irredeemably an instrument of superstition and cultural oppression. Rather than turning their backs on the kind of people who devised the Lambeth Walk song and dance routine, or the entrepreneurial skills of the dance hall proprietor who promoted it, democrats should themselves learn to use the new techniques of mass appeal, confident that in the right hands these techniques, like those of advertising and market research, could be used to promote active citizenship not passive conformity. The Communist Party, much more interested than Labour in the politics of culture, was more responsive to such arguments, breaking up a Moselyite demonstration in the East End by 'doing the Lambeth Walk', and adapting the song for the Tenant's Committee in Stepney.[19]

III

The close relationship that Harrisson had developed while in Bolton with the national Labour Party's 'propaganda experts' had brought him to London already in the spring of 1938. Invited by Transport House, Harrisson had

---

17. *Britain,* 140, 174, 182–3.
18. *Britain,* 169, 176. The song, intended as a model for use in by-election, had 'Worktown' as the constituency and 'Higgins' (TH's contact in Transport House) as the MP to be elected.
19. *Britain,* 175–6; Kevin Morgan, 'King Street Blues: jazz and the left in Britain in the 1930s–40s', in Andy Croft (ed.), *Weapons in the Struggle: essays on the cultural history of British communism,* 1998, 123–41.

moved the whole Bolton team temporarily to Fulham, where Edith
Summerskill was contesting a Tory seat in a by-election:

> Almost at the last moment, when the election campaign was already under
> way, I got an urgent telegram on Sunday morning asking that a Mass-
> Observation unit take part... and that full facilities for investigation would be
> provided by [the] Labour Party, in return for which we should deal with defi-
> nite problems from day to day that were set by [the] Labour candidate, London
> agent, etc. Agreed.[20]

Arriving in Fulham, about which they knew nothing, the Bolton team were
joined by volunteers from the local Labour Party, Julian Trevelyan and some
of his friends, and a group of people working in advertising. Instructed by
Harrisson—who felt it necessary to remind them that 'on this job—you are
NOT Labour'—this medley of researchers was sent out to observe meetings and record overheard conversations, to interview on the doorstep, the
street, in pubs and dance halls.[21]

It quickly became apparent that the Labour Party's strategy of treating
the election as 'a barometer of public opinion' on Chamberlain's handling
of Hitler (who had just occupied Austria) was a mistake. Early interviews
found those with a definite view evenly divided for and against the government, but the largest group (40 per cent) were simply bewildered by foreign
affairs, a state of mind summarized by Harrisson:

> As the world situation worsens and becomes less explicable, people feel that it
> is more and more a matter of each one for himself, or herself and her family.
> The WORLD is a machine which seems to have gone a spot crazy. And as this
> feeling tightens, home and self become more and more the conscious centre
> of the picture.[22]

In this situation, Harrisson argued, it made more sense for Labour to focus
their campaign on domestic issues. But this was not a message that his partners wanted to hear. At the end of the first week Harrisson recorded details
of a long discussion with MO's Labour activists, in which 'no one could
think of domestic slogans at all: all fixed on foreign affairs.'[23] In the later

---

20. 'West Fulham March 1938', nd (June 1938?), FR A7, 6.
21. 'Instructions to Observers', March 1938, TC 46/2/A; TH, 'Poverty of Freedom', 241–50; vari-
    ous documents in TC 46/2/C. About 7,000 of the 49,000 electorate were interviewed by
    MO.
22. Report, 23 March 1938, TC 46/2/c.
23. TH note, 25 March 1938, TC 46/2/c.

stages of the campaign the party did shift its emphasis away from foreign policy, and this may be one way in which MO contributed towards Summerskill's narrow victory.[24]

Their other contribution, putting MO's pursuit of the non-voter to practical use, was rather less straightforward. While in West Houghton Harrisson had justified stealing the Conservative canvass returns in the name of science; in Fulham he used these returns (presumably acquired by a similar subterfuge) to identify wavering Tory voters who were then targeted with leaflets composed of a bewildering juxtaposition of contradictory statements by Tory politicians designed to convince the recipient that their favoured party was in such a muddle that it was better not to vote at all. Using a control group, Harrisson established to his own satisfaction that the fake Tory leaflets had a significant negative impact on the propensity to vote.[25] But in so doing he had clearly shifted MO from researching the causes of non-voting to directly promoting it, a stance difficult to justify in the name of either science or democracy.

In the report he drafted for the Labour Party, Harrisson argued that MO's intervention had pioneered the way for a more 'scientific' approach to electoral mobilization than the 'hit and miss methods' traditionally employed:

> Today we can no longer afford to ignore the modern technique of finding out how to influence people, and no big business interest would think of trying to do so through any sort of propaganda channels without first spending a considerable amount of time and money on investigating the best ways of doing it.

His report—a detailed account intended to serve as 'an invaluable background of verifiable political technique'—was never completed.[26] Harrisson seemed to have fallen out with his Transport House sponsor, Michael Higgins, over the latter's insistence that the Labour Party, having facilitated MO's work, should have exclusive use of MO's findings. Although in the draft report Harrisson refuted this claim—'of course we are not able to withhold any result'—he later confessed to Madge that the reason he had not published a full account of MO's intervention in the by-election was

24. *The Times*, 6 April 1938.
25. In 1961 Harrisson gave a full account of 'The "Vote Killer": a London Experiment', *Britain Revisited*, 107–9.
26. 'West Fulham March 1938', nd (June 1938?), FR A7, 2.

that he had 'morally contracted not to use most of this material in other
ways for several years.'[27] The exercise in black propaganda, which was dubi-
ous legally as well as morally, was not referred to in print until Trevelyan
published his memoirs in 1957.[28] Harrisson's account of the by-election in
his (unpublished) 1939 book 'The Poverty of Freedom' makes no mention
of it. After West Fulham the pre-war Labour Party made no further attempt
to commission opinion research.[29] 'To see the Labour Party spending
£50,000 in propaganda, without the first bloody idea of what they are
doing, keeps me awake with intellectual diarrhoea,' Harrisson remarked in
a begging letter to his friend and occasional funder Naomi Mitchison
around this time.[30] While MO continued to monitor by-elections it was not
until 1940 that they found (in the Ministry of Information) a sponsor prepared to finance this work on a regular basis.

IV

The Munich crisis exemplified the deficiencies of democratic life in
Britain. Starved of reliable information about what was going on, public
opinion fluctuated wildly, ready to seize on Chamberlain's dramatic flights
and his scrap of paper as providing a fantasy reconciliation of conflicting
desires—a firm stand against Hitler, avoidance of war. With much of the
public convinced, by the end of September, that war was inevitable, the
Munich settlement triggered a tide of relief that momentarily swept all
before it. But while most of the media heaped praise on Chamberlain,
MO's interviews revealed growing bewilderment and shame; sentiments
which went unreported in any newspaper and unrecognized even by those
who privately harboured them 'until, at work and in the streets, by the
third day each had gradually found hundreds of others agreeing in this

27. TH to CM, 25 January 1940, 5, Org&Hist 1/1. There is no direct evidence that money
    changed hands on this occasion. But a remark in one of Madge's letters to Inez Spender does
    suggest that as late as December 1938 Higgins was a source of funding for MO: 'My Transport
    House Conference made it impossible for me to phone you at 12...Then there was a rush
    over lunch and to get some money from Michael Higgins' bank and I finally jumped on the
    train to Bolton just as it started to move' (CM to Inez, 12 December 1938, CMpap 8/3).
28. Trevelyan, *Indigo Days*, 100–1.
29. Laura Dumond Beers, 'Whose Opinion?: Changing Attitudes Towards Opinion Polling in
    British politics, 1937–1964', *Twentieth Century British History*, 17, 2, 2006, 193.
30. Heimann, *Most Offending Soul*, 137. The letter is undated and, although Heimann places it in
    the autumn of 1937, the contents suggest that July or August 1938 might be a better guess.

secret shame.'[31] Emphasizing the gulf between the leaders and the led, and the inability of the press either to inform the public about the real facts of the international situation so that realistic conclusions could be drawn, or to inform the politicians about the real state of public opinion (which, arrogantly, the newspapers pretended to represent while having no means of discovering what it actually was[32]), MO charted the impact of repeated international crises on the public attitudes. The predominant mood was divided between resignation about the inevitability of another great war, and wishful thinking about 'peace in our time'—both stances representing ways of accepting the powerlessness of ordinary people to do anything to influence events. In this situation, the urgent need was for leadership from those who *did* understand the facts. But the Labour Party, paralyzed by press representations of pro-Chamberlain feeling, did nothing to mobilize popular revulsion in the critical days following Munich, and MO reserved its praise for the Left Book Club's Victor Gollancz who got out nearly two million leaflets analysing 'The Great Betrayed' within three days of Chamberlain's return from Munich.[33]

Subsequently Harrisson drew a similar moral from the contrast between the fates of two of the popular front by-election candidates who attempted to capitalize on post-Munich shame. In Oxford, A. D. Lindsay, a university man unknown among working-class voters and aloofly contemptuous of populist electioneering, invited his own defeat: 'If we can't win on my own merits without being vulgar it's better to lose'.[34] In Bridgewater, by contrast, the success of the Liberal journalist, Vernon Bartlett, on an 84 per cent poll justified Harrisson's faith that 'democracy was not feeble or dead... its apparent apathy and confusion was not due solely to the attitude of the masses, but at least as much to the leadership available'. As an experienced journalist Bartlett knew how to get his message across. Despite concentrating exclusively on foreign affairs, which MO's election

31. *Britain*, 106.
32. With the exception of the *News Chronicle* which commissioned BIPO during the crisis to undertake regular surveys. Colin McDonald and Stephen King, *Sampling the Universe. The growth, development and influence of market research in Britain since 1945,* 1996, 98.
33. *Britain*, 97–8.
34. Harrisson, 'Poverty of Freedom', 260. In 'The Crisis By-Election', *Picture Post,* 5 November 1938, Harrisson attributed this remark not to Lindsay but to one of his academic supporters. On the Oxford by-election see Iain McLean, 'Oxford & Bridgewater', in Chris Cook and John Ramsden (eds) *By-Elections in British Politics,* 1997; Roger Eatwell, 'Munich, Public Opinion and the Popular Front', *Journal of Contemporary History,* 6, 4, 1971.

studies had repeatedly shown to be of minimal interest to most voters,
Bartlett's campaign effectively mobilized the non-voters, stimulating 'the
type of interest and citizen-cooperation which is the life-blood of a flourishing democracy.'[35]

No evidence survives about exactly what Harrisson's team did in
Bridgewater, or who (if anyone) paid their expenses, but it is clear that,
as in previous by-elections, there was nothing unpartisan about MO's
intervention.[36] Madge, while agreeing on the urgent need for a radical
popular front politics to mobilize opinion against the Chamberlain government, did not think that it was MO's job itself to provide such leadership, and he was alarmed by some of the more explicitly committed
language that Harrisson introduced into *Britain* at proof stage. As he
wrote a year later:

> you have a compulsion to attack and deflate those in authority. In the new
> phase this compulsion has added to it the slogan of "Active Leadership" for
> the "Bewildered" masses—a recommendation with which I absolutely agree,
> but I question whether MO should produce this recommendation as its dom-
> inant theme. The tendency first confronted me when we were finishing the
> Penguin book together. The passages you added then, were, you will admit,
> lively pamphleteering none the less political for not backing any political
> horse.

Harrisson's interventionist stance was, he feared, in danger of turning MO
into an instrument of a 'polemical crusade', diverting it from its original
goal of 'grappling with [the] social structures' underpinning the weaknesses
of British democracy.[37]

35. Harrisson, 'Poverty of Freedom', 153–4, 259, 272, 275. During the election itself, apparently,
  TH had advised Bartlett to speak more about agriculture (about which he knew nothing), but
  Bartlett later said that his attempts to do so only bored his audiences who really wanted to
  hear about foreign affairs. (Pimlott, *Labour and the Left in the 1930s*, 1986, 123–4). Pimlott's
  judgement coincides with Harrisson's: 'there are certainly grounds for saying that Bridgewater
  is a rare case in British electoral history of a by-election whose result can be ascribed to a
  foreign policy issue.'
36. It is curious that the account Harrisson gave in 'The Poverty of Freedom', written in the
  summer of 1939, made no mention of the role of the Left Book Club activists in
  Bridgewater whose work in reviving a moribund Labour Party and committing it to
  Bartlett's popular front candidature played, as Pimlott shows, a key role in winning the
  election. The contrast between this and the praise lavished on Victor Gollancz's Munich
  intervention in *Britain* is perhaps indicative of Harrisson's shift away from the left over the
  winter of 1938–9.
37. CM to TH, 21 January 1940, Org&Hist 1/1.

V

One claim the 1930s have to be years of social progress is in house building and slum clearance.[38] The rehousing of displaced slum-dwellers presented a challenge and an opportunity for reformers anxious to foster active citizenship among the poor; for experts involved in the design and construction of new working-class housing; and for the various commercial interests involved. When the blitz brought housing to the very top of the post-war political agenda, MO's capacity to contribute to the reconstruction debate owed much to its pre-war engagement with the housing problem. In Bolton Harrisson had learned about the resentment caused by insensitive rehousing schemes devised by 'men and women who can get off work in the afternoon to sit on the Worktown Housing Committee, reshuffling the citizens and altering their entire economy.'[39] It was no good rehousing people, he argued, if you did not take the trouble to ask them how they wanted to live.[40] MO's commitment to finding out what ordinary people wanted was music to the ears of rebellious students at the Architectural Association School in London who were contesting pedagogic tradition in the name of a socially aware modernism.[41] In the autumn of 1937 one such student bought a copy of the *Mass-Observation* pamphlet from a fellow student—John Madge, Charles' younger brother—and immediately saw the value of MO's accumulation of 'a large, comprehensive and accessible collection of facts about how we live, and how we want to live.'[42] In August 1938, encouraged by Mass-Observation, four architecture students took lodgings in Fulham in order to carry out a group project interviewing working-class residents in a street of run-down multi-occupied houses.[43] When they returned for a week to complete the work at the height of the Munich crisis, one of them wrote a daily diary for MO, vivid testimony to the febrile combination of wishful thinking (thrilling to suggestions that German

38. John Burnett, *A Social History of Housing, 1815–1985*, 1986, 249.
39. Harrisson, 'Poverty of Freedom', 99. Drinking after hours in the Irish club with Labour Party activists after a failed election, Harrisson recorded their conviction that Labour's ambitious re-housing programme had lost the party votes among slum dwellers ('Municipal Elections', 3 November 1937, W11/I).
40. Harrisson, 'Poverty of Freedom', 97–9, 291; *Britain*, 217–18.
41. Elizabeth Darling, *Re-forming Britain: Narratives of modernity before reconstruction*, 2007, 179, 186ff.
42. David Medd, DS 408. Medd became an active member of the MO panel, continuing to respond to directives throughout the war and beyond.
43. Darling, *Re-forming Britain*, 200–3.

workers were 'massing in the towns' to overthrow Hitler); resignation about
their personal futures (the 'general ending to a conversation is now becoming "see you in the army"'); and the careful, practical, mundane work of
finding out the domestic tastes and desires of the residents.[44] Nine months
later, not yet in the army, the same group of students were joined by others
on a more ambitious project in Stepney designing an alternative to an LCC
redevelopment plan incorporating what they had discovered about the
desires of the people being rehoused. The team, which this time included
John Madge, used a detailed questionnaire drawn up and analysed by MO,
which revealed, among other things, that it was overwhelmingly the men
who wanted to stay put while their wives aspired to better housing, together
with a strong preference for houses over flats.[45]

Alongside this relationship with the young rebels at the Architectural
Association, Harrisson gained financial support for MO's work from Clem
Leslie, a central figure in the interface between commerce, housing reform,
Labour politics, and architectural modernism.[46] In many ways Leslie was
Harrisson's ideal collaborator. As an advertising man at the London Press
Exchange, Leslie had managed the account of the Gas, Light and Coke
Company and subsequently became the company's publicity manager. An
inspired publicist (he invented the friendly 'Mr Therm') his task was to chal-
lenge the association between modernity and electricity, rebranding gas as
the fuel of the future. In association with the leading light of housing reform
in the voluntary sector, Elizabeth Denby, and the modernist architect,
Maxwell Fry, the gas company commissioned the Kensal House flats in
North Kensington. With no electricity, heated and lit entirely by coke and
gas, the flats were cheap to rent, but they were also designed to foster both
privacy for family life (and personal autonomy within it) and tenant participation in the management of the flats. Denby's recipe for turning ex-slum
dwellers into active modern citizens embodied values of individual liberty
and communal association not unlike those that Madge and Harrisson
found to celebrate in their account of the Lambeth Walk. Leslie promoted

44. David Goldhill, 'Crisis report', September 1938, DS 307. Goldhill was subsequently part of an
    MO team surveying towns in the south east during the last months of 1938 ('Brighton', 10–11
    December 1938, TC 66/2/A; Novy to Willcock, 27 July 1940, HNpap).
45. 'Preliminary analysis of brief investigation of certain elements in re-housing in the Borough
    of Stepney', TC 1/1/D; Darling, Re-forming Britain, 199, 205.
46. Obituary, The Times, 11 January 1980. Guy Hunter worked for Clem Leslie at the Gas, Light
    and Coke Company (CM, 'Autobiography', 374).

Kensal House imaginatively in press, pamphlet, and especially in the documentary film *Housing Problems* (1935) where working-class tenants were seen for the first time speaking direct to camera. Like the Peckham health centre—'where the working class look really nice diving into a very blue swimming bath', wrote Madge in self-parodic mode, 'drinking beer at sociologically-correct tables, dancing, having blood tests in a tremendously human, unbrassed (I hope USSR-like) atmosphere'[47]—Kensal House, became an icon of progressive user-centred planning in the late 1930s.[48]

It was not only a common interest in housing reform that made Leslie a likely source of funds for MO. As a leading progressive in the advertising world he had been instrumental in putting together a team of advertisers to help Herbert Morrison win the 1937 LCC elections, a behind-the-scenes operation not unlike Harrisson's own work with the Labour Party during the early months of 1938.[49] In October 1938, citing MO's findings on the non-voter, Leslie was urging the establishment of a 'Ministry of Public Enlightenment' whose job would be to 'use modern techniques of communication to help to articulate and bring alive the idea of democracy in the public mind.'[50] The affinity with Harrisson's ideas is obvious, and at some point during the winter of 1938–9 Leslie agreed to finance the MO project in Fulham. In the summer of 1939 the gas company was paying for a programme of interviews about home life on 'some fifteen new housing estates and tenements in the London area' which, as Harrisson told a Housing Centre meeting, 'has provided enough ammunition to blow a lot of architectural assumptions from here to Port Sunlight.'[51]

VI

When Harrisson took over from Madge in Blackheath he set out to build a new team of full-timers. Joe Wilcock had moved back to London in the

47. Madge to Inez, 20 August 1938, CMpap 8/3.
48. Peckham was singled out as a like-minded initiative in the *Mass-Observation* pamphlet, 62. On the affinities between MO and Peckham, see also Ben Highmore, 'Hopscotch Modernism: on everyday life and the blurring of art and social science', *Modernist Cultures*, 2, 1, 2006, 73–5.
49. B. Donoughue and G. W. Jones, *Herbert Morrison: portrait of a politician*, 1973, 209–10; Dominic Wring, *The Politics of Marketing the Labour Party*, 2004, 30–2.
50. *Western Daily Press*, 17 October 1938; S. G. Leslie, 'How the Public Thinks', *The Spectator*, November 1938.
51. 'Emergency Problems and Mass-Observation', 29 August 1939, FR A22; TH, 'notes for meeting at Housing Centre', 24 October 1939, TC 1/1/A.

summer and worked in Fulham during the Munich crisis, but Harrisson
had no money to pay him and the best he could do for Wilcock, and for
Eric Bennett who had also come to London, was to persuade his contacts
in the Labour Party to take them on.[52] Leslie Taylor, who left Bolton for
London towards the end of the year, timed things better and Harrisson, by
then, had the money to employ him full-time until he was called up at the
start of the war. Kathleen Box, a 26-year-old London School of Economics
graduate living with her father in Wandsworth and working as a copy typist,
had been angling for a job with MO since she joined the panel in August
1937.[53] Though drawn politically to the Communist Party she, like many
members of the panel, lacked 'the propaganding temperament…I tend
rather to look on people as specimens and to take a rather armchair and
academic view', preferring to assuage her guilty middle-class conscience by
working for MO.[54] Harrisson came to rely on her during the West Fulham
by-election, and employed her as soon as he could. By the turn of the year
he had taken on at least three more full-timers to work alongside Box and
Taylor.[55] Jack Atkins, aged 23 in 1939, had taught for a year in an elementary school, before doing a History degree in Bristol. He was an active
member of the Labour Party in Hammersmith. Brian Allwood, as a schoolboy communist in Loughborough, had sent reports to MO, and he was
only 19 when Harrisson recruited him to work full-time. Brought up in
West Africa as the son of a consular official, 'Tich', as he was affectionately
known, was short and very scruffy: he rarely shaved or bathed, had long
dank hair, and went around in a filthy mackintosh. But Harrisson described
him as 'the quickest minded' of all his staff: 'he had a kind of magpie brain,

52. Madge to Inez, 2 August 1938, CMpap 8/3. In December 1938 Brian Barefoot reported that
    Wilcock had 'a job in Transport House' (Barefoot memoir, December 1938, 201, Personnel/
    Barefoot); see also TH to CM, 25 January 1940, 21, Org&Hist 1/1. In the spring of 1939 TH
    referred to 'a special Mass-Observation unit' in the Labour Party, set up 'when they took over
    two of my whole time Observers. The results seem to be pleasing them, though the unit seems
    to me to be echoing more and more "socialist", less objective' (TH, 'Poverty of Freedom',
    395). Wilcock appears to have to use a continuing association with MO as a cover for solicit-
    ing information from his new employers' political adversaries (Woodford to Wilcock, 12
    August 1938, TC 46/2/a). During the war Wilcock worked for a time with Norwegian sailors
    in Newcastle, but nothing more is known about him after that (Cawson, interviewed by
    Calder, 29 February 1980).
53. CM, interviewed by Stanley, 23 March 1978; Box to CM, 20 September 1937, DS 018; 'West
    Fulham March 1938', nd (June 1938?), FR A7, 7.
54. Dorothy Sheridan (ed.), Wartime Women. An Anthology of Women's Wartime Writing for Mass-
    Observation 1937–45, 1990, 21 (Box anonymized as 'Miss Earnshaw').
55. TH 'Outline', 7 December 1938, TC 20/2/B.

detecting the bright glitter of interest and sympathy under dirt of dimness.'[56]
Allwood and Atkins became the closest of friends, both 'profoundly dissatisfied with the world we had been born into', and fizzing with incoherent
ideas about how it should be changed.[57] Both men were writers: Atkins
subsequently published biographies of various literary figures including
George Orwell; Allwood, a small book of poetry before his accidental death
serving in a non-combatant role with the RAF in 1944. Alec Hughes, the
third new recruit, who was rather less politically minded, had grown up and
gone to university in Liverpool before joining MO. He was seen by
Harrisson as the most objective of his field workers.[58] One further full-
timer, Priscilla Feare, had been inherited by Harrisson from Madge when
he took over in November. Brought up in Blackheath and Lewisham, she
had taken secretarial training before joining MO, aged 20, in response to an
advertisement in the local paper. Her father, an executive in a railway company, scorned her 'long-haired friends', but she felt herself among kindred
spirits, fond of Madge, able to cope with Harrisson (who came to rely heavily on her secretarial skills), and flourishing among the clever young men
most of whom fell in love with her: 'all this seemed what I had been looking
for—a university education in itself'.[59]

This was a very different group from Harrisson's Bolton team: younger,
better educated, and much more middle class. None of them had anything
approaching the experience of working-class life that Walter Hood, Wilcock,

56. TH, obituary of Allwood, *The New Saxon Review*, No 4, nd (1945?); Priscilla Macnamara,
    interviewed by Calder, 10 January 1980.
57. After his friend's death in 1944, Atkins described the bizarre ideas they had been dreaming up
    together, premised on the use of MO techniques to investigate irrational popular irritations
    with everyday inconveniences, with a view to launching a new politics of annoyance:

    Annoyance...is a quality which may be too small and petty to concern those
    [whose]...conception of politics is confined to so-called giants such as Churchill or
    Stalin, so their conception of psychology is confined to big and gawdy [sic] things like
    anger and retribution...Annoyance is like people; it consists of a myriad particles of emo-
    tion which scramble over the face of the earth in no particular order and with no notice-
    able purpose. It is too unimportant for important people to bother about. Yet if a group of
    people had the intelligence and determination to study the psychology of annoyance and
    apply their findings to the political scene, they could achieve power in a very short time.

    Playful, not altogether serious, these ideas were one version of a kind of middle-class politics
    of the everyday that appealed to Harrisson's clever young men. They bear an intriguing
    resemblance to the anti-noise and anti-smell leagues promoted by George Bernard Shaw in
    the 1930s, in concert with one of Tom's closest friends, the leading London lawyer Ambrose
    Appelbe (Obituary of Ambrose Appelbe, *The Daily Telegraph*, 20 March 1999).
58. FR 474, 30 October 1940; Novy to TH, 22 and 28 February 1940, HNpap.
59. 'Henry and Priscilla narrative', 12, Personnel/Macnamara.

or John Sommerfield brought to the Worktown project. But because they were young, idealistic, and, in several cases, had parents able to contribute to their support, they came cheap, needing 'only ... pocket-money and a nominal salary ... [and willing to] put up with considerable discomfort when funds have been low.'[60] Or, as an embittered Hughes was to put it many years later: 'A few of us ... bore the brunt of developing M-O in circumstances which amounted to exploitation.'[61]

VII

During the 12 months between the Munich crisis and the outbreak of war Harrisson kept his end of MO going with a series of rather miscellaneous projects, picking up commissions and funding as and when he could. The work during this period had none of the coherence of the initial Worktown project. Despite the initial focus on Fulham, successive weekends between November and January saw teams of observers, paid and unpaid, led by Box, descending on five southern towns (Canterbury, Aldershot, Ipswich, Windsor, and Brighton), observing dance halls, pubs, churches, and interviewing local leaders and people in the street.[62] One aim of this work was to discover what it was that people liked or disliked about the towns they lived in, perhaps as a way into investigating what Harrisson much later referred to as 'those tangled traditions, experiences, sentiments, relationships, emotive fantasies and ecological facts which determine local sentiment and the parameters of local loyalty.'[63] But the project was a disappointment, as Harrisson's scrawlings all over Box's report make clear: 'Very dull. Badly thought out, lacking any new idea, conclusion awful generalisation and rubbish. ... How DUMB after all that work.'[64] At the same time he was drawing up plans to commission ethnographic reports from several of the panel members about the villages in which they lived, perhaps as a preliminary to establishing a permanent rural unit to supplement the urban centres in Bolton and Fulham.[65]

60. Note on MO's history, nd (August 1939?), 4, Org&Hist 1/3.
61. Hughes to Calder, 4 February 1979, Personnel/Hughes.
62. TC 66/2/A.
63. Harrisson, *Living through the Blitz*, 208.
64. 'Weekend town survey', January 1939, TC 66/2/D.
65. One of these was Stebbing, who was later to publish his own MO war diary. Correspondence between TH and Stebbing, January–May 1939, TC 66/20/D.

Meanwhile the failure of 'politicians and "socially conscious" people' to take seriously the propagandist possibilities of popular music was a continuing source of frustration to Harrisson. In the autumn of 1938, analysing the 'mass-poetry' of jazz lyrics—'the hymns of young England'—he argued that 'the tremendous individualist, "selfish", and thus "anti-social" effect of jazz education now lavished on every boy or girl throughout adolescence' was creating among the young an escapist 'dreamworld' culture dangerously resistant to a 'realistic view of life and its meanings'.[66] Nevertheless, he was confident that there was an unmet demand for popular music with a less anti-social message, and he eagerly documented the Locarno organization's attempt to follow up the success of the Lambeth Walk with a song and dance routine embodying a conscious anti-fascist intent.[67] The importance Harrisson attributed to these issues was reflected in his decision to employ Hughes during the first eight months of 1939 to investigate 'ways in which jazz can contribute to the social good, rather than trading on escapism'.[68] Two other young men were also taken on to assist Hughes, one of them the future historian and industrial relations expert Hugh Clegg, for whom, it has been argued, this first encounter with working-class people was of abiding significance in fostering his democratic sentiments and inoculating him 'against the "servants of power" managerialism' characteristic of much post-war industrial relations research.[69] Like the Worktown books this project was also overtaken by the war, although the tone of Hughes' reflections on the material collected from the panel, from dance hall observations and door-to-door interviewing in south London, suggests that there would have been difficulties producing a worthwhile book. Having acquired 'a strong predilection for the intellectual pleasures of life at the university', Hughes' exposure to popular culture left him with a disappointed feeling that life was after all 'extraordinarily simple and rather depressing':

66. Tom Harrisson, 'Whistle While You Work', *New Writing*, Autumn 1938, 48–67.
67. Tom Harrisson, 'The Chestnut Tree', *Picture Post*, 7 January 1939.
68. Harrisson, 'Poverty of Freedom', 360; MO *Bulletin*, June 1939, FR A19; TH to Yarwood, 4 July 1939; AH to Blunden, 17 July 1939; both in TC/38/C.
69. Peter Ackers and Ruth Hartley, 'A Social Science Apprenticeship? Hugh Clegg at Mass-Observation, 1939', *Historical Studies in Industrial Relations*, 2008, 217. By contrast, Jennie Taylor ('Sex, Snobs and Swing: A Case Study of Mass-Observation as a Source for Social History', Mass-Observation Online) convincingly explores the sexually charged voyeurism of these middle-class young men. Taylor's approach closely follows Gurney's analysis, but, like him, she neglects the different dynamics of class and gender involved in the work of Hughes and his assistants, on the one hand, and those of the older men in Bolton, on the other.

Coming from 'varsity' with the hopes of conquering all sorts of problems and plunging deep into the mass of human activities I am now rather appalled to find out how little there is in it all—and I wonder whether most people deceive themselves into imagining life to be complicated or whether it is I who is being deceived.[70]

Moreover his conclusion that it was the tune rather than the words that explained the popularity of a song sat awkwardly with Harrisson's conviction that jazz lyrics had a major impact on the outlook of the young, as did his scepticism about the capacity of the professional lyricists to understand the minds of the masses.[71] Although the book came to nothing, Harrisson was to devote considerable effort during the war to cultivating jazz lyricists as potential agents of pro-war propaganda.

When he took over in Blackheath, Harrisson tried to raise money for the ongoing work on opinion formation from the Booksellers Association, who had already been approached in the summer by Madge. On this occasion he made it quite clear that there could be no exclusive rights to the results:

> It is understood that M-O undertakes this investigation not specifically FOR the book-interests concerned. M-O is an independent organisation which cannot sell its results to anyone. But it is directly concerned with reading as the biggest factor in influencing contemporary culture, and this research is in its direct line of work. It gladly directs its attention to special aspects of the subject in return for help from the book trade.

In addition to the material on reading habits accumulated from the panel, Harrisson had organized doorstep interviewing in Bolton and London and, in December, had taken on Allwood to observe people reading in the cafes, parks, streets, tubes, and buses of central London. The proposed new programme would have involved several more full-timers, and more work with the panel, but the deal came to nothing.[72]

A more successful attempt to marry MO's agenda of investigating opinion formation with commercial needs came in the summer of 1939, when Harrisson secured a contract from the Railway Companies Association (RCA) to monitor the impact of their 'Square Deal' campaign for changes in laws restricting their ability to compete with road transport. Bruce Watkin,

---

70. AH to Blunden, 1 May 1939, TC 38/8/C.
71. Hughes, 'Jazz—theoretical', 19 August 1939, TC 38/6/H.
72. TH 'outline', 7 December 1938; John Baker to CM, 1 November 1938; TH to Baker, 7 December 1938; Baker to TH, 16 December 1938; all in TC 20/2/B.

who had worked with Madge on the smoking study and with Sommerfield on the pub, was engaged to organize nearly 7,000 interviews—by far the largest interviewing project MO undertook in its first decade—to discover the impact of the RCA's press advertising and posters. Their finding—that the campaign passed very largely over the heads of its intended audience— provided ammunition for Harrisson's argument that advertising undertaken without proper preliminary enquiries into popular knowledge and opinion was largely a waste of money. It sufficiently impressed the RCA for them to commission further work piloting ongoing advertising, and probably contributed to the decision of the Ministry of Information to commission MO to monitor the impact of its own posters at the beginning of the war. But the methodology of the RCA work—its exclusive reliance on tick-box questionnaires—was a far cry from MO's normal modus operandi.[73]

VIII

Early in December 1938, confident that he could 'get a lot of money soon', Harrisson told Madge that he planned to transfer MO's headquarters from Blackheath to the East End early in the new year. Concerned about the growth of anti-Semitism, he set out to subject prevailing stereotypes about the Jews— flashy, mean, loud, salacious, and unusually politically minded—to 'objective' examination, and to investigate the extent and causes of anti-Semitism. The initial plan was for another Penguin Special, but the Jewish Board of Deputies, to whom he looked for funding, was wary of drawing attention to anti-Semitism and insisted, in return for a down payment of £250, that the enquiry and its results remain confidential for at least five years.[74] With the money secured, Harrisson, together with Leslie Taylor and Norman Cohn—an Oxford research student from a mixed Catholic/Jewish family in London who was later to become a distinguished historian of anti-Semitism—moved into three rented rooms in a bug-ridden tenement building off Commercial Road.[75]

73. 'Investigation of "Square Deal" for the Railways', July 1939, FR A23; 'Emergency Problems and Mass-Observation', 29 August 39, FR A22; TH to Richard Temple, TC 43/2/B; Bill sent to Temple, 19 October 1930, TC 70/1/b; BW, memo on questionnaires, 18 January 1947, Org&Hist 4/1; Bruce Watkin to 'Dear Sir', 21 January 1995, Personnel/Watkin.
74. CM to Inez, 4 December 1938, CMpap 8/3; TH to Laski, 21 April 1939, cited in Kushner, *We Europeans*, 85; 'Anti-Semitism Survey', nd (March 1939?), 1, FR A12.
75. TH to CM, 17 January 1939; Thomas diary 26 January 1939; TH to Laski, 12 June 1939 cited in Kushner, *We Europeans*, 85.

This was Davenport Street again, only more so: squalid, authentic, and (unlike Bolton) pleasingly exotic:

> Working in a tiny bug-infested room, uneven floor, one damp wall, winter's draft whistling through window cracks from the narrow blind-alley outside, the opposite houses only few feet away, empty, filthy and condemned. Down unlit steep steps to the family of Jews below, he crippled in bed all day fully dressed, playing dominoes with a Rabbi. Floor below that, onto the shelves on which pauper negroes crept and slept. In the cellar cocks for kosher killing. As a background the incessant vivid roar of Commercial Road, most dynamic of arteries, linking dockland to dreamland, Cockney to Chinatown, East India to the City of London.

By the time he wrote these words Harrisson had abandoned the East End for the house in Ladbroke Road that was to become MO's headquarters during the war. Here he was able to work in 'a big room with wide windows all along both sides, on to Spring and the trees, blackbirds on the lawn, my books...and china...around me'.[76] The house belonged to Biddy Clayton, a wealthy upper class socialite who he was to marry a year later as soon as her divorce came through, to the disgust of some of his friends who believed he was simply after Biddy's money.[77] However much he enjoyed the material comforts provided by this new relationship, the sentiments of February had been genuine enough, as a contemporary letter to Trevelyan testifies:

> At last I am a man again. This place, E. End, is terrific...I cannot even start to tell you...I'd love to come on Thursday to Whi[techapel] Art Gallery but I feel that to do so would be to undo all this. I *must* get away from people who make me compete and talk about my bloody self. Only in this simplicity— and it is that—can I escape an increasing urge to be harrison [sic] and powerful. Here life undoes its tremendous tendrils, and I forget the importance of success. It is enough to move among it knowing only the stranger. I can't explain.[78]

After an initial period of undirected immersion—Box wrote desperately to Harrisson begging for 'something definite' to investigate: 'I've been lurking

---

76. Harrisson, 'Poverty of Freedom', 10–11.
77. Heimann, *Most Offending Soul*, 152–3, 157–8.
78. TH to Trevelyan, JTpap. The letter is undated, but the reference to Whitechapel Art Gallery suggests that it was written early in February 1939. An exhibition organized by the Artists' International Association, including work by Trevelyan, opened on Thursday 9 February 1939 (Radford, *Art for a Purpose*, 106–7, 190).

about such a lot that I'm afraid of becoming conspicuous if I lurk much more'[79]—the team set about systematically observing the behaviour of Jews and Cockneys in the street, pubs, clubs, dance halls, and cinemas, recording overheards and conducting informal interviews. They also used doorstep interviews to probe feelings about anti-Semitism, and investigators infiltrated a number of local organizations—'always the most fruitful phase in our researches'—including the Christian Socialist League, the Stepney Tenants' Defence League, and the Young Jewish Communists.[80] One observer hung out for a week with a group of Jewish lads, faithfully recording their unsuccessful attempts to pick up Cockney girls (and the obscenities regularly traded in these encounters). Sommerfield, who had made an initial plan for the work, had suggested infiltrating fascist groups, but nothing came of this.[81] Equally abortive were plans made with Geoffrey Gorer for in-depth therapeutic sessions with selected individuals to explore individual Jewish life histories, and the unconscious roots of anti-Semitism among gentiles.[82] But a panel directive commissioned in February inviting respondents to examine the formation of their own attitude to the Jews threw a good deal of light on the psychology of latent anti-Semitism among MO volunteers throughout Britain.

The original plan was for a study lasting three months, but most of the £250 was used to pay off debts, and Harrisson, in a bid for more cash, submitted a preliminary report after six weeks. Jews and Cockneys, he reported, lived very separate lives, seldom mixing (except in the Tenants' League whose rent strike was enthusiastically reported as a rare example of inter-racial solidarity). Although this Jewish separateness was seen as an underlying cause of anti-Semitism, MO reported that most of the stereotypical notions of Jewish behaviour were without foundation and estimated that only about a fifth of the Cockneys were positively anti-Semitic. Most Cockneys, they reported, adopted a 'live and let live' attitude towards their Jewish neighbours, although resenting what they saw as the tendency of the Jews to consider themselves superior. Contrasting this finding with the sur-

79. Box to TH, nd (January 1939?), TC 62/1/a.
80. 'Anti-Semitism Survey', nd (March 1939?), 33a, FR A12.
81. Sommerfield to TH, nd (January 1939?), TC 62/1/B.
82. 'Anti-Semitism Survey', nd (March 1939?), 1, 42, FR A1; Brotman to TH, 15 February 1939, enclosing a memo from Geoffrey Gorer: 'Outline of Projected Psychological Study of Jews in relation to Wider Investigation of Anti-semitism', TC 62/1/b; TH to Laski, 19 June 1939, TC 62/1/b.

prisingly negative attitudes to the Jews revealed by the panel respondents, Harrisson concluded that 'anti-semitism appears to exist on a level not of fact but of fantasy', and that 'people who live in places where there are no Jews tend to be more anti-Semitic than people in Leeds or Whitechapel.'[83] Although much of the work rested on a questionable a priori assumption that East Enders could be neatly divided between Jews and Cockneys (and that investigators could tell them apart simply by observing their physical characteristics), the combination of fieldwork and panel responses enabled Harrisson to reach conclusions that anticipated the findings of much later research.[84] The normal MO spattering of bizarre statistics—Cockneys, for example, were found to be three times as likely as Jews to whistle while peeing in public lavatories (evidence apparently of their greater self-consciousness)—made the report an easy target for hostile members of the Board of Deputies, some of them no doubt alienated by the report's enthusiasm for the rent strikers and by Harrisson's acknowledgment of help from two well-known East End leftists, the author and artist, Pearl Binder (a founder member of the Artists, International Association) and Willy Goldman, autodidact son of Russian–Jewish immigrants taken up by Bloomsbury as a 'proletarian writer'. Nevertheless the Board agreed to supply funding for another two months.[85]

As the new deadline approached, in June 1939 Harrisson wrote to Laski listing a plethora of work he claimed to be organizing including more door-to-door interviews to discover 'the misconceptions on which Anti-Semitism is founded'; detailed studies of individual Jewish and Cockney families and of the 'Jewish way of speaking English' (by 'an expert in phonetics'[86]); 'objective field work in Hampstead' on the impact of recent Jewish immigration; 'personal visits by me and organisation of sub-units to study the problem in other towns' and test the inverse relationship between anti-Semitism and the presence of Jews; and a further directive to the panel.[87] Apart from the

---

83. 'Anti-Semitism Survey', nd (March 1939?), 1, 26, 44, 61.
84. For a full evaluation see Kushner, *We Europeans*, 86–91.
85. TH to Laski, 19 June 1939, TC 62/1/b; 'Anti-Semitism Survey', nd (March 1939?), 3; Kushner, *We Europeans*, 88–90. On Pearl Binder (1904–1990) see Tony Rickaby, 'The Artists' International', *History Workshop*, 6, 1978, 154–44. On Goldman see Valentine Cunningham's obituary, *The Guardian*, 6 July 2009; Jonathan Rose, *The Intellectual Life of the British Working Classes*, 2001, 450–2; Willy Goldman, *The East End My Cradle*, 1940.
86. Possibly Goldman's wife, the German-Jewish Communist Frieda Eisler, a psycholinguist who was briefly to work for MO during the war.
87. TH to Laski, 19 June 1939, TC 62/1/b.

last of these, no evidence survives in the archive that any of this work was ever undertaken, and no final report was written.[88] Instead Harrisson gave priority to a television documentary on the coexistence of 'Cockney and Jew, Lascar and Chinaman' in the East End, broadcast on 12 July.[89] Perhaps plans to complete the work later were overwhelmed by the coming of war, but several of the key investigators had already been moved onto other work in March 1939, and one cannot help wondering whether, in his anxiety to secure new funding from other sources, Harrisson had behaved in just the way that the Board of Deputies' most hostile member had predicted: 'The Jews have got the jitters, let's diddle 'em of their dough.'[90]

IX

In the spring of 1939, with the collapse of the Munich agreement and Hitler's occupation of Prague, MO's leaders were turning their thoughts to how the organization might find a role for itself in the event of war. Harrisson was commissioned by a 'high-up civil servant'—actually a retired academic working temporarily for the Ministry of Labour—to investigate the level of commitment among people who volunteered for Air Raid Precautions (ARP) work.[91] Between April and June 1939 Box, with help from five other full-timers, interviewed about 1,000 ARP volunteers in Fulham, probing their reasons for joining and their attitudes to the service.[92] The report, written by Box and Stanley Cramp (who did the statistics), argued that continuing enthusiasm among the volunteers was being frustrated by muddle and inefficiency in the organization of ARP and the absence of any mechanism by which the grass roots could make their

88. CM to TH, 21 January 1940, 2; Saloman to England, 7 July 1951, TC 62/2/F.
89. TC 62/1/E; for an account of the script see Kushner, *We Europeans*, 91–7.
90. Lian Franklyn, 12 April 1939, cited in Kushner, *We Europeans*, 85. Box and Taylor had been moved onto the Fulham ARP study in April. Kushner dismisses this accusation: and certainly TH's motivation was far more complex than a simple pursuit of money. In June TH protested to Laski, rather defensively, that his intentions must be honourable since he had a Jewish grandmother who he had greatly respected (TH to Laski, 19 June 1939, TC 62/1/b). But money may have been the reason he defaulted on the final report.
91. 'Speak for Yourselves', 1 June 1939, FR A26, 19. Dr A. E. Morgan had been hired by the Ministry of Labour to work on its National Service campaign (*The Times*, 22 May 1939). He had been principal of University College, Hull (1926–35) and vice-chancellor of McGill University (1935–37).
92. 'Fulham ARP: Method', nd, TC 23/1/H.

feelings known to the hierarchy; a finding expressed more forcefully elsewhere by Harrisson: 'Everyone knows that ARP was and is chaos at almost
every point.'[93] The message from Fulham—popular willingness undermined
by elite incompetence—anticipated the message that much of MO's work
was to deliver to the wartime state. No record survives of the Ministry of
Labour's reaction, but it is unlikely that the civil servants involved were any
keener to listen to such criticisms than were their wartime successors.

   While Harrisson was courting the Ministry of Labour, Madge made his
own, bolder move towards finding a role for MO in the event of war.
Believing that the work he had developed since moving to Bolton in
October 1938 had a potentially important contribution to make to the
understanding of contemporary economics, he offered his services to the
man who was to become Britain's leading wartime economist: John Maynard
Keynes.

93. Harrisson, 'Poverty of Freedom', 141; 'Report on ARP in Fulham', 3 September 1939,
    FR A24; CM to TH, 21 January 1940, 2, Org&Hist 1/1.

5

Saving and Spending

Having now completed...the first phase of work in Bolton—the phase of outlining the main institutions and the individual role in the total culture—we can turn to horizontal studies of a more far reaching kind. All through the work of the past two years, the confusion between economic needs, and social or personal-social needs has been getting across our work...In the literature of economics there is little that clarifies these issues, though some American work...indicates new lines of approach. The whole basis of our particular job is to SEE WHAT REALLY HAPPENS. As this seldom seems to have been done in the economic field of BEHAVIOUR, I decided that as soon as our first cycle of books was completed, we should concentrate our attention on two wide problems. One 'The Difference between Men and Women', two 'The Social Factors in Economics'.

(Tom Harrisson, draft memo on 'Social Factors in Economics', November 1938)[1]

I

The second phase of Mass-Observation's (MO's) work in Bolton began, not with Charles Madge, but with the arrival of a 33-year-old Austrian refugee, Gertrude Wagner, in July 1938. Brian Barefoot remembered her not only for her 'feminine influence'—by which he meant that she cleaned up the house—but also because she was able to stand up to Tom Harrisson without getting herself thrown out.[2] Older than the only other

---

1. Hubble, *Mass-Observation and Everyday Life*, 189, says that this memo, in W 1/C, is unsigned, but it is clearly marked as a 'memo from Tom Harrisson'. The same programme is flagged up in MO *Bulletin*, November 1938, FR A8. I have found nothing in the archive to suggest that any work was ever done on the proposed book about gender differences.
2. Barefoot memoir, 1979, Personnel/Barefoot.

woman to have spent time in Davenport Street (Sheila Fox, who *was* thrown out), Wagner arrived with previous research experience and a funded project of her own. After studying law and psychology in Vienna in the late 1920s she had participated in the *Marienthal* study.[3] Arriving in England in 1936, she found work through a fellow refugee—the economist Hans Singer—as an investigator on the Pilgrim Trust project on long-term unemployment, published in 1938 as *Men Without Work*.[4] In February 1938 she published a critical article on market research (of which she appeared to have some experience), arguing for the replacement of tick-box questionnaires with methods that allowed the skilled investigator to record 'as much as possible the exact words of the interviewed person' along with 'his own shrewd and trained observations.' The best results, she argued, would be obtained by in-depth interviews, preceded by preliminary study of 'the impact of social environment and social institutions'.[5] MO's Bolton project could have been designed to provide the 'preliminary study' Wagner needed to pursue her work in social psychology, although whether she was aware of it at this point is unknown. But in the summer of 1938, when the Pilgrim Trust gave her a two-year grant to do an MA thesis on 'The Psychological Aspect of Saving and Spending', she wrote to Harrisson proposing to do the research in Bolton as part of the MO team.[6] With the four Gollancz books nearing completion, Harrisson seized on this opportunity to reorient the Bolton project.

Within weeks of Wagner's arrival in Bolton, Harrisson departed for London to work with Madge on MO's coverage of the Munich crisis. But Bolton was not far from his mind and in October, having set Stanley Cramp to work in the London School of Economics (LSE) library finding out

3. TH, with characteristic exaggeration, boosted her as 'one of the pioneers in social research at Mariethal' (TH to Simon, nd (December 1938?), W1/C), while she claimed only to have 'taken part in the well-known survey of unemployment carried out in Marienthal.' (*Men Without Work*, Report to the Pilgrim Trust, 1938, x). Jahoda later told Sheridan that Wagner was only 'on the periphery' in Vienna and did not work at all on the Mariethal study (Wagner interviewed by Sheridan, 27 April 1988).
4. Wagner was responsible for the section on Blackburn, which reveals complex feelings among unemployed women weavers discovering the pleasures of full-time domesticity. (Liz Stanley, *An archaeology of a 1930s Mass-Observation project*, Manchester University Sociology Department, Occasional Paper, 1990, 18–19, 29).
5. G. W Wagner, 'Market research: a Critical Study', *Review of Economic Studies*, 5, 2, February 1938, 134, 138.
6. Wagner interviewed by Sheridan, 27 April 1988.

'what economic theorists have to say about the question of how and why people spend their money',[7] Harrisson revisited Bolton, presumably to discuss the project with Wagner. It is quite clear from Madge's own account of his move to Bolton that it was Harrisson who was initially responsible for the design of the new project:

> Kathleen and I parted, and I was rather upset. Tom Harrisson suggested—really a good suggestion—that I should go to Bolton and he would come to Grotes Buildings. So we swapped. And he suggested, which was also a good idea, that I should make a study of economic life...[8]

It was Harrisson, not Madge, who made the first approach to Ernest Simon, in November 1938, asking for money for the new project on 'Social Factors in Economics', and assuring him that two professors of economics (Percy Ford in Southampton and John Jewkes in Manchester) had already offered their support for work designed to subject economists' assumption of economic rationality to empirical investigation of the everyday working-class economic behaviour.[9] This was Harrisson in classic ornithological mode, anticipating 'six months of intensive fieldwork' to 'see what really happens'—or as Madge put it subsequently: 'I went up there with this very broad brief studying economic life in Bolton which was...conceived as trailing people round Woolworths and seeing how they behaved'.[10] To this end Harrisson dispatched Geoffrey Thomas—who had been working for MO in Fulham for a couple of months—to join Madge in Bolton to conduct 'objective fieldwork and detailed outdoor studies of behaviour.'[11] Between November 1938 and June 1939 a great deal of time was spent by Thomas—at the time an aspiring young novelist recovering his health after years of illness and, in later life, Director of the Government Social Survey[12]—following people around Bolton's shops and markets investigating how far the housewife 'knows beforehand exactly what she wants, how far...she [is] influenced by what she sees in the shop', noting down precise

7. 'The answer is not much' (Cramp to TH, 19 October 1938, W 1/B).
8. CM, interviewed by Calder, March 1976, 21–2.
9. Harrisson, draft memo on 'Social Factors in Economics', nd (November 1938?), W 1/C (quoted above).
10. CM, interviewed by Calder, March 1976, 22.
11. 'Spending and Saving in Worktown', nd, W 1/C.
12. Wagner interviewed by Sheridan, 27 April 1988; Chapman, interviewed by Stanley, 23 February 1979.

details of how she chose what (if anything) to buy, her interactions (if any) with shop assistants, and so on.[13]

It was, however, clear from the start that the work would go beyond Harrisson's notion of 'objective' fieldwork, if only because the other key player, Wagner, however much she valued MO's 'preliminary study', brought with her a social psychologist's focus on 'the individual side of this problem, the personal statements, interviews'.[14] As Harrisson conceded in December 1938, 'the best way to pursue this line of research will be by the combination of detailed interviewing with observation of shopping habits and standard of living attitudes.'[15] The innovation was not just that direct interviewing compromised MO's stance of 'unobserved observation': also crucial was where these interviews were conducted. Wagner established her credentials in Bolton by giving talks on life in Austria wherever she could gain entry, always concluding with a brief explanation of her research project and a request for people prepared to be interviewed at home. The response was friendly and many of her interviews were conducted over a big Lancashire tea.[16] By taking the fieldwork inside the household, Wagner did much to redress the male-centred focus of the earlier Worktown project, as is apparent in the contrast between John Sommerfield's romance of the masculine community of the pub, and Wagner and Madge's concern to probe the gender dynamics of the household economy: 'How is the weekly money divided up among the household? Does the housewife budget on a conscious plan and does she discuss it? ... Sex differences in the standard of living. The compromise of married life.'[17] Madge, of course, had already devised his own method of penetrating the private sphere (though predominantly the middle-class private sphere), and from the start it was envisaged that the Bolton work would be supplemented by directives to the panel on 'money habits, saving, shopping, betting, etc.'[18] In their commitment to getting behind the front door Wagner and Madge saw eye to eye on the need to move decisively beyond Harrisson's notion of 'objective fieldwork'.

13. 'Spending and Saving in Worktown', nd, W 1/C; see, for example, the analysis sheets in W 30/D and E, which also contain Madge's detailed reports on 'shop follows' in Woolworths and Marks & Spencer.
14. 'Outline of Social Factors in Economics', W 1/C.
15. 'Reactions to Advertising', December 1938, 4, FR A10.
16. Wagner 'Shopping expedition', 13 March 1939, W 29/A.
17. 'Spending & Saving in Worktown', W 1/C.
18. 'Outline of Social Factors in Economics' W 1/C; 'Reactions to Advertising', December 1938, 4, FR A10.

II

Anxious to counterbalance what he dismissed as 'the somewhat academic tendencies of Wagner and Madge',[19] Harrisson responded warmly to an approach from a second experienced researcher: Dennis Chapman (aged 29), the son of a West Country trade union organizer, who had himself served a craft apprenticeship and organized strikes as a shop steward. After graduating from LSE, Chapman spent a year working as a researcher for Rowntree in York, and then joined Oscar Oeser's team in Dundee providing expertise as an economic historian. He may well have been recommended to Harrisson by Oeser when the funding for the Dundee project ran out. Having met Madge early in 1937 when he had some involvement with the analysis of the first day surveys, Chapman took a dim view of the value of the panel material. He was equally critical of the market research methods employed by the British Institute of Public Opinion (BIPO) and later claimed to have turned down an offer to head the new organization 'on moral grounds: I didn't approve of the way in which they could manipulate public opinion in the form of the questions.'[20] Unemployed and with a wife and children to support, he wrote to Harrisson in October 1938 asking for work. Harrisson assured him that money would be forthcoming for his salary, and he arrived in Bolton early in November.[21]

Madge, confronted by two academically trained sociologists and well aware of his own ignorance—according to Chapman, speaking presumably about his first encounter with Madge 18 months earlier, he had not even heard of Booth or Rowntree[22]—wrote to Inez Spender on 15 November: 'I have a houseful of bloody experts here now, and I foresee that M-O is going to be a series of skirmishes and battles between them and me and

19. TH to Chapman, nd (October 1938?), Org&Hist 1.
20. Chapman, interviewed by Stanley, 23 February 1979. According to the DNB entry on Henry Durant, who got the BIPO job in 1935: 'Harry Field...an emissary from the pioneering American opinion pollster George H. Gallup, had contacted the LSE appointments bureau seeking a bright graduate who might be interested in setting up a British affiliate to Gallup's American Institute of Public Opinion. Of the six students recommended by the bureau, Field chose Durant.'
21. Chapman to TH, 11 October 1938, Org&Hist 4/1; telegram from TH to Chapman, 2 November 1938, Org&Hist 1/8.
22. Chapman, interviewed by Stanley, 23 February 1979. Madge confirms Chapman's account: 'It was pathetic how little I knew...I was more or less totally ignorant about methodology in the social sciences as it existed at that time' (CM, interviewed by Stanley, 23 March 1978).

Tom'.[23] With Chapman the battle did not last long. In January 1939, when Harrisson's promised salary had still not materialized, Chapman decided to leave.[24] At the outset Harrisson had expected him to take 'charge of the historical and statistical side of [the] investigation', but Madge seems to have given him responsibility for the research on shopping, and, before leaving, Chapman briefed Thomas with his ideas for developing this work, which included some rather over-excited notions about women shoppers, sexuality, and sock buying.[25] Madge was relieved when he decided to go, writing to Harrisson: 'Though not ANTI mass-observation, he is too deeply ingrained with the academic approach to get really right behind us in effort'—an ironic conclusion given Harrisson's original expectation that Chapman would counteract what he saw as the academicism of Wagner and Madge.[26]

With the other 'bloody expert', Wagner, Madge developed an altogether more fruitful relationship. Although the first begging letter to Simon had been sent by Harrisson, it was Madge and Wagner who conducted the subsequent negotiations, involving Manchester University as well as Simon himself.[27] Madge, as we have seen, was able to organize financial support from Unilever and the London Press Exchange, and he also dealt with Gollancz who eventually promised an advance of £150 for what he expected to be the fifth Worktown book.[28] But it was Wagner's links with Hans Singer,

23. CM to TH, 15 November 1938, CMpap, 8/3.
24. Chapman, interviewed by Stanley, 23 February 1979; Geoffrey Thomas, diary entry, 25 January 1939, Personnel/Thomas.
25. 'Outline of Social Factors in Economics', W 1/C; Thomas diary, 27 January 1939, Personnel/Thomas. Two days earlier Thomas recorded a visit to Davenport Street from a journalist working for the local Co-op who 'raised a good many interesting points, such as the sexual stimulation many women get out of shopping (including the remarks of two young married women, who, when asked by the 5 male assistants in one shop if they got any pleasure out of coitus, the males being sure that women didn't, answered that they enjoyed the first fortnight but that since then they wouldn't have cared if their husbands had been castrated).' This improbable story probably tells us rather more about the sexually charged atmosphere among the young men at Davenport Street than it does about the sexual significance of shopping.
26. CM to TH, nd (January 1938?), W 1/C. By contrast, Barbara Smethurst, another full-timer briefly with the project during December and January, quit after Madge told her that she was not academic enough, despite having done a social science degree at LSE. Daughter of a local mill-owner who had come down in the world, Smethurst told Madge that 'she couldn't understand the objectives of M-O and did not think there were any, she said she wanted to do things which were of immediate help to people, Charles of course remarked nastily that she ought to be a social worker, which annoyed her immensely because it is just what she wants to be...' (Thomas diary, 24 January 1938, Personnel/Thomas; Spending & Saving in Worktown, W 1/C).
27. CM to Inez, 3 and 12 December 1938, 5 and 15 January 1939, CMpap 8/3.
28. CM to Inez, 22 February 1938; Thomas diary, 11 February 1938, Personnel/Thomas.

now in the Manchester Economics department, which helped to establish the academic respectability of the project. In January Simon, despite several meetings with Madge, was still holding back, worried that none of the other Worktown books had yet appeared. Anticipating the departure of Chapman he proposed that Singer should be asked to act as a consulting economist to the project, along with his colleague Adolf Loewe, another German refugee, who had published a book in 1935 on *Economics and Sociology. A plea for co-operation in the social sciences*. Early in February, with the cash running out fast, Wagner clinched the deal with Simon, although it took another anxious month for his money actually to arrive.[29]

In February 1939 Geoffrey Thomas—who found Wagner difficult and was clearly disturbed by the presence of a woman acting on equal intellectual terms with a man—remarked in his diary that 'poor Charles is only secondary in her estimation ... She is a female who attempts to deal in the abstract, when she is not built for it.'[30] In fact, the same diary entry suggests a much more productive encounter, describing Wagner and Madge pulling apart Loewe's book. Later Madge recalled that, after an initial period of adopting the 'rather Tom Harrisson like approach' of 'following people round Woolworths', it was in Bolton that he sorted out his ideas on method.[31] In January he wrote to Inez Spender: 'My ideas about M-O have been developing very rapidly into more concrete shape during the last few days, and I foresee that in the next few months I shall be able to formulate much more satisfactorily why it is so important and valuable an activity just now'.[32] The intellectual collaboration between Madge and Wagner was enshrined in the four-page memorandum, 'A Basis for Social Fieldwork', probably written early in 1939:

> While we would agree that the ultimate aim in this kind of research is to produce an integrating theory which will embrace the whole field of social behaviour, we feel that it is premature to try to formulate such a theory and that enough harm has been done by sociological speculation based on

29. Thomas diary, 25 and 26 January, 11 February 1938, Personnel/Thomas; CM to Inez, 22 February and 22 March 1939.
30. Thomas diary, 11 February 1939. A year later he repeated this judgement to Henry Novy: 'GT says she is a very clever woman who wants to play the part of a man but just fails, lacking wide view and foresight' (Novy to Allwood, 9 February 1940, Novy papers).
31. CM, interviewed by Stanley, 23 March 1978.
32. CM to Inez, 15 January 1939, CMpap 8/3.

inadequate facts. At the same time we naturally recognise that our collection of facts must be guided by certain selective principles which constitute in effect the elementary working hypothesis of our research.[33] To clarify our approach to fieldwork, we have therefore drawn up this statement of the assumptions we are consciously making in selecting certain fields for observation.

Although this document is unsigned as well as undated, its contents appear to reflect a fusion, or compromise, between Madge and Wagner's perspectives:

> A team is at present making field observations in Bolton on the social-psychological factors influencing spending and saving at the income levels which include the great majority of people in England. The work is largely experimental and exploratory. Those taking part in it are concerned with immediate problems of collecting information, observing behaviour and recording attitudes as revealed by interviews, conversation and questionnaires.

The stress on social psychology and the mix of research methods involved shows how far Madge, under Wagner's influence, had moved from Harrisson's approach. It is now the interview and the questionnaire that take priority, while 'observation of behaviour' is seen as 'supplement[ary to] our questioning of people', justified only to the extent that people's unconscious motives may be seen to manifest themselves 'in socially standardized forms of behaviour, however embryonic.' Madge's concern with the processes by which informal 'social and imitative tendencies' become 'crystallised' in formal institutions is central to the document, while Wagner's input is evident in the suggestion, borrowed from her earlier article on market research, that by uncovering the processes of social change such research would eventually be able to obviate much 'wasteful and destructive' activity by predicting in advance which innovations—in products, fashions, and institutions—would succeed and which would fail. The document concludes with a warning, directed at Loewe, about 'the danger of generalising without any information on the behaviour of *homo economicus*.'[34]

33. Perhaps they had taken note of a footnote in a luminous article by Evan Durbin published in the summer of 1938 pleading for cooperation between economists and other social scientists. The footnote cited MO as an example of the illusion that the facts could be made to speak for themselves through 'the mere accumulation of information' (E. F. M. Durbin, 'Methods of Research—A Plea for Co-Operation in the Social Sciences', *The Economic Journal*, 48, 190, 1938, 188).

34. 'A Basis for Social Fieldwork', nd (February 1939?), W 1/C.

III

Although the presence of Wagner and Chapman served to link the project with the ideas of 'functional penetration' practiced in *Marienthal* and espoused by Oeser, Madge's Worktown team was in reality much less integrated in the life of the town than Harrisson's original team had been. His leading investigators were university trained and they lacked the kind of rapport with the subjects of their study that Joe Wilcock had with the Christians, Walter Hood with the Labour Party, or Sommerfield with the men in the pub. Certainly Wagner's interviews opened up realms of experience unreached by the earlier project, but the housewives who confided in her had no doubt about her superior status, as was brought home when one of them, meeting her in the street, was 'astonished to see me carrying a basket and I though it maybe not agree [sic] with my role I am acting in Bolton to be seen with a shopping basket.'[35] Aware of this, Madge aspired to supplement the team with, as he put it in a letter to Harrisson, 'a Walter-Hood-like prolet-obs'.[36] The nearest the team came to finding such a person was Bill Naughton, who drove a coal lorry for the Co-op and was a frequent visitor to Davenport Street after work. He and Wagner were lovers and, Chapman believed, she relied on him as her 'key informant . . . [on] the emotional substructure of working-class life', including information about the families he got to know in the course of his work. At the time, seeing her bedspread hung up to dry in the kitchen, he snidely remarked 'that it was a binding for a big portion of her thesis.' Chapman knew what he was talking about since he himself was carrying on with Joyce Mangnall, a constant source of contacts for MO since Harrisson first got to know her when working in a mill in 1936.[37] Both parties benefitted from these liaisons. For Naughton and Mangnall the encounter with MO contributed positively to their upward social mobility—Naughton becoming a well-known author and scriptwriter, Mangnall a social worker of some distinction in Melbourne.[38]

35. Wagner, 'Shopping Expedition', 13 March 1939, W 29/A. Germanic grammar often strives to assert itself in Wagner's written English.
36. CM to TH, nd (January 1939?), W 1/C.
37. Thomas diary, 27 January 1939, 11 February 1939, Personnel/Thomas. Mangnall appears in Humphrey Jennings' film, *Spare Time* (Thomas diary, 19 March, 23 April 1939).
38. Chapman, interviewed by Stanley, 23 February 1979; Chapman to Sheridan, 3 December 1997, Personnel/Mangnall. On Naughton see entry in DNB.

And, unlikely though it is that either Wagner or Chapman were consciously responding to Harrisson's notorious suggestion that the anthropologist should not hesitate to sleep with the natives, the presence of these two 'native informers' at Davenport Street certainly improved the team's understanding of the local working-class culture. Contact with a quite different section of the local community was provided by Gerald Edwards, a gay man of morose disposition from Guernsey employed by the local authority as drama organizer, who worked part-time for MO and lived rent-free in the Davenport Street attic, bringing in a flow of people involved in amateur theatre.[39] With all this going on life in Davenport Street, as is clear from Thomas' vivid diary, was at least as overcrowded, under-financed, dirty, and interesting as it had been during Harrisson's regime the previous year.

IV

It was to be Harrisson, rather than the 'bloody experts', who provided most of the 'skirmishes and battles' that Madge had feared when he arrived in November. If at first Madge was grateful to Harrisson for facilitating his escape from an impossible position in Blackheath, relations between the two men rapidly deteriorated. A series of accusing letters, long phone calls, and an emergency meeting halfway in Birmingham, left Madge feeling that he had re-established the dominance over Harrisson that the move to Bolton had temporarily disrupted. 'The funny thing', he wrote to Inez Spender early in December,

> is that in his letter [Tom] was pleading to be dominated again, which is a very revealing indication of his psychology...he said he was convinced by my letter that he was making a shit of himself, being got down by his power-complex, etc. A really amazing document.

Whatever was happening to Harrisson's 'power-complex' at this time, Madge's was clearly in fine fettle as he confessed (or boasted) to Inez Spender:

> I have always found that if I exerted by own personal influence on ANYONE they caved in. It is rather a dangerous power and one which I keep switched off most of the time, so much that I give most people the effect of mildness.[40]

---

39. Chapman, interviewed by Stanley, 23 February 1979; Thomas diary, 22 January 1939; Thomas, interviewed by Stanley, 26 November 1979.
40. CM to Inez, 4 December 1938, CMpap 8/3.

But Harrisson's desire to be dominated had its limits. Despite a 60-word telegram at Christmas proclaiming: 'I now feel perfectly happy about everything', by the new year the two men were 'trudging round a very cold St James' Park', while Harrisson offloaded 'an endless and largely neurotic series of grievances', and Madge, in 'violent discussions', stood his ground, confident that 'my policy of bloodiness to him was on a long view justified'. After a couple of days of this, returning to Bolton, Madge allowed himself to believe that he had 'finally established harmony with Tom', a sentiment echoed by a letter from Harrisson celebrating 'this new kindly spirit of our work which makes all so much nicer.'[41] Perhaps Harrisson's immersion in his East End project really did enable him, temporarily at least, to escape the 'urge to be harrisson [sic] and powerful.'[42]

One result of this outbreak of harmony was the establishment of a three-man group headed by Max Nicholson 'to act as advisors and if need be censors of... policy in regard to finance, organisation and publicity'. The other two members were James Fisher, assistant curator of London Zoo, like Nicholson an ornithological friend of Harrisson's and with whom Madge had worked closely while carrying on with his wife in the summer of 1938; and John Pudney, who wrote a column for the *News Chronicle* under the name of Henry Bean.[43] When this group held its first (and possibly its only) meeting on 21 February, it was agreed that Madge should take back responsibility for the panel, which had been run by Harrisson from Blackheath since November (although Madge had been drafting directives relevant to the Bolton work on spending and saving).[44] Harrisson was, no

---

41. CM to Inez, 20 December 1938, 2 and 5 January 1939, CMpap 8/3; TH to CM, 12 January 1939, Org&Hist 1/8.

42. TH to Trevelyan, nd (February 1939?), JTpap.

43. There had been an earlier attempt in the winter of 1937–8 to establish such a group, consisting of Malinowski and/or George Catlin, Stuart Legg, Charles' brother, John Madge, and a solicitor, Roderick Garrett, who was to act as treasurer (MO *Bulletin*, November 1937, FR A4; *First Year's Work*, 24; Madge to Catlin, 27 December 1937, Catlin papers, McMaster University). The main purpose had been to establish a joint bank account and a more formal basis for money-raising, but the committee folded after a couple of meetings (CM, interviewed by Stanley, 23 March 1978). The new group also intended to pool all MO's income in a separate account, with H.G. Wells and Lord Horder as trustees ('History of M-O 1939', nd (June 1936?), Hist&Org 1), but it is clear that this did not happen, since as late as 1942 M-O was still using TH's personal bank account (TH to Fitter, nd (1942?), Org&Hist 1/Fitter donation). In June 1939 TH assured a new commercial client that MO was 'independent of private obligations or any sort of private control. We have no governing body or official committee, but run the organisation quite freely with an Advisory Panel, which very seldom needs revising' (TH to Bagnall, 23 June 1939, Org&Hist 3/New Zealand).

44. CM to TH, 21 January 1940, 7, Org&Hist 1.

doubt, glad to be rid of the panel, but for Madge the meeting served to confirm his belief that he was now the dominant partner: 'at this point I take over the responsibility for M–O from Tom'.[45]

As the work progressed Madge became increasingly confident about his own intellectual development. 'Late last night,' he wrote to Inez Spender on 16 April, 'I had a sudden flow of ideas which I think may lead to a new kind of theory about society.'[46] In this self-assured mood, he wrote out of the blue to Maynard Keynes, who, he believed, was one of the few economists to have 'recognised... the relevance of psychological questions to economics'. Outlining the work they were doing on the working-class savings and enclosing a copy of their questionnaire, he asked whether Keynes thought 'that work like ours might help the economist in those of his forecasts which involve psychological assumptions.' In particular, with the international outlook becoming progressively more threatening, he wondered 'whether the crisis is likely to have a big effect on savings and, if so, for what psychological reasons.' What did Keynes think? 'We would gain immensely from having your opinion on these questions.... Possibly, by modifying our research on savings, we might make ourselves useful both during the "twilight" period and in wartime.'[47] Madge, expecting war to break out at any moment, was thinking hard about how MO might position itself.[48] Keynes responded positively, agreeing that very little was known about working-class saving habits and suggesting an addition to the questionnaire. In subsequent correspondence he agreed to look over the questionnaire for a follow-on enquiry he had proposed on how people spent their surplus income. He also had his publishers send a copy of his magnum opus, acknowledged gracefully by Madge: 'It is some time since I read the *General Theory*'.[49]

45. CM to Inez, 22 February 1939, CMpap 8/3.
46. CM to Inez, 16 April 1939, CMpap 8/3.
47. CM to Keynes, 18 April 1939, CMpap, 21. It may have been Hans Singer, who had been part of Keynes' circle in Cambridge (obituary, *The Times*, 28 February 2006), who encouraged Madge to contact the great man. If so he was sadly disappointed by the outcome: H.W. Singer, 'How Widespread are National Savings? A Critique of the Madge Enquiry', *The Manchester School*, 13, 2, August 1944, 61–79.
48. CM to Inez, 9 April 1939, CMpap 8/3.
49. Keynes to CM, 20 April 1939; CM to Keynes, 21 April 1939; Keynes to CM, 25 April 1939, CMpap, 21.

V

By June, with the end of the project in sight, Madge was planning to close down the Davenport Street house in the autumn. Wagner had secured a research post in the Liverpool Sociology department from 1 October, and Madge intended to move into the rooms Harrisson had rented in the East End of London, where he would write the book while Thomas read up the relevant literature at the LSE.[50] Because the war intervened, this never happened, and the closest we have to a report on the 'social factors in economics' project is Wagner's MA thesis on 'The Psychological Aspect of Saving and Spending', based largely on her Bolton interviews and panel responses to the directives.[51] While the section on saving anticipated the work that Madge subsequently undertook for Keynes, Wagner's treatment of spending was restricted to attitudes to clothes.

As war became ever more probable, the focus of Madge's interest in the 'social factors in economics' shifted from fundamental questions of social theory towards more narrowly policy-oriented research. On 23 August he wrote to Nicholson—who had been lined up for a senior post in the Ministry of Information—setting out his ideas about how MO could make itself useful in the coming war:

> We have been working as you know on the social psychology of everyday household expenses, and we have by now a good working knowledge of these in more or less 'normal' times, which puts us in a strong position for judging the alteration in times of emergency...I know you agree with our point of view that public money can be saved and efficiency increased by this sort of check up on the social impact of the new measures. [He had in mind 'the effects of a rationing system...on the ordinary family'.] There have been so many beautiful plans which have not worked owing to neglect of the social factor.

As evidence of the practical value of MO's work he pointed to the fact that 'Unilevers and London Press Exchange, having once subsidized our work,

---

50. Thomas diary, 17 June 1939, Personnel/Thomas; CM to Max Nicholson, 23 August 1939, TC 43/2/B.
51. The MO Archive has an incomplete draft of the thesis. The final version is in London University Senate House Library. It was a London University thesis, not Liverpool, as Hubble states (*Mass-Observation and Everyday Life*, 241), and an MA not a PhD, as Liz Stanley states: Liz Stanley, 'It has always known, and we have always been "other": Knowing capitalism and the "coming crisis" of sociology confront the concentration system and Mass-Observation', *Sociological Review*, 54, 6, 2008, 544.

found it of sufficient practical use to them to subsidize us a second time on an increased scale.'[52] The irritating chore of writing reports for these funders,[53] initially undertaken to provide resources for the more fundamental work, was now represented as central to MO's modus operandi.

Even when fired up with glimpses of 'a new kind of theory about society' in April 1939, Madge had been looking for immediate practical applications of his work, as was evident in his letter to Keynes. Between April and August, however, the balance shifted. In April he had presented MO's independence as essential to its effectiveness—'our approach is as personal as possible, since working-class people react strongly against any "official" inquiry'[54]; but, under war conditions, he now assumed, the reverse would be the case:

> we could only carry on provided we had some measure of official recognition, as otherwise there would almost certainly be resistance to giving interviews, or getting volunteer co-operation. We are prepared to be unreservedly at the service of the Ministry if this recognition is once given.

To this end he proposed, with Ministry support, to continue the Bolton operation, set up similar units in Newcastle, Liverpool, Manchester, Birmingham, Cardiff, and Bristol, 'while Tom would no doubt mobilise the London people.' The panel would be used to monitor the reactions of 'lower professional groups' to the crisis.[55]

Madge sent a copy of this letter to Harrisson, but had not consulted him in advance. The brief moment of harmony in the early months on 1939 had soon disintegrated and in April Madge was unloading his exasperation to Inez Spender:

> I had a bloody letter from Tom yesterday to which I replied very briefly that it seemed that we were making a mistake to collaborate. Probably there will be a shindy and it will all be very tiresome, but I'm really fed up with a policy

52. CM to Nicholson, 23 August 1939, TC 43/2/B.
53. CM to Inez, March 1939, CMpap, 8/3.
54. CM to Keynes, 18 April 1939, CMpap, 21.
55. CM to Nicholson, 23 August 1939, TC 43/2/B. MO's 'Wartime Directive, No. 1' (September 1939, FR A25) asked observers in these six towns, plus Leeds, to get in touch immediately with Davenport Street 'indicating how much time they will have for M-O in the near future, as it is hoped to set up special centres in these towns for work of national importance.' The plan to start new units was quickly dropped when the MOI made it clear that what interested them was MO's ability to compare pre-war and wartime attitudes in the two places it had studied before the war (TH to CM, 20 September 1939, Org&Hist 1).

of appeasement. I'm not getting any intellectual co-operation from him, and his stupid jealousy and self-built-up are just one long pain in the neck.[56]

Two days later he added: 'I think he wants a break too—in fact I think his letter was a deliberate provocation with this end in view…it would be a pity if M–O became simply a vehicle for his megalomania. So I expect before long I shall be in the thick of that fight'.[57] Nothing had changed by August, and in his covering note Madge issued an ultimatum:

> Our co-operation has clearly, become nominal only, and I can't even perform the function you once thought useful of criticising…all this I was hoping to get cleared up when I came to London in October, since only by frequent meeting could such a fog be dissipated: but supposing…we do get landed in a war, don't you think we had better pool our resources a bit more whole-heartedly or not at all?[58]

For a short time the outbreak of war brought the two men closer together again, but within nine months the final break anticipated by Madge had occurred.[59]

56. CM to Inez, 16 April 1939, CMpap 8/3.
57. CM to Inez, 18 April 1939, CMpap 8/3.
58. CM to TH, 23 August 1939, Org&Hist 1.
59. CM, interviewed by Nick Stanley, 23 March 1978.

6

War Begins

I should naturally be most grateful for any help you can give us in getting Mass-Observation accepted by the Ministry of Information. My attitude in wishing this is, I think, an honest one. I don't want to avoid any danger or risk. As you probably know from being married to Zita, I rather revel in anything of that sort. But I do think that during a war M-O could make observations of value. These observations could be of value to the authorities, and I am in favour of helping them in so far as to do so is to favour a better system than that of our 'enemies', and because, being British, I am to that extent automatically caught up in the spirit of these days. I think that properly co-ordinated study linked to propaganda, information and ARP [Air Raid Precautions] would materially increase the social and psychological happiness of the civilian population... Of course I also want to be able to carry on work through the war so that we may make a full and objective record of what war means in terms of individual and mass behaviour. This record, which would be collected incidentally and as an automatic part of the whole study, might prove an important record for history and for replanning after the war.

(Tom Harrisson, letter to Richard Crossman, 28 August 1939)[1]

At the outbreak of war, with its commercial income drying up, Charles Madge and Tom Harrisson were at one in looking to the new Ministry of Information (MOI) to keep Mass-Observation (MO) afloat.[2] For a few weeks they seemed to be succeeding, but the initial MOI commission was quickly withdrawn and it was not until April 1940 that Harrisson was able to negotiate a regular contract. During the winter of 1939–40 MO was close

---

1. TC 43/2/B. Zita had been his lover before she married Crossman.
2. In September Harrisson told the MOI that MO had 'lost the financial support of its clients (Gas, Light & Coke, Railways, Unilever, etc) and its patrons. It is now completely without resources.' (Report on Posters, 20 September 1939, INF 1/261.)

to collapse. The staff—irregularly paid and autocratically managed—became rebellious. Madge and Harrisson, casting around for alternative sources of funding, seldom saw eye to eye, and the uncertainties of these months did nothing to improve their relationship. By the time the MOI came to MO's rescue, the relationship between the two men had become unsustainable, and the deal that Harrisson struck with Whitehall in April 1940 became the occasion, though not the cause, for Madge's decision to abandon MO as soon as he had alternative funding in place.

I

In August 1939 Madge and Harrisson had good reason to believe that the MOI would be keen to make use of their services. In March, a senior figure in the planned Ministry, alert to the need for careful monitoring of public reactions if public opinion was to be 'shepherded' in the right direction, had taken the trouble to read MO's *Britain by Mass-Observation* and concluded that 'it might be worthwhile seeing the leaders of the movement and making discrete inquiries as to its future (probable) development.'[3] Max Nicholson, now secretary of the think-tank Political and Economic Planning (PEP), was asked for his opinion, and he would certainly have let Harrisson know about the Ministry's interest; although he would probably also have passed on considerable worries about the reliability of MO's methods and the political stance of its leaders (MI5 were asked to investigate), and fears of adverse reactions if Parliament and the press got to know that the Ministry was employing an outside agency to investigate public responses to its propaganda.[4]

The day after writing to Crossman, Harrisson followed up Madge's letter to Nicholson with an agreed plan 'to assist in national service in times of emergency', explaining in detail the work that MO was currently doing and offering either to 'work semi-independently and report confidentially to the authorities, or [to] make itself openly and directly at their disposal.' Summarizing MO's findings on public attitudes to the crisis so far, he rehearsed familiar themes—the gap between leaders and led, popular scepticism about whether they were being told what was really going on, apathy and hopelessness among the masses—while assuring the authorities

---

3. Macadam, 'Memo on Home Publicity', 18 March 1939, INF 1/711.
4. Publicity Division, *minutes*, 20 March 1939, INF 1/711; Ian McLaine, *Ministry of Morale*, 1979, 23.

that MO's services would be inexpensive, because its full-time workers were themselves so 'vitally interested in [the] objective study of British life' that they were prepared to work at rates 'deliberately [set] far below normal.'[5]

MO's prospects with the new MOI were greatly enhanced by the appointment of John Hilton as Director of Home Publicity: 'a long and Bolton friend of M-O,' an excited Harrisson wrote to Madge, 'no one else in the country could suit us so well'. When, three days after the declaration of war, Harrisson was summoned to the MOI's improvised offices in Senate House to explain himself he was delighted to be received by a sympathetic group of Hilton's advisers, typing an account in vivid detail for the record when he got home that evening. Crossman, representing Labour in the new ministry, expressed his horror at the way in which civil servants were recruiting their old tutors from Oxbridge to write propaganda directed at the masses about whom they knew nothing whatsoever and whose language they could not begin to speak. Gervas Huxley—who knew all about American opinion polling and sampling methods—was ready to be convinced 'that M-O offers a unique service, not statistical, but of a sort not available anyhow or anywhere else.' When Harold Rhodes—the civil servant in attendance to represent the official mind—suggested that MO's qualitative approach was unscientific, he was brutally put down by the geneticist J. B. S. Haldane (who had arrived early for another meeting): 'It's such nonsense to say M-O isn't scientific. These civil servants think science means mathematical. And they haven't been trained in mathematics anyway.' Nicholson, also present, explained that an earlier plan to use the BBC Listener Research panel had been dropped, leaving the Ministry with no means at all of monitoring responses to its propaganda. When the hapless Rhodes dared to respond that the Ministry was content to rely on cuttings from a censored press and feedback from the local notables being appointed to its regional committees, the meeting exploded in rage. Finally Hilton joined the group and, cutting through Rhodes' obstructive explanations of how long it would take to get authorization for any spending on MO, promised to take Harrisson's memo, redrafted there and then, directly to the Minister, which he did the next day.[6]

5. 'Emergency Problems and Mass-Observation', 29 August 1939, FR A22.
6. TH to CM, 7 September 1939, TC 43/2/D; TH to Crossman, 28 August 1939, TC 43/2/B; TH note, 30 August 1939, TC 43/2/D. Other members of the group included Gordon Selfridge, who had read *Savage Civilisation* and 'thought it wonderful', and Tom Stephenson, *Daily Herald* columnist and rambling enthusiast, who was 'already an admirer'.

Encouraged, Harrisson and Madge pressed ahead with their report on reactions to the crisis: 'a complete and detailed documentation of widespread and often hidden breakdown in civilian morale, and especially in the attitude of the masses to their leaders and to the instructions put out by their leaders'.[7] Within days of receiving the report Hilton—arguing that unless money could be provided very soon MO would probably disintegrate and its expertise be lost for good—secured Treasury approval and MO was given the go-ahead for a four-week trial, starting with a report on the Ministry's leaflets and posters.[8] Or so it appeared.

Harrisson and Madge leaped into action, recruiting more staff. Ambitious plans were drawn up for work in London and Bolton involving much counting of the number of people who looked at posters; direct and indirect interviews with people who had just passed the posters; 'statistical study of what people look at, at what height and angle'; following shoppers to observe their 'potentiality . . . to look at things'; testing people's memory of the words on the posters. Madge sent out a detailed questionnaire to the panel asking for a quick return. Harrisson mobilized London panellists who had volunteered part-time help, and got on the phone to solicit the opinion of various experts, including advertisers and poster distributors.[9]

Meanwhile, however, obstruction was continuing at the highest levels in the Ministry. Although Harrisson was assured that the delay in issuing a proper contract was just a formality, it was not until six days after being verbally commissioned to do the work that he learned that the deal had been blocked by the Minister, Lord Macmillan. At a time when the press were in full hue and cry against interference from the new Ministry, Macmillan was not prepared to take the risk of having to deal with accusations of 'political espionage'.[10] The cancelling of the contract left MO's

---

7. 'Memorandum from M-O', 4 October 1939, MApap 4/f; MO report, 20 September 1939, INF 1/261.
8. Waterfield to Beresford, 23 September 1939, INF 1/261; Kale to Waterfield, 24 September 1939, INF 1/261; Commission to M-O, nd (September 1939?), INF 1/261; 'Memorandum from M-O', 4 October 1939, MApap 4/f. MO was not the only string to Hilton's bow. Henry Durant, head of the British Institute of Public Opinion, whose sample surveys had been regularly published by the *News Chronicle* since the Munich crisis, had also offered his services, and by late September, Hilton had secured Treasury authorization to pay them (Durant to Hilton, 6 September 1939, INF 1/261; Hilton to Waterfield, 20 September 1939, INF 1/261).
9. 'Poster Investigation', 26 September 1939; TH, Further points', 27 September 1939; TH to CM, 27 September 1939, TC 42/1A; 'Memorandum from M-O', 4 October 1939, MApap 4/f.
10. 'Memorandum from M-O', 4 October 1939, MApap 4/f; Waterfield to Macmillan, 27 September 1939, INF 1/261.

finances in a dire state, but rather than abandoning the project they decided
to complete it and argue about the money afterwards. Under pressure from
Hilton the civil servants eventually accepted liability for the problems caused
by their 'sudden reversal of engines' and agreed to foot the bill, paying £200
to MO.[11] But questions in Parliament and continued attempts by MOI officials to persuade the Minister to change his mind on the long-term employment of outside agencies were unavailing.[12]

Not content with lobbying Whitehall on MO's behalf, Harrisson tried to
organize a joint approach with other non-governmental agencies. Early in
November, telling the Liberal MP Richard Acland that he was 'gradually
developing a pretty competent war-time listening machine, on the public
opinion front,' he claimed to be speaking not only for MO but also 'for a
number of other organisations... which I hope are shortly going to form a
co-ordinating... opinion research group.'[13] Aware that the British Institute
of Public Opinion (BIPO) and various market research organizations were
competing for contracts from the MOI, Harrisson had been talking since
the first weeks of the war to MO's main rivals about establishing some system of quality control and coordination among the more established bodies
offering their services to the wartime state. On 1 November he used a PEP
luncheon to propose the setting up of an informal grouping. Crossman,
presiding at the lunch, was supportive, as was Nicholson. Henry Durant (of
BIPO) and Robert Silvey (of BBC Listener Research) had already expressed
their support, and Harrisson was commissioned to draw up a paper on 'the
co-ordination of social research'. The objective was to educate civil servants
and politicians about the need for objective, scientific research on popular
attitudes and behaviour, both as a basis for immediate policy making but
also with the 'high purpose... of producing a unique documentary account
of a civilisation at war... to ensure the proper study of this war on the
Home Front, and to ensure that relevant records are kept, co-ordinated and
published in the future.' To this end the participating organizations should
coordinate their efforts, keep the long-term study of the war's social, economic, and psychological impact at the forefront of their concerns and resist
pressures to live hand-to-mouth on the 'higgledy-piggledy tit-bits' on offer

11. Hilton to Leigh Ashton, 8 November 1939, INF 1/261; TH to Hilton, 2 November 1939; CM
    to Thomas, 12 November 1939, Org&Hist 1.
12. TH to Mander, 17 November 1939, TC 25/5/G; TH to Adams, 7 October 1939, MApap4./f;
    Waterfield to Director General, 13 November 1939, INF 1/261.
13. TH to Acland, 6 November 1939, TC 25/5/G.

from Whitehall or commercial sources. Only by asserting an authoritative non-governmental voice on these issues, he argued, could the social science community hope to establish its value, and—not the least of his anxieties— protect its staff from conscription.[14]

Nothing came of this initiative, but the 'high purpose' he set out here was to remain central for MO throughout the war. The dream—never fully realized—was to gain a source of funding that would enable MO to focus on long-term social scientific work, rather than hustle for immediate returns. So long as they needed to hustle, Harrisson had written to Madge in late September, the guiding principle was clear: 'what we want is to do enough useful work to be allowed to keep going, so that after the war we may tell the truth for the first time.'[15] Meanwhile no work should be taken on that did not, in one way or another, contribute to the larger goal of document-ing the war for posterity; and, if short-term secrecy was sometimes unavoid-able, long-term publication rights must always be defended. In September 1939, explaining to the panellists the consequences of their new official status (somewhat prematurely as it turned out) Harrisson and Madge assured them that while 'much of our information will have to wait some time in cold storage before we can publish it . . . it will in time be published fully; and it will be analysed and used immediately.'[16]

With the collapse of the MOI contract, MO's financial position was des-perate. Madge tried unsuccessfully to persuade Cecil King, his ex-boss at the *Daily Mirror,* to come to the rescue,[17] while Harrisson appealed to Clem Leslie, who had funded MO work before the war and was now acting as a publicity officer for the National Savings Committee:

> I would be glad if you could find us any work since at present the organisation is threatened with bankruptcy, and if we do have to disband it is obvious that we shall loose our panel, our trained whole-time people, our continuity and our prestige. It would be dream-like to be able to carry on studying subjects like sav-ing and spending, or personal and home attitudes which are in line with our general studies, rather than the sort of work that we've been recently doing, which has been higgledy-piggledy tit-bits for various departments or politicians.

14. TH, 'Co-ordination of Social Research', 2 November 1939, FR 10; TH to CM, 23 September 1939, Org&Hist 1.
15. 'That is what is in my mind, anyway,' he added aggressively: 'What is in yours?' (TH to CM, 23 September 1939, Org&Hist 1).
16. 'Wartime Directive, No. 2', October 1939, FR 6a.
17. CM to Thomas, 26 October, 8 November 1939, Org&Hist 1; CM, chronology, 27 October 1939 and CM to his mother, 11 February 1940, CMpap 71/1/6.

Even more important than the money, however, was the need for some kind of official status, in order to protect his key workers against conscription:

> what we most need is a definite official status, even if unpaid. If you can make us an official unit available for assisting you, I should be everlasting ready when the war is over to do research for the Gas Light and Coke Co. [Leslie's company] free, gratis and for nothing![18]

Nothing came of this, but they did get some work monitoring public behaviour in the blackout for the Railways Executive, who had commissioned the largest of MO's pre-war surveys.[19]

II

One of Harrisson's selling points to the MOI had been that its full-time workers were well trained, highly motivated, and prepared to work for peanuts. Despite worries that in working for the MOI 'we may simply become snoopers with an evil purpose', the staff understood that a balance had to be struck between 'high purpose' and following the money: 'to catch contracts and gain official recognition...much of our ideals must be shelved for a while.'[20] At a staff meeting on 23 October, when payment from the MOI for the poster work still hung in the balance, Harrisson asked them to write down their own views about what MO should be doing during the war. Responses from 7 of the 14 London staff survive in the archive, providing a clear picture of the attitudes of Harrisson's staff at this early stage of the war.

John Atkins, the 23-year-old history graduate, was keen to investigate 'bitterness' aroused by the war, not only against Hitler but also against the ruling classes at home. Were the masses irritated by wartime restrictions, or did they take them lying down; and, if the latter, did that mean that the British public had given up on democracy and were ripe for fascism?[21] Brian Allwood, the scruffy 19-year-old, also focussed on the dangers of popular apathy and domestic authoritarianism. MO, he felt, should not confine

18. TH to Leslie, 11 October 1939, TC 57/2/A.
19. TH to Temple, 24 October 1939, TC 70/3/A.
20. Novy, 'M-O and the war', 29 October 1939, Org&Hist 4/5.
21. Atkins, 'General memo', 30 October 1939, Org&Hist 4/6.

itself to the study of popular attitudes, but also pay attention to what he expected to be the 'deadening and atrophying' impact of the war on intellectual life, science, and the arts.[22] Alec Hughes, the jazz specialist, favoured among other things 'a study of the development of hate', and the impact of the war on sexuality: 'Abnormalities may well manifest themselves—homosexuality; promiscuity on a wide scale after air raids... partial breakdown of the marriage convention, etc.'[23] Priscilla Feare, the railway executive's daughter, was living in Bloomsbury by the outbreak of war, working as Harrisson's secretary and developing her own project on the impact of war on fashion. Her broader programme for MO's wartime work stressed the importance of women to national morale, and proposed using the panel to monitor gendered responses to the violence and changing attitudes to sex, including to homosexuality (her over-possessive stepmother lived with her female lover in what Feare later described, surprisingly, as the 'lesbian hothouse of Blackheath').[24] Kathleen Box was equally concerned with the impact of war conditions on sexual behaviour, recommending observation of the 'amount and intensity of love-making in public places. Pick ups. Remarks between strangers of opposite sex'.[25]

Henry Novy, who had only just joined the staff, understood MO as an attempt 'to place every member of our society in the light of his own individuality; to find out problems he knows better than anyone else, those of his self': a view which owed more to his own quest for a philosophy of life than to anything authorized by MO's founders. But he went on to list many of the topics that MO was to investigate from 'love in the Parks and promiscuity', to religion, morale in war industry, and attitudes to Frenchmen.[26] The last of these was a personal concern since he himself was French, his mother having remarried an English businessman and brought him to England aged 15. After leaving school in the summer of 1938 he dismayed his parents by turning down the offer of a place at Oxford, refusing to take a job in the family firm, signing up for a correspondence course in journalism and trying to make it as a freelance writer. Allwood, who had been at grammar

---

22. Allwood, 'General memo', 28 October 1939, Org&Hist 4/5.
23. Hughes, 'Suggestions', nd (October 1939?), Org&Hist 2.
24. Feare, 'Suggestions', 30 October 1939, Org&Hist 4/5; 'Henry and Priscilla Narrative', Macnamara/Personnel.
25. Box, 'suggestions', 30 October 1939, Org&Hist 4/2.
26. Novy, 'General memo', 29 October 1939, Org&Hist 4/2.

school with Novy in Loughborough, persuaded Harrisson to take him on in October 1939.[27] The friendship between Allwood, Novy, Atkins, and Feare was to play an important role in the internal politics of MO during the next few months.

Other staff working for Harrisson in the autumn of 1939 included Stella Schofield who specialized in women and women's organizations;[28] and Margot Dulanty, who had earlier done historical research for the anti-Semitism study, and was now analysing periodical literature alongside going around stations '*seeing* how people behave in the blackout...I could have earned £s if it hadn't been for M-O!....No wonder all the lone women in stations were huddled together in small knots'.[29] Charles Pepper, aged 25, was working on economic topics with Jack Atkins before he joined up as an air gunner in 1940.[30] The youngest worker, Len England, who had joined the panel as a public schoolboy at Dulwich College where he edited the school magazine, was one of the less politically minded of the full-time staff. Like many another mass observer he had no difficulty in feeling superior to the alleged 'vacuity' of the suburban culture in which he had grown up: 'so drugged by cinema and wireless that they do not bother to think...a vast, efficient and uninteresting dormitory':

> I consider myself different from my neighbours in that I do not concern myself with the same petty things that they do. I am interested in the things that matter, such as religion and government, while they are interested in the latest fashions; I go to the pictures to see a good film, they go because of a favourite film star regardless of the picture...

But his responses were religious and aesthetic rather than political, and he professed a fondness for the public school virtues of 'team spirit' and 'sense of leadership', despite all the 'tommy rot' that was talked about them.[31] Harrisson, who may well have felt more comfortable with such attitudes than the leftism of most of his workers, took him on, aged 18, in October 1939 and allowed

27. Novy diary 1938–39, *passim*; Novy to Pedro, 29 September 1939; Novy to TH, 14 December 1939; Novy to Pedro, 3 January 1940 all in HNpap.
28. Schofield, 'Women in Wartime', 4 January 1940; Schofield, 'Memo on overheards and interviews', 10 May 1940, Org&Hist 4/6.
29. Margot Dulanty, diary letter to friend, 8 November 1939, Personnel/Dulanty; TH to Laski, 19 June 1939, TC 62/1/b; 'Anti-Semitism Survey', nd (March 1939?), FR A12.
30. He was killed in 1941. Richard Fitter, interviewed by TH, 1 October 1971; Humphrey Pease diary, 31 August 1940, Personnel/Pease; Pepper, reports and correspondence while in the airforce, TC 29/2/F.
31. England, June 1939, DR; 'Report of New Observer', nd, Personnel/England.

him to specialize in reporting on film.[32] After his call-up in January 1941 he reported extensively on army life.[33] Len England was to return to MO after the war and play the leading role in its development as a commercial market research organization in the 1950s and 1960s. To men like Atkins and Hughes, these later developments—led by a youngster who had never shared their own hopes for MO—represented a betrayal they could not forgive.[34]

Humphrey Pease—at 37 the oldest member of staff—was an old Etonian, a former art student at the Slade, an amateur ornithologist and, in Madge's rather condescending words, 'a well-off dilettante who had spare time. He did anything he was qualified to do.'[35] An early volunteer at Blackheath, he had worked briefly for MO in Bolton in April 1938 and again in London in the winter of 1938–9. Re-recruited by Harrisson at the end of September 1939 to work on the poster investigation, he noted in his diary:

> We and others have a high opinion of our value, but we are not yet 'placed' officially. The more independence we can preserve the better... but for such 'snooping' work we must have official protection. I don't much like to think of us becoming part of some British Gestapo or Ogpu, or even taking our orders from the present Government.[36]

Despite such unease, and the anti-war and anti-government attitudes shared by most of the MO staff, they were prepared to put their faith in Harrisson's ability to strike an acceptable bargain with the MOI.[37]

32. England, interviewed by Calder, 1 March 1979; Richards and Sheridan (eds), *Mass-Observation at the Movies*, 6–7.
33. Sandra Koa Wing, *Our Longest Days,* 2008, 65; England, reports and correspondence while in the army, TC 29/2/B.
34. Sheridan to Pullin, 6 August 1984, Personnel/Atkins; Hughes to Calder, 4 February 1979, Personnel/Hughes.
35. CM, interviewed by Calder, 23 March 1978.
36. Pease diary, 30 October 1939; Pease memoir, nd (1971?), both in Personnel/Pease.
37. In December 1939 TH and CM were employing 17 full-timers (listed by name in 'Wartime Directive, 4', December 1939, FR 15a). Two of these were working in Bolton and are discussed next. Arthur Ballard was helping Madge from London with the administration of the panel. Madge's lover, Inez Pearn, was also listed as a full-timer. Violette Bazalgette, an 'elderly and rather eccentric lady' who offered her services as a student of the theatre proved 'absolutely useless' and TH got rid of her after a few weeks during which she 'did virtually nothing and what she did showed that she had no understanding of either fieldwork methods or the theatre' (TH to Huxley, 30 October 1940, TC 16/4/M). Finally, of a certain Dr Kvergic nothing is known, and his stay with MO was short lived: but he may have been the Austrian scholar of Slovakian descent whose eccentric 1935 typescript on the *La psychologie de quelques éléments des langues Turques* had appealed to the Turkish dictator Ataturk in his quest for a useable nationalist past (Wendy M. K. Shaw, 'Whose Hittites and Why? Language, Archeology and the Quest for the Original Turks', in Michael L. Galaty and Madge Watkinson (eds), *Archaeology under Dictatorship*, 2004).

Madge, in Bolton, had rather more difficulty managing expectations. The outbreak of war put paid to his plans to close Bolton down, since having a northern as well as a metropolitan presence was important for MO's appeal to its friends in the MOI.[38] During the two weeks of the poster research six people were employed full-time in Bolton, but after that Madge moved back to London (and to Inez Spender). This left Geoffrey Thomas, the only surviving member of the pre-war team, to keep up the 'Worktown War Barometer'—routine observation of gas mask carrying, shopping habits, and war talk—assisted by weekend volunteers and a new full-timer, Jack Cornhill, a difficult 17-year-old from Margate.[39] In mid-October Madge, reluctant to go back north, wrote to Thomas hoping that 'you and Jack aren't feeling totally deserted', and promising to wire some money once an expected cheque came in from the BBC (which had broadcast a morale-raising play based on overheard conversations supplied by MO).[40] Five days later he wrote again, explaining that he was postponing his visit to Bolton 'until I have money to give you'.[41] When the MOI finally paid up on 12 November, Madge sent money to pay the outstanding bills 'with some left over for you'. A second instalment a week later included only £3 for Thomas despite the fact that he was owed £18 in back pay. When Thomas protested bitterly that the workers always seemed to come last, Madge acknowledged that 'you certainly have every right to expect some return for [your] long drawn out devotion in Siberia', but pointed out rather tetchily:

> Perhaps you didn't realise that for the past two months we've all been living precariously by borrowing from friends with enough discretion to prevent them from ceasing to be friends . . . I made a very careful study of how to meet £200 debts with the £100 [his share of the MOI money] . . . For instance, I've only been able to send my wife and children £4 10s in the past month . . .[42]

38. Hilton to Waterfield, 22 September 1939, INF 1/261.
39. TH, memo on expenses, 19 October 1939, TC 42/1A; CM to Thomas, 19 October 1939, Org&Hist 1; Thomas to TH, nd (November 1939?), Org&Hist 1; Thomas, 'Worktown War Barometer', 1 and 11 November 1939, W 50/B; Novy to Hughes and Thomas, 28 March 1940; Novy to TH 11 April 1940, HNpap. Cornhill had answered MO Directives since early 1939—respondent 1133.
40. CM to Thomas, 19 October 1939, Org&Hist 1. On the broadcast see TH to Potter, 27 September 1939, TC 74/3/F; CM to Potter, 30 October 1939, TC 5/1/K; 'War Directive, 3', November 1939, FR 11c; Stanley, Extra Dimension, 13.
41. CM to Thomas, 24 October 1939, Org&Hist 1.
42. CM to Thomas, 12 and 23 November 1939, Org&Hist 1.

When Harrisson asked Bolton to check out a mischievous *Daily Express* story on the Stockport Co-op—'we are making a special study…of the war between the Co-op and the *Daily Express*'—Thomas reminded him that he and Cornhill had to take care of the house and feed themselves as well as cope with the routine work. To keep up with this, and to implement whatever plans Harrisson and Madge might be making 'for the much-needed co-ordination of Worktown and Metrop', they needed more staff.[43] Harrisson and Madge agreed to send Allwood and Hughes to take over temporarily in Bolton in December, while Thomas came to London to work with Madge and spend some time in Ladbroke Road 'to compare notes with the now flourishing London unit, and so be fully equipped for running the Bolton unit.'[44]

III

During the summer of 1939, absorbed by the economic survey, Madge had done little to develop the panel. Plans to visit or phone the most regular correspondents were never implemented, and analysis of some of the most interesting directives was neglected.[45] At the outbreak of war, Madge solicited help from panel members for his ambitious plans for launching MO units in seven major provincial cities.[46] Harrisson, energetically mobilizing the London panellists to take on voluntary work for MO, proposed splitting responsibility for the panel between Madge in the North and himself in the South.[47] But Madge refused to be marginalized in the North, and, after coming back to London in October, turned his attention to building up the panel.

Ever since the autumn of 1937 members of the panel had been encouraged to keep daily diaries during periods of 'national emergency' and such material had been put to good use in MO's analysis of the Munich crisis.[48] As war

43. TH to Thomas, 13 November 1939; GT to TH, November 1939, Org&Hist 1.
44. CM to Thomas, 23 November 1939, Org&Hist 1.
45. Notably the June 1939 directive on 'class', on which see James Hinton, 'The "class" complex: Mass-Observation and cultural distinction in pre-war Britain', *Past and Present*, 199, 2, 2008. Presumably Madge had been intending to use this in preparing the book for Gollancz on economics, which was overtaken by the outbreak of war. On the plans for contacting panel members see MO *Bulletin*, Apr 1938, FR A8; TH to CM, 23 September 1939, 18 January 1940, Org&Hist 1.
46. 'Crisis Directive', September 1939, TC 66/12/A.
47. TH to CM, 23 September 1939, Org&Hist 1.
48. MO *Bulletin*, October 1937, FR A4; MO *Bulletin*, February 1938, FR A8; Calder, *Britain by Mass-Observation, passim.*

approached in August 1939 Madge sent out a new 'crisis directive' asking
people to keep diaries for 'the next few weeks... keeping political discussion
at a *minimum*, concentrating on the details of your everyday life, your own
reactions and those of your family and others you meet.' This work, panel
members were assured, was 'perhaps the largest contribution they can make at
the present time.' The diaries would ensure that for the first time ever future
'historians and social scientists' would be able to make use of 'a detailed,
authentic record of the effects of war on the civil population'.[49] In the last few
days of August 70 individuals responded by starting war diaries and a further
55 joined them during September. After this initial influx new recruits tailed
off sharply, and a quarter of the diarists dropped out after a single entry. By
January 1940 the number of people sending in a diary each month had stabi-
lized at around 80, where it remained until the summer of 1941.[50]

Madge was acutely aware that the panel—small and predominantly middle class—had been of little value for his work on social factors in economics,
and he was anxious to increase its size and representativeness. Working with
an assistant in Blackheath, Arthur Ballard, Madge sent personal letters to the
panellists, put the records in order, and brought the analysis up to date.[51]
Encouraged by evidence that growing popular distrust of the established
media during the early months of the war was stimulating an upsurge of
unofficial newsletters, Madge decided that a weekly newsletter reporting
MO's findings could serve not only to cement the loyalty of existing mass
observers and recruit new ones, but also appeal to a broader readership disillusioned with the representation of public attitudes by newspapers and the
radio. By participating in an anticipated flowering of unofficial anti-
establishment news media MO would be true to its original goals, and hopefully gain a regular source of income, releasing it from the need to cultivate
friends in high places.[52] Harrisson, busy doing just that, thought Madge over-
optimistic about the finances and worried that in the absence of substantial
initial capital the start-up costs would be unsustainable.[53] He was right. The

---

49. 'Crisis Directive', September 1939, TC 66/12/A 'Wartime Directive, 1', September 1939, FR
    A25.
50. J. Langley, 'Report on War diaries', 16 July 1940, Org&Hist 4/4; statistics calculated from MO
    Archive catalogue.
51. TH to CM, 18 January 1940, Org&Hist 1.
52. CM to Thomas, 8 November 1939, Org&Hist 1; CM to TH, 18 January 1940, Org&Hist 1. On
    the unofficial newsletters see Bob Willcock, 'Salvaging History', 11 September 1941; Harrisson,
    Living Through the Blitz, 36.
53. TH to CM, 25 February 1940, 27, Org&Hist 1; TH to Bond, 14 June 1940, Org&Hist 3/15.

newsletter, *US*, started in February 1940 but failed to attract anything like the 3,000 subscribers that it needed to make money. It was closed down at the end of May after 17 issues, leaving unpaid printers bills of £140.[54]

IV

Alongside his work on the panel, Madge spent most of the last three months of 1939 working with Harrisson on MO's first wartime book, *War Begins at Home*. It is a long and sprawling text, but its central purpose—to persuade the authorities to make use of MO—was stated with admirable clarity in the opening sentences:

> We believe . . . that one of the vital needs now in this war is that the Government should be fully aware of all the trends in civilian morale. They need an accurate machine for measuring such trends; a war barometer . . . It is not (yet) the job of any Ministry to collect information on the subject.[55]

In the absence of any such machinery, a political and administrative elite profoundly ignorant of the everyday life of the mass of the people was trying to organize home-front mobilization with little or no understanding of the impact of their measures on popular habits, norms, and prejudices. MO's work on the MOI posters had shown this clearly enough, but nowhere was it more apparent than in the handling of evacuation. The movement of millions of mothers and children out of urban areas had been carried out with mathematical efficiency on the outbreak of war, but little thought had been given to the social problems involved in uprooting people from their homes and billeting them in a radically different social environment:

> Like re-housing and other measures intended to benefit the people, it was conceived too abstractly, without taking into account the human factor of custom and prejudice. Once more the leaders thought of citizens as mathematical units, all alike, all more than ready to do the right thing.[56]

Making full use of the panel, and of a survey of Liverpool evacuation carried out by Gertrude Wagner,[57] *War Begins* provided a vivid account of the

---

54. Bond to TH, 10 June 1940, Org&Hist 3/15.
55. *War Begins*, v.
56. *War Begins*, 313.
57. Gertrude Wagner, *Our wartime guests: opportunity or menace? A psychological approach to evacuation*, 1940, with preface by T. S. Simey.

reasons why most evacuees went home again once it became clear that the devastating air raids anticipated at the outbreak of war were not occurring. The experience of evacuation demonstrated that Britain was far from being a united society, and the insensitivity with which the authorities handled the inevitable tensions arising from the attempt to superimpose incompatible ways of life left a legacy of distress and antagonism which, the book suggested, was likely to jeopardize the effectiveness of any future schemes of evacuation. Such ignorance and insensitivity, equally apparent in other aspects of wartime mobilization studied by MO (ARP, the black-out, the MOI's useless posters, the delay in introducing food rationing) was undermining the capacity of the wartime state effectively to mobilize the population for the effort that would be required of them when the deceptive inactivity of the 'phoney war' gave way to the real thing: 'It is impossible to impose new social machinery on a highly complicated industrial society without detailed investigation and understanding of its problems.'[58] While the book pulled no punches in its criticism of the MOI, it blamed much of the Ministry's ineffectiveness on the press campaign against it and on Lord Macmillan, its first Minister: his replacement shortly before the book came out by Lord Reith, who understood the value of opinion research because of his experience of Listener Research at the BBC, 'brings new hope, at last.'[59]

Reviewing *War Begins* in the *Daily Telegraph* Harold Nicolson—who shared Harrisson's anxiety about the fragility of popular morale—declared that 'the Ministry of Information...should be grateful' to Madge and Harrisson. Despite some reservations about the scientific status of MO's work he concluded: 'I have heard many professional sociologists deride M-O as a somewhat amateurish pastime of a poet and a biologist. Nobody could read this book without feeling that it was something far more useful, more important and more interesting than that.'[60] The book attracted nearly one hundred reviews in the press, including leaders in several national dailies, most of them favourable.[61]

58. *War Begins*, 347.
59. *War Begins*, 416; Harrisson, *Living Through the Blitz*, 297.
60. *Daily Telegraph*, 17 October 1940.
61. Adams to Macadam, 2 February 1940, INF 1/261; Adams to Macadam, 8 March 1940, MApap 1/B.

V

In November 1939, casting around for ways to keep MO going in the absence of contracts from the MOI, Harrisson had attended a meeting hosted by Rebecca Sieff, a wealthy Zionist and feminist campaigner, 'to discuss possibility of an informal committee to co-ordinate the private and lesser channels of information and propaganda in this country'.[62] Together with Michael Young (then working for PEP) he volunteered to investigate the wartime upsurge of unofficial newsletters. By December he had persuaded Sieff to stump up £150 towards his own project on propaganda and opinion formation,[63] and this immediately became 'the whole concern of my end of M-O at the present time':

> We are investigating in detail the way in which ordinary people form their opinions on current events. We are following this up by detailed individual analysis, by observation and overheards, by cross-section interviewing, and by a detailed study of the propaganda itself, everything ranging from BBC variety and newsreels, to parish magazines and dirty jokes. The whole panorama of war allusion, conscious and unconscious propaganda and opinion-forming, is our field... We hope by mid-March to have a complete report of how people are forming their opinions, and on the existing machinery of opinion-forming. I think I can truthfully say this will be a really basic and original piece of work...[64]

This was the account he gave to Mary Adams, who was to be MO's most influential friend in the MOI. Adams, 13 years Harrisson's senior, had been an academic biologist before joining the BBC as head of its Adult Education department in 1930. Her daughter described her as

> small, birdlike, always well dressed, with bright blue eyes and, in public, a knowing confidence. Her character, though full of contradictions, was magnetic. She was a socialist, a romantic communist, and could charm with her charisma, spontaneity, and quick informed intelligence... These qualities ensured she was the centre of attention in a social setting, and she involved herself with all the right people.[65]

62. TH note, 9 November 1939, TC 43/2/D; DNB entry on Sieff.
63. 400102 McEwen to TH, 2 January 1940, TC 32/1/b; Women's Publicity Planning Association, minutes, 19 December 1939. A good deal more money may have followed. In February Brian Allwood wrote: 'I don't know if he only got £100 out of the yid, but I cashed a cheque for him at Bheath [sic] of that amount. Jack [Cornhill] told me that up to now, according to Pris [Feare], he's had £1000 out of her. Where's it gone to?' (Allwood to Novy, 1 February 1940, HNpap).
64. TH to Adams, 16 January 1940, MO&MOI 2.
65. DNB entry on Adams.

Since first meeting him in Oxford in 1933, Adams had adopted Harrisson as a friend and protégé, commissioning him to broadcast both on radio and television.[66] He frequented her Regents Park house where he met all sorts of important people and got to know her husband Vyvyan, a maverick Tory MP who opposed Munich and supported the popular front. During the autumn of 1939 Harrisson had been in contact with Adams, sharing intelligence about the chaotic internal politics of the MOI.[67]

By December the Ministry's embryo Home Intelligence department had been closed down altogether, and it was only the persistence of Hilton, determined to achieve something before quitting Whitehall in disgust, that ensured its resurrection under a new leader. If the appointment of Hilton as the first Director of Home Publicity at the MOI had been a stroke of luck for MO, his parting gesture bordered on the miraculous. The person he appointed to establish a viable system of Home Intelligence was none other than Mary Adams herself.[68] When Harrisson wrote to her in January about his new project on opinion formation he was asking her to encourage Sieff to keep the funds flowing by letting her know that the MOI valued his work; but he was also hoping, as he explained to Madge, that Adams would be able to persuade her superiors in the Ministry to take over the funding for the project after its first two months.[69]

VI

The coming of war had done nothing to improve relations between Harrisson and Madge. In the midst of his late September negotiations with the MOI, Harrisson resisted Madge's desire to come down to London and get involved, pointing out that 'I know ... the people who are going to wing it for us, you don't'.[70] Isolated in Bolton, Madge worried about Harrisson's capacity to withstand the corrupting influence of his proximity to power, his 'obsequiousness to public figures' and his 'alternately bullying and buttering up of associates'.[71] Although the angry exchanges were interspersed

66. Heimann, *Most Offending Soul*, 38–9, 118.
67. TH note on phone conversation with Adams, 3 October 1939, TC 43/2/B.
68. McLaine, *Ministry of Morale*, 50.
69. TH to CM, 18 January 1940, 26, Org&Hist 1.
70. TH to CM, 23 September 1939, Org&Hist 1.
71. CM to TH, 21 January 1940, Org&Hist 1.

with declarations of undying love—'indestructibly, indivisibly and mutually indispensably, Madge'[72]— Harrisson put off the promised discussion of concerted future plans until the outcome of negotiations with the MOI was known, and, as we have seen, the two men pursued distinct and independent strategies during the winter with little or no mutual consultation.[73]

On 18 January Harrisson fired off a rambling 30-page broadside to Madge in Blackheath, reviewing the history of their collaboration, expounding his frustrations, grievances, and thoughts about the future. He and Madge, he wrote, had been ploughing separate furrows ever since the foundation of MO, repeatedly failing to coordinate the functions of the volunteer observer and those of the full-time investigator. 'We have never even attempted to assess, which would be easy, the difference between the answers of the panel to certain questions, and the answers of a cross-section of the population.' Despite an attempt to avoid personal feelings by writing about their relationship in the third person—M and H, not you and me—Harrisson interspersed his analysis with comments on differences of temperament (himself aggressive, outgoing, go-getting, and tending to take over; Madge geared to 'slower process of life…gentler thinking'). He was sharply critical of Madge's failure to make coherent use of the panel material, his abandonment of the Bolton unit, and the way he had allowed the crisis in his personal life to overwhelm his commitments to MO. As for the new regime with the panel, would this 'as in the past, be run energetically for a while, then decay again because M has personal, poetic or marital problems?'[74]

Madge responded with his own anxieties about the direction in which Harrisson seemed to be taking MO. Having himself done most of the writing for *War Begins* he was indignant about the fact that Harrisson, at proof stage and without consultation, had spiced up the text with shrill remarks about the need for 'active leadership' of the 'bewildered masses'. 'All our evidence suggests', Harrisson had written, that with 'active leadership' informed by accurate understanding of the popular mind, 'it would be easy to transform the present civilian attitude into something…more firmly based on long-term realities—therefore more able to stand tremendous strains which have not yet come, but may come.'[75] Pointing out that 'all our

72. CM to TH, 22 September 1939, Org&Hist 1.
73. CM to TH, 21 January 1940, 22, Org&Hist 1.
74. TH to CM, 18 January 1940, Org&Hist 1.
75. *War Begins*, vi, 8, 49.

evidence suggests' was a favourite Harrisson phrase usually deployed as 'prelude for a general statement which was in your head quite apart from the evidence,' Madge complained that Harrisson was allowing his own engagement with the task of mobilizing the masses for the war effort to interfere with the objective observation of popular attitudes. MO was in danger of being used by Harrisson as a vehicle for his overtly political ambitions, a means by which he could establish his authority to lecture politicians and civil servants about how best to sustain popular morale. Harrisson's conviction and drive might for the moment dazzle Sieff or Adams, but his claim to understand the formation of opinion was half baked, and his missionary zeal put in jeopardy one of MO's fundamental strengths: that, unlike the Communist Party or the Left Book Club, 'it has not claimed to offer a panacea, solution or millennium... its strong suit lay in being sensible'. In the end Harrisson's conviction that he knew what needed to be done would prove self-defeating. MO existed to ask questions, to probe shifting popular attitudes, not to provide ready-made solutions. If it was perceived to have a programme, a campaigning agenda, it would lose its appeal not only to 'the "ordinary" man in mills [and] mines', but also to the 'newspaper-business-administrative-middle class circles' on which 'inevitably' they relied for future funding.[76]

Brushing aside Madge's fear that he was trying to turn MO into a campaigning organization with a defined programme, Harrisson argued that any such attempt would be blown out of the water by the wide range of political standpoints among the staff, many of whom (he might have added) held communist or pacifist opinions totally at odds with his own pro-war stance. Though acute about Harrisson's excitement at the prospect of proximity to power via the MOI, Madge underestimated his colleague's capacity to combine the pursuit of personal political influence with the maintenance of relatively objective fieldwork. It was a high-wire balancing act for which Madge, craving the quieter waters of academically respectable social research, had nothing but distaste. Harrisson also yearned for secure funding and long-term projects, but it was what he described to Madge as 'the public, pushing, polemical, unreserved elements of myself which I think you mistake for "Political"' that held the key to MO's future.[77]

76. CM to TH, 18 and 21 January 1940, Org&Hist 1.
77. TH to CM, 25 February 1940, Org&Hist 1.

In his original memo Harrisson, doubtful that the distrust engendered by their methodological and temperamental differences, could be overcome 'by friendly discussions' alone, had proposed establishing a 'written and fairly rigid code of collaboration, on the rule of thumb laws to apply to given situations,' and, most importantly, on the coordination between his own agenda for the full-time units and Madge's directives to the panel. He also suggested that Madge should move his centre of operation from Blackheath—too far off the beaten track to facilitate easy day-to-day communication—to somewhere much closer to Ladbroke Road. Madge responded with his own make-or-break prescription, offering to come and live in the Ladbroke Road house, and to take overall responsibility for writing up results, while Harrisson organized the fieldwork. That was not at all what Harrisson had in mind. Madge on the premises would be too close for comfort, and he was certainly not going to accept a division of labour that gave Madge effective control of MO's output.[78] By the end of February the exchange of memos had petered out in stalemate. Overhearing 'Charles...giving Tom hell over the phone', Cornhill, newly arrived in London at the end of February, reported back to the Bolton staff that 'Charles has adopted a militant attitude to Tom and his eruptions, and intends to curb him as much as possible'.[79]

VII

When Thomas returned to Bolton early in the new year he found Hughes still there and in control, an arrangement approved by Harrisson since, in his view, Thomas 'has done little to help the others...[and] has not been trained to run a unit, and is in fact not a suitable person to do so.'[80] Madge had sent quite inadequate amounts of money and run up substantial debts to local tradesmen, who harassed the impecunious staff for payment. The routine work—cynically described by Allwood as 'getting cold feet counting blackouts and radios and getting tight on Saturday night'—suffered not only because there was no money to spend while listening in to other people's conversations in the pubs, but also because both Hughes and Cornhill were

78. TH to CM, 18 January 1940; CM to TH, 21 January 1940; TH to CM, 25 February 1940, Org&Hist 1.
79. Cornhill to Thomas et al, 27 February 1940, HNpap.
80. TH to CM, 18 January 1940, 26, Org&Hist 1.

reluctant to venture out when it snowed because their shoes leaked.[81] None
of the men had any domestic skills and the money would not stretch, as it
had in the past, to paying anyone to clean or cook, so the house was filthy—
'enough dirt on the floor to grow carrots'—and Cornhill, the 18-year-old,
overworked and underfed, was losing weight.[82]

Since Madge had now withdrawn entirely from responsibility for Bolton,
it was up to Harrisson to decide whether to close the operation down, or
relaunch it on a new basis. Visiting Davenport Street in mid-January he
decided on the latter course, proposing a monthly schedule of work in
which one week (which he would pay for) was spent collecting 'War
Barometer' material for comparison with London, another researching the
specialist topics agreed for each member of staff, leaving two weeks free
each month for work on 'the way in which ordinary people form their
opinions on current events'.[83] Novy, sent by Harrisson at the end of January
to join the Bolton unit, explained to his friend Allwood that by focussing
on a small area (14 streets, 276 houses) in an impoverished part of Bolton
the unit would be able to do 'real and thorough work... a great deal more
consistent and scientific than anything Tom has yet attempted.'[84]

> Our main purpose is to determine how far propaganda, direct and indirect,
> influences individual social life and the relative effect of institutions—cine-
> mas, wireless, pub-going, government propaganda, social clubs, sport, etc—on
> the social attitude of Bolton's workers. To this end we must share the life and
> come into close contact with the people around us, and at the same time
> make a thorough analysis of all the sources of propaganda.[85]

During February the team made copies of 'every single poster in our special
area... goggled [at] by the inhabitants as we stood for hours in front of a
silly hoarding', and conducted preliminary house-to-house interviews with
72 people in the area (over 10 per cent of the total population): 'We wanted
to know what external influences contributed to their way of thinking.
What they think, and why they think it.' Following Harrisson's advice no
notes were made during these interviews, the purpose of which was to

81. Novy to Allwood, 27 January 1940; Allwood to Novy, 1 February 1940; Thomas, 'Observer
    Meeting: Worktown', 25 February 1940, HNpap.
82. Novy to Allwood, 27 January 1940; Allwood to Novy, 1 February 1940; Novy to TH,
    21 January, 28 February 1940, HNpap.
83. TH to Adams, 16 January 1940, MO&MOI 2; Novy to TH, 27 January 1940, HNpap; TH to
    CM, 18 and 25 January 1940, Org&Hist 1.
84. Novy to Allwood, 9 February 1940, HNpap; list of houses, etc., 17 February 1940, W 41/A.
85. Novy to Denham, 5 February 1940, HNpap.

select a smaller number of friendly and articulate people for more intensive study.[86] For Novy this was a 'captivating' experience, which gave him 'real contact with the working class':

> in each home men and women pour out their grievances in their clumsily sincere way. It's a great pity that men should be labelled as hopelessly ignorant just because they happen to be inarticulate. They know their own lives... I feel each man is just as thoughtful... as their more fortunate leaders.[87]

Through 'close study of working class personality' he felt it would be possible to bridge the gulfs of misunderstanding separating the elites from the masses. Wagner, now working in Liverpool, agreed to help supervise the new project with a weekly visit to Davenport Street,[88] and her influence was evident in Novy's concern to push forward the 'social factors in economics' agenda:

> When I did economics at school I always felt something was missing. Isn't the whole problem one of psychological reaction to imposed economic circumstance?... Marshall and Keynes worked down from their figures... I feel they ought to have worked up from the other end.[89]

The staff's enthusiasm for the project was tempered by their knowledge that it could only go ahead if Harrisson succeeded in raising new funds to pay for it, and while an application to the Rockefeller Foundation hung in the balance, they remained insecure and desperately short of money.[90]

After his arrival at the end of January Novy cleaned up the house and took over the shopping and cooking. Harrisson, unable to find money he had promised for Bolton, urged the team to look for new sources of funding. Novy approached newspaper editors across Lancashire, but, despite moments of unrealistic optimism, this had more to do with preparing a personal escape route if Harrisson decided to close down the operation than it did with keeping it alive.[91] Meanwhile the staff decided to hire a cook and to give Harrisson an ultimatum: they would stay until the funds ran out and then 'scram leaving Tom with the bills'.[92]

86. 'Preliminary report on selected area', W 41/B; 'Posters. Special Area', 20 February 1940, W 41/H; Novy to Horner, 4 March 1940; Novy to TH, 28 February 1940; Novy to Allwood, 20 February 1940, HNpap.
87. Novy to Allwood, 22 February 1940, HNpap.
88. TH to CM, 18 January 1940, 26, Org&Hist 1; Novy to Allwood, 9 February 1940, HNpap.
89. Novy to Horner, 4 March 1940, HNpap.
90. Novy to Allwood, 22 February 1940; Novy to TH, 28 February 1940, HNpap; Thomas, 'The Files', nd (February 1940?), W 1/C.
91. Novy to Denham, 8 February 1940; Novy to Allwood, 9 and 22 February 1940, HNpap.
92. Novy to Allwood, 30 January, 9 February 1940, HNpap.

The survival of Novy's correspondence during this period provides an unusually intimate portrait of relations among the full-time investigators, Harrisson's managerial style and the chaotic hand-to-mouth conditions under which so much of MO's work was conducted. Waiting for the axe to fall in Bolton the staff got on each other's nerves: 'we dissect each other's characters like guinea pigs in a laboratory.'[93] Keen though he was on the new project, Novy had little time for his colleagues. Cornhill, the callow youth, was transferred to London, where Harrisson saw his limitations and got rid of him.[94] Thomas seemed uncommitted and determined to leave as soon as he found something else. Novy complained of his 'strict introversion' and 'completely selfish approach to everything.'[95] And Hughes, nominally in charge since January, was variously condemned as pedestrian, officious, ineffectual, and pathetically anxious to ingratiate himself with Harrisson, who, Allwood wrote, kept him in thrall with the promise of a 'bloody book on jazz with his name on the front':

> I know you were beginning to feel fed up with Alec [Hughes] before you went up, and I agree. I think we all are. He will never make anything out of life if he goes on like this, and it's really no use to bother with him...in a Soviet state I'd have him digging canals...M–O is full of hopeless cases. I think you and I and Pris[cilla Feare] and Jack [Atkins]...are about the only live ones.[96]

Apart from criticizing each other's attitude to the work, the young men in Davenport Street spent much of their time talking about sex. Novy was the expert, a 'happy-go-lucky sensualist' and already, at 20, a practised womanizer. In Bolton, however, he seems to have abstained, if only because (as he explained in letters to Allwood and Feare) the local women were not to his taste: 'I have kissed one, just to be on really good terms with her, but it won't go any further—her breath is awful. It took me days to recover...I have adopted Tom's idea of field glasses for all below 30, it is safer.'[97] Thomas and Hughes, who were both still virgins, believed themselves to be in love with Pris (as Feare was generally called) but were too timid to declare their

93. Novy to Allwood, 9 February 1940, HNpap.
94. Novy to Hughes and Thomas, 28 March 1940; Novy to Thomas, 2 April 1940; Novy to TH, 11 April 1940, HNpap.
95. Novy to Feare, 4 March 1940; Novy to TH, 11 April 1940, HNpap.
96. Allwood to Novy, 6 February 1940; Novy to Allwood, 27 January 1940; Novy to TH, 11 April 1940, HNpap.
97. Novy to Allwood, 22 February 1940; Novy to Feare, 4 March 1940; Novy to Pedro, 29 September 1939, HNpap.

feelings to her—a situation that provoked a good deal of mockery in the correspondence between Novy, Allwood and Pris herself. But Allwood and Pris were hardly in a position to pull rank in such matters. Although the closest of friends—'he goes to her home to listen to Mozart and Bach on the gramophone'—they were both still virgins and, as Allwood explained to his uncomprehending friend, the attachment was strictly 'intellectual':

> The sexual act is quite outside the range of his ideas. He gives the impression of someone very hungry who sits at the top of a basement kitchen, inhaling the delicious odours...[98]

The phoney war, it appears, was full of phoney sex. It was only after Hitler struck to the West that these various sexual tensions became resolved. Now that the war was serious, perhaps, it was a case of 'if not now, when?' Novy, back in London by the end of March, finally realized that it was himself, not Thomas, Hughes or even Allwood, who was really in love with Pris, and he lost no time in (as he might have put it) taking possession. By May they had decided to get married. Allwood, distressed at this turn of events, nevertheless volunteered to fill Novy's place in Bolton (enabling Novy and Pris to be together in London). In late May Allwood finally discovered the joys of sex with a local girl from the Co-op.[99] Meanwhile Thomas had found a girl of his own, and Hughes had teamed up with Annie Barlow who had been working for some time as a volunteer with the Bolton team.[100] By August Barlow and Hughes had married, one among several pairings among MO's investigators that summer.[101]

A month after his arrival in Bolton, Novy was organizing a renewed ultimatum to Harrisson. Writing to Allwood, in London, 'about the last piece of Tom buggery', Novy reported:

> Alec [Hughes] is at present ringing up Gertrude [Wagner], asking particulars about the truthfulness of Tom statements, and we have just had a conference at which we decided to launch the greatest offensive yet attempted against the leader of swines. Alec is boiling over with righteous indignation, Geoffrey [Thomas] cold and angry, Jack [Atkins] and I are ready to leave the organisation.[102]

98. Novy to Pedro, 3 January and 20 February 1940, HNpap.
99. Novy to Allwood, 19 May 1940, Allwood to 'Heloise and Abelard', 21 May 1940, HNpap; 'Henry and Priscilla Narrative', Macnamara/Personnel.
100. Allwood to Novy and Feare, 3 and 14 May 1940, HNpap.
101. As Humphrey Pease noted in August (diary entry, 31 August 1940, Personnel/Pease), Jack Atkins had also married an observer, and Betty Ward, Harrisson's new secretary, had married Charles Pepper. Harrisson himself married Biddy in August, but the best Pease himself could manage was to get very drunk at the wedding and 'loudly try...to seduce John Sommerfield's wife'.
102. Novy to Allwood, 30 January, 28 February 1940, HNpap.

Pris, working as Harrisson's secretary, supplied inside information to the rebels: 'Very entertaining... you will be getting a full memo on your last one, which Brian showed me, next week, nicely swatting at the three of you as though you were troublesome flies.'[103] Novy was planning to threaten to expose Harrisson with 'a nice little article' in the local press about 'social science unable to pay its way in West Lancs.'[104] But there was no point, and when the rebels met with Harrisson in Manchester, he convinced them that there really was no money, recalling Novy (and subsequently Hughes) to London and leaving Thomas alone in Bolton while they waited to see if the Rockefeller application would succeed.[105]

VIII

The reason Harrisson had initiated a show-down with Madge in January was that he wanted to clear the decks for a new bid for an ongoing contract from the MOI now that Adams had been appointed to run Home Intelligence. On 22 January, when Adams submitted her first outline of the 'Functions of Home Intelligence', Harrisson's fingerprints were all over it. From the outset it was clear to Adams that there were two possible ways in which the Ministry could gather evidence about public attitudes. Its existing regional machinery had been set up, as the new minister, Lord Reith, explained to the Cabinet, 'to present the national war effort by every available medium of local publicity and to keep people in good heart', and Adams doubted whether this propagandist brief was compatible with objective observation of what ordinary people actually thought and believed. At the very least that would require 'the attachment to each of our regional offices of special investigators charged with the supervision of field work', and such machinery would take time and considerable expense to establish. Moreover its findings would be vulnerable to the kind of self-censorship that ordinary people would be likely to exercise when questioned by investigators known to be working for the government. So she decided to leave the establishment of any official opinion-testing machinery for a possible future, while making immediate use of outside agencies—notably MO,

103. Feare to Novy, 2 March 1940 HNpap.
104. Novy to Feare, 4 March 1940, HNpap.
105. Novy to Peter, 7 March 1940; Novy to Thomas, 2 April 1940, HNpap.

BIPO and the London Press Exchange. For the time being her own department would be developed as a small central unit commissioning research,
and analysing and interpreting the results.[106]

It took Adams a month to get approval for MO's first commission for
Home Intelligence: a token payment of £20 towards the study of the second by-election of the war, on 22 February in Silvertown, a safe Labour seat
in the East End of London, where the official Labour candidate was challenged by Harry Pollitt, the Communist Party leader, and by one of Mosley's
fascists.[107] Since Madge's venture in Ilford in June 1937, MO had studied
every subsequent by-election, including the first wartime one in Southwark
early in February 1940 when a dissident Labour pacifist fighting with
Communist support had significantly dented the Labour majority.[108]
Convinced by Harrisson's argument that by-elections presented a unique
opportunity to probe the relationship between private and public opinion
on the war and to reveal 'latent trends of opinion', Adams gained approval
for the employment of MO in future by-elections, starting with a payment
of £60—the full cost—for a study of the next one in Leeds on 13 March.[109]
'I am becoming their by-election machinery,' Harrisson wrote, confidently.[110]
Subsequently he was also commissioned for a quick report on attitudes to
the conclusion of the Russo–Finnish war, and to observe picketing by anti-
war bodies at Labour Exchanges on the day (6 April) when 25-year-olds
were required to register for military service.[111]

Nervous about being seen to involve itself in partisan politics, the Ministry
approved the by-election studies on condition that MO gave no indication
that they were paying.[112] To forestall criticism if the press discovered that the
Ministry was employing MO, Adams suggested that it would be wise to
inform the political parties (if not the public in general) with 'a frank statement of our objectives and [a] written account of the instrument we propose
to use in obtaining results'; but her advice was not followed. She was careful

106. MA, 'Functions of Home Intelligence', MApap 1/A; Lord Reith, 'Propaganda: Appreciation
     of Action Taken and its Effects', 24 January 1940, CAB 68/4/35.
107. Waterhouse to Adams, 19 February 1940; minute, 20 February 1940; Adams to TH, 21
     February 1940, INF 1/286.
108. US 4, 24 February 1940, FR 34; Allwood to Novy, 12 February 1940, HNpap.
109. Adams to Waterfield, 5 March 1940; Adams to TH, 8 March 1940, MApap 1/B; Adams to
     Leigh Ashton, 8 March 1940, INF 1/286.
110. TH to Potter, 15 March 1940, TC 74/3/F.
111. Adams to Macadam, 13 March 1940, INF 1/286; Bentley to MO, 5 April 1940, TC 27/1/F.
112. Adams to TH, 21 February 1940, INF 1/286; Adams to Macadam, 8 March 1940, INF 1/262.

not to exaggerate the value of the MO material, echoing the evaluation drawn up by Crossman in October, which had balanced praise for 'the astonishing ingenuity of Mr Tom Harrisson and the fertility of his ideas for new techniques of investigation', against his tendency 'to try to turn a hint which they have discovered into a scientifically demonstrated fact.'[113] The subjective element in MO's qualitative findings would need careful inter- pretation by her own staff and, where appropriate, independent statistical testing by one of the commercial polling organizations, BIPO or the London Press Exchange.[114]

Confronted by official worries that MO itself might be seen as a subver- sive organization, Adams pointed out that press reviews of *War Begins at Home* had been generally favourable, with the exception of the *Daily Worker* which had condemned its authors as 'right wing, in favour of the war, and anxious to instruct the Government!'[115] In any case, she wrote:

> What does one mean by 'subversive'? The results of M-O are, not unnaturally, *critical* of certain social happenings, and I do not think that criticism is subver- sion. The use to which criticisms are put may lead to subversive actions. But it is our business to acquaint ourselves with criticisms and to direct the atten- tion of those in authority to the causes of discontent. By doing so we hope to prevent unfortunate consequences.

The fact, well known no doubt to MI5, that many of MO's full-time staff held left-wing and anti-war opinions could, she suggested, be a positive advantage when the organization was used to investigate Communist election campaigns or pacifist picketing of Labour Exchanges: 'If observ- ers are to fade into any background special personal qualifications are necessary, and the observer most acceptable to the situation being studied must be chosen.' There was, of course, a slippery slope here towards home- front espionage, and some of the arguments used by Adams to persuade her superiors of the value of MO to the Ministry would have worried not only the MO staff but also Harrisson himself had he been privy to them at the time: 'by financing the investigations and supervising them', she argued, they would be able 'to control the activities of the organisa- tion . . . It would be useful if their resources were mobilised for our purposes

113. Richard Crossman, 'Report on the work of Mass-Observation', 26 October 1939, INF 1/261.
114. Adams to Macadam, 8 March 1940, INF 1/262.
115. Adams to Col. Crutchley, 22 February 1940, MApap 2/E.

rather than for their own.'[116] But that was not at all what Harrisson intended to happen.

By late March 1940 a significant proportion of MO's work was being financed by the Ministry, and Harrisson and Adams agreed that the time was ripe to press for a more permanent arrangement. Adams needed flexibility and a quick response, but remembering September's 'unfortunate experience', Harrisson was reluctant to begin any work 'until it has been finally and fully sanctioned from your end.'[117] With the Treasury holding back on payment for work already done, and negotiations for a more permanent contract due to be finalized, Harrisson was postponing payment of wages for all but the most impecunious of the staff.[118] When he returned from Bolton on 28 March, Novy, determined not to be once more 'swatted like a troublesome fly', got together with Atkins, Feare and Allwood to mobilize the rest of the London staff. On 7 April, the day before Harrisson's scheduled meeting with the MOI, 14 of the staff met unofficially, formulated plans to hold regular meetings ahead of Harrisson's weekly staff meetings to share views, appoint a spokesperson and 'ensure that the wishes of the majority of observers are considered by the organisers.' They also demanded that Harrisson and Madge present financial accounts periodically to the staff meeting, and that no new staff should 'be taken on without the organisers previously consulting permanent observers, who must be satisfied that this will not entail any cuts or delays in receiving their salaries, either at present or in the future.'[119]

Next morning Harrisson responded with a long memorandum accepting the idea of unofficial meetings, but rejecting any suggestion that he should present accounts: 'observers who don't have general confidence in my judgement and integrity on such matters should I think better work in some organisation where they have confidence in the person in charge'. Nor was he prepared to consult existing staff before making new appointments:

> I think it is now necessary to get quite clear that M-O cannot be an organisation which is run by votes, and that the wishes of the majority of the observers are not necessarily the best things for M-O. I am sure that most of

116. Adams to Macadam, 8 March 1940, INF 1/262.
117. TH to Adams, 26 March 1940, INF 1/262.
118. Novy to Hughes and Thomas, 28 March 1940, HNpap.
119. Agenda for unofficial meeting, 2 April 1940, HNpap.

you will agree with this fundamentally. After all...I built up my end of the thing and have given it all my attention and brains and money-making ability for the last three years, and my judgement must inevitably be worth rather more than others.... While observers have a very natural wish to control M-O democratically...in practice so much depends on...my own initiative and drive, that it would in end be unsatisfactory if I bound myself by any resolution of a meeting.

Revealing that his crucial meeting with the MOI was scheduled for that afternoon—'the culmination of months of effort, work and memorandising on my part'—Harrisson warned that the future of MO depended on the outcome:

> I don't feel able any longer to carry on maintaining the unit under the terrific financial and psychological strains which I have been going through since the outbreak of war in making both ends meet, not including all my personal obligations, in involving myself deeper and deeper in my personal debts in order to support M-O etc...But at this meeting this afternoon I shall either succeed in getting a certain sum of money guaranteed, or I shall fail. If I succeed, everyone will be guaranteed a certain wage for a year, and everyone will be immune from conscription. If I fail...I don't think we can carry on.[120]

That afternoon a three-month contract was finalized with the MOI under which, in return for £100 a week, Harrisson put most of MO's resources at the disposal of the Ministry. The Ministry agreed to take steps to prevent the police interfering with MO's work, and to do what it could to protect key staff against conscription. By mutual consent these arrangements were to be kept confidential, and MO was to retain its status as an independent organization, undertaking other work as it saw fit, and continuing to publish articles in the press and to broadcast. Harrisson did his best to retain the right to publish work commissioned by the Ministry, if only after the war; but he was forced to accept that 'publication rights depend absolutely on the permission of the Ministry and that nothing which may in any way affect the Ministry may be contributed to any publication. The Ministry has the sole right of veto on this question.'[121] The issue of home-front espionage was covered by a guarantee that the Ministry would not expect any work to be done 'which is liable to offend the susceptibilities of the personnel, who are

---

120. TH to 'Dear Observers', 8 April 1940, HNpap.
121. Leigh Ashton to TH, 9 April 1940, INF 1/262; TH to Leigh Ashton, 11 April 1940, INF 1/286.

doing work with certain scientific principles in mind', and Harrisson insisted that in any use of the panel 'particular care must be taken ... not to offend the susceptibilities of any of the many different sorts of persons who help us in this voluntary way.'[122]

These protections for the susceptibility of the staff, newly organized and self-assertive following Novy's return from Bolton, were crucial to Harrisson's management of MO's internal crisis.[123] At the end of April 1940 Pease wrote in his diary: 'There was nearly a collapse of the whole M-O organisation owing to rebellion of Observers at not getting regular pay and being treated undemocratically.'[124] Despite the regular weekly staff meetings, it seems likely that Harrisson played the negotiations with the MOI close to his chest and it may not have been until the hours before the formal contract was agreed on 8 April that he informed the staff that they were already spending most of their time working for the state.[125] Pease later recalled:

> one day Harrisson announced that M-O was going to be taken over by the MOI and that henceforth much of our work would be pressurised, if not ordered by them. We were mostly inclined to anti-govt and anti-war feelings but it was chiefly the restriction on the organisation's independence that was the trouble.[126]

On 9 April, the day after the contract was agreed, Harrisson demanded a vote of confidence. 'Put up against the wall,' Novy reported to the Bolton staff, 'we had to give him the vote.'[127] During the next two weeks the staff

122. TH, 'Special Points', 8 April 1940, INF 1/286.
123. Novy felt able to reassure his colleagues that 'the clause which has to do with work for the ministry is very elastic, and there is ample room to refuse undertaking any work which isn't fair, such as snooping, etc ... Refusal can be made by Tom and also by individual observers if they have a conscience case' (Novy to Thomas and Hughes, 13 April 1940, HNpap).
124. Pease diary, 29 April 1940, Personnel/Pease.
125. Early in March Adams had assured her boss that 'for our own protection, and in the interests of the objectivity of the report, the field workers employed by M-O are not informed that their results are for the use of the MOI' (Adams to Macadam, 8 March 1940, MApap 1/B). Although there was no mention of the MOI in the instructions Harrisson gave for the Registration Day (6 April) investigation, the staff were surely capable of reading between the lines: 'for God's sake don't say anything about Mass-Observation having ever done any official work or anything of that sort ... I have had to do some awful wrangling as it is about this thing with the Ministry of Labour, so for God's sake keep all Government or official names out of it' (TH, 'Points for everyone', 5 April 1940, HNpap).
126. Pease memoir, nd (1970?), Personnel/Pease.
127. Novy to Thomas and Hughes, 13 April 1940, HNpap.

agreed to drop their demand for democratic control of MO's policy—
'except on fundamental issues' (unspecified)—in return for a procedure
involving a monthly meeting of all observers to be held in the absence of
Harrisson and Madge to put items on the agenda of the official staff meeting, which would be held immediately afterwards 'in order to prevent
intimidation and wavering of individuals'. In the same suspicious spirit the
staff also insisted on electing a new 'delegate' each month to handle issues
that arose between meetings on the grounds that a more permanent spokesperson would inevitably be co-opted by what they described as too 'frequent Tom contact'—a backhanded testimony to Harrisson's charismatic
powers of leadership.[128]

Alongside this 'more efficient democratic machinery', which Harrisson
hoped would prevent any future 'private agitations' like that led by Novy
since his return from Bolton, each of the full-timers signed an individual
contract setting out their rights and duties for the term of the MOI agreement. Previously rates of pay had been arranged individually by Harrisson,
but now all full-timers were to receive the same amount, £3 per week—
enough for a single person to live on, though hardly generous.[129] Nina
Masel, then a 17-year-old new recruit, recalled the crisis as:

> three weeks in which there was no money, no wages. Harrisson urged us to
> stay on; said he was pretty sure he could do a deal which would double our
> wages and backdate over the three weeks. He did. Wages were upped from
> £1.10s to £3 a week…We each got £12 that week, including back pay. So
> we were thrilled, at first, to be on a sound financial footing.[130]

Security of employment was guaranteed, an issue given added importance
now that the MOI promise to seek exemption from conscription for MO's

128. Novy to Thomas and Hughes, 13 April 1940; 'From TH and CM to all who are working
     whole time for M. O.', nd (April 1940?), putting forward their plan for 'a more efficient
     democratic machinery' for MO, HNpap.
129. Fremlin, interviewed by Calder, 17 March 1980; 'Draft contract', 22 April 1940, INF 1/286.
     Interviewers for the Wartime Social Survey were paid twice as much ('Home Intelligence:
     Wartime Social Survey, Mass-Observation, etc', OEPEC Paper 530, 9 October 1940, INF
     1/286). Moreover the contract added that this was to be 'inclusive of all expenses'. In May
     TH spelt out what this meant: the £3 should not be thought of as a salary, it had to cover
     expenses, although for fieldworkers away from home for more than eight days he would pay
     return fares, rent of (unused) room in London (if any), and a small extra allowance (TH to
     Novy, Atkins and England, 21 May 1940, HNpap).
130. Masel to Sheridan, 12 May 1984; draft article for *New Statesman,* nd, Personnel/Masel.

key staff had placed increased power in Harrisson's hands.[131] He did, however, reserve the right to dismiss any member of staff who violated 'the spirit or intention of the organisation or introduces into it emotional and neurotic complications which have nothing to do with the work.'[132] This curious formulation was probably linked to his difficulties with Box. Whether the passion she conceived for Harrisson was ever reciprocated is unknown; but in the spring of 1940, distressed at the news of Harrisson's forthcoming marriage to Biddy, she had thrown a very public jealous fit after which Harrisson refused to let her enter the Ladbroke Road house.[133] In line with Harrisson's agreement on confidentiality with the MOI, the field workers undertook 'to exercise the utmost discretion in regard to our official relationship, not to mention it, even when challenged by police, in which case the procedure is to refer back to me.' They also agreed to 'show similar discretion in private political and similar activities. The observer is entirely at liberty to carry on these according to his own views, but it is necessary to be careful that he does not make himself conspicuous and indirectly involve or embarrass the organiser or the organisation.' The main gain for Harrisson was acceptance by the staff that any of them might be sent anywhere at a moment's notice: the 'flying squad... which has in the past been concentrated on a few individuals

131. Before the contract was agreed TH had indicated that everyone would get exemption (TH to 'Dear Observers', 8 April 1940, HNpap): but all that the MOI actually promised was to use its influence to try to secure exemption for 'you key men while engaged on Ministry work' (Leigh Ashton to TH, 9 April 1940, INF 1/262). On 13 April Novy, while still optimistic, noted that 'the exemption clause was not very clear when we were told about the ministry...' (Novy to Thomas and Hughes, 13 April 1940, HNpap). Already in January 1940 CM had expressed concern that fear of conscription placed a dangerously authoritarian weapon in the hands of MO's management (CM to TH, 21 January 1940, 9, Org&Hist 1).
132. 'Draft contract', 22 April 1940, INF 1/286.
133. Macnamara (née Feare), interviewed by Calder, 10 January 1980. Box's version of events is contained in a letter she wrote 'to all Observers' on 16 April 1940 (HNpap): 'I hear that... TH made certain accusations against me... I trust that observers will regard them impartially in the light of their knowledge of TH's previous record for honesty, whatever that may be. I deny the accusation made in my presence that I was "rude" to anyone at 82 Ladbroke Road.' See also TH to CM, 2 August 1940 (MO&MOI 1, 11/F): 'there is absolutely no question of my employing K Box... there is no question of her ever working with any part of the organisation with which I am concerned.' Subsequently she worked for some months for Madge, but, despite the efficiency of her work, he also came to find her impossible to deal with, writing despairingly to Inez: 'she was insidiously awful... simply blots any landscape... such a lot of the time is occupied getting away from her' (400811 CM to Inez, 11 August 1940, CMpap, 8/3). In 1941 she joined the Wartime Social Survey where she had a distinguished career alongside a number of other former mass observers, before committing suicide in the 1970s (Louis Moss, *The Government Social Survey. A History*, 1991, 17; Thomas, interviewed by Stanley, 26 November 1979).

would now be distributed all round, on a fair basis, as everyone is now of exactly the same status.' In return he guaranteed that each member of staff would be given time to pursue their own particular line of research, something that he had been encouraging since the autumn.[134]

A subsidiary goal of the rebels had been 'to save the unity of M-O'. Initially their acceptance of the MOI agreement was conditional on the achievement of 'a real unity of purpose between Tom's end and Charles' end.'[135] Harrisson dismissed as unrealistic their desire for a 'hearty all-in-it-together collaboration', turning the tables on Madge's criticism of his sexing-up of *War Begins*, by registering his 'violent disagreement' with the 'journalistic principles' on which Madge ran the newsletter. This, he felt, did more harm than good to MO's reputation as a serious research organization: instead they should 'pile up material for books to be published after the war, when thoroughly digested and thought over'.[136] But the panel and the newsletter were no longer the only strings to Madge's bow. In March, very hard up—according to one staff member who had been staying in the Blackheath house 'poor Charles has been hawking his old belongings around to raise enough money to live'[137]—Madge had renewed contact with Maynard Keynes, who responded enthusiastically to his offer to test out the public acceptability proposals for financing the war through compulsory saving.[138] Giving Madge an immediate subsidy of £50 from his own pocket, Keynes urged the National Institute of Economic and Social Research (NIESR) to fund the project. Harrisson and Madge, he wrote, 'are live wires, amongst the most original investigators of the younger generation and well worth encouraging', and this was 'an enquiry of first class importance, which I have long wished to see undertaken...more purely economic-scientific [in] character than some of their previous enquiries', and 'vastly more deserving' than many of the dreary and fruitless academic projects customarily financed by the NIESR.[139] Waiting for the outcome of

134. 'Draft contract', 22 April 1940, INF 1/286; Wartime Directive, 4, December 1939, FR 15a.
135. Novy to TH and CM, 10 April 1940; Novy to Thomas and Hughes, 13 April 1940, HNpap.
136. Novy to Thomas and Hughes, 13 April 1940, HNpap. And see TH to CM, 30 April 1940 (TC 25/18/A): 'I do think that there is an unconscious tendency to make things very dramatic for the newsletter, as indeed we did for the book.'
137. Cornhill to Thomas et al, 27 February 1940, HNpap.
138. CM to Keynes, 17 and 26 March 1940; Keynes to CM, 28 March 1940, Donald Moggridge (ed.), *The collected writings of John Maynard Keynes, Vol.22, Activities 1939–1945, internal war finance*, 1978, 810–11.
139. Keynes to Crowther, 28 March 1940, Moggridge (ed.), *Collected writings of Keynes*, 22, 812–13.

his grant application, Madge was reluctant to engage with the rebellious staff, leaving them exasperated by a 'wavering uncertainty' which made it clear to them that that MO's future, if it had one, depended mainly on Harrisson: 'There is no talk of joining Charles as we feel we can't trust him to raise the money.'[140] Attempts to bring the two ends of MO together were further frustrated by Harrisson's refusal to allow Box—now working on the newsletter in Madge's new headquarters in central London—to attend joint staff meetings at Ladbroke Road.[141]

Although Madge was not party to the agreement with the MOI, Harrisson expected to pay him £5 a week 'for facilities in sending of questions to his panel, and in generally getting a check up through this nationwide system of part-time observers.'[142] Despite his initial enthusiasm for a deal with the MOI, Madge later recalled Harrisson's April contract as the final straw:

> I didn't want to be drawn into a thing which consisted in an activity which was rather like spying on our own side. That was the thing we broke on. He wanted me to be involved in it and I said I didn't want to and that was really the breaking point.[143]

But the existence of alternative funding was at least as important, and the final break did not come until that was assured. Harrisson took over responsibility for recruiting new diarists and set up a new system for classifying incoming diary material; and the decision to close down the newsletter, *US*, at the end of May effectively put an end to Madge's involvement with the panel.[144] Madge, hearing from Keynes that the NIESR was looking favourably on his grant application, pressed ahead with his new project employing five workers in intensive door-to-door interviewing on saving and spending in London and Coventry.[145] Although Harrisson and Madge were still

140. Novy to Thomas and Hughes, 13 April 1940, HNpap.
141. Box to 'all observers', 16 April 1940, HNpap.
142. TH, 'Particulars of Costing', 8 April 1940, INF 1/286.
143. In retrospect, however, Madge conceded that Adams had used the MO material 'rather intelligently without it degenerating into a system of spying' (CM, interviewed by Stanley, 23 March 1978).
144. 'Decisions reached at meeting between TH, CM etc.', 26 April 1940, Org&Hist 1; TH, 'Ideas about diary analysis', 19 April 1940, Org&Hist 4/4; CM, interviewed by Stanley, 23 March 1978; TH to Radcliffe, 29 May 1940, MO&MOI 2.
145. Keynes to CM, 16 April 1940, Moggridge (ed.), *Collected writings of Keynes*, 22, 814; CM, 'Economic Effects of the War', 14 July 1940, FR 267; 'General Report for July', July 1940, FR 322.

describing the work of the 'Economic Unit' as an integral part of MO's work in August 1940,[146] Madge had already decided that if the NIESR renewed the grant (which they did in August) he would receive it 'as a private individual, not as M-O'.[147] But it was not until December that Madge publicly announced that 'since July 1940 I have no longer shared the responsibility for "Mass-Observation" '.[148] Madge's subsequent work on saving and spending, which was to provide important evidence in support of Keynes' policy recommendations on how to pay for the war, fully justified his belief that the approach he and Wagner had developed in Bolton had a serious contribution to make to grounding economic theory in the empirical study of popular attitudes.[149] But that contribution was made only after he had decided to break with MO, a decision, he wrote later, which 'helped me . . . to do work which came much nearer to being scientific than any I had done before'.[150]

IX

In January Madge had remarked that 'the direction of whole-time field-work by penniless but enthusiastic young men and women needs special drive and stimulation'—something he knew to his cost from his own difficulties in managing the Bolton staff.[151] Harrisson's ability to ride out rebellion in the spring of 1940 was all the more remarkable given the fact that most of his more dynamic staff held political views on the war sharply at odds with his own. Hughes had registered as a conscientious objector, and both Atkins and Pease were intending to plead conscientious objection when their age group was required to register.[152] Novy, Allwood, Fremlin, and Masel were all Communists, and by June 1940 Box, abandoning her earlier detachment, was applying to join the Party.[153] Given the weight of

146. *US* 18, August 1940, FR 360; 'Wartime Saving and Spending', 10 August 1940, FR 335.
147. Madge to Inez, 14 July and 29 August 1940, CMpap 8/3.
148. CM, 'The propensity to save in Blackburn and Bristol', *Economic Journal*, 50, 200, December 1940, 410.
149. The impact of Madge's wartime work is discussed in Hubble, *Mass-Observation and Everyday Life*, 194–9.
150. CM, 'Autobiography', 122.
151. CM to TH, 18 January 1940, 2, Org&Hist 1.
152. Atkins to TH, 11 June 1940, TC 66/21/A; Pease diary entry, 31 August 1940, Personnel/Pease.
153. 'Kay is trying to join the CP, I heard that from Celia Fremlin who now works quite full time for us. She wanted to know what kind of a girl Kay was. For the Party' (Novy to Allwood, 12 June 1940, HNpap).

anti-war opinion among the staff, it is striking how little controversy was caused by *War Begins at Home*, correctly identified by the *Daily Worker* as a thoroughly pro-war text. Box, clutching at the only concession to the views of their staff that Harrisson and Madge provided in the book—a remark that 'it may be a very good thing' that 'the whole structure of society' was under threat—was pleased to note that this showed MO was not biased in favour of 'the present system'. And the criticism she voiced, in a letter to Harrisson, was mild to the point of absurdity: 'I think some people might get the impression that the book was a little bit pro-war in tone.'[154] Novy, while deploring Harrisson's more strident calls for 'active leadership' of the 'bewildered masses'—'a strong fascist tinge, uncompromising rigidness of attitude which I dislike'—nevertheless conceded that 'I can't help admitting that something must be done'.[155] Despite his membership of the Communist Party, Novy was politically inactive and wrote cynically that, far from mobilizing the masses, the Party merely provided for the enlightened few 'a comfortable refuge in simulated activity and the mental ease of being led'.[156] His own politics were a curious mixture of mystical communitarianism and recalcitrant individualism, and his 'budding philosophy of life' owed more to Aldous Huxley, whose 1937 book *Ends and Means* preached the Buddhist virtue of 'detachment', than to Karl Marx.[157] Allwood, a much more seriously committed Party member—'the *Daily Worker* is his bible and revolution his watchword'—was sickened by *War Begins*, telling Novy: 'if that's what's meant by mass observation then, as Tom said somewhere, I'd rather be a fish-monger.'[158] But even Allwood was far from being an orthodox Communist: according to Novy he harboured a secret belief in 'Chestertonian Christianity'.[159]

These were clever young people searching for meaning in a world collapsing into chaos, and MO's commitment to documenting everyday life in extraordinary times provided them with a sense of purpose that outweighed their dislike of Harrisson's pro-war stance, or their indignation about his arbitrary methods of management. In December 1939, apologizing to

154. Box to TH, 9 February 1940, Org&Hist 1; *War Begins*, 11–12.
155. Novy to Pedro, 20 February 1940, HNpap.
156. Novy, 'M-O and the war', 29 October 1939, Org&Hist 4/2.
157. Novy to Pedro, 29 September 1939, 3 January and 20 February 1940.
158. Allwood to Novy, 1 and 12 February 1940; Novy to Pedro, 3 January and 20 February 1940, HNpap.
159. Novy to Pedro, 20 February 1940, HNpap.

Harrisson for some sharp (but effective) notes demanding payment of expenses, Novy had pleaded for a more inclusive style of management: 'Make us feel that we are part of M-O, give us access to some of your ideals... We should have more discussion of the ideals of M-O, because many of us still have ideals'. Too often, he complained, the investigators' relationship with Harrisson was characterized by 'obedient acquiescence on the one hand and lack of consideration on the other'.[160] But there *were* ideals to be shared, and those who stood up for themselves in face of Harrisson's bullying found that they could win his respect. 'If you put up with the initial outbursts things will clear themselves and you may have a good time,' Novy counselled young Cornhill when he went to work in London in March 1940.[161] It was a rough way of managing people, but it worked.

For all their anger and rebelliousness, in the end the staff deferred to Harrisson, and not just because he was the source of their bread and butter. Even at his most cynical, Novy continued to feel that 'life in M-O is very active and damned interesting. With the war on and everything upside down it's about the best way of wasting time... I see and talk to more people in a week than I did before in six months.'[162] Opposition to the war effort in no way undermined the value of recording its impact: social research, as Hughes explained when applying for exemption as a conscientious objector, provided a means of serving the community whatever one's view of the war.[163] Harrisson frequently made the same point, sending what Allwood described as 'keepyourendupallforscience' missives to his staff.[164] When in June 1940 Atkins changed his mind about the war and asked Harrisson to stop trying to get him exempted from conscription—'I want to be in the van because I hate watching'—Harrisson responded:

> your mind is working in a slightly out-of-date way. The van is coming to you and to all of us. And actually the work you are doing is a much more real, energetic and unique contribution both to democracy and the course of the war than if you join up and start training. That is my view. We are doing something which is more permanent than most things, and even if we were to lose

160. Novy to TH, 14 December 1939, HNpap.
161. Novy to Cornhill, 4 March 1940, HNpap; Heimann, *Most Offending Soul*, 71.
162. Novy to Pedro, 3 January 1940.
163. Hughes, 'Statement of Conscientious Objection to Military Service', nd (April 1940?), HNpap.
164. Allwood to Novy and Feare, 3 May 1940, HNpap.

the war and be overrun, all our essential stuff is getting over to America now through official channels, including much of your work. So it will not die.[165]

The argument seems to have worked. Atkins got his exemption, and was not called up until April 1944.[166] Whether they were for or against the war, MO's staff could see the research as having a longer term purpose, and it was this that justified the compromises necessary to keep the organization alive. And, as Harrisson pointed out to Feare in the autumn of 1940, they should all appreciate their good fortune in having war work that was 'really useful and constructive. Nothing about it is destructive, unlike practically every other form of war activity.'[167] Several of the MO investigators who joined up early in the war subsequently came to appreciate Harrisson's belief that they would have made a more vital contribution to democracy by remaining with MO: 'Please convey my remembrance to observers,' wrote Charles Pepper, languishing in menial tasks in the RAF, 'and tell them that they are far more useful where they are than in this racket.'[168] As a thoroughly browned-off Sommerfield put it, trapped in 'absolutely fool activities' in Cumberland during the London blitz: 'no-one seems to have learned anything since the Boer war ... I wish to Christ I was around and about London doing M-O stuff. If ever there's a time when what's really happening and what people are really saying and thinking about it should be recorded, now is it.'[169]

165. TH to Atkins, 14 June 1940; Atkins to TH, 11 June 1940, TC 66/21/A. In the summer of 1940 TH arranged for 'the best part of our first year's work' (i.e. 1939–40) to be typed out and sent for safe keeping in the United States (TH to Novy, 9 July 1940; TH to Investigators, nd (October 1940?), HNpap).
166. Willcock to Ivey, 17 April 1944, TC 66/6/A.
167. TH to Feare, 28 September 1940, HNpap.
168. Pepper to TH, nd, TC 29/2/F.
169. Sommerfield to TH, 27 November 1940, TC 29/2/I.

7

The Summer of 1940

'When Hitler comes over here he'll shoot all the capitalists, anyway.'
'Yes, and the Jews.'
'Oh no. They'll get away. So will the King. They'll all get away and leave us
poor buggers to face it.'

(Conversation between two women in a Bolton pub,
18 June 1940, overheard by Brian Allwood)[1]

I

As well as ongoing coverage of by-elections, Tom Harrisson's April contract
with the Ministry of Information (MOI) committed Mass-Observation
(MO) to undertaking studies on whatever subjects the Ministry required—
'provided it does not involve "espionage"'.[2] Writing to Harrisson, the *Daily
Mirror* columnist Cassandra worried: 'Isn't it a short step from reporting
people's conversations (including the subversive ones) to taking their
names?'[3] That was a step that MO never took, but the ban on 'espionage' did
not prevent one of its regular tasks being to report on pacifist and defeatist
sentiment. Covering public meetings sponsored by the MOI was another
part of the brief, alongside advance checking and testing of MOI publicity.[4]

---

1. BA, 'Bolton Crisis', 18 June 1940, W 50/H.
2. TH, 'Work to be done', 8 April 1940, INF 1/286.
3. Cassandra to TH, 1 August 1940, MO&MOI 11/f.
4. Taylor to Parker, 15 April 1940, INF 1/101. In October 1939 officials had wanted to circulate to
   the 'academic copywriters'—the Oxbridge dons whose secondment to write MOI leaflets
   had so outraged Richard Crossman (TH note, 30 August 1939, TC 43/2/D)—a list previously
   broadcast by MO of 'hoity-toity' words that the general uneducated public did not understand,
   but, embarrassed by the 13th hour cancellation of MO's contract, they had felt unable to ask for
   a copy (Stewart to Dickey, 5 October 1939; Lady Grigg, 6 October 1939; ED to Charles, 3
   November 1939 all in INF 1/261). The list in question survives in the MO Archive, FR A26 5a.
   But MO's understanding of this was not infallible, as Allwood pointed out, citing words defined
   by TH and CM as incomprehensible to ordinary people which were in fact used by Bolton
   people in everyday conversation (BA, 'Talk in General', 19 July 1940, W 11/F).

But MO's main job for the MOI was the everyday monitoring of morale as the phoney war came to an end by direct interviewing of a small stratified random street sample (usually about 60 interviews) using open-ended questions—e.g. 'What do you think of the news today?'; 'What did you think of Churchill's broadcast last night?'—and recording verbatim answers in full. The so-called 'News Quota' was conducted every Monday and Thursday morning until the end of the European war, providing a mass of suggestive information about public attitudes.[5] The daily morale reports instituted by Mary Adams on 18 May were based mainly on information supplied by MO's News Quota.[6]

Part of MO's appeal to the MOI was that its activities were not confined to the capital, and regular reports from Bolton were envisaged in the April contract. Henry Novy refused to go back and work with Alec Hughes, but Brian Allwood, perhaps in an effort to escape his sense of displacement by the romance between his two close friends, agreed to take his place.[7] The 'special area' project was now sidelined, and the main excitement arose from the difficulty of interviewing for the News Quota in the increasingly paranoid atmosphere of May 1940.[8] Alarmed by questions from a stranger (Allwood) about whether or not she thought Britain was going to win the war, an elderly working-class woman, shouting 'Rule Britannia', rallied her neighbours to seize hold of Geoffrey Thomas (canvassing the same street) and call the police. Well aware of MO's activities, the police quickly calmed things down, and in any case they were much more interested in the same woman's allegation that her nextdoor neighbour, a 'Bolshevik', was working in a local munitions factory.[9] A few days later a man from the same area was arrested and charged with saying that it would be a good thing if Hitler came.[10] Harrisson, noting that his

5. 'War Morale Chart', 6 February 1946, FR 2346; Memo on News Quota, nd (1945?), Org&Hist 4/1; GM, 'Meaning and Limitation of News Quota Statistics', 28 March 1944, FR 2060; TH, 'To All Observers', 21 May 1940, HNpap.
6. Adams to TH, 2 September 1940, INF 1/286. For example, the conclusions of the first HI morale report (reproduced in Paul Addison and Jeremy A. Crang, *Listening to Britain. Home Intelligence Reports on Britain's Finest Hour*, 2010, 5–6) were simply copied with minor verbal alterations from the conclusions of MO's report to the MOI of the same date: 'Morale', 18 May 1940, FR 125. Similar borrowings occur in subsequent reports.
7. Novy to TH, 11 April 1940; Allwood to Novy and Feare, 3 May 1940, HNpap.
8. Allwood to Novy and Feare, 21 May 1940, HNpap.
9. Hughes, Thomas, and Allwood, 'Spy Scare: Bolton', 29 May 1940, W 52/A.
10. JF, 'Spy Stories: Bolton', 1 June 1940, W 52/A.

investigators had no such problems in London, suspected that it was
Allwood's scruffy appearance that lay at the root of the incident, but for
Allwood it simply confirmed that 'Lancashire is full of blue-coated class
enemies.'[11] Early in July, after a blazing row with Harrisson on the phone,
Thomas resigned to take up a local government job in Bolton, though he
stayed on for a time in the Davenport Street house, much to Harrisson's
fury.[12] In August the Bolton unit was closed down. Hughes and his new
wife were relocated, at the MOI's request, to Middlesbrough, where air
raids had begun, thus sustaining for a few more months MO's northern
presence.[13] Allwood left MO shortly afterwards, probably because he was
called up.[14] A rural outpost established in Humphrey Pease's cottage in an
East Suffolk village collapsed after a few months when Richard Picton,
the young man Harrisson had sent to live and observe there, was conscripted.[15] Slightly more long lived was a second 'rural' unit, consisting of
Jack Atkins and his wife outposted to the market town of Worcester from
June to November 1940.[16]

Worcester had been chosen probably because of its proximity to Malvern
and the nearby village of Leigh Sinton, where Harrisson established a
'Western HQ' for MO in a ten-bedroom manor house belonging to a
friend from Cambridge days. Arranged jointly with Adams in the weeks
following Hitler's western offensive, when the prospect of invasion seemed
all too real, the Malvern house was initially intended to serve two purposes.
On the one hand, it would house MO's records and some of its staff in a
location suitably remote from any anticipated blitz or battle front. On the
other hand, in the event of invasion, the house was admirably suited to act
as a bolt-hole for Harrisson and his wife, Biddy, Adams and her four-year-
old daughter, Gandar Dower (an old friend of Harrisson's briefly on the

11. Allwood to Novy and Feare, 14 May and 5 June 1940, HNpap.
12. Thomas, interviewed by Stanley, 26 November 1979, tape in MO Archive; AH, 'Interviews
    with refugees', 17 July 1940, W 52/C.
13. TH to Adams, 5 September 1940, INF 1/262. They sent in regular weekly morale reports from
    Middlesbrough from 24 August to 13 October 1940, TC 66/13/J.
14. His final report, on evacuees in High Wycombe, was written on 11 October 1940, TC
    66/14/C.
15. Reports in TC 66/19/A and B; Pease diary, 29 April and 31 August 1940, Personnel/Pease.
16. TC 66/21/A; 'Worcester', October 1940, FR 475. See also TH to Feare, 12 November 1940,
    HNpap.

MO pay-roll[17]), and two more of Adams' friends, both now working for her in Home Intelligence: Stephen Taylor (of whom more later), and the cartoonist Nicholas Bentley, all with wives and some with children and/or servants. In a post-invasion Britain, Harrisson and Adams seem to have envisaged Leigh Sinton doubling as an ongoing centre for Home Intelligence work as well as a refuge, 'a dream oasis in a dark world.' To this end MO paid half the rent, while the prospective tenants shared the remainder. Later on the MOI underwrote some of the costs and Adams used her influence to prevent the house being requisitioned for evacuees.[18] The 'Western HQ' survived until April 1941, when, with the threat of invasion now remote, the records were moved to Letchworth, where Biddy was now living.[19] Thereafter MO's 'national' presence depended almost entirely on the volunteer panel and flying-squad visits by full-time staff based in London.[20]

II

Harrisson's energy, charisma, and authoritarian style of leadership might make MO appear, after Charles Madge's departure, something of a one-man band. But he could not run the organization without investing significant authority in several other key figures. Already in January 1940, in an attempt to offload some of his day-to-day responsibilities and give himself 'more intellectual privacy, more time to think out what I am doing and M-O is doing', he had taken on a deputy to coordinate the office work and organize the files.[21] Bob Willcock—a 27-year-old Oxford English graduate who had resisted pressure

---

17. In May 1940 Harrisson had recruited Cecil Gandar Dower, a fellow adventurer he had known at Harrow and Cambridge, and a writer of travel books on Africa. But the half-baked scheme they cooked up for using MO materials as a basis for 'humanitarian propaganda' overseas was insufficient to persuade Adams to press for his exemption from conscription, and Gandar Dower was quickly whisked off by the Colonial Office to act as a press representative in Kenya ('Immediate International uses of Mass-Observation', 2 June 1940, FR 225; Adams to Charles, 20 July, 7 August 1940, MApap 1/B; and the entry on Gandar Dower in DNB).
18. TH to Adams, 14 June 1940, TC 74/3/F; Richard Fitter, interviewed by TH, 1 October 1971; 'Henry and Priscilla narrative', Personnel/Macnamara. On Bentley, see DNB entry.
19. MO *Bulletin*, 7 April 1941, FR 678; TH to Gauntlett, 8 April 1941, TC 29/4/C; Heimann, *Most Offending Soul*, 163.
20. Although in April 1941 there were three paid investigators living permanently in the provinces: Miss Harrisson, TH's cousin in Oxford; Mollie Tarrant in Portsmouth; and Priscilla Novy (née Feare) in Winchester (memo on personnel, 21 April 1941, INF 1/286).
21. TH to CM, 25 January 1940, 27–8, Org&Hist 1.

to join his father's successful Midlands building company—had worked with
MO before the war, when he was teaching in a north London private school.[22]
A rare attempt to 'mass observe' the Ladbroke Road house in the summer of
1940 describes Willcock 'giving instructions to observers; answering phone;
dealing with correspondence; preparing directives for next day; filing', leaving
Harrisson free to spend his time 'clearing up messes' and dictating articles and
letters to his new 19-year-old secretary Betty Ward.[23] Priscilla Feare remembered Willcock as 'a bit bumbling', but 'quiet and dependable.'[24] From the
autumn of 1940 he specialized in handling the panel, working initially in the
Malvern house, and then in Letchworth, before returning to Ladbroke Road
in February 1943 to take charge as acting director following Harrisson's conscription. Adams' initial efforts to get Willcock exempted were unsuccessful,
but he was deferred on medical grounds and was able to stay with MO
throughout the war, running things unsupervised during the two years that
Harrisson was out of the country.[25]

The stabilization of MO's finances following the deal with the MOI
enabled Harrisson to expand his management team, and two other lynch-
pins of the office were recruited at this time, both graduates in their late
twenties, and both at various times taking charge of the daily organization
of the team of observers, planning their deployment and issuing instructions. Like Willcock, John Ferraby was exempt from call-up for medical
reasons. Son of a West Country Jewish businessman, he had been educated
at Malvern College and Cambridge, where he read maths and experimental
psychology.[26] This academic background was apparent in his work for MO
from the outset in a methodologically sophisticated report on tribunal hear-
ings for conscientious objectors whose agnostic conclusion provoked a
characteristic scrawl from Harrisson: 'Typical of psychologists, proving after
three days research that NOTHING can be done.'[27] Despite such outbursts

22. Telegram from Willcock to TH, 31 July 1939, TC 70/5/B; Willcock to TH, 23 November
    1940, TC 66/4/C; Willcock, letter to *The Times*, 13 May 1938; correspondence with Ninka
    Willcock, January 2012, Personnel/Willcock. Willcock had been educated at Gresham's School
    in Norfolk where he briefly overlapped with W. H. Auden, playing a sprite to Auden's Caliban
    in a 1925 production of *The Tempest*.
23. Richard Fitter, notebook, nd (August 1940?), Personnel/Fitter.
24. Macnamara (née Feare), interviewed by Calder, 10 January 1980.
25. Adams to Charles, 27 January 1941, MApap 1/C; 410221 Adams to Admiral Godfrey, 21
    February 1941, MApap 2/E; Admiral Godfrey to Major-General Davidson, 19 July 1941, ADM
    223/476.
26. Barron Harper, *Lights of Fortitude*, 1997, 449–50.
27. Ferraby, 'CO Tribunal. Analysis and Suggestions', 22 April 1940, TC 6/1.

Harrisson respected his expertise, and Ferraby put his grasp of statistical method to good use both in digesting fieldworkers' reports and in taking issue with the number-crunching positivism of MO's rivals and critics among the practitioners of market research and opinion polling.[28] Years later he was remembered by one of the staff as the man who 'used to lurk in the basement working out figures and emerge from time to time like a troglodyte, asking Harrisson questions and getting shouted at.'[29] He does not seem to have had a lot in common with the other staff. In 1941 he became a member of the Bahá'í faith, and after the war he worked full-time for the Bahá'í, eventually becoming one of their best known leaders.[30] Richard Fitter, also a businessman's son, was more on Harrisson's wave length—if only, like Pease, as an enthusiastic ornithologist: he is best known as the author of the *Collins Pocket Guide to British Birds,* first published in 1952. After studying economics at the London School of Economics (LSE), he had worked for Political and Economic Planning (PEP) whose director, Max Nicholson, persuaded Harrisson to take him on when PEP had to cut down on staff in July 1940. Harrisson was able to use his Whitehall connections to get Fitter exempted for a couple more years, during which time he wrote up many of MO's reports.[31] Celia Fremlin—daughter of a scientist, with a Classics degree from Oxford, and a member of the Communist Party—had first come to Harrisson's notice when he read a review of her book, *Seven Chars of Chelsea,* a vivid study based on months working in various kinds of domestic service which she had undertaken in search of the 'real' working class who she could not find in communist circles.[32] She had been encouraged to write the book by Cecil Mace, a London University specialist in the study of work incentives and a member of Bartlett's Social Psychology Group.[33] Fremlin was active in the Psychological Society, joining

28. See Chapter 11.
29. Macnamara (née Feare), interviewed by Calder, 10 January 1980.
30. Harper, *Lights of Fortitude,* 449–54; Ferraby, *All Things Made New. A Comprehensive Outline of the Bahá'í Faith,* 1957.
31. Memo on Personnel, 21 April 1941, INF 1/286; Fitter to TH, 21 April 1941, TC 25/12/A; Fitter, interviewed by TH, 1 October 1971; TH to Adams, 17 January 1941, TC 74/3/F; obituary in *Daily Telegraph,* 6 September 2005.
32. Fremlin, interviewed by Stanley, 18 September 1981; Celia Fremlin, *Seven Chars of Chelsea,* 1940, preface. Fremlin's book is discussed in Judy Giles, *The Parlour and the Suburb: Domestic Identities, Class, Femininity and Modernity,* 2004, 81–7. On her Communist Party affiliation see Novy to Allwood, 12 June 1940, HNpap.
33. On Mace see Antony Flew, *The Philosophical Quarterly,* 23, 93, October 1973, 371–2. He had been Oeser's predecessor at St Andrews.

a small group set up in June 1939 to undertake work in social psychology. After the outbreak of war Fremlin and her group collaborated with MO to investigate expectations about air raids, and by January 1940 they were jointly planning work on one of Harrisson's central concerns: the psychology of 'wishful thinking'.[34] At the time of his contract with the MOI, Harrisson listed Fremlin, aged 26, as one of the people 'who help when necessary', and shortly afterwards he took her on full-time.[35] During the London blitz, short of cash for her wages, Harrisson persuaded her to repeat her direct observation of working-class women by getting a job as a waitress (a 'Nippy') in Lyon's Corner House, but she returned to full-time work in November.[36] Alongside Willcock, Ferraby, and Fitter, Fremlin became an important part of the management team that Harrisson relied on as the work expanded during 1940–1.

Other new recruits included an older woman, Doris Hoy (b. 1904), who had previously worked as an interviewer in the commercial world of market research.[37] Nina Masel, by contrast, was an intense and idealistic young Communist who had joined MO's volunteer panel as 'a tiny escape-hole from the dead-end tedium of small-town home and school', and was guiltily delighted when the outbreak of war gave her an excuse to abandon her studies. She started a war diary, but her ambition—much to the distress of her Jewish parents who ran a corner shop—was to 'mix with all those bohemians and writing folk' at MO. So after a few weeks, 'with a self-confidence I now look back on with envy I sent Harrisson an ultimatum: "Either you give me a fulltime job or else I stop writing my diaries." He took me on'; but initially only for temporary work on the poster investigation for the MOI. For a time she found work in an office, but joined the permanent staff, aged 17, in the spring of 1940.[38] Her self-image as 'a slightly foreign looking young woman with a taste for colourful gear' was amply confirmed in a semi-fictionalized account published at the time by a man who

---

34. *War Begins*, 12–13, 128; TH to CM, 27 September 1939, TC 42/1A; TH, 'Possible collecting techniques for wartime', 27 September 1939, TC 43/2/D; TH to CM, 18 and 25 January 1940, Org&Hist 1.
35. 'M-O's Personnel', 7 April 1940, INF 1/262; Novy to Allwood, 12 June 1940, HNpap.
36. Fremlin, interviewed by Stanley, 18 September 1981; Harrisson, *Living Through the Blitz*, 75.
37. Novy to Thomas and Hughes, 13 April 1940; memo on personnel, 21 April 1941, INF 1/286; 'Memorandum on Mass-Observation', 29 October 1942, FR 1450.
38. Novy to Hughes and Thomas, 23 March 1940, HNpap; Masel to Sheridan, 12 May 1984; draft article for *New Statesman*, nd, Personnel/Masel; Masel war diary (5370), September 1939.

witnessed her arrival (by bicycle) in an Essex village, looking for people to interview about evacuees:

> She was dressed in dark blue slacks, a red jumper partially covered by a green corduroy cardigan, red woollen socks, and sandals. She seemed absurdly young. Her complexion was like crushed blackberries; dark alive eyes flickered above the snub nose smeared with bicycle grease. A bandana encased frizzy black hair.[39]

Harrisson had sent her to live in the East End to report on anti-Semitism, and, despite her flamboyant appearance, she turned out to be a highly effective observer and was the author of MO's influential exposé of conditions in air raid shelters at the beginning of the London blitz.[40] Jimmy Stevens, recruited in July 1940, was even younger than Masel. A surviving fragment of his MO diary from February 1940 shows him, aged 16, mixing with intellectual, musical, cultured young people in Mill Hill, while working as an assistant on a bookstall.[41] By July the number of staff had risen to 22, not counting the five people employed by Madge. Reckless as always, Harrisson spent every penny that came in on hiring new staff, keeping nothing in reserve.[42] But this was the peak of MO's numbers, which fell back from the summer as military conscription began to claim the younger men.

III

Back in September 1939 Harrisson had sought to reassure Madge about the putative deal with the MOI on the grounds that John Hilton and Richard Crossman, the men most directly in charge, were sufficiently sympathetic to MO's purposes to leave them 'a quite pleasant margin of liberty'.[43] The same went for Adams, and Harrisson was determined to make good use of this 'margin', and not to allow Whitehall's needs entirely to dominate MO's agenda. Thus he continued to make time to collect detailed descriptions of daily life in London intended purely for the historical record. During the

---

39. Michael Williams, 'It's Nice to Know', *Modern Reading*, 2, 1941, 25, copy in Personnel/Masel.
40. See Chapter 8.
41. Stevens diary (5206), February 1940; TH to Box, February 1940, TC 30/3/A; Stevens to Box, TC 20/3/D.
42. 'General Report for July', July 1940, FR 322; TH to Adams, 2 July 1940, INF 1/262.
43. TH to CM, 20 September 1939, Org&Hist 1.

week that the MOI started producing its morale report, with consequent intensification of its demands on MO's services, he sent seven investigators out with instructions to 'describe, observe, detailedly [sic] report' on 14 different sites, including 'atmosphere in an evening in an ordinary pub in central area'; 'atmosphere and incidents in a typical afternoon in West End store—John Lewis'; 'any typical sporting event this week, full factual description'; 'description of an evening on some allotment in London'; 15 minutes at a bus stop in the rush hour; a Locarno dancehall; and an 'evening strolling along the river at Putney or Fulham.' The brief was to 'describe fully, factually, what *is*...Just as they are. Don't look for any particular war aspects. Describe as if explaining to someone who had never seen it before, e.g. a young American.'[44] One of these observers, Masel, remembered how 'occasionally we were all dispersed to public places—a market, a railway station, an airport—to write detailed descriptions, as if for a Martian'. She was pleased that historians were now (in the 1980s) making use of material she had helped to gather deliberately for their use: 'although', she added, 'I believe we had the twenty-second century in mind at the time.'[45] A similar spirit of laying down data for the historical record was common among the volunteer war diarists.

Apart from such everyday background work Harrisson continued to pursue his work for Rebecca Sieff. Early in April she had been planning a luncheon for 'key people' to launch MO's 'comprehensive report on propaganda', but when MO's mainstream work on opinion formation was taken over by the MOI she was happy to continue funding more focussed research on opinion formation among women; research that was directly relevant to her plans to launch a new feminist journal.[46] Adapting his tone to his audience, Harrisson wrote to Sieff: 'In practically every channel of propaganda and appeal women are inadequately dealt with...Few people realise how much this is still essentially a male society...run by men for men. This is not a conscious process, but it underlies the whole structure of our culture, and comes out in every sort of publicity and propaganda.'[47] Over the summer and autumn, recovering from glandular fever in the peace of Malvern, Feare worked on the women project, frustrated by the gender-blindness of some

44. TH, minute of meeting, 20 May 1940, Org&Hist 4/2.
45. Nina Hibbin, 'I Was a Mass Observer', *New Statesman*, 31 May 1985.
46. Women's Publicity Planning Association, minutes, 5 April, 1 May, and 28 June 1940; TH to Feare, 16 July 1940, HNpap.
47. TH to Sieff, 19 April 1940, TC 32/1/B.

of MO's earlier work, inspired by the richness of the diary material, and spurred on (or perhaps discouraged) by highly critical feedback from Harrisson.[48] She completed the report in December, shortly before resigning as an MO full-timer following her marriage to Novy and his conscription. The Penguin book on 'Women in Wartime' that Harrisson had been planning was never produced, but Fitter reworked Feare's material for an article for the feminist journal *Time and Tide*.[49]

IV

For Harrisson, as for Adams, the overriding concern from the spring of 1940 was with what he later described as 'those amorphous marshlands of the mind which in wartime are dubbed "morale"'.[50] As Paul Addison has pointed out, while Westminster and Whitehall talked obsessively about morale, 'no one knew how to define [it], measure it, or affect it.'[51] This was what Harrisson set out to do: the job of social science in wartime, he asserted in July 1940, was to 'analyse morale into its constituent parts, to foresee the tension points and to suggest solutions.'[52] Ever since the first weeks of the war, he had been pointing to the danger of a sudden breakdown of morale: 'the enormous mass of evidence we have collected', he wrote to Adams in October 1939, 'suggests imminent collapse on the Home Front.'[53]

Ian McLaine, the MOI's historian, writes somewhat scornfully about the Ministry's failure to comprehend popular feeling, dismissing pervasive fears of collapse and defeatism as a product of upper class ignorance of the essential soundness of working-class Britain.[54] While this may accurately describe the mentality of much of the MOI establishment and their political masters, such ignorance can hardly be seen as the source of Harrisson's anxiety. In

48. Feare to TH, 31 July, 4 and 11 August 1940, HNpap.
49. Feare, 'Women and Morale', 10 December 1940, FR 520, reproduced in Sheridan (ed.), *Wartime Women*, 110–22; Fitter, 'Women and the War Effort', 30 December 1940, FR 533; TH to Adams, 9 January 1941, MApap 4f; Feare to TH, 26 November 1940, HNpap.
50. Harrisson, *A World Within*, 163.
51. Paul Addison, *The Road to 1945*, 1977, 44. And, in retrospect, Harrisson agreed: 'those confusions of thinking were, of course, fully shared by this writer and M-O generally' (Harrisson, *Living Through the Blitz*, 360).
52. TH, 'Science, Morale and Propaganda', July 1940, FR 297.
53. TH to Adams, 3 October 1939, MApap 4/f.
54. McLaine, *Ministry of Morale*, 10–11, 95–7, 100–2, 139, 226, 280–1.

June 1940 he was reporting that upper class anxiety following the fall of France was not shared by 'ordinary working people', who 'simply cannot conceive of anything else but outright victory.' What this confidence reflected, however, was neither a sober assessment of the situation, nor a defiant Churchillian martial vigour, but mere 'wishful thinking': the 'mental resistance of the mass of the people to the dangerous realities of war' that had been a keynote of MO's findings ever since Munich. Rooted in psychological mechanisms of avoidance, and encouraged by a newspaper press whose advertising backers had a vested interest in encouraging people to spend money by fostering optimism about the future,[55] popular complacency was revealed by the widespread failure to take elementary domestic air raid precautions or to carry gas masks. But the real danger was the lack of psychological preparation. Every crisis served to reinforce popular scepticism about the veracity of what they read in the papers or heard on the BBC, and the efforts of the Ministry of Information to inform and instruct the population, when they were not (as in the initial poster campaign) simply inept, were systematically undermined by ferocious opposition to the Ministry's operations from much of the press. With the channels of public discourse so corrupted, it would be difficult for even a democratically minded leadership—let alone the class-ridden structures of the British polity—to establish the kind of rapport with the masses that would be needed to persuade them to face up to the realities of war and hold steady in an emergency.

When events appeared to shatter the foundations of popular wishful thinking, there was nothing for the 'bewildered masses' to fall back on. At such moments—in September 1939 (before it became clear that the war was, for the time being, 'phoney'); in May 1940 (before Churchill's assumption of power 'restored complacency' following the shock of failure in Norway); or in June following the collapse of France—the sudden exposure to reality threatened a collapse into hopelessness, defeatism, and the kind of fatalism apparently widespread among those women who secretly admired Hitler as a 'mystical astrological figure' endowed with unstoppable force.[56]

The explosion Harrisson feared was not the spectre of revolution haunting some Whitehall offices, but the kind of panic, disintegration, and chaos

55. A point strongly made in 'Poverty of Freedom', Ch. XI. See also Alan Hodge, 'Control of the Press', May 1940, 15–17, FR 126.
56. TH, 'General Points on Morale', 22 June 1940, FR 222.

triggered in France by the advance of Hitler's armies. What would happen in Britain when the invasion came? His response to Dunkirk was not to endorse the myth-making sentimentality of heroic little paddle steamers sailing to the rescue—according to MO's researches, many listeners to J. B. Priestley's famous 'Postcript' of 5 June found it 'too romantic' or 'too unreal'[57]—but to send his fieldworkers to conduct extensive interviews with French and Channel Island civilian refugees who had made it to England in an attempt to learn lessons from a disaster that might soon be repeated in Britain. He concluded optimistically (and in flat contradiction to what he was being told by at least some of his investigators):

> Many of these people would have stayed and fought if they had been given clear and firm leadership…If they had had some task that they believed was worthwhile doing, any task that implied discipline…then it is possible that eight million of them would not have cluttered up the roads and lost the war for France.[58]

This work on morale brought Harrisson as close to the centre of power as he was ever to come. In April Adams had set up a committee of outside experts to advise Home Intelligence on its methods and conclusions, and provide some public authentication of its work. Headed by Julian Huxley, the group included Crossman, Tom Hopkinson (the editor of *Picture Post*)—all long-standing friends of MO—together with Francis Williams (ex-editor of the *Daily Herald*) and the leading psychologist, Edward Glover.[59] Though not formally a member, Harrisson attended most of the meetings, was part of a deputation to the Minister after which he drafted a follow-up memorandum[60] calling for 'bold leadership and a forceful, imaginative use of propaganda.' On 12 June a memorandum—allegedly written by five (unnamed) men 'with a wide experience in newspaper and magazine work (editing and owning them), in advertising and publicity', but, judging by its language and the annotations on the copy in the MO Archive, actually drafted by Harrisson—expressed alarm at the state of the government's relationship with the civilian population:

57. 'Morale Today', 6 June 1940, FR 173.
58. 'Immediate International uses of Mass-Observation', 2 June 1940, FR 225; 'Refugees', 30 June 1940, FR 238; 'Refugees', 11 July 1940, FR 262; Hughes to Gandar Dower, 18 July 1940, W 52/C. And see Hughes' interviews with Channel Island refugees in the same file.
59. McLaine, *Ministry of Morale*, 85; Harrisson, *Living Through the Blitz*, 286; Adams to Clarke, 29 June 1940, MApap 1/B.
60. 'Notes on Present Morale Situation', 3 June 1940, FR 165.

A government which may require citizens of one town to sit quiet and not leave their houses while enemy tanks rumble through the streets—the citizens of another to take to the woods—of another to wait their turn and be gradually evacuated over two days—must have real control, over its people. It must know that its orders will be carried out and that people must be in the habit of acting on the Government's advice.... There are many disturbing signs...which go to show that the Government at the present time has no such grip on the reins of the Home Front...

What was needed was a coherent and coordinated policy on home-front morale cast in 'the language of leadership':

Since the war entered its more serious phase, the ordinary democratic citizen has been longing and asking for stronger Government leadership and instruction...the general public [is] amazingly receptive to sensible, coherent, patriotic instruction.

Giving everybody clearly defined tasks, explicitly related to the needs of the overall war effort, was the key to preventing a sudden collapse of morale in the face of blitz or invasion.[61] The degree to which Harrisson, at this moment of crisis, had come to see firm leadership as the key to national survival was apparent in a letter published in *Picture Post* in which he attacked those calling for Chamberlain's dismissal from the government on the grounds that 'one of the biggest factors in the tremendous mess we find ourselves in today, is the habit of Prime Ministers to bow to superficial public opinion. Now Mr Churchill is a man of tougher stuff, and if he has made up his mind to have Chamberlain in the Cabinet, that ought to be good enough for us.'[62]

It is not possible to establish how much influence Adams' morale committee had on Duff Cooper (brought in by Churchill in May 1940 to replaced Lord Reith as Minister of Information), but by early June the Ministry's high-level Home Morale Emergency Committee was also reporting that 'what the public now desired was not so much exhortation as guidance, not so much words of comfort as words of command', and warning that in the absence of coordinated propaganda on positive war aims significant sections of the public might be dangerously susceptible to any peace

61. 'A New Attitude to the Problems of Civilian Morale', 12 June 1940, FR 193. Next day TH told Clem Leslie that the memorandum was being considered by the Minister (TH to Leslie, 13 June 1940, FR 197).
62. *Picture Post*, 12 July 1940. For Madge this seemed to provide conclusive evidence that Harrisson was 'going down the drain' (CM to Inez, 15 July 1940, CMpap 8/3).

offensive that Hitler might launch.[63] By the end of the month Cooper had been persuaded to take a paper urging these arguments to his Cabinet colleagues: 'People want to be ordered about, to have sacrifices imposed on them, to be provided with occupation obviously related to national defence...unless the demand for compulsion is met, the public will feel that the Government lacks energy and efficiency.' But Churchill was not prepared to face down Whitehall resistance to the subordination of departmental work to a centralized propaganda-driven home-front strategy, and Duff Cooper's intervention fell on deaf ears.[64]

V

Although she remained convinced of the value of MO's approach, rejecting descriptions of its work as 'misleading' or 'amateurish' as products of the 'professional jealousies' rife in the world of opinion research,[65] Adams had always intended to supplement and check MO's suggestive, qualitative findings with quantitative investigation based on statistically reliable random samples. A week before she concluded the £100-a-week deal with Harrisson in April, she had been given the green light to investigate ways of spending far greater sums of money (£40,000 a year) on a programme of continuous investigations on a statistical basis to provide a 'barometer of public opinion'.[66] At first she had thought of using one of the commercial firms for this purpose, probably Mark Abram's London Press Exchange, but by early May she had settled on the academics at LSE, led by the Professor of Commerce, Arnold Plant, as best suited to developing the project, and it was agreed, to lend still further academic weight, that the new organization, Wartime Social Survey (WSS), would run under the auspices of the National Institute of

63. 'Report of the Home Morale Emergency Committee', 4 June INF 1/250; 'Report of Planning Committee on a Home Morale Campaign', 24 June 1940, INF 1/250.
64. PRO1-14, 'Draft covering note by Minister', 24 June 1940, INF 1/250; Harrisson, *Living Through the Blitz*, 285–6.
65. Adams to Nicholson, 24 June 1940, MApap 1/B.
66. OEPEC Paper 374, 12 June 1940, INF 1/286. Adams probably picked up the term 'war barometer' from MO, though what MO usually meant by it was the News Quota, not the large-scale interviewing that Adams intended. In March TH made the distinction, telling Adams that what he could offer was 'a thermometer to morale rather than a barometer' (TH to Adams 26 March 1940 INF 1/262). Terminological confusion arose from the 1970s when TH repossessed the term in *Living Through the Blitz* (281) to describe MO's News Quota results.

Economic and Social Research (NIESR).[67] The initial contract was issued on 13 May for surveys on food and air raid precautions, and fieldwork on the former started a week later. By the end of the month Adams had persuaded the Ministry's Policy Committee to agree that WSS should also conduct 2,500 interviews a week to monitor public morale.[68] Nothing, however, appears to have been done about this, and the large sums of money authorized for such work were never spent.[69]

None of these plans was any threat to MO, which had never aspired to do quantitative work on this scale. Nevertheless a threat was emerging, and one which would eventually put paid to MO's work for the MOI. Harrisson was not the only bright young man whose ideas about researching popular opinion had impressed Adams. In May 1940 Stephen Taylor, another of her protégés, started work in Home Intelligence. Harrisson and Taylor, born in the same year, had both first come into contact with Adams in 1933 when she was in charge of talks at the BBC and they were ambitious 22-year-olds anxious to make their voices heard on radio. In the later 1930s they probably met at Adams' Regents Park flat, where Taylor often felt out of place among the left-wing intelligentsia with whom Adams and her maverick Tory husband surrounded themselves—though he got on well with Crossman. Taylor had trained as a doctor and practised as a psychiatrist, but his interests were as much in journalism and social reform as in medicine. In 1938 he published an influential article in *The Lancet* on 'The Suburban Neurosis', dealing with the psychosomatic symptoms affecting the bored and isolated housewives that he met in his practice in suburban London.[70] He was active in PEP before the war, formulating ideas for the creation of a national health service. During the first half of 1939 he worked as assistant editor of *The Lancet*, and Adams (now in television) had him lined up for a job as a BBC producer. The war killed the infant TV service, and Taylor joined up as a naval neuro-psychiatrist working in a mental hospital.[71] When Adams joined the MOI at the end of the year she was immediately in touch with

67. Adams to Macadam, 8 March 1940, INF 1/262; Brown, 'statistical surveys', 2 May 1940; Adams, 'Statistical Surveys During the Crisis', 4 May 1940; Home Intelligence, 'Statistical Surveys', 4 May 1940, INF 1/263; OEPEC Paper 374, 12 June 1940, INF 1/286.
68. Waterfield to LSE, 13 May 1940, MApap 2/E; Macadam to Welch, 7 June 1940, MApap 1/B.
69. According to OEPEC Paper 530, 9 October 1940 (INF 1/286) the actual spending on WSS was as follows: May £247; June £1,003; July £1,460; August £1,545; September £990.
70. Stephen Taylor, 'The Suburban Neurosis', *The Lancet*, 26 March 1938.
71. Taylor, *A Natural History of Everyday Life*, 146–9, 256, 259–60, 264–5; Adams to Waterfield, 9 March 1940, MApap 1/B.

him, seeking comments on her initial ideas and advice on how to establish 'a service of medical reports on the physical and mental health of the community'. Encouraged by his considered, sympathetic, and lengthy responses, she quickly decided to recruit him, but it took months of lobbying to wear down Admiralty resistance to his transfer.[72]

Taylor fully shared Adams' belief in the need for qualitative research, but he was irritated by MO's habit (apparent in *War Begins*) of giving percentage results without stating the number of observations, and he was less impressed than Adams by Harrisson's intuitive genius, more by his 'facility for interpreting the results with greater enthusiasm than accuracy.'[73] In his memoirs, Taylor was condescending about Adams—'a sweet, energetic, liberal minded but muddled lady'—and dismissed Harrisson as a charlatan whose reports fed alarm and despondency about morale, describing this as 'the conventional attitude . . . of the intellectual left at that time.'[74] Within weeks of his appointment he was advising Adams that MO's reports were 'tendentious, and completely at variance with the unimaginative but accurate reports of chief constables to the Home Office and of postal censorship'.[75] Although he records that she 'found it impossible to believe this', it may have been Taylor's pressure that prompted Adams in mid-June to press for the extension of the WSS brief from quantitative to qualitative work on morale:

> After the most detailed analysis I have come to the conclusion that the market research methods employed by the Survey are too slow for the present tempo of events and I would propose that new investigators be appointed who, while carrying out house to house enquiries on a statistical basis, should make their observations and reports of a much higher qualitative value.[76]

Plant, who was interested in nothing but figures, resigned over this (and the NIESR subsequently withdrew its sponsorship), but Adams got her way and, with help from Sibyl Clement Brown—part author of the Cambridge Evacuation Survey and a leading figure in the introduction of US-inspired psychiatric social work in Britain—ten social psychologists were recruited

72. Taylor to Adams, 12 and 19 January,? February,? March 1940; Adams to Taylor, 18 January, MApap 2/A Adams to Taylor, 18 and 25 April 1940, MApap 2/E; Adams to Woodburn, 18 April 1940, Adams to Macadam, 11 May 1940, MApap 1/B; Taylor, *Natural History of Everyday Life*, 260–1.
73. Taylor to Adams, 11 February 1940; Taylor to Adams, nd, Sunday, MApap 2/A.
74. Taylor, *Natural History of Everyday Life*, 259–60, 261.
75. Taylor, *Natural History of Everyday Life*, 261.
76. Adams to Macadam, 29 June 1940, MApap 1/B.

by WSS to carry out fieldwork designed to probe 'the more fundamental attitudes behind the purely verbal' questionnaire responses.[77] By September the Survey had a 'Team B' tasked to investigate rumours, evacuation, attitude to shelters, class feeling, attitudes to the news media, and 'peace petitions (are there any?)'.[78] This clearly was MO terrain, and Adams was explicit in spelling out that Team B's role in an emergency would 'be similar to that of Mass-Observation... investigating hearsay evidence of deteriorating morale at first hand'.[79] While Adams wanted the WSS to duplicate Harrisson's work, and thus act as a check upon its accuracy, she saw this new departure as complimentary to MO rather than as a replacement for it.[80]

Towards the end of July 1940, press hostility to the MOI boiled over in a concerted attack on the work of the WSS, whose fieldworkers were lambasted as 'Cooper's Snoopers', mischievously doorstepping busy housewives with intrusive questioning, and posing a totalitarian threat to privacy, freedom of opinion, and democracy. Started by the left, the attack was quickly taken up by the right-wing press, diehard Tories, and members of the MOI's own local information committees who had always seen Home Intelligence as an impertinent encroachment on their own terrain.[81] Adams had been warning from the start that by making a secret of its intelligence activities the Ministry made them appear sinister, inviting scandal and exposure.[82] Eventually Cooper was forced to defend the WSS in a full scale parliamentary debate, which he did successfully, convincing most MPs and

---

77. Adams, memo on WSS, 16 September 1940, INF 1/101; Sibyl Clement Brown, 'Looking Backwards: Reminiscences, 1922–1946', *British Journal of Psychiatric Social Work*, 10, 4, 1970, 161–9; 'The Work of HI Division', INF 1/290.
78. The team was led by E. J. Lindgren, an American social anthropologist from Cambridge, who before the war had been a member of Bartlett's social psychology group (Alan Costall, 'Pear and his peers', in Bunn et al (eds), *Psychology in Britain: historical essays and personal reflections*, 2001; Bartlett, et al, *The study of society; methods and problems*, 1939).
79. Adams, memo on M-O and WSS, 12 September 1940, INF 1/262.
80. The competitive relationship between M-O and WSS was sharpened by personal antagonism between Harrisson and Lindgren whose work had been ridiculed by Harrisson and Madge in *Britain* (230–1). She took her revenge in 1940 by attacking Harrisson's work on the blitz (TH, 'Report from Social Survey', 14 October 1940, FR 455; 'Comparison', 15 October 1940, FR 456).
81. McLaine, *Ministry of Morale*, 84–6; Laura Dumond Beers, 'Whose Opinion?: Changing Attitudes Towards Opinion Polling in British politics, 1937–1964', *Twentieth Century British History*, 17, 2, 2006, 188–90; Adams, memo on WSS, 16 September 1940, INF 1/101; ASG, *An Appeal to Reason. Social Surveys Surveyed*, 1940 (copy in Org&Hist 1/2).
82. 'Only ten days ago I begged the Minister, in answering Acland's question in the House, to say that our methods were not secret and to give a brief resume of our machinery. But deaf ears were turned.... We have been having a horrid time' (Adams to Deedes, 29 July 1940, INF 1/697 cited in McLaine, *Ministry of Morale*, 86). See also McLaine, *Ministry of Morale*, 51.

the more intelligent sections of the press that it made sense for the government to use 'an established method of social research...to find out what
ordinary people are thinking about current events.'[83]

A surprising feature of these events was how little attention was paid to
MO. Quizzed about the Ministry's use of MO, Cooper replied: 'We have
once or twice applied to it for statistical information on certain subjects on
which it has been able to furnish information which it was not worthwhile
setting up a special inquiry to obtain.'[84] Press hostility was focussed on the
WSS and no one questioned this bare-faced lie.[85] Writing to Madge the day
after the parliamentary debate, Harrisson claimed 'that with infinite suffering and nights without sleep, I have managed to steer the row right off MO.
Indeed we have even come out of it with some credit.'[86] Well briefed by
Harrisson, several MPs mentioned MO 'in a nice way', including Richard
Acland who drew a sharp line—over-generous in the circumstances—
between the WSS, whose findings provided the state with a secret weapon
for the manipulation of public opinion, and the MO, who published its
results for all to see.[87]

The 'Cooper's Snoopers' agitation had worrying implications not only
for the WSS but for market research as a whole, particularly if continued
press agitation created resistance among the public at large to doorstep
interviewing. On 2 August Harrisson was invited to address a regular luncheon hosted by the Advertising Service Guild (ASG), a group of advertising
agencies 'violently dissatisfied with behaviour of the Press' who felt that
advertisers and government should make common cause to force the press—
heavily dependent on them for revenue—to desist.[88] MO's own findings
were reassuring. As Harrisson delighted in pointing out, despite intensive

83. *Economist*, 3 August 1940; see also *The Manchester Guardian*, 1 August 1940: 'this method of
    substituting research into public opinion, instead of depending on the "hunches" of individu-
    als or cliques, for the information on which policy should be formed is in itself laudable.'
    Similar testimonials appeared in the *Evening Standard* and *Picture Post*, the latter written by TH.
    'Report on the "Coopers Snoopers" press campaign', 5 August 1940, FR 325; Beers, 'Whose
    Opinion?'.
84. 'Report on the "Coopers Snoopers" press campaign', 5 August 1940, FR 325.
85. TH later sought to excuse Cooper by suggesting that he was probably unaware of the extent
    of M-O's involvement with the MOI at the time (Richard Fitter, interviewed by TH, 1
    October 1971). This is improbable. Tom Harrisson was in close contact with Cooper: indeed
    he later recalled that after the debate he travelled back to the MOI with Cooper (TH, Sixth
    Report on the M-O Archive, 1970, 12–13, MOA 29/2/2/4).
86. TH to CM, 2 August 1940, MO&MOI 1.
87. Hansard, 363, 1535, 1541.
88. *Advertiser's Weekly*, 1 August 1940; TH to Adams, 2 August 1940, MO&MOI 1.

efforts throughout the 'Cooper's Snoopers' agitation, no journalist was able even to locate anyone who had been interviewed by a WSS fieldworker, let alone find evidence that people objected to such interviews.[89] Nevertheless, the assembled advertisers asked their secretary to 'draft and have printed a statement on market research and doorstep methods.' In the event it seems to have been Harrisson himself, not the ASG secretary, who wrote the resulting 16-page pamphlet—*An Appeal to Reason. Social Surveys Surveyed*— which analysed the press campaign, outlined the history of market research, and argued that only professionals using scientific techniques could reliably assess public opinion. Delighted to be at the centre of things, Harrisson wrote to Adams of the Guild's 'keen desire to keep up this unorthodox contact with outside sources, through me. It asked me to come again to their next meeting next Friday, and they warmly welcomed my suggestions that I should bring you.'[90] Taylor, when he read the pamphlet, wrote to Harrisson: 'You really are a proteus. I never know what you are going to appear as next! Congratulations on being the ASG. It really is a jolly good bit of work, though I must say if I'd looked at it more carefully I think I ought to have spotted its authorship'.[91] Perhaps, at this point, Taylor really did admire Harrisson's 'protean' energies, or perhaps he was just being polite to his boss's other protégé. In either case, in the longer term he remained MO's most dangerous enemy. But, as we shall see, in the ASG, Harrisson had found a source of support that would allow MO to survive the eventual loss of its contract with the MOI. In the end the advertisers turned out to be far more congenial paymasters than the state.

VI

As the fuss over 'Cooper's Snoopers' died down Harrisson made time to write an article for *The Political Quarterly* in which he pulled together the work MO had done on opinion formation since the outbreak of war.[92]

89. 'Press Campaign Against Duff Cooper', 8 August 1940, FR 333.
90. TH to Adams, 2 August 1940, MO&MOI 1.
91. Taylor to TH, 9 August 1940, MO&MOI 1.
92. TH, 'What is Public Opinion?', *The Political Quarterly*, August 1940. FR 361 contains various drafts of this article. Unless otherwise indicated the quotations to follow are from the published version. This article, Harrisson wrote later, was 'largely stimulated by the questions raised in the Coopers Snoopers attacks' (TH, Third Report the MOA, 1970, 33, MOA 29/2/2/4).

'What is Public Opinion?' presented his conclusions about a question that had been at the centre of MO's concerns since its foundation: the role of the press in the formation of popular attitudes. Many of the issues that Madge had attempted to address with his theory of the three social areas were reformulated by Harrisson in a dynamic model of the way in which 'public' opinion (what people will say to a stranger) was determined by the inter-play between 'private' opinion and 'published' opinion (for these purposes understood as what the newspapers, more or less dishonestly, declared pub-lic opinion to be). Two insights about the nature of popular attitudes were fundamental to this analysis. The first, hardly controversial, was that most people harbour a range of half-formulated, often self-contradictory beliefs and opinions. The second was that, because of a profound need to conform to the norms of the group, they were reluctant to reveal opinions they believed to be unconventional to anyone outside their most intimate circle. Acknowledging that 'readers of the *Political Quarterly* will not always recog-nise their own behaviour here'—since education prized the free play of opinion—Harrisson insisted that the Worktown evidence left no room for doubt about the 'overwhelming importance of the done thing' among the mass of the population who had left school at 14. Shifts in public opinion (as measured, for example, by the 'stranger interviews' conducted by opin-ion pollsters) occurred when the press gave legitimacy to views which, while they may well have previously existed widely in private opinion, remained invisible since those who held such views believed them to be unconventional and therefore unrespectable. Unless and until the press gave 'social sanction' to such views they remained unexpressed: 'public opinion is only a part of private opinion and only that part which, so to speak, dare show itself at any moment.'[93] This was the pattern that MO had described during the Munich crisis, and Harrisson had seized on the sudden swing of public attitudes against Chamberlain following the Norway disaster in May 1940 as an opportunity to confirm that analysis, urging his staff 'to get to the roots' of the process of opinion formation 'its mechanism and theory side.'[94] Opinion polls showed majority support for Chamberlain until the very last moment, but the subsequent swing, he argued, could only be explained by the fact that many people had harboured private doubts which they would

93. TH, 'What is Public Opinion?', 374.
94. TH to Willcock, Novy and Hodge, 13 May 1940, Org&Hist 4/4.

not express in a stranger interview. MO, however, had been able to pick up this undercurrent of hostile feeling by observing the reaction of cinema audiences to newsreels (because, so the argument ran, the darkened cinema provided an anonymous space within which people could express their private opinions in public). The upsurge of anti-alien feeling in the summer of 1940 provided another example, in which widely held xenophobic views, previously hidden because believed to be unrespectable, were suddenly given legitimacy by a press campaign.

While the power of the press was substantial, it was not without limits, as the lack of public response to the 'Cooper's Snoopers' campaign had just demonstrated. The processes of social sanctioning only worked to the extent that there were latent currents of feeling down in private opinion waiting, as it were, to be released into public opinion. That had been MO's argument about the spread of the Lambeth Walk in 1938, and Harrisson cited press campaigns against rationing in the winter of 1939–40, or for retributive bombing of German cities after the first air raids in the summer of 1940, as examples of attempts to shift public opinion which failed to connect with any genuine current of feeling in private opinion. It was also possible for opinions germinating in private to force their way into the public sphere despite a press blackout, as had occurred in the aftermath of Munich; but in 1940 Harrisson was less inclined than he and Madge had been two years earlier to celebrate this as evidence of popular self-assertion. The moral to be drawn was that wise democratic leaders should give no credence to newspaper claims to represent public opinion (at least not until the press itself took genuine steps to discover what that opinion actually was) but should try to find out as much as possible about private opinion so that they could sanction and encourage those parts of it that were constructive and discourage those parts that were not. Implicit in this argument was the claim that the methods of MO could provide such leaders not only with reliable information about current public opinion, but also with knowledge about that 'private opinion of September' from which 'comes the public opinion of October…The deeper question for democracy and far seeing leadership,' Harrisson concluded, 'and one needing a regular, accurate, objective answer: "What is Private Opinion?"' [95]

95. TH, 'What is Public Opinion?', 373, 382.

Harrisson's model of opinion formation rested on a substantial body of empirical work, but in his concern to establish the uniqueness and indispensability of MO to the functioning of an enlightened democracy, he pushed the argument beyond anything that the evidence could sustain. Harrisson was careful to define 'private' opinion narrowly: 'It is at the level of wife, self and dream that the most significant... assessment of opinion can be made.'[96] Views expressed in conversation with friends and acquaintances—i.e. in the kinds of situations where MO techniques of the 'overheard' and the 'indirect interview' could be deployed—were likely to be subject to self-censorship in much the same way, Harrisson suggested, as views expressed in interviews with strangers: 'A man's public conversation is confined in the same sort of conventional boundaries as his bowler hat or the rigid routine of standing rounds when drinking beer with his friends.'[97] It was only in its relationship with the panel that MO could claim (with considerable justification) to have access to private opinion. However, as MO was usually careful to acknowledge when using this material, the panel could not be seen as representative of the 75 per cent of the population who left school before they were 15, the 'masses' whose processes of opinion formation Harrisson's model set out to illuminate. The only members of these 'masses' who participated in the predominantly middle-class panel were, more or less by definition, exceptionally articulate individuals many of whom prided themselves precisely on their ability to hold unconventional opinions. However sensitive a tool MO might provide for understanding the complexities of public opinion, it was no more equipped than anyone else to provide a 'regular, accurate, objective' picture of the 'private opinions.... prides and prejudices, personal antagonisms and loyalties' which ordinary working-class people expressed freely only to themselves, their wives or in their dreams. In claiming that MO was 'in touch with the masses at the level of wife and dream', Harrisson was allowing the logic of his model to obscure the limits of his method.[98] That he was well aware of the

96. TH, 'What is Public Opinion?', 368.
97. TH, 'What is Public Opinion?', 370. Moreover, as TH pointed out, 'wartime's compulsive loyalty' tended to reinforce such conventional boundaries, making defeatist views something 'that may only be whispered to wife or self' (TH, *Living Through the Blitz*, 331). See also 'Morale in 1941', 15 February 1941, FR 568.
98. TH, draft for 'What is Public Opinion?', FR 361, 3, 10. The implication that private opinion was an exclusively male affair was an unintended consequence of conventional sexist language. Harrisson was as interested in discovering the private opinions of women as he was of men.

fragility of his claims to access 'private opinion' among the masses is apparent in later formulations in which he widened the category of 'private' to
include overheard conversations. Thus by the autumn of 1941 he was defining private opinion as 'what people say *to each other* and to their wives and
themselves, rather than what they say to the interviewer, the stranger'.[99]
Bidding for an MOI contract at this time he claimed that MO could access
people's 'private hopes and fears' about the post-war world by methods of
direct and indirect interviewing.[100] MO's eventual book on reconstruction,
which referred to the 'fears, desires and hopes, long mediated and talked
over in the privacy of home and pub',[101] led one sympathetic reviewer to
summarize the distinction between public and private opinion as the difference between the products of direct interviewing and 'statements made
either amidst a circle of friends or in the more complete privacy of the
diary'.[102] It was of course perfectly legitimate to conceptualize opinion in
this way, on a sliding scale from public to private. But that was to put to one
side Harrisson's initial insight about the conventional nature of the views
expressed even in conversation among friends.

VII

Towards the end of August 1940, a new director general at the Ministry,
Frank Pick, called into question both WSS and MO. Under pressure to
economize to appease the press, and surrounded by civil servants who saw
the WSS as left wing and 'dangerous', Pick sacked half the WSS staff and put
pressure on Harrisson to fill the resulting gap, which would have involved
doing 'the sort of work which M-O is not prepared to undertake'—
presumably the kind of quantified national random samples that WSS had
been set up to conduct.[103]

Adams mounted a vigorous defence of the WSS, arguing that, if they
were abandoned, Cooper's earlier statements to Parliament would be made
to look foolish; that there would be an outcry from those sections of the

---

99. TH, draft letter to *New Statesman*, 5 September 1941, Org&Hist 3/1, my emphasis, JH.
100. 'M-O work on Reconstruction', nd (October 1941?), TC 2/2/D.
101. *Journey Home*, 101.
102. Elwyn Jones review of *Journey Home*, *Leisure*, 20 October 1944, M-O Press Cuttings.
103. McLaine, *Ministry of Morale*, 87–8; 'Minutes of London Meeting', 18 September 1940, HNpap;
     Adams to Pick, 5 October 1940, MApap 1/A.

press that supported them; that Home Intelligence would be forced to rely on hearsay evidence; and that the 'other Ministries which have relied upon Home Intelligence for Market Research work and other public investigations will be forced to use commercial organisations, at a considerably greater cost to the Government.'[104] At the same time she proposed reconstructing WSS under the leadership of 'a man of some independent scientific status' with an interest in qualitative work. Her first suggestion was the psychologist Edward Glover and, when he wouldn't play, the professor of social science at Liverpool, Tom Simey. Once there was a new director the services of MO, with its 'special qualifications (both in personnel and methods) for undertaking ad hoc investigations', and its corps of experienced male investigators (which the WSS, staffed by female social psychologists, did not possess), should be brought 'within the framework of the survey'.[105] In reality it was the speed and effectiveness of MO's response to crises, not the gender of its staff, that recommended it. Citing an MO report on unofficial evacuation from the East End—which contradicted press reports that people were cheerfully staying put despite the bombing—Adams claimed that this had enabled the authorities to put in place an organized scheme ahead of recognition of the problem in the press. This was a classic case, as she explained, echoing Harrisson's *Political Quarterly* article, of the discrepancy between published opinion and true public opinion: 'In emergency, M-O is the most valuable piece of machinery Home Intelligence possesses.'[106]

Pick took her point and it was agreed to proceed with WSS and MO 'co-ordinated under one Director'.[107] On 17 September—the day on which Adams recommended Glover for the job—Pick offered Harrisson the directorship of a combined WSS/MO. Harrisson, according to the account he gave the next day to MO's staff, turned the offer down on the grounds that 'he was only interested in M-O'.[108] I have found no independent evidence that this surprising offer was ever made, and we may suspect

104. 'Home Intelligence: M-O and WSS', 12 September 1940, INF 1/262.
105. Memo on WSS, 17 September 1940; Adams to Pick, 23 September 1940, INF 1/101; Adams to Simey, 15 November 1940, 5 January 1941, MApap 2/E; Adams to Macadam, 3 January 1941, MApap 1/C.
106. 'Home Intelligence: M-O and WSS', 12 September 1940, INF 1/262; 'Evacuation and other East End Problems', 10 September 1940, FR 392; Masel, 'Stepney. Evacuation', 9 September 1940, TC 5/2/G; 400000 PRO1-43 'The Work of HI Division', 4, INF 1/290.
107. OEPEC Paper 530, 9 October 1940, INF 1/286.
108. 'Minutes of London Meeting', 18 September 1940, HNpap.

Harrisson of over-egging whatever had been said in his conversation with Pick.[109] But the meeting left him convinced that he was now very well placed to insist on a speedy decision on MO's future position.[110] Early in October MO's contract was renewed for a further six months, a significant advance on its previous three-month contracts.[111] Spending on WSS, by contrast, had been cut back and its staff reduced from 60 to 20, and Pick insisted that in future it should concentrate on 'purely factual studies' and surveys for other ministries.[112] Despite this ruling, Adams did her best to use the WSS staff to do qualitative work on morale, but her efforts were undermined by the inability of the WSS staff themselves to respond to crisis situations with anything approaching MO's speed and efficiency,[113] and by the absence of any suitable candidate prepared to take on the role of director and knock them into shape.[114] It was MO not WSS that provided Home Intelligence with the information it needed to keep abreast of public reactions during the months of blitzing that followed.

By cutting the WSS down to size, Pick had protected MO. But, as we shall see, Taylor was busy developing a quite different alternative to the Ministry's dependence on MO, one which was to enable him—when he eventually took over from Adams in the spring of 1941—pretty much to dispense with Harrisson's services. At that point it was Harrisson's friendship with the radical advertising men of the ASG that was to keep MO afloat.

109. A year later, however, there was talk within the Ministry of offering Harrisson a senior post in the reorganised WSS: 'Apparently the new proposals regarding Intelligence work do not provide for more that the occasional use of MO. Increased use will, however, be made of WSS and more staff will be necessary. If the new proposals are approved and Mr Harrisson is offered one of the wartime posts, the question of seeking further deferment of military service will arise' (memo from ?? (indicipherable) to Welch, 1 September 1941, INF 1/286).
110. 'Minutes of London Meeting', 18 September 1940, HNpap.
111. After Pick left the MOI Harrisson was fulsome in his appreciation of the former Director's support, and continued to seek his 'advice and criticism' (TH to Pick, 16 January 1941, Frank Pick collection, London Transport Museum, PF 18 125).
112. McLaine, Ministry of Morale, 87; Memo on WSS, 1 March 1941, INF 1/101; Adams to Macadam, 3 January 1941, MApap 1/C; 'Report on the "Coopers Snoopers" press campaign', 5 August 1940, FR 325.
113. Adams to Edkins, 7 December 1941; Adams to Clement Brown, 4 January 1941; Adams to Frederick Brown, 8 February 1941; Adams to Silvey, 7 March 1941, MApap 2/E. Dennis Chapman, one of the first people to be appointed to WSS when it was reorganized by Louis Moss in May, alleged that in 1941 the social psychologists had seen WSS as 'simply a means of providing them with a salary while they went on doing their academic work' (Chapman, interviewed by Stanley, 23 February 1979; Louis Moss, The Government Social Survey: a history, 1991, 5).
114. No Director had been found when Mary Adams resigned, and it was not until May 1941 that her successor appointed Louis Moss—a quantifier—as head of WSS.

8

Blitztown

In the case of air raids observers will not be expected to stand about... it will be entirely satisfactory if observers take shelter, so long as they are able to take shelter with *other people*. Preferably *with a lot of other people*... air raids are a unique opportunity for M-O to observe the underlying levels of behaviour... we ought to get something of first-class importance and permanent interest to social and psychological theory as well.

(Tom Harrisson, to all observers, 24 May 1940)

I

As always Tom Harrisson's instructions to his staff—this example sent out two weeks after the invasion of Holland in May 1940—sought to balance the immediate value of their work as a way of monitoring civilian morale with his longer term ambitions for Mass-Observation (MO). Anticipating chaos, the memorandum continued with detailed contingency plans for staff deployment 'in the case of more drastic developments, e.g. sudden invasion, dislocation through parachutes, internal revolution, or what have you.' Harrisson would move to the Western HQ, announced here for the first time, with several of the staff, leaving Bob Willcock in charge in London.[1] In September Harrisson circulated detailed plans, based on individual discussion with each member of staff. Those allocated to London were to stay there whatever happened, except for Nina Masel who would leave before the Germans arrived, travelling on her bike with other refugees, and seek to make contact with Doris Hoy (relocated in Oxford) or the Western HQ. Alec Hughes and his wife should stay put in

---

1. TH to all observers, 24 May 1940, HNpap.

Middlesbrough, but Brian Allwood—in whose 'toughness, timing and initiative' Harrisson placed especial trust—would leave Bolton as soon as invasion 'looks serious', travel 'by lorry, on foot, etc' to Birmingham and make contact with Jack Atkins in Worcester.[2] The invasion, of course, never came, but by the time these plans were circulated the London blitz had started in earnest.

The heroine of the London blitz was Masel, who sent in vivid reports on air raids and shelter life, cycling round to observe the damage, and keeping a detailed record of the reactions of her neighbours and the Jewish family with whom she lodged in Stepney.[3] On 10 September Harrisson, with characteristic exaggeration, told the Ministry of Information (MOI) that Masel was 'now practically the only person living and sleeping in her particular street'.[4] With Harrisson's approval she worked with a *Picture Post* photographer, showing him round and writing the commentary for a photo-essay on 'Shelter Life'.[5] Ironically, given the general tone of MO's reports on the blitz, including Masel's, this article helped to construct the myth of the cheerful Cockney soldiering on through the blitz with 'patience, cheerfulness, resignation, friendship, even gaiety, and, most of all, helpfulness'.[6] But her most celebrated contribution was a report on the so-called Tilbury shelter (close to Liverpool Street station, not in Tilbury), which Harrisson published in the *New Statesman* at the end of September, describing it, imaginatively, as the work of 'an East End working girl'.[7] A colossal, cavernous warehouse and goods depot—the roof of which (supported by metal girders and massive brick arches) gave a misleading impression of security—had been almost fully occupied (without official approval) by upwards of 10,000 people each night: 'When you get over the shock of seeing so many sprawling people', wrote Nina Massel, 'you are overcome with the smell of humanity and dirt... People are sleeping on piles of rubbish', and the only

2. TH to 'Dear Investigator', 13 September 1940, HNpap.
3. Masel reports in TC 23/9/T.
4. 'Evacuation and other East End Problems', 10 September 1940, FR 392. In fact only about a fifth of the street had left permanently, and many of the others were temporarily evacuated pending the explosion of a time bomb (Masel, 'Stepney', 11 September 1940, TC 23/9/T).
5. TH to Adams, 25 September 1940, FR 418; *Picture Post*, 26 October 1940.
6. Stephen Brooke, 'War and the Nude: The Photography of Bill Brandt in the 1940s', *Journal of British Studies*, 45, 1, 2006, 118.
7. 'War Adjustments', *New Statesman*, 28 September 1940. As Michael Williams remarked sardonically a few weeks later, in his thinly disguised account of an encounter with Masel: 'Well, well.. it's nice to know what an East End working girl is really like' (Michael Williams, 'Its Nice to Know', *Modern Reading*, 2, 1941).

lavatories were screened-off pails.[8] Much visited by journalists and other blitz tourists from the West End, Tilbury became a cause célèbre in the agitation for improved welfare in the public shelters.[9]

Harrisson warned Home Intelligence that his *New Statesman* article was about to appear, reassuring Mary Adams that it contained nothing new or significant and was mainly intended to encourage members of the panel, on whose reports it was based.[10] In fact he roundly attacked the failure of the authorities to deal more rapidly with the human problems of the blitz, and quoted at length from Masel's account of the Tilbury shelter. Adams' boss in the MOI picked up on the article immediately, demanding to know what useful work MO did for its £100 a week.[11] More significant was Churchill's reaction. The minutes of the War Cabinet for 2 October read:

> *The Prime Minister* referred to a statement by the Editor of *The New Statesman and Nation,* which had been brought to his notice, giving an account of conditions in the large shelter at Stepney.[12] In parts of this building, which had not been thought suitable for a shelter, and had not therefore been recognised as such, and suitably equipped, indescribable conditions had prevailed. The Prime Minister urged the need for strong action to prevent large numbers of people crowding into this building until the necessary work had been done to make it safe. From all he learnt of the position, drastic action was called for, and the Air Raid Precautions [ARP] Officer in Stepney should be immediately superseded.[13]

Two days later the Home Secretary made an order forcing Councillor Davis, the Stepney ARP officer, to step aside.[14] When the War Cabinet minutes

---

8. Masel, 'Stepney', 14 September 1940, TC 23/9/T. This passage was cited accurately in TH's *New Statesman* article (28 September 1940). But when, thirty years later, Harrisson wrote his own history of the blitz, he could not resist doctoring the quote for effect. The following words attributed to Masel—'The floor was awash with urine ... only two lavatories for 5000 women, none for men'—appear to have been invented by Harrisson. Nothing like them occurs in the copy of Masel's report surviving in the archive, from which the rest of the passage cited in *Living Through the Blitz* (117), is taken. He also misdates, by nearly a month, Masel's later report on how the shelterers kept order among themselves: the passage on page 119 derives from the same report cited on page 118, and was written on 29 September, not 21 October.
9. Calder, *People's War*, 211. On blitz tourism see also Report of ARP controller, 21 January 1941, HO 207/1026.
10. TH to Adams, 25 September 1940, FR 418.
11. Macadam to Adams, 30 September 1940, INF 1/262.
12. Churchill conflated the editorial (which called for swift action to prevent the spread of disease in unsanitary deep shelters), with Harrisson's article in the same issue which contained Nina Masel's account of the Tilbury shelter (*New Statesman*, 28 September 1940).
13. War Cabinet Conclusions, 2 October 1940, CAB 65/9/26.
14. 'Stepney: Transfer of control of civil defence organisation from local council to Ministry of Home Security', 29 October 1940, HO 207/1026.

were opened in 1971, Richard Crossman seized on this incident as evidence of the power of the pen in wartime Britain, and Nick Hubble, working from Crossman's account, highlights this incident as representing 'a greater success in bridging the gap between the leaders and the led than any of M-O's work for the MOI.'[15] In fact, as the Home Secretary reported to the same cabinet meeting, steps were already in train to remove Councillor Davis (who, later in the war, was to be jailed for corruption[16]), and the main effect of Churchill's intervention was to embolden the police to block entry to the shelter while work was done to strengthen the roof, an action that led to a violent clash between Communist leaders of the unofficial shelterers and the police: 'Police Baton Crowd at Office of ARP Dictator', headlined the *Daily Worker*.[17]

No evidence survives of Masel's reaction to this unexpected outcome of her Tilbury report. She was well aware of the potential conflict between her work and her politics, and she had been careful to declare her interest in her report on the Tilbury shelter: 'Inv[estigator] has a biased view of political activity, but this evening the only activity that came to her view was that of the Stepney Tenant Defence League [a Communist-led organization] collecting signatures on petition for better shelter conditions.'[18] It was not impossible to reconcile the Communist Party's agitation for better air raid protection with MO's declared goal of closing the gap between the leaders and the led. Adams, who used MO sources to report regularly on Communist activity (but not on the inner life of the Party[19]), advised her superiors that what the situation in the East End required was not anti-Communist propaganda but a 'positive constructive answer to Communist agitation. Deeds not words answer Communists.'[20] But, as the outcome of the Tilbury report suggested, such a benign relationship between pressure from below and

15. Hubble, *Mass-Observation and Everyday Life*, 187; 'London Diary', *New Statesman*, 5 February 1971.
16. Maurice Harold Davies, leader of the majority Labour group on the Council and ex-mayor of Stepney was sentenced to 6 months in November 1944 for having tried to suborn various officers of the council into issuing him with a false identity card after he had given a false name when caught travelling on the railway without a ticket. 'Grave allegations of bribery and corruption have been made against Davis in the past, but unfortunately these cannot be proved and therefore we are not in a position to place this information before the court' (Chief Inspector Davis to Chief Constable, 8 November 1944, MEPO 3/2357).
17. War Cabinet Conclusions, 21 October 1940, CAB 65/9/36; 'Brief Outline of Incident', 21 October 1040, HO 207/1026; *Daily Worker*, 21 October 1940.
18. Masel, 'Stepney', 14 September 1940, TC 23/9/T.
19. Adams to Macadam, 18 January 1941, MApap 1/C.
20. Adams to Macadam, 1 October 1940, MApap 1/B.

reform from above could not always be counted on. In the East End there was widespread scepticism about the value of brick-built surface shelters (which provided protection against flying glass and splinters but could not withstand a direct hit), and the Communists made great play with this in their agitation for deep shelters.[21] Within weeks of the Tilbury incident, Masel discovered that her reports about popular hostility to the surface shelters were being used by the MOI, not to press for their replacement, but to finesse leaflets designed to reassure people that the shelters were safe. She was 'shocked to the core...I was terribly ashamed of the part I had unwittingly played in this act of betrayal. I left soon afterwards in a blaze of indignation and fury.'[22] Within six months, however, she was happily sending in vivid reports of her new life in the Women's Auxiliary Air Force.[23]

II

Masel's troubles were small beer compared with the difficulties confronting Harrisson in his efforts to establish MO as a democratizing agent within the apparatus of the wartime state. At the end of September, just as MO's relationship with Adams' Home Intelligence department was being placed on a more secure basis, the department's own status and influence was itself radically downgraded. Adams' reports, which since May had been seen by ministers and top civil servants, were henceforth to be circulated only within the MOI.[24] While MO's work could still inform MOI propaganda it would have no effect on the authorities' practical handling of the blitz unless Harrisson could find some other way of getting it into the hands of those with the power to act. When the ambiguities of MO's relationship with the state became too much for Masel's conscience, she could opt out. But Harrisson was determined to tough it out; fighting to maintain MO as an effective advocate for the unmet needs of civilians in the front line.

21. K. Morgan, *Against War and Fascism,* 204.
22. Masel, 'I Was a Mass Observer', *New Statesman,* 31 May 1985. In fact the MOI seems to have been a most reluctant player in the attempt to rehabilitate surface shelters in the public mind (Planning Committee, *minutes,* 21 April 1941, INF 1/249, cited in McLaine, *Ministry of Morale,* 126).
23. TC 32/3/E. Some of these reports are reproduced in Calder and Sheridan, *Speak for Yourself,* 130–5. See also TH to Masel, 2 January 1942, Personnel/Masel.
24. 'Notes of decision taken by Director General', 27 September 1940, in MA 1/A.

As the war came ever closer to home, blowing out the windows in Ladbroke Road,[25] Harrisson—awaiting the outcome of his negotiation with the new MOI Director General, Frank Pick—sought to rally the staff, stressing the long-term purpose of MO's work, as he always did on such occasions:

> I deeply appreciate the way in which everybody has made the best of the temporary new financial arrangements...[i.e. pay cuts] I am determined that whatever happens, M-O shall come through the war and bring out a complete record of it...But we have got to expect scars, wounds, casualties...I do not think I need to issue any special instructions to cover any sudden military circumstances that may arise. The main thing, under all circumstances, is to carry on observing, and keeping up notes, if necessary in pocket notebooks, each page carefully dated and timed...To meet all...difficulties we must keep open minds, and good natures, tough hearts and whole skins...After the war...a lot of people are going to be really grateful to us for all we have done now...and when it is properly written up by four or five people, going through the material steadily for two or three years in peace, we are going to have quite new things to say and perhaps quite new solutions to very, very old and previously terrifying problems. I would not say this to anyone outside the organisation because it might sound conceited. But I believe it is true. That is why I am sweating my guts and nerves out night and day in order to keep things going...It makes me feel fine to know that other people are keen on the job too, and ready to give up a lot, and in several cases to go voluntarily on very dangerous jobs...Whatever happens, we can be sure that a nucleus will come through thick and thin.[26]

Two months later, shocked by accusations from two of his most trusted staff that MO's relationship with the MOI had compromised its ability to do 'disinterested, objective work', Harrisson protested that 'nothing ever can or will make me do less than independent or honest [work]', denying that the fact that some of MO's work was of immediate value to the authorities in any way contradicted the long-term goals of accumulating material for a scientific account of the impact of the war on ordinary people.[27]

On the night of 14 November the Luftwaffe switched its attention from London to Coventry. Alerted by Adams, Harrisson summoned Humphrey

---

25. TH to Feare, 28 September 1940, HNpap. In late October there was a direct hit next door (TH to Waddington, 21 October 1940, TC 34/1/D). And in a draft article written in May 1941, TH added that 'a large piece of another bomb came through the roof and two floors to land beside my chair' ('A Public Demand for Reprisals?', May 1941, FR 694).
26. TH to Investigators, nd, HNpap.
27. TH to Feare, nd, responding to Feare to TH, 26 November 1940, HNpap.

Pease and George Hutchinson (a 20-year-old observer recently recruited from the *Yorkshire Post*[28]) and set out for the blitzed city. Arriving the day after the blitz, the three men found 'more open signs of hysteria, terror, neurosis…than during the whole of the past two months together in all areas.' Their report attacked as counterproductive to local morale the usual unrealistic newspaper stories of civilian unflappability under fire, praised the efficiency with which the emergency services had responded to the catastrophe, and focussed on the need for 'much more powerful and imaginative organisation to deal with the purely psychological and social' aftermath of bombing.[29] On Saturday 16 November, two days after the blitz, Harrisson somehow persuaded the BBC to give him its popular 9.00 p.m. 'Postscript' slot:

> I've been chasing air raids in this country ever since they began: often I've heard awful stories of the damage and arrive to find them grossly exaggerated. But about Coventry there hasn't been much exaggeration.

But overall his tone was upbeat and his criticism of post-blitz services was restrained. After two days, he reported, the devastated city was beginning to recover its wits. Those who had not fled the town ('the frightened, nervous ones') were now 'beginning to feel tough—just as the people of London had felt tough before them.'[30] The broadcast, he told Priscilla Feare, 'raised uproar among the high-ups', confirming his reputation as 'the best hated thing at the MOI'.[31] When the War Cabinet met two days later Anthony Eden, Secretary of State for War and MP for Coventry's neighbouring towns, Leamington and Warwick, led the uproar: 'This had been a most depressing broadcast, and would have a deplorable effect on Warwickshire [military] units.'[32] The Cabinet's response to Harrisson's broadcast was to tighten government control of the BBC.[33]

In the weeks and months following the Coventry blitz MO's 'mobile squad'—usually consisting, as in Coventry, of Harrisson, Hutchinson, and

28. TH recalled Hutchinson as the most regular member of the blitztown team apart from himself (Harrisson, *A World Within*, 63). Hutchinson had left school early for the *Yorkshire Post*, where he was still working in September 1940 and sending reports to M-O about attitudes to the London blitz (Hutchinson diary, 11 June 1941, TC 29/2/K; Diarist 5117, September 1940).
29. 'Coventry', 18 November 1940, FR 495.
30. TH, broadcast on Coventry, 16 November 1940, FR 497.
31. TH to Feare, nd, responding to Feare to TH, 26 November 1940, HNpap.
32. War Cabinet Conclusions, 18 November 1940, CAB 65/10/10.
33. British Broadcasting Corporation. Memorandum by the Chancellor of the Exchequer, 26 December 1940, CAB 66/14/21; War Cabinet Conclusion, 30 December 1940 CAB 65/10/31.

Pease—chased around the country in Pease's car following each major raid. Harrisson usually started by interviewing local officials while the others observed in pubs, dance halls, and rest centres; inspected shelters; and counted how many people joked or whistled in the street, carried gas masks or hung out Union Jacks; listened in to everyday talk and struck up conversations with policemen, wardens, shop assistants, etc. Three or four hours after starting work, the observers would meet to pool impressions: 'by that time I have . . . usually managed to see several high-ups and get their views, while the others have got a good quantity of working-class stuff'. This, Harrisson claimed, was sufficient for the team to have a sense of where public faith in local administration was at its weakest, so that they could organize their work for the remainder of the visit to probe these gaps between leaders and led. The team was usually in town for two or three days, working at high pressure from 7.00 a.m. to 11.00 p.m., sometimes with help from panel members living in the area.[34] The reports, written up as soon as the team got back to London, were designed to provide the MOI with a comparative picture of morale in each town, and to identify perceived inadequacies in the provision of post-blitz services.[35]

These flying visits, often to places of which MO had little previous knowledge, were clearly not the ideal way to study the effects of bombing on civilian morale. At the end of August 1940 Celia Fremlin had opposed the setting-up of any special unit to study the effect of air raids, arguing that this could be done far more fruitfully by staff already engaged in longer term work on the area affected: 'any journalist or psychologist who happens to wake up and think of air raids as interesting' could study air raids in isolation. MO's unique strength lay in its ability to bring to bear knowledge and understanding of pre-blitz conditions in the affected locality.[36] This was good

34. TH to Adams, 8 January 1941 specifies a team of three, including himself. Other full-timers involved in blitz-chasing included the three young men Jimmy Stevens, Len England and Eric Gulliver. Celia Fremlin, in a document heavily amended by TH ('Plan for Survey of Blitzed Town', 8 January 1941, TC 23/8/a), proposed, among other things, that a woman should always be included in the team. This advice does not appear to have been followed.

35. Brad Beaven and John Griffiths ('The blitz, civilian morale and the city: mass-observation and working-class culture in Britain, 1940–41', *Urban History*, 26, 1, 1999) rightly criticise the MO analysis as relying on rather stereotyped notions of regional and local character. At the same time, however, their own argument that variations in working-class responses to the blitz closely reflected the degree to which town or city centres were destroyed assumes (perhaps unwisely) that MO's measurement of underlying morale was sufficiently accurate to provide a reliable basis for comparison.

36. Fremlin, 'interviewing during air-raids', 31 August 1940, TC 66/12/A.

advice in London, where MO's previous work on anti-Semitism in the East End provided a sound base for its post-blitz reporting. But Hitler did not oblige by following up the London blitz with a raid on Bolton, or confining his bombs to places previously studied by MO, so, for what came to be known as the 'blitztown' work, there was no alternative to a specialized flying squad. Where resources permitted, however, Harrisson took the opportunity to commission longer term work on post-blitz recovery. Priscilla Novy— Feare had married Henry Novy in December just before he was called up— did a report on Southampton.[37] And a new observer, Mollie Tarrant, a 31-year-old spinster living with her widowed mother in Havant, did a detailed study of four working-class streets in Portsmouth over a period of six months following the first large-scale attack on the town in January 1941.[38] After the attentions of Hitler's bombers had shifted to the Eastern front, the Ministry of Home Security set up a well-funded team under the scientist Solly Zuckerman to conduct retrospective research on the impact of the bombing. The main purpose of this was to assess the value to the war effort of concentrating manpower and resources on blitzing German civilians, although neither Bomber Harris nor Churchill took any notice of its largely negative conclusions.[39] But these longer term studies—whether by MO or the Home Office team—were of little use to Home Intelligence, which needed quick results for its weekly morale reports.

Adams was pleased with Harrisson's work, recommending MO's Coventry report as a model to others engaged in assessing post-blitz morale.[40] It rapidly became clear to MO that there were repeated patterns of failure by the local authorities in charge of post-blitz services and that they were failing to learn from each other's experience, or from the experience of the London blitz. But local autonomy remained central to Britain's unwritten constitution,[41] and the Home Office—unwilling to challenge the pride and parochialism of provincial elites—was reluctant to second-guess the judgement of local civil defence chiefs. Moreover, while Harrisson's zeal in ferreting out dysfunctional relationships between the leaders and the led rested on a belief in the desirability and possibility of more open, rational, and

37. 'Southampton', March 1941; 'Memorandum on Mass-Observation', 29 October 1942, FR 1450; Reports in TC 66/16/B, C & E.
38. Living Through the Blitz, 181–2, 187–8, 355.
39. Max Hastings, Bomber Command, 1979, 131–2.
40. Adams to Edkins, 7 December 1940; Adams to Palmer, 30 November 1940, MApap 2/E.
41. Jim Bulpitt, Territory and Power in the United Kingdom, 1983.

democratic ways of organizing social life, to many of those in authority such obsessive probing of weak points appeared at best unnecessary, at worst positively dangerous. To keep the show on the road it was better not to dwell on the everyday pains and resentments of a profoundly unequal society. Some things, they believed, are better left in obscurity.

The Home Office (and, behind the scenes, MI5) had always resented Home Intelligence as a trespasser on their patch, but during the crisis summer of 1940 the two ministries had been sharing information on public feeling and morale.[42] When, in September, Pick queried the duplication of effort, Adams pointed out that the Home Office Intelligence Department had 'not produced detailed reports solely concerned with *the attitude of the public* to the Civil Defence services, nor indeed are they in a position to do so, since their reports are drawn solely from Civil Defence personnel.'[43] With no fieldworkers of its own and dependent on the self-evaluation of local civil defence chiefs, the Home Office had no way of picking up the kind of information about grass-roots feeling that MO specialized in ferreting out. But nor did they show any interest in such information, and they certainly did not relish unsubstantiated criticism of their work being circulated to all and sundry in the corridors of power. In the summer of 1940 the Home Office had been exasperated by the way Adams' weekly morale reports gave currency to public criticisms of the civil defence organization regardless of their validity: 'it was found by this Department', minuted one senior official, 'that whenever criticisms... were examined and evidence required... the criticisms were ill-founded.'[44] As Stephen Taylor pointed out, reviewing the history of Home Intelligence after he had taken over from Adams:

> the reports were often highly critical of the work of the Government departments concerned with meeting the physical needs of the public. Where these criticisms could not be substantiated—as was often inevitably the case, since the raw material was opinion only—distrust of the daily reports was generated

---

42. Adams to Bamford, 17 July 1940, MApap 1/A; 'Report on history, functions and administration of Home Intelligence Division', 1944, 3, INF 1/290. Harrisson seems to have had his own private arrangement with someone in the Home Office, since copies of the Police Duty Room reports, summarizing police and other HO sources of information on public attitudes, can be found in the MO archive (TC 54/1) for the whole period from October 1939 to February 1941. In December 1940, Adams, complaining that she was no longer being supplied with these reports, told Pick that 'we collect the information by more devious routes' (Adams to Pick, 7 December 1940, MApap 1/A). Perhaps she was getting them from Harrisson.
43. Adams to Pick, 19 September 1940, MApap 1/A.
44. Gater to Minister, 27 January 1941, HO 199/442, cited in McLaine, *Ministry of Morale*, 125–6.

outside the Ministry. And the good they might have done was stultified by the strong emotions they engendered in harassed and overworked officials.

The Home Office was never able to understand that MO was dealing not in authenticated fact about official performance but in popular perceptions. It was pressure from the Home Office that had led Pick to put an end to the circulation of daily reports to the Cabinet.[45] When, within days of this decision, Herbert Morrison took over as Home Secretary, Adams was initially hopeful that he might understand the value of the kind of material only MO could supply.[46] But Morrison was a local government man, no more inclined than his officials to listen to dangerously irresponsible voices from outside the hierarchy: he 'regarded any criticism of ARP anywhere as a personal insult'.[47] 'The interests of the public', Harrisson wrote shortly after the war, '... were deemed less important than the interest of the good name of the Minister among his Cabinet colleagues.'[48] Relations between Home Intelligence and the Home Office went from bad to worse and, by February 1941, Adams was describing them as 'nonexistent and/or deplorable.'[49] By then, however, Harrisson had taken steps to bypass the Home Office-inspired ban on the circulation of his reports.

III

When Harrisson moved in with Biddy Clayton in 1939 he not only acquired use of the Ladbroke Road house as MO's headquarters, he also got to know many of her upper class Mayfair friends. One of these, Charles Lambe, became godfather to the couple's son, born at the end of September 1940.[50] Lambe was at that time an up-and-coming naval officer in Whitehall, and before the end of the year he had introduced Harrisson to Admiral Godfrey, Director of Naval Intelligence, who was concerned about the impact of the

45. 'Report on ...Home Intelligence Division', 1944, 4, INF 1/290.
46. Adams to Huxley, 3 October 1940, MApap 2/E. One reason for optimism was that Morrison took with him to the Home Office his right-hand publicity man, Clem Leslie, a pre-war supporter of MO. But Adams was not sure where Leslie stood, and matters cannot have been improved by the accidental transmission to him of Harrisson's highly critical opinion of some of Leslie's own work (TH, memo, 23 October 1940, TC 43/2/D).
47. Godfrey, 'Mass Observation', April 1947, ADM 223/476.
48. TH to Godfrey, 22 January 1947, ADM 223/476.
49. Adams to Silvey, 28 February 1941, MApap 1/C.
50. Heimann, *Most Offending Soul*, 161–2.

blitz on the morale of service personnel whose wives and families now found themselves in the front line.[51] Godfrey—an unusually liberal-minded sailor whose uncompromising insistence that intelligence work should be carried out in a 'critical, sceptical and scientific' spirit and presented 'without fear or favour' made him many enemies in establishment circles—was already familiar with Harrisson's *New Statesman* articles, and appreciated MO's ability to get beneath the surface of official complacency.[52] Harrisson, of course, was delighted at the interest in his work shown by 'someone who really matters', and, starting with the report on the Coventry blitz, happily supplied Naval Intelligence with copies of the reports he did for Adams. He also undertook commissions specifically for Godfrey.[53] Godfrey circulated the reports, suitably vetted 'from the point of view of expediency and good taste', to naval commanders in the port towns in the belief that a 'more or less unexpurgated...account of the reactions of local inhabitants to heavy bombing could not but be of value especially as they provided the background for letters which would be sent from parents and others to personnel afloat.'[54]

Godfrey also sent copies of the reports to the Home Office.[55] Wing-commander John Hodsoll, in charge of ARP, drew up a forensic six-page riposte to the MO reports, concluding:

> The impression that we got was of a small band of people who seemed to be themselves defeatists, who got hold of all the defeatist people that could be found, went round trying to find something which broke down, and then condemned everything on the strength of it.

51. Merrett, Notes for A.D.N.I., 23 February 1946, ADM 223/476.
52. Godfrey, 'Mass Observation', April 1947, ADM 223/476. Eventually the 'establishment' got him and he was moved on at the beginning of 1943, much to the detriment of the British war effort, according to the naval historian Stephen Roskill (entry on Godfrey in DNB).
53. TH to Hopkinson, 4 May 1941, Org and Hist 3/Hopkinson; TH to Godfrey, 12 February 1947, ADM 223/476. Adams knew he was doing this, and approved (Adams to Macadam, 27 January 1941, MApap 1/C). Hubble, *Mass-Observation and Everyday Life* (186), is mistaken in suggesting that TH's work for the Admiralty 'was just beginning' in March 1941.
54. Godfrey's personal secretary recalled: 'There was a drill for dealing with the copies of Harrisson's reports when they came to hand. They were usually very verbose, strongly in the manner of the journalist, and at times highly coloured and dramatic. I was frequently instructed by [Godfrey] to reduce these reports into some short factual form which would be acceptable to Commanders-in-Chief' (Merrett, Notes for A.D.N.I., 23 February 1946, ADM 223/476). But Godfrey recalled that 'the more sulphurous portions might be passed to Sea Lords, and selected directors' (Godfrey, 'Mass Observation', April 1947, ADM 223/476).
55. HO 199/442 contains MO reports on Bristol, Southampton and Cheltenham, retyped by Naval Intelligence on 22 December 1940, and sent to Commanders-in-Chief at naval bases and dockyards; and on Liverpool and Manchester dated 6 January 1941 and sent out by Naval Intelligence on 10 January.

Objecting to MO's allegations of 'a dangerous lack of imaginative leadership' in Bristol, Hodsoll asserted that in fact the Bristol authorities 'did extremely well', incautiously adding 'far better than the Southampton ones'. On second thoughts he crossed out the comparison with Southampton, presumably because it conceded too much to MO's case.[56] Hodsoll knew very well what had happened in Southampton since he himself had been sent to sort things out after the town clerk fled the bombing and the local civil defence system broke down completely. In his retrospective account, *Living Through the Blitz*, Harrisson went out of his way to praise Hodsoll as an honest and dedicated civil servant whose desire to take a tough line with failing local authorities was frustrated by Morrison's excessive respect for the autonomy of local government.[57] But Hodsoll, however ready he might be to criticize ineffective services, had no patience with what he saw as MO's dangerously negative reporting:

> We all know that [shelter] conditions [in Liverpool] were bad...but at the same time every effort was made to improve them as quickly as possible. We did not broadcast to the world that they were bad, and comments made in this report, which reflect directly on the arrangements made by the Department, were unfortunate even though they might have been to some extent true.[58]

Had he been privy to this document Harrisson might have been rather less positive about the qualities of a man whose class-conscious blindness to popular mentalities was best revealed in his objection to MO's statement, again about Liverpool, that 'a considerable proportion of dockers are showing very little interest in winning the war or working hard to win it... There is a major emotional conflict from the dockers against the employer class.' Such statements, wrote Hodsoll, 'amount to more than a suspicion of class warfare', and their circulation, particularly with the blessing of the Admiralty, was 'dangerous'. In any case, he added for good measure, the suggestion 'that dockers as a race... [could] suffer from "major emotional conflicts"' was self-evidently absurd. In Hodsoll's worldview dockers were unthinking beasts of burden, and MO's staff were written off, in the words of another Home Office official, as members of 'what [is] known as the "intelligentsia"... [who] would be very much better employed in doing something useful for the community.'[59]

56. Hodsoll to Scott, 23 December 1940, HO 199/442.
57. *Living Through the Blitz*, 153–4, 178, 299, 325.
58. Hodsoll to Scott, 23 December 1940, HO 199/442.
59. ?? (indecipherable) to Mabane, 21 January 1941, HO 199/442.

In January Victor Warrender, Parliamentary Private Secretary to the First Lord of the Admiralty, A. V. Alexander, sent the MO reports to several senior ministers with an accompanying note explaining:

> I understand that this Observation Group has done some very useful work for the Ministry of Information. It seems to me a pity that these valuable reports should hide their light under a bushel in the Admiralty . . . In many cases these reports are outspoken and critical, but I am sure that no offence will be taken if by this means a real defect can be remedied. As other reports are produced I will circulate them in like manner.[60]

Whether Warrender's naivety was genuine or affected is unknown, but the response from the Home Office to this attempt to overturn its previous success in suppressing the Home Intelligence reports was instantaneous and furious. Morrison wrote to Alexander (a fellow Labour MP) demanding immediate withdrawal of the newly circulated MO reports, described by one of his advisers as 'a most extraordinary mixture of fact, fiction and dangerous mischief.'[61] Alexander retreated on the circulation to ministers, but continued to send the reports to naval commanders in the port towns.[62] With angry exchanges flying back and forth between senior ministers, and even Adams being uncharacteristically critical of his reports,[63] Harrisson kept his head down, withdrawing articles he had planned for the *New Statesman* and Edward Hulton's *World Review*:

> my work . . . has precipitated a crisis in high quarters, and this has put me in a difficult position as regards publishing anything about it at the moment . . . for the last few days, I have been the principle blitzed town in England![64]

Warned off 'by my official contacts', Harrisson thought it politic to delay publication 'until the fuss has died down', adding defensively that this was 'not a matter of censorship but . . . of my necessary moral obligations to those who partly support the organisation and make it possible to continue in wartime'.[65]

60. Victor Warrender to Lord President, 18 January 1941, HO 199/442.
61. ?? (indecipherable) to Mabane, 21 January 1941, HO 199/442.
62. Morrison to Alexander, 31 January 1941, HO 199/442.
63. TH to Adams, 9 January 1941, MApap 4/f.
64. TH to Kingsley Martin, 29 January 1941, Org and Hist 3/1.
65. TH to Edward Hulton, 29 January 1941, Org and Hist 3/World Review. This was much the same formulation that he had used in 1940 to justify his failure to publish the results of the work he did before the war for the Labour Party. See pp. 47–8.

Despite Morrison, Godfrey continued to commission work from MO until the middle of 1942, during which time the Admiralty was instrumental in protecting Harrisson himself against conscription.[66] One advantage of using MO, as Godfrey later explained, was 'that they commit one to nothing, whereas an official survey of naval conditions implies resultant action, and breeds disappointment if action does not follow enquiry... The merit of "observation" as distinct from "survey" is that people are unconscious that it is being carried out'. Moreover, Harrisson had 'a remarkable gift of nosing out anything that is in the least out of the ordinary'; as he showed in reports on dockyard security (or rather the lack of it) in Dover and in Hull.[67] Within hours of arriving in Hull, Harrisson had penetrated the dock area through holes in the fence, and made a map showing the location of each ship. 'Inv. could have placed dummy bombs at many key points, and had extensive opportunity for pilfering unobserved.'[68]

IV

Expressing his fury at MO's trespassing on his patch, Morrison wrote to Alexander demanding to know how the First Lord of the Admiralty would feel if the Home Office were to employ MO to report on morale on the lower deck.[69] There was, of course, no question of the Home Office doing this, but since the outbreak of war Harrisson had been attempting to interest the armed forces in MO's services. When his staff were called up, he kept in touch, sending them MO literature, cash, cigarettes, and, in some cases, subscriptions to the *New Statesman* or *The Spectator*; and encouraging them to write reports.[70] He also urged conscripted panellists to respond to directives and continue their diaries.[71] In December 1940, Henry Novy—newly conscripted and aware that the Army

---

66. Godfrey to Major-General Davidson, 19 July 1941; Godfrey to Alexander, 20 May 1942, ADM 223/476.
67. Godfrey to Admiral Sir B H Ramsay, 13 January 1941; Merrett, Notes for A.D.N.I., 23 February 1946, ADM 223/476.
68. 'The Port of Hull', 22 April 1942, FR 1211; TC 66/10/C.
69. Morrison to Alexander, 31 January 1941, HO 199/442.
70. See correspondence in TC 29/2. Most of this contact ceased, however, once they were posted overseas. 'We have had numerous enquiries from soldiers stationed in India, Africa, Palestine and elsewhere who are anxious to help with our work. But we have always advised enquirers not to report to us on matters connected with army life while the war is on, in case of accidental breaches of security regulations' (*Journey Home*, 53).
71. TH to Langley, 12 August 1940, Org&Hist 4/2.

Council was worried about the number of men going absent without leave—decided to write to his commanding officer to 'propose some sort of enquiry on M-O lines...and see whether he thinks it worthwhile.' Harrisson, he suggested, should think about 'doing something similar your end? It might be a reasonable good chance of making M-O workable in the army if we seize the opportunity. What do you think about it?'[72] In February 1941, encouraged no doubt by the success of his relationship with Naval Intelligence, Harrisson contacted Dermot Boyle (later to become Chief of the Air Staff) with a report prepared by a volunteer observer on an RAF base, replete with quotations in the filthiest language—'it was half the fun for the questioners that I promised to report their words verbatim.'[73] Although Harrisson was confident of Boyle's broad-mindedness, nothing seems to have come of this initiative. It was Len England, stationed at the Royal Army Ordinance Corps' supply depot in Donnington, who came closest to exploiting the possibilities identified by Novy, persuading the colonel in charge to set up what was effectively an MO unit on the base: 'to facilitate the airing of grievances...with or without foundation, on the part of the staff generally... The object', the colonel explained, 'was twofold in that he had the interests of the Staff in mind, and also the efficiency of the sub-depot.'[74] Two groups of volunteer 'counsellors' were recruited, one among the military personnel, the other among civilians working on the base, to be instructed by England in techniques of listening and recording the views of the staff. The colonel provided typing facilities for their reports, which, apart from the usual complaints about unnecessary spit and polish, picked up extreme discontent over an increase in weekend working (which was quickly reversed).[75] Jumping the gun, as usual, Harrisson told Kingsley Martin that War Office, 'already peculiarly conscious of the fact that we have several hundred voluntary informants scattered throughout the military machine...have just given me some jobs to do.'[76] Whether he had already been in touch with the War Office is unclear—England certainly thought that he had—but he was waiting for the results from Donnington before pressing the case for a wider MO scheme in the army. After three weeks, however, England's experiment collapsed. Trade

72. Novy to TH, 27 December 1940, TC 29/2/D.
73. 'Surveys conducted by Observer D Douglas at RAF Marston', 21 February 1941, TC 29/4/A. On Boyle see DNB entry.
74. 'Notice for Notice Board', 6 June 1941, TC 29/2/B.
75. 'Meeting of counsellors', 29 May, 6, 12, 14 June 1941; 'Morale report (1), 14 June 1941, TC 29/2/B.
76. TH to Kingsley Martin, 31 May 1941, Org&Hist 3/3. See also Papineau to TH, 8 June 1941, TC 29/2/G.

union activists among the civilian workers, seeing the scheme as an attack on
their own functions, dismissed it as 'Gestapo' espionage; military officers resented
the men's voices being given direct access to the Commanding Officer, undermining their own authority; and the enlightened colonel moved on to another
job. Hesitating about whether to take his superior's advice and go for officer's
training, England wrote to Harrisson asking whether 'there is any hope at all of
the M-O War Office plans maturing, and, in that case, if there is any chance of
a job for me.'[77] But, if such plans had ever existed, the implosion at Donnington
seems to have put an end to them, and the archive holds no further evidence of
MO's involvement in monitoring morale in the army on behalf of the authorities.[78] In the navy, however, Hutchinson, who joined up in June 1941, wrote
reports on naval authority as seen from the lower deck.[79]

V

Nine months of blitz-chasing had done nothing to reassure Harrisson about
the state of civilian morale or about the effectiveness of existing leadership in
combating the bewilderment of ordinary people shocked and disoriented by
the destruction visited on their towns, if not their own homes. Harrisson's
understanding of the impact of bombing on morale was cast in terms of the
model of opinion formation that he had sketched out before the blitz started:

> The social pressure operates in the familiar way towards making people show
> publicly the best side of their morale. It is our job to try to penetrate the sur-
> face layer and map the strata of underlying feeling.[80]

Politicians and the media, at one in their classically 'pastoral' celebration of
the heroism of simple working people (about whose complicated sentiments

77. England to TH, 20 June 1941, TC 29/2/B; England, M-O Diary, 29 May, 3 June 1941.
78. In 1944, however, MO claimed, presumably with reference to the Forces Parliament in Cairo,
that: 'There is an independent MO unit operating in Cairo, we understand, with the full sanction of the authorities, and results of enquiries have been published in Egyptian papers'.
(*Journey Home*, 53).
79. 'First two months in the Navy', 11 August 1941, FR 821; 'Notes from an Aircraft Carrier', FR
1179, 30 March 1942; Hutchinson's extensive diary and correspondence are in TC 29/2/K.
After the war he caused a flurry of anxiety in the Admiralty when he co-authored, with the
Daily Herald journalist Hannen Swaffer, a highly critical book attacking caste distinction in the
Navy (Hannen Swaffer, *What Would Nelson Do?*, Gollancz, 1946, 13). Swaffer's campaign
caused consternation in the Admiralty, and questions were asked about Hutchinson and his
association with MO (Merrett, Notes for A.D.N.I., 23 February 1946, ADM 223/476).
80. Report on Portsmouth and Plymouth, 20 January 1941, 1, FR 559.

they knew little and understood less), created an atmosphere in which it
had become 'practically disloyal to suggest that morale is not perfect.'[81]
Adams complained of 'the terrific pressure everywhere to say . . . that everything is alright, that morale is splendid',[82] and MO's own investigators,
unwittingly affected by the press 'ballyhoo', found themselves doubting the
evidence of their own eyes and ears.[83] Boldly trespassing on well-guarded
professional territory, Harrisson wrote to the *British Medical Journal* to suggest that psychiatrists, lulled into complacency by all the talk of good
morale, were tending 'to gloss over the serious psychological effects that air
raids have on people, and to insist that the neurotic effects are negligible.'[84]
The saturation of public discourse with this message of the indomitable
spirit of the masses, he argued, was breeding a dangerous complacency
among Britain's leaders about the state of popular morale. Since the people
could 'take it', there was no urgent need for new efforts to ameliorate post-
blitz suffering, or for new ways of explaining the meaning and purpose of
the war. Down in private opinion, on the other hand, the mismatch between
sanitized press accounts of the bombing and the raw terror of those exposed
to it, bred resentment and confusion: 'emotions have been bottled up, and
the gulf between public opinion and private opinion is . . . becoming dangerously enlarged.' In public people did their best to maintain the stance of
cheerfulness—'the superficial smile, the thumbs up to a movie camera'—
partly because they knew it was required of them, partly because the very
performance of cheerfulness could operate as a way of evading a deeper
unarticulated pain.[85] But, as Harrisson argued at the beginning of April
1941, behind the superficial smiles

> the private desire for the war to be over and done with [is becoming] greatly
> amplified. People [in the blitzed towns] do not want to give in or make terms
> with Hitler; they do not think it out like that. But *in their guts* they want it to
> end, it being the constant threat of future blitzes, and in so doing, in the

81. 'Morale in 1941', 15 February 1941, FR 568.
82. Adams to Nicholson, 15 March 1941, MApap 2/E.
83. 'Morale in 1941', 15 February 1941, FR 568.
84. TH, *British Medical Journal*, 1, 4188, 12 April 1941, 573 and 4195, 31 May 1941, 832. In recent
    years historians have been challenging the 'no neurosis myth' propagated by much of the
    psychiatric establishment during the war. Lyndsey Stonebridge, 'Anxiety at a time of crisis',
    History Workshop Journal, 45, 1998; Hazel Croft, 'Psychiatrists and the making of the "no neu-
    rosis myth"', Paper delivered to conference on 'The Second World War: Popular Culture and
    Cultural memory', Brighton, 13–15 July 2011.
85. 'Morale in 1941', 15 February 1941, FR 568.

absence of any specific aims or focus for enduring it, there is a real (though so far inconspicuous, because held down in private opinion and not sanctioned in public opinion) tendency for the main war aim of the individual to become PEACE.[86]

Given this discrepancy between public and private opinion, it was 'mad folly' to discount the possibility of that military reversals might trigger a catastrophic collapse of morale: 'the whole opinions structure might suddenly explode'.[87] As events in France had demonstrated 'there can be a sensationally rapid swing from cheerfulness and confidence into mass evacuation and uttermost despair.'[88] But the French collapse was triggered by invading troops on the ground, and Harrisson's fears of a subterranean current of defeatist sentiment, however plausible they might seem when seen through the lens of his model of opinion formation, actually rested on thin and impressionistic evidence. Discussing the situation in Manchester in January 1941, for example, he wrote:

> While plenty of...people were determined and courageous, and few were openly defeatist, careful analytical discussions with sample people, confirmed by talks with trained sociologists and social workers...pointed to a considerable private opinion of real depression and despair. Manchester people are definitely on edge, are afraid of the next raid, are beginning really to worry about the future with a feeling of crime [sic – grim?] semi-despair. All this is under the surface.[89]

The 'careful analytical discussions' remained undocumented and the opinions of social workers about working-class attitudes were no more or less reliable than Harrisson's own intuitions. The problem, of course, was that it was in the nature of 'private opinion' to be private, and apart from the diarists (distributed too thinly in any one place to be helpful for the blitztown work) MO really had no reliable way of accessing what was going on 'under the surface'.

In the event there was no sudden collapse of morale and, when he came to write *Living Through the Blitz* in the early 1970s, Harrisson was more concerned to argue that bombing was generally ineffective as a

---

86. 'The Need for an Offensive Morale', 4 April 1941, FR 633.
87. 'Morale in 1941', 15 February 1941, FR 568; 'The Morale Situation: notes for Clement Davies', 21 April 1941, FR 675.
88. 'Preliminary Report on Morale in Glasgow', 7 March 1941, FR 600.
89. Report on Liverpool and Manchester, 6 January 1941, HO 199/442.

means of breaking civilian morale than to uphold his wartime view that it might prove all too effective. In line with this shift of perspective his view of the value of reprisal raids on German cities had also changed.[90] When he broadcast on the Coventry blitz, Harrisson remarked that he had found no call for reprisals among the victims.[91] At least one listener found this 'most heartening... [it] came like a breath of fresh air... All who remind us, as you did, that destruction and the spirit of revenge cannot make peace, are doing the nation a great service.'[92] Others, like the *News Chronicle* columnist A. J. Cummings, were outraged at what they took to be pacifistic propaganda on Harrisson's part.[93] But both reactions confused Harrisson's observation of attitudes in Coventry with his own opinion of the desirability or otherwise of reprisal raids; an opinion he spelled out forcefully in a second broadcast a few days later on the BBC's European News Service:

> Total war between Britain and Germany is bound to be total for both sides... The people of Coventry... buried 200 dead yesterday... in a common grave... They did not shout about reprisals. They did not scream for the annihilation of a German cathedral. They knew that these things could be left to our air force, who would decide the best moment and the best place to strike with fury in the language of total warfare and broken homes.[94]

Even while conjuring visions of sudden collapse in the spring of 1941, Harrisson acknowledged that 'such things will probably never happen',[95] focussing his analysis instead on the danger that by viewing morale in terms of cheerfulness and an ability to 'take it', official opinion was failing to grasp the need to foster something more positive than a spirit of merely passive endurance. The urgent need was for leadership capable of:

90. *Living Through the Blitz*, 288, 300–1, 328–34.
91. 'Coventry', 16 November 1940, FR 497.
92. Letter to 'the broadcaster of the Postscript on Coventry', 18 November 1940, TC 66/4/E.
93. TH, 'A Public Demand for Reprisals?', *The Cambridge Review*, 30 May 1941, 454–6, FR 671; TH to Cummings, 25 November 1940; Cummings to TH, 27 November 1940, TC 66/4/E. In his *Cambridge Review* article, Harrisson refuted press claims that blitzed populations were demanding reprisals, using the findings of a BIPO poll to demonstrate that the number of people demanding reprisals varied regionally in inverse proportion to the extent to which the area had been bombed. In this article Harrisson declared that he had 'no particular feeling... either way' about the merits of reprisals and was happy to defer to the judgement of the government on their utility or otherwise.
94. Script for broadcast on BBC European News Service, 21 November 1940, TC 66/4/E.
95. 'Preliminary Report on Morale in Glasgow', 7 March 1941, FR 600.

crystalliz[ing] passive emotions into active, aggressive channels, using the elementary principles of individual and mass psychology, sublimating the [sense
of] defeat into a counter-attack, externalising the shock onto emotional
objectives (enemies) . . .

However sound this advice, Harrisson's own proposals for applying the 'elementary principles of psychology' were unimpressive. The reason why
working-class people who suffered the worst of the blitz were much less
responsive than the middle classes to newspaper demands for reprisal bombing of German cities was to be found, he suggested, not so much in fear of
provoking further German bombing, still less in any humanitarian resistance
to calls for revenge, but rather in the parochialism of workers to whom for-
eigners and 'abroad' seemed too remote for what happened there to connect significantly with their own feelings:

> Most working-class people have never travelled abroad, and the names of
> German towns to them do not signify any reality, anything which can be
> visualised as a ruin. And the disaster has fallen on their town. It doesn't seem,
> to most unsophisticated people, to do much good if the same thing happens
> to a place called Dusseldorf. This disaster comes from the skies in a random,
> 'senseless' way.[96]

To counter this, and to draw the full value of reprisal raids as a means of
boosting 'an offensive morale', he proposed, among other things, that representative working-class figures should be invited to accompany the RAF on
bombing raids so that they could report back to towns meetings on what
they had seen.[97] It was one of his sillier thoughts.

Above all, he argued towards the end of April 1941, good morale meant
'the physical and psychological determination to work on and on and
on . . . the real criterion is *work*'.[98] After the Nazi invasion of the Soviet
Union in June 1941 put an end, for the time being, to the blitzing of British
cities—and with it the danger of sudden collapse—it was the need to opti-
mize war production that came to occupy the centre ground in Harrisson's
thinking, turning his attentions from the social consequences of bombing
to the still more dysfunctional human relations characteristic of Britain's
war factories. By then, however, MO's relationship with MOI had changed
drastically.

96. TH, 'A Public Demand for Reprisals?', *The Cambridge Review*, 30 May 1941, 454.
97. 'The Need for an Offensive Morale', 4 April 1941, FR 633.
98. 'An Offensive Morale', draft article for *Evening Standard*, 21 April 1941, FR 666.

VI

Following the end of Pick's brief and unhappy tenure as the MOI's director general at the end of 1940, Adams lobbied for the restoration of her department's pre-Pick position or, better still, the recognition of Home Intelligence as an independent unit operating under the control of the Cabinet Office.[99] All too aware of the unpopularity in official circles of her commitment to probing underlying weakness in public morale, she had little hope of a successful outcome, and when the director of intelligence at the Home Office, Parker, who represented precisely the 'complacency' against which she and Harrisson had been fighting, was moved into the MOI with powers to supervise her work, she gave up the battle and resigned. She was succeeded in April 1941 by her deputy (and one-time protégé), Taylor, who had long been critical of what he saw as the alarmism of MO's reports.[100]

Shortly before Adams resigned MO had been granted a further six-month contract,[101] and Taylor's initial intention was to find a way of making use of the organization:

> If the work of M-O is subjected to rigid scientific control, it is possible that it may prove valuable. Tom Harrisson is full of energy and ability, but also of prejudices. If he can be made to control his own feelings and to allow his observations to speak for themselves, I think M-O should be worth retaining as a part of HI [Home Intelligence].[102]

But his did not happen. Instead Harrisson was left to swing in the wind, denied access to Taylor or other senior personnel; given few instructions or feedback on MO's continuing work for the Ministry; and left with the impression, as he told Martin early in June, that the MOI 'really seem to be practically paying me to keep quiet.'[103] When, in July, he wrote to Taylor

99. Adams, memo on need for reorganisation of Home Intelligence, 11 March 1941, INF 1/101. Harold Nicholson, Duff Cooper's PPS, shared Adams and Harrisson's view of morale (Nicolson to Clark, 5 March 1941, INF1/252) and told Adams that he would try to persuade Attlee to press the case for Home Intelligence to be transferred from MOI control. Attlee's personal assistant, Grant Mackenzie, drafted several memos pressing the case (Mackenzie to TH, 26 August 1941, TC 43/2/E). Harrisson pushed for the same solution in a paper drafted jointly with Adams for the Home Policy Committee of Cabinet, 27 May 1941, FR 716.
100. Adams to Harold Nicholson, 15 March 1941, MApap 2/E; 'Office circular,' 9 April 1941, MApap 2/G; Taylor, *A Natural History of Everyday Life*, 261.
101. Monkton to TH, 7 April 1941, INF 1/286.
102. Taylor to Parker, 15 April 1941, INF 1/101.
103. TH to Kingsley Martin, 6 June 1941, Org&Hist 3/3.

pleading for some regular liaison, his letter went unanswered.[104] By then Taylor was busy building up machinery—including a panel of volunteer informants not dissimilar to the MO panel—which would enable the MOI to monitor public opinion independently and, he believed, more reliably than anything Harrisson could offer.[105]

In the early summer of 1941, before Hitler's invasion of the Soviet Union took the pressure off Britain's towns, Harrisson was becoming more and more alarmed about the state of popular morale. The mishandling of evacuation during the April raids on Plymouth provoked an unusually frank outburst about those responsible: 'disgusting, degrading and tantamount to sabotage of the war effort'[106] (Harrisson's blitz reports were usually written with at least a pretence of measured calm and objectivity). 'I am now intensely anxious about the morale situation,' he wrote to Tom Hopkinson (the editor of *Picture Post*), which was now worse than it had been at the height of the crisis of May–June 1940.[107] A few weeks later events in Liverpool produced a complete breakdown, 'unprintably violent comments on local leadership', and, for the first time in any blitzed town, 'publicly expressed signs of disgruntlement moving towards a willingness to surrender.'[108] On 21 May Harrisson wrote again to Hopkinson: 'the inefficiency and dis-organisation in Liverpool exceeds anything else I have seen, which is saying a terribly great deal. After three days there, I felt in real and deep despair about the whole possibility of our winning'.[109] 'For the first time since last summer,' he wrote of the situation in the weeks preceding Hitler's invasion of the Soviet Union, '*several* investigators picked up openly defeatist remarks. Real doubt about the outcome was increasing. And with it some *impatience* with the war, a desire to get it over with at all costs.'[110]

With little now to lose in his relationship with the MOI, Harrisson had no reason to continue to 'keep quiet'. By early June, after talking things over with Martin, he was ready to throw caution to the winds and go

104. TH to Taylor, 11 July 1941, INF 1/286.
105. See Chapter 11.
106. 'Plymouth', 4 May 1941, FR 683, 19.
107. TH to Hopkinson, 29 and 30 April 1941, Org&Hist 3/5. He commended Hopkinson on being 'the only journalist who hasn't written a book about the blitz and our superb courage in it. I hope you are not remedying this defect.' Ploughing through these war books for an article he had promised Cyril Connelly for *Horizon* served to reinforce his sense of official complacency. The *Horizon* article eventually appeared in December 1941.
108. *Living Through the Blitz*, 240.
109. TH to Hopkinson, 21 May 1941, Org&Hist 3/5.
110. 'Third Weekly Report', 23 Jue 1941, FR 753.

public with a series of full length articles in the *New Statesman* using his blitztown material:

> obviously it is difficult stuff to publish with the possible charge of giving information useful to the enemy... But really, the time has come when the facts of the blitztown situations ought to be widely publicised. When we might as well face up to the fact that people are fed up... My interest in the matter is purely constructive, and I have the strongest feelings that the war is simply slipping away from us, and that we're deluding ourselves into thinking that with a free press, etc etc... we get out the facts and get things done, whereas in fact we are surrounded by the ballyhoo we make ourselves, the fear of ever saying anything which fringes upon the possibilities of defeat, the powerful pressure of social sanctions on "inevitable victory", "national unity", etc, which sterilise candour... I would readily spend all the time I could in preparing for you any information along the above lines, even if it meant, as it well might, serious trouble for me from official sources...[111]

Nothing came of this, but in August the journal of the National Association of Local Government Officers published a lengthy and constructive article by Harrisson arguing the need for improvements in post-blitz services: above all in the provision of public information.[112] Most responses to the article were favourable, and the journal subsequently reported that 'many authorities are preparing or amending their scheme in accordance' with Harrisson's recommendations.[113] The response from Parker in the MOI, by contrast, was a last attempt to silence Harrisson by alleging that he was in breach of his contractual obligation not to publish material acquired while working for the Ministry.[114] While Harrisson protested

111. TH to Kingsley Martin, 6 June 1941, Org&Hist 3/3.
112. 'Blitzinformation', *Local Government Service*, August 1941. The spadework for this article, bringing together the results of the blitztown reports, had been done by Fitter and paid for by an American investigator working for Chicago University's Public Administration Clearing House who conveniently approached MO for information on how British local authorities had responded to the blitz. Fitter to TH, 5 May 1941; TH to Fitter, 21 May 1941, TC 25/12/a; 'Biddle Survey', August 1941, FR 840; TH to Sylvester Gates, 14 March 1942, INF 1/286; Eric H. Biddle, *The mobilization of the home front: the British experience and its significance for the United States...*, American Public Welfare Administration, 1942; William Anderson and John M. Gaus, *Research in Public Administration*, Chicago, 1945.
113. *Local Government Service*, December 1941. See also various responses published in the journal in September, October and November; Lambe to TH, 22 and 29 August 1941; Watson to TH, 20 September 1941, TC 23/11/O; TH to Parker, 7 October 1941; TH, Memo on MO publications, 20 October 1941, INF 1/286.
114. Hanson to Ainsley, 13 October 1941; Parker to TH, 16 October 1941; Taylor to Parker, 20 October 1941, INF 1/286.

his innocence—incidentally playing fast and loose with the wording of
the original contract[115]—Parker took legal advice. Eventually, however,
he backed off, advised that there would be difficulties in prosecuting,
particularly since the contract had finished in September, and realizing
that legal action would only serve to advertise what the MOI was most
anxious to keep secret: the extent to which it had made use of MO in the
past.[116] Despite these ructions, however, Harrisson continued to press
Taylor to make use of MO's services, and Taylor responded by commissioning reports on an ad hoc basis, notably one on Auxiliary Territorial
Service recruitment in November 1941 and a major report on reconstruction in August 1942.[117] But these were crumbs from the table compared with the regular contract that MO had enjoyed between April
1940 and September 1941. To fill the resulting gap Harrisson turned to a
quite different source of funding: the advertising industry.

115. TH to Parker, 17 October 1941, INF 1/286. TH wrote: 'of course the information we have
      ourselves collected in field work is our own property, as it has always been; and there has
      never been any question of written permission about that', a statement, as Parker pointed
      out, that appears to directly contradict the agreement he had signed about publication rights
      in the original contract with the MOI in April 1940 (TH to Parker, 7 October 1941; Parker
      to TH, 16 October 1941, INF 1/286).
116. Gates to TH, 11 November 1941, INF 1/286.
117. TH to Taylor, 3 and 29 October 1941; Taylor to TH, 16 October, 5 and 7 November 1941,
      INF 1/262; TH to Taylor, 6 August 1942, MO&MOI 2. Other commissions from the MOI
      included £60 for a report on the use of 'Towels in Pubs' and £135 for 'Attitudes to Americans'
      (Consultative Committee, minutes, 16 November 1942 and 1 January 1943, Hist&Org 1).
      Hubble (*Mass-Observation and Everyday Life*, 187) is mistaken in suggesting that the ATS com-
      mission in November 1941 was MO's 'last main collaboration with the MOI'.

9

Production

When Mass-Observation's (MO's) contract with the Ministry of Information (MOI) finally ended in September 1941, Tom Harrisson, in the course of a scorching critique of the Ministry, was able to announce: 'Happily we have been able to replace the MOI's financial support by a far more active and public spirited support of the Advertising Service Guild.'[1] Since June the Guild had been paying MO a retainer of £30 a week,[2] and for the remainder of the 1940s much of MO's output was to be delivered in association with the Advertising Service Guild (ASG), two of whose leading figures eventually became directors of MO when, in 1949, it transformed itself into a limited company. It would be easy to see MO's involvement with the ASG simply as the means by which Harrisson and Charles Madge's democratic experiment of 'an anthropology of ourselves' was transformed by the 1950s into a more or less conventional market research organization. But that would be a considerable oversimplification of the relationship between the two organizations.

I

The ASG had been established in February 1940. A consortium of seven advertising agents[3] concerned about the impact the war was having on their businesses, the Guild was designed both to drum up business by pooling the agencies' creative resources, and, more broadly, to promote 'the widest

---

1. TH letter to *New Statesman*, 5 September 1941, Org&Hist 3/3.
2. ASG, minutes, 14 November 1941. The initial proposal had been a payment of 'approximately £100 a month' (ASG, minutes, 16 June 1941). By March 1942, when the initial contract expired, MO had been paid a total of £1450 (ASG, minutes, 27 February 1942).
3. Basil Butler Co, Ltd; Arthur S. Dixon, Ltd; Cecil D. Notley Advertising, Ltd; Rumble, Crowther and Nicholas, Ltd; C. R. Casson, Ltd; Everetts Advertising Ltd; Stuart Advertising Agency, Ltd. An eighth member (Alfred Pemberton, Ltd) joined in August 1941 (ASG, minutes, 26 August 1941).

recognition of the usefulness of advertising in the world of commerce and in the social and civic life of the nation.'[4] One way they did this was to host fortnightly lunch parties, inviting politicians, civil servants, bankers, industrialists, military leaders, academics, journalists, and others, networking across institutional boundaries. In the course of the war the ASG lunches became prestige occasions, the names of those attending duly recorded on the court page of *The Times*.[5] The ASG leaders, who had all established successful advertising agencies in the interwar years, shared a belief in the social purpose of advertising, and they saw the Guild as a means of promoting 'idealistic aims' alongside their commercial activities.[6] A similar combination of business acumen and social reformism had characterized several of the advertising men who had sponsored MO before the war—notably Jack Beddington at Shell, T. O. Beachcroft at Lintas, and Clem Leslie at the Gas, Light and Coke Company—so this was a milieu of which Harrisson already had a good deal of experience. Unlike the relationship with the MOI, working for the ASG posed no threat to MO's independence: publication of MO's findings was not only welcomed by the Guild, but guaranteed in advance. Moreover the Guild's aim of charting wartime changes of social habit as a contribution to wartime governance and post-war reconstruction (as well as to the advertising industry) was at one with MO's own broader ambitions.[7]

Marcus Brumwell and A. Everett Jones—the two ASG leaders later to become directors of MO—were responsible respectively for the Guild's internal and external relations. Brumwell, in charge of 'creative liaison' among members of the Guild, was a patron of modernist art and a leading player in the movement to raise design standards in the world of industry, and was responsible with Misha Black for the establishment of the Design Research Unit in 1944, one of the most influential design practices in post-war Britain.[8] A close friend of the Communist crystallographer J. D. Bernal since the 1930s, Brumwell was as much at home among scientists as among

4. ASG Constitution, January 1942. See also Brumwell's 1944 article 'Tell the people: is advertising social? Has it a place in the planned economy?' in Nicholas Kaldor papers, NK/1/60.
5. *The Times*, passim.
6. ASG, minutes, 6 May 1941.
7. *People in Production*, iii; *People's Homes*, iii.
8. Robin Kinross, 'Herbert Read and Design' in David Goodway, *Herbert Read Reassessed*, 151–4; Sophie Forgan, 'Festivals of Science and the Two Cultures: Science, Design and Display in the Festival of Britain, 1951', *The British Journal for the History of Science*, 31, 2, 1998, 223; *Design*, 240, 1968, 25.

artists, and in the 1950s he was to play a central role in promoting the discussions between Labour politicians and leading scientists which culminated in Harold Wilson's 'white heat of technology' stance in the 1964 election.[9] In 1960 Brumwell described himself as having been involved 'all my life...with advertising of all kinds, mass communication, journalism, editing, industrial design and social survey' and most particularly with fostering 'the application of the skill of the artists in this country to large scale industry and...of our scientists...in industry and politics.'[10] The range of Brumwell's interests made him a man after Harrisson's own heart, and the two men established an enduring relationship.

Everett Jones (generally known as EJ), who was responsible for the Guild's 'parliamentary liaison', saw his job as being to cultivate links with those MPs who 'were seeking to get rid of the dead wood in the Government and to really start organising the war.'[11] Both Everett Jones and the ASG's chairman, J. B. Nicholas, were Liberal Party activists, and it was primarily through Liberal MPs that the Guild sought influence at the parliamentary level.[12] This suited Harrisson well. Always the popular frontist, he was keen to consolidate his links with those radicals—of whatever party—who had opposed appeasement and worked for the overthrow of Chamberlain in 1940. Alongside his journalistic links with such popular front organs as Tom Hopkinson's *Picture Post* and Kingsley Martin's *New Statesman,* Harrisson was keen to involve himself and MO during 1941–2 with radicals ready to break with the electoral truce and promote independent by-election candidates committed to gingering up the war effort and rooting out incompetence, complacency, and vested interest in high places.

The closest Harrisson had to a party political affiliation was with the more radical members of the Liberal Party. When, in their bitter exchanges in January 1940, Madge complained that Harrisson was trying to use MO

9. David Horner, 'The Road to Scarborough: Wilson, Labour and the scientific revolution', in R. Coopey, S. Fielding and N. Tiratsoo (eds), *The Wilson Governments, 1964–1970,* 1993, 51–4, 56, 58–62, 66; M. W. Kirby, 'Blackett in the "White Heat" of the Scientific Revolution: Industrial Modernisation under the Labour Governments, 1964–1970', *The Journal of the Operational Research Society,* 50, 10, 1999, 986.
10. Particulars of members proposed, 18 May 1960, 1944 Association papers, Labour Party archive.
11. ASG, minutes, 2 February 1940, 26 June 1940.
12. J. P. McNulty, who replaced Everett Jones as secretary in May 1940, and left to join the MOI later in January 1941, may well have been another radically minded Liberal. In September 1947 *The Times* published a letter from him supporting grass-roots trade union militancy and attacking both employers and the TUC leadership (*The Times,* 20 September 1947).

as a basis for launching himself as a political leader, he denied any such intention, insisting that he was 'quite happy to be as far in politics as I am now, that is to say knowing what's going on and watching what's going on.'[13] In fact it was rather more than that. In November 1939 he had offered MO's services to Richard Acland, suggesting 'some definite association' between MO and the Liberals with whom Harrisson had previously collaborated 'in several elections'.[14] Acland, the leading advocate of a popular front in the pre-war Liberal Party, had little pull with his fellow Liberal MPs and was already well on the way towards breaking with them to establish the new Common Wealth Party. In February 1940, following the publication of the book in which he announced his conversion to the principle of common ownership *(Unser Kampf)*, Acland commissioned MO to pre-test his 'Manifesto of the Common Man'. This was to little effect since he chose to disregard MO's finding that the word 'common' had a far from positive meaning among working-class people.[15] It was not with Acland but through his association with the ASG that Harrisson was able to consolidate his links with Liberal supporters of popular front politics.

One trusted sponsor of the ASG's political initiatives was Clem Davies, who had played a leading role in the cross-party manoeuvring that brought down the Chamberlain Government in May 1940, and was later to become leader of what was left of the Liberal Party after 1945.[16] The links between the Guild and radical Liberalism were further strengthened by the recruitment of Tom Horabin, a businessman returned in a 1939 by-election as a popular front, anti-appeasement candidate, who was paid a retainer to lobby the Department of Overseas Trade on the Guild's behalf.[17] Following their failure to carry a resolution against the political truce at the June 1941 Liberal Assembly, Liberal activists set up a group, Radical Action, to press their case within the party. Everett Jones was at the forefront of this

13. TH to CM, 25 January 1940, Org&Hist 1/1.
14. TH to Acland, 6 November 1939, TC 25/5/G.
15. TH to Acland, 26 March 1940; Acland to TH, 27 March 1940, TC 25/8/A.
16. Malcolm Baines, 'The Survival of the British Liberal Party, 1932–1959', Oxford DPhil, 1989, 56–7.
17. ASG, minutes, 7 May 1940. Horabin had been elected to Parliament as an anti-appeasement popular front candidate in the North Cornwall by-election in January 1939. Consistently on the left of Liberal politics, he defected to Labour (and its Keep Left grouping) in 1947. His political credo, spelt out in a 1944 Penguin Special, already put him well to the left of mainstream Labour opinion (J. Reynolds and I. Hunter, 'Liberal Class Warrior', *Journal of Liberal Democrat History*, 28, Autumn 2000, 17–21).

movement and was instrumental in persuading Davies and Horabin to lend their support.[18] It was Everett Jones who first proposed that Harrisson should be commissioned by the ASG, and six years later MO was still doing research for Radical Action, while Harrisson was personally contributing to its funds.[19] From the outset Harrisson's association with the ASG was underpinned by his political affinity with some of its leading members.

II

One of the Guild's first acts had been to offer their services to the MOI on a non-profit basis, an offer turned down because it would have undercut existing relationships between the Ministry and other advertising agents.[20] Those in charge of advertising in the MOI, however, liked the idea of agencies working together, and they were happy to go along with the ASG's proposal that the Guild itself should decide which of its constituent firms would be entrusted with coordinating any particular campaign and how the proceeds should be shared.[21] In June 1940 the Guild received its first major commission: an anti-gossip campaign intended to combat the threat of a sudden collapse of morale by creating 'a large group of people pledged to stop the spreading of ill-founded rumours', a 'Silent Column' to frustrate the 'Fifth Column' rumour-mongering of defeatists and pro-Nazi agents. Personally authorized by Churchill, the Silent Column advertisements carried the punch line: 'If you know anyone who makes a habit of causing worry and anxiety by passing on rumour and who says things persistently that might help the enemy—tell the police', adding, as if in anticipation of the storm to come, 'but only as a last resort.' Issued in the context of well-publicized prosecutions under the Emergency Powers Act for spreading alarm and despondency, the totalitarian implications of the campaign seemed to confirm fears that the government had lost faith in the popular will to resist and was turning to Gestapo methods to enforce it. Faced with mounting

18. Baines, 'Survival of the Liberal Party', 49, 56–7, 63; David Dutton, *The History of the Liberal Party*, 2004, 145; Donald Johnson, *Bars and Barricades*, 1952, 214–17.
19. ASG, minutes, 4 July 1940; Lancelot Spicer, 'To members of the Radical Action Executive Committee', 18 November 1946, annotated by TH, FR 1128; TH to Everett Jones, 22 May 1947, TC 61/10/b.
20. ASG, minutes, 28 June 1940.
21. Rodgers to Davidson, 8 June 1940, INF 1/533.

outrage in press and Parliament, Churchill announced the cancellation of the Silent Column campaign on 23 July.[22] Tasting blood, the press launched its campaign against Cooper's Snoopers a few days later.

As we have seen, Harrisson's involvement with the ASG began when he drafted their pamphlet defending market research during the Cooper's Snoopers agitation.[23] Subsequently he arranged for Mary Adams to advise the ASG chairman, J. B. Nicholas, about how best to add his voice to the pressure for a more coherent and coordinated propaganda policy, something that Harrisson had been arguing for since the summer of 1939.[24] Nicholas blamed the failure of the Silent Column campaign (about whose authoritarian implications several ASG members had expressed serious doubts[25]) on the fact that 'we were instructed to put a plaster on a running wound' rather than treat the wound itself. Different ministries were running their own campaigns, competing for diminishing advertising space in the press, and confusing the public with rival and sometimes contradictory appeals and instructions. What was needed, argued Nicholas—in a memo approved by Adams and submitted to the director general in August 1940—was a single strategic plan for all media, focussed around a daily 'call to the nation' by the government.[26] Harrisson approved the plan, although he joined Tom Hopkinson in taking a suitably repentant Nicholas to task for his nostalgia for 'the old fighting symbols of the British people'—John Bull, St George—lecturing him on the low salience of such patriotic symbolism among the masses, and stressing the need for any propaganda strategy to be informed by independent research into public attitudes.[27]

22. McLaine, *Ministry of Morale*, 82–4; 'Prosecutions under Defence Regulations', 29 July 1940, TC 43/2/E.
23. In fact Everett Jones's first proposal to 'enlist...the aid of Harrison [sic] and his "mass-observation" people' was made earlier in July to advise on the formulation of the Silent Column campaign (ASG, minutes, 4 July 1940). Nothing seems to have come of this: if it had, perhaps Harrisson would have steered them away from the heavy-handed tone which caused so much offence.
24. 'Note concerning Mr Nicholas's Memo re MOI', ASG, minutes, 12 August 1940.
25. ASG, minutes, 8 and 15 July 1940.
26. J. B. Nicholas, memo, 13 August 1940, MO&MOI 1.
27. Hopkinson to TH 15 August 1940; TH to Nicholas, 16 August 1940, MO&MOI 1; TH to Hopkinson, 16 August 1940, TC 43/2/D. Two years later Nicholas, having swapped old-fashioned English symbolism for new-fangled Soviet brutalism, gave full reign to his patriotic fervour in a relentlessly philistine attack on contemporary British artists for failing to rise to the needs of war with the necessary 'hate, anger and ferocious determination'. Henry Moore's 'Tube Shelter perspective' was dismissed as 'a vista of corpses in a catacomb, not cockneys in a tube. These pallid ghosts will never rise again, but the cockneys will be back at their jobs next morning'. As for the namby-pamby belief 'that even under the stress of war we must keep alive the things we are fighting for [including] our pre-war art, I suppose'; it was, he ranted,

III

In the summer of 1939 MO had started some work on shopkeepers' grievances on behalf of a Liberal Party enquiry into the position of 'the independent trader', and when, in January 1941, the ASG was asked by the MOI to develop a campaign to address the problems caused for shopkeepers by rationing they approached Harrisson 'to see if he could give us some information concerning the small retailers present reactions to the limitation of supplies.'[28] Harrisson—himself commissioned by the Board of Trade to look into relations between shoppers and retailers—was happy to supply the ASG with copies of his reports,[29] and this gesture paved the way for a contractual relationship between the two organizations. In June 1941 the ASG decided to expand its operations, pooling profits to finance the setting-up of a Film Unit and to employ MO to produce a series of reports on wartime social change:

> The world is changing before our eyes. Old habits and customs are disappearing; new social standards and aims are emerging. All of us who hope to live and work usefully in the world that is forming must be interested in the signs of change, social, political, commercial and industrial that show us what kind of world will be.

The idea was to publish an occasional bulletin, *Change*, based on MO's work, to be sent out initially without charge to a couple of thousand people: 'friends of Guild members or any other influential people. This would be very good propaganda for the Guild'. Once established, it was hoped that the bulletin could be distributed commercially, making the whole operation self-financing.[30] By the end of June 1941 the ASG minutes recorded that 'Tom Harrisson is now functioning, will write to the Guild every Monday

---

deeply disturbing 'that such escapist arguments should be seriously put forward to defend one of the nation's hobbies when the nation's life is in danger...' ('Is British Art Fighting?', *Art and Industry*, May 1942, 122–4). An incensed Herbert Read responded with an all-out attack on 'Mr Nicholas and his friends in the ASG', who were trying to use their own pre-war expertise in the 'creation of artificial wants...to degrade the ideals we are fighting for to the same level of commercial vulgarity...' (*Art and Industry*, July 1942, 2–4). Harrisson, of course, did not share Nicholas's philistine attitudes, and it is perhaps remarkable that within a year of this exchange Read was cooperating with Brumwell and the ASG in founding the Design Research Unit (*Art and Industry*, June 1943, 161).

28. 'Report on the Liberal Party's National Enquiry into the Position and Difficulties of the Independent Trader', 19 November 1941, FR 949; ASG, minutes, 3 January 1941.
29. ASG, minutes, 25 April 1941.
30. *Clothes and Clothes Rationing*, June 1941, preface; ASG, minutes, 9 and 16 May, 16 June 1941.

telling us what he is doing, will present his report once a month, and will from time to time, say once a month soon after the arrival of each report, attend a Guild luncheon probably bringing guests with him'.[31]

The first issue of *Change* was an analysis of reactions to the introduction of clothes rationing, for which the Board of Trade had hired the ASG to organize, in great secrecy, the initial press publicity.[32] Based on street interviewing in Bolton, Worcester, and London, conducted a few weeks after the introduction of rationing in June, and on the results of a directive to the panel on wartime changes in clothing habits, the survey concluded that most people had not yet thought about how rationing might change their clothes-buying or wearing habits. This provided some, rather meagre, evidence for Harrison's refrain of 'bewildered masses' and the need for governmental 'leadership'. Drawing on earlier MO work on the social psychology of clothing—one of Gertrude Wagner's central concerns—Harrisson argued that the main anticipated difficulties were a product of popular conservatism not of absolute shortages. Appropriate government propaganda, he suggested, could 'sanction' changes in established social habits, persuading women that they had no need for stockings, and clerks that they could do their work perfectly well without collars and ties.[33] Circulating copies of this report to 200 of the most active panel members, Harrisson revealed that MO had also done other work for the ASG over the summer of 1941, including a study of the effect of the war on dogs and their owners, a survey of displays in shoe shop windows, and an analysis of directive replies about the impact of war on smoking habits.[34] Probably, these were undertaken for clients of ASG agencies and funded separately from the *Change* series, and the link with the ASG continued to bring in other work, notably, in 1941, a substantial study of working-class attitudes to saving for the National Savings Committee, whose advertising was being handled by the Guild.[35]

31. ASG, minutes, 26 June 1941.
32. Meynell to Royd, 8 April 1942, INF 1/341.
33. *Clothes and Clothes Rationing*, 34 and *passim*.
34. MO *Bulletin*, 10 October 1941, FR 854. Reports on this work include FR 754, 779, 804, 838, 979. See also TC 79/1 and TC 4/2.
35. 'A Savings Survey', January 1942, FR 1053. Keynes (to whom he sent a copy) took a dim view of the report: 'I had no ideas that his people also were working at this subject,' he wrote to Madge, 'But the result seems to me rather a flimsy affair. He has not aimed, you will find, at any quantitative results, and, indeed, I am not quite sure what he has aimed at' (Keynes to CM, 12 January 1942, CMpap 21). An ASG member also commissioned MO to report on public attitudes to a bus company operating north of London ('Report on Birch Busses', January 1942, FR 1049; Waddicor to TH, 13 November 1941, TC 70/5/C).

IV

Ever since the fiasco of the Silent Column campaign the ASG had been pressing the case for a more coherent approach to home propaganda.[36] In April 1941 the Guild was encouraged by the outcome of a meeting with Sir Walter Monckton, Pick's successor as director general at the MOI.[37] Matters came to a head after Monckton threatened resignation unless the MOI was given authority to 'direct the form, timing and treatment of official news; the right of access to all information available to service departments and the Foreign Office; and the control over propaganda to enemy countries.'[38] With Beaverbrook also in support, Duff Cooper took his case to the Cabinet on 24 June, arguing that his job was impossible without the power 'to ensure complete co-ordination though unity of command'. If this could not be granted then it would be best to break up the Ministry and allocate its various responsibilities elsewhere.[39] Churchill, unwilling to face down the service departments' insistence on controlling the release of military news, not only refused to budge but further weakened the powers of the MOI by affirming the right of other departments to conduct their own relations with the press as well.[40] Within weeks Brendan Bracken had replaced Cooper as Minister of Information.

It was in the aftermath of these events that the ASG published the second issue of *Change* in October 1941. Drawing on MO material since the outbreak of war, *Change 2* laid out the now familiar case for a coordinated approach to propaganda, the danger of complacency about morale, and the fact that (unlike commercial advertising) 'people look to official propaganda to tell, not to ask; to lead, not plead.'[41] In September, when his contract with the MOI came to an end, Harrisson had given vent to his feelings in a draft letter to the *New Statesman*:

the whole of this tremendously important work of preparing weekly report [sic] on morale and propaganda impacts, grievances, industrial worries, air-

---

36. ASG, minutes, 16 December 1940.
37. ASG, minutes, 3 March, 2 April, 25 April 1941.
38. McLaine, *Ministry of Morale*, 234.
39. Cooper, 'Future of the Ministry of Information', 24 June 1941, CAB 66/17/12.
40. McLaine, *Ministry of Morale*, 238; Churchill, 'Information and Propaganda', 26 June 1941, CAB 66/17/15; Beaverbrook, 'Information and Propaganda', 28 June 1941, CAB 66/17/20; Churchill, 'Information and propaganda', 2 July 1941, CAB 66/17/22.
41. *Report on Official Home Propaganda, Change 2*, 64.

raid reactions, administrative breakdowns, and so on, will be left within the closed circle of people in Home Intelligence, and without any sort of external, scientific, standard or check. That would not matter so much if the personnel within Home Intelligence was itself of a high standard and expert. But I think I am right in saying that the three main people responsible for writing the Weekly Intelligence report are a cartoonist, lady novelist and a little known painter, and that none of them have any training in scientific method or any intimate knowledge of elementary things like local administration, or working-class economy.[42]

He appears to have thought better about such a personalized attack and the letter was never published, but he probably revealed as much in his talk to the ASG luncheon a few days later where he and the *New Statesman* editor, Kingsley Martin, spoke about official propaganda.[43] Fearing the worst, Steven Taylor, in charge of Home Intelligence since Adam's departure, lent his weight to official attempts to silence Harrisson.[44] In the published report, however, Harrisson was careful to avoid any reference to his treatment by Taylor, declaring that MO had always had the 'the most friendly and cordial relations' with the MOI, and blaming 'difficult circumstances' and 'the dark areas of inter-departmental jealousy' for the failures of official propaganda, rather than the Ministry itself. When Harrisson sent Taylor two copies of the report—'one privately and one for tearing up into small pieces!'— Taylor, reassured, responded by commissioning MO to report on a recruitment campaign for the Auxiliary Territorial Service.[45] In a report prepared for internal use in the Ministry a few days later Taylor summarized *Change 2*, endorsing many of its arguments, and appending a note which, in contrast to his later dismissal of Harrisson as a charlatan peddling mere prejudice, was measured in its appreciation of the strengths and weaknesses of MO methods.[46]

   Change 2 was well received in the press,[47] and, as Harrisson told Adams, the book was 'working nicely' for MO itself—a lunch invitation from Shell's Beddington (now responsible for the Crown Film Unit), and overtures from

---

42. TH draft letter to *New Statesman*, 5 September 1941, Org&Hist 3/3.
43. TH to Kingsley Martin, 3 September 1941.
44. Hanson to Aynsley, 10 October 1941, INF 1/286.
45. TH to Taylor, 31 October 1941; Taylor to TH, 5 November 1941, INF 1/262.
46. 'HI report on Home Front Propaganda. A Note on MOs Methods', November 1941, MApap 4/A.
47. *Manchester Guardian*, 1 November 1941; *The Times*, 3 November 1941; *News Chronicle*, 7 November 1941.

ICI about 'an interesting job on a possible long-term basis.'[48] In the report Harrisson had taken care to praise the 'imagination and energy' shown by Bracken as Cooper's successor at the Ministry, and in December Bracken was invited by the ASG directors to lunch with them, Harrisson, and the MP, Tom Horabin, in order to 'discuss the implications of home propaganda.'[49] Bracken had backed Cooper's case in July 1941, and in April 1942 he was to succeed where Cooper had failed, insisting that the cabinet discussed and approved a monthly MOI paper on morale and propaganda policy so that all departments could be kept to a uniform line.[50] Although the arguments he used held strong echoes of those regularly deployed by Harrisson ever since the summer of 1940, he presented them as novel:

> At this stage of the war public feeling and the public's reactions to the war cannot any longer be taken for granted. To study them, to assess them and to adjust our publicity to meet them is now a much more important concern of the Government than it was two years ago...

Ironically, one way in which Bracken was able to win over ministers sceptical about 'the various techniques of taking the public pulse' was by contrasting the procedures of his own department's Home Intelligence with the 'overstatements and obsessions', the tendency to 'exaggerate disquieting features' characteristic of other, unnamed, public pulse-takers.[51] This coded reference to MO was made explicit during the Cabinet discussion of Bracken's proposal in 'unfavourable comments' passed (by whom is not recorded, but there is reason to suspect Ernest Bevin[52]) on the third, and most substantial, of Harrisson's *Change* reports, *People in Production*.[53]

V

In October 1941, as questions about inefficiency in war industry moved to the forefront of British politics, the Guild decided to commission a two-volume

---

48. TH to Adams, 12 November 1941, TC 74/3/F; MO *Bulletin*, 10 November 1940, FR 938.
49. ASG, minutes, 14 November 1941.
50. McLaine, *Ministry of Morale,* 257.
51. Braken, 'Home Propaganda', 10 April 1942, CAB 66/23/35. McLaine's argument (*Ministry of Morale,* 10–11 and *passim*) that unlike his predecessors Bracken had no doubt about the state of public morale exaggerates the contrast.
52. Heimann, *Most Offending Soul,* 168.
53. War Cabinet Conclusions, 15 April 1942, CAB 65/26/10.

'Enquiry into Production'.[54] One volume was to be written by Thomas Balogh, a young protégé of Maynard Keynes, who the AGS had recently hired as their 'economic expert'.[55] While Balogh would deal with structural and economic aspects, MO was commissioned to deal with the psychological issues.[56] Balogh's volume was never produced,[57] but MO's report—an exhaustive survey of wartime factory life—was published by the Guild in April 1942, reprinted for general circulation by the publisher John Murray, and reissued in an abridged version as a Penguin Special in October.[58]

The world of work had not previously been a major theme in MO's output. The little that had been done on Bolton factories—participant observation by Penelope Barlow and Harrisson himself, some interviews and direct testimony from cotton operatives—was never intended to do more than provide material for a background chapter to the planned volume on how workers spent their spare time.[59] It was Harrisson's work for the Admiralty, particularly surveys of the highly problematic industrial relations in the shipyards of Clydeside and South Wales in March and July 1941, that stimulated his interest in workplace life and helped to feed a growing conviction that, as the threat of a blitz-induced collapse of morale receded, it was poor morale in war industry that constituted the biggest threat to the British war effort.[60] 'Divorced', as he saw it, from 'the common current of our culture', the conditions of factory life bred attitudes deeply dysfunctional to efficient war production: 'nowhere else in our war effort is the unity of feeling and purpose necessary to any war effort less satisfactory than in war industry.'[61] Approaching the industrial world as outsiders, Harrisson and his staff produced vivid accounts of the raw bitterness at

54. *People in Production*, iii, 13.
55. ASG, minutes, 26 August and 20 October 1941. A leading objective of the ASG was to secure advertising contracts for British exports from Whitehall, and Balogh was publishing on the future of the export trade in *The Economic Journal*. In June 1941 he was invited to an ASG luncheon and by July he was exchanging views with Harrisson on the production situation (ASG, minutes, 17 April 1940, 16 June 1941; TH to Kingsley Martin, 10 July 1941, TC 75/4/H).
56. *People in Production*, iii–iv.
57. Early in 1943 the ASG was still hopeful that Balogh would produce it (*People's Homes*, viii).
58. All quotations in the text of *People in Production* are from the Penguin Special, unless otherwise indicated.
59. See various drafts of this chapter in W40/A.
60. 'Morale in Glasgow', 7 March 1941, FR 600, 'The South Wales Waterfront', 10 July 1941, FR 781.
61. *People in Production*, x, 59.

the heart of much of British industrial relations: something which more seasoned observers took for granted.

Writing in July 1941 to Kingsley Martin from a Cardiff hotel, 'with the smoke of the Rhondda strong in my nose', Harrisson expressed his astonishment at the 'inefficiency and inadequacy which still prevails':

> bad labour relations growing worse, declining work effort, personal interests put before war interests both by management and men, delays, muddles, red tape, pettiness, lack of any central drive or real incisive policy. Unions, firms, shop stewards, individual men, foremen pulling in an inapposite higgeldy-piggeldy so that to listen to the point of view of one after another (as I have done for day after day) is a continuous objective bombardment of subjective selfish stupidity.

Though well aware of his ignorance of the industrial world, the underlying causes of this situation seemed clear enough to Harrisson. While wartime full employment had undermined employers' disciplinary powers, the workers' memory of interwar unemployment ensured that they would use their brief period of wartime indispensability to maximum sectional advantage, shoring up defences for the renewed insecurity that they fully expected to encounter as soon as the war was over:

> Behind all this lies the sickening anarchy of the Jarrow years, when working men were treated as dirt and when without hesitation whole industries were sabotaged in the interests of directors, whole areas were rendered 'special', whole populations forced to live by the yardstick of means test and meanness. Today when South Wales and Clyde boom again, it is fantastic...to expect these skilled, proud, intelligent workmen to forget the ten years they lived in the shadow of slagheaps.[62]

For both the workers and their bosses the need to defend sectional interest in this 'war within a war' was more real, more immediate, more pressing than the demands of the war against Germany.[63]

During the six months following October 1941 most of MO's staff were deployed at one time or another on the production enquiry. Harrisson himself concentrated on getting the view from above, seeking out contacts in Whitehall, meeting representatives of the main employers' federations, and talking to industrialists up and down the country.[64] By February 1942 he

---

62. TH to Kingsley Martin, 10 July 1941, TC 75/4/H.
63. 'The South Wales Waterfront', 10 July 1941, FR 781.
64. *People in Production*, 19, 22.

had personally visited more than 50 factories and, altogether, managers from about 80 firms, large and small, were interviewed, sometimes inviting investigators to visit them at home and stay overnight: 'The principal persons in industry have time for discussion (their work is largely talking, reading, pondering and wondering), and have been kind enough to spend a great many man hours in talking about their problems and principles.'[65] Guaranteed anonymity, many, including some of Britain's leading industrialists, were prepared to speak frankly.[66] Stanley Walpole, a London industrialist and a close associate of the ASG, invited Harrisson to attend his own series of lunches, where he could witness, and participate in, the efforts of reform-minded businessmen to tackle what they saw as the obstacles to industrial efficiency.[67] Walpole himself was sufficiently impressed by Harrisson's project to contribute £100 towards MO's costs.[68] In many firms employers facilitated MO interviews with supervisory staff, but few were prepared to give MO direct access to their shop-floor workers. Norman Kipping—works manager of the Standard Telephone and Cable, a leading player in London industrial circles and, later, director general of the Federation of British Industries—was keen on the project, and happy to talk to Harrisson and to give MO contacts in other firms, but he would not let them investigate shop-floor relations in his own factory.[69]

The only employer to invite MO to place an investigator on the shop floor was Michael Lipman, a most unusual businessman who had grown up as 'a ready-made socialist-atheist' in the radical milieu of Russian Jewish immigrants in early 20th-century Leeds.[70] Lipman had made a career in radio manufacture, and was responsible at the beginning of the war for

65. *People in Production*, 17–18; 'War Production', 6 February 1942, FR 1078.
66. None of the notes TH must have written up on these interviews survives in the archive, although there is a good deal of correspondence arising from them. TH's notes on an earlier meeting with Sir Charles Craven, one of Britain's leading arms manufacturers (19 October 1939, TC 25/5/E), gives a glimpse of the kind of indiscretions that he was adept at collecting.
67. *People in Production*, (Murray edition), 73. The seating plan for the Walpole lunch on 20 November 1941 survives in the MO Archive, along with a good deal of relevant correspondence, TC 75/6/A.
68. ASG, minutes, 14 November 1941.
69. *People in Production*, 34; TH to Kipping, 3 December 1941; Kipping to Waddicar, 20 November 1941, TC 75/4/H. On Kipping's wartime role see James Hinton, *Shop Floor Citizens: Engineering democracy in 1940s Britain*, 1994, 128–34.
70. Michael Lipman, *Memoires of a Socialist Business Man*, 1980. Harrisson's statement in his preface to *War Factory* (5) that he had been approached 'on the basis of "People in Production"' is clearly mistaken, since Fremlin arrived in the factory several months before *People in Production* was published and some of her reports are cited in the book.

setting up a new and top secret factory in the grounds of a country house
near the Wiltshire market town of Malmesbury to make radar equipment
for the RAF. Most of the 1,000 workers were women with little or no previous industrial experience, many of them away from home and engaged on
boringly repetitive work. It was to investigate what could be done to raise
the morale of these women that Celia Fremlin was sent by Harrisson, at
Lipman's request, to work incognito in the factory between February and
April 1941.[71] Looking back from the 1980s she believed that there had been
no prior arrangement with Lipman and that when she arrived no one knew
she was an MO investigator:

> It had long been agreed among us that as soon as we got called up we would
> send in reports to M-O of wherever we were . . . It just happened that that was
> where I was sent. I sent in reports which Tom liked for some reason—he got
> in touch with the management and asked whether they would mind if he
> published a book about it, because it was all rather secret . . .[72]

It is clear, however, from the contemporary record not only that Lipman
had arranged for her to be directed to the factory to provide a 'worm's eye
view' of shop-floor morale,[73] but that she knew that this was the case, noting
in the account she wrote of her first day that 'the following description is
typical of the arrival of any new employee: anything that happened owing
to the special capacity in which Inv. came down has been left out.'[74] Fremlin
and Harrisson did not get round to writing their report until months after
the publication of *People in Production*.[75] Lipman believed he had commissioned a confidential report, and when Harrisson sent him the draft manuscript for his comments, he was unaware that MO intended to publish the

71. According to Lipman (161) she was there for three months. That is compatible with surviving
    records of her activity in the MO Archive, which has no other work from her until May
    1942.
72. Fremlin, interviewed by Nick Stanley, 18 September 1981. See also CF's preface to Cresset
    Library's 1987 edition of *War Factory*.
73. *War Factory*, 6.
74. Fremlin, 'Arrival of a New Employee', 7 February 1942, FR 1081. The welfare manager had
    arranged with Harrisson to meet her from the train (Garland to TH, 5 February 1942, TC
    75/4/F). She may not have been called up at all. If she was, she somehow secured her release
    and was back working for MO by May 1942 shortly after which she married (Fremlin, interviewed by Stanley, 18 September 1981). By October, when she *was* threatened with conscription, she was expecting a baby and was therefore allowed to continue working with MO
    ('Memo on Mass-Observation', 29 October 1942, FR 1450).
75. Fremlin spent three weeks writing up her experience, probably in the autumn of 1942 when
    she revisited the factory (Fremlin, interviewed by Stanley, 18 September 1981; Lipman to
    Harrisson, 3 November 1942, TC 75/4/H).

material and was astonished (and astonishingly forgiving) to receive a copy
of the book (*War Factory*) in the post. Although the location of the 'war factory' was not disclosed, its identity was perfectly apparent to those who
worked there and the local W. H. Smith's was overwhelmed with orders for
the book. Lipman feared a backlash over having placed a 'spy' in the works,
but (according to his memoirs) most of the employees were delighted to
find themselves 'in a book'.[76] Fremlin seems never to have known that the
book was seen by the people she had observed, and convinced herself,
despite evidence to the contrary in the published text, that none of the
individuals she discussed could have been identified by the management.[77]

War Factory provides a vivid antidote to romanticized accounts of wom-
en's involvement in war production. The unskilled repetitive work required
of the women in the Malmesbury factory did nothing to enhance their self-
esteem or to foster pride in their contribution to the war effort. To her
surprise, Fremlin discovered that the boredom was ameliorated by a 'curious, almost exhilarating sense of the slipping away of all responsibilities that
come over people after a few days in this sort of work', and she saw this lack
of responsibility—'from eight in the morning till eight at night life is taken
off one's own hands, completely and absolutely'—as the root cause of the
women's 'apathy about the factory and everything to do with it'; an apathy
further reinforced by the fact that the younger women, all living in hostels
or lodgings, had no domestic responsibilities to give meaning and purpose
to their lives.[78]

However interesting Fremlin's observations, Malmesbury was remote
from the mainstream of British industrial life, and the combination of
enlightened management and inexperienced (and largely un-unionized)
workers that characterized Lipman's factory was far from typical of war
industry in general. In search of a more representative view from below,
MO investigators interviewed several leading trade unionists and the
Communist leader of the unofficial shop steward's movement.[79] But their
main sources for working-class opinion were questionnaire-based interviews with people accosted in the street in factory districts of London,

76. Michael Lipman, *Memoires of a Socialist Business Man*, London, 1980, 161.
77. Fremlin, preface to the Cresset edition of *War Factory*, 1987.
78. *War Factory*, 43, 47, 49, 95–6, 109–12.
79. *People in Production*, 19; Note on Interview with Jack Tanner (General Secretary of the
    Amalgamated Engineering Union), 4 February 1942; Interview with Len Powell, 26 January
    1942, TC 75/6/D.

Coventry, Luton, Welwyn Garden City, Oldbury (in the Black Country),
Chester, and Malmesbury. Investigators tried to match respondents with the
factories where Harrisson or others had interviewed the management,
catching people as they left work. This led to complications in Luton when
the Vauxhall management complained that their workers were being stopped
in the street and quizzed by a woman who wanted to know if they were
'happy at work'. Tracked down to her flat in central London, the MO investigator told the police that 'her instructions were to make her investigations
unofficially without the knowledge of factory managements'.[80] A less experienced investigator, Eric Gulliver, an idealistic young Communist who
spent two years with MO between leaving school aged 16 and his call up in
1943, found it difficult to locate any workers at all on a cold January day in
Watford:

> In all cases entrances to workplaces were barred, and the few cafes encoun-
> tered after much walking and looking around seemed to contain few peo-
> ple who even looked as if they were war workers. To say the least of it this
> time spent endeavouring to find suitable points and people together with
> the extremely disagreeable nature of the weather concerned proved a sever
> dampener on my enthusiasm for the first approach at an Industrial
> Questionnaire . . .[81]

Despite such discouragements, however, around 1,200 street interviews
were conducted.[82] The most intensive work was done in Coventry, the
cockpit of conflict in British war production during the winter of 1941–2.
Five investigators (including Fremlin before she went to Malmesbury)
worked there, attending meetings, observing demonstrations, interviewing
workers, talking to all the leading players, and providing the material for
some of the most vivid passages in *People in Production*.[83] Further information came from members of MO's panel, both in the form of directives
soliciting views about the production crisis and in direct testimony solicited by MO from panellists working in one capacity or another in war
industry.

---

80. Luton Borough Police report on Cecilia B. Mackintosh, 22 January 1942, INF 1/286.
81. Report by EG, 16 January 1941, TC 75/1/B.
82. *People in Production*, 20.
83. *People in Production*, 46–7, 26–8, 102–3. For a full discussion of these events see J. Hinton,
    'Coventry Communism. A study of factory politics in the Second World War', *History Workshop
    Journal*, 10, 1980, and Hinton, *Shop Floor Citizens*.

People in Production provides convincing evidence against the view that
wartime national unity had put an end to class conflict. But that is not how
Harrisson chose to describe his findings. Although the bitter antagonisms
that characterized industrial relations in much of British industry are carefully observed and vividly described, Harrisson's analysis of these dysfunctional human relations is cast primarily in psychological terms, rather than
in the structural language of class. His avoidance of the word 'class' when
discussing relations between workers and management is a striking feature
of the book. Harrisson had always rejected Marxist approaches to the understanding of social relations, and his exposure to the bitter world of British
industrial relations did nothing to change this view. He reserved the concept of 'class' for the minutiae of status differentiation, operating as much
within the 'working classes' as between them and the rest of society.[84] Within
days of the publication of *People in Production* Harrisson was expounding
this view to a meeting of the British Psychological Society.[85] His paper, later
published in *The Sociological Review,*[86] argued that the notion that society
was structured by a fundamental conflict between capital and labour was 'a
psychological simplification' which appealed to no more than 'a small section', particularly those skilled workers in war industry who had 'gone up
rather suddenly and [are] at present in a "strong position", while at the same
time afraid that after the war [they] will slide down again.' Despite the fact
that wartime conditions were fostering more critical attitudes to the social
order, the class war rhetoric of the militants—'unusually intelligent and
often ambitious persons'—had not, or not yet, displaced hierarchical social
imagery in the minds of the mass of the workers among whom 'there is little solidarity or observable consciousness of mutual identity and interest.'
His observation of sectionalism in the shipyards, where the boilermakers
lorded it over lesser breeds,[87] had served to reinforce what he had learned in
the cotton mills: that competition for status ran right through working-class
life.[88] The great majority of working people, he argued, drawing on
Worktown evidence, saw the stratification of British society as a ladder to

84. *The Listener*, 13 October 1938, 765–6.
85. 'Report for *Nature*', 17 April 1942, FR 1214.
86. 'Notes on Class Consciousness and Class Unconsciousness', *The Sociological Review*, 34, 1942.
87. 'The South Wales Waterfront', 10 July 1941, FR 781.
88. Contrast Madge's 'Marxist' comment in 1937: 'I think it queer that you should expect me to
    draw back in a shocked manner at your observations on sectionalism in the working class...It
    would however be mere negative turnabout to say down with the workers because the poor
    bastards have been split into warring sections' (CM to TH, 17 September 1937, Org&Hist 1/7).

be climbed, not a system to be overthrown. The main class struggle in Britain, he asserted in a striking phrase, was 'the struggle to be more class': to move up a little in the pecking order. The complex differentiations of status which characterized British society provided, he argued, a structure that served to satisfy 'an almost universal and usually "healthy" human urge: the urge and incentive of personal progress, symbolically upward.'[89] As though responding in advance to Angus Calder's retrospective characterization of the 'People's War'—'the people surged forward to fight their own war, forcing their masters into retreat'—Harrisson insisted that 'the men from below do not surge up and overthrow; they take their gradual places near the top.'[90]

There *was* danger in the current situation, but it derived less from class feeling among the masses than from the 'ignorance and prejudice' of wealthy people who attributed to those less fortunate than themselves 'an exaggerated envy and menace', unable to believe that the newly empowered masses were not bent on depriving them of their privileges. This class consciousness among employers was potentially self-fulfilling, inducing a mentality of resistance to the, actually very modest, aspirations of working people that lent credence to the language of class war. Socialist propagandists saw industrial conflict as evidence of the reality of class war: capital and labour locked in a fundamental clash of interests. For Harrisson, in an unlikely simile, strikes were like lovers' quarrels, no more evidence of a fundamental conflict of interest than a lovers' tiff was of sexual incompatibility. In a passage breathtaking in its optimism, he argued that 'a few words will often remove a clash of interests', citing the astonishment he had witnessed among industrialists who had been persuaded to put to one side fears of encroachment on managerial prerogative and set up joint production committees. 'An hour or two a month round a table,' they discovered, could transform the whole atmosphere of a factory:

> An increasing number of 'progressive-minded' firms are finding how much they can reduce industrial friction within their factories by welfare schemes, by developing loyalties within the firm and producing a group consciousness around the factory unit, reaching from the Managing Director down to the lowest unskilled girls. These loyalties—which can now be found in a number

89. 'Notes on Class Consciousness', 152.
90. 'Notes on Class Consciousness', 159; Calder, *People's War*, 21.

of the biggest concerns in the country—cut vertically across the horizontal interests of income groups.[91]

So extreme was Harrisson's denial of the conflict of interest between capital and labour that it provoked a defence of Marxist perspectives from the doyen of the London School of Economics' Sociology Department, a liberal moral philosopher, Morris Ginsberg.[92]

For Harrisson the ill-feeling that pervaded the war industry reflected not any irreconcilable antagonisms of class, but a failure of leadership; and he had no time for the muddled but practical logic of those who understood that 'wartime national unity' was, at best, a series of compromises and evasions:

> The yardstick against which we measure our remarks [he wrote in his July 1941 report on the South Wales shipyards] is one of a reasonable unity and efficiency such as might be expected in a time of great crisis, when employer and men are fighting for Britain instead of, as in peacetime, for nothing broader than their own interests.[93]

A few 'simple if drastic measures' would be sufficient to create such 'unity and efficiency'—including a more direct controlling presence of the Admiralty to bring home to the workers the larger context of their work. To dissolve the appalling influence of 'the past and petty' on Clydeside's industrial relations he proposed in March 1941 the publication of 'some kind of... report on the local situation, admitting some of the mistakes on all sides and clearing the air for a new start.'[94] While Harrisson conceded that it was 'perhaps Utopian' to expect the voice of pure reason to carry all before it, the above-the-struggle stance adopted in *People in Production* had similarly utopian underpinnings. Wage incentives were not the answer, if only because there was little to spend the money on in wartime. Joint consultation, along with practical measures to improve welfare provisions, reduce excessive hours of work, provide support for working mothers, and so on, would go some way to remove obstacles to greater productive effort. But there was a limit to what could be achieved by even the most powerful and enlightened of managing directors. Only appropriate leadership at the national level could create the conditions necessary to unleash maximum effort from the workers.[95] And the main obstacle here was

91. 'Notes on Class Consciousness', 163.
92. 'Report for *Nature*', 17 April 1942, FR 1214.
93. 'The South Wales Waterfront', 10 July 1941, FR 781.
94. 'Morale in Glasgow', 7 March 1941, FR 600; *People in Production*, 265.
95. *People in Production*, 266; *War Factory*, 121–2, 125.

the familiar tendency of official propaganda, confusing cheerfulness with good morale, to foster complacency about the progress of the war. Workers were all too ready to believe in the certainty of victory, allowing them to focus on pursuing their war with the bosses rather than maximizing production. The propaganda of events (Dunkirk), or the kind of bull-in-a-china-shop propaganda stunts at which Beaverbrook excelled, were effective in stimulating effort in the short term, but only at the expense of the steady, continuous long-term effort that industrial work required: 'Production has to be based on steady rhythms, routines, methods, moods. It does not lend itself to catch-phrases and sudden spurts.'[96]

Despite extensive documentation of allegations of inefficiency in war production from a plethora of different sources, Harrisson was at pains to distinguish MO's approach from that of the critics whose views he reported. While allegations of managerial incompetence abounded, cases of proven inefficiency were difficult to come by, and as public discourse about the scandal of production grew it became ever more difficult to separate 'fact' from 'feeling and fantasy'.[97] Much of what was said and written about inefficiency reflected nothing more than 'personal experience multiplied by temperamental prejudice, divided by degree of understanding of all the factors involved.'[98] As an outsider he did not feel competent to assess complaints of technical inefficiencies arising from managerial muddle, confusion, and the competitive structure of industry. Perhaps he was deliberately leaving discussion of such things to Balogh's planned parallel study of economic factors in war production. It was, however, perfectly apparent to him that many of the hold-ups and interruptions in production that triggered so much bitterness on the shop floor were an unavoidable consequence, not of managerial incompetence, but of technical innovation and changing demands from the military. The problem, as he saw it, lay not in the disruptions themselves, but in the antagonistic industrial relations that prevented them from being sensibly handled. Instead of sitting down together to see how to minimize hold-ups in production, everybody concerned looked for someone else to blame, generally those above them in the industrial hierarchy. Shop stewards blamed management, small firms blamed the subcontracting arrangements of the big arms producers, employers in general

96. *People in Production*, 59.
97. *People in Production*, 32–3; *People in Production*, (Murray edition), 383.
98. *People in Production*, 73.

blamed red tape in the supply departments, and meanwhile the press had a field day magnifying this chorus of discontent into the kind of scandal that sold newspapers.[99] The sense of scandal and the 'carping criticism' of those using it, with the best of intentions, in their campaigns for reform fed back in turn to the shop floor, helping to create inefficiency 'though a general feeling of dissatisfaction and distrust, bad morale.'[100] Inefficiency in war production had become an *idée fixe,* believed in regardless of any evidence, and Harrisson's central concern was not with the reality or otherwise of such beliefs, but with the processes by which they were created: as always it was the processes of opinion formation, rather than the opinions themselves, that interested him most. At the core of *People in Production* was an analysis, not of the scandal of production, but of the production of scandal:

> The facts are frequently coloured by feelings, derived from the traditional pattern of industrial hostilities, multiplied by the additional tensions of war industry, and sanctioned by general published opinion criticism of industrial efficiency...It is necessary to have this complicated point clear before one can go far in any study of war industries today...[101]

This emphasis on the process of opinion formation, rather than on facts, worried some of Harrisson's friends among the employers, notably George Dickson, a member of the Walpole group and a leading critic of inefficiency caused by the unplanned proliferation of subcontracting resulting from the cosy relationship between the supply ministries and the big arms firm. Commenting on the proofs of the book, Dickson worried that Harrisson's interest in the 'fantasy' was leading him to lose sight of the 'facts': 'I think I can see the point that is developing, but so far the writing does certainly imply that there has been far too much talk about bad production in relation to the actual facts.'[102] But Harrisson, characteristically biting the hand that fed him, dismissed the Walpole group's 'engrossment in detail of Government machinery for passing out orders to firms' as a diversion from the real psychological issues of leadership and human relations. Unimpressed by what he had heard at the Walpole lunches, Harrisson preferred to believe what he had been told in his meetings with 'key people in some of the big

99. *People in Production*, 31, 48–52, 63–5, 67, 226.
100. *People in Production*, 46, 60, 266.
101. *People in Production*, 30.
102. Dickson to TH, 11 March 1942, TC 75/6/A.

firms'. It was these people, who had the widest overview, whose views on industrial efficiency carried the most weight with Harrisson and 'they tended on the whole to be the least critical of war production.'[103] For these captains of industry the talk of managerial inefficiency was overdone, blown up out of all proportion by a mischievous alliance between shop stewards delighting in wrong-footing management and newspapers with a nose for scandal; the grievances of smaller firms sidelined by the 'arms ring' were beside the point. Moreover the fears of the reactionary leaders of the Engineering Employers' Federation, who spent the winter of 1941–2 bitterly resisting the combined pressures of shop floor and Whitehall to establish joint production committees, were without foundation. It was among the biggest industrialists, the men at the commanding heights of war production, that Harrisson located the clear-sighted power of leadership that he believed was needed to overcome the crisis of industrial morale. Despite the fact that Walpole and Dickson had both been at the forefront of experiments in 'industrial democracy' in their own factories, it was Lloyd Roberts, the architect of ICI's labour relations who had been brought in by Bevin to force through the establishment of joint production committees across war industry, who Harrisson singled out for approval as the pioneer of joint consultation.[104] As with his uncritical embrace of Churchillian authority in the summer of 1940, Harrisson's democratic sentiments took second place to his belief in the need for clear-sighted leadership.

Launched at the height of a political crisis over war production and the conduct of the war, the book was extensively and favourably reviewed in the press, including leaders in *The Manchester Guardian*, *The Observer* and the *British Medical Journal*, the latter insisting that it merited 'the most careful study by the authorities'.[105] Writing in *The Economic Journal*, the economist Philip Sargant Florence (a longstanding friend of MO), insisted that Harrisson had no need to apologize for the journalistic vividness of his presentation— 'as absorbing as any novel with plenty of dialogue'—since something more than dry statistics was needed to educate 'a ruling class of politicians [and] employers' cut off from the masses about the realities of shop-floor life.[106]

103. *People in Production*, 105.
104. *People in Production*, (Murray edition), 84. On Lloyd Roberts, Dickson, and Walpole see Hinton, *Shop Floor Citizens*, 107ff.
105. *British Medical Journal*, 1, 4245, 16 May 1942, 612; *Guardian* and *Observer* cited in H. D. Willcock, 'Mass-Observation', *American Journal of Sociology*, 48, 4, 1943, 453–4.
106. P. Sargant Florence, *The Economic Journal*, 52, 206/207, 232–4.

True to form, Britain's actual rulers—the War Cabinet—responded by minuting their irritation at what they (mistakenly) took to be a tiresome exercise in subversive propaganda.[107]

VI

A few weeks before the publication of *People in Production* in April 1942, the ASG had decided to ask Harrisson

> to name the figure that he would require to work solely for the Guild and to become the director of a Guild research institute should we establish it after the war or sooner. [It was] pointed out that this might not cost us much more than we are paying him now and that we should then reap the benefit of any other work he is now doing outside the Guild and that we should hope thereby to gain prestige, publicity and new advertising accounts.[108]

Whether this proposition was ever put to Harrisson is not known, but if it was it would have been clear to him that he could not have accepted such a proposal without seriously jeopardizing MO's independence. Moreover, however positive the Guild may have felt about MO's work, there were some important potential clients for whom their association with Harrisson brought anything but 'prestige... and new advertising accounts'. Early in April 1942, for example, the ASG was excluded from a major new contract with the Board of Trade, at the insistence of the Board's head of publicity, Francis Meynell, who complained to the committee allocating advertising contracts that:

> we are embarrassed by the Guild's relations with Tom Harrisson and Mass-Observation. He has been making an unhelpful running commentary on the Board's surveys as a means of glorifying his own, and I should not feel able to trust his associates with the consumer survey data which as Agents they must have to inform their work for the Board.[109]

---

107. War Cabinet, *Conclusions*, 15 April 1942, CAB 65/26/10. It was suggested later that Bevin's fury at the book—which actually went out of its way to praise his handling of the production crisis (*People in Production*, Murray ed. 383–4)—played a central part in the decision to conscript him and other MO workers a few weeks later (Heimann, *Most Offending Soul*, 168). As we shall see, however, other factors contributed to this decision.
108. ASG, minutes, 27 February 1942.
109. Advisory Committee on the appointment of Agents, minutes, 8 April 1942, INF 1/341. Among other things he had no doubt been irritated by an article in *Tribune* ('Bracken's Trackers', 13 March 1942) in which TH cited a Board of Trade enquiry as evidence of how misleading direct interviewing of representative samples could be in discovering real public opinion. On Meynell see DNB entry.

Meynell—one-time Communist and a distinguished typographer and publisher—had become a leading figure in the advertising world during the
1930s. Like MO's enemies in the Ministry of Labour, the MOI, and the
Home Office, Meynell did not take kindly to Harrisson's gadfly attacks on
the competence of established authority.

Perhaps it was this incident that took the gloss off the idea of a Guild
Research Unit, although it would have faded in any case as the various
partners in the ASG fell out over the amount of their money being spent on
MO and the Film Unit. In April 1942 the Guild agreed to ask Harrisson
'what...minimum retaining fee he would expect from the Guild in order
that the Guild may be in a position to renew working with [MO]...at a
suitable opportunity'.[110] The answer, it seems, was £20 a month, in return
for which MO supplied the ASG with copies of their regular morale reports,
reports paid for by other agencies, and agreed to undertake small surveys
free of charge and to hold itself in readiness for other work as and when the
need arose.[111] In the meantime, however, MO had still to deliver on a further report commissioned by the ASG—Change 4—dealing with the central
issue of post-war reconstruction: housing. As in his approach to war production, Harrisson's take on reconstruction planning was to put him at odds
with much conventional progressive opinion.

110. ASG, minutes, 14 April 1942.
111. Consultative Committee, minutes, 6 February 1943, Org&Hist 1.

10

Reconstruction

Tom Harrisson was well aware that one reason for the antagonistic nature of relations in war industry was the workers' belief that as soon as the war was over large-scale unemployment would return, enabling employers to cut wages and restore autocratic control on the shop floor. But *People in Production* had little to say about the need to combat such fears with visions of a new and fairer post-war world. Harrisson's concern was to focus people's attention on the urgent demands of war fighting and he was unconvinced by the growing tide of reformist opinion pressing for post-war reconstruction planning to be seen as an integral part of the war effort. In its initial May 1941 agreement with the Advertising Service Guild (ASG), a third volume of *Change* dealing with attitudes to reconstruction had been planned, but Harrisson was happy in the autumn to postpone this in favour of what both he and the ASG saw as the more urgent issue of war production.[1]

Advocates of reconstruction planning argued that a positive vision of a new post-war social order was essential to the war effort, that it would be difficult to maintain popular morale if the war was perceived as being fought merely in defence of the status quo. A famous *Times* leader, written by the diplomat and historian E. H. Carr two weeks after the fall of France, captured this mood:

> If we speak of democracy, we do not mean a democracy which maintains the right to vote but forgets the right to work and the right to live. If we speak of freedom, we do not mean a rugged individualism which excludes social organisation and economic planning. If we speak of equality we do not mean a political equality nullified by social and economic privilege. If we speak of economic reconstruction, we think less of maximum production (though this too will be required) than of equitable distribution.[2]

1. *People's Homes*, 4.
2. *The Times*, 1 July 1940.

It is not surprising that the left seized on this line of argument, insisting that only a People's War—a war fought to establish a new, planned, more egalitarian social order—could unlock the popular energies necessary to sustain Britain in its long struggle against Nazi Germany. But Mass-Observation (MO) remained silent about this supposed link between reconstruction planning and wartime morale. Despite Harrisson's close association with left-wing critics of the Churchill coalition, and despite the socialist views of most of MO's staff and volunteer panellists, at no time in Harrisson's voluminous writing about morale between 1939 and 1942 did he press the case for firm government commitments to post-war social reform as a vital ingredient of wartime morale-building.[3] On this issue Harrisson was at one with Churchill: the important thing was to focus minds and energies on maximizing Britain's war-fighting efficiency, not on planning for a New Jerusalem. While this certainly involved addressing immediate causes of social discontent (excessive hours of work; perceived inequalities in the distribution of food, fuel, and other necessities of life; inadequate post-raid provision; etc.), Harrisson was sceptical about the proposition that talk about a bright new post-war future would do anything to boost popular morale. Two things underlay this scepticism. In the first place, he believed, most of the advocates of reconstruction planning showed little understanding of—or even interest in—the expectations or desires of ordinary people. And secondly MO's own researches suggested that popular anxieties about the post-war future were too complex and too deeply rooted to be susceptible to any quick New-Jerusalemist fix.

I

As the tide of reconstruction talk mounted in the early months of 1941, Harrisson was 'gradually sifting ideas in my mind on the general approach to reconstruction from our point of view.'[4] Ever since his observation of working-class hostility to rehousing projects in Bolton, Harrisson had been critical of the tendency of architects and town planners to assume that they

---

3. Everett Jones, in his preface to *People's Homes* (iii), referred to 'the open secret that the war incentive of the ordinary people of Britain is not merely to defeat the common enemy and draw his fangs, but to create for themselves a better society', but no such linkage between post-war hopes and 'war incentive' (morale) is made in the body of the book.
4. TH to Fitter, 20 March 1941, TC 25/12/A.

knew how ordinary people *ought* to live without going to the trouble of asking them how they *wanted* to live. It was not, as he explained to a meeting of the Housing Centre in October 1939, that people's wants were necessarily the same as their needs. Popular aspirations were often restricted by ignorance and low expectations, and enlightened expertise certainly had a role to play in the education of desire. But without the knowledge of existing aspirations, which only careful objective sociological enquiry could supply, the planners were all too likely to confuse their own chatter and mutual back-scratching with a genuine raising of public awareness: 'the successful reformer must know the *is* before he can dictate the *ought*.'[5] The same dangers were apparent in the burgeoning 'reconstruction racket', notably in G. D. H. Cole's Nuffield Reconstruction Survey, set up with Treasury funding in February 1941:[6] 'a sort of Fabian Club for the higher idealism of pseudo-popular understanding,' Harrisson wrote sourly in April, aware that the Oxford academics in charge were unlikely to commission MO to supply any genuine understanding of popular attitudes.[7] Richard Fitter, attending a conference of the Garden Cities and Town Planning Association in March, fully endorsed Harrisson's views:

> The outstandingly depressing fact about the conference was the general failure to realise the importance of the human factor in planning and reconstruction... The general impression of the conference was to confirm the worst fears about the way in which the reconstruction racket is being run at present by idealists out of touch with reality.[8]

Since December 1940 Fitter had been devoting his time to a hugely ambitious project to 'condense into readable form illustrated by maps, diagrams and tables, the available information and statistics relating to human behaviour in Great Britain... As complete an account of the habits and customs of the British islanders as any anthropologist has ever done of the habits and customs of a Melanesian tribe.'[9] Harrisson wanted this to be 'the most authoritative, accurate, scientific and serious thing M-O has done... our

5. TH, Notes for a Housing Centre meeting, 24 October 1939, TC 5/2/U. And see TH, letter to *Architects Journal*, 20 October 1941: 'I am concerned with what people need. But need is a composite thing, including the want... We can only get effective planning if the prejudices of people are taken into account.'
6. Addison, *Road to 1945*, 181.
7. TH to Fitter, 8 April 1941, TC 25/12/A.
8. Fitter, 'Garden Cities and Town Planning Association Conference', 7 April 1941, TC 2/1/M.
9. Fitter, 'The Public. Note on Implementation', 6 March 1941, TC 25/12/A.

chef d'oeuvre, the flower of all past years' work',[10] and Fitter, with a side-swipe at the 'arbitrary categories' employed by the Cole's encyclopaedic *Condition of Britain* (1937) ('production', 'distribution', etc.), set out to organize the material around time cycles: daily activities, weekly, monthly, annual, irregular, once in a lifetime.[11] When this didn't work he drew on his (and Harrisson's) ornithological background, taking as his model a handbook of British birds with 'sections on numbers and physical distribution, habitat and ecology and the time factor, followed by sections on physical, mental and co-operative activities and finally a section on the life cycle.'[12] Something of the spirit of this enterprise can be imagined from the following note for a section on 'breathing':

> how often do people breath? How long can a man live without breathing?; habits relating to open windows; bad breath—advertising campaigns; excreting—frequency, psychological inhibitions and significance; constipation; types and distribution of closets and urinals. Toilet paper, use of; perspiration, BO.[13]

But Fitter, who had been responsible for Political and Economic Planning's authoritative pre-war report on the press, was no fool, and by the beginning of March it was clear to him that the project would be impossible without major new resources. Since December his salary had been funded by a grant from Rebecca Sieff, but 'if we are to proceed with the project I shall clearly have to have an office, a secretary, and two or three research assistants. This would involve a budget of £2–3,000.' Fitter envisaged the bulk of the money coming from Whitehall (because the report, he believed, would be invaluable to those planning reconstruction, and both Mary Adams and a contact at the Ministry of Health had already expressed an interest), topped up with smaller payments from market research agencies, major businesses, newspapers, and social research organizations in return for pre-publication access to the data.[14] While Harrisson's marginal notes suggest that he at least

10. TH to Feare, nd (27 November 1940?), HNpap.
11. Fitter, 'The Public. Note on Implementation', 6 March 1941, TC 25/12/A; Fitter to TH, 31 January 1941, TC 25/12/A. This was an idea that Harrisson and Madge had toyed with from the early days of MO: CM to TH, 21 January 1940.
12. Fitter, 'The Public. Summary of New Arrangement of Material', 6 March 1941, TC 25/12/A. Later in life Fitter wrote the acclaimed *Collins Pocket Guide to British Birds* (1952).
13. 'Notes on breathing', nd (February 1941?), TC 25/12/A.
14. Fitter, 'The Public. Note on Implementation', 6 March 1941, TC 25/12/A. Comparing the project to the London Press Exchange's pre-war *The Home Market*, which consisted mainly of population and other statistics 'likely to be useful to manufacturers and others planning future

toyed with the idea of trying to raise money on this scale, within two weeks
of this memorandum he was instructing Fitter to put the project to one side
in order to concentrate on a quick publication dealing with reconstruction:

> Very much more than our own interests may depend on getting out some-
> thing rapidly and effectively, which will make people think again about what
> they are reconstructing, who they are reconstructing, why they are doing it.
> I see major new problems and tensions arising from this uncontrolled wave of
> liberal replanning…I think we can do a lot of good, real social good, if we
> produce an intelligent and well thought out, conservatively worded critique
> on reconstruction at the moment.[15]

The immediate aim was a 20,000-word pamphlet on 'Reconstruction: What
the people want', perhaps a Penguin Special, cobbled together from existing
MO material and ending with a critique of 'the whole reconstruction racket
and all the groups engaged in it'.[16] Although some draft chapters exist in the
archive, the project was put on hold in May when Fitter was again moved
on to more urgent (and independently funded) work, pulling together the
lessons of MO's blitztown reports on post-raid services.

Plans for the Penguin Special on reconstruction were briefly revived in
the autumn of 1941, when Harrisson explained to the staff that MO's
objective was 'to find out what people really feel about events after the
war, what their private hopes and fears are about their homes, their jobs,
the political mechanism designed to make their wants known, as distinct
from what planners, politicians and press-men would like them to feel.'[17]
In a *New Statesman* article in September 1941, he took Richard Titmuss to
task for optimistically suggesting that the war 'could be seen as "a climax
in the upward development of many towards co-operation"'. Not only
had MO's work shown that 'the degree of community feeling in the
massive urban populations is much lower than has been supposed', but

---

production,' Fitter explained the far wider scope of his intended volume which would cover
'such important aspects of human behaviour as feeding, dressing and leisure habits, how long
people sleep, what attitudes they adopt towards aliens and Jews, how climatic conditions affect
them, and how many of them need special treatment because they speak Welsh, Gaelic, Yiddish
or some Continental language.'

15. TH to Fitter, 20 March 1941, TC 25/12/A.
16. 'Reconstruction: What the people want', nd (March 1941?), TC 25/12/a; TH to Fitter, 24
   March 1941; Fitter, 'Progress Report on Penguin', 4 April 1941, TC 25/12/A.
17. TH, 'M-O work on Reconstruction', nd (October 1941?), TC 2/2/D; Fitter, 'Planning for
   What. Revised plan for a Penguin on Reconstruction', 29 October 1941; Fitter, 'Memo on the
   Penguin on Reconstruction', 9 November 1941, TC 2/2/D.

reconstruction planners would need to confront the fact that 'behind eve-rything, there is a very strong pessimism about the post-war economic and security set up, which is colouring people's attitudes to all plans, per-sonal and national.'[18] Just as the question of political apathy and the non-voter had been at the core of Harrisson's work in Bolton, so analysis of popular pessimism about post-war prospects was to be central to MO's work on reconstruction.

II

MO's first major publication on reconstruction dealt with housing. Although not published until March 1943, most of the work for *People's Homes* had been done between August 1941 and April 1942.[19] As the young men were called up, MO's fieldwork came increasingly to rely on female investigators, particularly a group of four women led by Celia Fremlin. Doris Hoy was later described by Fremlin as unintellectual, 'big and bouncy and warm'. She had joined MO in the spring of 1940, aged 36, and had previous experi-ence in market research work.[20] Marion Sullivan, aged 32 when she joined MO in July 1941, came from a rather humbler background than most of the other investigators (her father worked as foreman in a sewage works), but as a telephonist in the Stock Exchange she acquired a boyfriend sufficiently well-heeled to take her to the fashionable Cafe Royal, where she bumped into Harrisson (it was one of his favourite haunts) 'who thought she'd do very nicely for M-O'. During the blitz she shared a flat for a time with Fremlin in Hampstead, and the two women became lifelong friends.[21] The youngest of the team, 24 in 1941, was Veronica Tester, a vegetarian ex-ballet dancer and acrobat who lived with her brother in a caravan.[22] These four women, with occasional help from young men awaiting call-up like Jimmy Stevens and Eric Gulliver, did the bulk of the fieldwork for *People in Production*, working as a team in Coventry, or sent off independently to observe tin-mining in Cornwall (Fremlin), the Bettshanger miners' strike in

18. TH 'Human Planning', *New Statesman*, 27 September 1941, 301–2.
19. *People's Homes*, 6.
20. Fremlin, interviewed by Calder, 17 March 1980; 'Memorandum on Mass-Observation', 29 October 1942, FR 1450.
21. Sullivan, interviewed by Calder, 17 March 1980.
22. Fremlin, interviewed by Calder, 17 March 1980.

Kent (Tester), or industrial life in Chester (Hoy).[23] Sullivan and Tester both spent several weeks in the summer of 1942 as participant observers working at Tube Investments in Birmingham where Harrisson's ASG contacts had secured a commission from the management.[24] Alongside this work on industrial topics, it was this group of mobile, single women in their twenties and thirties who undertook almost all the fieldwork for *People's Homes*.

In the aftermath of the blitz, housing lay at the centre of public debate over post-war reconstruction. During 1941–2 several women's organizations were circulating rival questionnaires intended to inform planners about 'what the British housewife wants in her post-war home'. MO was highly critical of the amateurish nature of some of these questionnaires—far too many detailed questions, many of them leading (e.g. 'would you like a refrigerator?')—and the restricted range of opinion likely to be reached by the organizations concerned. By contrast MO's own questionnaire was brief, open-ended, and designed to capture 'the points *spontaneously* raised by housewives... irrespective of outside suggestion'.[25] As usual, investigators recorded a large amount of verbatim material. About 1,100 interviews were conducted with a random sample of working-class housewives (every 11th dwelling) living in 12 selected areas. Five of these involved old houses in working-class districts of Birmingham, Fulham, Ilford, Portsmouth, and Worcester; three were on London City Council estates (Dagenham, Roehampton, and Watling); two in blocks of flats (York Rise, Highgate and some flats in Fulham); and two in garden cities (Bournville and Letchworth).[26] All the selected areas had either been previously studied by MO, or, as in Watling and Becontree, been the subject of substantial pre-war surveys by others.[27] Interviews were supplemented by direct observation: 'mapping the community interests, studying the shopping and working journeys, pub and

23. Fremlin's and Tester's work was written up in the Murray edition of *People in Production*, but did not make it into the Penguin Special.
24. TH, 'General Memo on Organisation', 16 July 1942; Executive Committee, *minutes*, 10 October 1942, Org&Hist 1. Their results, written up as 'Tube Investments Ltd', FR 1390 and 1393, August 1942, were disappointing, displaying none of the psychological insight apparent in Fremlin's work.
25. *People's Homes*, 2–3; Ledeboer to Fitter, 20 July 1942; Fitter to Ledeboer, 3 August 1942, TC 1/8/K.
26. The following pseudonyms were used in the book: Midtown (Birmingham), Metrotown (Fulham), Subtown (Ilford), Seatown (Portsmouth), Churchtown (Worcester), Metroflats (in Fulham), Newflats (York Rise, Highgate), Modelville (Bournville), Gardenville (Letchworth), Becontree (Oak Estate), Roehampton (Elm Estate), Watling (Ash Estate) (Fitter, memo on proposed pseudonyms, 26 March 1942, TC 1/4/H).
27. Ruth Durant, *Watling*, 1939; Terence Young, *Becontree and Dagenham*, 1934.

cinema foci, and so on.'[28] Fitter supervised the work jointly with Fremlin, and was responsible for writing it up.

While it contains a mass of valuable material about the attitudes of working-class women to their homes, *People's Homes* resists easy summary. Irene Barclay, the housing reformer, remarked of an early draft that 'you are throwing your notebook at your readers'... heads',[29] and despite substantial pruning, the final text, organized around each room or feature of the house in turn, reads more as a compendium of interesting information than as a sustained argument. Perhaps the most notable finding was the 'high degree of acceptance of conditions as they are'. While the housewives were full of practical suggestions for improvement within the home—putting 'out of court once and for all' the planner's shibboleth 'that ordinary people have no idea what they want in housing'—three quarters of them liked their existing home and only one in seven actively disliked it. The investigators paid particular attention to the kitchen, as the centre of the housewife's existence and the most important source of satisfaction or dissatisfaction with the dwelling as a whole.[30] The report stressed the diversity of people's housing needs ('so irritating to planners'), dismissing as 'fundamentally *absurd*' the 'barren old controversy between houses and flats'. While the majority would prefer a house with a garden, well-equipped flats closer to the workplace also had their appeal: 'Flats are for some; Welwyns for others.'[31]

The investigators sometimes found it hard not to read high satisfaction levels as evidence of low aspirations, as in the 'grim and parade ground atmosphere' of the 'large, austere five-story blocks' of flats in Fulham, which were nevertheless liked by 74 per cent of their inhabitants.[32] Moreover, prolonged exposure to the mentality of working-class housewives did nothing to reassure Fremlin and her co-workers about the capacity of these women for active citizenship, as is clear from a remarkably judgemental passage towards the end of the book:

> The basic idea of democracy is that each individual citizen should feel personal responsibility for the management of the affairs of the community. Unless this is so, there is no full democracy, for the affairs of the community

28. TH to Cloag, 10 October 1941, TC 2/2/E.
29. Barclay to Fitter, 5 May 1942, TC 1/4/H.
30. *People's Homes*, x, 3–5, 53, 82, 84, 99.
31. *People's Homes*, ix; 'M-O work on Reconstruction', nd (November 1941?), TC 2/2/D.
32. *People's Homes*, 47–9.

are in fact managed by that minority which is sufficiently interested to take part in the various public activities essential for the government of the community. It is therefore a fact of importance that when people were asked whether they liked the neighbourhood or not, *less than one person in a hundred mentioned any form of activity that involved co-operation with their fellow citizens.* The idea of living in a neighbourhood thus appears virtually to have no connection with any responsibility for its good government in the minds of the *average housewife*... To an extent unbelievable to those who have not investigated it, many people are passive-minded, letting things be done to them, hardly thinking of what they could get done, if they would co-operate with their neighbours and fellow citizens.[33]

People's Homes was unusual among MO's publications in making no use at all of the panel. Intended to influence planners and architects building the working-class housing of the future, the book remained silent about middle-class housing aspirations. In their more general work on attitudes to reconstruction, by contrast, MO writers paid more attention to the views of panel members than they did to the results of street or door-to-door interviewing. And one result of this was to produce a considerably more complex picture of attitudes among the citizenry than that suggested by their work with working-class housewives.

III

In the early summer of 1942, with the ASG subvention reduced to £20 a month, Harrisson cast about for alternative sources of income. Odhams Press paid for a study of reading habits, library use, and book buying, involving interviewing, observation, and directives to the panel.[34] In June Harrisson managed to interest the Ministry of Information (MOI) in a survey of attitudes to reconstruction and a deal worth £250 was concluded with Stephen Taylor by the beginning of August. In addition to extensive work on the diaries and panel responses to directives, the new MOI contract paid for street interviews conducted in various parts of the country in September 1942.[35] This work dovetailed well with a project (worth a further £80 a

---

33. *People's Homes*, 208.
34. 'Book Reading Survey', 22 April 1942, FR 1222; 'Books and the Public', July 1942, FR 1332; Shard to TH, 29 April 1942, TC 20/5/B; 'Note on meeting with Surrey Dane', 12 June 42, TC 20/5/B.
35. TH to Taylor, 6 August 1942, MO&MOI 2.

month) monitoring changing public attitudes to Stafford Cripps, which Harrisson had set up with Cripps's parliamentary 'bagman', George Strauss, who, along with Cripps and Aneurin Bevan, had been expelled from the Labour Party in January 1939 for their advocacy of a popular front. After serving as British ambassador in Moscow, Cripps re-entered British politics, at a moment when public satisfaction with Churchill was at a low ebb, with a hugely popular BBC Postcript broadcast in February 1942, contrasting Britain's half-hearted war effort with the heroism and self-sacrifice he had witnessed in Russia. Overnight, hopes were invested in Cripps as a politician untainted by party spirit and a possible alternative to Churchill. In July, despite having accepted office in the government as leader of the House of Commons, and subsequently headed a doomed mission to negotiate peace with Indian nationalism, Cripps was still getting very high levels of support in MO's street surveys.[36] But this support was fragile and could evaporate very suddenly. Behind the stable approval figures, material from the panel indicated that 'some of the most ardent of Cripps followers are already fore-armed against disappointment', all too ready to believe that the faith they had placed in his integrity had been misplaced.[37] Lacking a base in the parliamentary Labour Party, and therefore more dependent on his standing with public opinion than any other leading politician, Cripps had a unique need to know what people were saying and thinking about him; a need that Harrisson proposed to meet with weekly street interviewing, monitoring of spontaneous references in the diaries, and occasional directives to the panel as a whole. In addition, since Cripps's 'prestige is particularly tied up with people's hopes for the future,' MO would provide him with monthly reports on 'developments in public opinion and private feeling about the future.'[38] This project, as Harrisson explained to Strauss, while of benefit to Cripps, would also help to consolidate MO's own work:

> In the ordinary way these investigations are made for our own private interests and files, though sometimes circulated to the few people who seem to take any live interest in what the ordinary chap thinks. If we had some regular psychological incentive ourselves to prepare these reports month by month,

36. Steve Fielding, 'The Second World War and Popular Radicalism: The Significance of the 'Movement away from Party', *History*, 80, 258, 1995, 38–58; Peter Clarke, *The Cripps Version. The Life of Sir Stafford Cripps, 1889–1952*, 2002, 263ff.
37. 'Third Report on Stafford Cripps', 31 August 1942, FR 1394; 'Fourth Report on Stafford Cripps', 4 September 1942, FR 1411.
38. 'Second Report on Stafford Cripps', 6 August 1942, FR 1375.

we should do them more regularly, more analytically, and with more feeling
of usefulness.

The upshot was a complex and nuanced analysis of attitudes to reconstruction that was to inform much of MO's work for the remainder of the war.
The starting point of this analysis was the assertion that the civilian experience of war was producing a substantial 'growth of social consciousness':[39]
'Enormous numbers of citizens' Harrisson told the Housing Centre in
March 1942, 'were being re-educated in citizenship and being made aware
that they each had a function in society, whereas before the war it was possible to live in this country without fulfilling any obligation for society.'[40]
Bob Willcock, who was mainly responsible for the work on reconstruction
during 1942 and beyond, reported 'an increased consciousness of moral and
spiritual things', together with 'growing ideas of happiness in service, simplicity and a change of heart; of scope for everyone in equality of opportunity and equally distributed sacrifice', suggesting that this represented 'a
new direction of thought about the post-war world which may have considerable potentialities if it develops.'[41] Harrisson, rather more sceptical, put
a large question mark against Willcock's most purple passage, and warned
that such feelings might be 'swept away by the excitement and forgetfulness
of peace'.[42]

   In sharp contrast to Fitter's work on housing, Willcock's approach to
reconstruction was primarily informed not by the street interviews organized to satisfy the MOI's need for quantitative data, but by evidence drawn
from the panel.[43] Since November 1940 Willcock had been the main analyst
both of the diaries and of the directive replies, supplying statistics and quotes
relevant to whatever MO was working on at the time, and his enthusiastic
reports of a new social consciousness reflected the wartime flourishing of
the spirit of service among the unusually publicly spirited and disproportionately left-wing people who volunteered to write for MO. When MO
asked the panel directly whether the people they knew had become more
or less public spirited during the war, the responses faced both ways: those
inclined to be public spirited had become more so, while the selfishness of

39. 'Third Report on Reconstruction', September 1942, FR 1414.
40. TH talk at Housing Centre, 18 March 1942, FR 1162.
41. 'Third Report on Reconstruction', September 1942, FR 1414; 'Report on Reconstruction',
    16 October 1942, FR 1452.
42. TH, 'Answering You', 29 June 1942, FR 1326.
43. Willcock to Behrens, 18 July 1942, TC 25/14/H.

others had also increased.[44] Willcock didn't know quite what to make of this polarization, although he might have read it as evidence of a characteristic sense of moral superiority—and pessimism about the general run of people—among the more active citizenry.

For all the excited talk about 'the decay of selfishness and the growth of co-operative citizen-conscious ideas',[45] MO also detected deep currents of pessimism about the post-war future. As early as January 1941 the panel's response to the question 'What social changes do you expect to be brought about by the war?' showed that alongside those confidently expecting radical social change there was a large group who 'half-expect their hopes, half-expect their fear... that change will not be as great as desired.'[46] Expectations of the return of large-scale unemployment after the war were widespread, and with it anxiety and pessimism about the prospects for personal security and advancement. Planners, Harrisson warned the Housing Centre in March 1942, should not assume too much on the basis of wartime advances in active citizenship: 'a striking number of people... were thinking not in terms of helping to make this country better to live in, but of getting out... after the war and going to America, Australia, etc. A strong feeling was growing up that people should have less planned and ordered lives and could be themselves more.'[47] Individualism of this kind, however, owed less to reaction against wartime regimentation—indeed MO detected a significant increase in the willingness to accept restrictions on personal liberties during 1941–2[48]—than to a realization that the existing political system was unlikely to deliver the kind of planned, egalitarian future to which many people aspired. Thus initial enthusiasm for Cripps as a vehicle for such hopes was qualified by the feeling that he would 'never be allowed to do all that... the privileged ones and the vested interests will take good care that things go on the same'; a view borne out in the spring of 1942 by the government's refusal to nationalize the mines or impose fuel rationing. Implicitly dissenting from Harrisson's view of class, Willcock detected a shift away from the earlier wartime belief that class distinction was lessening: 'Class differences are seen not so much as differences in behaviour and understanding as differences in vested interest and power. People want, in 1942, to

44. 'Third Report on Reconstruction', September 1942, FR 1414.
45. TH, 'Answering You', 29 June 1942, FR 1326.
46. 'Report on Portsmouth and Plymouth', 5 March 1941, FR 599.
47. TH talk at Housing Centre, 18 March 1942, FR 1162.
48. 'Report on Reconstruction', 16 October 1942, FR 1452.

eliminate class privilege rather than class distinction.' But, confronted by the evidence that the 'old gang' remained in control in politics, finance, and big business, and that the Labour Party leadership was not prepared to risk national unity by taking them on, the dominant mood was pessimistic: 'under the unity to win the war,' wrote one private in the army, 'there are still those sectional interests which flourished before the war ready to spring to life again and destroy all those things which we are supposed to be fighting for.' Willcock summarized these negative feelings about the political elite as 'a decline in the prestige of leadership in its widest sense, and with this declining belief in the likelihood of current social trends carrying over into peacetime.' The memory of the disappointed hopes of Lloyd George's 'homes fit for heroes' after the First World War was pervasive, acting as a powerful check on hopes for significant post-war social change.[49]

Not content to explain this mismatch between hope and expectations simply in terms of a realistic appreciation of the continuing power of vested interests, Willcock mined the panel material for some deeper, psychological source of pessimism. Looking back over the war diaries he detected powerful guilt feelings driving the initial upsurge of enthusiasm for Cripps in February 1942. When Cripps compared the British war effort unfavourably to that of the Soviet Union and called for greater austerity and self-sacrifice, he struck a chord: 'The feeling that both personally and nationally more sacrifices were needed was very strong.' To illustrate the point Willcock seized on a passage in Nella Last's diary, written early in 1942:

> Will a clarion call *never* come that will make us all the 'one determined body' that speakers are so fond of talking about? Are the rest of the people in Britain so 1% about the war? I work as hard as I can, yet it's so doll-eyed, so futile. What after all do I do? Raise at most £3 a week with my raffling and tea-making at the [Women's Voluntary Service] Centre and keep things together there as best I can.... I felt critical and severe with myself.[50]

Cripps's broadcast established him as a leader overnight because, Willcock argued, he articulated

---

49. 'Report on Reconstruction', 30 July 1942, 15–25, FR 1364; 'Third Report on Stafford Cripps', 31 August 1942, FR 1394; 'Third Report on Reconstruction', September 1942, 5, 23, FR 1414; 'Report on Reconstruction', 16 October 1942, 74–5, FR 1452.
50. 'Second Report on Stafford Cripps', 6 August 1942, FR 1375, 2–3. I have been unable to locate this passage in Nella Last's diaries or directive replies. Some of her writing around this period is missing from the archive. Perhaps the relevant pages were misplaced by Willcock himself while he was writing this report.

feelings of national and personal inadequacy and inferiority which [were] craving for expression in action...the sense of inadequacy among old people who are doing all that they can for the war, the widespread feeling of guilt among younger citizens about being out of uniform...the feelings of theirs that they are too comfortable, too well paid, working too short hours.[51]

Summing up his argument in a section labelled 'Guilt, liberty and leadership', Willcock argued: 'We are atoning for...the suffering of the Russians and occupied Europe by—in effect—being as uncomfortable as we can persuade the authorities to make us. The vicarious guilt of war brings out vicarious urges for self-immolation, basically self-centred in origin.'[52]

The implications of this analysis for post-war reconstruction were rather depressing. The 'general post-war fear fantasy...is that things will not change fundamentally after the war, and that the same old politicians and governments will carry on in a mildly modified form.'[53] Given the divergent 'reality-horizons' of hope and expectation, 'it will not be difficult for quite moderate legislation and change to give people a pleasant surprise and make them feel that as much or more is being done than they thought at all likely.'[54] But any such satisfaction would be short-lived:

> The implication is that unless some lead and hope is given to clarifying ideas about social change, people will be apt to think that a little change is considerably more than there might have been. But these studies clearly show that these changes will not satisfy people, though in the present mood they may pacify them. Apathetic discontent is the post-war mood if present trends continue.

Most worrying of all was the possibility that 'the impulse to self-immolation, while immediately useful for purposes of war, may well, if it lasts into the peace, prove as easy to exploit for totalitarian ends as it is now in the interests of total effort... In this sense, in the writer's opinion, the present welcoming of restrictions is important and ominous.'[55]

Willcock's report was submitted to the MOI shortly before the publication of the Beveridge Report[56] which, rather like the Cripps phenomenon

---

51. 'Third Report on Reconstruction', September 1942, 19, FR 1414.
52. And, he argued, similar guilt feelings about the Empire informed popular reactions to the fall of Singapore: 'We are atoning for our past sins in the Empire by losing it, to the Japanese' ('Third Report on Reconstruction', September 1942, 21, FR 1414).
53. 'Seventh report on Stafford Cripps', 20 October 1942, FR 1443.
54. 'Third Report on Reconstruction', September 1942, 2, FR 1414.
55. 'Report on Reconstruction', 16 October 1942, 20–1, 71, FR 1452; 'Third Report on Reconstruction', September 1942, 19, FR 1414.
56. Consultative Committee, minutes, 16 November 1942, Org&Hist 1.

in February 1942, produced an immediate upsurge of hope for a rosy post-war future quickly followed by cynical reflection about the power of vested interests to block reform, a cynicism fed by Churchill's public resistance to any move to legislate for the post-war implementation of Beveridge's plans. Charting public responses to these events, Home Intelligence reached very similar conclusions to MO, without, however, the psychological speculation underpinning Willcock's understanding of popular pessimism about the post-war future.[57] MO's own work on responses to Beveridge during the winter of 1942–3 was slight, consisting largely of rehashes of Willcock's September 1942 report on reconstruction.[58]

IV

Harrisson had been called up in June 1942. Although no longer in day-to-day control of MO, he remained closely involved until he was sent overseas two years later. In his absence the range and pace of MO's work shrank, only picking up again on his return from military service in the Far East in September 1946. Before examining the history of the organization during the four years of Harrisson's military service, his call-up provides an opportune moment to interrupt the narrative and look back over what had been achieved since Charles Madge and Harrisson first set out to lay bare the habits and customs of the British islanders in 1937. The next chapter does this in the form of a discussion of the evolution of MO's methodology. First, however, in further illustration of the range of Harrisson's interests and the energy with which he pursued them, we round off this chapter with brief accounts of two initiatives he undertook alongside his work with MO.

In the original *Mass-Observation* pamphlet, Madge and Harrisson had deplored the isolation of science from popular culture:

The scientist engaged in research prefers to work in isolation and without publicity until he has completed his investigation...If his results ever do win a wider publicity, they will be diffused in the form of 'popular science'...in the process [assuming] the very superstitiousness which it was to supersede. Individual scientists deplore this state of affairs, but there is nothing they can

57. McLaine, *Ministry of Morale*, 182–5.
58. 'Précis of Post', 6 January 1943, Org&Hist 4/4; 'Public Reactions to the Beveridge Report', 1 January 1943, FR 1565; 'Public Reactions to the Beveridge Report', 12 January 1943, FR 1568

do about it, so long as the mass remains so naturally superstitious that it will only swallow science in the form of superstition.[59]

Popular perceptions of the scientist either as a magician capable of solving all the world's problems, or a monster bent on devising ever more powerful means of destruction, needed to be broken down before scientific rationality could take its proper place in public discourse. To this end Harrisson devised a scheme for regularly supplying the newspapers—none of which had full-time science correspondents—with well-written reports of the latest scientific research. In September 1940 he presented his 'Memorandum on Propaganda for Science' to Solly Zuckerman's scientific dining club—known as the 'Tots and Quots'—of which he was a member alongside Max Nicholson, Julian Huxley, Desmond Bernal, J. B. S. Haldane and other leading scientists.[60] The upshot, Zuckerman explained to Huxley, was the formation of a small group 'to enquire into the possibility of forming what amounts to a science news service. That vigorous man Harrisson is in charge of it.'[61] Despite initial enthusiasm from *Picture Post* and the *Sunday Express* the scheme failed to get off the ground, with the latter paper dropping what was billed as a regular column of 'Notes from the Laboratories' almost as soon as it was launched.[62] This was the end of Harrisson's involvement, although other members of the Tots and Quots did have some success in promoting scientific journalism during the war.[63]

Enabling scientists to popularize their research activities was one way of pursuing MO's mission of combating 'the sway of superstition in the midst of science'.[64] Another was to tackle the problem from the other end, by working directly with those 'large new groups of semi-intellectuals and semi-creative persons' employed in commercial entertainment, whose work played a central role in encouraging superstitions and escapist modes of thinking among the masses. As in his attitude to the technical expertise of advertisers, Harrisson was not content simply to condemn these 'marginal

59. *Mass-Observation*, 39–40.
60. TH, 'Memo on Propaganda for Science', 3 September 1940; Zuckerman to TH, 4 September 1940; TH to Julian Huxley, 11 September 1940; TH, paper for Tots & Quots, 28 September 1940, TC 34/1/E.
61. Zuckerman to Huxley, 9 October 1940, TC 34/1/E.
62. Crowther to TH, 6 October 1940; TH to Waddington, 21 October 1940; TH to Bernstein, 2 November 1940; Zuckerman to TH, 7 November and 3 December 1940; Waddington to TH, 30 November 1940, TC 34/1/E.
63. Ralph J. Desmarais, 'Tots and Quots', DNB.
64. *Mass-Observation*, 10.

creative personnel'—romantic novelists, songwriters, astrologists. Instead, practical as ever, he tried to engage directly, encouraging them to use their access to the mass mind to foster responsible and realistic, rather than escapist, attitudes. In a memo intended for the Fabian Society, written shortly before his conscription in June 1942, Harrisson claimed that:

> while quite a lot of the people who turn out slush for the millions are beyond hope, a very large minority are ripe and ready for some sort of political reorientation... [They are] only too well aware of the lack of seriousness in their work and there is growing appreciation among them that writing slushy novels and escapist songs may actually be doing harm in the world as it is today... One of the most successful of cheap novelists said to me the other day, quite out of the blue: 'I wish you'd tell me something that I've always wanted to know about. What is socialism?' It wasn't a joke; it was a heart cry.[65]

Ever since MO's work on the Lambeth Walk, Harrisson had been keen to cultivate lyricists working in popular music. In the summer of 1940 he had persuaded the well-known singer/writer, Annette Mills, to join him in a 'scheme to make some new sort of popular song in keeping with the spirit of the moment,' with songs including 'United we Stand', based on a Churchill speech, and 'I'm so mighty glad that you're away', designed to encourage evacuation of women and children.[66] Despite the best efforts of Adams and Kenneth Clark, however, the MOI refused to intervene in the music industry, leaving 'wide areas of potential social propaganda... virtually untapped.'[67] The Communist Party, Harrisson complained, was the only organization prepared to take seriously the propaganda potential of popular music, systematically targeting dance band leaders.[68] In the spring of 1940

65. TH, 'Marginal Creative Personnel', 16 June 1942, FR 1314. The novelist in question may have been Denise Robins, author of about 170 gothic romance novels and, in 1960, founding president of the Romantic Novelist's Association.
66. Mills to TH, 24, 27 July 1940; TH to Cowl, 4 August 1940, TC 38/8/C. On Annette Mills, sister of the actor John Mills, see DNB. The music hall artist Leslie Henson was equally obliging, sending Harrisson a song on the theme of 'Careless talk Costs Lives', 'Careless Talk', 11 July 1940, TC 16/4/G.
67. Adams to Mills, 17 March 1941, MA papers 2/E; TH, 'Marginal Creative Personnel', 16 June 1942, FR 1314. On TH's efforts to get the MOI to take popular music seriously see also 'Notes on Present Morale Situation', 3 June 1940, FR 165; TH to Leslie, 13 June 1940, FR 197.
68. TH, 'Marginal Creative Personnel', 16 June 1942, FR 1314. On the Communist Party's intervention in the music industry see Kevin Morgan, 'King Street Blues: jazz and the left in Britain in the 1930s–40s', in Andy Croft (ed.), *Weapons in the Struggle: essays on the cultural history of British communism*, 1998, 123–41.

Richard Acland had responded enthusiastically to Harrisson's suggestion of a meeting with

> some people in the dance music world...I wonder if it would be worth try-
> ing to convert any of these to our ideas and try to get them to express them
> in dance tunes. I can imagine for example an immense popularity for some-
> thing with the refrain 'When are they going to let us build that better world?'
> Do you think I could meet any of them and put the idea to them? Would you,
> for example, invite three of four to meet both of us at the House of Commons
> for lunch or for drinks, on me?

The House of Commons was probably not the best venue for such a meeting, and nothing seems to have come of this. But even the most archetypal
purveyors of superstition were not beyond the reach of Harrisson's reformist zeal, as Edward Lyndoe, who wrote the astrology column in *The People*,
insisted in a private letter responding to Harrisson's attack on newspaper
astrologers in a 1941 *New Statesman* article.[69] Describing himself as 'an
enthusiastic disseminator of MO literature, and an admirer of your work
from its inception' he urged Harrisson not to 'alienate men like myself...We
want to help you and all those who are trying to make the world better. Ask
me for help of any kind and you will realise that I am sincere'.[70] Although
Harrisson's response to this letter has not survived, it can be imagined from
his insistence a year later that 'even among astrologers there is much insight
into human nature...they understand...the great non-voter public in a
very special way. That makes them all the more valuable and important as
allies.'[71]

69. TH, 'Mass Astrology', *New Statesman*, 16 August 1941.
70. E. Lyndoe to TH, 16 August 1941, TC 8/1/A. Lyndoe took issue with TH's claim that astrol-
    ogy was 'opposed to the trend of scientific thought in the past century...it is an astonishing
    fact that I am at present engaged on research with scientists of great repute (unpaid) covering
    mental disorders, certain developments of photographic investigation connecting up with
    work being done by Einstein—whom I am invited to go over and see later on; fieldwork in
    astronomy...in company with a brilliant young astronomer and physicist; investigation of
    certain economic cycles, in which a socialist-minded scientist's labours figure largely.
    "Opposed"? Only to that modern science which has played into the hands of those who wish
    men *not* to live fully, *not* to desire changes in society, *not* to undertake their full citizenship...I
    have spent my life in the scientific field (astronomy and experiential psychology)...I follow
    the tradition of Tycho Brahe, and Newton, not the tatterdemalion notoriety of Old Moore.'
    TH had already pointed out the accommodation with science characteristic of modern
    superstition in his *New Statesman* article, locating the appeal of astrology in its combination of
    'an element of "science" and scientific validity [with] an element of mystery and history and
    myth.' TC 8/1/A also contains an interview by Bob Willcock and an official from the MOI
    with the other most widely read newspaper astrologer, Naylor of the *Sunday Express*.
71. TH, 'Marginal Creative Personnel', 16 June 1942, FR 1314.

Although neither of these two initiatives succeeded, the range of contacts involved, from distinguished scientists to music hall singers, was characteristic of Harrisson's restless search for influence at all levels of British cultural life. It was through his own journalism, probably, that he had most impact: a regular outpouring of articles based on MO findings which did more than anything else to bring MO to the attention of a wide public, as well as to raise much needed funds for the organization. His articles, John Ferraby noted in 1941, were 'sought by most of the daily and weekly papers with any pretensions to intellectual content'.[72] And in March 1942, alongside everything else, Harrisson became Britain's first ever newspaper radio critic, contributing a weekly column to *The Observer*, a job he kept up until the Army sent him overseas in July 1944. Among his qualifications was the fact that 'during most of my life I have listened to the radio for several hours a day.'[73] How he found the space for this is clear from Len England's memory of Harrisson in 1942 at work in his study, surrounded by a mass of papers, dictating memorandums, reports or articles to his secretary, constantly interrupted by enquiries from the staff or phone calls from clients; all the time with the radio playing in the background and 'at the very end of the morning he would dictate an article about what he had been listening to.'[74] There were few areas of British cultural life that did not, at one time or another, engage the attention of 'that vigorous man Harrisson.'

72. FR 550, 22.
73. TH, *The Observer*, 8 July 1944; Heinmann, *Most Offending Soul*, 168–9.
74. Len England, 'Stranger than Fiction', MO Archive.

II

Method

Much of the contemporary criticism of Mass-Observation's (MO's) methods, even that published after the war, rested on the experience of pre-war Bolton and took no account of the professionalization of the organization during the war.[1] When, in April 1940, it seemed that Gollancz might at last get round to publishing *The Pub and the People,* Harrisson insisted on rewriting the preface which 'was written when M-O was in embryo' and 'gave a flagrantly out of date...[and] misleading idea of our methods'.[2] Although under constant pressure to earn their keep by producing substantive results, many of the MO staff saw themselves as pioneering a new kind of social investigation, and were keenly interested in discussing technical and methodological questions. During the later war years, MO made time to publish accounts of its methods in several academic journals,[3] although as John Ferraby pointed out:

> from the start...these methods have been developed chiefly by trial and error. If Mass-Observation had an endowment to draw on, even if interest in opinion research in Great Britain was sufficient for it to be highly paid commercially, it would be possible to improve and schematize them experimentally. But as things are, it is possible to progress only by trying out new methods in the conducting of ordinary investigations, and judging by experience which are good and which are bad.[4]

Ferraby may have been remembered by Celia Fremlin as a rarely seen 'troglodyte' grinding out statistics in the basement of Ladbroke Road, but

1. The two most considered critiques were Firth,'An Anthropologist's View of Mass-Observation', *Sociological Review*, 31, 2, April 1939 and Mark Abrams, *Social Surveys and Social Action*, 1951, 105–13. On Abrams' experience of MO in Bolton before the war, which clearly influenced his later critique, see Stanley's interview with him, 9 September 1982.
2. TH to Miss Horsman, 4 April 1940, Org&Hist 3/Gollancz.
3. H. D. Willcock, 'Mass-Observation', *American Journal of Sociology*, 48, 4, 1943, 445–56; J. G. Ferraby, 'The Problem of Propaganda', *Agenda*, August 1944; J. G. Ferraby, 'Planning a Mass-Observation Investigation', *American Journal of Sociology*, 51, 1, 1945, 1–6; J. G. Ferraby, 'Observations on the Reluctant Stork', *Public Opinion Quarterly*, 9, 1, 1945, 29–37.
4. Ferraby,'Recording and classifying verbatim information', FR 2146, August 1944.

in fact he spent a good deal of his time reflecting on methodological issues. Engaged on an intellectual journey which took him from statistics and experimental psychology in 1930s Cambridge to a leading position in the Bahá'í faith by the later 1940s, Ferraby's writing, discussed at the end of this chapter, provides the most sustained contemporary defence of the MO approach.

I

Complaints about the amateurishness of MO's work often alleged that the investigators were given no training. Certainly Harrisson believed in throwing new investigators in at the deep end—'you either sank or swam', Fremlin recalled.[5] But that did not mean that he did not take their training seriously. On their first assignments people were apt to 'wander around not knowing what to write down, what to observe', coming up either with subjective impressions rather than the verbatim quotations or the objective counting that MO needed, or, like young Jimmy Stevens on his early assignments, behaving like the comic stereotype of the mass observer, noting down anything that came to hand—'the least gesture or overheard remark'—with no focus or feel for what might be of significance.[6] One oft-repeated criticism of MO methods was this tendency to indiscriminate observation, jackdaw-like collecting of information with no agenda or principles of selection. In practice, while 'receptive intelligence'[7] and openness to the unexpected was a virtue to be cultivated, most of the time observers were sent out with specific issues to investigate and questions to ask. Finding an appropriate balance between focus, detail, and generalization was a skill learned by experience, but also nurtured by the verbal feedback that Harrisson gave to his fieldworkers.

The nature of such feedback can be glimpsed from letters he wrote to his cousin, Ann, who worked during the spring of 1941 as MO's outpost in Oxford:

...not sufficiently detailed...Your opening paragraph is the sort of thing journalists are regularly writing, and which is so regularly proved to be wrong.

5. Fremlin, interviewed by Stanley, 18 September 1981.
6. Jimmy Stevens, 'Mass Observing in Wartime', *Seven Magazine of People's Writing*, 2, 2, August 1941, FR 853A.
7. Novy, interviewed by TH and Calder, 1 March 1979.

I suspect in this case it is based on facts, but what I want in such cases is what 10 to 15 people actually said, then your generalisations...It is useless when you say 'the queue of most prodigious length.' I get a mental picture of something like 300 yards, but other people might think of them as 20 yards only. Long experience has shown that if a person is permitted simply to generalise without giving supporting data, you can get four people in the same place, all making quite different generalisations about the same subject. In fact it is precisely because this happens that organisations and official interests employ us, knowing that however indigestible and complicated, we will give them a picture based on the external phenomena and not on personal synthesis and highly selected observations.[8]

But such personalized attention was time consuming, and in August 1941 Harrisson complained to Cyril Connelly—who had recommended a young woman who turned out to be most unsatisfactory, interested in working for MO merely as a way of avoiding the threat of conscription— that while 'in peacetime I had the time myself to supervise new staff, talk to them, train them...nowadays that isn't possible.'[9] By 1944 the Wartime Social Survey (WSS) had developed systematic and formalized training for its fieldworkers, but MO lacked the resources to develop any such programme of its own.[10] Unlike the WSS, which concentrated on collecting factual information by direct interviewing, MO's fieldworkers required a broader and more flexible range of skills, and it was still the case at the end of the war, as Harrisson had written in 1940, 'that no form of training at present exists which makes people better at the kind of observing, interviewing and recording which is needed'.[11] Ferraby had attempted to draft a handbook on fieldwork technique, but his generalized guidelines seemed abstract and mechanical compared with the instructions to investigators prepared by Harrisson or, indeed, by Ferraby himself for particular projects.[12] In any case, as Ferraby explained, it was futile to lay down rules for those things—like the knotty problem of how best to record verbatim comments in the days before portable recording machines—which depended on the particular aptitudes of each investigator.[13] So training continued to depend

8. TH to Ann Harrisson, 19 March 1941, TC 66/14/D.
9. TH to Connelly, 6 August 1941, Org&Hist 3/Horizon.
10. Kathleen Box and Geoffrey Thomas, 'The Wartime Social Survey', *Royal Statistical Society*, iii–iv, 1944, 160.
11. TH to CM, 18 January 1940, Org&Hist 1.
12. Ferraby, 'Draft handbook', 21 March 1941; Ferraby, 'Concerning the Draft Plans for investigations', 29 March 1941, Org&Hist 1.
13. Ferraby, 'Recording and classifying verbatim information', August 1944, 3, FR 2146.

on personal feedback, accumulated experience, and, of course, help from other fieldworkers. Marion Sullivan—sent out by Harrisson for the day to find out what people thought about the use of the Chislehurst caves as an air raid shelter—came back with 85 interviews, as against the normal daily quota of 25 to 30, and had to be warned about rate-busting by the rest of the team.[14] More positively, investigators swapped tips about the best techniques for approaching strangers and encouraging them to talk freely. Henry Novy's three-page 'Notes on Interviewing', reflecting on his own experience, was a good deal more user-friendly than Ferraby's exhaustive compendium.[15]

Harrisson was on the lookout for observer bias, cross-checking the material collected by different fieldworkers (on a weekly basis, he claimed in April 1941), and resisting pressure to allow observers to live together at Ladbroke Road (as they had in Davenport Street) for fear that this would encourage the formation of group opinions that might 'seriously invalidate' the reliability of the fieldwork.[16] Some of the early experiments with the News Quota were casual in the extreme—'collect any 10 people's opinions... on the Hore-Belisha business... between now and Tuesday'[17]—and Harrisson should have been alarmed by the implications of Alec Hughes' complaint that staff in Bolton found it more difficult to fulfil the quota than their colleagues in London 'because they can interview friends and acquaintances'.[18] But as the News Quota became established, investigators were given specific instructions about where to conduct street interviews and the appropriate balance to aim at of sex, age, and class.[19]

Deliberate falsification of results by investigators was probably less of a problem since, as Fremlin later claimed: 'We were all very committed... [so] the question of cheating didn't arise because we wanted to know the answer'; unlike the employees of market research organizations most of

14. Rickards (née Sullivan), interviewed by Angus Calder, 17 March 1980.
15. Novy, 'Notes on Interviewing', 15 May 1940, Org&Hist 4/2.
16. 'Memo on Personnel', 21 April 1941, INF 1/286; TH to CM, 25 January 1940, Org&Hist 1/1; 'They Speak for Themselves', 1 June 1939, 20–1, FR A 26.
17. TH to Dualty, 8 January 1940, HNpap.
18. Hughes, 'Interviews in wartime', 27 September 1939, Org&Hist 1.
19. Behrens, 'Street Counts', 25 January 1943, FR 1571. For a balanced assessment of the validity of the News Quota data see GM, 'Meaning and limitation of News Quota statistics', 28 March 1944, FR 2060. But the following entry by a diarist who applied for a job with MO nicely indicates the difficulty of assessing age by sight: 'Priscilla Novy, explaining M-O technique to me, said one must guess a person's age to the nearest five years. I asked her to guess mine and she said 40–5; I am, of course, 31' (Diarist 5233, May 1942).

whom were in it for the money and, it was said, regularly 'cooked' their results.[20] In December 1940 the acting head of the British Institute of Public Opinion (BIPO), Louis Moss, had explained to Fremlin his own techniques for catching 'cookers', including requiring investigators to add their own general impressions to their findings, which, he claimed, showed up those who had no real interest in the work.[21] This was normal practice in MO, although it was not a foolproof method of spotting cheating. Nina Masel wrote years later of her dislike of doing street interviews 'so I took to making the answers up. Nobody at HQ spotted any discrepancy between my phoney reports and the real ones from the rest of the team.' After several weeks of this she marched into Harrisson's office and confessed her guilt: 'That just shows how well I've trained you,' he responded, 'I've given you a true nose for the public mood.' It is a story that probably says more about Harrisson's management style in dealing with a clever but difficult young woman, than about any indifference to the reliability and honesty of his investigators.[22]

For some, like Kathleen Raine's astrologer friend Gay Taylor, who came back to work for MO from 1942, interviewing was an unalloyed delight— 'enchanting dancing interviews with strangers':

> Today, delicious interviews with working-class women off the Portobello Road...my days are full of sparkling surprises, given and received...Nothing else on earth had ever freed me from melancholy or inward loneliness, or brought that continuous flow of blessed daily contact that makes life worth living.[23]

But for most, interviewing was not the favourite part of the job. Novy wrote of 'the gradual hatred of interviewing which eventually overcomes *all* observers',[24] and Humphrey Pease found it so uncongenial and produced such unsatisfactory results that Harrisson agreed to exempt him from direct interviewing altogether.[25] A couple of the men found it hard to fulfil their News Quotas because they hesitated to approach young women, especially

20. Fremlin, interviewed by Stanley, 18 September 1981; Fitter, interviewed by TH, 1 October 1971; Fremlin, 'Report on market research', 8 December 1940, Org&Hist 4/2.
21. Fremlin interview with Louis Moss (BIPO), 11 December 1940, Org&Hist 4/2.
22. Nina Hibbin, 'I Was a Mass Observer', *New Statesman*, 31 May 1985; see also draft of this article in Personnel/Masel.
23. Loran Hurnscot [Gay Taylor], *A Prison, a Paradise*, London, 1958, 209, 215.
24. Novy, 'Notes on Interviewing', 15 May 1940, Org&Hist 4/2.
25. Pease to Fremlin, 26 December 1940, Org&Hist 4/2.

attractive ones, for fear of their intentions being misunderstood.[26] Nina Masel, on the other hand, worried about how to escape from 'someone who is trying to recount his complete life history to you.'[27] Generally people were happy to talk and showed little curiosity about who the interviewer was working for; and those who did enquire were usually content with a vague reference to freelance reporting or market research.[28] As the crisis deepened in 1940, however, there was a perceptible increase in people's unwillingness to submit to questioning by strangers in the street, and more frequent complaints to passing policemen. Novy tried to solve this problem by always interviewing the policeman first, if there was one in sight.[29] But the fifth column paranoia of the spring of 1940 encouraged an emphasis on the more indirect methods of sounding out opinion which Harrisson had, in any case, always favoured, and which most of the investigators much preferred.

'The direct technique gives quantitative results,' Harrisson wrote in October 1939, comparing results of the Ministry of Information (MOI) poster investigation from fieldworkers using different methods, 'but the indirect, though much slower, gives a deeper quality.'[30] Slower, and also more skilled. The use of the 'overheard' captured what people were saying to each other without any interference from the observer. Overheards could be done in the street, but this was expensive in shoe leather: 'One must be ready to turn around, follow, go back, stop etc, and be quite worn out by the time one reaches Oxford Circus from Marble Arch.'[31] The main problem was to find inconspicuous ways of writing down what was said. Masel did her overheards in Romford by walking a triangle between her father's shop, the library and the post office, nipping in to take her notes to whichever 'base' was closest or, if caught short, to a telephone kiosk.[32] Leonard England,

26. 'I couldn't stop a reasonably attractive girl in the street. I just couldn't. An unattractive girl, perhaps—but she'd have to be very unattractive and I'd have to feel that she was conscious of her unattractiveness', George Hutchinson, 'Interviewing', 21 December 1940, Org&Hist 4/2; Pease to Fremlin, 26 December 1940, Org&Hist 4/2. Novy noted the tendency to select more sympathetic and intelligent-looking people for street interviewing, adding 'could this be discussed at meeting?' Novy to TH, 8 January 1940, HNpap.
27. Masel, 'Memo on method', 2 May 1940, Org&Hist 4/2.
28. Jack Atkins, 'Memo on interviewing', 4 October 1939; George Hutchinson, 'Interviewing', 21 December 1940, Org&Hist 4/2.
29. Alec Hughes, 'Memo on interviewing' 30 September 1939; Novy, 'Notes on Interviewing', 15 May 1940, Org&Hist 4/2.
30. TH, 'Memo on posters', TC 42/1A.
31. Novy, 'Overheards', 15 May 1940, Org&Hist 4/5.
32. Masel, 'Memo on method', 2 May 1940, Org&Hist 4/2.

who felt that snatches of conversation overheard in the street were pretty meaningless, preferred to do his overheards on bus journeys.[33] But best of all were places where people met together and talked: in pubs, workmen's cafes, dance halls, sporting, social or political clubs, where the 'overheard' could be mixed with the 'indirect interview', engaging people in conversation without setting the agenda or leading the witness. This became easier to the extent that observers became habitués of particular social spaces—for Humphrey Pease, a regular at more pubs and West End clubs than was good for him, this was no hardship[34]—and, recognized as regulars, indirect interviewing shaded over into participant observation.

Pitching to the MOI at the outbreak of war, Harrisson explained that: 'Observers have been trained to observe without being observed. They record and register facts without upsetting the environment in which they record them.'[35] In pre-war Bolton, as we have seen, this cult of invisibility had often given way to the observer's urge to get involved; and such lapses did not entirely cease in wartime. Observing a by-election rally in Leeds for the MOI, Novy became so incensed by Hugh Dalton's speech ('cynical and awful') that he 'yelled at him several times, and an old pot-bellied man behind me hit me in the back of the neck saying "Be quiet young man!"'[36] For those engaged in participant observation the skill was to remain inconspicuous, to participate without influencing the atmosphere, and to find ways of taking notes without being rumbled. Fremlin, with her experience among charwomen, waitresses, and later factory workers, became particularly adept at this kind of work, cultivating a reputation as an obsessive letter writer, using speedwriting to take down the gossip as it occurred on paper headed 'Dear Aunt Emma'.[37] Her friend, Marion Sullivan, also mass observing on the shop floor, spent more than her fair share of time sitting on the loo, where she could write unobserved.[38]

33. England, memo, 2 May 1940, Org&Hist 4/2.
34. Pease, diary, 8 January, 5 October 1940, Personnel/Pease.
35. 'Emergency problems and mass-observation', 29 August 1939, FR A22.
36. Novy to Thomas, 10 March 1940, HN pap. Two months later, sent to cover a trade union demonstration in London, Novy confessed (or boasted) to his Communist friend Brian Allwood: 'I felt like taking part, and so forgot M-O for a while,' heckling the platform speakers in Hyde Park (Novy to Allwood, 4 May 1940, HN pap).
37. *War Factory*, 2nd edition, 1987, Preface. The same technique was used by one of the MO diarists, Edith Oakley, a Glasgow office worker, who sometimes typed office dialogue as it happened in 'the guise of private letters', giving the speakers invented names, annotated when she got home with the real ones (Diarist 5390, October 1944).
38. Rickards (née Sullivan), interviewed by Calder, 17 March 1980.

II

Alongside information collected by the investigators, most of MO's wartime enquiries also made extensive use of the volunteer panel. Regular monthly directives had been sent to the panel since January 1939, when more than 300 people responded.[39] The publication of *Britain by Mass-Observation* brought in 200 new recruits in February and numbers kept up during the first half of 1939, rising to a peak of over 442 responding to a directive on 'race' in June (as well as nearly 400 to the 'class' directive in the same month). By the outbreak of war it would have been reasonable, totting up the new recruits since January 1939, to assume that the panel had about 1,000 effective members, though, even at best, fewer than half of these could be expected to respond to any one directive. After the disruption caused by the outbreak of war the numbers responding revived, peaking at over 300 early in 1940. In the crisis months of June–August numbers fell sharply, but revived again to some extent in the autumn. What happened in 1941 we do not know, since none of the directive reports have survived, but there were several effective appeals for new members in various journals.[40] By the beginning of 1942 the numbers responding to individual directives were back up to 400 and stayed high until the autumn, peaking at 533 in May 1942. From the autumn of 1942 numbers fluctuated around a declining trend, averaging 290 in 1943, 230 in 1944 and 190 in the first two months of 1945.

Altogether over 1,200 people were recruited to the panel during the war years, in addition to the 1,000 or so participating before the war. The archive holds returns from 2,324 respondents, a figure close to the 2,500 that MO occasionally liked to claim.[41] That is, however, a very misleading figure, since it takes no account of those who left. Each year, between 1939 and 1945, about a quarter of the panellists responded to only one directive (except during 1940 when this proportion increased to nearly 40 per cent). Over the six years as a whole nearly a quarter of those volunteering for the panel dropped out after a single response, and 58 per cent answered no more than four directives. The remainder were divided more or less evenly between

---

39. Most of them presumably already members of the panel. According to the archive's catalogue 295 of the day survey respondents eventually became directive respondents.
40. MO, *Bulletin*, 12 August 1941, FR 809; MO, *Bulletin*, 10 October 1941, FR 891.
41. The catalogue actually gives 2,393 directive respondents, but 69 of those registered apparently sent in no responses.

those submitting between four and nine responses (499) and those submitting ten or more (483). These figures suggest that, once we allow for those who had dropped out as well as for the new recruits, the effective size of the panel was much the same as before the war: never more than about 1,000, of whom between a third and a half responded to any particular directive.

Many of those who sent in responses to the directives also became war diarists. Over a third of the 474 diarists listed in the archive catalogue were recruited during the first four months of the war, and a further 91 came in during the first ten months of 1940. From October 1940 recruitment virtually ceased until a new drive between July and November 1941, which brought in another 85 diarists. After that recruitment came in dribs and drabs averaging about eight people a month for the remainder of the war. As with the panel more generally, a large proportion of diarists quickly dropped out, a fifth after their first posting and another fifth after two to four postings.[42] Only 38 per cent of those volunteering to write war diaries sent in more than ten entries. The number of diaries received never regained the peak of 141 in the first month of the war, quickly falling below 80 per month until the second surge from July 1941 and reaching a second peak of 137 in November 1941. It then fluctuated around 120 until July 1942; fell steadily over the next two years to half that number; staged a brief small upturn to 85 in September 1944; and fell back to around 60 by the closing months of the war.

Before the war the MO panel had been drawn disproportionately from young men. Table 11.1 compares the average age of the panel in 1939 and 1945 with that of the population as measured by the National Register in 1939.[43] (People of 18 or younger have been omitted from this table, and the percentages adjusted accordingly.)

Compared with the general population MO in 1939 had recruited nearly four times as many people in the 19–24 age group and a third more

---

42. These figures, derived from the archive catalogue, are roughly compatible with the figures given by the woman in charge of communication with the panel during much of 1940 (JL, 'Report on War Diaries', 16 July 1940, Org&Hist 4/2). For JL's identity—Miss Langley—see 'M-O Personnel', INF/1 262, 7 April 1940.

43. The National Register figures have been taken from Stanley, 'Extra Dimension', 159. The MO figures are derived from the archive catalogue, which gives the year of birth for around 90 per cent of respondents. The 1939 figures average the eight DRs between January and June 1939. The 1945 figures average the five DRs between January and December 1945. Stanley's discussion of the age profile ('Extra Dimension', 159–61) although based on only about 60 per cent of respondents for whom he had ages, reaches much the same conclusions as my own.

Table 11.1 Age distribution of MO panel, 1939–1945

	1939 National Register (%)	1939 Mass Observers (%)	1945 Mass Observers (%)
19–24	10	36	10
25–34	23	33	23
35–44	21	17	23
45–54	18	9	23
55–64	15	4	13
65 and over	13	2	7
	100	100	100

Figures are rounded

among 25–34 year olds. Older groups, on the other hand, were under-represented on the panel. During the war this relative youthfulness disappeared. By 1945 the age distribution of the panel was broadly representative of the population as a whole, the only anomaly (apart from among the elderly) being the slight over-representation of the 45–54 age group. In part, of course, this change was due to the ageing of the original recruits: substantial new recruitment failed to compensate for this. Most strikingly, people of 18 or less, who had constituted 17 per cent of respondents before the war, had disappeared altogether from the panel by 1943. As Table 11.2 reveals the great majority of these young pre-war recruits had been male, and the absence of schoolboy recruits during the war contributed not only to the ageing of the panel, but also to a shift in its gender composition.

Before the war only 30 per cent of respondents had been women, but this had risen gradually to an average of 39 per cent during 1942 and then jumped close to 50 per cent in the spring of 1943, where it remained until the end of the war. The women panellists had always been significantly older than the men, although before the war even the women were younger than the female population as a whole. The convergence of the panel's age distribution with the national pattern by 1945 was partly a product of this continuing gender difference. The 1945 female respondents were substantially older than the population as a whole: well over half were between 45 and 64 compared with only a third of the general population (excluding children). Among the men, on the other hand, only a fifth were between 45 and 64, while the younger age groups continued to be over-represented, although less so than in 1939. Although MO was aware that its female

Table 11.2 Gender/age distribution of MO panel, 1939–1945

	1939	1939	1945	1945	1939
	Male	Female	Male	Female	National Register
	%	%	%	%	%
18 and under	12	3	0	0	X
19–24	37	21	15	5	10
25–34	29	31	29	16	23
35–44	12	24	28	19	21
45–54	5	16	9	38	18
55–64	3	5	11	16	15
65 and over	1	1	7	6	13

observers tended to be older than its male ones,[44] I have found no contemporary attempt to explain why this was so.

Age and gender were not the only respects in which the panel was unrepresentative of the population at large. There were considerably more mass observers in London and the South East per head of population than in the rest of the country, and Scotland and Wales were especially poorly represented.[45] But the outstanding characteristic of the panel was its class composition. Charles Madge had initially been reluctant to accept that the panel was, and would remain, disproportionately drawn from the middle classes.[46] By the end of 1938 he was conceding that the panel was 'predominantly lower middle class', but at the same time insisting that 'in social habit and attitude' they could be taken as representative of a stratified sample of the population as a whole.[47] Pitching to the MOI in August 1939 he made the even more outlandish claim that 'the lower professional groups (shopkeepers, clerks, civil servants)' who made up the bulk of the panel 'probably dominate the country numerically'.[48]

44. Willcock cited in Stanley, 'Extra Dimension', 170.
45. Stanley, 'Extra Dimension', 161–4.
46. See, for example, the misleading class balance of the quotations used in Madge and Jennings, 'They Speak for Themselves', *Life and Letters Today*, 9 February 1937, in *First Year's Work*, 68–79 (despite the figures cited on p. 65 of the same book showing clearly the middle-class domination of the panel), and in the script for MO's radio broadcast, 'They Speak for Themselves', in June 1939, FR A26, 3. Also note the assertion in *Britain* (217) that a long extract from a working-class panellist was 'typical enough in the direct outlook and language which predominates in the millions of words of this sort of material now in Mass-observation's files'.
47. 'Reactions to Advertising', December 1938, FR A10.
48. CM to Max Nicholson, 23 August 1939, TC 43/2/B.

Harrisson's version, at the same time, was that the panel was 'slightly weighted in the direction of the upper working and lower middle classes'[49]: a characteristically (and surely deliberately) befuddling way of summarizing the figures MO itself had published in 1938, which showed that of 429 panel members analysed, 215 were either working or lower middle class, as against 214 who were 'middle middle' or upper middle class.[50]

They should have known better. In June 1939 nearly 400 panellists had responded to a directive asking them, among other things, to what class they felt they belonged. Table 11.3, based on the 87 per cent of respondents who applied conventional class labels to themselves, shows the result.[51]

At a time when the manual working class accounted for up to three-quarters of the population and the middle class around a quarter, the latter are clearly over-represented.[52] Strikingly, there were almost twice as many upper and upper middle-class mass observers as there were working-class ones. And even that proportion of working-class respondents was exaggerated, since most of those defining themselves as working class held white collar jobs.[53] Moreover, less than a third of the middle class saw themselves as belonging the 'lower middle class'. Far from being 'slightly weighted' towards

Table 11.3 Self-attributed class of MO panel, 1939

	All (%)	Male (%)	Female (%)
Working class	19	22	11
Lower middle class	25	26	23
Middle class	27	25	33
Professional	11	9	14
Upper middle class	15	15	16
Upper class/gentry	3	2	4
Total	100	100	100

Figures are rounded

49. 'Emergency Problems and Mass-Observation', 29 August 1939, FR A22.
50. *First Year's Work*, 65.
51. For a full analysis and discussion of these responses see Hinton, 'The "class" complex': Mass-Observation and cultural distinction in pre-war Britain,' *Past and Present*, 199, 2, 2008.
52. R. McKibbin, *Classes and Cultures. England 1918–1951*, 1998, 45–6, 106.
53. Including 13 clerks most of whom were young men living at home with working-class parents and probably destined to acquire an identity more in keeping with their occupations when they left home. Several others (e.g. 2070, 1372, 1362) used the term 'upper working class' to describe situations—a 'collar and tie job'—that would more conventionally be classified as lower-middle class.

the 'upper working and lower middle classes' the panel was heavily weighted towards the higher strata of British society, to which almost two-thirds of respondents felt they belonged. An occupational analysis of nearly 500 mass observers who sent in ten or more directive responses during the war tells a similar story. Leaving aside housewives, members of the armed forces, and a small number of miscellaneous groups, most of the remaining 382 people were either owners (4.5 per cent), managers (2.9 per cent), professionals (46.6 per cent), or students (9.7 per cent); while white collar (21.5 per cent) and manual workers (13.6 per cent) made up little more than a third of the total.

In the assessment he made of MO's value for the MOI in October 1939, Richard Crossman wrote off the panel as 'merely a chance collection of individuals interested in mass observation, and for that very reason uncharacteristic of the common man.'[54] At the time Harrisson was similarly dismissive, and in private even Madge agreed that, so long as the panel remained so small and unrepresentative, it would be unwise to place too much reliance on the material it supplied.[55] But as Harrisson took control of the panel his view of its usefulness shifted: it was, after all, the resource that enabled MO to lay claim to knowledge of private as well as public opinion.

To encourage the observers to keep going each of the monthly directives was accompanied by a bulletin giving feedback on previous directives and summarizing MO's ongoing work. When time permitted directives were accompanied by appreciative comments on the observer's previous response. 'Letter from M-O this morning', wrote one panellist, 'with the usual personal remark in violet ink, I should like to say how that personal remark made month by month makes all the difference, and brings into the work the feeling of friendship, rather than a pure scientific job.'[56] Panellists were regularly asked to consider starting diaries: and diarists were advised to prioritize their diaries over directive replies if they felt they had no time to do both.[57] The more regular respondents were rewarded with book tokens at Christmas and free copies of some of the *Change* books.[58] 'It has opened my eyes a great deal to the work that is being done and has made me feel more

54. R. Crossman, 'Trial Employment of M-O and BIPO', 26 October 1939, INF 1/261.
55. CM to TH, 21 January 1940, Org&Hist 1.
56. Diarist 5110, June 1944.
57. Langley to TH, 12 August 1940, Org&Hist 4/2; MO *Bulletin*, May 1943, FR 1671; MO *Bulletin*, August 1944, FR 2145; MO *Bulletin*, Willcock to panellists, December 1944, FR 2190F.
58. MO *Bulletin*, 10 September 1941, FR 854; *Bulletin*, 10 November 1941, FR 938; *Bulletin*, 14 February 1942, FR 1096.

enthusiastic,' wrote one grateful recipient of *People in Production*: 'It is such a new experience to find someone interested in the trivial happenings in one's life—and to a good purpose'.[59]

From the outbreak of the war MO had presented the monthly directives to the panel as being of 'immediate and practical' value in 'sorting out the facts which will help to find a human non-bureaucratic solution for problems of civilian morale.'[60] To this end early wartime directives probed panellists' attitudes to wartime innovations: rationing, evacuation, the black-out, war savings, etc. In the autumn of 1940 Harrisson experimented with ways of using the panel to 'supplement [the] objective systems of measurement already in use' for assessing morale, asking selected panellists to chart the ups and downs of their feelings over a week and to identify things that made them more cheerful or more depressed.[61] By the spring of 1941 Bob Willcock, who had been in charge of the panel since the previous November, was producing regular analyses of responses to directives, often based on a balanced sample of 100 replies selected to equalize the numbers of men and women.[62] While some of these were geared to publications or commissioned projects that MO was working on at the time, others belonged among the many hundreds of 'file reports' intended not for immediate use but as a data-bank of 'sifted research material' to be 're-analysed and more fully digested' after the war when, hopefully, MO would have the time and resources to write the considered social history of the war, preparation for which had been MO's primary purpose ever since September 1939.[63]

Even more so than the directive replies, the diaries were seen primarily as a resource for later historians: 'Not a lot of work to be done on diaries', Harrisson minuted in November 1940, 'but put in well-prepared cold storage.'[64] Nevertheless, within two weeks of his contract with the MOI

59. Diarist 5261, 16 May 1942.
60. MO *Bulletin*, November 1939, FR W3.
61. 'Experiment in gauging any daily morale fluctuations', 30 October 1940, FR 473a; Directive, November 1940, FR 509; 'Attitude scales', December 1940, FR 515, MO *Bulletin*, January 1941, FR 565 The results were unimpressive. In *Living Through the Blitz* (279–81) Harrisson used daily charts on what determined day-to-day feelings to show that air raids were very low down the list. But this was all rather fanciful, as Fremlin, editing the text after Harrisson's death, pointed out (footnote, 280).
62. e.g. 'Holidays', May 41, FR 715; 'Influences on opinions', August 1941, FR 852; 'Superstition', November 41, FR 975; 'Religion', April 1942, FR 1200; 'Death & Supernatural', June 1942, FR 1315.
63. 'Home-Front History and M-O', May 1944, FR 2092.
64. TH 'Points from meeting', 6 November 1940, HN pap.

in April 1940 he had been drawing up headings under which the content of the diaries could be indexed for immediate use.[65] Over the summer he had Miss J. Langley indexing incoming diaries in London, while, in Malvern, Novy sorted out the chaotic piles of diary material bequeathed by Madge, enabling Priscilla Feare to use it for her work on women and war.[66] By November, despite Ferraby's view that 'reading these [diaries] at present seems to me a great deal of work for very small rewards,'[67] Willcock was producing weekly analyses of 'The War in M-O diaries' classified under the same headings as those used in the MOI's weekly reports.[68] 'Each week,' he assured the diarists in January 1941, 'we read every word and report on outstanding features'.[69] Harrisson tried out a short version of the digest on Mary Adams in February, 'done to get quick result. Any use?'[70] The problem, inevitable with material derived from the panel, was that it was too retrospective to be of immediate use in monitoring morale.[71]

Although some of MO's projects did make extensive use of material derived from the diaries,[72] the most extensive wartime work on the diaries—undertaken by Yoni Lane, a young psychologist in 1941, and by Celia Fremlin in 1944—was seen more as a preliminary to their eventual use as the basis for the post-war social history of the war, than as a contribution to MO's immediate output.[73] And that was in line with the emphasis that MO had always placed in communications with the diarists on the central purpose being 'to store up material for history'.[74] In January 1942, commenting on Harold Nicolson's remark that 'no good diary was ever conceived as a purely private diary', Harrisson wrote to *The Spectator* outlining MO's 'scheme for private-public diarists', explaining that:

65. TH, 'Ideas about diary analysis' 19 April 1940, Org&Hist 4/4. By the end of the month he and Madge had agreed that a mark should be made 'against anything of outstanding interest in the diaries. Each entry analysed to have a special mark round it according to whether subject was heard, seen, said, thought or done' ('Decisions reached at meeting between TH, CM etc . . .', 26 April 1940, Org&Hist 1.)
66. TH to Langley, 12 August 1940, Org&Hist 4/2; Feare to TH, 31 July 1940; Novy to Willcock, 31 July 1940, HN pap.
67. Ferraby, note on diaries, 23 October 1940, Org&Hist 1/1.
68. FR 510, 1 December 1940; FR 523, 10 December 1940; FR 574, 13 January 1941.
69. MO *Bulletin*, January 1941, FR 565.
70. TH to Adams, 4 March 1941, FR 598.
71. Adams to TH, 11 March 1941, MApap 2/E.
72. e.g. *War Begins at Home* and *People in Production*.
73. MO *Bulletin*, 9 June 1941, FR 721.
74. 'Wartime Directive No 1', September 1939, FR A25.

we suitably file and index the diaries, keeping them…safely down in the
country, where they are valuable both for the diarist personally after the war,
and for the social student. This gives a diary incentive and interest, bridges a
private-public gap, and at the same time provides what will, I believe, be
sociological material of interest and value in the years to come…As Harold
Nicolson remarks, 'a good diary is the raw material of history'. We are
energetically accumulating this raw material.[75]

Early on Harrisson had understood that the panel material had the potential
of revealing the evolution of individual attitudes and behaviour. It was on
these grounds that in January 1940 he criticized Madge for 'not thinking sufficiently about his panel as *people*', and for filing the material in a such a way
that 'the cross-correlation of material from the same individual would be an
appalling task.'[76] In March 1941 he set Lane to write a study of the early
months of the war based on the responses of just four of the diarists.[77] But
nothing much came of this, and the urgent needs of the present ensured that
incoming diaries and directive responses would be filed and analysed separately. Even if Harrisson had found the time and resources to 'think about the
panel as *people*'—as individuals—any resulting publication (as Lane apparently
was planning) would have run into insuperable problems over the anonymity
guaranteed to panel members, and flown in the face of the pledge made by
Harrisson and Madge in their original 1937 explanation of MO's objectives
that 'we do not intend to intrude on the private life of any individual, as individual. Collective habits and social behaviour are our field of enquiry, and
individuals are only of interest in so far as they are typical of groups.'[78]

    Willcock, who knew more about the panel than anyone else, was happy
to concede Crossman's point that the volunteers, precisely because they
were volunteers and prepared to write at length about their views, could
not possibly be representative of 'the common man'. What they did represent, Willcock argued, was a minority of 'thinking' people, spread across a
wide range of social and geographical locations. While it was undeniable

75. TH, letter to *The Spectator*, 6 January 1942, Org&Hist 3/Spectator.
76. TH to CM, 18 January 1940, 15, 20–1, Org&Hist 1.
77. Lane to TH, 28 March 1941, Org&Hist 1/2. 'I am working on the book on the diaries on the
    lines you indicated. I read a number of diaries and have selected four for main use: O. Smith
    (dramatic narrative); R. Nicholls (quiet stuff); T. Smallbones (typifying proletarian progressive
    mind); N. Satterthwaite (a working class woman of remarkable courage and cheerfulness)'.
    The disproportionate selection of three working-class diarists to one middle-class one
    (Nicholls was a park keeper) suggests that Lane (and perhaps Harrisson) were still not recon-
    ciled to the overwhelmingly middle-class composition of the panel.
78. *Mass-Observation*, 1937, 30.

that this thinking minority was to be found disproportionately within the educated middle class, it was by no means co-extensive with that class. Plenty of middle-class people were unreflective creatures of habit, while working-class communities harboured their share of thoughtful and articulate people. The 'mental stratification' of society, Willcock asserted (on the evidence of the panel membership), 'is correlated to quite a high degree with social, economic and educational stratifications, but at the same time it is none of these things, and possesses an independent existence of its own.'[79] That, certainly, was how many mass observers saw themselves: members of a group of self-consciously enlightened individuals located across the class spectrum.[80] The value of their testimony, Willcock argued, lay in their readiness to explore and articulate their private thoughts about the exhaustive range of contemporary issues that MO sought to probe through the monthly directives. The loss of statistical representativeness was more than compensated for by this articulation of opinion in formation: the 'why' as well as the 'what' of public attitudes.[81]

> Anyone who cares to examine his own *private* opinion on a number of subjects will quickly see that it often differs markedly from his *public* opinion on the same subjects. But opinion is only the top, most rational, layer of the whole complex of feeling, emotion, fear, hope, and finally of unconscious driving force, which determines a person's attitude and behaviour. Public opinion may serve as a disguise for private opinion, but private opinion is often itself a compromise with *feelings* which have not yet had time to translate themselves into opinion at all... The value of the Panel lies in a relationship which enables its members to write about these deeper levels which they recognize in themselves, but about which they, like anyone else, would be unwilling to talk in detail to a strange interviewer, or, often, to their own personal friends.[82]

Reflecting in 1947 on his experience of analysing scores of directive replies since 1940, 'in close conjunction with field survey data', Willcock claimed that on any particular issue the panel 'will reflect all the *main* outlooks and attitudes to be found among the general popula-

79. 'Report on Reconstruction', 16 October 1942, FR 1452, appendix 2.
80. J. Hinton, 'The "class" complex', *Past and Present*, 199, 2, 2008.
81. Madge's formulation in *War Begins*, 20.
82. MO *Bulletin*, February 1947. Philip Ziegler, who reproduced this text in *Crown and People*, 208, assumed that it had been written by Harrisson, but Mollie Tarrant (Tarrant to Wainwright, 31 October 1978, Personnel/Tarrant) thought that Willcock was the author, which seems likely.

tion... [although] not, of course... in the same proportion as the general population'. In interpreting this data the analyst could make allowance of the inbuilt biases of panel members, biases that the observers could be relied upon to reveal with an honesty born of their motives for volunteering and MO's cultivation with them of a trusting relationship 'of friendly informality... it [is] improbable that members of a volunteer panel will indulge in social evasions and personal camouflage. They know that to do so would make their work valueless.'[83]

In practice, Willcock's handling of the panel material was not always as measured as his theoretical gloss indicated. His 1942 report on reconstruction for the MOI outlines the theory in an appendix. But one of the leading claims in the body of the report—that popular opinion in general was likely to follow the trend of panel responses away from particular material concerns like jobs and housing, and towards the general principles that should underpin post-war reconstruction—rested on a surprising failure to allow for the fact that, more or less by definition, the 'thinking minority' were always likely to reflect on current issues at a more abstract level than the population in general.[84] Willcock, like Harrisson before him, was not immune to the temptation to allow his excitement about the insights provided by the panel into the processes of opinion formation to override the fact that the mass observers were radically atypical of the population as a whole. His confident claim that the panel responses reflected, however disproportionally, the range of attitudes in the population at large, is difficult to sustain against the evidence supplied by the 240 panellists who responded to a September 1943 directive asking 'What part do politics play in your life nowadays?'[85] True, there were a few committed conservatives—four, to be precise, all women—and five ageing Liberals. But 60 of the 69 people who stated a preference for a particular party identified with parties of the left, and a further 59 people outlined political views that clearly belonged to the left without identifying with any particular party.[86] Among those identifying

---

83. Willcock, *Polls Apart*, 62–3.
84. 'Report on Reconstruction', 16 October 1942, 13–14, FR 1452.
85. DR, September 1943.
86. Half of the respondents (117 people) gave answers that could not be classified as 'left' or 'right'. Sixty-one of these made it clear that they took an interest in politics, and among the remaining 56 who said politics played no part in their lives, several gave answers that implied political engagement in a non-party sense. In addition to the Conservatives there was only one respondent who stated political views clearly belonging to the right. But perhaps Nella Last should be added to this group, although in her September 1943 response she said she had no interest at all in politics.

with parties of the left, the Communist Party had almost as much support as the Labour Party, and more than three times as many people looked to Richard Acland's new Common Wealth Party as to either of the two older parties. Although Willcock acknowledged the disproportionate leftism of the mass observers, he did not attempt to quantify it: had he done so it would have been difficult to sustain the view that a panel including only a handful of supporters of the dominant political party (and hardly more of its coalition partner and main rival) could adequately reflect 'all the main outlooks and attitudes' among the public at large.

III

MO did not invent panel research, nor was it the only panel operating during the war.[87] When, in February 1941, Harrisson got wind of plans for Home Intelligence to solicit reports on morale from Listener Research—the panel of correspondents started by the BBC in September 1937—he wrote anxiously to Adams, rehearsing reasons why the BBC would be unsuited to this purpose. The volunteer correspondents of Listener Research, he argued, would be likely to deliver far too cheerful a view of morale, telling the BBC ('the most "official" source of opinion formation') what they thought it wanted to hear.[88] The real rival to the MO panel, however, came not from Listener Research but from within the Ministry itself. Stephen Taylor, who took over from Adams as head of Home Intelligence in April 1941, had always been sceptical of the alarmist tone of MO's morale reports.[89] But he was fully persuaded that qualitative research based on a nationwide panel could reveal aspects of popular opinion beyond the reach of the interview and sampling methods used by BIPO or the WSS.[90] So he set out to construct an in-house version of the MO panel, but one better designed to get at a broad range of opinion, and whose findings were not refracted through what he saw as the over-dramatizing mind of Harrisson. Adams had made use of MO partly because she was sceptical about the capacity of the

87. P. Lazarsfelt and M. Fiske, 'The "Panel" as a new tool for measuring opinion', *Public Opinion Quarterly*, 2, 4, October 1938.
88. TH to Adams, 14 February 1941, TC 74/3/F.
89. Taylor to Adams, February 1940, MApap 2/A.
90. Stephen Taylor, 'The Study of Public Opinion', *Public Administration*, October/December 1943, 115.

Ministry's regional information officers and their committees of local notables to provide reliable evidence about public opinion: 'The prediction of
public opinion by amateurs, and those who "think they know", is often
faulty, and skilled and scientific cross-checking is essential.'[91] Not only did
the Ministry's regional apparatus lack the necessary expertise, but, since it
had been established to foster good morale, its officers were unlikely to
report negatively on the effectiveness of their efforts. In May 1940, when
Home Intelligence was first asked to produce daily reports on morale, the
regional information officer's contribution consisted of impressionistic
accounts cobbled together 'partly by discussions with their own staff, partly
by casual conversations initiated or overheard on the way to work, and
partly by a hurried series of visits to public houses, and other places where
the public foregathered.'[92]

According to a historical account of the development of Home
Intelligence written in 1944 (presumably by Taylor himself), efforts to
improve the regional intelligence-gathering machinery began in London
from the spring of 1940:

> Those in Home Intelligence who were doubtful about the representativeness
> of the Mass-Observation reports were anxious to provide some system of
> studying the feelings of the public more directly and impartially. So it was
> decided to make contact with a number of people in London in all strata of
> society, who would be prepared, in response to a telephone call or a personal
> visit, to report the feelings of those with whom they were in contact...
> doctors, dentists, parsons, publicans, small shopkeepers, newsagents, trade union,
> officials, factory welfare officers, shop stewards, Citizen's Advice Bureaux
> secretaries, hospital almoners, business men, and local authority officials.[93]

These contacts, Taylor later explained, were not supposed to be a typical
cross-section: 'if it were, it would be useless, since a considerable part of it
would be completely inarticulate'. Like Willcock he believed that 'the trends
of thought of the non-articulate follow closely those of their articulate
friends', and that 'articulate opinion is not a perquisite of any social class.'[94]
The Home Intelligence 'contacts' were, as Brendan Bracken described them
to a sceptical Churchill, 'people reputed to be sensible and level-headed, and
whose occupation brings them into contact with a large number of people

91. 'Mass-Observation and Wartime Social Survey', 12 September 1940, INF 1/262.
92. 'The Work of Home Intelligence Division', 1944, 2 and 5, INF 1/290.
93. 'The Work of Home Intelligence Division', 1944, 3, INF 1/290.
94. Taylor, 'The Study of Public Opinion', 114–15.

every day.'[95] Because London was initially administered directly from the Ministry, rather than through its own regional office, these reports could be digested by headquarters staff. The regions, lacking intelligence officers with the necessary skills, were unable to provide reliable analyses of opinion, even when they cultivated contacts similar to those being used in London. Taylor moved swiftly to put this right, persuading the Treasury to underwrite the appointment of 'Intelligence Officers' in each region to develop panels similar to the London one.[96]

Eventually at least 2,400 contacts were recruited, each submitting a report once a month on a staggered cycle, so that 600 reports came in each week.[97] These were digested by the regional intelligence officers, and the resulting reports were edited by Taylor and other headquarters staff to weed out the bias; remove subjective phrases like 'it is surprising to find' or 'contrary to what one might expect'; and ensure that 'where personalities were involved' the reports presented a 'true picture without being gratuitously offensive.' The latter task, he remarked, 'has often taxed the ingenuity and literary skill of the authors.'[98] Taylor took a lot more care than Harrisson to avoid unnecessarily antagonizing his paymasters, and each weekly report carried a clear statement designed to limit any offence that might be caused to other Whitehall departments:

> In reading this report, it is important to bear in mind that it does not set out to record facts, except in so far as public opinion is itself a fact. It is a record and reflection of the public's views and feelings about the war in general. Therefore, on matters on which public opinion is ill informed, prejudiced or inconsistent, the report does not imply any endorsement of the views which are expressed in it.[99]

When not (as in his memoirs) polemicizing against Harrisson, Taylor was happy to acknowledge his debt to MO for having pioneered the use of a

---

95. 'The Assessment of Public Feeling at Home', Memo by the Minister of Information, 25 November 1942, Cab 66/31/28. Churchill thought that the weekly reports contained 'hardly anything which could not have been written by a man sitting in a London office and imagining the echoes in the country of the London press' (Mclaine, *Ministry of Morale*, 258–9).
96. 'The Work of Home Intelligence Division', 5, INF 1/290.
97. These are the figures given by Taylor in his memoires (Taylor, *A Natural History of Everyday Life*, 273). The 1944 official history (2) gives a higher figure of 4,000 contacts. Bracken's report to the War Cabinet in November 1942 (CAB 66/31/28) says that each regional intelligence officer received at least 30 reports from his contacts each week, which would imply about 1,500 contacts overall.
98. 'The Work of Home Intelligence Division', 1944, 16, INF 1/290.
99. Mclaine, *Ministry of Morale*, 257.

national panel in opinion research. But the MOI panel was superior to MO's, he claimed, since its members were responsible people from all sections of society, people 'whose judgement and discretion can be relied upon',[100] invited, instructed, and carefully vetted by the regional officers. The MOI had the resources to implement 'a more scientific build-up' of its panel, avoiding the inbuilt bias of those self-selected enthusiasts who were drawn to MO, many of whom would have been familiar with its publications and in sympathy with their critical tone.[101] No analysis of the political views of the Home Intelligence panel survives, and as far as we know no such analysis was ever undertaken: but, given the method of selection, the MOI's 'contacts' may well have veered as much to the establishment as the MO panel veered to the left. Moreover, they were being asked to report on other people's opinions rather than their own. This was a procedure fraught with difficulty, as Harrisson had explained to Adams: generalizations made by untrained observers about other people's views or behaviour were, in MO's experience, '80 per cent generalisation about themselves.'[102] A further problem was that the contacts were expected not only to report on public opinion, but also to act as a channel of communication between individual members of the public and the authorities, supplying 'full details about any grievances they want investigated, [and] passing back... information to the people with whom they are in touch.'[103] To the extent that they were thus engaged in the business of influencing, rather than just reporting on, public opinion, the objectivity of the contacts was open to the same objection that Adams had originally made about the objectivity of the regional officers themselves. The questions posed by Home Intelligence were less wide ranging than those posed by MO, and Taylor was not interested in soliciting the subjective data about the thoughts and feelings of its own panellists, so much more reliable than their attempts to report the thoughts of others, which constituted the central strength of MO's method.

From the standpoint of the historian, however, by far the biggest limitation is that Taylor's approach was strictly present-minded. Unlike MO, with its mission to document the social history of the war, the MOI saw no purpose in collecting and preserving their contacts' reports. Just two individual

100. Letter from London regional intelligence officer recruiting a new correspondent, cited in 'The Work of Home Intelligence Division', 1944, 30, INF 1/290.
101. Taylor, 'The Study of Public Opinion', 115.
102. TH note on Listener Research, 14 February 1941, TC 74/3/F.
103. 'The Work of Home Intelligence Division', 1944, 27–8, INF 1/290.

reports are reproduced in an appendix to the 1944 history of Home Intelligence, one of them a typed report from a worker at the railway works in Derby, reporting low morale and rampant anti-Semitism among his fellow workers in a manner comparable to many an MO report, but without explicit discussion of the writers' personal opinions. The other, flagged up as a 'specimen of a typical average report' was written by a middle-aged female teacher in Keswick whose impressive range of activities—maternity and child welfare, Liberal Party, League of Nations Union, Mothers' Union, Workers' Educational Association, Townswomen's Guild, National Savings—make her characteristic of the kind of local social leaders that the regional officers set out to recruit.[104] Alongside dutiful reports on responses to the war news, petrol shortages, etc., she writes at length about what is evidently her own disappointment at a sub-standard Churchill speech—'the wine must have been circulating very freely'—and her indignation at the attempt of a group of local councillors to have all books dealing with Germany (most of them written by anti-Nazis) removed from the local library. These two reports read remarkably like the MO directive replies, hinting at a parallel treasure trove of material which, had it survived, would have complimented the MO material, providing a perfect comparator and check upon its inbuilt biases. As it is, all we have are Taylor's digests, which, as we have seen in the case of attitudes to post-war reconstruction, were in fact very similar to MO's own findings. In this way, ironically, one long-term result of Taylor's successful efforts to outflank and marginalize Harrisson was that the rival panels tended to confirm each other's reliability as a means of assessing popular attitudes.

IV

A key feature of MO's approach was to operate with a mix of methods, and it was constantly experimenting with ways in which its various resources could most productively be deployed and combined. Debating with BIPO's director, Henry Durant, at the British Psychological Society in April 1942, Harrisson rehearsed the weaknesses of the sample interview: 'we are still

---

104. The one mass observer I know of who doubled as an MOI 'contact', a Warwickshire Women's Institute leader and member of the Coventry Information Committee, had a similar profile. On this woman, Gertrude Glover, see Hinton, *Nine Wartime Lives*, 51–71.

completely ignorant of the relationship between what people say to a stranger and what they say to a friend'; or between what they 'say, think and do.' Interviews, he argued, needed to be supplemented with 'observational technique', 'individual analysis', and 'penetration study of institutions'.[105] MO's particular concern, Willcock explained, was to investigate 'people's behaviour, their subjective feelings, their worries, frustrations, hopes, desires, expectations and fears.' Since the outbreak of war MO had improved its 'complex machinery for recording these things', enabling it to investigate intimate topics like religious faith, feelings about death, or attitudes to sex on which questionnaire-based surveys would never produce more than superficial answers. Freely admitting that 'the technique for this qualitative study of behaviour and opinion at a more intimate level than that recorded by the doorstep interviewer is at present in an early experimental stage,' he presented MO as vigorously engaged in developing this new dimension of social science.[106]

From the outset MO had been experimenting with the possible uses of the panel. Where there were local concentrations of observers, Madge was keen to use them for intensive local studies, although he worried that pre-mature contact between individual observers could lead to group thinking and undermine the subjective value of their directive responses.[107] During 1938 groups of London panellists had observed visitor behaviour at Kew Gardens and London Zoo, but, on reflection, Madge concluded that organizing volunteers for such work was more trouble than it was worth.[108] During the war Harrisson frequently made use of panellists as temporary fieldworkers to supplement the work of the full-time staff. Scores of volunteers all over the country participated in an exercise for the MOI watching for pacifist activity outside Labour Exchanges on the day in April 1940 when 25-year-olds were required to register for military service.[109] Local panellists were recruited to help the blitztown team in Manchester and Liverpool, and the work for the Admiralty on dockside security in Hull.[110]

---

105. Report of 11 April meeting of British Psychological Society, *Nature*, 149, 9 May 1942.
106. H. D. Willcock, 'Mass-Observation', *American Journal of Sociology*, 48, 4, 1943, 456.
107. Directive, September 1937, FR A4.
108. CM to TH, 18 January 1940, Org&Hist 1.
109. Willcock to panel members, 29 March 1940, TC 27/1/G, and see the reports in this file.
110. 'Report on Liverpool and Manchester', 6 January 1941, HO 199/442; TH, 'The Port of Hull', 17 April 1942, TC 66/10/C.

Special reports were often solicited from observers with experience relevant to particular investigations, as for example, those working in industry whose testimony features prominently in *People in Production*.[111]

Before the war Madge had encouraged observes to report systematically on other people's opinions, before realizing that the panel was at its best when engaged in self-observation.[112] Willcock returned to this issue in 1941–2, experimenting with the use of panel members to supplement the regular bi-weekly News Quota carried out by the full-time staff. Volunteers from among the panel were recruited to ask three News Quota-style questions of 12 people each week, a target that proved excessive and was quickly dropped to six. The interviewing was to be done indirectly, slipping in the questions in the normal course of conversation with friends and acquaintances, and in this way getting something closer to private opinion than the material produced by the fieldworkers' direct interviewing of strangers in the street.[113] Analysing 200 such responses sent in by the volunteers during the week following Pearl Harbour in December 1941, Willcock concluded that 'this method of collecting a large body of information by indirect non-interview methods holds considerable possibilities. For a small number of investigators opinion-sampling on a large scale is only practicable by direct interviewing, because of the very large amount of time spent in entering into conversation with people and introducing the questions naturally.' The technique, however, 'is not perfected, and it is doubtful whether it can be perfected in wartime when almost everyone's time is so limited.'[114] One problem was that the panellists' friends and acquaintances were, like themselves, disproportionately middle class. In theory this could have been corrected when selecting responses for analysis, although the large category of 'housewife' could not be analysed in class terms, and in practice many volunteers failed to specify either the class or occupation of their acquaintances.[115] By February 1942, when Willcock was soliciting further volunteers for the News Quota, the exercise had been further reduced from a weekly to a fortnightly basis, and from the summer it seems to have been dropped altogether.[116]

111. *People in Production*, 21 and *passim*.
112. Directives, November and December 1937, FR A4; Directive, February 1938, FR A8; CM to TH, 18 January 1940, Org&Hist 1.
113. *Bulletin*, 29 November 1941, FR 938; Directive and *Bulletin*, 19 December 1941 FR 1003.
114. 'Panel News Quota', 30 April 1942, FR 1233.
115. 'The provincial News Quota', 17 May 1942, FR 1264.
116. Directive, 14 February 1942, FR 1096.

Plans drawn up for an ambitious, but never completed, 'study of youth' provide a good example of the energy with which Harrisson fostered MO's methodological catholicism. As the London blitz began in the autumn of 1940, work by Masel and Richard Fitter on attitudes to politics in the East End alerted Harrisson to problems of alienation among the young.[117] With the prospect of conscription looming, young men were unable to make the plans for their future that they would normally be doing in their late teens. Torn between apathetic resignation and wishful thinking that the war would be over before their turn came, they were, even more so than in peacetime, drifting, restless, and cynical. The paucity of leisure facilities for the young after they left school at 14 left up to 70 per cent of them (according to a study conducted by Gertrude Wagner for the Manchester Council of Social Service) cut off from the civilizing influence of 'church, party, voluntary organisation, club or night school'; a situation aggravated by the conscription of adult youth leaders and the blitz, which closed many of the clubs and societies catering to youth.[118] Sensing an opportunity for a major study, Harrisson sent Ferraby off to do library research; secured Wagner's cooperation; directed Stevens (aged 17) and England (aged 20) to conduct more interviews in London; and tried to persuade the Marxist sociologist, Francis Klingender, to 'undertake the planning and supervision of the enquiry.'[119] Though initially interested, and prepared to give MO four days a week of his time at a guinea a day, Klingender withdrew after a few days.[120] More successfully, Harrisson approached Dr A. E. Morgan, whose 1939 survey of *The Needs of Youth* had painted a depressing picture of feral adolescents corrupted by the pools and urged the need for greater state support for educational and leisure provision for young people.[121] Morgan, who had commissioned MO's work on Air Raid Precautions in Fulham before the

---

117. 'Survey of voluntary and official bodies during bombing of the East End', 27 September 1940, FR 431.
118. TH, 'The Hope of Youth', 21 November 1940, FR 499.
119. Ferraby to TH, 16 October 1940, TC 51/2/A; TH to Wagner, 29 October 1940, Wagner to TH, 1 November 1940; Klingender to TH, 1 November 1940; TH to Klingender, 11 November 1940; LE to TH, 2 November 1940, all in TC 51/1/C.
120. Although later in November TH was still hoping to use Klingender on another research project (TH to Feare, 27 November 1940, HN pap). Klingender, whose 1935 book, *The Conditions of Clerical Labour in Britain since 1918,* had predicted the radicalization of the lower middle class, was a leading intellectual in the Artists' International Association, writing and lecturing on Marxist approaches to art history. Harrisson had been in touch with him since at least 1937 when he consulted him about the social effects of film (Stuart Legg to TH, 27 October 1937, W 36/A).
121. *The Times*, 23 June 1939.

war, was himself writing a report on the problems of youth for a committee of club organizers, social workers, and churchmen in London, and he persuaded them to fund a two-week comparative study of two London boroughs.[122] Supervised by Ferraby, England and Stevens were to spend the first week of 1941 observing the behaviour of young people in Paddington, while Fremlin and George Hutchinson did the same in Bermondsey, and Fitter spoke to officials in the two boroughs. To ensure the comparability of the two studies Harrisson drew up a detailed schedule of tasks, which included: 'penetration of every type of institution, organisation, shelter, etc; counts and census of activities; detailed collection of overheard conversations; follows of young people by day and night; and so on.'[123] At the end of the week he convened a meeting of all the investigators 'to pool total experience for the first phase and... discuss plans for the next week, which', he promised, 'will be less hectic.'[124] During the second week the fieldworkers got into informal conversation with young people, as well as doing 100 questionnaire-based direct interviews. Unsurprisingly, perhaps, Harrisson's report concluded that 'something around half the youth in each area is vaguely drifting along with a minimum of cultural, ideological or other guidance or interest... the huge majority are hardly touched by the organised social and moral forces.'[125]

Harrisson was still hopeful of securing more extensive funding. In January he drew up plans for a much more extensive study of youth at work, home, and play in London (central and suburban), a provincial industrial town, an agricultural centre, and a non-industrial country area of small scattered villages. Direct interviewing would be kept to a minimum, used mainly to estimate the proportions involved in different leisure activities. Instead, the investigators would 'infiltrate into the life of the youth community, record behaviour [and] spontaneous comment.' They would take factory jobs, join youth clubs, or 'make personal contact with non-organised youth in street, pub, etc.' They 'will live in typical family households as lodgers and participate in family life, recording home behaviour and the actual problems which arise.' This would have involved six fieldworkers over six months, plus two analysts, at a total cost of £650. Alongside the fieldwork, the war diaries

122. 'Plan for a 2-week study', 1 January 1941, TC 51/2/A; 'Young People', FR 553, 24 January 1941.
123. 'Youth Report', 5, nd (1941?), TC 51/2/A.
124. 'Plan for a 2-week study', 1 January 1941, TC 51/2/A.
125. 'Youth Report', 35, nd (1941?), TC 51/2/A.

would be trawled for information concerning youth, and members of the panel would be asked for their views which would show 'what the more thoughtful part of the population believes to be the outstanding problems now, and how they would like to see them solved.'[126] A significant number of mass observers were themselves engaged in youth work, and they would be asked to write detailed accounts of their experience. No funder with £650 to spare came forward, and, perhaps overwhelmed by his relentless blitz-chasing in the provinces during the early months of 1941, Harrisson let the project drop. Two years later he picked it up again when a possibility arose of funding from the Birmingham Council of Social Services.[127] But this too came to nothing, as did the contract he agreed with Gollancz in July 1942 to write a short book on 'The Young Man's War'.[128]

V

MO struggled to convince the social science community that its methods were worth attention. Living from hand to mouth, kept afloat by Harrisson's brilliance as a journalist and entrepreneur, lacking time, resources, or indeed inclination to proceed carefully with academic rigour, it was easy for outsiders to dismiss MO as, at best, a superior kind of journalism (Taylor's view) or, at worst, 'a sociological dustcart' sweeping up, in its amateurish enthusiasm, so much worthless junk.[129]

From his earliest days with MO, Ferraby strove to theorize the MO practices that he observed; to flesh out, more systematically than Harrisson or Madge had done, the claim that MO was pioneering a new approach to the scientific study of society.[130] Central to his thinking was MO's prioritization of qualitative over quantitative methods. Ferraby did the statistics for MO, and he understood their limitations better than anyone else. In an intellectual

126. 'Projected Study of Youth', January 1941, TC 51/2/A.
127. See Chapter 12.
128. The contract (3 July 1942) and relevant correspondence (14 March–13 July 1942) is in Org&Hist 3/Gollancz.
129. Thomas, interviewed by Stanley, 26 November 1979. For Taylor's view see 'HI statement re M-O' attached to TH to Bracken, 20 April 1943, MO&MOI 2.
130. Ferraby's early interventions include: 'A method of establishing socio-economic groupings', nd (February 1940?), FR 41a; 'Report on Tribunals', April–May 1940, TC 6/1; 'Methodological criticism', 2 August 1940(?), Org&Hist 4/4; 'Concerning the Draft Plans for investigations', 29 March 1941, Org&Hist 1/6.

climate where quantification was often seen as the hallmark of scientific method, Harrisson and Willcock, neither of whom had much grasp of statistics,[131] were sometimes tempted to place more weight on MO's own statistics than they could bear.[132] Such slapdash deployment of figures—percentages with no indication of the size of the sample, conclusions drawn on the basis of statistically insignificant differences—did much to justify those who dismissed MO's methods as hopelessly unscientific. But rather than kowtowing to 'the current mania for expressing everything in terms of figures', Ferraby took the battle to the enemy, spelling out why, in the field of public opinion research, it was mistaken to equate quantitative precision with scientific accuracy:

> It would always be possible for M-O to treble or quadruple the size of sample without affecting time and costs by using cross-off questionnaires, part-time interviewers and tabulating machines. We should then have figures of indubitable veracity, and no means of interpreting them. In fact, of course, we invariably record verbatim replies, which takes at least four or five times as long per interview; which means employing skilled interviewers; analysis by hand instead of machine; saturation of the analyst and report-writer in millions of words instead of hundreds of figures. We use this costly and laborious method because we consider we get much nearer the real answer that way.[133]

The effort put by pollsters into refining sampling techniques and statistical method was, he argued, disproportionate to the results obtained. However appropriate such techniques were to forecasting voting patterns or consumer buying—predicting *actions* rather than future trends in *opinion*—the pursuit of numerical precision was only as valuable as what was being measured. Standard tick-box polling techniques gave no more than a snapshot of attitudes artificially lumped into pre-determined categories, and were therefore of little value in getting at 'the intensity with which opinions are held, the reasons why they are held, the diversity of opinion, the nature of

---

131. TH, 'Note on M-O opinion samples, rough, confidential, for use of BW,' 30 August 1939, TC 43/1/B. In 1942 Willcock wrote to a statistically educated colleague: 'Don't give me correlation coefficients etc without a brief explanation, if it's desirable to give them me at all, I know practically nothing at all about them' (Willcock to Behrens, 18 July 1942, TC 25/14/H).

132. Ferraby, 'Representative sampling and the qualitative approach to public opinion research', 27 August 1943, FR 1886.

133. *Britain and her Birth-rate*, 11 (the manuscript of this book is in Ferraby's handwriting: TC 3/2/O).

unexpressed opinion'.[134] By using pre-determined categories the pollster achieved an appearance of precision and accuracy quite at odds with the real validity of his figures.[135] MO, by contrast, preferred to ask open-ended questions, record verbatim responses, and hold back from categorization until the analyst could get a feel for the true variety and ambiguities of opinion by reading through the whole range of responses.[136]

The fullest elaboration of this point was made after the war by Willcock in an article setting out the variety of states of mind lumped together in the pollster's category of 'Don't Know'. As with the non-voter, MO resisted the conventional assumption that the 'Don't Knows' were simply ignorant or indifferent. Even the stereotypical older working-class women—the 'eff-six-tiddees' (F60Ds) as they were known among MO investigators—who had no time for political questions, had firm opinions on the domestic issues that touched them directly and on questions of ethics and belief. Far from indicating indifference, the 'Don't Know' response, on further probing, often revealed people who for one reason or another were reserving judgement, perhaps because they were 'too worried about the issue to commit themselves to a decision'; or because they were reluctant 'to criticise the status quo . . . . [like] the hesitant woman, unwilling to commit herself against something she doesn't feel she understands very well, but about which she feels vaguely uneasy'; or because, as in psychoanalysis, they were unconsciously using ignorance to block out an unresolved conflict of ideas. After elaborating 11 different categories among the 'Don't Knows', Willcock concluded:

> Where there is a high ratio of Don't Knows [on an issue people care about] . . . it is probable that many are reserving judgement because they are veering towards a pessimistic or critical view which they would prefer to avoid. In such cases the balance of positive opinions is often misleading . . . It is when an issue is alive but puzzling, or when changing events begin to force people's minds into an unaccustomed way of thought, that the Don't Knows embrace the most diverse and incompatible elements. In such cases they may be the most important group of all, an index of tension and a key to tomorrow's opinionated outlook.[137]

134. Ferraby, 'Representative sampling and the qualitative approach to public opinion research', 27 August 1943, FR 1886.
135. Ferraby, 'Validity of public opinion survey results', August 1944, 3, FR 2144.
136. Ferraby, 'Recording and classifying verbatim information', August 1944, FR 2146.
137. Mass-Observation, 'Don't Know, Don't Care', in *The Adventure Ahead*, Contact Books, March 1948, 59–60.

While the polling firms had a vested interest in dismissing the MO approach as 'slapdash and slovenly', Ferraby believed that MO's substantive results should be sufficient to demonstrate that its methods deserved serious attention from 'University [social] Scientists'.[138] In April 1943 he presented a paper to the Manchester Statistical Society on 'The Limitations of Statistics in the field of Public Opinion Research', laying out reasons why the focus on accuracy in sampling and statistical method was less important to discovering real public opinion than the qualitative methods developed by MO.[139] But none of this made much impression on his academic audience, who were more inclined to agree with MO's ex-workers at the WSS—whose work was largely concerned with matters of fact rather than opinion—that Ferraby's attitude was simply perverse:

> Mr Ferraby's argument about there being less need for an accurate technique in some problems than in others is rather obscure. The Survey takes the point of view that reliable results can be obtained only if the sample chosen is representative of the parent population, and this seems to hold good whether the subject of the enquiry is simple or complicated. Qualitative information about attitudes can be of use only if the proportions of the population having different broadly defined attitudes are known, and for this reason statistical treatment is the first essential.[140]

That, for Ferraby, was to put the cart before the horse. However accurately the distribution of 'broadly defined attitudes' was counted, the meaning of the resulting figures could serve only to obscure the variety of states of mind lurking beneath the analyst's pre-determined categories.

Underpinning Ferraby's attack on mindless quantification was a more fundamental critique of the positivistic methods adopted by academic sociologists who, he believed, were seeking respectability by aping the methods of the physical sciences. MO's founders—more concerned with understanding contemporary society than with establishing academic credentials—had been the pragmatic pioneers of a new kind of social

---

138. Ferraby, 'Mass-Observation methods', 20 February 1943, 2, FR 1597.
139. 'The Limitations of Statistics in the field of Public Opinion Research', 14 April 1943, FR 1666.
140. Box and Thomas, 'The Wartime Social Survey', *Royal Statistical Society*, iii–iv, 1944, 189. And see Abrams' subsequent comment on Ferraby's 'admission' that 'an element of subjectivity' was involved in the analysis of MO's data, which he contrasted with the scientific objectivity achievable by 'a quantitative classification of a given body of content in terms of a system of categories . . . defined so precisely that different analysts can apply them to the same body of content and secure the same results . . .' (Abrams, *Social Surveys*, 112).

science.[141] As yet untheorized and still experimental, MO's methods had the potential 'to emancipate [sociology] from the curbs of physical science', liberating social research from constricting models of deductive reasoning. The key fallacy of academic sociology, he argued, was to seek objectivity by distancing the researcher from the behaviour under observation. In the study of human affairs, however, such distancing was achievable only by suppressing 'a major portion of the equipment with which man comes into the world.' Reason, as modern psychology had demonstrated, is subordinate to other mental qualities, and the scientific exploration of social reality would remain drastically restricted until the sociologist found disciplined ways of deploying the whole range of resources with which human beings are endowed for understanding one another. As things stood, the 'common sense' methods of the journalist or the novelist—intuitive understanding informed by close contact and worldly experience—had more to offer to the understanding of social life than the deductive reasoning of the social scientist. Suspicious of participant observation, because of the danger that by making himself part of the material he is studying the investigator will lose that detachment necessary to making objective judgements, the academic remained an outsider, cut off from the knowledge and understanding acquired intuitively by insiders whose everyday business required them to make sense of the world around them.[142]

Intuition played a key role in Ferraby's model of social scientific enquiry. By their immersion in the milieux under investigation MO's investigators opened themselves up to intuitive ideas about what was going on. The analyst and report writer—Ferraby himself in many instances—might lack the personal experience of participation, but would have the investigators' impressions to work from, alongside the verbatim quotations the collection of which was the basis of MO's method. Saturated 'in millions of words instead of hundreds of figures' the analyst was able to categorize and synthesize the material in a process which, while admittedly 'still rather mysterious', seemed to have more in common with the diagnostic techniques of the medical practitioner than the deductive reasoning of the statistician. Above all, for Ferraby it was the psychiatrist who had done most to advance understanding of the human mind, deploying a balanced combination of

141. 'It could be said that the basic idea of M-O was not an idea concerning sociological method, but a determination to get results at all costs', 'Ferraby, 'Sociology in Great Britain', FR 550, 22 January 1941.
142. Ferraby, 'Mass-Observation methods', 20 February 1943, FR 1597, 11–15.

observation, intuition, reason, and verification so much more productive
than the positivistic methods of the experimental psychologists who had
taught him as a Cambridge undergraduate.

> There is a capacity of the human spirit to which little attention has so far been
> paid by scientists. Given a mass of material, an investigator invariably forms
> ideas about the material before he has applied the process of reason to
> it ... There seems to be a quality in the human mind which allows it [given
> sufficient immersion in the material] to synthesise intuitively the implications
> of facts.[143]

Such intuitions, tested and elaborated against the accumulated material,
produced knowledge of social reality far superior, Ferraby insisted, to that
delivered by deductive reasoning from statistically reliable tables of numbers
bled of nuance and human ambiguity by the reductive processes of quantification. As a description of Harrisson's method of working this seems
entirely appropriate, and Ferraby was probably justified in suggesting that
much contemporary social science would benefit by acknowledging that
'the basis of [their] work should be more a synthesis of observation, developed intuitively, and less an analysis of observations, developed by the use of
reason, than is usual at present'.[144] But Ferraby was in danger of overreach-
ing himself in offering MO's methods as the basis for 'a reorientation of
[the] scientific approach'. Harrisson, although impressed by Ferraby's
work,[145] was well aware of this danger, and used his editorial pen to tone
down Ferraby's more aggressive formulations.[146] This may explain why
Ferraby's more far-reaching ideas never appeared in print.

   It was in relation to the problem of sustaining objectivity while immers-
ing oneself in the activity being observed that Ferraby was at his most original. The investigator should seek objectivity by detaching himself not from
the subjects of his study but from his own ego, his own wants and desires.
By cultivating detachment from the self the investigator could avoid the
trap of seeing only those things which bore out his preconceptions and
resist the self-aggrandizing rush to establish premature generalization, the
tendency to 'delude ourselves that we are obtaining certainty when we are

---

143. Ferraby, Draft for Handbook, March 1941, Org&Hist 1.
144. Ferraby, 'Mass-Observation methods', 20 February 1943, FR 1597, 31.
145. 'Valuable and thoughtful', Harrisson wrote on Ferraby's paper 'Mass-Observation methods',
     adding 'Comments follow separately'. Frustratingly I could find no trace of these comments
     in the archive.
146. Ferraby, 'Sociology in Great Britain', FR 550, 22 January 1941.

doing nothing of the sort [which] can never lead us anywhere but to a morass of conflicting schools', disrupting collaborative processes of advancing knowledge. To this end he recommended that social scientists should undergo 'training in detachment from the self' as 'taught by the various mystical schools of the different religions'. Techniques of detachment developed by Eastern mysticism could be adapted to enable social scientists to report objectively on what they observe, to open their minds to intuitive ideas arising from their immersion in the evidence, and to bring into consciousness the mysterious processes underlying the capacity of the human mind for intuitive synthesis.[147] One of MO's first historians aptly summarized Ferraby's approach as a kind of 'sociological Quakerism' in which 'a quiet and attentive attitude provides the best environment for the spirit to speak as it will.'[148] The statistician had moved far from the scientism of his Cambridge undergraduate training in his journey towards the Bahá'í faith. To ears attuned to later 20th-century ethnographic and post-structuralist approaches to the production of social knowledge, Ferraby's ideas may seem obvious enough, but it is easy to imagine the scorn with which they would have been received by the social science community in the 1940s, especially given the religious inflexion of his thinking. He was probably well-advised not to attempt to publish at the time.

147. Ferraby, 'Mass-Observation methods', 20 February 1943, FR 1597, 25–7.
148. Stanley, 'Extra Dimension', 40.

12

Interregnum

I

Since the outbreak of war conscription had taken a steady toll on Mass-Observation's (MO's) male staff. Brian Allwood, Alec Hughes, and Henry Novy had all been called up before the end of 1940. By February 1941 Jack Atkins was working for a demolition firm in blitzed London, perhaps as an alternative to military service.[1] Len England was called up in January 1941, and George Hutchinson in June. Jimmy Stevens, being younger, lasted until February 1942, and Humphrey Pease, being older, until May 1942. While Bob Willcock and John Ferraby both gained permanent exemption on health grounds, the two remaining senior men, Richard Fitter and Tom Harrisson himself, were both conscripted in July 1942.

Fitter had been exempted when he worked for Political and Economic Planning and Harrisson had been thankful for Mary Adams' support in getting his deferral extended: 'It greatly lightens the burden of running M–O to know that I have a really good male in charge of the administrative and directing side.'[2] Fitter, knowing that the six-month deferral Harrisson obtained for him in January 1942 was unlikely to be renewed, used the breathing space to secure service work appropriate to his talents: joining the RAF to edit a journal in the Operational Research Section of Coastal Command.[3] Harrisson, by contrast, went into the army as a private soldier. A year earlier David Astor, believing his friend's conscription imminent, told him that it would 'certainly do you good to live the socialistic life of the armed forces and to...have first hand experience of what "armed

---

1. 'Demolition in London', 1 July 1941, FR 768.
2. TH to Adams, 17 January 1942, TC 74/3/F.
3. Fitter, interviewed by TH, 1 October 1971; Obituary in *Daily Telegraph*, 6 September 2005.

might" means: discipline, routine, crudity, repetition…the grimly slow machinery of which a battle is just a momentary spark.' Nevertheless, Astor insisted, Harrisson's real vocation lay on the home front, doing his '16 hours a day at the MOI (reformed).'[4] Harrisson had said much the same to Atkins in 1940, when Atkins wanted to volunteer.[5] By 1942, however, according to his memoirs, Harrisson was increasingly feeling that 'a person with energy, impatience and high opinion of self, could hardly feel good if he stood outside the full consequences of war indefinitely.'[6] At the time he told Victor Gollancz 'I have now decided to become a private soldier,'[7] and within a year of his conscription he wrote that he had been 'anxious to get into the army and become a soldier, which very well suits my temperament.'[8] Given the gusto with which Harrisson took to army life and indeed to the 'momentary spark' of combat when parachuted into Borneo to organize the tribesmen as a guerrilla fighter against the Japanese occupiers, there is no reason to doubt that a good part of Harrisson welcomed this change in his life.[9] But it is also unlikely that he would have been able to avoid conscription even if he had wanted to. According to Stephen Taylor the decision to conscript Harrisson was taken 'after consultations at the highest level'.[10] As we have seen, Ernest Bevin, infuriated by *People in Production*, probably had a role in this.[11] But what seems to have been decisive was the attitude of his patron in Naval Intelligence. In September 1941 the Admiralty had secured a further six-month exemption for Harrisson, but when their attempt to extend this was turned down by the Ministry of Labour, Admiral Godfrey's initial intention to appeal was abandoned after he learned that Harrisson, on a secret mission to Dublin for Naval Intelligence in May 1942, had revealed who he was working for, confirming earlier reports that 'if ever [he] had too much to drink, he became very voluble and indiscreet'.[12] This may well be a more accurate version of events than Harrisson's own retrospective claim to have been demoralized by the fact that 'more and more of

---

4. Astor to TH, 20 May 1941, TC 43/2/D; TH to Kingsley Martin, 28 July 1941, Org&Hist 3/3.
5. See Chapter 6.
6. Harrison, *A World Within*, 164.
7. TH to Gollancz, 24 June 1942, Org&Hist 3/10.
8. TH to Bracken, 20 April 1943, MO&MOI 2. But he omitted this sentence from the final draft of his letter.
9. Heimann, *Most Offending Soul*, Part Four.
10. 'HI statement re M-O' attached to TH to Bracken, 20 April 1943, MO&MOI 2.
11. See Chapter 9.
12. Merrett, Notes for A.D.N.I., 23 February 1946; Godfrey to the First Sea Lord, 20 May 1942, ADM 223/476; TH to Adams, 11 May 1942, TC 74/3/F; *World Within*, 163.

the things I was being asked to do were moving over the borderline of objective description and honest analysis towards provocative partisanship or actual espionage.'[13] Whatever the truth in these murky waters, there is no doubt that Harrisson was relieved to be out of it, embracing his commando training with all his usual passion for new experience. He gloried in the toughness of his 'killer-driller' unit, and found time to organize a variety show, boasting characteristically: 'Having no previous experience of this, I am amazed at what a good show it looks like being.'[14]

But he certainly did not believe that joining the army meant abandoning MO. Until he was sent overseas, Harrisson did much to keep up MO's public profile through his work as a journalist and broadcaster—the latter including the BBC's accolade of a session of Desert Island Discs.[15] At first, Harrisson did everything he could to remain in control of the organization's day-to-day activities. Fearful that in his absence MO might descend into civil war—as, he alleged, had occurred among staff left without benefit of his leadership in both Bolton and the Malvern house during 1940—he set up a Byzantine system of checks and balances.[16] Willcock, though running the panel from his home in Letchworth, was to be in overall control. Day-to-day work at Ladbroke Road would be directed by Derek Behrens, a physicist who had joined the MO staff in February 1942 to replace the temporarily absent Ferraby as the chief statistical analyst, and who was to spend a year with MO before taking up a job at the Atomic Energy Research Division at Harwell.[17] Fitter, like Harrisson, did not see his service commitments as excluding a continuing involvement with MO, and agreed to become the organization's treasurer, acting 'in a supervisory capacity.' What this seems to have meant was that while Willcock would 'take all important decisions', he would need Fitter's approval to spend any money. As if this was not confusing enough, Harrisson, anxious about how the staff would respect the fabric of the Ladbroke Road house itself, persuaded one of his

13. Harrison, *A World Within*, 164. Or than his claim in a letter to Bracken that: 'I found it embarrassing and undignified to continue with senior admirals fighting to protect me from two or three people in the Ministry of Labour . . . I therefore requested that no further action should be taken in this matter' (TH to Bracken, 20 April 1943, MO&MOI 2).
14. TH to Lean, nd (December 1942?), 1/6; TH 'Aggressive Mentality in the Army', 8 January 1943, TC 20/7/A.
15. Heinmann, *Most Offending Soul*, 168.
16. Except where otherwise noted this paragraph derives from TH, 'General Memo on Organisation', 16 July 1942, Org&Hist 1/6.
17. Tarrant to Sheridan, 12 October 1981, Personnel/Tarrant. D. J. Behrens was working for MO between February 1942 and Mar 1943.

closest friends, 'a person whom I rate highest in honesty and commonsense', to move in, taking over his study, drawing room, and bathroom. The friend was Tangye Lean, a *News Chronicle* leader writer now working for the German service at the BBC, who Harrisson had got to know in the early 1930s when Lean was a precocious undergraduate in Oxford, editing *Isis*, publishing novels, and founding the Inklings, a literary club subsequently famous as the place where Tolkien and C. S. Lewis shared their fantasies.[18] As well as keeping an eye on the property, Lean was expected to give MO the benefit of his experience in the media and to represent Harrisson's 'general point of view'; and in the event of disagreements among the management team they were to turn to Lean for arbitration. Although insisting that he would have 'no responsibility for M-O', Harrisson instructed Willcock, Fitter, and Behrens to show Lean everything that they would previously have shown to Harrisson, so that he could 'read everything before it goes out for a final veto on ordinary tactical and public relations grounds.' None of these elaborate and overlapping arrangements were, however, intended to supersede Harrisson's own authority, and to ensure that he would be able to exercise it he arranged for a two-page 'daily digest' of correspondence and activity to be posted to him.

Of course it couldn't work. By October, in an attempt to coordinate things, the leading office staff, plus Fitter and Lean, had established a weekly Executive Committee (rapidly renamed Consultative Committee, presumably in deference to Harrisson's authority). Lean gave in his notice after a few weeks and was replaced (as both tenant and adviser) by another of Harrisson's trusted friends, James Fisher, assistant curator at London Zoo and a leading ornithologist whose influential 1940 book *Bird Watching* had advocated 'the Mass Observation of birds'.[19] Writing to Fisher in November, Fitter proposed a 'joint demarche to Tom' to demand the appointment of an

18. Humphrey Carpenter, *The Inklings: C. S. Lewis, J.R.R. Tolkien, Charles Williams and their friends*, 1978, 56–7; Obituary of Lean, *The Times*, 30 October 1974. Tangye Lean (younger brother of the film director David Lean) had a distinguished career in the BBC external service where he ended as director before retiring early to return to his first love, writing. He published an enormous study of English 'traitors' who supported Napoleon. In 1942, at Harrisson's request, he had asked his psychoanalyst to read Churchill's first (and only) novel for clues to the great man's personality. The psychoanalyst was unforthcoming, but, learning of Harrisson's decision to join up, Lean asked: 'Can I live in your London house and look after your interests while you're careering in the Army?' (420101 TH Lean, 1 and 20 January 1942; Lean to TH, nd (July 1942?), TC 74/3/F).

19. Matless, *Landscape and Englishness*, 1998, 259; Consultative Committee, minutes, 16 November 1942, Org&Hist 1/6.

executive head with full authority: 'Whatever happens the present system of diarchy must cease.' No one, for example, knew whether or not the Committee had the power to take on new jobs without Harrisson's explicit approval; a situation bound to lead to delays and risk the loss of much-needed contracts.[20] Eventually, in January 1943, after Fisher resigned (and moved out), defeated like Lean before him by Harrisson's impossible brief, the Committee proposed that it should be given 'real authority to take decisions'.[21] Harrisson, who saw 'Committee rule' as institutionalized dithering, responded by persuading Willcock to move from Letchworth into Ladbroke Road where he could exercise effective control as acting director general, with the Committee in an advisory role 'suggesting, stimulating, pooling ideas and criticisms'. At the same time, Atkins (now working as a journalist with *Tribune*) replaced Fisher as the representative of Harrisson's 'general point of view', taking on various office jobs in his spare time.[22] Later on, in the summer of 1943, when the side effects of an operation for an abscess on his appendix put Willcock out of action for several months, Atkins was to step in temporarily as acting director, and he continued to help out in the office until his eventual call-up in April 1944.[23]

The financial arrangements, however, remained obscure. Previously everything had been done by Harrisson, and, although Fitter was acting as honorary treasurer, it was Harrisson's personal account that held the organization's money; so that when, for example, he restocked his wine cellar, he had to remember to warn Fitter, who was struggling to find enough in the account to pay the wages. Fitter and Fisher pressed for the separation of MO 'from the person Tom Harrisson', and its reconstitution as a limited company, with Harrisson's position guaranteed by making him the managing director on leave of absence.[24] Under pressure from the senior staff Harrisson agreed, and by February 1943 draft articles of association had been drawn up by another of Harrisson's long-standing friends, Ambrose Appelbe, a high-profile London solicitor of pacifist and feminist convictions who was later to defend (and befriend) the serial killer John Christie, guide

20. Fitter to Fisher, 19 November 1942, Org&Hist 1/6.
21. Consultative Committee, minutes, 1, 16 January 1943, Org&Hist 1/6.
22. TH to Willcock et al, 5 February 1943; Fitter to TH, 6 February 1943 (misdated in source as 1942); Consultative Committee, minutes, 16 February 1943, Org&Hist 1/6.
23. Atkins to Jones, 26 July and 13 September 1943, TC 85/1/C; Willcock to Marston, 26 April 1944, TC 20/8/B.
24. TH to Fitter, nd (1942?); Fitter to Fisher, 19 November 1942; Consultative Committee, minutes, 2 December 1942, 1 January 1943, Org&Hist 1/6.

Mandy Rice-Davies through the Profumo Affair, and help to establish War on Want, the Marriage Guidance Council, and Help the Aged.[25] Appelbe also agreed to take over as MO's treasurer when, in February, Fitter resigned.[26] By then Adams, Basil Nicholson and Gertrude Wagner had been approached to serve as members of an advisory council for the incorporated body, alongside Fitter and Lean. Although in April arrangements were being made for an inaugural meeting to set up the limited company, all existing accounts of MO's history agree that it did not become a limited company until 1949, so we have to assume that the plans made at the beginning of 1943 came to nothing.[27]

II

These organizational questions were the least of MO's worries in the months that followed Harrisson's conscription. In the autumn of 1942 the local Labour Exchange received instructions that employment by MO should no longer be accepted as an alternative to war work for women eligible for conscription.[28] Anticipating the worst, the office launched a premature recruitment drive that left MO with considerably more staff than it could afford. 'The recent large additions to the staff', Fitter reported in November, 'had been made rather precipitately on instructions from TH and with the mistaken idea that the latter was willing to cover part of the additional expense involved.' Barely able to meet the weekly salary bill, and with existing contracts coming to an end, MO was forced to sack half the people it had just taken on. Meanwhile urgent requests for support were sent to MO's various friends among the great and the good. The Minister of Information, Brendan Bracken, lobbied by Harold Laski, was sympathetic, but Bevin, lobbied both by the Advertising Service Guild's (ASG's) Liberal MP Tom Horabin, and by Stafford Cripps's fixer George Strauss, was unyielding.[29] By February 1943 Veronica Tester, Doris Hoy, and Marion

---

25. Obituary, *The Daily Telegraph*, 20 March 1999.
26. Fitter to TH, 6 February 1943 (misdated in source as 1942); Consultative Committee, minutes, 2 February 1943, Org&Hist 1/6.
27. Loeb to Everett Jones, 6 April 1943, TC 1/4/I.
28. 'Memorandum on Mass-Observation', 29 October 1942, FR 1450.
29. Consultative Committee, minutes, 12 and 16 November 1942, Org&Hist 1/6; Tarrant, letters to Crowther, Bernal and Zuckerman, 12 November 1942, Personnel/Tarrant; Taylor, 'Reservation of Mass-Observation', 23 January 1943 INF 1/262.

Sullivan had all been conscripted, and Celia Fremlin (now married) was spared only because she was about to have a baby.[30] Mollie Tarrant, who had done innovative blitztown work in Portsmouth (where she looked after her sick mother) and subsequently operated independently of Fremlin's team as a mobile investigator entrusted with responsibility for negotiating important MO contracts, was also called up early in the new year.[31]

For the rest of the war MO's fieldwork depended on older women not subject to conscription or exempted on health grounds, and more or less temporary staff, often young men awaiting call-up. Among the former the most important were Lena Bleehan, a married woman who had been working for MO since February 1942 but about whom I have found out very little;[32] and Gay Taylor, Kathleen Raine's astrologer friend, who, after escaping from a soul-destroying job in postal censorship, worked part-time for MO from the autumn of 1942 and full-time from the spring of 1943.[33] The longest-serving among the young men was Eric Gulliver who later recalled being 'mothered' by Celia and Doris when he started with MO in 1941, aged only 16 and overflowing with youthful enthusiasm for all things Soviet. After his call-up in the summer of 1943, Gulliver continued to send material to MO, at first from the RAF and, from 1944 to 1946, from the Nottingham coalfield where he worked as a 'Bevin boy'.[34] One of MO's reactions to the impending loss of its core female investigators had been to solicit help from members of the panel willing to work full-

30. Another stalwart, Cecelia Mackintosh, who had worked for MO since the autumn of 1941, also resigned in February 1943. Hoy and Sullivan were both placed in administrative jobs in the War Office (Consultative Committee, minutes, 6 and 16 February 1942, Org&Hist 1/6; Sullivan, interviewed by Angus Calder, 17 March 1980; 'Memorandum on Mass-Observation', 29 October 1942, FR 1450).

31. 'Memo on personnel', 21 April 1941, INF 1/286; Harrison, *Living Through the Blitz*, 181–2, 187–8, 355; Consultative Committee, minutes, 25 November 1942, Org&Hist 1/6; Tarrant to Sheridan, 2 April 1979, Personnel/Tarrant.

32. Consultative Committee, minutes, 16 November 1942, Org&Hist 1/6. Her work first appears in the MO catalogue in February 1942, and is prolific between then and the end of the war. See also Harrisson, *Britain Revisited*, 268. The surname Bleehan is extremely unusual, so it is possible that that she was the woman responsible for the following small advertisement in *The Times* (26 November 1937, 3): 'Swiss or Austrian Lady required to look after two boys, 8 and 10 years: light house duties; as family: happy home assured—Bleehan, 132 Hanover Road, NW10.'

33. Consultative Committee, minutes, 16 November 1942, Org&Hist 1/6; Loran Hurnscot [Gay Taylor], *A Prison, a Paradise*, 1958, 204–10.

34. Gulliver, interviewed by Stanley, 8 September 1982; Diarist 5091, November 1940–December 1941, *passim*; various reports on Communist Party meetings, etc. in TC 25/8/1; 'Coal mine survey', 1944–7, TC 64/2/B. After the war he became a school teacher, but, as we shall see, his involvement with MO was to continue into the 1970s.

or part-time. Some who responded found they had little to offer, notably Noel Willmett, a rather ineffectual young man medically unfit for military service and, his diary suggests, psychologically unfit for more or less any employment. After a couple of months working for MO early in 1943 he was laid off, rather to his relief: 'I found the work interesting but a great strain. I am extremely shy and diffident and my heart would sink every time I talked to a stranger'. It was this diffidence, no doubt, which invited aggressive responses, like that of the man whose reaction to being asked 'Do you believe in astrology?' had been to threaten to throw poor Willmett into the ruins of a nearby bombed-out house.[35] Other temporary young men, like the future political philosopher Maurice Cranston, who worked for MO briefly before joining the Friends' Ambulance Service in the autumn of 1942, were altogether more useful.[36] By mid-February the number of fieldworkers (excluding the ones known to be leaving shortly) was down to ten, compared with 26 at the height of the panic recruitment drive in November 1942 and around 18 at the peak of MO's fortunes in the summer of 1940.

The office was also hit by conscription. Behrens, who played a central role after Harrisson and Fitter left, had moved on to Harwell by the spring of 1943. Edith Loeb, a young Jewish refugee who had been helping with filing and analysis since joining the staff early in 1941 was threatened with transfer under the aliens regulations but seems to have survived with MO until the summer of 1943.[37] This left Willcock and Ferraby, protected by their ill-health, and (possibly) a Mrs Hasse, who worked as a typist.[38] But there was also an important new recruit. Diana Brinton-Lee, who had served with Humphrey Jennings on the committee organizing the 1936 surrealist exhibition and saw herself as part of the 'urban intelligentsia', had been part of Charles Madge's circle in the early days of MO, alongside her film-director husband. She became Harrison's secretary in the summer of 1942, taking over from Priscilla Novy

35. Diarist 5233, May 1942; Willmett to Tarrant, 4 April 1977, Personnel/Tarrant: 'I met you at Tom Harrisson's house in 1943. I was hoping to be a regular Mass-Observer but I could not make the grade. I was too shy with strangers.' His wife, who also kept an MO diary, was long suffering but made of much tougher stuff. They were the only married couple, apart from the Walton's (see Hinton, *Nine Wartime Lives*, Chapter 9) to both write war diaries for MO.
36. Consultative Committee, minutes, 16 November 1942, Org&Hist 1/6; DNB entry.
37. TH, 'General Memo on Organisation', 16 July 1942, Org&Hist 1/6.
38. Consultative Committee, minutes, 16 November 1942, 16 February 1943, Org&Hist 1/6.

who had returned to the job a few month's earlier.[39] By November 1942 she was responsible for the office administration, a post she filled for the remainder of the war.[40] Another figure from MO's infancy, Madge's ex-wife Kathleen Raine, also put in a brief appearance over the winter of 1942–3, turning the odd shilling for MO by writing articles on its findings for the weeklies.[41]

III

Financially, MO needed all the help it could get. In November 1942 Fitter was paying out £130 a week in wages and petty cash, a sum barely covered by the income from existing contracts. Although the clear-out of newly recruited staff reduced the weekly bill by £30, MO's income fell even faster, and by early January the organization was being kept afloat by an overdraft of £120. Searching for further economies, Fitter sought to limit MO's contribution to the costs of the Ladbroke Road house (rent, rates, housekeeper, gardener, etc.) which totalled £8 a week, while Brinton-Lee looked around for cheaper accommodation in central London.[42] Eventually, in the autumn of 1943, MO was to move to 21 Bloomsbury Street, round the corner from the British Museum.[43] Back in January, however, with no prospect of further help from the bank manager, both Fitter and Harrisson feared that, in the absence of any major new commissions, MO would 'hardly last the spring.'[44] At the time of Harrisson's conscription in July 1942, in addition to the ASG retainer of £5 a week, there were four major ongoing contracts—the work for Cripps; various projects for the publishers Odhams; an investigation of

---

39. CM, 'Autobiography'; Jackson, *Humphrey Jennings*, 168; DR 1060, June 1939. Her diaries of the months between August 1940 and May 1941 are deposited in the Imperial War Museum. Harrisson's opinion of them, when she asked him for advice about publication, was robust: 'She is representing herself as a British housewife. Her! Hardly...surrealist (a founder member in UK) dilettante and all. Clearly this is a diary composed afterwards...and later largely re-written...from the raw entries of an original not here presented. It is just what an M-O diary, ideally, is not.' TH, note appended to the typescript, 27 July 1973; Brinton-Lee to TH, 14 July 1973.
40. Consultative Committee, minutes, 16 November 1942.
41. Consultative Committee, minutes, 2 December 1942; Raine, 'Have You A Mind Of Your Own?', 7 December 1942, FR 1536; Consultative Committee, minutes, 16 January 1943.
42. Consultative Committee, minutes, 16 November 1942, 1, 8, and 16 January 1943, Org&Hist 1/6; 'Précis of Post', 6 January 1943, Org&Hist 4/4.
43. MO *Bulletin*, September 1943, FR 1911; Jones to Atkins, 2 February 1944, TC 85/1/C.
44. Fitter to TH, 6 February 1943 (misdated in source as 1942), Org&Hist 1/3.

'multiple shops' in Ealing, Chester, and Bolton; and the participant observation study of the Tube Investments factory in Birmingham being undertaken by Sullivan and Tester.[45] In October MO landed a contract from the Ministry of Fuel for a series of nine weekly reports on attitudes to fuel economy through to December.[46] These contracts brought in over £75 a week through the autumn, but apart from the ASG retainer, and possible new work from Odhams, none of it was expected to last into the new year.

Watching, with mounting anxiety, the unsuccessful efforts of MO's leaders to find new sources of income, Harrisson condemned them as 'feeble and naïf'.[47] When Fitter contacted Julian Huxley for advice about raising academic grants from Rockefeller, Carnegie, or Leverhulme, Harrisson revealed that he had previously made four unsuccessful applications to Leverhulme and that, in any case, the application process took far too long to be relevant to immediate needs. On the other hand, he harangued the team; they seemed to be doing nothing to go out and grab 'the MANY current job chances, especially in the BUSINESS, press, advertising etc fields'. Well aware that none of them had his own energy, flair, experience, or connections, he suggested trying to persuade Cyril Connolly, who was quitting a short-lived job as literary editor of The Observer, to stand in for him as MO's public relations officer: an improbable substitute given Connolly's reputation for extreme sloth.[48]

By February 1943 Harrisson was pinning his hopes for the future on two major bids: one to the Birmingham Education Committee for a six-week survey of youth, following up MO's earlier work in London; the other, which Everett Jones was keen on as the basis for a further volume in the Change series, to the Health Education Council (a non-statutory body) for a six-month study of attitudes to health and sickness using a research design already worked out the previous year and expected to bring in at least £1,000.[49] In the event neither of these bids succeeded. Harrisson was particularly upset by the fate of the health project, which was awarded to the

45. TH, 'General Memo on Organisation', 16 July 1942; Brinton-Lee to Fitter, 19 November 1942, Org&Hist 1/6.
46. 'Suggested service by M-O for Ministry of Fuel', October 1920, FR 1446. The reports are in FR 1447, 1448, 1449, 1487, 1488, 1489–90, 1526, 1527.
47. TH to Willcock et al, 5 February 1943, Org&Hist 1/3.
48. Consultative Committee, minutes, 2 December 1942; DNB entry on Connolly.
49. Consultative Committee, minutes, 16, 25 November, 2 December 1942, 16, 23 January 1943, 16 February 1943, Org&Hist 1/6; Fitter to TH, 6 February 1943 (misdated in source as 1942), Org&Hist 1/3; 'Précis of Post', 6 January 1943, Org&Hist 4/4.

Wartime Social Survey (WSS). Taylor was so anxious to get the job (which did much to establish the reputation of the WSS) that he not only offered to do it for free, but also circulated members of the Health Education Council with a letter knocking MO's capacity to do objective work.[50] Nevertheless, it was a series of contracts from Taylor that helped to keep MO afloat during these difficult months: the November 1942 report on reconstruction, a report on attitudes to American servicemen in January 1943, and a survey of the use of towels in pub lavatories.[51]

Some of the jobs MO took on during the war were difficult to distinguish from market research. In 1941 there had been research on likely attitudes to a scheme for re-sharpening old razor blades and another, commissioned by a bus company, on public perceptions of its services.[52] While both of these could be justified, just about, as contributions to war efficiency, that was a more difficult argument to make in respect of the 176 interviews conducted in July 1942 with West End dog owners on their use of 'Bob Martin's dog powder', or Gay Taylor's work for Weston's on biscuit brand name recognition in March 1945.[53] In all of these cases the commissions came from clients of the ASG, whose members referred them on to MO: and in the case of the dog powder, Robert Martin was both very rich and addicted to the company of intellectuals, which was, perhaps, why Harrisson thought it worthwhile cultivating him even at the expense of MO's purity of purpose.[54]

But there *were* limits. Mollie Tarrant earned Harrisson's fury when she negotiated a deal with a Cardiff engineering firm introduced to MO by Jones to write a company history, particularly since she agreed to the firm's demand that it should keep control of the historical material and the publication rights:

50. TH to Bracken, 20 April 1943, MO&MOI 2; Lewis Moss, *Government Social Survey*, 9–10.
51. Consultative Committee, minutes, 16 November 1942, 1 January 1943, Org&Hist 1/6; TH to Bracken, 20 April 1943, MO&MOI 2. But these were MO's final commissions from the MOI. In August 1943, when Taylor proposed commissioning MO to report on the effectiveness of an army exhibition in central London—'a task eminently fitted for MO and their methods'— he was overruled by higher authority (Taylor to Gates, 31 July 1943, INF 1/286). On 5 August 1943 Gates minuted: 'I have spoken to Mr Royds. By general consent this idea is to be abandoned.' This is the last item in the MOI file on MO.
52. TH to Everett Jones, 17 September 1941, TC 78/2/A; Waddicor to TH, 13 November 1941, TC 70/5/C; 'Razor Blade Scheme', October 1941, FR 911; 'Report on Birch Busses', 22 January 1942, FR 1049.
53. 'Bob Martin Powder', 7 July 1942, TC 78/1/A; 'Interim Report on Public Knowledge of Biscuit Brand Names', 1 May 1945, FR 2240; Taylor to Willcock, 17 November 1945, TC 67/7/A.
54. England to Cunard, 14 October 1997, Personnel/England.

This...is a negation of all M-O principles...Our job is to study people, not dig up a firm's history for its private reasons...It would be fatal if we started taking on jobs just for *money* instead of for the *value* of the *sociological results*... We are *not* an organisation out to make money by doing jobs for big business. We only do these jobs if we can, in some small way, advance the sum of knowledge.[55]

That job was refused, but the guiding principle that any contract should enable MO to pursue its sociological interests was sufficiently elastic to allow the organization, a few weeks later, to accept £150 from Rothman's for a survey comparing the popularity of two brands of cigarettes. Ferraby's objection that this was pure market research work was overridden, presumably on the rather flimsy grounds that MO had from its early days been interested in the sociology of smoking.[56]

In June 1944, appealing for funds from the public, Willcock claimed that at least a third of the work that MO had done during the war had been of purely historical interest, not paid for by any client. Moreover, much of the commissioned work had been 'done at cost price or considerably below it, because we feel it is of particular sociological value, and there is no-one in a position to pay "commercial" rates for it.'

M-O [he continued] could easily have been built into a prosperous market research concern over the past years, had we confined our activities to the limited field of statistical research in which most units are interested, and for which they will pay. Instead we have used our resources for keeping up a continual study of the impact of war on ordinary people.[57]

Harrisson's insistence, in September 1939, that MO's wartime strategy should be 'to do enough useful work to be allowed to keep going, so that after the war we may tell the truth for the first time' continued to inform the organization throughout the war. Although most of the 2,000-plus 'file reports' accumulated by 1945 were the product of commissioned surveys or drafts for MO's various wartime publications, a good many represented a preliminary analysis of material intended for post-war use. In the instructions he

---

55. TH to Lean, nd (August 1942?); TH, minute of meeting with EJ, 19 September 1942, Org&Hist 1/6.
56. Consultative Committee, minutes, 1 and 8 January 1943. Three months later Ferraby wrote: 'Smoking habits...are of sociological interest, but the popularity of a particular type of tobacco is of interest only to the manufacturer' ('The Limitations of Statistics in the Field of Public Opinion', April 1943, 4, FR 1666).
57. 'Mass-Observation and Home-front History', May 1944, FR 2092.

wrote at the time of his conscription Harrisson stressed the importance not only of seeking new contracts but also of 'keep[ing] up the regular routines of work on the historical side... record[ing] descriptive material for post-war use'.[58] Wartime by-elections continued to be covered, despite the absence of any paying client for this work: unlike Adams (and most subsequent historians), Taylor dismissed by-elections as irrelevant to the assessment of public attitudes.[59] The practice of sending investigators out periodically to observe daily life simply for the historical record continued even when finances were at their most exiguous.[60] Alongside the directive replies and war diaries Willcock encouraged panellists (as well as investigators and other contacts) to send in cuttings from the local press, printed ephemera, and private letters for a 'War Library' which he classified and stored as a 'service to social scientists... historians and writers in the future'. In the 1950s this collection was transferred to the Imperial War Museum, which in 1940 had encouraged MO to undertake the work on the grounds that no one else was collecting 'unofficial mass propaganda'. Despite later attempts to reclaim the material for the Sussex archive it has now disappeared without trace, presumably dispersed among the Museum's general collections.[61]

The papers deposited in the MO Archive by Fitter in 1988, which have made possible the foregoing detailed account of MO's organization, staffing, finances, and contracts in the months following Harrisson's conscription, only cover the period from July 1942 to February 1943. How long Harrisson continued to receive a 'daily digest' from the office is unknown. Already by December 1942 things were slipping, provoking a desperate *cri de coeur*: 'digest is Friday to Tuesday—4 days !!! My God.'[62] Even after he departed for the Far East in June 1944 Harrisson, having arranged for a monthly statement of MO's doings to be sent to him in Melbourne, was harassing

58. TH, 'General Memo on Organisation', 16 July 1942, 1/6.
59. Taylor to TH, 16 January 1941, INF 1/262.
60. For example the Consultative Committee, minutes, 2 December 1942, Org&Hist 1/6, which list subjects to be covered—including a day in Hyde Park, a day at the zoo, 'bridges and embankments. Report on people looking at the water, feeding gulls etc, and on conversation'.
61. Willcock, 'War Library', 16 September 1940, TC 20/12/B; Willcock, 'Salvaging History', 11 September 1941, FR 896; 'War-Library', 3 September 1946, Org&Hist 4/1; H. D. Willcock, 'Mass-Observation', *American Journal of Sociology*, 48, 4, 1943, 455; MO *Bulletin*, 19 December 1941, FR 1003; Willcock to TH, 7 August 1971, Personnel/Willcock; England to Cunard, 24 June 1997, Personnel/England; Imperial War Museum to Sheridan, 2009, MO Archive.
62. TH to Brinton-Lee, (?)nd, December 1942, Org&Hist 1/6.

Willcock for a fortnightly report.[63] By then, however, he had long since been forced to hand over day-to-day control and, despite his continuing involvement, MO's output in the later war years owed as much to the concerns of Willcock and his chief report writer, Ferraby, as it did to Harrisson himself.

63. Willcock to TH, 1 July 1944, TC 66/15/A.

13

The Willcock Years

I

A count of the file reports completed during the three and half years of Bob Willcock's regime suggests a sharp fall in activity, and this trend is broadly confirmed by the number of (dated) documents listed in the archive's catalogue of the wartime 'topic collections'.[1]

The number of Mass-Observation (MO) publications also declined, although less sharply. In the six years between its foundation and the end of 1942 MO published eight books, and a further two—*War Factory* and *People's Homes*—both published in 1943, were substantially underway before Tom Harrisson ceded day-to-day control to Willcock. Between then and the end of the war only two new books were published: *The Journey Home* (on attitudes to demobilization and post-war reconstruction) in May 1944, and *Britain and her Birth-rate* in the spring of 1945. Work on three other books—*Puzzled People*, *Exmoor Village*, and *Browns and Chester*—was virtually complete before the end of the war, but post-war paper shortages and perhaps a

Table 13.1 MO activity, 1940–1945

	No. of file reports	No. of topic collections
1940	469	1,663
1941	414	1,277
1942	320	1,040
1943	193	258
1944	106	267
1945	78	210

1. The dating of the documents in the catalogue is usually rendered in the form '1.9.42'. Documents dated in a different form will not have been included in this count.

certain lack of energy in bullying publishers delayed their appearance until 1947, when *Peace and the Public* (based on a survey undertaken before Harrisson's return in the autumn of 1946) was also published. One further book, a study of the South Wales mining town, Blaina, drafted in October 1942 and completed by August 1944, was subsequently abandoned by its publisher (Warburg) and never saw the light of day.[2] As well as the books, MO published a series of methodological articles (discussed in Chapter 11) and Willcock drafted much of a book on MO's history and methods. The manuscript of *Polls Apart* survives in the MO Archive, but the American publisher for whom it was intended failed to produce the book.

II

Since September 1939 MO's major publications had been focussed on issues of wartime mobilization. While challenging complacency about the state of popular morale, MO had consistently argued that the key to effective mobilization lay in improving communication between the leaders and the led. Pessimistic warnings of imminent disaster were balanced by optimism about the capacity of intelligent leadership, informed by MO's understanding of the masses, to sustain popular morale. It was an argument well crafted by Harrisson to establish the indispensability of MO itself to the successful prosecution of the war. From 1942, Willcock and John Ferraby, who were largely responsible for writing MO's books after Harrisson's call-up, spoke with much the same voice. As attention turned from wartime mobilization to post-war reconstruction, MO repeatedly warned that profound popular scepticism about promises of a post-war New Jerusalem was going to undermine the collective spirit necessary for successful post-war reconstruction unless politicians found effective ways of addressing the real hopes and fears of the masses; which, of course, MO alone understood correctly.

If the basic structure of argument remained the same, there was nevertheless a shift of emphasis. While both *The Journey Home* and *Britain and her Birth-rate* had specific recommendations to make to the politicians, the emphasis of both texts was more on analysing deep structures

---

2. Consultative Committee, minutes, 1 January 1943, Org&Hist 4/3. The manuscript, with an introduction by Leonard Woolf, is in TC 64/1/D. See also Brian Roberts, 'Welsh identity in a former mining valley: social images and imagined communities', *Contemporary Wales*, 5, 7, 1995.

of popular disaffection than on giving immediate policy advice. Unlike Harrisson, Willcock and Ferraby had no personal connections with members of Britain's political elite and no active engagement with political life. As a result they were less tempted than Harrisson had been to compromise MO's independence, or to offer facile solutions to deep-seated cultural problems. Willcock's dealings with Common Wealth— the new left-wing party whose mushroom growth in the later war years struck a chord with many of MO's volunteers (and with Willcock himself)—were a model of propriety, in sharp contrast to Harrisson's courtship of the Labour Party during the Bolton years.[3] The new regime's remoteness from political engagement meant that the balance Harrisson had tried to strike between pessimism of the intellect and optimism of the will tended to give way to a more thoroughgoing cultural pessimism, relieved only by vague calls for national spiritual renewal. In fleshing out the analysis of attitudes to reconstruction that Willcock had initiated in 1942, MO's later wartime writing painted a picture of what was happening to British culture under the impact of war profoundly at odds with the heroic and nostalgic myths that came to dominate popular memory of the war.

III

The Journey Home—the fifth volume in the Change series—dealt with attitudes to post-war demobilization. The main fieldwork for the study, carried out in the summer of 1943, consisted of 570 interviews balanced for sex, age, and class distribution, with half of them conducted in London, half in provincial towns or villages.[4] This was supplemented by interviews with a group of civil defence workers and with women war workers at the Osram-GEC lamp factory in Hammersmith, where Harrisson earlier in the war had established a close relationship with the manager.[5] A good deal of the

---

3. See the correspondence in TC 83/1/B between Willcock and Norman Hidden, Common Wealth's prospective Parliamentary candidate in Harwich, over the conduct of an opinion poll in the constituency by MO.

4. Journey Home, 8–9: Manchester, Bolton, Newark, Bishop's Auckland, and a cluster of Hampshire villages.

5. Journey Home, 9, 55; Chelioti to MO, 3 May 1943, TC 27/2/H; TH correspondence with Chelioti in TC 75/4/F, TC 75/3/A; Effects of the Exhibition, 20 October 1943, FR 1945.

report, devoted to attitudes in the armed forces, was based on material supplied by mass observers serving in the forces, including ex-full-timers like Nina Masel, Henry Novy, Len England and, of course, Harrisson himself. In March 1944, when *The Journey Home* was in proof, MO's offices were raided by MI5, alarmed by the security implications of a directive asking panel members to report 'either from their own knowledge or from enquiries, where, when and how the Second Front would commence'. All replies to the offending directive were confiscated, but when they turned out to contain 'nothing dangerous or improper', Churchill's security adviser, Desmond Morton, had to accept that there were no grounds for closing MO down, despite his and the Prime Minister's conviction that it was 'an infernal nuisance and a potential danger.'[6] If Willcock—said to have been 'warned and frightened' by the raid—was nervous about going ahead with the publication of servicemen's views on demobilization, Harrisson had no hesitation in urging him to stand firm against MI5 pressure.[7]

MO's findings on the ostensible subject of the book—the management of post-war demobilization—were relatively reassuring. Soldiers understood that the return to civilian life would have to be phased over a lengthy period; and women conscripted into wartime factories were generally keen to return to domestic life. Despite a pervasive fear of unemployment, most people felt that things would work out alright for themselves, although greater clarity by the authorities about the timetable and priorities for demobilization would help to allay existing anxieties. These findings, however, were embedded in a wider analysis of post-war hopes and expectations which was far from reassuring.

In the autumn of 1942 Willcock had reported that popular hopes for a better post-war world coexisted with widespread pessimism about the likelihood of such hopes being realized. This gap between hope and expectation was breeding a spirit of cynicism and apathy which threatened to

6. 'Leakage of Information re Overlord', 2 March 1944; Churchill to Secretary of State for War, 5 March 1944; Norton to Churchill, 9 March 1944, PREM 3/345/6. Morton told Churchill that MO was 'a dirty affair. It obtains its "volunteer observers" by posing as a group with Left Wing tendencies...but actually sets its enthusiastic supporters to finding out free of charge how people like Mesrs. Unilever's margarine and things of that sort.... At the same time, as a result of free information provided by his dupes, HARRISSON has published several booklets [from] which he has made money and acquired a reputation for being a research student.' Although MI5 kept 'a constant watch' on MO none of the resulting files has as yet been released or even catalogued. The quality of the information about MO supplied by MI5 to Churchill on this occasion suggests that the contents of these files, if they do ever surface, may not add much of value to our knowledge.

7. TH, 'Note on Change V', 19 May 1944, FR 2102.

undermine popular morale both during the war and after.[8] A year later the gap between hope and expectation had, if anything, intensified as initial popular enthusiasm for the Beveridge Report, published in December 1942, had come up against Churchill's 'delaying ambiguity' about its implementation. While people were now clearer about the kind of post-war world they desired, they were also more convinced of the 'power of vested interest to prevent change' and this 'darkens [their] horizons.'[9] The 'Beveridge sequence'—'enthusiasm, incredulity, cynicism, apathy'—was acting to foster pessimism about the post-war world 'in spheres only remotely connected with the proposals of the report itself,' reinforcing a 'generalised distrust of leadership', cynicism about the political elite, and post-war expectations grounded in the popular memory of mass unemployment and the betrayal of First World War promises of a new social order.[10] Fatalistic attitudes were further reinforced, Willcock suggested, by a more profound unease:

> It seems quite probable, from much of the information which M-O has collected during this war, that many post-war ideas and fears and plans are rooted in war-guilt, in a sort of diffuse underlying belief that collectively and individually the sin of war has to be expiated. We may not be going nearly deep enough in explaining the desire to 'get away from it all' as predominantly individualistic, opportunistic or self-centred. There is an element of self-immolation and fatalism about many post-war ideas which is not explained entirely satisfactorily by external factors, but which private expiatory motives might largely illuminate.[11]

No less than effective war fighting, successful post-war reconstruction was going to require popular discipline, effort, and participation; and this would have to be achieved without 'the welding stimulus of war'. The evidence, however, was that the 'journey home' dreamed of by war workers and military personnel had little space for the strenuous building of a New Jerusalem. People were preparing themselves not for the world that they wanted, but for the world they expected: 'What people will *do* as they take the first step down civvy street will be conditioned, not by impotent idealistic hope, but by potent realistic anxiety.' And if they assumed that the cooperative and collectivist spirit of wartime was going to be replaced by 'a general return to the competitive struggle for personal security that existed before the

8. See Chapter 10.
9. *Journey Home*, 21.
10. *Journey Home*, 11, 14, 105.
11. *Journey Home*, 48.

war', then their own behaviour would help to ensure that this would indeed
be the outcome:

> The more deeply people believe that the motto of the post-war world will be
> each for himself, the more difficult it will be for them to adjust their actions to a
> social pattern when the time comes... To make it like last time because they are
> afraid it will be like last time, and because the past is the only future on which they
> can build, the only future they can clearly visualise. That is the danger today.[12]

All, however, was not yet lost. Popular acceptance of wartime restrictions
suggested a move away from selfish individualism. People feared the loss of
'the communal values of war' precisely because 'the sense of common cause
and effort for an end beyond self... has captured very many minds.'[13] They
were 'not so cynical as they say they are'—a paradoxical statement resting
on MO's claim to a superior understanding of the deep currents of private
opinion. Publically expressed cynicism was, in reality, 'a protective device for
guarding against further disappointment', no more than 'a thin crust' and
'not yet impenetrable'. There was still time for 'dynamic forward leadership'
to turn back the tide of apathy and secure the enthusiastic popular participation necessary for effective post-war reconstruction.[14] With the Labour
Party locked up in the coalition government, and only Common Wealth or
the Communist Party to choose from as vehicles for the expression of popular hopes for a new social order, the well-attested wartime shift to the left
in popular opinion remained for the time being unfocussed and leaderless.
But 'this very set-up favours the emergence of new, dynamic grouping and
political appeal—so that some quite fresh line might rapidly emerge.'[15]

In an article written shortly before the publication of *The Journey Home*
Harrisson stressed the positive features of this situation, asserting that the
war had seen a significant expansion of the 'active minority' who took an
interest in public affairs:

> Whatever government is in power [post-war] will work under the critical eye,
> the watchful scrutiny of many men and women who know today roughly
> what ought to be done. Plenty will remain apathetic, but not nearly so many
> as heretofore. Even in a democracy, much is eventually left to an active minor-
> ity. The larger the minority, the healthier the democracy...[16]

12. *Journey Home*, 23, 105, 111.
13. *Journey Home*, 52.
14. *Journey Home*, 14.
15. *Journey Home*, 106.
16. TH, 'The mood of Britain—1938 and 1944', 20 April 1944, FR 2067.

The 'active minority' were, of course, the public-spirited people from whom
the MO panel was disproportionately drawn, and *The Journey Home* can
perhaps better be understood as an analysis of the mentality of this minority
than of the population as a whole.

Willcock was a good deal less confident than Harrisson about the
health of British democracy. Talk of the sudden emergence of a new
political force was all very well, but any such force would have to contend
not just with popular pessimism about the ability of politicians of any hue
to overcome the resistance of vested interests, but also with something
much more deeply rooted: 'the virtual collapse of the idea of inevitable
progress'.[17] Underlying popular anxiety about the post-war world was a
more general crisis of faith in the future. While Harrisson put the emphasis on political solutions, Willcock was more inclined to direct MO's
efforts towards mapping this deeper crisis of faith; an approach encouraged by his second-in-command, Ferraby, who combined methodological rigour with a concern with the spiritual dimensions of life rooted in
his Bahá'í beliefs.

IV

Ferraby was the main author of MO's next book, *Britain and her Birth-rate*,
the sixth volume of the surveys sponsored by the Advertising Service
Guild (ASG) on wartime social change.[18] Since the 1930s British demog-
raphers had become increasingly worried that the fall in the birth rate
would lead to long-term population decline. *The Journey Home* pointed to
'the failure to have sufficient children to keep up the race'[19] as indicative
of a general crisis of the culture: 'Battledress to sports suit; overalls to
frocks. For many the future stops there [rather than looking] willingly
forward from sports suits to boiler suits, from frocks to maternity gowns'.[20]
Women, like men, were indifferent to their social duties, looking forward

17. *Journey Home*, 13.
18. Although Mollie Tarrant later suggested that Willcock had written the book (Tarrant to
    Wainwright, nd, 'MO Publications and Author', Personnel/Tarrant), the original manuscript
    in TC 3/2/O is in Ferraby's handwriting, and it was Ferraby who authored articles written on
    the subject at the time: Ferraby, 'Observations on the Reluctant Stork', *The Public Opinion
    Quarterly*, 9, 1, 1945, 29–37; 'Why women don't have more children' and 'Sex, Morality and the
    Birth-rate', 1945, TC 3/2/H.
19. *Journey Home*, 12.
20. *Journey Home*, 102–3.

to 'a future of relaxation, of less responsibility, more leisure, more private adventure',[21] and this militated against any reversal of the declining birth rate. To explore the reasons why women were reluctant to have more children MO interviewed around 1,000 housewives on the doorstep and in the street, mainly in London. Other sources included interviews with 56 married women working in the Osram factory; detailed observation in two lower middle-class families; 500 letters written to a birth-control clinic; the postbag of the Radio Doctor during 1943; and, of course, extensive use of panel responses to a directive on the subject.[22] The book provides much fascinating testimony to women's attitudes to childbirth, contraception, family size, and the responsibilities of motherhood, but the wealth of material was more than Ferraby could cope with, and of all MO's books this was probably the one most in need of editorial pruning. It was also the most polemical, 'frankly partisan' in its advocacy of larger families.[23] Much space was devoted to refuting the belief, particularly strong among MO's own middle-class panel respondents, that there was nothing to be feared from population decline. Ferraby's concern with methodological questions was displayed not only in frequent pedantic asides speculating about the precise meaning of the statistics but also, and more usefully, in his use of the qualitative data to explore his assumption that the reasons women gave for limiting family size—insufficient income, poor housing, etc.—were mainly rationalizations for an underlying determination not to subordinate their own life chances to the demands of motherhood in the way that, as many of them saw it, their own mothers had done. At this point the thrust of Ferraby's polemic faltered. While disinclined to argue explicitly against 'the emancipation of women', and careful to put their 'selfishness' in inverted commas,[24] he was nevertheless convinced that some means had to be found to persuade them to undertake their citizenship duty of procreating in sufficient numbers 'to perpetuate the English race.'[25] Progressive opinion eagerly seized on pro-natalist anxieties to promote better housing, family allowances, nursery schools, home helps, and other social reforms. But, however desirable these things were in themselves, Ferraby argued, they were unlikely to reverse the

21. *Journey Home*, 123.
22. *Britain and her Birth-rate*, 9, 243, 153ff.
23. *Britain and her Birth-rate*, 7.
24. *Britain and her Birth-rate*, 119, 199.
25. *Britain and her Birth-rate*, 200.

316 THE MASS OBSERVERS

long-term trend towards smaller families. Despite what women said to interviewers, all the evidence suggested that the falling birth rate was a consequence not of poverty, but of rising living standards. It was, after all, the poor who were the slowest to limit family size, although one could hardly advocate increased poverty as the best way to reverse the falling birth rate. The ultimate cause of the decay of 'maternal instinct', Ferraby suggested, lay in 'feelings of insecurity and purposelessness in the modern world', themselves a result of the decline of religion and the loss of faith in secular progress. The poor bred recklessly because they were badly educated and prone to wishful thinking about the future. The better off and better educated had a more realistic understanding of the state of the world and a more pessimistic view of the dangers ahead. 'To what extent,' Ferraby asked, 'is the will, even the ability, to perpetuate the race linked deep with the sense of life's purposefulness and point?'[26] If 'the deepest explanation of the falling birth-rate is the state of culture,' he wrote elsewhere, then 'the way to raise the birth-rate is not so much specific governmental actions, but the development of a new philosophy, a new religion, a new framework of life'.[27] This, he acknowledged, was not a proposition susceptible of statistical proof: 'We shall never know to what extent child-bearing is related to faith in the future until a new faith arises and can be measured against birth-rate trends.'[28] In the meantime, however, MO intended to throw further light on the subject by exploring 'the aims of ordinary people in life'.[29] They did this in their next major enquiry—a study of attitudes to religion commissioned by the secularist Ethical Union in 1944—and eventually published, as *Puzzled People*, in 1947.

V

While the work for *Puzzled People* was getting underway in the autumn of 1944, Celia Fremlin, who had done some of the interviewing for *Britain and her Birth-rate*,[30] made her own attempt to explore what she took to be the profound psychological crisis at the core of contemporary civilization.

26. *Britain and her Birth-rate*, 192.
27. 'Observations on the Reluctant Stork', *The Public Opinion Quarterly*, 9, 1, 1945, 37.
28. *Britain and her Birth-rate*, 198.
29. *Britain and her Birth-rate*, 191.
30. See interviews reproduced in Sheridan (ed.), *Wartime Women*, 206–14.

Announced by MO as 'a book on the life of middle-class housewives, based on wartime diaries',[31] her ambitions for the book went far beyond its ostensible subject, offering an approach to MO's central concerns which, had Fremlin possessed the intellectual confidence to sustain the analysis, might have added depth to Willcock's and Ferraby's account of 'the state of the culture'. Her decision to abandon the draft was symptomatic of a tendency to subordinate genuine feminine insight to misguided masculine self-confidence, which MO found it easier to acknowledge when analysing questionnaire responses than it did in reflecting on its own internal structures of authority.

Starting from MO's well-established theme of the decline of faith, whether in God or in Progress, Fremlin rehearsed 1930s fears of the coming war, the age old fantasy of apocalypse 'reappearing in modern guise' as scientists painted 'a picture of such horror and devastation, such bloodshed and torment, as resembles nothing more than the early Christian picture of Hell.'[32] When war finally arrived, housewives, expecting doom, had thrown themselves into blackout preparations; preparations which, while in the event they turned out to be sensible enough, were absurdly disproportionate to the scale of the expected catastrophe. 'When people get to the point of relying on strips of sticky paper to stave off the collapse of civilisation,' she remarked, 'we may be sure there is something more behind their actions than rational foresight.'[33]

The clue to what lay behind the housewives' irrational busyness in the face of the apocalypse, lay, she argued, in the psychological strategies that middle-class housewives had adopted in the 1930s to fend off a growing terror, not of poison gas and high explosives, but of the inescapable fact that they were becoming as functionless and unnecessary, as superfluous to the needs of society, as the Victorian spinster was popularly supposed to have been. 'From time immemorial,' Fremlin wrote, 'a woman's security has depended on the fact that she is indispensable to some man or men of her society'—and not just to satisfy his sexual needs or to bear his children. The middle-class Victorian housewife, however leisured, had a household of servants to manage. Since then, however, the commodification of everyday needs—store-made clothes, public laundries, restaurant meals, service flats—had been stripping away her

31. *Bulletin*, 9 September 1944, FR 2157.
32. Fremlin, 'War in Diaries', September 1944, FR 2181, 1.
33. 'War in Diaries', September 1944, FR 2181, 9.

functions: 'the middle-class man of today has very little need of a woman to provide his material wants'. As no woman 'in her heart of hearts' could possibly believe that running a small modern labour-saving house needed her full-time labour, she was forced to invent tasks to keep herself busy; and then prided herself on being 'rushed off her feet'. Like the Victorian spinster, the modern housewife was 'engaged on that same soul-destroying occupation of trying to find some way of being needed by the society to which she belongs.' She might find a job, sit on committees, organize whist drives, or—an alternative playfully close to Fremlin's own experience but one which would surely have been edited out of any published text—undertake 'to sell *Daily Workers* in Willesden High Road'.[34] But none of these were going to satisfy the feminine need to be needed, and needed personally, by a man.

Anticipating the objection that the problem of the functionless housewife was largely confined to the middle classes, Fremlin argued that sooner or later rising living standards and the impact of welfare reform would reproduce the crisis in working-class homes as well. So MO's middle-class war diarists could be seen as 'guinea pigs', prefiguring a psychological crisis that, in the coming era of affluence, would eventually affect the whole of society. Of course working-class housewives deprived (by progress) of full-time domestic responsibilities might, like their middle-class sisters, seek identity by going out to work. But Fremlin's experience of participant observation in both domestic service and factory work did not suggest that the employments available to working-class women would provide a satisfactory substitute for the sense of worth and fulfillment they had (she believed) traditionally acquired from the demanding work of mother, wife, and household manager.

Anyone familiar with the sociological literature on the late 20th-century family will understand the flaw in this argument; the exaggeration of the degree to which men no longer relied on the services of women. Nevertheless Fremlin had a point. The functionless middle-class housewife, she argued, was symptomatic of a still larger social problem: 'how to reconcile personal, individual relationships as we know them at present with a state of society which is aiming at reducing individual interdependence to a minimum.' What she had in mind was the encroachment on the household by the emerging welfare state, driven by an ethically incontrovertible desire to protect the rights of the individual:

34. 'War in Diaries', September 1944, FR 2181, 4–6.

There is agitation on foot to put wives in a position in which they will not
suffer financially for the extravagance or selfishness of their husbands;[35] there is
legislation proposed to ensure that no child shall suffer in health or education
though the poverty, ignorance, or carelessness of his parents; there are many
who advocate family allowances so that parents who have a lot of children will
not thereby have to work any harder or lower their standard of living.

But to the extent that such reforms are achieved, 'we shall be making each
individual of the family materially independent of the rest of the family',
sweeping away 'the hard fact of mutual interdependence' on which 'the ties
of affection and emotion [have] for centuries ... been based.'[36] It worried her
that the future life of comfort, ease, and peace planned by progressives like
herself was unlikely to leave much room for the virtues she most admired:
toughness, endurance, and family solidarity rooted in the mutual interdependence compelled by a harsh environment. What would happen to 'the
ties of affection and emotion' once the material needs of the family had been
taken over by business and the state? This was a question that was to preoc-
cupy critics of late 20th-century individualism. Fremlin had got there early,
but she did not know how to complete the analysis, and rather than build on
her insights, Willcock and Ferraby filed them away in favour of their own,
rather less promising, preoccupation with the decline of religious faith.

Fremlin herself was partly responsible for this outcome, abandoning the
draft because she felt that the sources she was using, so rich in psychological
insight, were invalid because they were unrepresentative of the population
at large. In September 1944 she sent the uncompleted draft to Willcock with
an accompanying note:

> I think by now you will have come to the same conclusions that I have - to
> wit: that it is no use trying to publish this masterpiece as it stands. The longer
> I work on the diaries the more definite becomes my opinion that they should
> *not* be used on their own. They are essentially *supplementary* to more detailed
> investigations. Used thus they provide invaluable quotations, sidelights, etc.
> But when you try to use them by themselves you continually come up against
> the fact that you can't prove anything from them. Thus all you can do is to

---

35. The Married Women's Association, led by the feminist Labour MP Edith Summerskill, was
campaigning for legislation to protect the right of the married woman to a share of her husband's income (Catherine Blackford, 'Wives and Citizens and Watchdogs of Quality: Post-War
British Feminism', in J. Fyrth (ed.), *Labour's Promised Land. Culture and Society in Labour Britain,
1945–51*, London, 1995, 60–70).
36. 'War in Diaries', September 1944, FR 2181, 8–9.

illustrate from them points which are so obvious or well known as not to need any proving: it is clearly impossible to bring in any novel or controversial matter within those limitations... So I think it would be best if you kept this (as much of it as is of any use) to incorporate in some bigger and better work which you will doubtless be undertaking in the near future.[37]

While it is true that several generations of historians, contemplating the MO war diaries, came to much the same conclusion, with more intellectual self-confidence Fremlin might have been able to resist the methodological demands of positivist social science, and argue that the individual case study, by its nature unrepresentative, provided a route to truth as valid in its own right as any other. Stephen Taylor, after all, had found no difficulty in doing just this in his celebrated pre-war article on the 'suburban neurosis'.[38] And, of course, nor had Freud.

VI

While Fremlin was puzzling about how the diaries might be used to throw light on the state of the culture, Willcock set about organizing MO's follow-up to *Britain and her Birth-rate*: an enquiry into 'the aims of ordinary people in life' commissioned by the humanist Ethical Union.[39] During the autumn of 1944 MO interviewed 500 people in Hammersmith, talked with clergymen and youth leaders in the borough, and issued a directive to the panel soliciting details of their religious beliefs, if any.[40] Willcock wrote up the results in the new year,[41] but although the manuscript was submitted to Gollancz in August 1945, and revised in the summer of 1946, publication was delayed until May 1947.[42] Implicitly rejecting Ferraby's approach in *Britain and her Birth-rate*, Willcock declared that 'this is not a technical book', promising to 'avoid excessive methodological discussion' and to do his best 'to present the facts as simply and clearly as possible.'[43]

37. Fremlin to Willcock, 14 September 1944, 'War in Diaries', September 1944, FR 2181.
38. Stephen Taylor, 'The suburban neurosis', *The Lancet*, 26 March 1938.
39. *Puzzled People*, 191; Ethical Union, Executive Committee, minutes, 3 June, 19 August, 23 September, and 25 November 1944.
40. *Puzzled People*, 12; DR November 1944. David Kynaston (*Austerity Britain*, 1945–51, 2007, 126) is mistaken in placing the fieldwork two years later.
41. MO *Bulletin*, 20 January 1945, FR 2200.
42. Printed card from Victor Gollancz acknowledging receipt of manuscript, 8 August 1945; Hodges to Willcock, 1 and 19 March, and 24 April 1946; Willcock to Hodges, 5 March 1946, Org&Hist 3/10.
43. *Puzzled People*, 12.

Puzzled People painted a picture of doubt and confusion about ultimate existential realities, tempered by indifference. While most people thought that there probably was a god, their personal religious beliefs were 'exceedingly vague and unorthodox', curious mixtures of half-understood Christian doctrine and ideas (notably about reincarnation and astrology) derived from the pagan past. The great majority were neither regular churchgoers (10 per cent) nor convinced atheists (5 per cent); and their generally benevolent attitude towards Christianity had less to do with belief in god than with the idea that religion was useful as a way of inculcating ethical behaviour among the young.[44] This, however, was likely to prove a vain hope. As the tide of faith ebbed away, the ethics of Christianity, stripped of divine sanction, no longer carried 'the conviction they once had'. But there was no sign that they were being replaced by any new, rationalist, basis for an ethical life capable of sustaining social solidarity, which was what the Ethical Union existed to promote: 'We are not, today, witnessing the replacement of an old ethic by a virile new one, but the simple decay of a considerable number of guiding principles, replaced by no clear principle at all.'[45] To the extent that a perceptible 'new ethic is arising among those who doubt the existence of a Deity', Willcock argued, 'it is an ethic of "independence", not only of God, but of other people, a concentration on more purely personal aims and pleasures.'[46] Willcock's depressing diagnosis of the state of the culture turned on much the same distinction between 'interdependence' and 'independence' that Fremlin had worked with: 'a distinction between those who spontaneously look upon their fulfilment in life as dependent on their relation with others, and those who look upon it as dependent on what they can do for themselves.'[47] Like Fremlin and Ferraby, he argued that the trend was towards a society that valued independence over interdependence, personal autonomy above social solidarity. Whereas Fremlin and Ferraby had both placed married women in the vanguard of this process, *Puzzled People*, put men at the centre, suggesting that 'one way of looking at many of the attitude and habit-changes which have taken place over recent years would be to say that people generally are thinking and behaving more like young men.' There was no necessary contradiction between these two viewpoints.

44. *Puzzled People*, 156–7, and *passim*.
45. *Puzzled People*, 75.
46. *Puzzled People*, 126–7.
47. *Puzzled People*, 114.

Young men had always been 'less co-operative, more personal-pleasureful' than their sisters. What was now changing was that the women were increasingly demanding the same rights to personal autonomy and independence as the men.[48] And, all three MO writers agreed, the results of this process were going to pose major problems for the maintenance of any coherent cooperative social order.

Ever since Bolton days, MO analysis had linked religious decline and political apathy in a more general picture of 'social apathy'. *Puzzled People* elaborated Willcock's assertion in *The Journey Home* that 'more and more people find life meaningless today', but its conclusions—to which the reader was directed from the start—were as much about the political consequences of 'meaninglessness' as about the existential crisis itself: 'It is not chiefly that people are losing faith in ideals and objectives, but that they are losing hope of the capacity and desire of those in prominent positions to help realise those desires.'[49] Running through *Puzzled People* is an unresolved tension between the evidence of widespread indifference to ultimate questions about the meaning of life, and Willcock's insistence that the decline of faith, not only in religion but also in political routes to a better life, had left a dangerous vacuum in the popular mind, an opportunity for some new fascism to offer its ersatz belief in the future to people hungry for purpose in their lives: 'ordinary people are looking for something to believe in. As the need becomes more urgent, so their capacity for discrimination is likely to diminish... The starving spirit is not hypercritical of new food.'[50] In fact the report contains no evidence that ordinary people were urgently searching for some new panacea, and most commentary on these years stress exhaustion and resignation rather than hunger for change as the dominant mood. Willcock acknowledged that 'the subject is peculiarly one on which personal beliefs are liable to have a distorting effect,' and claimed that 'particular care has been taken not to publish any interpretation which the material will not fully bear'.[51] But there was nothing in the report to bear out his assertion that 'people cannot carry on for long in the profoundly negative frame of mind which characterises the short-term outlook of so many today,' and his claim to have demonstrated that 'the need for faith, whether religious or secular, is... acute, though only partly articulate as yet' was

48. *Puzzled People*, 126.
49. *Puzzled People*, 151.
50. *Puzzled People*, 155, 158.
51. *Puzzled People*, 6.

equally unfounded.[52] Willcock's own beliefs shine through the treatment, framing MO's findings in an alarmist picture of the return of the past:

> Events in the past two decades have shown what crazy, sinister, and elaborate structures can be built in minds empty of firm aims and ideals...Someone is going to cash in on these wide open spaces in the mind...This report is a diagnosis of a social malady whose ultimate consequence may be disastrous if its course is not checked...[53]

Reviewers, the most scathing of whom was Steven Taylor writing in *Tribune*, were unanimous in rejecting Willcock's alarmism: 'there is no present indication', wrote *The Manchester Guardian*, 'that "desultory living" amounts to an invitation to the emergence of an English Hitler.'[54] The point had already been forcefully made in the preface to the book by the secretary of the Ethical Union, Harold Blackham, who had commissioned the study. The danger was not that the masses, anxiously seeking meaning in life, would be swept away by revolutionary panaceas. They were no more receptive to fascist ideology than they were to the ideas offered by Christians, Marxists, or indeed the 'independent rationalists in the liberal tradition' for whom Blackham spoke. The real danger lay in the apathy which made the masses, unlike the active minority, deaf to ideologies of all kinds: 'The hard core of the problem is in the many who are permanently indifferent to any doctrine, not in the few who have lost their beliefs'; and to confuse these two groups would, Blackham suggested, 'lead to radical errors of diagnosis and prescription.'[55] But this was just what Willcock had done.

Puzzled People was explicit in discussing the difference in outlook between the educated and activist minority disproportionately represented in the MO panel, and the less educated masses. It was the former who were in danger of losing faith in science and progress, and whose orientation to life required a belief in the future and their own role in making it. By contrast the less educated were untroubled by doubts about progress, and, though puzzled like everyone else about the larger existential questions, unanxious about resolving them, their expectations modest, their desires limited, just as Harrisson had argued from Worktown evidence before the war:

52. *Puzzled People*, 158.
53. *Puzzled People*, 17, 19.
54. *Manchester Guardian*, 27 May 1947; Stephen Taylor, *Tribune*, 27 June 1947; H. L. Beales, *The Plain View*, July 1947; *Times Literary Supplement*, 12 July 1947.
55. Blackham, *Puzzled People*, Preface, 7–8.

> The lack of wide idealisms, concentration on the simple, the immediate, the unorganised personal side, neighbourliness, non-interference; or on fun, and money for fun, on keeping clear of too many obligations and ties, keeping the home together and the home relationships bright—these are the normal everyday strivings of most people's lives.[56]

These people were not about to be swept away by any new panacea. It is difficult to understand how Willcock, in his more alarming predictions, came to lose sight of the distinction he himself made clearly in the same text. Whatever the explanation, within months of the publication of *Puzzled People* he was responding to criticism, grudgingly conceding that: 'the possibility of a continuing stability-in-apathy cannot be altogether discounted.'[57]

This admission was made in *Peace and the Public*, a book based on a survey undertaken in Hammersmith and Shrewsbury early in 1946 for the New Commonwealth Society, but not published until June 1947. Despite widespread support for collective security through the United Nations, the survey showed deep scepticism about the capacity of politicians to construct a new world order capable of preserving peace, with nearly half the sample expecting another world war within 25 years. Those wishing to mobilize popular energies in relation to international affairs needed to start from a recognition that the superficial support for the pooling of sovereignty shown in opinion polls hid an undercurrent of 'negative nationalism' rooted in the belief that, however desirable, internationalist solutions to the problem of war were impractical.[58]

Between 1939 and 1942, Harrisson had sought to establish MO's indispensability to the war effort by constant repetition of the possibility that a collapse of popular morale might be just around the corner; a danger buried deep beneath public conformism and revealed only by MO's capacity to penetrate to the unspoken and half-formulated fears germinating in private opinion. *Peace and the Public*, summing up MO's message in relation to post-war reconstruction, hammered home the same point:

> High ideals and low expectations (the protective armour of cynicism which has enabled people to take disappointment in their stride), have helped to make the first 18 months of post-war a time of apathetic acceptance of the apparently inevitable. It is difficult to be angry when things turn out just as you thought they would . . . [It is] only though an appreciation of the depth to which this fatalistic outlook has penetrated that something can be done to

56. *Puzzled People*, 116.
57. *Peace and the Public*, 48.
58. *Peace and the Public*, 31.

release the underlying energies masked by current apathy. During the past years M-O has described again and again the symptoms that would lead to post-war apathy if the disease were allowed to run its course.[59]

Harrisson had certainly believed that popular morale was a good deal more fragile than those in authority would publicly admit, and no doubt Willcock too was genuinely worried that popular disillusion could open the way for the advocates of ugly right-wing panaceas. But for both of them the Cassandra voice served the same functional purpose: establishing the indispensability of MO's services to the authorities if catastrophe was to be avoided. The Labour Government, Willcock wrote, had not yet succeeded in bridging the 'great gulf of distrust stretch[ing] between leaders and... disorientated mass.'[60] If Labour was going to succeed in 're-establishing a dynamic relationship with the people of Britain in the next two or three years,'[61] they were going to need help, his argument implied, from MO. In the early years of the war, when national survival seemed to be at stake, the British state had opened itself up—cautiously, reluctantly, temporarily—to the advice offered by radical populists like Harrisson and Mary Adams. After the war, however much the Labour Government needed to mobilize popular energies, it faced no such existential crisis, and MO's message to the authorities fell on deaf ears. If MO was to survive it would need to look for support from commercial interests like the ASG, voluntary organizations like those which had commissioned *Puzzled People* and *Peace and the Public*, or profitable publishing initiatives of its own.

VII

In 1942, as we have seen, Harrisson had been forced to drop his grandiose plan for a book on *The Public*, intended to make a lot of money for MO by superseding the London Press Exchange's standard digest of statistics about *The Home Market* with a far more wide-ranging 'account of the habits and customs of the British islanders.'[62] By the early months of 1944 MO was involved in a rather more modest project in cooperation with Adprint, a

59. *Peace and the Public*, 11–12.
60. *Puzzled People*, 158.
61. *Puzzled People*, 159.
62. Fitter, 'The Public. Note on Implementation', 6 March 1941, TC 25/12/A.

pioneer of high-quality colour printing, and the Austrian refugee, philosopher, and political economist Otto Neurath, whose Isotype picturegrams—developed in 1920s socialist Vienna as a way of communicating social facts to the less educated—came to be widely used in the 1940s to display social and economic statistics for a popular audience.[63] Since the early days of the war Adprint (and Neurath who was employed by them) had been cooperating with the publisher Collins on an extensive series of books, 'Britain in Pictures', designed to celebrate the national heritage 'in the face of [our] book-burning foes'.[64] James Fisher's *Birds of Britain* was published in this series in 1942, and several of MO's scientific promoters—Julian Huxley, John Gilmour, Richard Fitter and Fisher himself—were involved with Neurath in planning Collin's follow-up 'New Naturalist' series.[65] MO's involvement, a sociological spin-off from the biologists' initiative, came early in 1944 when agreement was reached to launch a sub-set of 'Britain in Pictures'—to be known as 'British Ways of Life'—reporting on small-scale communities each selected to illustrate a different aspect of life in contemporary Britain. Intended for a popular audience the texts would provide a 'quite new kind of "guide book"',[66] based on the work of experienced mass observers, written up by established authors, and lavishly illustrated with colour photographs and Isotype charts.[67]

Although *Exmoor Village*, the first—and, as it turned out, the last—of these books, was not published until 1947, the research was carried out in 1944. The chosen village, Luccombe, was a tiny, introverted place on the edge of the moor with a population of just 74 people, an elementary school, no pub, and, despite MO's best efforts to discover one, no 'lovers lane' for courting couples.[68] In the summer months most of the residents took in holiday guests, but for the rest of the year they had little contact with, or interest in, the world

63. Paul Rennie, 'British picture books for grown-ups from the 1940s', September 2005, <www.rennart.co.uk/web%20site%20pdfs/books.pdf> (accessed 22 October 2010); Christopher Burke, 'Isotype: representing social facts pictorially', *Information Design Journal*, 17, 3, 2009, 210–21.

64. David Kerr, *The House of Collins*, 1952, 267.

65. Tom Rosenthal, 'Walter and Eva Neurath: Their Books Married Words with Pictures', in Richard Abel and Gordon Graham (eds), *Immigrant Publishers. The Impact of Expatriate Publishers in Britain and America in the 20th century*, 2009, 112–13. One of the first of the New Naturalist volumes was a book on London's Natural History written by Fitter (Kerr, *House of Collins*, 278).

66. *Bulletin*, 9 September 1944, FR 2157.

67. Isotype Institute, 'General remarks on Series', 15 April 1944, TC 66/6/A. Judging by remarks he made in the preface to the book, Harrisson was probably representing MO at the April 1944 meeting reported in this document (*Exmoor Village*, 11–12).

68. 'Instructions to Investigator', 6 March 1944; Ivey to Atkins, 11 April 1944, TC 66/6/A.

outside. The book claimed that the research had been done by skilled observers living 'inconspicuously' in the village 'gather[ing] information in [the] slow, roundabout way which gives a truer insight'.[69] In fact most of the work was done by a single observer, Desiree Ivey, who had little previous MO experience and who was known locally to be collecting material for a book on the village.[70] For six of the seven weeks she was there she worked alone, supervised by post from London by Jack Atkins until his sudden call-up forced Willcock to take over, and it is clear from their extensive correspondence that she found it very difficult to understand what MO was after:

> I told you before that I was not at all sure I would be able to do this job in M-O style as I was not at all sure what was wanted. Some of the details you ask for are very personal and the people resent it especially knowing it will be published and they can't see the necessity for it.[71]

In an effort to explain, Willcock sent her a copy of Celia Fremlin's *War Factory* as 'an example of the sort of information which can be obtained from a small community without anyone knowing they're being surveyed at all'.[72] But it was not until Nina Masel arrived during the last week of the project that Ivey felt that she understood 'exactly what is needed. I realize now what a lot of information I have let pass by not knowing it was of value.'[73] John Hinde, a pioneer of colour photography working with Adprint,[74] came to photograph the villagers, and Compton Mackenzie, a flamboyant character and prolific writer subsequently famous for the novel (and Ealing comedy) *Whisky Galore,* was commissioned to write the text.[75] The eventual author, however, was not Mackenzie but W. J. Turner, a poet and music critic and editor of the 'Britain in Pictures' series.[76]

69. *Exmoor Village*, 12.
70. Ivey had worked briefly for MO in Chester.
71. Ivey to Atkins, 20 April 1944, TC 66/6/A.
72. Willcock to Ivey, 21 and 25 April 1944, TC 66/6/A.
73. Ivey to Willcock, 26 April 1944, TC 66/6/A.
74. Obituary, *The Independent*, 3 February 1998.
75. Des to Willcock, 3 May 1944; 'Memo to Mrs Ivey and Nina', nd; Isotype Institute, 'General remarks on Series: "British ways of life". Vol 1. A Wessex Village, by F. Compton Mackenzie', 15 April 1944, TC 66/6/A. Mackenzie had been involved with Adprint earlier in the war (Mackenzie, *My Life and Times, 1939–1946*, 160).
76. Wayne McKenna, *W.J. Turner: Poet And Music Critic,* 1990, 55–7; Rennie, 'British picture books for grown-ups from the 1940s'. It is not clear when the text was written. In September 1944 MO anticipated completing the work within 'a few months' (*Bulletin,* 9 September 1944, FR 2157). It must have been in production by the time Turner died in November 1946, since his death is not mentioned in the book, published four months later.

The book was eventually published in April 1947, to a mixed reception. While Hinde's photographs were splendid, Turner's text, an odd mixture of pedestrian detail and nostalgia, lent itself easily to John Betjeman's satirical pen:

> Go to the Inn on any Friday night
> And listen to them while they're getting tight
> At the expense of him who stands them drinks,
> The Mass Observer with the Hillman Minx.
> (Unwitting he of all the knowing winks)
> The more he circulates the bitter ales
> The longer and the taller grow the tales.
> 'Ah! this is England', thinks he, 'rich and pure
> As tilth and loam and wains and horse-manure,
> Slow—yes. But sociologically sound.'
> 'Landlord,' he cries, 'the same again all round.'[77]

While Ivey's researches produced nothing to match the vivid insights of *War Factory*, her concern about the invasion of privacy involved was shared by several reviewers.[78] No attempt was made to disguise the identity of individual villagers—an impossibility given the photographs—and many of them were outraged when they saw their private lives displayed for all their neighbours to peruse. Although they had known that a publication was being prepared, it had been widely believed in the village that the book was intended exclusively for export.[79] A mass observer who visited Luccombe in November 1947 in connection with a national survey boarded incognito in the house that Masel had used three years before. 'All the other people in the other villages got to know about our private affairs and that's not right,' he was told by his host: 'They had better not come here again.' There had been a meeting and talk of a libel action, 'but ... it just faded out like most things. You see we did not have anybody who really knew what to do about it in the village here.'[80] It was, perhaps, just as well that no further books in the series appeared:

77. John Betjeman, *A Few Late Chrysanthemums*, 1954, 79; first published in *Harper's Bazaar*, July–August 1947.

78. Notably R. C. Churchill who used the book to launch a broadside attack on MO as a bunch of public school boys incapable of understanding that respect for privacy was not just a petty bourgeois prejudice (*Tribune*, 4 April 1947).

79. Ivey to Atkins, 20 April 1944; Willcock to Ivey, 21 April 1944, TC 66/6/A; Howard to JG, November 1947, TC 66/6/G: 'They said that the book was to go to Russia and would not be printed here. We did not mind it going to Russia but it was all over the place here, in the papers and everywhere.'

80. JG, 'Report on the effects of the publication of the book', November 1947, TC 66/6/G. The local Labour MP, who was friendly to MO, had advised the solicitor contacted by the villagers to drop the case. TH, 'Luccombe Reactions', 5 May 1947, FR 2487.

other intended subjects might have had a better grasp than these unsophisticated villagers of their right to resist MO's intrusion. While Ivey was at work in Luccombe, Willcock had been looking around for a suitable community to study in the Potteries,[81] and in the summer of 1944 he had started work for a third volume, placing observers with a touring circus troupe which Hinde was photographing.[82] But MO's involvement in this project seems to have been short-lived, and there was no mention of them in the book, *British Circus Life*, in which Hinde's photographs were eventually published.[83]

VIII

The final book written during the Willcock years was something of an anomaly. *Browns and Chester* is a rather conventional history of a department store catering to Cheshire's wealthy middle class; essentially a celebration of the firm decked out as social history. When, in 1942, Mollie Tarrant had negotiated a similar commission from a Cardiff engineering firm, Harrisson intervened to abort the project, furious at the suggestion that MO should prostitute its services in this way. The difference with *Browns and Chester* was that its managing director, Leonard Harris, was not only a good customer of market research services from MO, but also a leading light in Chester's Liberal Party and a close friend of the ASG's Everett Jones, who became a member of Brown's board of directors in 1945 and stood as the Liberal Party's candidate for Chester in the general election.[84] When the idea was mooted of commissioning a history of the firm for its 150th anniversary, Harrisson's

81. Correspondence in TC 33/1/H; Willcock to Ivey, 21 April 1944, TC 66/6/A.
82. Two observers went in succession: Lola Meichtry and Margaret Holland. Surviving correspondence in the archive (TC 16/1/F) shows that their relations with Recio—'the main personality'—were difficult. See also typed notes dated 21 June 1944 re. 'British Ways of Life' referring to Hinde and the need for MO research on circus in the Isotype archive at Reading University. I am grateful to Diane Bilbey (Collections Officer, Typography & Graphic Communication, University of Reading) for this information.
83. The book was written by Lady Eleanor Furneaux Smith and edited by W. J. Turner.
84. Memo of TH meeting with Everett Jones, 19 September 1942, Org&Hist 4/3; Atkins to Harris, 17 September and 5 October 1943; Harris to Atkins, 8 and 21 January, and 23 March 1944; printed circular from Harris to the Brown's staff, 24 April 1945, TC 24/6/B; Note written on back of undated letter from Irene (Browne) to Willcock, TC 20/10/E. Harris subsequently became a director of Mass-Observation Ltd, and (with Mollie Tarrant's help) wrote *Long to Reign Over Us*, an undistinguished book on the 1953 coronation based on MO material. England described him as 'a millionaire with a social conscience which M-O fitted rather neatly. Was very generous to funds, but commissioned "Browns" which really didn't fit with M-O', England to Cunard, 14 October 1997, Personnel/England. See also DNB entry on Harris.

political and business connections converged to make the project unavoidable. However reluctant he may have been at first, Willcock soon warmed to the idea, explaining to Harris that he had felt, while writing up the market research, 'that here was an almost ideal situation for studying the way in which a tradition is built up and an organisation becomes part of the life of the community.'[85] The initial idea, on the model of *Exmoor Village*, was for MO to assemble material on the basis of which a well-known author would be commissioned to write the book. By the time the research was being done in the autumn of 1944, however, Willcock had secured 'a free hand to write the first Mass-Observation historical survey our own way.'[86] Having found a publisher prepared to take on the project Willcock had high hopes for what he saw as 'the incursion of Social Survey into Social History' represented by the book, and Diana Brinton-Lee tried to interest her uncle, heir to a dynasty of carpet manufacturers in Kidderminster, in commissioning a similar study. This was not advertising, she explained, but a form of public relations thoroughly compatible with the 'dignity' of his long-established firm.[87] As Harris, who funded the history to the tune of over £600, had put it 'in my view the main advertising value of the book to the Company will not be the number of people who actually read it, but those who will refer to Brown's of Chester as the Firm about which a book has been written.'[88] But what Willcock saw as a happy convergence of public relations and social science produced a dull book, and nothing came of the Kidderminster initiative.

In April 1947 Willcock wrote to Humphrey Pease: 'We're prospering hectically since Tom's return turning out masses of publications'.[89] Harrisson's return from the Far East in September 1946 was to see a step change in the level of MO's activity. But although only one book—*Britain and her Birth-rate*—had been published during Harrisson's absence, the clutch of publications in 1947 were the result of work already more or less completed under Willcock's management. The pace may have slackened, but Willcock had been effective in keeping things ticking over. When the warrior returned, it was to a viable organization, a solid base for the 'hectic prospering' that he had every intention of promoting.

85. Willcock to Harris, 23 June 1944; Diana Brinton-Lee to Cecil Brinton, 13 April 1945, TC 24/6/B; Willcock to Radvanyi, 4 July 1946, Org&Hist 2/Mexico.
86. Willcock, 'Specimen for the Treatment of History of Browns' of Chester', 9 November 1944, TC 24/6/C; BW to Harris, 26 April 1945, TC 24/6/B.
87. Brinton-Lee to Brinton, 13 April 1945, TC 24/6/B.
88. Harris to Willcock, 6 March 1945, TC 24/6/B.
89. Willcock to Pease, 7 April 1947, TC 20/12/B

14

Harrisson's Return

I

Within three weeks of his return from the Far East in September 1946 Tom Harrisson was giving his first impressions of the state of post-war England to *New Statesman* readers. What struck him most forcibly was the privateness of the culture:

> After Australia, Manila, a Sarawak long house, or the easy friendship of soldiers, it is horrid to stand solitary in a city pub, or face your fellows in the train speechless, almost ashamed...Each day that passes one's orientally acquired easiness and directness of manner shrink back a little further into the unsatisfied apparatus of the civilised ego...the restricted circle of private western experience.[1]

The domestic political temperature seemed tepid, pragmatic, un-idealistic; the people tired and retreating into whatever 'molecular content' they could muster, with only an outbreak of organized squatting by homeless families in army camps and upmarket flats, closely observed by Mass-Observation (MO) investigators, providing a brief moment of domestic drama.[2]

Intent on stirring things up, Harrisson re-engaged with Everett Jones and others in Radical Action to resist the efforts of Liberal free marketeers to realign the party with the Tory opposition.[3] Shortly before leaving for Borneo he had accepted nomination as the Liberal parliamentary candidate for Watford, although he did not come back to fight the election in 1945.[4] In November 1946 he helped to draft a letter from Radical Action to the emerging Keep Left grouping among Labour MPs, offering to work jointly with them around a social programme designed to enhance individual freedom

---

1. TH, 'Demob Diary', *New Statesman*, 28 September 1946. See also TH, letter to Panel, October 1946, FR 2429A.
2. 'The Squatters', November 1946, FR 2431 and material in TC 48/1.
3. Everett Jones, TH et al, letter to *The Observer*, 24 November 1946.
4. Heinmann, *Most Offending Soul*, 197.

within a planned economy.[5] Within a year several of the Liberal MPs involved had joined the Labour Party, where they felt most at home as members of Keep Left.[6] Speaking as someone 'actively associated with the Radical Action group' and a former Liberal parliamentary candidate, Harrisson intervened in a by-election in Paddington to support Labour, telling voters that 'we Liberals have a fair amount in common with the less doctrinaire, more intelligent, younger section of the Labour Party to which [the Labour candidate] belongs.'[7] As did Woodrow Wyatt, elected Labour MP for the Aston division in Birmingham in 1945. An admiring acolyte in the late 1930s, Wyatt had kept in touch with MO while in the army, and one of Harrisson's first initiatives on his return was a trip to Aston to set up a study of 'A Constituency and its Constituents'.[8] Margaret Quass, a graduate student at the London School of Economics (and later director of the Council for Education in World Citizenship), made a start on the work and Harrisson invited Julian Trevelyan, Michael Wickham, and other 'old comrades of M-O' to join him for a weekend to observe, paint, and photograph what he described as 'a great amorphous, colourless, planless, chunk of working-class Birmingham, but with, as always, under the undertones, lots of corners of excitement and beauty.'[9] This was Bolton again. The anticipated book came to nothing, but a survey of leisure activities in Aston (disguised as 'Blacktown') made at this time featured in a later MO report.[10]

At the same time other 'old comrades' were called in as Harrisson, scenting scandalous incompetence in Whitehall, set out to foster a parliamentary campaign against the widespread closure of day nurseries. In late September, going straight to the top, he wrote to Aneurin Bevan, now in charge of the Ministry of Health, requesting departmental help and proposing 'a short talk about things in general... to renew our acquaintance.'[11] Although Bevan put off the proposed meeting, he provided an introduction to the official in charge, a man whose evident hostility to day nurseries convinced Harrisson

5. TH to Spicer, 18 November 1946, attached to 'The British Public's Feeling about Liberalism', March 1942, FR 1128. In May he was among 'a small but influential group of Leftist political journalists' invited to Keep Left's launching party (News Review, 8 May 1947).
6. Acland, Horrabin, Mander et al, letter to The Times, 11 May 1950.
7. TH, 'to the electorate of North Paddington', 16 November 1946, TC 46/16/E.
8. Peace and the Public, 1947, flyleaf.
9. TH to Wickham and Trevelyan, 14 November 1946, JTpap; 'Draft for first fortnight of Aston Survey', 1 October 1946; Willcock to Meadows, 1 October 1946, TC 66/1/B; Quass, obituary in The Guardian, 24 December 2003.
10. Lord Beveridge and A. F. Wells, The Evidence of Voluntary Action, 1949, 41–3.
11. TH to Aneurin Bevan, 28 September 1946, TC 19/1/E.

that Whitehall, while disclaiming any responsibility for the closures, was in fact encouraging local authorities to close nurseries down: 'I am sure we are on to something really fishy,' he wrote to Wyatt, '... my investigator nose tells me that we are on to something very queer indeed.'[12] Primed by Harrisson, Wyatt was prominent in harassing the Ministry with parliamentary questions and, by early December, Harrisson was telling Britain's leading campaigner for day nurseries that Zita Crossman, acting as 'our representative', was collecting material for an MO study of day nurseries.[13] Whether she did is unknown, but no evidence of such a study survives in the archive.

II

While these immediate initiatives soaked up some of Harrisson's formidable energy, they were soon overtaken by far more ambitious plans as he set about establishing a long-term post-war programme for MO, while Willcock continued to take care of the day-to-day administration.[14] At the end of October, corresponding with Dennis Chapman, who had moved on from the Wartime Social Survey to a senior lectureship in Liverpool, Harrisson gave vent to his frustration:

> It makes me green with envy that you can write in terms of research for three [years]. If we could only get enough money to think in that sort of horizon, instead of working along from month to month, financing the work that interests us out of the profits from work which means nothing at all to us.[15]

But he was optimistic that by taking things in hand he would eventually be able to 'put the whole unit on a firm financial and scientific basis',[16] freeing it to undertaking 'more solid, detailed, penetrative research than we attempted before the war.'[17] In the meantime the publication programme, held up by acute paper shortages, shifted into a new gear: *Puzzled People, Exmoor Village,* and *Browns and Chester,* which had languished since the end of the war, all came out within eight months of Harrisson's return. And, with a view to future books, Harrisson launched several new projects.

12. TH to Wyatt, 22 October 1946, TC 19/1/E.
13. TH to Einthoven, 4 December 1946, TC 19/1/E.
14. TH letter to Panel, October 1946, FR 2429A.
15. TH to Chapman, 31 October 1946, cited in Chapman to TH, 18 December 1946, Org&Hist 1/8.
16. TH to Chapman, 15 December 1946, Org&Hist 1/8.
17. TH letter to Panel, October 1946, FR 2429A.

Pursuing a long-standing ambition to document the inner workings of working-class family life,[18] he made contact with Judith Henderson, a recent Cambridge anthropology graduate and daughter of Virginia Woolf's psycho-analyst brother. She was living in a working-class street in Bethnal Green as part of a research project set up by the warden of the University House set-tlement, and running a course—'Discover your Neighbour'—for doctors, clergy, probation officers, and other professionals working in the area designed to offer them an anthropological approach to understanding the local cul-ture.[19] Keen to practice what she preached, Henderson agreed to keep a detailed record of the life of a neighbouring family, the Samuels, while her husband, Nigel (another child of Bloomsbury, who was to be prominent in the 1950s as an experimental artist), took Humphrey Spender-like photo-graphs of street life in the area.[20] 'Extremely fascinating stuff', Harrisson commented on Judith's initial report. He was particularly impressed by the information she had gleaned from the Samuels' children who had befriended her, and urged her to use this contact to spend more time inside her neigh-bour's house.[21] 'It is easier to observe in public places than in the home', he wrote at this time, 'but with ingenuity it is extraordinary what can be achieved—as I hope to demonstrate in a study now being made of one working-class family over a year.'[22] By June 1947 Henderson's study of the family was expected to continue for two years, but little survives of this project in the archive. At some point anthropological observation gave way to friendship, and by the late 1950s the Samuels had joined the Hendersons' *avant garde* print-making business in Judith's family home in rural Essex.[23]

18. The abortive 'Projected Study of Youth' (January 1941, TC 51/2/A) included plans to place investigators 'in typical family households as lodgers and participate in family life, recording home behaviour and the actual problems which arise.' Similar plans, equally unfulfilled, were outlined in 'Why People Marry', 9 February 1944, FR 2015.
19. Ben Highmore, 'Hopscotch Modernism: On Everyday Life and the Blurring of Art and Social Science', *Modernist Cultures*, 2, 1, 2006, 73.
20. Henderson to TH, 20 November 1946, TC 26/5. On Nigel Henderson see Victoria Walsh and Peter Smithson, *Nigel Henderson: Parallel of Life and Art*, 2001 and Anne Massey, *The Independent Group: Modernism and Mass Culture in Britain, 1949–59*, 1995.
21. 'Notes on the S family', November 1946; TH to Judith Henderson, 4 December 1946, TC 26/5.
22. TH, 'The Future of Sociology,' *Pilot Papers*, 2, 1 March 1947.
23. SRP, minutes, 24 June 1947, TC 11/2/A; Willcock to Henderson, 29 May 1947, TC 26/5. Walsh and Smithson, *Nigel Henderson: Parallel of Life and Art*, 54–5, 148. Thanks also to Ben Highmore for the information about the subsequent history of the two families. According to Walsh and Smithson the target family did not discover that they had been observed for MO until 1978, when Nigel used extracts from Judith's diary to accompany an exhibition of his photographs.

By December 1947 Harrisson had raised £1,100 from Rowntree's League for Education Against Gambling for a project on mass gambling.[24] The brief, drafted by MO, stressed 'analytical, documentary, qualitative and penetrative' approaches, rather than any attempt to provide a statistically representative national sample. The work, mostly done during the spring of 1947, involved a panel directive, a postal questionnaire sent to various opinion formers from clergymen to bookmakers and members of the British Psychological Society. But the bulk of the work consisted of direct observation and indirect interviewing by investigators based in Middlesbrough, York, Bolton, Aston, Blaina, Glasgow, and several villages including Luccombe, alongside formal interviews with nearly 3,000 individuals in the same places.[25] Willcock's lengthy report, which showed clearly just how out of touch the anti-gambling lobby was with popular attitudes, horrified its sponsors who dismissed it out of hand—'utter tosh and tripe'—and used their contractual option to prevent its publication for a year.[26] Although a publisher had been arranged by the spring of 1949 the book never appeared—perhaps because by that time, as we shall see, the people running MO were anxious to avoid publishing controversial findings based on qualitative research.[27]

A second attempt to raise non-commercial money came to nothing. Doing his best to deliver on the wartime promise to make full post-war use of the diaries, Harrisson commissioned Pam Vince, a 24-year-old educational psychologist who had been helping Willcock draft MO reports while working part-time at the Maudsley, to revisit the project abandoned by Celia Fremlin in 1944 and write a book on 'the impact of the war on the everyday lives, habits, attitudes and opinions of people in Britain, as evidenced from personal diaries kept during the period 1939–47'. The project would start with 'a complete indexing of these diaries and an analysis of their contents.'[28] But, despite backing from Lord Horder and C. A. Mace, the academic psychologist who had encouraged Fremlin's work before the

---

24. TH to Chapman, nd (December 1946?), Org&Hist 1/8; England to Sheridan, 17 September 1991, Personnel/England.
25. 'Mass Gambling', January 1948, FR 2560; 'Postal Questionnaires', December 1948, FR 3072.
26. David Dixon, From prohibition to regulation: bookmaking, anti-gambling, and the law, 1991, 307–10. The report was, however, submitted in evidence to the 1949–51 Royal Commission on Gambling, which found it 'of great assistance in the early stages of our enquiry.'
27. 'Reports to be published shortly', March 1949, TC 12/2/H.
28. The 1947 grant application and Vince's CV are in Org&Hist 1/1. Her referees included Fremlin's academic sponsor, C. A. Mace.

war, Vince's grant application—presumably to a research foundation—was unsuccessful and the work was never done.

This failure did not bode well for the old dream, which Harrisson was still pursuing in December 1946, of securing long-term academic grants to make MO 'fully ... independent of patronage in any form (publishers, advertisers, political groups etc)'.[29] Nor did the 1946 report of the Clapham Committee, set up to advise government on future public financing of the social sciences. Despite hearing evidence from Political and Economic Planning (PEP), the report focussed exclusively on research carried out in government departments and universities, making no mention of the role played by independent, non-university bodies.[30] Chapman, who continued to be supportive of MO despite his very considerable reservations about the validity of its methods, was among those urging the Association of Scientific Workers to campaign against what Harrisson hoped was just an unfortunate 'oversight'.[31] Early in 1947 Harrisson was part of an informal grouping of social researchers hosted by PEP—including Chapman, Mark Abrams, Charles Madge and his brother John, Munro Fraser (an industrial psychologist), and A. T. M. Wilson of the Tavistock Institute—who resolved to meet regularly to share their concerns about the development of the social sciences.[32] It was in this context that, in March, Harrisson published a wideranging article in *Pilot Papers*, a short-lived journal edited by Madge, reviewing the state of the social sciences in post-war Britain and deploring the continuing weakness of sociological fieldwork. While conceding the value of wartime advances in quantitative methods, Harrisson rehearsed MO's arguments against the Clapham Report's reduction of 'realistic and practical' social research to that which could be quantified. 'University and other academic sociologists,' he remarked unkindly, 'experience difficulty in mixing in with many aspects of mass life, distrust their ability to observe objectively in such situations...The armchair sociologist's ideal is to sit back and direct a large number of...less qualified person(s) to stand on every sixteenth doorstep...so that higher-grade "computors [sic] and sort-

29. TH to Chapman, nd (December 1946?), Org&Hist 1/8.
30. Report of the Committee on the Provision for Social and Economic Research, July 1946, Cmd 6868.
31. Chapman to England, 12 August 1949; Chapman/TH correspondence, Org&Hist 1/8; TH, 'The Future of Sociology,' *Pilot Papers*, 2, 1 March 1947, 23; ASW, *The Social Sciences. A case for their greater use*, 1947.
32. TH to Abrams and Fraser, nd (February 1947?), Org&Hist 1/8; TH, 'New Synthesis', *Public Opinion Quarterly*, Fall 1947, 327.

ers" can prepare results for holes punched and answers given by Hollerith.' The kind of penetrative, observational, and informal interviewing work undertaken by MO 'has barely been exploited in Britain, largely because it takes more time, requires a higher standard of interviewer training, and produces answers less easy to analyse and mechanize for punch-card calculation.'[33] Madge published the article with a rather condescending editorial caveat urging readers offended by Harrisson's polemics to remember that 'without such intellectual gadflies we should never overcome our very strong resistance to direct social fieldwork.'[34] But while the gadfly might irritate some sensitive academic skins, he could make little headway against the advancing tide of quantification in academic social science.

III

In the commercial world too, the quantifiers were consolidating their position. On 5 November 1946 the major market research and polling organizations—led by Mark Abrams (who now had his own firm, Research Services Ltd) and Henry Durant of the British Institute of Public Opinion—established the Market Research Society, intended in its 'jealously guarded' membership to embrace 'all existing research talent'. As well as representatives from Lintas, the London Press Exchange, the Institute of Incorporated Practitioners in Advertising, and various other market research firms, there were research directors from the Ministry of Food, the Co-operative Wholesale Society, the British Export Trade Association, Louis Moss from the Government Social Survey, Robert Silvey from BBC Listener Research, and Ruth Glass from the Association for Planning and Regional Reconstruction. *Advertiser's Weekly* welcomed the new organization as a group of 'like minded' researchers committed to 'the passionless atmosphere of the laboratory' who would be able to convince a sceptical business world of the scientific value of market research and isolate 'the wishful thinkers and charlatans.'[35]

Had Harrisson been in Britain during the preparatory stages of this initiative it is difficult to believe that he would not have bullied his way into the meeting. In the absence, at least for the time being, of public or foundation

---

33. TH, 'The Future of Sociology,' *Pilot Papers*, 2, 1 March 1947, 16, 17–18, 22.
34. CM, *Pilot Papers*, 2, 1 March 1947, 4.
35. McDonald and King, *Sampling the Universe*, NTC Publications Ltd in association with the Market Research Society, 1996, 24–7.

money MO needed commercial contracts to survive, and relegation to the ranks of the excluded charlatans would certainly have been fatal. To avoid this Harrisson carried the fight for qualitative fieldwork into the competitive world of market research. Determined to refute rumours that MO was not interested in doing commercial work which, he alleged, were being spread by 'some of the market research boys', he placed advertisements in the *Advertiser's Weekly*.[36] That he had some success in establishing MO's relevance is suggested by the fact that in May 1947, shortly before his return to Borneo, he was invited to make the keynote speech at the annual conference of the Advertiser's Association.[37] He used the occasion to assert that advertisers, having paid little attention to the means of testing the impact of their publicity on an increasingly sceptical public, were going to be in for 'a horrible shock' when post-war shortages gave way to a buyer's market.[38]

In an undated brochure, produced shortly after the war, outlining its approach to consumer research, MO asserted that the qualitative methods it had pioneered were now being adopted by progressive market researchers around the world, especially in the United States. Crucial to this 'more intensive' approach was the attention given to the environment in which consumers made their choices. The borderline between commercial and social research, MO argued, was indistinct: the more a commercial survey probed the wider social characteristics of consumers of a particular product, the more useful it would be to the client:

> many of the surveys which we make on behalf of commercial concerns are just as much social surveys as are those we make on behalf of social, political, religious and suchlike organisations...A marketing survey to be of greatest practical value *is* a social survey...Consumer research in the future will be practically indistinguishable from social research.[39]

While this last prediction all too conveniently airbrushed the disadvantages for MO of dependence on commercial contracts, it was Harrisson's ability to convince hard-headed businessmen that MO's qualitative methods were appropriate in the field of market research that underpinned his success during the winter of 1946–7 in securing a raft of new commissions for MO which were to be largely responsible for keeping the organization afloat for

---

36. TH to EJ, 7 May 1947; EL to TH 12 May 1947, TC 61/10/B.
37. TH to EJ, 14 May 1947, TC 61/10/B.
38. *Newspaper World*, 24 and 31 May 1947; *World Press News*, 22 May 1947.
39. 'Services available from MO', nd (1945?), Org&Hist 4/1.

the next two years. Some of these commercial contracts amounted to little more than conventional market research, although even in these cases MO's use of informal interviews and verbatim quotation made for a more nuanced investigation of consumer attitudes than the tick-box questionnaires preferred by its rivals. Others, however, were designed to contribute directly to MO's broader agenda of social research.

The most profitable of the commercial contracts was a survey of drinking habits commissioned by Sir Hugh Beaver, the managing director of Guinness, who had read *The Pub and the People* and been impressed.[40] In January 1947 members of the Guinness management team were reading some of the more recent MO studies to get 'a better idea of your methods and the kind of results that can be achieved,' and in February a detailed plan for a one-year study 'to map, analyse and document British alcoholic drinking habits with particular reference to Guinness and related products' was agreed at a cost of £8,000: considerably more than MO had been paid by the Ministry of Information during 1940–1, even allowing for inflation. While insisting, as always, that MO should retain copyright of the material with a view to future publication, Harrisson accepted that the involvement of Guinness in funding the survey would be kept confidential and that the firm would have the right to veto publication of any findings that they considered 'private to them or likely adversely to influence their own or other interests': a substantial sacrifice of MO's founding principles to the requirements of commercial funding.[41]

Contacting other old patrons, Harrisson secured a substantial commission from Clem Leslie, now director of the Council for Industrial Design, to survey responses to the Britain Can Make It Exhibition. The work, completed by the end of 1946, involved 15 fieldworkers over two weeks following, observing, and interviewing visitors to the exhibition, and demonstrated conclusively, according to Harrisson, that far from preferring bad taste, the masses appreciated

40. Harrisson, *Britain Revisited*, 1961, 168.
41. Phillips to TH, 17 January 1947; 470207 TH 'Drinking Survey', 7 February 1947, TC 85/2/A. In the event Guinness raised no objection to the incorporation of material from this survey into a planned (but never published) revised edition of *The Pub and the People*, but they did refuse MO's request to reveal their sponsorship in promoting their own market research services. (Phillips to England, 1 March, 13 May 1949, England to Phillips, 7 March 1949, TC 85/2/A). Confidentiality about the sponsorship had its uses for MO since it helped to secure cooperation in the survey from the Pub Users' Protection Society who were led to believe (by Sommerfield acting of Willcock's behalf) that the survey was a straightforward update of *The Pub and the People*, an unsponsored 'impartial collection and study of facts about pubs and pub goers' (questionnaire sent to PUPS members; Sommerfield to England, 1 April 1947, TC 85/2/A).

good domestic design when they saw it.[42] Allen Lane was equally obliging, commissioning a major survey of public book-buying and reading habits involving 1,000 formal interviews; a panel directive; observation; informal interviews in libraries, bookstalls, shops, and homes; and analysis of fan mail to Penguin authors. Alongside this, MO interviewed retailers, wholesalers, and librarians about their attitudes to Penguin books.[43] The report, completed in December 1947, ran to over 350 pages, nearly a third of which were devoted to a detailed account of life among the staff at Penguin's Harmondsworth works written by Irene Browne, a bright young woman filling in time between jobs, who had posed for a month (unbeknownst to anyone but Lane himself) as a trainee there. Harrisson did his best to recruit her for MO more permanently, but she went off to Paris to work for an Anglo-French weekly.[44]

In December 1946, having just been appointed advertising agent for the *Daily Mirror*, Marcus Brumwell encouraged Harrisson to put together a proposal for a study of the paper's readership:

> I could imagine a damned interesting survey by you into newspaper reader-ship in general, and the influence of newspapers on politics if any, etc, etc. The whole thing published as a Penguin (having been paid for by the *Daily Mirror*) and given with their compliments to the 10,000 most important business executives in this country. What do you say?

Within a week Harrisson came back with a plan for the intensive study of a random sample of readers in MO's usual localities designed to investigate how far the *Daily Mirror* influenced everyday life:

> families, homes, gardens, tastes, clothes, political and religious associations, social organisations, hobbies, amusements, educational and artistic interests, intelligence, alertness, ambition, general knowledge of outside affairs, etc.[45]

This was very much in line with Harrisson's long-standing project of under-standing precisely how the press influenced opinion formation, and he was

42. P. J. Maguire and J. M. Woodham, *Design and Cultural Politics in Postwar Britain*, 1997, 174–5; 'The Public's Progress', *Contact*, April 1947. The CID proved to be a long-term client for M-O which 'continued to generate research reports into the effectiveness of its...propaganda on behalf of design, the last of which appeared in 1984' (Lesley Whitworth, 'Getting Beneath the Surface of Things: Mass-Observation and Material Culture', Mass-Observation Online).
43. 'A Report on Penguin World', December 1947, FR 2545; 470219 Willcock, 'Interim Report on Penguins', 19 February 1947, TC 20/10/E; TH to Lane, 20 and 26 February 1947; Willcock to Lane 23 June 1947, TC 20/10/B.
44. TH to Browne, 1 January 1947; Browne to Willcock, nd (1947?), TC 20/10/B; England to Browne, 10 January 1947, TC 20/10/E.
45. Brumwell to TH, December 1946, TC 61/10/B.

convinced that the study would represent a major advance on the standard statistical readership surveys:'I really think I shall have to go into competition in that field. The thing can be done so much better, so much cheaper'. The *Mirror's* own marketing people, however, thought they knew their readers well enough already, and Cecil King, who discussed the project with Harrisson at an Advertising Service Guild (ASG) lunch in February, proved as resistant to Harrisson's charms as he had been when Madge tried to persuade him to come to MO's rescue in October 1939.[46] By May, giving up on the *Mirror*, Brumwell was 'all fired up' by the idea that the ASG itself should put up £1,200 to finance 'a really intelligent newspaper survey, including the whole influence of the press, as a piece of public relations' for themselves.[47] Although *The Press and its Readers*, published (not by Penguin) in 1949, was mistakenly attributed to Harrisson on the cover, the research—over 3,000 interviews, supplemented by directive replies from the panel and some observation in libraries and newsagents—was carried out over the winter of 1947–8, after Harrisson's departure. Building on recent authoritative statistical surveys of press readership the report sought to probe 'the *attitude* of readers to their newspapers...the words and moods of people behind the decimal point.'[48] Analysing the ways in which readers of different papers consumed the news, editorial, feature articles, sports sections, cartoons, and correspondence columns, the report concluded with a restatement of MO's long-standing argument that newspapers (chosen largely for their political orientation) served more to reinforce existing attitudes than to inculcate new ones. Despite the new research, *The Press and its Readers* added little to the arguments that MO had been making about the role of newspapers since Harrisson's 1940 article on the relationship between published, public, and private opinion.

IV

Academic research funding might be unavailable, but there were other non-commercial channels worth exploring. An attempt to re-engage with Naval Intelligence came to nothing.[49] But when Clem Leslie moved from the Council of Industrial Design to the Treasury's Information Division in May

46. Brumwell to TH, 11 February 1947; TH to Brumwell, 29 April 1947, TC 61/10/B.
47. Brumwell to TH, 2 May 1947, TC 61/10/B.
48. *The Press and its Readers*, 7.
49. TH to Godfrey, 22 January 1947, ADM 223/476.

1947, MO won a contract to study the reception of the government's 'Work
or Want' campaign.[50] In April 1947 MO was commissioned by Conservative
Central Office to gauge public reactions to the party's reformist policy document, *The Industrial Charter*. The eventual report, framed in MO's familiar
arguments about public indifference, ignorance, apathy, and cynicism was so
dispiriting that one party official minuted: 'one might almost be excused for
coming to the conclusion that Mass-Observation is some subversive Fascist
or Communist organisation formed with the object of undermining confidence in the democratic way of life!'[51] Like a number of recent historians,
the Tory agent could see only the present facts, the evidence of apathy, not
the potential for change that MO's methods were designed to probe and
reveal.[52] A more appreciative client in this respect was William Beveridge,
whose Liberal links with Harrisson may have played a role in his decision
to commission MO to write a series of six reports for his 1947 enquiry into
Voluntary Action, and to give them pride of place in the volume of evidence
published alongside his final report.[53] As well as quizzing the general public
and the panel on their attitudes to voluntary work and charity, MO investigated a wide range of organizations, from pensioners' associations to political parties, interviewing activists, observing meetings, talking with members,
and compiling a picture of an often vigorous associational life alongside the
wider reality of popular apathy and indifference to public affairs. Commenting
on the fact that, despite the small size of its sample, MO's conclusion that
less than a third of people took any regular part in voluntary social service
was in 'notable agreement' with a national representative survey of 3,000
people undertaken by Mark Abrams' Research Services Ltd, Beveridge
pointed out that, in contrast to Abrams' purely quantitative study, MO's
investigators were able to supplement the brute fact of non-involvement
with evidence of 'an incipiently positive attitude'—'most of those who do
not help others commonly feel that they should do so, and make excuses of

50. *The Times*, 23 May 1947, 'Work or Want', June 1947, TC 42/4/G.
51. Cited by Harriet Jones, '"New Conservatism"? The Industrial Charter, Modernity and the
    Reconstruction of British Conservatism after the War', in Betty Conekin, Frank Mort and
    Chis Waters (eds), *Moments of Modernity. Reconstructing Britain 1945–1964*, 181–2.
52. Hinton, '1945 and the apathy school', *History Workshop Journal*, 43, 1997.
53. Lord Beveridge and A. F. Wells (eds), *The Evidence for Voluntary Action*, 1949. The full text of the
    six reports, dealing with friendly societies, mutual aid and the pub, voluntary services, charity,
    holidays and the Co-op, can be found in FR 2505–2510 and FR 2551. Beveridge was a sup-
    porter of the Liberal Party's left-leaning Radical Action ginger group (David Dutton, *The
    History of the Liberal Party*, 245; Jose Harris, *William Beveridge. A Biography*, 1997, 448).

lack of time and means', a finding Beveridge seized upon to argue that to focus only on those already active would be to underestimate the extent to which 'the spirit of service' was diffused among the people, and to insist, in MO's words, that 'there is a reserve of willingness to be drawn upon.'[54]

What Beveridge responded to was the abiding MO aim of documenting not just existing active citizenship, but the potential for engagement among the mass of the population, if only the activists could learn to appeal to them in a language that they understood. This was Harrisson's consistent message whether he was discussing politics and the non-voter, the activist minority and the passive majority, or self-improving Penguin readers and the consumers of popular fiction. Refusing to halt the analysis at the point of difference between the educated elite and the masses, Harrisson stressed the potential for 'public progress' within a common culture in which 'you can gamble *and* listen to Beethoven...Let us not take the Littlewoods obsession or the Robert Taylor mania *too* seriously. The engineer who gets drunk on Saturday night is not thereby a drunkard or inefficient.' For all their disengagement, apathy, and ignorance the masses, he argued, possessed a degree of 'common sense and self-discipline' that made them 'steadier and in some respects wiser than their half-elected leaders.'[55] MO might specialize in reality testing the self-serving rhetoric of those who posed as spokesmen for the popular will, but there was nothing anti-democratic about its central message. Always, for MO, diagnosis was the beginning of cure. Democracy was certainly a long way from being realized in Britain, but it was not a lost cause.

V

While Harrisson drummed up new contracts, Willcock did most of the writing up and remained in overall charge of the office, assisted by Len England, back from the army by the autumn of 1946, who coordinated the research and Mollie Tarrant, back from her teaching job in 1947, who supervised the fieldworkers.[56] Apart from Willcock, England, and Tarrant, the only members of the wartime staff to continue full-time were Lena Bleehan, Doris Hoy (who later sent in some intriguing accounts of sadomasochistic behaviour among

54. Lord Beveridge, *Voluntary Action. A Report on Methods of Social Advance*, 151; Beveridge and Wells (eds), *Evidence for Voluntary Action*, 34, 69f.
55. TH, 'The Public's Progress', *Contact*, April 1947.
56. Tarrant to Brumwell, 30 July 1947, TC 61/10/B; TH letter to panel, October 1946, FR 2429A.

her lesbian acquaintances),[57] and (with occasional breaks) Gay Taylor, who continued to relish the mundane counterpoint that the MO interviewing provided to the mystical journey she shared with Kathleen Raine in search of life's deeper meaning.[58] Some other former staff now otherwise employed, including Fremlin, took on occasional jobs.[59] Eric Gulliver—released from the mines and working as a primary school teacher in Kent—came in at weekends to help sort the panel material, as well as doing a good deal of field-work in his holidays.[60] Altogether about 90 different individuals contributed to the fieldwork during 1946–7, most of them doing only a few days' work, and a good many of them probably unpaid volunteers from among the panel. But the bulk of the fieldwork was done by new full-time staff. Ivan Piercy, at a loose end after the war, joined MO in 1946, living at first in the Willcocks' house and later spending a year at the MO unit in Middlesbrough working on various surveys. Described by Tarrant as 'undoubtedly the best of the field-workers of the new lot', he stayed with MO until 1950, and subsequently became a director of the American cigarette firm Rothman's.[61] John Golley, who joined MO for a year on his release from the air force in 1946, worked in the mining town of Blaina where, according to his obituarist, 'he developed first-rate interviewing skills'. He moved on into advertising, becoming sales manager for ATV at the launch of commercial television in 1955, and setting up his own PR firm in 1957.[62] Michael Lyster, a statistician who joined MO in 1946, became part of the management team before leaving in 1951 for a career in advertising and market research. In 1957 he was elected chair of the Market Research Society.[63] The new intake brought a very different ethos from that of MO's pre-war origins, and the commercial trajectory of these leading new full-timers, which mirrored that of MO itself, was much resented by some of the earlier staff.[64]

57. Hoy, 6 and 14 January 1949, TC 12/15/H.
58. Loran Hurnscot, [Gay Taylor], *A Prison, a Paradise*, London, 1958, 226–7 and *passim*.
59. TH to Chapman, nd (December 1946?), Org&Hist 1/8.
60. Gulliver, survey of Wickham Common School, 30 January 1947; Gulliver, interviewed by Stanley, 8 September 1982; Tarrant to Wainwright, 2 April 1979, Personnel/Tarrant.
61. Tarrant to Wainwright, October 1980; Piercy to Tarrant, 5 April 1984, Personnel/Tarrant.
62. England to Robertson, 24 March 1948, TC 64/2/D; obituary of John Golley, *The Daily Telegraph*, 16 December 2000.
63. *The Incorporated Statistician*, 8, 1, 1957, 43. I have been unable to discover anything about Kay Butcher, another full-timer who did a good deal of work during 1947, including some fasci-nating reports on associational life for the Beveridge enquiry (TC 53/2/E and F). TH later identified her as among those who helped to keep MO going in this period (Harrisson, *Britain Revisited*, 268).
64. Hughes to Calder, 4 February 1979, Personnel/Hughes.

The full-timers were much better paid than in wartime, the leading people getting up to £15 a week, experienced fieldworkers up to £10, and,
Harrisson claimed in December 1946, no one getting less than £6, 'except
novices on trial'.[65] In the past the full-timers had to be ready to turn their
hands to whatever needed doing, but the easing of the acute labour shortages of wartime made possible a greater division of labour among the investigators, and Willcock was able to employ people to work exclusively on
formal interviewing while allowing his best fieldworkers to specialize in
qualitative research, 'free from work which they find irksome.'[66] Aware that
the tedium of doorstep interviewing could lead to the kind of cheating that
was allegedly commonplace in market research companies, MO developed
its own routines for checking up on interviewers.[67]

By the end of the war the number of panellists responding to each directive had fallen to well below 200. Reliable figures for the immediate post-
war years have not been compiled, and it may now be impossible to discover
them since a good deal of material from that period was damaged by flood
water. Early in 1947 an effort was made to rebuild the panel, and an appeal
in the *New Statesman* brought in nearly 1,000 responses.[68] How many of
these turned into regular contributors is unknown, but it appears that after
a purge of inactive members in the spring of 1948 the number of panellists
had fallen to less than 500.[69] Over the next year the number increased again
to over 1,000, of whom between 600 and 800 regularly sent in material: a
better rate of return both relatively and absolutely than MO had achieved
previously at any time in its history.[70] The panel was an important source for

65. TH to Chapman, nd (December 1946?), Org&Hist 1/8. During 1947 one new recruit, Bernard
    Latham, was paid twice the going fieldwork rate because, as an out of work actor with a family
    to support, he needed the money.
66. Willcock, *Polls Apart*, Chapter 7.
67. 'Capital Punishment: Progress Report', 27 April 1948, 3 May 1948; 'MO and Opinion Polls',
    12 May 1948, TC 72/1/B.
68. FR 2479.
69. Mary to Faith, 18 May 1948, TC 47/11/A.
70. Although 'Notes on M-O Services and Techniques', November 1948, FR 3060 and 'Mass-
    Observation: A Nation-wide Intelligence Serivice', 1950, FR 3197 both claimed 'some 2000
    voluntary part-time correspondent observers' the more precise figures given in 'MO Panel on
    Television', April 1949, FR 3106 are probably more reliable. According to England the 642
    replies received from the 1,000-member panel to a directive for the 'Little Kinsey' report in
    1949 represented 'roughly our usual return' (Liz Stanley, *Sex Surveyed, 1949–1994. From M-O's
    'Little Kinsey' to the National Survey and the Hite reports*, 1995, 194). Towards the end of the same
    year he wrote: 'Panel strength at the time of writing is about 1200, and an average reply in any
    one month is 750–800' (Len England, 'Little Kinsey: an outline of sex attitudes in Britain',
    Public Opinion Quarterly, 13, 4, 1949–50, 592).

MO reports throughout the later 1940s, although it appears to have been neglected from 1951 onwards. There was a brief revival in connection with MO's study of the coronation in 1953, when panel members were re-contacted and 150 responses secured.[71] By the mid-1950s, however, the panel had been abandoned altogether.[72]

VI

There had long been talk of establishing MO as a limited company, although an attempt to do this in 1943 had come to nothing. In the spring of 1947 Harrisson took a major step in this direction, setting up a limited company to operate alongside the existing organization, Social Research Publications (SRP). The company rented an office from MO—the address given was actually Willcock's own house in Hampstead—and paid MO for the services of a secretary. Alongside Harrisson and Willcock, two long-standing supporters of MO served as directors: Woodrow Wyatt and Arthur Calder Marshall, later joined by Harrisson's friend and lawyer, Ambrose Appelbe.[73] The primary purpose of the new company was 'to make it possible for original social research of general interest to be given the widest possible distribution among the public, instead of... being kept locked up exclusively in academic journals and University archives.' To this end it proposed to act as a literary agent for MO and other sociological researchers, advising on the presentation of findings, and seeking to persuade 'reputable publishing firms' that 'a very wide public can be interested in serious sociological field reports'.[74] SRP placed Willcock's book on *Juvenile Deliquency*, which drew heavily on records kept by Harrisson's godfather, Reverend D. B. Kittermaster, of his work as a Borstal chaplain.[75] But the publisher was a minor one, and Calder Marshall's attempt to persuade Allen Lane to launch a social sciences programme on

71. Letter to Panel, May 1953, TC 69/1/B. See TC 69/7/F for Murielle Hartman's 1996 analysis of the Coronation DR responses.
72. Derek Roberts' experience was probably typical: see his response to an Mass-Observation Project directive in June 1990: 'I rejoined in 1988 after being dropped from the Panel in 1955' (R2143). Roberts, a leading cycling enthusiast, deposited his papers in the Modern Records Centre at Warwick.
73. SRP, minutes, 21 May 1947; Willcock, Draft explanation of SRP Ltd, 30 December 1947, TC 11/2/A.
74. Draft letter from SRP to selected publishers, 23 July 1947, TC 11/2/A.
75. Kittermaster, 'A Critical Survey'; correspondence between Kittermaster, TH, and Willcock in TC 11/2/A.

the model of Penguin's very successful 'New Biology' series fell on deaf ears. Equally unsuccessful was an effort by SRP to build on contacts MO had made with a Mexican journal to set itself up as a distributor of sociological journals published overseas. The American *Public Opinion Quarterly*, which had published several MO articles, expressed interest in shifting its UK distribution from Oxford University Press to the SRP if favourable terms could be negotiated. But the Board of Trade refused SRP's application for an import licence, so this initiative also came to nothing.[76]

The other string to SRP's bow was the marketing of the MO Archive. For the princely sum of £48 the company bought all MO's records, with the exception of the panel material which continued to be located in Letchworth, looked after by Monty Ward, who had taken over the administration of the panel from Willcock, a job he retained until all contact with the remaining panellists was abandoned in the mid-1950s.[77] The material was stored in Willcock's Hampstead house:[78] the American sociologist Harold Orlans later recalled 'a large heap of unsorted paper on a Hampstead floor' when he visited MO in the autumn of 1948.[79] Gulliver came in at weekends to file and sort the material, and anyone could arrange to consult it on payment of a fee of 10s. 6d. The protocol, which might surprise a modern archivist, laid down that 'no notes may be taken by the person consulting the material, but passages of interest may be marked in the manuscript, and will then be copied and forwarded to him' at charge of 3s. 6d. per 1,000 words. The researcher would then be free to quote without further charge, so long as individual names and places were disguised and the usual acknowledgement was made. Anyone wishing to use MO material 'as the sole or main data for a substantial publication', however, might be required 'to enter into ... an agreement to pay a certain percentage of the author's royalties'.[80] Whether these carefully thought-out arrangements made any money for MO in the 1940s is unknown, but they did establish a precedent for the future exploitation of the archival material. Although SRP seems to have disappeared almost as soon as it was born and the current archivist does not encourage researchers to mark up the manuscripts, MO still sees the archive

76. SRP, minutes, 6 December 1947; Faith to Willcock, 19 January 1948, TC 11/2/A.
77. SRP, minutes, 21 May 1947, TC 11/2/A; Tarrant to Wainwright, 2 April 1979.
78. 471230 BW Draft explanation of SRP Ltd. Present 'temporary storage depot' is 11 Heath Street.
79. Orlans to Sheridan, 19 August 1990, Personnel/Orlans; Willcock, Draft explanation of SRP Ltd, 30 December 1947, TC 11/2/A.
80. Willcock, Draft explanation of SRP Ltd, 30 December 1947, TC 11/2/A.

as a marketable commodity, and it employs a long-established literary agency, Curtis Brown, to negotiate contracts with authors wishing to use the archive as the main source of their work. Back in 1947, when Kittermaster told MO that he intended to use Curtis Brown to find a publisher for his own material, Harrisson advised him to use SRP instead because Curtis Brown would 'just treat it like any other book.'[81] Later he changed his mind, since Curtis Brown were already acting for the archive when it came to Sussex in the early 1970s.

VII

Despite Harrisson's polemics against the quantifiers he was well aware that MO's future depended on being able to deliver, alongside its qualitative findings, the apparently 'hard' data which clients increasingly demanded. 'Since August,' Willcock remarked in January 1947, 'we've done proportionately more straight questionnaire work and larger numbers of questionnaires than at any time since the Square Deal for the Railways in 1939.'[82] During the war MO had occasionally sent material out to be analysed by a Hollerith machine, but now they decided to buy one of their own and do this work in-house.[83] Concerned that they should not be doing this quantitative work merely as 'a concession to the clients' simplicity', Willcock and Harrisson looked into new and more sophisticated questionnaire techniques involving the use of attitude scales developed by psychologists which, they hoped, would enable them to get at the 'why' as well as the 'what' of respondents' thinking, techniques which would further increase their reliance on number-crunching since they required 'the longest and most elaborate type of alternative-answer questionnaire, whose results are solely a matter of machine statistical calculation.'[84] Although they did not try to compete with rivals in using representative national samples, and continued to base their surveys on places they knew well— the most commonly used being Fulham, Tottenham, Hammersmith; Aston,

---

81. TH to Kittermaster, 12 May 1947, TC 11/2/A.
82. Willcock, memo on questionnaires, 18 January 1947, Org&Hist 4/1.
83. Tarrant to Sheridan, 2 November 1986, Personnel/Tarrant; England to Hubback, 24 January 1949, TC 12/2/G.
84. Willcock, memo on questionnaires, 18 January 1947, Org&Hist 4/1; England, interviewed in 'Stranger than Fiction', MO Archive.

Bolton, Blaina, Middlesbrough, Malmesbury, Worcester; and Luccombe—
they were increasingly concerned to ensure the representativeness of these
local samples. This led to experiments which were not always welcomed by
the fieldworkers. Taylor, normally the happiest of interviewers, erupted in
fury when MO decided to abandon quota sampling (which allowed the
fieldworker to select individual respondents) in favour of respondents
selected at random from Food Office registrations:

> I am working on a survey in Wigginham [i.e. Tottenham] about the use made
> of the public library. For the first time, *Bomp* [i.e. MO] is experimenting with
> the governmental method of what's called 'pre-selected addresses', several of
> which are not there... Today a long telephone conversation, with *Bomp*, con-
> cerning their new method of interviewing. Yes, they said, theoretically speak-
> ing it is scientific and impeccable, but in practice it isn't accurate and it costs
> three times as much as any other method. For instead of choosing our victims
> according to our own sweet will and an age and class quota, we have to seek
> out special persons, of whom the percentage of blind, deaf, dumb, illiterate,
> mentally deficient or over ninety amounts to more than half, which the
> meanest statistician would find unlikely.[85]

Even without indignant investigators, no amount of increased attention to
the representativeness of their samples was going to consolidate MO's reputation for objective and reliable work if they were caught out cheating. In
January 1947 Willcock threatened to quit unless Harrisson pledged:

> never again to publish deliberately misleading statements about the repre-
> sentativeness of a questionnaire sample... I think you have been utterly
> unscrupulous about this in the past... It is one thing to inform one's intuition
> thorough reliable data, and publish controversial interpretations which have
> intuitive backing: quite another to cook the data up to back one's intuition
> (even if it's right) and then publish as if scientifically proved.

The occasion for this outburst was a newspaper article by Tom Driberg
which used figures supplied by Harrisson to argue that public opinion was
becoming increasingly pro-Russian, a conclusion derived from an obviously
illegitimate comparison between the results of an earlier national survey
with a recent survey of Hammersmith, a Labour stronghold. 'I look upon
this', Willcock wrote, 'as a particularly blatant example of the wish being
father to the thought'; or, even worse, as deliberate cheating, since Harrisson

---

85. Loran Hurnscot [Gay Taylor], *A Prison, a Paradise*, 1958, 221–2. This is a fictional account. But
it closely mirrors her furious written complaint ('Notes on Tottenham Inquiry', 16 July 1946,
TC 20/13/C). Other investigators also complained.

had warned England 'not to give Driberg any details of the sample . . . which suggests that you were quite well aware of the tendentiousness of the results.'[86] Harrisson's response does not survive in the archive, but within months both men had withdrawn from the leadership of MO and a new generation, more oriented to the norms of the commercial world, was in the driving seat.

Towards the end of February 1947 Harrisson told Lane that he was 'going back to Borneo in a few weeks time to do a special job for the Colonial Office', filling the vacant posts of official ethnologist and curator of the Sarawak museum. At this stage, expecting the job to last only a few months, he planned to keep a close eye on MO while he was away: 'I shall . . . receive weekly carbons of draft material,' he wrote reassuringly to Lane.[87] Plagued with malaria and amoebic dysentery, he was unable to leave for Borneo until late May. Still anticipating a short stay, he explained to Everett Jones and Brumwell that he would 'be keeping in close touch by air mail and cable, and if there are any things you want to put to me personally, I will be right there.' In the meantime 'everything has been left properly in Bob Willcock's hands'.[88]

Within weeks of Harrisson's departure, however, Willcock himself collapsed and was out of action for several months: overwhelmed, he later explained, by the difficulties he faced in keeping MO going without selling out to market research.[89] Towards the end of 1947 he recovered sufficiently to spend a couple of months working from home, but relapsed again in the new year.[90] Restored to health in the spring of 1948, his return to MO was short lived. By the end of May he had taken a job alongside Geoffrey Thomas and Kathleen Box with the Government Social Survey where he was to spend the remainder of his working life.[91] This did not prevent him, however, from continuing to cooperate with the organization in his spare time, revising the manuscript of his (never published) book on MO's research methods.[92] From June 1948 England took over formally as acting director, a job he had been doing in practice since the previous summer, with Tarrant as his second-in-command.

86. Willcock, memo on questionnaires, 18 January 1947, Org&Hist 4/1. See TC 14/1/J for the offending *Reynolds News* article.
87. TH to Lane, 26 February 1947; Heimann, *Most Offending Soul*, 243; TH to Abrams and Fraser, nd (February 1947?), Org&Hist 1/8.
88. TH to Everett Jones and Brumwell, 22 May 1947, TC 61/10/B; TH to Einthoven, 4 December 1946, TC 19/1/E; TH to Firth, 5 March 1947, Firth papers.
89. Ninka Willcock to Hinton, 6 January 2012, Personnel/Willcock.
90. England to Brumwell, 18 November 1947, 11 February 1948, TC 61/10/B; England to Hume, 13 November 1947, TC 12/2/C.
91. England to Brumwell, 28 May 1948, TC 26/1/C; Moss, *Government Social Survey*, 17, 28, 37, 47.
92. He had been working on *Polls Apart* since 1945, but some of the extant manuscript refers to literature published or events occurring after he left MO.

15

A New Regime

Len England's takeover was not the final betrayal portrayed by most accounts of Mass-Observation's (MO's) history. Throughout the 1950s and 1960s a cash-strapped MO continued to make space for occasional non-commercial work, and to preach and practice qualitative approaches to opinion research. By the 1970s MO's contribution to sustaining qualitative work through the quantitative years was beginning to be appreciated in the market research industry itself.[1] England, however, never matched Tom Harrisson's ability to raise commercial (or other) cash for basic social research: and, even when he did, his overriding concern to establish MO's reputation in the eyes of potential commercial clients stood in the way of the publication of controversial findings. More concerned with commercial respectability than with cultural innovation, he allowed some of MO's very best work—work for which he himself was responsible—to languish unpublished.

England also brought a new and quite distinct angle of vision to MO's ongoing study of British society. From MO's foundation until 1947 Cassandra had been the ruling spirit. The MO analysis of the state of the culture was framed by an anxiety and pessimism about the erosion of (presumed) traditional values, the (presumed) fragility of democracy, and the gulf between the leaders and the led. In Harrisson's hands this standpoint underpinned an activist orientation, an optimism of the will capable of sloughing off repeated disappointments and turning to the next opportunity for MO to facilitate dynamic, democratic social change. In the hands of lesser men—Bob Willcock and John Ferraby—the Cassandra stance came close to the promotion of cultural despair: the bold statements of opportunity for dynamic change, informed (for Ferraby at least) by improbable expectations of some future religious revival, sounding increasingly formulaic and unconvincing.

---

1. McDonald and King, *Sampling the Universe*, 1996, 71–2; Joe Moran, 'Mass-Observation, Market Research, and the Birth of the Focus Group, 1937–1997', *Journal of British Studies*, 47, 2008, 850.

England, by contrast, was well adapted to the coming world, at ease with the growing individualism of the enlightened middle-class vanguard who made up most of MO's panellists. Unlike the previous generation of MO leaders, England was not haunted by disappointed hopes for a more solidaristic society. He had never shared the leftist sympathies of most of MO's staff, nor, although himself a practising Christian, did he have any time for the religious revivalism underpinning Ferraby's outlook.[2]

MO had always been ready to take on a certain amount of market research to help to make ends meet. By the late 1940s, however, market research had become its main *raison d'être*. In 1950 MO issued a leaflet designed to explain the value of its approach 'to manufacturers, advertisers, advertising agents, retailers; to publishers, newspapers and all public and private bodies; to civic authorities.' The ordering of this list was significant, clearly intended to invert previous understandings of the relationship between MO's study of society and the services it offered to business:

> M-O observes and reports on what people are thinking and doing. Business men need market research as the essential basis of their merchandising plans. Government departments and many other bodies also require information of this nature, when it is often called social research. The long-established MO method of market research, social research, and all other aspects of social investigation is unique. It aims not merely to study the frequencies of people's habits and behaviour, but at the same time, as a necessary part of all and every research, to discover something of the reasons for people's actions and opinions.

Outlining MO's distinctive techniques, the leaflet stressed the skill and training involved in the verbatim recording of interviews, informal and indirect interviewing, or incognito participant observation designed to find out the difference between what people say and what they do. At the same time, however, they took care to reassure potential clients who might be worried by the cost of all this skill and training that 'when a more usual and simpler technique of straight counting, or questionnaire and statistical analysis, is sufficient to serve the purpose, then, of course, M-O is entirely ready to do this'. While stating that surveys were 'produced for the confidential information of the client', the suggestion that clients might agree to publication—as ICI had done recently with a survey of housewives' views of its products under the exciting title *People and Paint*—provided a

2. England, M-O Diary, *passim*.

faint echo of MO's founding principle (much compromised from the earliest days) that its findings should be open to all.[3]

In the competitive world of market research, many of the relationships built up by Harrisson continued to be a source of new work. Leonard Harris, the owner of Browns of Chester, commissioned a confidential survey of his customers, disguised by MO's investigators as part of a fictional national shopping survey. Gay Taylor complained about the difficulty of locating the exclusively middle-class clientele that Harris was interested in, describing the job as 'quite the nastiest enquiry I've ever done for M-O', but cheered up on discovering that the pub in which she was staying harboured its very own poltergeist.[4] Bob Martin commissioned further work on dog food, and, like Harris, joined the MO board during the 1950s.[5] A host of other market research jobs—many of them coming to MO through the good offices of the Advertising Service Guild members—are reflected in the surviving file reports from the late 1940s, including surveys dealing with face cream, custard powder, skirts, soup, wine cocktails, baby foods, washing machines, detergents, TV and radio sets, toothpaste, and cigarettes.[6]

Funding for more serious work came largely from newspapers. In April 1948 Michael Berry, editor of the *Daily Telegraph*, anxious to establish that proposed legislation to suspend the operation of the death penalty was out of line with popular feeling, commissioned a survey which marked a significant move by MO towards a more robustly quantitative approach. Unlike the work on drink or on gambling, which relied predominantly on classically MO methods of observation and indirect interviewing, the capital punishment survey was exclusively questionnaire based.[7] Needing rapidly to recruit large numbers of temporary, part-time staff, MO solicited help from panel members, reassuring them that although 'it is not a purely sociological survey' it was 'equally not a market research survey' and offering payment 'if you so desired'.[8] To get statistically reliable data on various groups in the population a total of 6,000 interviews were conducted over a three-week period in various parts of the country, and the results analysed

3. 'A National Wide Intelligence Service', FR 3197.
4. England to Everett Jones, 16 January 1950, England to Leonard Harris, 27 March 1950, TC 24/8/D; Taylor to Vince, 24 and 31 March 1950, TC 24/8/C.
5. TC 78/1/C & D; England, interviewed by Stanley, 14 October 1997.
6. FR 2546, 2547, 3047, 3097, 3098, 3106, 3171, 3173, 3192.
7. 'Instructions to Investigators', April 1948, TC 72/1/E.
8. 'Letter to Panel members who volunteered for direct interviewing,' April 1948, TC 72/1/E.

with MO's recently acquired tabulating machine.[9] Delighted with the outcome—which showed large majorities in favour of keeping the death penalty—the *Daily Telegraph* splashed the story on the front page. Marcus Brumwell wrote to congratulate England on a 'first class' job, 'particularly from the point of view of increasing the reputation of M-O.'[10] While both men regretted that the findings were being used in support of a cause which they deplored, and worried about the implications for democracy of government by opinion poll, England confirmed that the *Telegraph*'s presentation of the material was doing wonders for MO's reputation:

> We have never seen anywhere a more concise and accurate account of Mass-Observation's work from anybody outside the organisation. I quite agree with you about the prestige factor. The impact has already been felt considerably in this office—a large number of people who have always had suspicions of our 'oddness' seem at last to be beginning to believe that we are a genuine organisation![11]

Prominent among the new believers was the editor of the mass circulation *Daily Graphic* which, as it happened, belonged to Berry's uncle, Lord Kelmsley. From August to November 1948 MO undertook a series of orthodox national opinion polls—genuinely national representative samples of around 2,000 people—for the *Daily Graphic* dealing with attitudes to churchgoing, education, sport, leisure, and the cost of living.[12] Willcock, who had been involved in the *Daily Graphic* deal just before he resigned, later remarked that by entering the field of national opinion polling at this time MO 'narrowly missed the opportunity to say "told you so"' to the quantifiers when, in November 1948, voters in the American presidential election dramatically failed to act as the US pollsters had predicted.[13] As it was, the fiasco of the American poll predictions seem to have put paid to MO's adventure into direct competition with the orthodox opinion pollsters: there was no more work for the *Daily Graphic* after November 1948.

The newspaper funding was not restricted to purely quantitative work. Close to England's heart was a commission from *The British Weekly*, a non-denominational non-conformist paper, for a survey of the regular churchgoers

9. 'M-O Survey on Capital Punishment', 19 April 1948; Progress reports on survey, 27 April, 3 May, 12 May 1948; final report, May 1948, TC 72/1/B.
10. Brumwell to England, 28 May 1948, TC 72/1/B.
11. England to Brumwell, 1 June 1948, TC 26/1/C.
12. FR 3025, 3027, 3045, 3063a, 3067.
13. Willcock, *Polls Apart*, 'Section 4. Range and Weight', 139.

who had been largely neglected in *Puzzled People*'s description of bewilderment and confusion about religion among the population at large. England, himself a churchgoer, had given talks to various church-based groups about MO's earlier findings, and his own introduction to MO's articles on the churchgoers—published as though written by the newspaper's own editorial staff—was unashamedly directed at identifying what could be done to maximize church attendance.[14] His initial intention had been to use the *British Weekly* commission to launch a larger project, supplementing the survey with 'more intensive observation of some particular Church or church group', with a view to a more upbeat book on the faithful as a companion text to the bewildered and apathetic denizens of *Puzzled People*.[15] The book was never written, perhaps because, as the survey indicated, it would have contained too many 'nasty shocks' about the attitudes of religious people.[16] Potentially much more shocking, however, was the book England did write at this time, on sexual attitudes and behaviour. And the fate of this book, which had all the qualities of MO's very best work, speaks eloquently about the priorities of the new regime.

In November 1947 Marjorie Hume, Quaker chair of the Marriage Guidance Council, suggested to MO that they should undertake a survey on sex and marriage.[17] MO was keen, but when Willcock discussed the project with her it became clear that she was not able to raise the necessary money.[18] Following the publication of the Kinsey Report in January 1948, England approached the Rockefeller Foundation to fund a study of British attitudes to sex. At this point, despite the evidence of a wartime survey of attitudes to venereal disease which revealed a surprising willingness among people approached in the street to talk frankly about sexual matters, England assumed that 'the direct questionnaire method used by Dr Kinsey could not be duplicated in this country.'[19] Rockefeller declined to find the money, but by the end of the year England had found a sponsor in the *Daily Mirror*'s stable companion, the *Sunday Pictorial*, whose editor,

14. 'Contemporary Churchgoers', FR 3068, December 1948; 'Editorial Preface', FR 3071, 6 January 1949; correspondence in TC 47/11/A. MO's new secretary, Faith Lawson, was a Methodist and she made full use of her family connections to solicit responses to the postal questionnaire that MO sent to a large number of clergymen to supplement its interviews with ordinary churchgoers.
15. England to Hellicar, 31 May 1948; England to Griffiths, 28 May 1948, TC 47/11/A.
16. England to Brumwell, 1 June 1948, TC 26/1/C.
17. England to Hume, 13 November 1947, TC 12/2/C.
18. England to Hume, 4 March 1948, TC 12/2/C.
19. England to Hume, 4 March, 30 April 1948, TC 12/2/C.

Hugh Cudlipp, offered £1,200.[20] Billed as 'a survey on sexual morality',
England was now proposing a questionnaire with a national representative
sample dealing with both attitudes and habits, alongside 'executive interviewing', of parsons, policemen, MPs, doctors, film stars, and teachers,
designed 'to assess the difference between the "common man" and those
in authority in their attitudes to sexual matters.' The panel, whose trusting
relationship with MO would ensure frankness, were to be asked to write
about their own sexual lives, and investigators in London and some of
MO's regional centres would observe sexual activity in public places. They
would be assisted by 'a prostitute who has been fully trained in M-O
methods' who would be 'sent from London to all regions studied in detail,
with the intention of obtaining information from the prostitutes . . . on the
costs and types of clients, frequency of clients, differences in technique,
differences in prostitutes' taboo and ritual.'[21] While the Sunday Pictorial
would have exclusive newspaper rights to the findings, MO was left free
to make its own arrangements for the book that England had every intention of producing.[22]

    Given the sensitivity of the subject, England decided to establish a group of
expert assessors to advise on the research. In addition to Hume, the group was
joined by David Mace, a former non-conformist minister and secretary of the
Marriage Guidance Council; Gilbert Russell of the Church of England Moral
Welfare Council; Eva Hubback, feminist founder of the Townswomen's Guild
and a leading campaigner for family planning;[23] Clifford Allen, a Harley Street
doctor and writer on 'sexual perversions and abnormalities'; and Cyril Bibby,
educationalist, biologist, and British editor of the International Journal of
Sexology. Claude Mullins, a recently retired lawyer well known for his campaigns to humanize the judicial handling of marital disputes but a conservative in sexual matters, declined to join the group, strongly advising MO to
drop the project because 'we in this country adopt a very reserved attitude
to sex.' The only people likely to respond were those who had already
abandoned 'traditional morality', leading to sensational results which the
Sunday Pictorial was all to likely to 'dish up . . . in a way that might make your
organisation sorry that you had ever had any contacts with them.'[24] Some of

20. Cudlipp to England, 22 December 1948, TC 12/2/A.
21. England, 'Some Notes on a Survey of Sexual Morality', 10 December 1948, TC 12/2/A.
22. Cudlipp to England, 22 December 1948, TC 12/2/A.
23. She died suddenly before the articles were published in July 1949.
24. Claude Mullins to England, 14 January 1949, TC 12/2/J; DNB entry on Mullins.

the other assessors also worried that publication in a popular newspaper would add to the difficulty of 'persuading certain people that this piece of research...should be taken seriously', a fear entirely shared by England himself who was 'anxious... to do everything we can to increase the reputation of M-O...as a scientific organisation.'[25]

Initially England calculated that the book, which Allen & Unwin agreed to publish, would overcome any doubts about MO's scientific credentials caused by the tie-up with the *Sunday Pictorial*.[26] Harrisson, back in London since April on his first leave from Sarawak, wrote an enthusiastic preface, seizing the opportunity to lay into his favourite enemies by stressing how much the survey owed to traditional MO methods, presenting 'the actuality, the real life, the personal stuff of the problem...freed from [the] excess of methodological and statistical background' which, he implied, marred Kinsey's work: 'gigantic tables of correlations...[the] superficial and easily misleading validity of the exact percentage...fractional differences and decimal distractions in place of deep meanings and detailed understanding.'[27] England can hardly have been pleased by this Harrissonian provocation, but he also was keen to pursue the qualitative approach, making an unsuccessful attempt in July to persuade the *Sunday Pictorial* to fund further work based on 'a detailed study of two or more areas in which functional penetration and observation could be carried out over as long a period as possible,' perhaps involving following an individual woman 'through her life dealing particularly with such events as her first love affair, marriage, birth, etc'.[28] In the autumn, declining an uninvited offer from the crusader for sexual freedom, Eustace Chesser, to co-author the book, England claimed it was already almost complete and would be published in the spring.[29] Two articles appeared in serious journals over the winter outlining the methodology and findings of the study.[30] But writing the book turned out to be far more difficult than he had anticipated. In April 1950 he told Hume that 'three entire drafts have been prepared and thrown away,' although he still hoped

25. Mace to England, 17 March 1949; England to Mace 18 March 1949, TC 12/2/E.
26. England to Mace, 18 March 1949.
27. Stanley, *Little Kinsey*, 67–8; England to Cudlipp, 8 June 1949: 'This is a preface I propose for the Sex report in final form (eventually)', TC 12/3/A.
28. England to Murtough, 12 July 1949, TC 12/2/A.
29. Chesser to England, 3 October 1949; England to Chesser, 12 October 1949, TC 12/2/J.
30. England, 'An Outline of Sex Attitudes in Britain', *Public Opinion Quarterly*, 13, 4, 1949–1950, 587–600; Len England, 'A British Sex Survey', *International Journal of Sexology*, III, 3, 1950, 148–54.

to have a final version for the assessors to look at in the near future.[31] Ten months later, no further forward, he wrote to them:

> I do not know if you have been wondering whether you were ever going to hear from us again, but our intention of writing a book on our material still exists. We have now produced an entirely different version from the one made last year, and we are no more satisfied with the results than we were with those of the first draft. Despite the fact that we made it quite clear to ourselves and to you at the beginning of this survey that we were only intending to produce a sketch map, we think the results are too flimsy to be anything but rather dangerous... We feel as strongly now as ever that nothing would be more calamitous than to produce a book which is not worthy of us or of the subject, solely because of the sensational possibilities of the material.

By this point he had decided that publication, if it happened at all, should be confined to a 50-page pamphlet 'giving little more than the basic tables on attitudes and habits together with their interpretation.' Although both Allen and Bibby agreed with this suggestion, neither the pamphlet nor the book ever appeared.[32]

In his draft preface, Harrisson had stressed that the study was 'a prelimi-nary reconnaissance of the field', designed less to establish authoritative findings than to open the way for more rigorous exploration if and when somebody came up with the necessary funding. Such things had often been said about previous MO studies, but had not prevented them from being published. Moreover the draft manuscript that survives promised a book as good as any of MO's previous publications. England wrote clearly and economically; unlike Willcock and Ferraby, whose books look wordy and muddled by comparison, and indeed Harrisson himself who was often in sore need of a good editor. England expounded MO's findings, their limita-tions, and complexities without losing himself in speculation. But he seems to have regarded his own text with the same hypercritical eye that is appar-ent in the scathing marginal comments (probably made in 1949 by Michael Lyster) on the report that Willcock had written on 'Mass Gambling'; com-ments which resulted in that book also being withdrawn from publica-tion.[33] Harrisson, no doubt, would have published and been damned. But for the new regime nothing was more important than refuting their

31. England to Hume, 14 April 1950, TC 12/2/C.
32. England to Assessors, nd (February 1951?), TC 12/2/D; Allen to England, 6 March 1951, TC 12/2/F; Bibby to England, 9 March 1951, TC 12/2/E.
33. FR 2560. In March 1949 John Murray had been due to publish the report 'shortly'.

competitors' attempts to sideline MO as 'oddities' and 'charlatans'. What England was up against is clear from Mark Abrams' *Social Survey and Social Action*, published in May 1951, which singled out MO as a bunch of sloppy amateurs incapable of serious scientific work.[34] In the face of such attacks England's commercial caution trumped his creativity, and one of MO's most impressive studies languished unseen in the archive until Liz Stanley rescued it half a century later.[35]

As MO came to rely on market research for its core income other planned books were also abandoned,[36] and the only books actually to appear under the new regime (apart from Willcock's volume on *Juvenile Deliquency*) were two money-spinners aimed at a popular market—*Meet Yourself on Sunday* and *Meet Yourself at the Doctor*—both published in November 1949. Despite being lavishly illustrated with cartoons by Ronald Searle, and the involvement in the writing of a future Booker-prize winning novelist—Ruth Jhabvala, author of *Heat and Dust* and screenwriter for Merchant Ivory's films who, in 1949, was a 22-year-old graduate student of English Literature[37]—neither book sold well enough to justify the effort involved. As one reviewer observed, MO's earnestness got in the way of the 'admirably facetious' tone of Searle's cartoons and 'somehow the facts run away with the fun.'[38]

Harrisson's visit to Britain in 1949 provided the occasion for the establishment of MO as a private limited company, something much discussed but never achieved in the past.[39] England became managing director, and the other board members were Tarrant, Lyster, Brumwell, A. Everett Jones and Ambrose Appelbe. Despite being clear by now about the long-term nature of his commitment to Sarawak, Harrisson had no intention of losing control altogether and had himself appointed as permanent chairman, with Everett Jones chairing in his absence and Appelbe being entrusted with a

---

34. Mark Abrams, *Social Survey and Social Action*, 1951, 105–13.
35. Stanley, *Sex Surveyed, 1949–1994*, 1995.
36. In March 1949 MO was anticipating a book, *The Middle Classes*, to be published by Falcon Press.
37. Ruth Prawer did several other writing jobs for MO in 1949 (MT to DW, nd; MT notes, Personnel/Tarrant).
38. *Birmingham Mail*, 23 November 1949.
39. According to Heimann, Harrisson arrived in London in mid-April and returned to Sarawak in May (*Most Offending Soul*, 267–8). However, the minutes of the first board meeting of MO Ltd place him in London on 10 June, and during the same week the *Sunday Pictorial* gossip columnist went to a party hosted by Harrisson to celebrate the establishment of the new company (*Sunday Pictorial*, 12 June 1949). Heimann (268) is also mistaken in dating the formation of MO Ltd as 21 November 1949.

proxy vote to use on his behalf. Each director held a single share in the company, except Harrisson, who held an additional 4,000 shares.[40]

The formation of the limited company has often been seen as marking MO's final capitulation to commercial pressures, its definitive embrace of market research and abandonment of the original agenda of disinterested social research. But this is to oversimplify the relationship between market and social research. Central to the new regime's strategy since 1947 had been the attempt to promote MO's qualitative research methods and its concern with the wider social context of consumer habits as positive features of the services it could offer in competition with more orthodox market research companies. While the representative sample and the quantitative analysis of questionnaires accounted for 'the vast bulk' of MO's work in the 1950s and 1960s, qualitative methods continued to be employed, including verbatim recording of questionnaire responses and overheard conversation, indirect interviewing, and observation of behaviour.[41] Among the non-commercial clients who commissioned work from MO were Willcock, who subcontracted work on road safety from the Government Social Survey,[42] and Viola Klein and Alva Myrdal for their research on married women's work.[43] Alongside the commercial work the new regime also tried to pursue some of MO's traditional concerns, adding their own 'social' questions into market research surveys, and occasionally finding the resources to undertake uncommissioned surveys of their own. These included work on the 1950 and 1955 general elections in London, and a major study of the 1953 coronation. Mollie Tarrant, who seems to have been much keener on maintaining this aspect of MO's work than England,[44] was the moving spirit behind the coronation study which, she hoped, would bring the organization 'a little nearer our original aim, in which the study of *verbal* behaviour is only one part of the general study of behaviour.'[45] To this end she circulated a detailed memorandum on observational technique among the full-time staff, some of whom 'have had a fair amount of

40. MO Ltd, minutes of the first meeting of directors, 10 June 1949, in Personnel/Tarrant; *World Press News*, 16 June 1949; *Newspaper World*, 18 June 1949.
41. Tarrant, commenting on errors in Philip Ziegler, *Crown and People*, 31 October 1978, in Personnel/Tarrant.
42. Tarrant, 12 October 1985, in Personnel/Tarrant.
43. Alva Myrdal and Viola Klein, *Women's two roles: home and work*, 1968.
44. Tom Punt, 'Mass-Observation. The first seventy years', *The Research Network*, 2007, in Personnel/Punt.
45. Tarrant, 'Coronation', nd (1953?), TC 69/1/A.

observational experience, but have done little recently—and . . . others who have not had the opportunity of doing much work like this at all'.[46] She also wrote to the panel, sadly neglected during the previous two years, asking them to keep diaries ('to check the impact on daily life of the Coronation'), send in cuttings from the local press, record jokes about the event, and respond to a directive modelled on the one sent out in 1937. Teachers were asked to solicit essays from schoolchildren, and anyone witnessing people dressing up as animals, an ox-roasting, 'or any similar "folk" ceremony' was urged to write a full account.[47] All this was very much in the spirit of the original MO coronation study and many of the diarists were happy to re-engage.[48] The book that Tarrant intended to write never appeared, although 20 years later Philip Zeigler made use of the survey in a dull and conventionally obsequious account, quite deaf to the ironical and subversive undertones that a Charles Madge or a Harrisson would have detected in the material.[49] In the meantime, a vivid account of the common carnivalesque characteristics revealed by MO's two coronation studies, drafted by Tarrant, had been published as part of a short-lived revival of MO's social research work led by Harrisson, back in Britain on leave during the summer of 1960.[50]

To document social change and 'unchange' since pre-war days, Harrisson called on old friends to take time out between July and September 1960 to spend time in Bolton and Blackpool, revisiting the streets, churches, pubs, and other public spaces whose life MO had documented in the 1930s. Seduced by the old magic, John Sommerfield, Julian Trevelyan, Michael Wickham, Humphrey Spender, Woodrow Wyatt, Celia Fremlin,

46. Tarrant, 'Coronation Day Observations', nd (1953?), TC 69/1/A.
47. Draft letter to Panel, March 1953; Directive and letter to Panel, May 1953, TC 69/1/B; 'Coronation: what we are doing or have done', 12 May 1953, TC 69/1/A. The 1937 Hindu complaint about ox roasting was echoed in 1953 by a vegetarian's letter to a local newspaper (Harrisson, *Britain Revisited*, 233).
48. Including four of those represented in Hinton, *Nine Wartime Lives*: Gertrude Glover (irritated by the militarism of the procession, but pleased to have persuaded her fellow school managers—'left-wing people (miners)'—to issue bibles instead of coronation mugs to the children); Nella Last (thrilled, and surprised that even her reclusive husband kept the radio on all day; but only momentarily distracted from her depressing fate: 'I often feel of late I'm a goldfish in a bowl—never "achieving" anything in my round of days. The bowl a little wall that shuts out every outside interest or dims and distorts . . .'); Ernest van Someren (delighted when his son spotted an Eton school friend among the page boys in the Abbey, and sufficiently reconciled to the status quo to 'toast the Queen's health, formally, in white wine from South Africa; another thing we have never done before'); and Lillian Rogers, now a widow and working as a clerk.
49. Philip Ziegler, *Crown and People*, 1978.
50. Harrisson, *Britain Revisited*, Chapter 14.

and Bill Naughton, all responded to the call. The result was an impressionistic book, *Britain Revisited*, stressing continuity as much as change, padded out with material from Harrisson's unpublished 1939 analysis of 'the non-voters' who were still neglected in British election studies ('the best examination I know of this very important field,' remarked Raymond Williams[51]); Tarrant's chapter on royalty; and an enthusiastic account of a recent MO study, commissioned by tobacco companies, designed to call into question the assumption that the statistical link between smoking and lung cancer was also a causative link. Hans Eysenck, who supervised this study, used it to argue that it was personality (extrovert versus introvert) rather than the physical effects of smoking as such that underlay the link: another clear demonstration, Harrisson proclaimed rather too confidently, of the superiority of qualitative research over mere number crunching.[52]

It is unclear whether, at this stage, Harrisson saw *Britain Revisited* as the beginning of a new active engagement with MO, or simply as a way of doing something amusing with old friends during his summer leave. He concluded the book, in prose execrable even by his own lax standards, explaining that, despite the predominance of market research since the late 1940s,

> we have [not] neglected non-commercial and long-term interests, though they have been kept up in a seldom (after 1950) published way; this book further indicates that facet—and we hope to continue in the 'public' sphere with further activity to come.... cheerfully ... visualis[ing] a welding of the best of the past with the best of present, in our own particular—and, by now you may be entitled to say, peculiar—way.[53]

It is easy to imagine the fury with which England must have read these words, potentially so damaging to his efforts to establish that there was nothing 'peculiar' about MO. The old enemy, Abrams, seized on the publication of *Britain Revisited* to deliver another forensic attack: 'snatches of quasi-relevant statistics ... pages of verbatim quotations from barely articulate morons ... "plugs" for the author and all his friends ... hints of caches of raw material waiting to be used'.[54] It must have been a relief to England when Harrisson left for Sarawak in October 1960, accepting—as he put it in a

51. *Tribune*, 21 April 1961.
52. Harrisson, *Britain Revisited*, 202–3; H. J. Eysenck, Mollie Tarrant, Myra Woolf and L. England, 'Smoking and Personality', *British Medical Journal*, 14 May 1960, 1, 1456–60.
53. Harrisson, *Britain Revisited*, 268.
54. *The Financial Times*, 27 March 1961.

playful comment on the fact that only 1 per cent of those interviewed had heard of 'Tom Harrisson'—that 'it is nicer to be a forgotten man of the thirties, overtaken by time, and live quietly in Borneo, than bustling in Blackpool or Bloomsbury'.[55]

In reality, of course, Harrisson could not live without 'bustling'. His life and work in Sarawak provided sufficient bustle to keep him off England's back for the next few years,[56] and when he was compulsorily retired on his 55th birthday in 1966, he initially arranged to continue his work there from an academic base in the Anthropology department at Cornell University. These plans were undermined, however, when his many enemies in Sarawak, now part of newly independent Malaysia, succeeded in having him refused a visa to return.[57] At the same time two young research students working on Britain during the Second World War, Paul Addison and Angus Calder, were looking for a home for the MO Archive which Addison had discovered 'all higgledy-piggledy under layers of dust' in the basement of MO's South Kensington headquarters. Addison's Oxford college, Nuffield, snootily declined to house the papers—'dodgy stuff', he was told, 'amateurish and unscientific'—but Calder's supervisor, the historian and vice-chancellor of Sussex University, Asa Briggs, immediately understood the value of the material.[58]

During 1969 a deal was struck under which Harrisson, who owned the pre-1950 MO material, agreed to bequeath it to Sussex, in return for the university providing accommodation and supporting a bid for a three-year grant from Leverhulme, which enabled him to employ a series of assistants to start sorting and cataloguing the archive.[59] Harrisson became a member of the university as a research fellow and eventually, in 1974, a professor. Although both positions were honorary, they gave him the seal of academic approval he had always craved, and he could afford the luxury of working for nothing because, as his biographer explains in some detail, his third wife, like his first one, could afford to pay his bills.[60] Writing to a disapproving Mary Adams he sought to excuse the brutal dumping of his second wife (who did not have a private income) on the grounds that:

55. Harrisson, *Britain Revisited*, 266.
56. Everett Jones to Harrisson, 28 January 1965, MOA 29/2/6.
57. Heimann, *Most Offending Soul*, 350–1, 361–2.
58. Heimann, *Most Offending Soul*, 367–8, Paul Addison, 'Angus Calder', *History Workshop Journal*, 70, 2010, 300–1.
59. Heimann, *Most Offending Soul*, 367–8; *The Times*, 24 April 1970.
60. Heimann, *Most Offending Soul*, 368–73.

'I felt life was slipping away and that before I die I must take one more cruel chance to see if... I cannot somehow achieve that youthful promise of semi-genius'. Maybe there was still time to crystallize his polymath interests, 'to bridge, in a fresh way, that old savage civilisational gulf... linking... prehistory... to the Renaissance, Iron technology, Magellan, Niah Caves, Worktown 1971, etc'.[61]

Five years later, in January 1976, Harrisson and his new wife were both killed in a road accident in Thailand. During those five years Harrisson produced no magnum opus to bridge the savage-civilization gulf, but he did establish the archive, formally opened in October 1975, on a secure basis and he was able finally to deliver on the wartime promise to use the MO material to 'tell the truth' about the home front. *Living Through the Blitz*—'the hardest job I ever tackled'[62]—was written with help from Willcock, Fremlin, Nina Masel (now the *Daily Worker* film critic, Nina Hibbin) and Marion Sullivan, and published posthumously in 1976. It remains the best single book on the blitz, documenting popular resilience under fire while exposing the 'massive... cover-up of the more disagreeable facts of 1940–41' embodied both in wartime propaganda and in nostalgic post-war memory: 'a form of intellectual pollution: but pollution by perfume.'[63] Harrisson's view of the dismal ineptness of local leadership in many of the blitzed cities remained unrevised, but his wartime warnings of the fragility of morale were replaced by a powerful argument—informed as much by the experience of allied bombing of Germany and subsequent American behaviour in Vietnam as by the blitz itself—that air power alone was never likely to destroy popular morale. Fremlin, who saw the book through its final stages after Harrisson's death, had urged him to abandon this polemic, feeling that it detracted from the authenticity of the book's account of MO's wartime findings, imposing on the material a 'burden of definitive certainty' which it could not sustain.[64] But, as always, Harrisson's writing was driven by his need to engage with contemporary controversy, and the more neutral mode favoured by Fremlin would have to await later compliers of MO material.

61. Cited in Heimann, *Most Offending Soul*, 374.
62. Harrisson to Rolph, 3 November 1975, Personnel 8/7.
63. Harrisson, *Living Through the Blitz*, 16.
64. Fremlin to Harrisson, 4 May 1973, Personnel/Fremlin; Fremlin, interviewed by Stanley, 18 September 1981.

Harrisson remained a political animal, and his ambitions for MO in the 1970s went beyond his work with the archive. During the 1950s and 1960s Mass-Observation Ltd, despite establishing itself as a recognized player in the market research industry—England had been elected chair of the Market Research Society in 1961[65]—never found it easy to balance the books.[66] By the late 1960s the business was in deep financial trouble, and the company was reconstituted in November 1970 as M-O (UK) Ltd in a manoeuvre that appears to have been designed not only to write off debt but also to consolidate Harrisson's continuing influence as the largest shareholder in the new company.[67] There was a good deal of bitterness, and England left to set up his own company, taking with him some other leading staff and a number of clients,[68] and predicting (as it turned out, correctly) that the new management would be less concerned than he himself had been to retain 'any of the spirit of the original Mass-Observation'.[69] At the same time, however, he assured Harrisson of his continuing personal interest 'in your reported efforts to revive . . . the original concept': a reference, no doubt, to a *Times* report a couple of weeks earlier that 'there is a sneaking suspicion among Tom Harrisson's friends that he is considering reviving Mass-Observation as well as putting its archives in order.'[70] The suspicion was well founded.

In 1970 Harrisson had written to George Hutchinson, his right-hand man during the Blitztown investigations, explaining that alongside developing the archive 'as a unique source for social history . . . I am thinking of re-entering the research field, with special reference to politics.'[71] Encouraged by Briggs to explore possibilities for a 'Contemporary Social Archive', he considered contacting the war diarists and reconstituting the panel. At the same time he was 'experimenting with new field-work',

---

65. McDonald and King, *Sampling the Universe,* 1996, 45. He was later to be one of only four individuals to have been awarded a gold medal by the Market Research Society by the mid-1990s for their 'contributions to the theory and practice of market research', alongside Abrams. Another of the medallists, Elizabeth Nelson, had also worked for MO in the 1960s.
66. Everett Jones to Harrisson, 28 January 1965, MOA29/2/6; Tarrant comment on *Speak for Yourselves,* 12 October 1985, Personnel/Tarrant.
67. *The Times,* 27 November 1970; Parfitt to Harrisson, 28 September 1973, MOA 29/2/6; Appelbe to Harrisson, 30 June; Everett Jones to Harrisson, 25 June and 2 July 1971; Hale memo, 29 July 1971, all in Personnel 8/1.
68. Novy to Harrisson, 22 October 1975, MOA 29/2/3/4: TH papers 1970–6 Box 5. Mollie Tarrant had left to set up on her own in the mid-1960s.
69. England to Harrisson, 4 July 1971, MOA 29/2/6.
70. *The Times,* 1 April and 21 May 1971.
71. Harrisson to Hutchinson, 8 July 1970, Personnel/Hutchinson.

taking a unit to observe a by-election in Bromsgrove, and, with help from a couple of graduate students, 'testing revised observer method... studying pebble-throwing on the beach, the speed of blind beer drinkers,' and differences in appearance between university and polytechnic students.[72] Never missing an opportunity to polemicize against the superficiality of orthodox opinion polls,[73] he urged Hutchinson—now a journalist with excellent connections with the Conservative Party hierarchy[74]—to use his influence to persuade the Party to commission opinion research using MO methods. Four years later, a month after the collapse of the Heath Government, Harrisson was still pressing the case for

> at least one big initial experiment with new methods to see what we can come up with over, say, the next year... It is now becoming clear... that the [quantitative] methods which won out [after the war]... are not delivering the goods satisfactorily, and that what we and others tried to do in the 30s was clearly valid and should not have been discontinued.

As in the later 1940s he was happy to work for the Conservative Party, provided that his results would not be 'exclusive and secretive over any long period of time. This is the basis for our non-profit stance, and this is how to make ourselves known and powerful in a new way in this area of concern.'[75]

By October 1975, having got nowhere via Hutchinson, Harrisson was in discussion with Henry Novy, now a wealthy management consultant and a close friend of Angus Maude, the Conservative Party deputy chairman responsible for research, 'to sell to the Tories some electoral attitude research on the broadest possible basis.' Novy spelt this out as a survey of the evolution of popular attitudes to politics which would put together contemporary work to be undertaken by M-O (UK) Ltd with material from the archive. The prospects for this initiative did not look good, if only because John Parfitt, the managing director of M-O (UK) Ltd, was viscerally hostile to Harrisson and, even more than his predecessor, England, saw any public association between his organization and the original MO as commercially

72. Harrisson to Madge, 20 May 1971, Personnel/Madge.
73. e.g. *The Times*, 20 January and 21 May 1971.
74. In 1963 Hutchinson became Chief Publicity Officer for Conservative Central Office, leaving after the 1964 election to become Managing Director of *The Spectator* (Lord Windlesham, 'The Communication of Conservative Policy, 1963–64', *Political Quarterly*, 36, 2, 172). In 1970 he published a biography of Edward Heath.
75. Memo from Harrisson to Novy and Hutchinson, 26 March 1974, MOA 29/2/3/4.

counterproductive.[76] Harrisson's 1970s overtures to the Tory Party were probably doomed, but they do make it clear that right up to his untimely death he was looking for ways to re-launch the MO project, convinced that the qualitative methods of opinion research pioneered by MO in the 1930s would be no less relevant in the era of Edward Heath and Harold Wilson.

76. Novy to Harrisson, 22 October 1975, MOA 29/2/3/4.

16

Conclusion

I

From 1937 until the late 1940s Mass-Observation (MO) operated as an independent social research organization, financed by whoever could be persuaded to pay: wealthy benefactors, publishers, government departments, advertising agencies, newspapers, etc. Despite repeated attempts, Tom Harrisson never succeeded in attracting stable, long-term funding from one of the major research institutes. Nevertheless, with a succession of books analysing aspects of contemporary life, and a regular presence in the newspaper and periodical press, MO was able to make a significant contribution to the ways in which the British understood themselves in a tumultuous period of their history.

In its early years MO was really two organizations. While both Harrisson and Charles Madge set out to establish 'an anthropology of ourselves', their ideas about how this could be achieved were radically different. Moreover the ethos and social origins of Harrisson's initial Bolton team could hardly have been more different from the metropolitan intellectuals grouped around Madge in Blackheath. Madge's revolutionary and surrealist excitement gave birth to the national panel. But, unable to find any coherent use for the material sent in by MO's volunteers, Madge eventually abandoned his pursuit of 'popular poetry' for a rather more down-to-earth research project in Bolton, opening the door to the academic funding which allowed him to go his own way in 1940. Meanwhile, Harrisson, setting up in London after his two-year expedition to the North, had shifted the mainstream of MO's work away from anthropological immersion in a particular local culture towards an investigation of the influences determining popular opinion. In the study of opinion formation the panel became a vital resource, giving Harrisson the access to 'private' opinion which underpinned his insistence that popular morale was more fragile and changeable than public protestations of national unity in face of Hitler would suggest. The investigation of popular morale remained at the forefront of MO's work throughout the war, the focus shifting from the danger of a sudden collapse in the early years, via attitudes to war production, to a wider diagnosis of the state of the culture and its capacity to meet the demands of post-war reconstruction.

The nature of MO as an organization shifted significantly during the war. Harrisson's management of the Bolton operation had been entirely informal and autocratic, as was Madge's. In London, confronted by a larger, younger, and better educated group of full-timers, Harrisson held regular staff meetings, formalized his contractual relationship with the staff, and devolved some of the day-to-day management onto a small team of trusted subordinates. Conscription removed most of the men and, from the end of 1941, the younger women too, leaving MO's fieldwork largely in the hands of older women, supplemented by very young men awaiting call-up. Following his own conscription in July 1942 Harrisson had no option but to hand over day-to-day control to the management team, who formalized their authority in what was in effect, though not in name, an executive committee. But Harrisson retained the strategic direction of MO until he was sent overseas in July 1944, and it was only then that his deputy, Bob Willcock, took full responsibility for the organization.

II

The main purpose of this book has been to provide a rounded description of MO as an organization: the aims, methods, and attitudes of its leaders and workers; the internal routines, external sources of support, and relationships with other organizations. But MO was always something more than the sum of these things. Because so much of its work depended on the panel of volunteers, MO's significance is also to be found in the uses to which it was put by members of the panel. For a few of the observers MO was one aspect of a wider active engagement in left-wing politics, but for many more writing for MO offered the satisfaction of contributing to the creation of a more democratic and scientifically minded society, while allowing them to stand back from commitment to the dogmas or the disciplines involved in active membership of a political party. Several historians, seeking to capture this aspect of MO, have seen it as a kind of 'social movement', while acknowledging that this is a problematic concept to apply to an organization which never mobilized more than 1,000 people at any one time, and whose members operated in isolation and with no direct contact with one another.[1] But what the 'movement' characterization of MO registers is that the specific social research aims of the organization appeared to many of its members to fit neatly with the broader currents of anti-fascist and progressive politics represented by the Left Book Club, Penguin Books, *Picture Post*, and the wartime anti-Blimp patriotic radicalism evoked most powerfully in Orwell's 1941 polemic, *The Lion and the Unicorn*. Orwell saw the roots of this radicalism in the emergence of a new social stratum cutting across established class distinctions:

> the people who are most at home in and most definitely *of* the modern world, the technicians and the higher-paid skilled workers, the airmen and their mechanics, the radio experts, film producers, popular journalists and industrial chemists. They are the indeterminate stratum at which the older class distinctions are beginning to break down.[2]

For Tom Jeffery, working with a critique of pre-war and wartime populist radicalism developed in the 1960s by Stuart Hall and the Birmingham Centre for Contemporary Cultural Studies, the left-wing sympathies of most of the mass observers were to be understood as part of the self-assertion of a lower middle class newly radicalized by the catastrophic events of the 1930s. This was a leftism that, because it rallied behind the banner of national unity in face of fascism rather than all-out class struggle against capitalism, was, like MO itself, all too easily co-opted into a reformist politics which, as Orwell himself was to conclude before the end of the war, left the power of established elites largely untouched.[3] The popular frontist attempt to crystallize an oppositional national unity had a special appeal to middle-class radicals who saw themselves as more efficient than the Blimpish elites, and more progressive and constructive than an organized working class entrenched in negative defensive trade union structures.

1. See especially Penny Summerfield, 'Mass-Observation: Social Research or Social Movement?', *Journal of Contemporary History*, 20, 1985, 439–52.
2. George Orwell, *The Lion and the Unicorn. Socialism and the English Genius*, 1982, 69.
3. Jeffery, *Mass-Observation—A Short History*, 1978, 45; Stuart Hall, 'The Social Eye of *Picture Post*', *Working Papers in Cultural Studies*, 2, Centre for Contemporary Cultural Studies, University of Birmingham, 1972; George Orwell, 'London Letter', *Partisan Review*, December 1944, in Sonia Orwell and Ian Angus, *The Collected Essays, Journalism and Letters of George Orwell*, vol 3, 1970, 335–6.

For Jeffery, and those who followed his approach,[4] this characteriza-tion of the volunteers seemed to make sense of MO's post-war decline. As the popular front mentality disintegrated in the face of a backlash against what was seen as the Attlee Government's fostering of working-class interests at the expense of a middle class whose living standards had declined since the 1930s, the kind of people who had been attracted to MO's democratic and scientific agenda before the war tended to abandon left-wing and progressive politics. According to the opinion polls the proportion of middle-class people intending to vote Labour fell from a high-point of 40 per cent in January 1946 to less than 20 per cent four years later.[5] While there is no doubting the middle-class back-lash, the equation between this and MO's decline is problematic. As we have seen, the MO panel, in decline since the mid-war years, was suc-cessfully reinvigorated after the war. More than twice as many readers of the *New Statesman* responded to an MO appeal for new observers in the early months of 1947 than had done so in response to the original appeal in 1937.[6] Despite the disintegration of the popular front politics within which MO had originated, the panel was alive and well in the later 1940s. Indeed its effective membership was larger than ever before.[7] MO had certainly served as a means of expression for middle-class radi-calism in the 1930s, but Mike Savage's analysis of directive responses in the later 1940s suggests that it was equally attractive to middle-class people in full retreat from progressive views and deeply worried by what they saw as the swamping of their privilege—and with it, some of them felt, civilization itself—by the combination of working-class advance and state expansion.[8] The reason that the panel declined in the early 1950s was that MO's organizers were no longer making use of it, not that there were fewer people willing to involve themselves in such an exercise.

---

4. Summerfield, 'Social Research or Social Movement?' and see Hubble, *Mass-Observation and Everyday Life*, 215: 'It was the social change that turned the new middle class from an emergent force in the late 1930s into an oppositional fraction in the late 1940s which ultimately did for M-O.'
5. James Hinton, 'Women and the Labour Vote', *Labour History Review*, 57, 3, 1992, 64.
6. '*New Statesman* Panel Composition, 1937–47', FR 2479, 1947.
7. See Chapter 14, note 70.
8. Mike Savage, *Identities and Social Change in Britain since 1940. The Politics of Method*, 2010, 73ff.

III

MO's evolution into a market research organization had more to do with the departure of the only man with the skills and connections necessary to raise money for the organization to undertake social research than it did with any deep-seated cultural shift. In the early 1950s the work of the Institute of Community Studies—originating from a very MO-like belief that politicians and administrators were devising social policy with little understanding of the actual needs and aspirations of working-class people— was to demonstrate that it was possible to conduct serious sociological research outside the academy. It also showed that MO was far from being alone in its advocacy of qualitative as against quantitative approaches to research. Willmott and Young's *Family and Kinship in East London* rapidly established itself as a sociological classic, despite academic disapproval of its suspiciously journalistic dependence on vivid quotation from informal interviews and its deliberate avoidance of the strategies by which contemporary academic sociologists were endeavouring to establish the scientific nature of their discipline: the specialized language of engagement with grand theory and the sophisticated statistical manipulation of quantitative data. Peter Townsend's Harrissonian assault on the 'absurd mathematics of the survey exponents' can only have served to confirm the quantifiers' view of the Institute as closer to journalism than to genuine social science.[9] But even within the academy the quantifiers were far from having it all their own way. Despite MO's losing battle in the field of market research, qualitative approaches remained dominant in British sociology as it emerged in the post-war years: it was not until the 1960s that the representative national sample survey became, briefly, the gold standard of sociological method. Among the many local ethnographic studies being produced by university sociologists during the 1950s, Margaret Stacey's path-breaking study of Banbury was, like Harrisson's work in Bolton, partly inspired by the Lynd's *Middletown* attempt to document the life of 'ordinary' people; as distinct from the pathological, 'social problem' agenda of much academic sociology.

---

9. Significantly, Madge, by then a professor of sociology at Birmingham, was to succeed Richard Titmuss as chair of the Institute's trustees. Peter Willmott, 'The Institute of Community Studies', in M. Bulmer (ed.), *Essays on the History of British Sociological Research*, 1985; Halsey, *History of Sociology*, 110; Savage, *Identities and Social Change*, 166, 178–9, 210.

And Stacey was as militant as MO had been in resisting the quantifiers' claims for the national representative sample as the only reliable route to sociological knowledge.[10]

This is not to argue that MO could have produced work of the quality of *Family and Kinship* or Stacey's *Tradition and Change*. Harrisson's restless and undisciplined imagination could never have alighted on one topic or approach for a sufficient length of time to produce a sociological classic. Addicted to the premature publication which was endemic to his method of work, Harrisson lacked the patience to work to rigorous academic standards. In 1941, complaining that 'University Scientists' misjudged MO when they dismissed it as 'an amateurish effort not worthy of serious consideration', John Ferraby had claimed that

> we have by our refusal to be tied by existing methods, and often by existing prejudices, achieved a technique which, although still immaturely developed, has within it the germs of several ideas of the greatest value to sociological science.[11]

The claim was not unreasonable. But under-developed 'germs' were all that MO's methods were ever likely to deliver. Even if his dream of securing long-term research funding for the organization had been realized, it is difficult to imagine Harrisson settling down to the patient work of producing a scholarly text. And it was to be several decades before any academic social scientist was to show an interest in developing techniques pioneered by MO.

IV

Historians treating MO as a social movement have tended to exaggerate the degree to which the panel represented a particular section of the middle class. Because he was primarily interested in exploring the history of the lower middle class, Jeffery's pioneering history gave the impression that most of MO's volunteers belonged to this stratum.[12] As we have seen, however,

---

10. Margaret Stacey, *Tradition and change: a study of Banbury,* 1960; Savage, *Identities and Social Change,* 151–3, 163.
11. Ferraby, 'Sociology in Great Britain', 22 January 1941, FR 550; Ferraby, 'Mass-Observation methods', 20 February 1943, 2, FR 1597.
12. Jeffery, *Mass-Observation—A Short History,* 1978, 28–30.

only a quarter of MO's 1939 respondents saw themselves as belonging to the *lower* middle class, while well over half claimed a higher social status. Similar problems arise with attempts to equate the volunteers with Orwell's picture of a new technologically minded stratum. Analysis of the June 1939 directive replies on 'the class complex' makes it clear that a significant proportion of panellists were anxious to distinguish themselves not only from the workers and the established elites but also from the general run of suburban middle-class people among whom they found themselves living. Mike Savage, taking his cue from Orwell and Nick Hubble, has seen these claims to distinction as symptomatic of the emergence of a new kind of middle-class identity, 'which creatively sought to use Mass-Observation to distance itself from gentlemanly, artistic, highbrow motifs in favour of a more "technical", scientific intellectual vision.'[13] Savage places the mass observers in the context of a broader argument about the emergence of a new technically minded middle class, a development which he associates with the post-war advance of the social sciences at the expense of arts and humanities, disciplines shaped by the 'gentlemanly' culture of the established intelligentsia.[14] Whatever the merits of this larger argument, the presumed opposition between science and culture is far from apparent among the pre-war mass observers. In fact most of those individuals cited by Savage as exemplars of the new scientific mentality turn out, on further examination, to have invested a significant part of their claims to distinction in their appreciation of literature and the arts. They saw no contradiction between their commitment to social science as mass observers and their love of high culture, both serving equally to distinguish them from their philistine neighbours.[15]

What is apparent is that, despite MO's democratic rhetoric of enabling ordinary people to speak for themselves, many of the panel members did not think of themselves as 'ordinary'. They tended to see themselves as unusual people, distinguished by their desire to self-fashion their lives free from the conventions of their social milieu. Their claims to distinction were as likely to rest on an unusual engagement with high culture as with science

13. Mike Savage, 'Affluence and Social Change in the Making of Technocratic Middle-Class Identities: Britain, 1939–55', *Contemporary British History*, 22, 4, 2008.
14. Savage, *Identities and Social Change, passim.*
15. The evidence for this is presented in my review of Savage's book in *History Workshop Journal*, 75, Spring 2013.

and technology (and in some cases on a combination of the two); but what above all characterized them was their willingness to devote time and effort to the self-reflection required to respond honestly to MO's probing directives. It is in this regular practice of self-reflection, rather than in any preference for technical or scientific as against humanistic cultural modes, that the mass observers can be seen as symptomatic of broader processes of social change.

The anthropologist Raymond Firth concluded his 1939 critique of MO with the patronizing thought that, despite its limitations as a form of social science, 'it has still a value in providing a recreative outlet for its thousand or so Observers, and enabling them to learn something about the behaviour of others than themselves.'[16] That was spectacularly to miss the point. While many observers might, modestly, have agreed with Firth's assessment, in a longer perspective it is clear that the value of MO to the observers lay primarily in what they learned about themselves rather than about others, and that far from being a trivial hobby, their practice of self-observation was symptomatic of an increasingly individualistic culture in which reflexivity and active self-fashioning were believed to be displacing older sources of selfhood embedded in kinship, neighbourhood, class, and other forms of collective identity. While the disembedded self-fashioner may be an illusory construct of some late 20th-century theorizing, the aspirations that this theorizing registered were real enough.[17] When he revived the MO panel in 1981 the anthropologist David Pocock was primarily interested in using the observers to gather factual data about everyday life. But Dorothy Sheridan, who worked with him and took over responsibility for the project after his retirement in 1990, came to understand the enterprise as part of a broader movement towards greater reflexivity: 'writing ourselves' for MO providing one means, alongside oral history, feminist consciousness raising, or, later, the blogosphere, by which individuals could tell their own stories, and by so doing assert their agency in the face of received cultural norms.[18] The sociological significance of

16. Firth, 'An Anthropologist's View of Mass-Observation', *Sociological Review*, 31, 2, 1939, 193.
17. For contrasting accounts see Anthony Giddens, *Modernity and Self-identity: Self and Society in the Late Modern Age*, 1992 and Lynn Jamieson, *Intimacy. Personal Relationships in Modern Societies*, Cambridge, 1998.
18. Dorothy Sheridan, 'Writing to the Archive: M-O as Autobiography', *Sociology*, 27, 1, 1993, 27–40; Dorothy Sheridan, Brian Street, David Bloome, *Writing Ourselves. Mass-Observation and Literary Practices*, 2000; D. Sheridan, *'Damned Anecdotes & Dangerous Confabulations. MO as Life History*, MO Archive Occasional Paper, 1996.

the MO Project—which, especially between the mid-1980s and early 1990s, attracted similar numbers of respondents as the original MO panel—has yet to be adequately investigated. But, as with the earlier phase, it probably makes more sense to associate it with the growth of a more self-reflexive regime of (predominantly middle-class) identity, than with the technically minded, anti-Blimp middle class so seductively evoked by Orwell, which—as the evidence of MO's own panel responses in the later 1940s suggests—was a short-lived reflection of a popular front politics which disintegrated after 1945.

By fostering self-observation and life-writing, MO opened up to scientific enquiry aspects of subjectivity and everyday life that were only to emerge into the academic mainstream half a century later. However clumsy Madge's early efforts to handle the panel material, he was right to see that their scientific potential lay primarily in what they revealed about the subjectivity of the panellists.[19] In the intellectual climate of the late 1930s and 1940s the subjectivity of the panel's responses was a source of embarrassment for MO: by the 1980s and 1990s feminism, cultural studies, oral history, the cultural turn in anthropology, and the post-modernist attack on positivism in the social sciences combined to revalue the subjectivity of such sources as a gateway to understanding, rather than an obstacle to be overcome. It was precisely the uniqueness and complexity of the individual life stories revealed in autobiographical writing, oral history, and in-depth interviewing that enabled the investigator to identify the gaps and misunderstandings embedded in received social theory and open the way to more adequate conceptualizations.[20] The re-launch of the MO panel and the rediscovery of the archive were themselves significant moments in this re-evaluation of individual life history.

V

Much of existing writing about MO focuses on the pre-war years, and tells it as a story of decline. An aura of failure hangs over the received narrative: a slide

19. CM to TH, 21 January 1940, 5, Org&Hist 1.
20. The literature is extensive, across many disciplines. Key texts include Ken Plummer, *Documents of Life. An Introduction to the Problems and Literature of a Humanistic Method,* 1983; the essays collected in Prue Chamberlayne, Joanna Bornat, and Tom Wengraf (eds), *The Turn to Biographical Methods in the Social Sciences,* 2000; and Carol Smart, *Personal Life. New Directions in Sociological Thinking,* 2007.

from whatever utopian aims there were in the late 1930s towards mere market research by the 1950s. At its crudest this story presents MO as an organization whose original revolutionary ambitions were fatally compromised by the loss of independence involved in taking money from government and advertising agencies. It is true that ideas which could be described as revolutionary played a role in MO's early years: notably Madge's poetic exaltation, spun from a heady mixture of communism and surrealism, or the leftism of most of MO's fieldworkers between 1939 and 1941. But Madge rapidly moved to a sober empiricism; and the anti-war Communist fieldworkers were no less willing than their pro-war Liberal chief to accept funding from the wartime state on the grounds that this enabled them to do work of lasting value. Given his commanding role in the organization, the intentions that counted most were Harrisson's, and—as we have seen—these were never revolutionary. He wanted to bridge a gulf, to enlighten the elites about the attitudes of the masses, to usher in, not revolution, but more effective liberal democracy. Working for the Ministry of Information gave him an opportunity to push in this direction and while far from immune to the seductions of proximity to power, he did not hesitate to tell his paymasters what he took to be the truth about popular mentalities, even when this got him into hot water. Nor can his subsequent cooperation with progressive advertising men be understood as a sell-out of some earlier anti-capitalist stance. Marcus Brumwell and A. Everett Jones were of a similar cast of mind to Harrisson, and their funding gave him the freedom to continue to accumulate the material that would ultimately provide the central justification for MO's wartime role.

It was neither the end of the war nor the election of a Labour Government that put an end to the original MO. When Harrisson returned for nine months during 1946–7 he was able to re-energize the organization and find new sources of funding. We can only speculate about how far, had he per-severed, he would have been able to move towards his goal of putting 'the whole unit on a firm financial and scientific basis'.[21] As it was, his decision to return to Borneo, quickly followed by Willcock's nervous breakdown, left the organization in the hands of a generation of full-timers whose priorities lay elsewhere. The establishment of Mass-Observation Ltd in 1949 registered the shift from a social research organization funding itself oppor-tunistically with market research to a market research organization

21. TH to Chapman, 15 December 1946, Org&Hist 1/8.

undertaking some social research on the side. Even this, however, does not have to be told as a story of failure. As an organization engaged predominantly in conventional market research, MO Ltd continued to preach and practice qualitative approaches which were eventually to be recognized by its commercial rivals as having a significant contribution to make to the development of market research methods.[22]

Much more important, however, was the eventual re-evaluation of the MO approach by the academy. For all the charlatan in Harrisson's make-up, his genius lay in an ill-disciplined but marvellously fruitful sociological imagination; an imagination that pushed his small team of workers into what they always understood as being preliminary (and desperately under-resourced) investigations of issues with which the academy was only to engage as cash and talent poured into social research during the second half of the 20th century. The archive accumulated by MO was prophetically attuned to approaches that future academics—responding to theoretical and methodological issues which only emerged into intellectual life decades later—were to bring to the study of the social history of mid-20th century Britain. Sociologists, anxious to establish the scientific credentials of their work, were generally unwilling to acknowledge the pioneering role played by this ramshackle bunch of amateurs. 'A wild gypsy crusade... operating in the half-world of journalism and politics' was how Edward Shils, a dominating figure in the post-war development of academic sociology in Britain, chose in the mid-1980s to dismiss MO.[23] Historians, more assured, or perhaps more complacent, about the value of their discipline, could afford to be more generous. Shifts in the intellectual climate from the late 20th century opened up for both historians and social scientists lines of enquiry capable of exploiting to the full the kind of material accumulated by MO. This is just what Harrisson, Madge, the MO staff, the volunteer diarists, and panel respondents had always intended: to provide future historians with the means to go beyond conventional sources generated by the operations of power, and, in so doing, to deliver a democratic people's history from below. Hopefully this book, by providing a detailed account of the generation of the archive, will be useful in helping historians and social scientists to fulfill the hopes vested in them by the original mass observers.

22. For a persuasive account of MO on these lines see Joe Moran, 'Mass-Observation, Market Research, and the Birth of the Focus Group, 1937–1997', *Journal of British Studies*, 47, 2008.
23. Edward Shils, 'On the eve: a prospect in retrospect', in M. Bulmer (ed.), *Essays on the History of British Sociological Research*, Cambridge, 1985, 166.

Bibliography

I. ARCHIVES

Mass-Observation, University of Sussex Special Collections
Day Surveys
Directive Replies
File Reports
Former Personnel
MO and MOI
Organisation and History (Org&Hist)
Press Cuttings
Tom Harrisson papers 1970–6
Topic Collections
Worktown

Other Papers in University of Sussex Special Collections
Charles Madge papers
Henry Novy papers
Mary Adams papers

Modern Records Centre, University of Warwick
Trades Union Congress
Bevin papers

National Archives
ADM 223/476
CAB 65
CAB 66
CAB 68
FO 371/40839
HO 199/442
HO 207/1026
INF 1/101
INF 1/250
INF 1/255
INF 1/261

INF 1/262
INF 1/263
INF 1/286
INF 1/290
INF 1/291
INF 1/331
INF 1/341
INF 1/533
INF 1/697
INF 1/711
MEPO 2/4928
MEPO 3/2357
PREM 3/345/6

Tate Britain Archive
Brumwell papers
Graham Bell papers

British Library of Economic and Political Science
Bronislaw Malinowski papers
Raymond Firth papers

Other Archives
1944 Association papers, Labour Party Archive, Manchester
Bolton Unemployed Welfare Association, Bolton Archives
Ethical Union, Bishopsgate Institute, London
Nicholas Kaldor papers, King's College, Cambridge
Trevelyan papers, Trinity College, Cambridge
Women's Publicity Planning Association, Women's Library, London

2. STATE PAPERS

Hansard
Report of the Committee on the Provision for Social and Economic Research, July
    1946, Cmd 6868

3. MO BOOKS (IN CHRONOLOGICAL ORDER)

Mass-Observation, Frederick Muller, London, 1937
May the Twelfth: Mass Observation Day-Surveys 1937 by over two hundred observers, Faber,
    London, 1937
First Year's Work, 1937–38, Lindsay Drummond, London, 1938
Britain by Mass-Observation, Penguin, Harmondsworth, 1939
War Begins at Home, Chatto and Windus, London, 1940

Clothes and Clothes Rationing, Change, Bulletin of the Advertising Service Guild, 1, 1941

Home Propaganda, Change, Bulletin of the Advertising Service Guild, 2, 1941

An Enquiry into British War Production, John Murray, London, 1942

People in Production, Penguin Books, Harmondsworth, 1942

War Factory, Gollancz, London, 1943 (2nd ed., The Cresset Library, London, 1987)

The Pub and the People: A Worktown Study, Gollancz, London, 1943

An Enquiry into People's Homes, John Murray, London, 1943

The Journey Home, John Murray, London, 1944

Britain and her Birth-rate, John Murray, London, 1945

Puzzled People: A Study in Popular Attitudes to Religion, Ethics, Progress and Politics in a London Borough, Gollancz, London, 1947

Browns and Chester. Portrait of a Shop, 1780–1946, Lindsay Drummond, London, 1947

Turner, W. J., *Exmoor Village. A General Account based on Factual Information from Mass-Observation*, George G. Harrap & Co, London, 1947

Peace and the Public, Longmans, Green & Co, London, 1947

The Press and its Readers, Art and Technics, London, 1949

Meet Yourself on Sunday, The Naldrett Press, London, 1949

Meet Yourself at the Doctor's, The Naldrett Press, London, 1949

Willcock, H. D., *Report on Juvenile Delinquency,* Falcon, London, 1949

People and Paint, Imperial Chemical Industries, Slough, 1949

Voters' Choice: A Mass-Observation Report on the General Election of 1950, Art and Technics, London, 1950

4. BOOKS AND ARTICLES (CONTEMPORARY)

Abrams, Mark, *Social Surveys and Social Action*, London, 1951

Association of Scientific Workers, *The Social Sciences. A case for their greater use*, London, 1947

Bartlett, F. C., Ginsberg, M., Lindgren, E. J., and Thouless, R. H., *The Study of Society: Methods and Problems,* London, 1939

Bell, Graham, *The Artist and his Public*, London, 1939

Beveridge, Lord, *Voluntary Action: A Report on Methods of Social Advance*, London, 1948

Beveridge, Lord and Wells, A. F., *The Evidence of Voluntary Action*, London, 1949

Box, Kathleen and Thomas, Geoffrey, 'The Wartime Social Survey', *Royal Statistical Society*, iii–iv, 1944

Cantril, Hadley, 'The Social Psychology of Everyday Life', *The Psychological Bulletin*, 31, 5, May 1934

Durant, R., *Watling*, London, 1939

Durbin, E. F. M., 'Methods of Research—A Plea for Co-Operation in the Social Sciences', *The Economic Journal*, 48, 190, 1938

England, Len, 'Little Kinsey: an outline of sex attitudes in Britain', *Public Opinion Quarterly*, 13, 4, 1949–50

——, 'A British Sex Survey', *International Journal of Sexology*, III, 3, 1950

——, 'An Outline of Sex Attitudes in Britain', *Public Opinion Quarterly*, 13, 4, 1949–50

Eysenk, H. J., Tarrant, Mollie, Woolf, Myra and England, Len, 'Smoking and Personality', *British Medical Journal*, 5184, 14 May 1960

Ferraby, J. G., 'The Problem of Propaganda', *Agenda*, August 1944

——, 'Observations on the Reluctant Stork', *Public Opinion Quarterly*, 9, 1, 1945

——, 'Planning a Mass-Observation Investigation', *American Journal of Sociology*, 51, 1, 1945

Firth, Raymond, 'An Anthropologist's View of Mass-Observation', *Sociological Review*, 31, 2, 1939

Fremlin, Celia, *Seven Chars of Chelsea*, London, 1940

Goldman, Willy, *The East End My Cradle*, London, 1940

Harrisson, Tom, 'A Public Demand for Reprisals?', *The Cambridge Review*, LXII, 1529, 30 May 1941

——, 'Blitz information', *Local Government Service*, 25, 5, August 1941

——, 'New Synthesis', *Public Opinion Quarterly*, 11, 3, Fall 1947

——, 'Notes on Class Consciousness and Class Unconsciousness', *The Sociological Review*, 34, 1942

——, 'The Future of Sociology,' *Pilot Papers*, 2, 1 March 1947

——, 'The Public's Progress', *Contact*, April 1947

——, *Letter to Oxford*, Wyck, 1933

——, *Savage Civilisation*, London, 1937

Hilton, John 'Why I Go In For the Pools. By Tom, Dick and Harry—also Peggy, Joan and Kate', London, 1936

Klingender, Francis, *The Conditions of Clerical Labour in Britain since 1918*, London, 1935

Lazarsfelt, P. and Fiske, M., 'The 'Panel' as a new tool for measuring opinion', *Public Opinion Quarterly*, 2, 4, 1938

Lipman, Michael, *Memoires of a Socialist Business Man*, London, 1980

Madge, Charles and Jennings, Humphrey, 'They Speak for Themselves. Mass-Observation and Social Narrative', *Life and Letters Today*, 9, February 1937

Madge, Charles, 'Magic and Materialism', *Left Review*, February 1937

——, 'Oxford Collective Poem', *New Verse*, 25, May 1937

——, 'Press, radio and social consciousness', C. Day-Lewis (ed.), *The Mind in Chains*, London, 1937

——, 'The propensity to save in Blackburn and Bristol', *Economic Journal*, 50, 200, December 1940

Mass-Observation, 'Don't Know, Don't Care', in *The Adventure Ahead*, Contact Books, March 1948

Men Without Work, Report to the Pilgrim Trust, Cambridge, 1938

Oeser, O. A., 'Methods and Assumptions of Field Work in Social Psychology', *British Journal of Psychology*, General Section, 27, 4, 1937

——, 'The value of team work and functional penetration as methods of social investigation.' in Bartlett et al, *The Study of Society*, London, 1939

Orwell, George, *The Lion and the Unicorn. Socialism and the English Genius*, Harmondsworth, 1982

Pear, T. H., *Voice and Personality*, London, 1931

——, *The Psychology of Conversation*, London, 1939

——, 'Some problems and topics of contemporary social psychology' in Bartlett et al, *The Study of Society*, London, 1939

——, 'Psychologists and Culture', *Bulletin of the John Rylands Library*, 23, 1939

Priestley, J. B., *English Journey*, London, 1934

Singer, H. W., 'How Widespread are National Savings? A Critique of the Madge Enquiry', *The Manchester School*, 13, 2, August 1944

Sommerfield, John, *Volunteer in Spain*, London, 1937

——, *May Day*, London, 1984

Swaffer, Hannen, *What Would Nelson Do?*, London, 1946

Taylor, Stephen, 'The Study of Public Opinion', *Public Administration*, October/December 1943

——, 'The Suburban Neurosis', *The Lancet*, 231, 5978, 26 Mar 1938

Thouless, R. H., 'Scientific method and the use of Statistics', in Bartlett et al, *The Study of Society*, London, 1939

Wagner, G. W., 'Market research: a Critical Study', *Review of Economic Studies*, 5, 2, February 1938

——, *Our wartime guests: opportunity or menace? A psychological approach to evacuation*, Liverpool, 1940

Willcock, H. D., 'Mass-Observation', *American Journal of Sociology*, 48, 4, 1943

Young, Terence, *Becontree and Dagenham*, London, 1934

5. OTHER BOOKS AND ARTICLES

Addison, Paul, *The Road to 1945*, London, 1977

——, 'Angus Calder', *History Workshop Journal*, 70, 2010

Addison, Paul and Crang, Jeremy A., *Listening to Britain. Home Intelligence Reports on Britain's Finest Hour*, London, 2010

Beaven, Brad and Griffiths, John, 'The blitz, civilian morale and the city: mass-observation and working-class culture in Britain, 1940–41', *Urban History*, 26, 1, 1999

Beers, Laura DuMond, 'Whose Opinion?: Changing Attitudes Towards Opinion Polling in British politics, 1937–1964', *Twentieth Century British History*, 17, 2, 2006

Bennett, Tony and Watson, Diane (eds), *Understanding Everyday Life*, Oxford, 2002

Betjeman, John, *A Few Late Chrysanthemums*, London, 1954

Blackford, Catherine, 'Wives and Citizens and Watchdogs of Quality: Post-War British Feminism', in J. Fyrth (ed.), *Labour's Promised Land. Culture and Society in Labour Britain, 1945–51*, London, 1995

Brooke, Stephen, 'War and the Nude: The Photography of Bill Brandt in the 1940s', *Journal of British Studies*, 45, 1, 2006

Bulmer, Martin, 'The development of sociology and of empirical social research in Britain', in M. Bulmer (ed.), *Essays on the History of British Sociological Research*, Cambridge, 1985

Bulmer, M., Bales, K., and Sklar, K. K., *The Social Survey in Historical Perspective, 1880–1940*, Cambridge, 1991

Bulpitt, Jim, *Territory and Power in the United Kingdom*, Colchester, 1983

Burke, Christopher, 'Isotype: representing social facts pictorially', *Information Design Journal*, 17, 3, 2009

Burnett, John, *A Social History of Housing, 1815–1985*, London, 1986

Buzzard, James, 'Mass-Observation, Modernism and Auto-Ethnography', *Modernism/Modernity*, 4, 3, 1997

Calder, Angus, *The People's War. Britain 1939-45*, London, 1969

Calder, Angus and Sheridan, Dorothy, *Speak for Yourself*, London, 1984

Carey, John, *The Intellectuals and the Masses: pride and prejudice among the literary intelligentsia, 1880–1939*, London, 1992

Carpenter, Humphrey, *The Inklings: C.S. Lewis, J.R.R. Tolkien, Charles Williams and their friends*, London, 1978

Chamberlayne, Prue, Bornat, Joanna, and Wengraf, Tom (eds), *The Turn to Biographical Methods in the Social Sciences*, Abingdon, 2000

Clarke, Peter, *The Cripps Version. The Life of Sir Stafford Cripps, 1889–1952*, London, 2002

Clement Brown, Sibyl, 'Looking Backwards: Reminiscences, 1922–1946', *British Journal of Psychiatric Social Work*, 10, 4, 1970

Costall, Alan, 'Pear and his peers', in G. C. Bunn, A. D. Lovie and G. D. Richards (eds), *Psychology in Britain: historical essays and personal reflections*, Leicester, 2001

——, 'Why British psychology is not social: Frederic Bartlett's promotion of the new academic discipline', *Canadian Psychology*, 33, 1992

Cunningham, Valentine, *British Writers of the Thirties*, Oxford, 1989

Darling, Elizabeth, *Re-forming Britain: Narratives of modernity before reconstruction*, London, 2007

Davies, Sam and Morley, Bob, *County borough election results, England and Wales, 1919–1938: a comparative analysis. Vol. 1. Barnsley – Bournemouth*, Aldershot, 1999

Desmarais, Ralph J., 'Tots and Quots', DNB

Dixon, David, *From prohibition to regulation: bookmaking, anti-gambling, and the law*, Oxford, 1991

Donoughue, B. and Jones, G. W., *Herbert Morrison: portrait of a politician*, London, 1973

Dutton, David, *The History of the Liberal Party*, Basingstoke, 2004

Eatwell, Roger 'Munich, Public Opinion and the Popular Front', *Journal of Contemporary History*, 6, 4, 1971

Feaver, William, *Pitman Painters. The Ashington Group, 1934–1984*, Ashington, 2009

Ferraby, John, *All Things Made New. A Comprehensive Outline of the Bahá'í Faith*, London, 1957

Fielding, Steve, 'The Second World War and Popular Radicalism: The Significance of the "Movement away from Party"', *History*, 80, 258, 1995

Forgan, Sophie, 'Festivals of Science and the Two Cultures: Science, Design and Display in the Festival of Britain, 1951', *The British Journal for the History of Science*, 31, 2, 1998

Fryer, David, 'Introduction to Marienthal and Beyond', *Journal of Occupational & Organizational Psychology*, 65, 4, 1992

Giddens, Anthony, *Modernity and Self-identity: Self and Society in the Late Modern Age*, Cambridge, 1992

Giles, Judy, *The Parlour and the Suburb: Domestic Identities, Class, Femininity and Modernity*, Oxford, 2004

Gurney, Peter, '"Intersex" and "Dirty Girls": Mass-Observation and Working-Class Sexuality in England in the 1930s', *Journal of the History of Sexuality*, 8, 2, 1997

Haffenden, John, *William Empson: among the Mandarins*, Oxford, 2005

Hall, Stuart, 'The Social Eye of *Picture Post*', *Working Papers in Cultural Studies*, 2, Centre for Contemporary Cultural Studies, University of Birmingham, 1972

Halsey, A. H., *A History of Sociology in Britain. Science, Literature and Society*, Oxford, 2004

Harper, Barron, *Lights of Fortitude*, Oxford, 1997

Harris, Jose, *William Beveridge. A Biography*, Oxford, 1997

Harris, Leonard, *Long to Reign Over Us. The Status of the Royal Family in the Sixties*, London, 1966

Harrisson, Tom, *A World Within. A Borneo Story*, London, 1959

——, *Britain Revisited*, London, 1961

——, *Living through the Blitz,* Harmondsworth, 1978

Hastings, Max, *Bomber Command*, London, 1979

Heimann, Judith, *The Most Offending Soul Alive. Tom Harrisson and His Remarkable Life,* Honolulu, 1997

Highmore, Ben, 'Hopscotch Modernism: On Everyday Life and the Blurring of Art and Social Science', *Modernist Cultures*, 2, 1, 2006

Highmore, Ben, *Everyday Life and Cultural Theory: an introduction*, London, 2002

Hinton, James, 'Coventry Communism. A study of factory politics in the Second World War', *History Workshop Journal*, 10, 1980

——, *Protests and Visions*, London, 1989

——, 'Women and the Labour Vote', *Labour History Review*, 57, 3, 1992

——, *Shop Floor Citizens: Engineering democracy in 1940s Britain*, Aldershot, 1994

——, '1945 and the apathy school', *History Workshop Journal*, 43, 1997

——— , 'The "class" complex: Mass-Observation and cultural distinction in pre-war Britain,' *Past and Present*, 199, 2, 2008

——— , *Nine Wartime Lives,* Oxford, 2010

Horner, David, 'The Road to Scarborough: Wilson, Labour and the scientific revolution', in R. Coopey, S. Fielding and N. Tiratsoo (eds), *The Wilson Governments, 1964–1970*, London, 1993

Hubble, Nick, *Mass-Observation and Everyday Life,* Basingstoke, 2006

Hurnscot, Loran, pseud. [Gay Taylor], *A Prison, a Paradise, etc. Reminiscences in the form of a diary*, London, 1958

Jackson, Kevin, *Humphrey Jennings*, London, 2004

Jahoda, Marie, 'Reflections on Marienthal and after', *Journal of Occupational & Organizational Psychology*, 65, 4, 1992

Jamieson, Lynn, *Intimacy. Personal Relationships in Modern Societies*, Cambridge, 1998

Jeffery, Tom, *Mass-Observation – A Short History*, Birmingham, 1978

Johnson, Donald, *Bars and Barricades*, London, 1952

Jones, Harriet, '"New Conservation"? The Industrial Charter, Modernity and the Reconstruction of British Conservatism after the War', in Betty Conekin, Frank Mort, and Chris Waters (eds), *Moments of Modernity. Reconstructing Britain 1945– 1964*, London, 1988

Kerr, David, *The House of Collins*, London, 1952

Kinross, Robin, 'Herbert Read and Design' in David Goodway (ed.), *Herbert Read Reassessed*, Liverpool, 1998

Kirby, M. W., 'Blackett in the "White Heat" of the Scientific Revolution: Industrial Modernisation under the Labour Governments, 1964–1970', *The Journal of the Operational Research Society*, 50, 10, 1999

Koa Wing, Sandra, *Our Longest Days,* London, 2008

Kuklick, Henrika, *The Savage Within. The Social History of British Anthropology, 1885– 1945*, Cambridge, 1991

Kuper, Adam, *Anthropologists. The Modern British School*, London, 1983

Kushner, T. *We Europeans? Mass-Observation, 'Race' and British Identity in the Twentieth Century*, Aldershot, 2004

Kynaston, David, *Austerity Britain, 1945–51*, London, 2007

Lewis, Jane, Clark, David, and Morgan, David H. J., *'Whom God hath Joined Together'. The work of marriage guidance,* London, 1992

Lipman, Michael, *Memoires of a Socialist Business Man*, London, 1980

MacClancy, Jeremy, 'Mass-Observation, Surrealism, Social Anthropology: A present-day assessment', *New Formations*, 44, Autumn 2001

Macdonald, Helen, '"What makes you a scientist is the way you look at things": ornithology and the observer 1930–1955', *Studies in the History and Philosophy of the Biological and Biomedical Science,* 33, 2002

Macdonald, I., *History of The Times*, Vol 5, London, 1984

Mackay, Marina, *Modernism and World War II*, Cambridge, 2007

Mackenzie, Compton, *My Life and Times, 1939–1946*, London, 1969

Maguire, P. J. and Woodham, J. M., *Design and Cultural Politics in Postwar Britain*, Leicester, 1997

Marcus, Laura, 'The Project of Mass-Observation', *New Formations*, 44, Autumn 2001

Massey, Anne, *The Independent Group: Modernism and Mass Culture in Britain, 1949–59*, Manchester, 1995

Matless, D., *Landscape and Englishness*, London, 1998

McDonald, Colin and King, Stephen, *Sampling the Universe. The growth, development and influence of market research in Britain since 1945*, Henley-on-Thames, 1996

McKenna, Wayne, *W. J. Turner: Poet And Music Critic,* Gerrards Cross, 1990

McKibbin, R., *Classes and Cultures. England 1918–1951*, Oxford, 1998

McLaine, Ian, *Ministry of Morale; Home Front Morale and the Ministry of Information in World War II*, London, 1979

——, 'Oxford & Bridgewater', in Chris Cook and John Ramsden (eds) *By-Elections in British Politics*, London, 1997

Moggridge, Donald (ed.), *The collected writings of John Maynard Keynes, Vol. 22, Activities 1939–1945, internal war finance*, London, 1978

Moran, Joe, 'Mass-Observation, Market Research, and the Birth of the Focus Group, 1937–1997', *Journal of British Studies,* 47, 2008

Morgan, Kevin, *Against War and Fascism. Ruptures and Continuities in British Communist Politics,* Manchester, 1989

——, 'King Street Blues: jazz and the left in Britain in the 1930s–40s', in Andy Croft (ed.), *Weapons in the Struggle: essays on the cultural history of British communism*, London, 1998

Moss, Louis, *The Government Social Survey. A History*, London, 1991

Mulford, Jeremy (ed.), *Worktown People. Photographs from Northern England 1937–38*, Bristol, 1982

Nixon, Edna, *John Hilton: the story of his life*, London, 1946

Orwell, Sonia and Angus, Ian, *The Collected Essays, Journalism and Letters of George Orwell*, Harmondsworth, 1970

Oxford Dictionary of National Biography, online edition, 2004

Pahl, R., review of Mike Savage, *Identities and Social Change since 1940, Sociological Review*, 59, 1, 2011

Pimlott, Ben, *Labour and the Left in the 1930s,* London, 1986

Plummer, Ken, *Documents of Life. An Introduction to the Problems and Literature of a Humanistic Method,* London, 1983

Punt, Tom, 'Mass-Observation. The first seventy years', *The Research Network*, 2007

Radford, Robert, *Art for a Purpose: the Artists' International Association, 1933–1953*, Winchester, 1987

Raine, Kathleen, *The Land Unknown*, London, 1975

Rennie, Paul, 'British picture books for grown-ups from the 1940s', September 2005, <http:www.rennart.co.uk/web%20site%20pdfs/books.pdf> accessed 22 October 2010

Reynolds, J. and Hunter, I., 'Liberal Class Warrior', *Journal of Liberal Democrat History*, 28, Autumn 2000

Richards, Jeffrey and Sheridan, Dorothy (eds), *Mass-Observation at the Movies*, London, 1987

Rickaby, Tony, 'The Artists' International', *History Workshop*, 6, 1978

Roberts, Brian, 'Welsh identity in a former mining valley: social images and imagined communities', *Contemporary Wales*, 5, 7, 1995

Rose, Jonathan, *The Intellectual Life of the British Working Classes*, London, 2001

Rosenthal, Tom, 'Walter and Eva Neurath: Their Books Married Words with Pictures', in Richard Abel and Gordon Graham (eds), *Immigrant Publishers. The Impact of Expatriate Publishers in Britain and America in the 20th century*, London, 2009

Savage, Mike, 'Affluence and Social Change in the Making of Technocratic Middle-Class Identities: Britain, 1939–55', *Contemporary British History*, 22, 4, 2008

——, *Identities and Social Change in Britain since 1940. The Politics of Method*, Oxford, 2010

Shaw, Wendy M. K., 'Whose Hittites and Why? Language, Archaeology and the Quest for the Original Turks', in Michael L. Galaty and Madge Watkinson (eds), *Archaeology under Dictatorship*, London, 2004

Sheridan, Dorothy (ed.), *Wartime Women. An Anthology of Women's Wartime Writing for Mass-Observation 1937–45*, London, 1990

——, 'Writing to the Archive: Mass-Observation as Autobiography', *Sociology*, 27, 1, 1993

——, *Damned Anecdotes & Dangerous Confabulations. Mass-Observation as Life History*, Mass-Observation Archive Occasional Paper, 1996

Sheridan, Dorothy, Street, Brian, Bloome, David, *Writing Ourselves. Mass-Observation and Literary Practices*, New Jersey, 2000

Shils, Edward, 'On the eve: a prospect in retrospect', in M. Bulmer (ed.), *Essays on the History of British Sociological Research*, Cambridge, 1985

Smart, Carol, *Personal Life. New Directions in Sociological Thinking*, Cambridge, 2007

Spender, Humphrey, *Worktown People. Photographs from Northern England, 1937–38*, Bristol, 1982

Stacey, Margaret, *Tradition and change: a study of Banbury*, Oxford, 1960

Stanley, Liz, *An archaeology of a 1930s Mass-Observation project*, Manchester University Sociology Department, Occasional Paper, 1990

——, *Sex Surveyed, 1949–1994. From Mass-Observation's 'Little Kinsey' to the National Survey and the Hite reports*, London, 1995

——, 'MO's Fieldwork Methods', in Paul Atkinson et al (eds), *Handbook of Ethnography*, London, 2001

Stonebridge, Lyndsey, 'Anxiety at a time of crisis', *History Workshop Journal*, 45, 1998

Summerfield, Penny, 'Mass-Observation: Social Research or Social Movement?', *Journal of Contemporary History*, 20, 1985

Taylor of Harlow, Lord, *A Natural History of Everyday Life. A biographical guide for would-be doctors of society*, Cambridge, 1988

Thompson, Edward, 'Time, Work Discipline and Industrial Capitalism', *Past & Present*, 38, 1, 1967

Toogood, M., 'Modern observations: new ornithology and the science of ourselves, 1920–1940', *Journal of Historical Geography*, 37, 2011

Trevelyan, Julian, *Indigo Days*, London, 1957

Vaughan, Dai, *Portrait of an invisible man: the working life of Stewart McAllister, film editor*, London, 1983

Walsh, Victoria and Smithson, Peter, N*igel Henderson: Parallel of Life and Art*, London, 2001

Walton, J. K., 'Mass-Observation's Blackpool and some alternatives', in Gary Cross (ed.), *Worktowners at Blackpool. Mass-Observation and popular leisure in the 1930s*, London, 1990

Whitehead, Frank, 'The Government Social Survey', in M. Bulmer (ed), *Essays on the History of British Sociological Research*, Cambridge, 1985

Whitworth, Lesley, 'Getting Beneath the Surface of Things: Mass-Observation and Material Culture', Mass-Observation Online

Willmott, Peter, 'The Institute of Community Studies', in M. Bulmer (ed.), *Essays on the History of British Sociological Research*, Cambridge, 1985

Windlesham, Lord, 'The Communication of Conservative Policy, 1963–64', *Political Quarterly*, 36,2, 1965

Wring, Dominic, *The Politics of Marketing the Labour Party*, Basingstoke, 2005

Wyatt, Woodrow, *Into this Dangerous World*, London, 1952

Ziegler, Philip, *Crown and People*, Newton Abbot, 1979

6. JOURNALS

Advertiser's Weekly
Art and Industry
Daily Worker
Economist
Evening Standard
Fords and Bridges
Horizon
Left Review
Life and Letters Today
Light and Dark
Man
Modern Reading
Nature
New Statesman
New Verse
New Writing
News Chronicle

News Review
Newspaper World
Picture Post
Poetry Review
The Bolton Citizen
The Daily Telegraph
The Economic Journal
The Guardian
The Highway
The Independent
The Listener
The Manchester Guardian
The New Saxon Review
The Spectator
The Times
Times Literary Supplement
Tribune
World Press News

7. UNPUBLISHED

Baines, Malcolm, 'The Survival of the British Liberal Party, 1932–1959', Oxford DPhil, 1989
Calder, Angus, 'The Mass-Observers' (MO Archive)
Croft, Hazel, 'Psychiatrists and the making of the "no neurosis myth"', Paper delivered to conference on 'The Second World War: Popular Culture and Cultural memory', Brighton, 13–15 July 2011
Harris, Paul, 'Social Leadership and Social Attitudes in Bolton, 1919 to 1939', Lancaster PhD, 1973
Harrisson, Tom, 'The Poverty of Freedom', 1939 (MO Archive)
Madge, Charles, 'Autobiography', in CMpap, 71/1/6
Stanley, Nick, 'The Extra Dimension: A study and assessment of the methods employed by Mass-Observation in its first period, 1937–1940', CNAA PhD thesis, 1981
Willcock, Bob, *Polls Apart,* 1947 (MO Archive)

Index of Mass Observers

General Index